T0215814

Lecture Notes in Computer Science 12737

More information about this subseries at http://www.springer.com/series/7409

Xingming Sun · Xiaorui Zhang ·
Zhihua Xia · Elisa Bertino (Eds.)

Artificial Intelligence and Security

7th International Conference, ICAIS 2021
Dublin, Ireland, July 19–23, 2021
Proceedings, Part II

 Springer

Editors
Xingming Sun 📵
Nanjing University of Information Science
and Technology
Nanjing, China

Xiaorui Zhang 📵
Nanjing University of Information Science
and Technology
Nanjing, China

Zhihua Xia 📵
Jinan University
Guangzhou, China

Elisa Bertino 📵
Purdue University
West Lafayette, IN, USA

ISSN 0302-9743   ISSN 1611-3349 (electronic)
Lecture Notes in Computer Science
ISBN 978-3-030-78611-3   ISBN 978-3-030-78612-0 (eBook)
https://doi.org/10.1007/978-3-030-78612-0

LNCS Sublibrary: SL3 – Information Systems and Applications, incl. Internet/Web, and HCI

This Springer imprint is published by the registered company Springer Nature Switzerland AG
The registered company address is: Gewerbestrasse 11, 6330 Cham, Switzerland

Preface

The 7th International Conference on Artificial Intelligence and Security (ICAIS 2021), formerly called the International Conference on Cloud Computing and Security (ICCCS), was held during July 16–19, 2021, in Dublin, Ireland. Over the past six years, ICAIS has become a leading conference for researchers and engineers to share their latest results of research, development, and applications in the fields of artificial intelligence and information security.

We used the Microsoft Conference Management Toolkits (CMT) system to manage the submission and review processes of ICAIS 2021. We received 1013 submissions from authors in 20 countries and regions, including the USA, Canada, the UK, Italy, Ireland, Japan, Russia, France, Australia, South Korea, South Africa, Iraq, Kazakhstan, Indonesia, Vietnam, Ghana, China, Taiwan, and Macao, etc. The submissions covered the areas of artificial intelligence, big data, cloud computing and security, information hiding, IoT security, multimedia forensics, encryption and cybersecurity, and so on. We thank our Technical Program Committee (TPC) members and external reviewers for their efforts in reviewing the papers and providing valuable comments to the authors. From the total of 1013 submissions, and based on at least three reviews per submission, the Program Chairs decided to accept 122 papers to be published in two Lecture Notes in Computer Science (LNCS) volumes and 183 papers to be published in three Communications in Computer and Information Science (CCIS) volumes, yielding an acceptance rate of 30%. This volume of the conference proceedings contains all the regular, poster, and workshop papers.

The conference program was enriched by a series of keynote presentations, and the keynote speakers included Michael Scott, MIRACL Labs, Ireland, and Sakir Sezer, Queen's University of Belfast, UK. We enjoyed their wonderful speeches.

There were 49 workshops organized as part of ICAIS 2021 which covered all the hot topics in artificial intelligence and security. We would like to take this moment to express our sincere appreciation for the contribution of all the workshop chairs and their participants. We would like to extend our sincere thanks to all authors who submitted papers to ICAIS 2021 and to all TPC members. It was a truly great experience to work with such talented and hard-working researchers. We also appreciate the external reviewers for assisting the TPC members in their particular areas of expertise. Moreover, we want to thank our sponsors: Association for Computing Machinery; Nanjing University of Information Science and Technology; Dublin City University; New York University; Michigan State University; University of Central Arkansas; Université Bretagne Sud; National Nature Science Foundation of China; Tech Science Press; Nanjing Normal University; Northeastern State University; Engineering Research Center of Digital Forensics, Ministry of Education, China; and ACM SIGWEB China.

April 2021

Xingming Sun
Xiaorui Zhang
Zhihua Xia
Elisa Bertino

Organization

General Chairs

Martin Collier	Dublin City University, Ireland
Xingming Sun	Nanjing University of Information Science and Technology, China
Yun Q. Shi	New Jersey Institute of Technology, USA
Mauro Barni	University of Siena, Italy
Elisa Bertino	Purdue University, USA

Technical Program Chairs

Noel Murphy	Dublin City University, Ireland
Aniello Castiglione	University of Salerno, Italy
Yunbiao Guo	China Information Technology Security Evaluation Center, China
Suzanne K. McIntosh	New York University, USA
Xiaorui Zhang	Engineering Research Center of Digital Forensics, Ministry of Education, China
Q. M. Jonathan Wu	University of Windsor, Canada

Publication Chairs

Zhihua Xia	Nanjing University of Information Science and Technology, China
Zhaoqing Pan	Nanjing University of Information Science and Technology, China

Workshop Chair

Baowei Wang	Nanjing University of Information Science and Technology, China

Organization Chairs

Xiaojun Wang	Dublin City University, Ireland
Genlin Ji	Nanjing Normal University, China
Zhangjie Fu	Nanjing University of Information Science and Technology, China

Technical Program Committee Members

Saeed Arif	University of Algeria, Algeria
Anthony Ayodele	University of Maryland, USA
Zhifeng Bao	Royal Melbourne Institute of Technology, Australia
Zhiping Cai	National University of Defense Technology, China
Ning Cao	Qingdao Binhai University, China
Paolina Centonze	Iona College, USA
Chin-chen Chang	Feng Chia University, Taiwan, China
Han-Chieh Chao	Taiwan Dong Hwa University, Taiwan, China
Bing Chen	Nanjing University of Aeronautics and Astronautics, China
Hanhua Chen	Huazhong University of Science and Technology, China
Xiaofeng Chen	Xidian University, China
Jieren Cheng	Hainan University, China
Lianhua Chi	IBM Research Center, Australia
Kim-Kwang Raymond Choo	University of Texas at San Antonio, USA
Ilyong Chung	Chosun University, South Korea
Robert H. Deng	Singapore Management University, Singapore
Jintai Ding	University of Cincinnati, USA
Xinwen Fu	University of Central Florida, USA
Zhangjie Fu	Nanjing University of Information Science and Technology, China
Moncef Gabbouj	Tampere University of Technology, Finland
Ruili Geng	Spectral MD, USA
Song Guo	Hong Kong Polytechnic University, Hong Kong
Mohammad Mehedi Hassan	King Saud University, Saudi Arabia
Russell Higgs	University College Dublin, Ireland
Dinh Thai Hoang	University of Technology Sydney, Australia
Wien Hong	Nanfang College of Sun Yat-sen University, China
Chih-Hsien Hsia	National Ilan University, Taiwan, China
Robert Hsu	Chung Hua University, Taiwan, China
Xinyi Huang	Fujian Normal University, China
Yongfeng Huang	Tsinghua University, China
Zhiqiu Huang	Nanjing University of Aeronautics and Astronautics, China
Patrick C. K. Hung	University of Ontario Institute of Technology, Canada
Farookh Hussain	University of Technology Sydney, Australia
Genlin Ji	Nanjing Normal University, China
Hai Jin	Huazhong University of Science and Technology, China
Sam Tak Wu Kwong	City University of Hong Kong, China
Chin-Feng Lai	Taiwan Cheng Kung University, Taiwan, China
Loukas Lazos	University of Arizona, USA

Yongjun Ren	Nanjing University of Information Science and Technology, China
Arun Kumar Sangaiah	VIT University, India
Di Shang	Long Island University, USA
Victor S. Sheng	University of Central Arkansas, USA
Zheng-guo Sheng	University of Sussex, UK
Robert Simon Sherratt	University of Reading, UK
Yun Q. Shi	New Jersey Institute of Technology, USA
Frank Y. Shih	New Jersey Institute of Technology, USA
Biao Song	King Saud University, Saudi Arabia
Guang Sun	Hunan University of Finance and Economics, China
Jianguo Sun	Harbin University of Engineering, China
Krzysztof Szczypiorski	Warsaw University of Technology, Poland
Tsuyoshi Takagi	Kyushu University, Japan
Shanyu Tang	University of West London, UK
Jing Tian	National University of Singapore, Singapore
Yoshito Tobe	Aoyang University, Japan
Cezhong Tong	Washington University in St. Louis, USA
Pengjun Wan	Illinois Institute of Technology, USA
Cai-Zhuang Wang	Ames Laboratory, USA
Ding Wang	Peking University, China
Guiling Wang	New Jersey Institute of Technology, USA
Honggang Wang	University of Massachusetts Dartmouth, USA
Jian Wang	Nanjing University of Aeronautics and Astronautics, China
Jie Wang	University of Massachusetts Lowell, USA
Jin Wang	Changsha University of Science and Technology, China
Liangmin Wang	Jiangsu University, China
Ruili Wang	Massey University, New Zealand
Xiaojun Wang	Dublin City University, Ireland
Xiaokang Wang	St. Francis Xavier University, Canada
Zhaoxia Wang	A-Star, Singapore
Sheng Wen	Swinburne University of Technology, Australia
Jian Weng	Jinan University, China
Edward Wong	New York University, USA
Eric Wong	University of Texas at Dallas, USA
Shaoen Wu	Ball State University, USA
Shuangkui Xia	Beijing Institute of Electronics Technology and Application, China
Lingyun Xiang	Changsha University of Science and Technology, China
Yang Xiang	Deakin University, Australia
Yang Xiao	University of Alabama, USA
Haoran Xie	The Education University of Hong Kong, China
Naixue Xiong	Northeastern State University, USA

Wei Qi Yan	Auckland University of Technology, New Zealand
Aimin Yang	Guangdong University of Foreign Studies, China
Ching-Nung Yang	Taiwan Dong Hwa University, Taiwan, China
Chunfang Yang	Zhengzhou Science and Technology Institute, China
Fan Yang	University of Maryland, USA
Guomin Yang	University of Wollongong, Australia
Qing Yang	University of North Texas, USA
Yimin Yang	Lakehead University, Canada
Ming Yin	Purdue University, USA
Shaodi You	Australian National University, Australia
Kun-Ming Yu	Chung Hua University, Taiwan, China
Weiming Zhang	University of Science and Technology of China, China
Xinpeng Zhang	Fudan University, China
Yan Zhang	Simula Research Laboratory, Norway
Yanchun Zhang	Victoria University, Australia
Yao Zhao	Beijing Jiaotong University, China

Organization Committee Members

Xianyi Chen	Nanjing University of Information Science and Technology, China
Zilong Jin	Nanjing University of Information Science and Technology, China
Yiwei Li	Columbia University, USA
Yuling Liu	Hunan University, China
Zhiguo Qu	Nanjing University of Information Science and Technology, China
Huiyu Sun	New York University, USA
Le Sun	Nanjing University of Information Science and Technology, China
Jian Su	Nanjing University of Information Science and Technology, China
Qing Tian	Nanjing University of Information Science and Technology, China
Yuan Tian	King Saud University, Saudi Arabia
Qi Wang	Nanjing University of Information Science and Technology, China
Lingyun Xiang	Changsha University of Science and Technology, China
Zhihua Xia	Nanjing University of Information Science and Technology, China
Lizhi Xiong	Nanjing University of Information Science and Technology, China
Leiming Yan	Nanjing University of Information Science and Technology, China

Li Yu   Nanjing University of Information Science
                         and Technology, China
Zhili Zhou   Nanjing University of Information Science
                         and Technology, China

Contents – Part II

Big Data

Cloud Computing and Security

Encryption and Cybersecurity

Information Hiding

IoT Security

Multimedia Forensics

Contents – Part I

Big Data

Big Data

Big Data

Research on Optimization of Data Balancing Partition Algorithm Based on Spark Platform

Suzhen Wang[✉], Zhiting Jia, and Wenli Wang

Hebei University of Economics and Business, Shijiazhuang 050061, Hebei, China

Abstract. Aiming at the data skew problem in the Spark system caused by the unbalanced distribution of the input data and the default partition algorithm, this paper proposes an optimized partition method to solve the data skew problem. Firstly, the parallel cluster sampling algorithm is used to sample the intermediate data processed by each Map task to predict the data distribution. Then, the frequency of each Key is obtained according to the sampling prediction, and the weight is assigned to each Key. Finally, combining the greedy algorithm to divide the intermediate data to make the amount of data in each partition more balanced. Compared with the Hash and Range partitioning methods of the Spark platform and the SCID algorithm proposed by predecessors, experiments show this method effectively reduces the load deviation and reduces the task execution time.

Keywords: Data skew · Data partition · Load balancing

1 Introduction

Spark is the mainstream big data processing platform, and load balancing is one of the important indicators to measure the performance of the big data platform. Generally, the load balancing problem is solved by optimizing task scheduling [1] and data partitioning [2], etc. In the Shuffle stage of the Spark platform, data with the same key value will be allocated to the same partition by using a hash partition strategy, which will make the amount of data falling into each partition uneven, resulting in slow execution of certain subtasks and affect the overall task execution efficiency.

The current methods to solve this problem: (1) Increase the number of partitions to improve the parallelism of tasks, thereby reducing the problem of data skew; (2) Use virtual partitions to reduce the formation of over-large partitions [3]; (3) User-defined partitions Device [4]. Literature [5] proposed a dynamic partitioning scheme based on the combination of pond sampling algorithm and dynamic data partitioning algorithm, using different partitioning algorithms to partition data with different degrees of inclination. Literature [6, 7] proposed an iterative data balancing partition strategy, which adjusts the data skew generated by each iteration [8]. Literature [9] proposed an algorithm for splitting and combining intermediate data blocks (SCID Splitting and Combination), sampling the input data and partitioning according to the SCID algorithm.

© Springer Nature Switzerland AG 2021
X. Sun et al. (Eds.): ICAIS 2021, LNCS 12737, pp. 3–13, 2021.
https://doi.org/10.1007/978-3-030-78612-0_1

2   Analysis of Spark Shuffle Mechanism

Shuffle is the intermediate stage of the Map task and the Reduce task in MapReduce [5]. It breaks up the data processed by the Map and distributes the intermediate data to the corresponding Reduce nodes according to the partition strategy. Spark draws on MapReduce's data processing and calculation framework, and there is also Shuffle operation. Spark's Shuffle is divided into two stages, Shuffle write and Shuffle fetch, and the process is shown in Fig. 1. Operations performed in the Shuffle write phase: the Map task processes the input data to obtain intermediate data, that is, a series of key-value pair data, and then partitions these intermediate data through a partition strategy and distributes them to the corresponding partition buckets [10]. The color of the bucket in the figure represents the amount of data allocated in it. Operations performed in the Shuffle fetch phase: the Reduce task pulls the data in the bucket in the Shuffle write phase, performs a Reduce operation, and calculates the result.

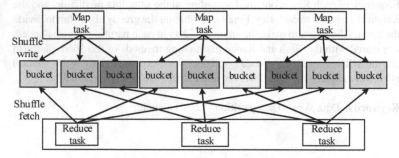

Fig. 1. Spark Shuffle process

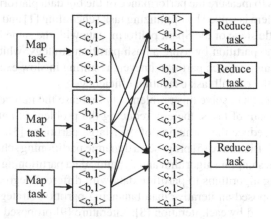

Fig. 2. Schematic diagram of data skew

The partition strategy in Spark includes Hash partition and Range partition. Hash partition is based on the intermediate key-value pair to modulo the number of partitions, and get the same hash value into one partition. This algorithm can ensure that Keys with the same Hash value are divided into the same partition. However, the intermediate data itself may be skewed, so data skewing will occur after partitioning, which will affect the efficiency of task execution, as shown in Fig. 2. In the Range partition algorithm, the data is first sampled in ponds, and then the range is divided according to the sampling results, and the divided data is mapped to the corresponding partition [11].

3 Research on Optimization of Spark Data Partition Strategy

3.1 Problem Description

During the operation of Spark, due to the uneven distribution of the input data itself and the uneven distribution of the default partitioning algorithm in the Spark system [12], the problem of data skew will occur. When the data is skewed, the execution time of some tasks will be significantly longer than other tasks. Since each task is executed in parallel, the final time is the execution time of the largest task, which affects the execution efficiency of the entire task [13]. Therefore, in order to solve the problem of data skew caused by the Spark Shuffle process, this paper studies and improves the data partition strategy.

3.2 Building the Model

After the Map stage is completed, the intermediate data is obtained, assuming that the intermediate data contains n keys. The data form of the intermediate data is $<K_i, V_i>$, and the data volume of each Key is $Q_1, \ldots, Q_j, \ldots, Q_n$. Assuming there are N partition buckets, the intermediate key-value pair data is allocated to the corresponding partition buckets, and the Key placed in a partition bucket j can be expressed as $\{(K_{1,j}, K_{2,j}, \ldots, K_{n,j})\}$, so that the amount of data in each partition bucket can be obtained as $q_1, \ldots, q_j, \ldots, q_N$, $1 \leq j \leq N$, q_j represents the total amount of data allocated in the j-th partition bucket.

Load balancing refers to whether the amount of data allocated on each partition bucket is balanced. This paper uses the coefficient of variation to calculate the data slope of each partition bucket after the intermediate data partition. As shown in the following formula.

$$D = \frac{\sqrt{\frac{1}{N} \sum_{j=1}^{N} (q_j - \bar{q})^2}}{\bar{q}} \tag{1}$$

$\bar{q}$ is the average value of the data volume, the calculation formula is a follows.

$$\bar{q} = \frac{\sum_{j=1}^{N} q_j}{N} \tag{2}$$

When D is larger, it means that the difference in the amount of data allocated between partition buckets is larger, and the data slope is larger. On the contrary, it means that the difference in data amount between partition buckets is smaller. When D is as small as 0, then indicates that the amount of data in each partition bucket is the same, reaching the optimum, that is, the amount of data is completely balanced.

When all the intermediate data is allocated, the task execution time $\max\limits_{1 \leq j \leq N} (T_j)$ is obtained.

By analyzing the data partition problem in the MapReduce stage, a multi-objective function based on load balancing and task execution time is proposed to design and verify the algorithm [14]. The objective function formula of the algorithm is as follows.

$$\text{Fit} = w_1 \cdot D + w_2 \cdot \max\limits_{1 \leq j \leq N} (T_j) \tag{3}$$

Among them, w_1 and w_2 are adjustable parameters, $w_1 + w_2 = 1$. The smaller the load balancing value and task execution time, the better the data partitioning strategy.

3.3 Optimization of Data Partition Method Based on Cluster Sampling-Greedy Algorithm

A cluster sampling algorithm is proposed to sample the data with the intermediate key values obtained after the Map task is processed, and the histogram is constructed by predicting the overall characteristics of the input data distribution and estimating the slope of the data by the sampling results [15]. According to the frequency of the Key obtained from the sampling results, weight is assigned to it, and the intermediate data is divided in combination with the greedy algorithm, so that the amount of data in each partition tends to the optimal, so as to achieve the result of balanced allocation and reduce the execution time.

Data Cluster Sampling. This paper chooses a cluster sampling algorithm and uses the parallelism of MapReduce in Spark to change this sampling. Since cluster sampling divides the overall data set into several non-overlapping groups for sampling[16], this paper regards the number of Map tasks in the Map stage as a set of groups, and performs simple random sampling of the data in each group according to the set sampling rate s to estimate the distribution of each Key. Among them, the higher the sampling rate is set, the higher the accuracy rate, and the more accurate the predicted data distribution, but the more time it consumes.Therefore, before experimenting, test each sampling rate and select an appropriate sampling rate. The algorithm process is described as follows:

(1) Calculate the total data mapPartitionsRddSize of all Map tasks through the RDD operator, that is, each computing node calculates the number of records contained in each Map task according to the number of Map tasks included, and finally transmits mapPartitionsRddSize to the Driver end.
(2) Calculate the total sample size that needs to be sampled according to the sampling rate set by the user, that is, sampleSize = mapPartitionsRddSize*sampling rate, and then calculate the sample size to be sampled from each Map task according to the number of Map tasks sampleSizePerPtion = Math.ceil(sampleSize/N), where N represents the number of partition buckets.

(3) Each computing node calls the sample function of RDD through the size of sampleSizePerPartition to sample the RDD data partition, counts the number of records of each Key value in the local sample, and transmits (Ki,Qi) to the Master node.

(4) The Master node summarizes the total number of samples of each Map task, estimates the overall distribution of the data, and obtains the intermediate data set Tuples = {(K$_1$,Q$_1$), (K$_2$,Q$_2$),..., (K$_n$,Q$_n$)} according to the setting of the sampling rate.

Through the above sampling method, the types and total number of Key values in the intermediate data can be estimated. Through this information, the characteristics of the approximate data and the slope of the key can be estimated. Thus, the ideal capacity in each partition bucket can be obtained, as shown in the following formula.

$$\bar{q} = \frac{Q}{N} \tag{4}$$

By calculating the frequency of each key, the slope of each key is estimated. As shown in the Fig. 3.

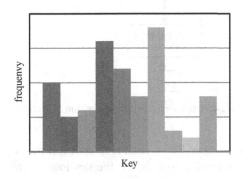

Fig. 3. Key skew histogram.

Greedy Algorithm Partition Method. Using the greedy algorithm, the total amount of data allocated in the partition buckets is regarded as a whole, and the average amount of data in each partition bucket is regarded as a sub-problem, so that the load in each partition bucket tends to the optimal solution as far as possible, so as to better solve the problem of data tilt.

First, estimate the set Tuples = {(K$_1$,Q$_1$), (K$_2$, Q$_2$), ..., (Kn,Qn)} of intermediate data by sampling, sort Qi from large to small, and assign weights to it. The greater the frequency, the greater the weight assigned, and the weight represents the order of processing. Then according to the set number of partition buckets and the total load of the Key type in the sampling result, the approximate average value of the data load of the score area is obtained. See Eq. (4), which is used as the threshold of the partition to adjust the load in each partition the amount. Then partition and allocate the data, which can be divided into three situations: One is to get the Key load equal to the average value, then directly allocate it to the partition bucket no.0, and record this Key and the

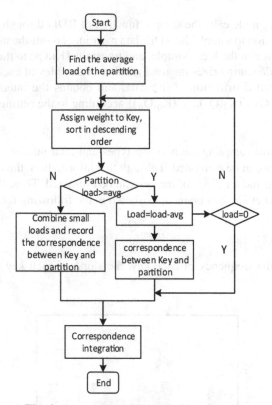

Fig. 4. Improved partition algorithm flowchart

corresponding partition number. The second is to split it if the key load is greater than the average value. The second is to split it if the key load is greater than the average value. Use the total load to subtract the average value to split, put the average part into the corresponding partition, record the Key and the corresponding partition number, and put the remaining part of the data back into the queue. Re-sort the Key through the half-and-half insertion algorithm, and then judge the load of the Key. If the remaining part is still greater than the average value, continue to split it until all are placed in the corresponding partition; The third type is that if the Key is a small load, it is directly allocated to the N-th partition, the Key and the corresponding partition bucket number are recorded, and the remaining capacity of the partition is modified. The flow chart of the partition algorithm is shown in Fig. 4.

4 Experimental Verification and Result Analysis

4.1 Experimental Configuration and Test Data Information

This paper verifies the proposed optimized data balancing partitioning algorithm in the Spark cluster environment through load balancing and task execution time. The Spark

Table 1. Software version information

Software	Version
Centos	6.5
JDK	1.8
Hadoop	2.7.7
Spark	2.4.5
Scala	2.11.8

cluster used in this article has a total of 5 nodes, one is a master node, and the rest are slave nodes. Table 1 shows the software version information.

The experimental data set adopted the comment information of various products provided by SNAP(Standford Network Analysis Project), from which 0.5G, 1G, 1.5G and 2G were selected as the experimental data set and 3 data sets with inclination a of 0.2,0.6,1 were generated through Zipf distribution. The size of each text was 1.5G. The partition method proposed in this paper was verified through Word Count experiment.

4.2 Experimental Results and Analysis

Since this paper involves sampling, it is necessary to determine the sampling rate first. This article selects four sampling rates of 10%, 15%, 20%, and 25% for experiments to select an appropriate sampling rate. Using Zipf distribution to generate three sets of 1.5G data sets with gradients of 0.2, 0.6 and 1, respectively, the execution time of the four cases of sampling rates of 10%, 15%, 20% and 25%. As shown in Fig. 5.

It can be seen from Fig. 5 that under the same data volume and the same inclination, the execution time is less when the sampling rate is 10% and 15%; Under the same data volume and different inclination, the sampling rate is relatively stable at 15%, and it can be concluded that the sampling rate at 15% has little effect on the subsequent data partitioning strategy. Therefore, this paper sets the sampling rate at 15% in the improved cluster sampling algorithm.

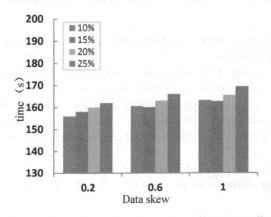

Fig. 5. Comparison of execution time under different sampling rates

The 0.5G, 1G, 1.5G, and 2G data volumes selected from the data set provided by SNAP are used to verify the improved partitioning method proposed in this paper (CSGA, Cluster sampling greedy algorithm) in the two dimensions of partition load deviation and task execution time Whether the effect is better, and compared with the two partition strategies in the system and the SCID partition strategy [9], the experimental results are shown in Fig. 6 and Fig. 7.

It can be seen from Fig. 6 that when the amount of data is small, the optimized partitioning strategy (CSGA) is not much different from the two partitioning strategies and SCID partitioning strategies in the system. With the gradual increase in the amount of data, the load deviation of the four partitioning strategies is gradually increasing. However, the SCID partition strategy and the CSGA partition strategy are rising slowly. When the amount of data exceeds 1.5, SGAP shows an advantage over the other three algorithms.

The execution time of the task is also an important evaluation index to measure the quality of the partition strategy. It can be seen from Fig. 7 that the improved partition algorithm can effectively balance the load of each partition, thus shortening the completion time of the task.

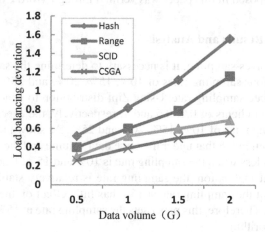

Fig. 6. Comparison chart of load deviation under changing data volume

To verify the same amount of data on different data sets inclination, the experimental results shown in Fig. 8 and Fig. 9.

It can be seen from Fig. 8 that when the data slope is 0.2, the load deviation of the four algorithms has a small difference. When the slope reaches 0.6, the load deviation of the Hash partition increases, but the SCID partition strategy and strategy of CSGA partition load deviation degree of the increase is not big, When the slope reaches 1.0, the CSGA partition strategy has achieved good results, making the load balance a good relief.

It can be seen from Fig. 9 that in the case of different data slopes, the improved partitioning algorithm balances the partition load, thereby shortening the task execution time.

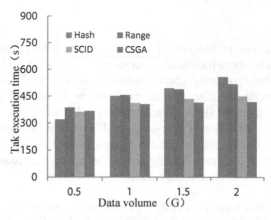

Fig. 7. Comparison chart of task execution time under changing data volume

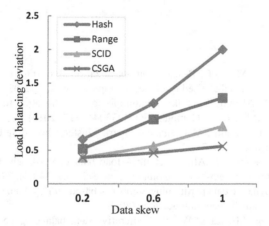

Fig. 8. Comparison chart of load deviation under changing data skew

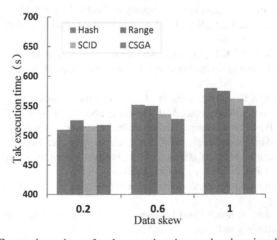

Fig. 9. Comparison chart of task execution time under changing data skew

5 Conclusion

By studying the data skew problem caused by the two partitioning algorithms in Spark, this paper proposes a balanced partitioning method based on the parallel cluster sampling greedy algorithm. The algorithm proposed in this paper is verified under different data sizes and different inclination data. The results show that this method effectively solves the problem of data partition skew, reduces the overall running time of the task, and improves the resource utilization. The research in this paper is carried out under homogeneous cluster, which is not comprehensive enough. In the next step, we will optimize the partition strategy in the Spark Shuffle process in a heterogeneous environment to make the data partition allocation more balanced and efficient.

Acknowledgements. This paper is partially supported by the Social Science Foundation of Hebei Province (No. HB19JL007), and the Education technology Foundation of the Ministry of Education (No. 2017A01020).

References

1. Hu, Y.H., Sheng, X., Mao, J.F.: Research on optimization algorithm for task scheduling in spark environment with unbalanced resources. Comput. Eng. Sci. **42**(02), 203–209 (2020)
2. Liu, Z., Zhang, Q., Ahemd, R., et al.: Dynamic Resource Allocation for MapReduce with Partitioning Skew. IEEE Trans. Comput. **65**(11), 3304–3317 (2016)
3. Xia, Y.C.: Research on Shuffle Mechanism of Spark Cluster. Chongqing University of Posts and Telecommunications (2017)
4. Zaman, S.K.U., Maqsood, T., Ali, M., et al.: A load balanced task scheduling heuristic for large-scale computing systems. Int. J. Comput. Syst. Sci. Eng. **34**(02), 79–90 (2019)
5. Yan, Y.F.: Spark dynamic data partitioning algorithm based on Key-Value tilt model. Beijing University of Posts and Telecommunications (2019)
6. Zhang, Y.M., Jiang, J.B., Lu, J.W., et al.: Iterative data balancing partition strategy for MapReduce. Chinese J. Comput. **42**(08), 1873–1885 (2019)
7. Jiang, J.B.: Research on MapReduce-oriented Intermediate Data Partitioning Strategy and Transmission Optimization. Zhejiang University of Technology (2019)
8. Zhang, Z.F., Wang, W.L., Geng, S.S., Jia, Z.T.: Research on spark data skew problem. J. Hebei Acad. Sci. **37**(01), 1–7 (2020)
9. Tang, Z., Zhang, X.S., Li, K.L., Li, K.Q.: An intermediate data placement algorithm for load balancing in Spark computing environment. Future Gen. Comput. Systems **78**(01), 287–301 (2016)
10. Wang, S.Z., Geng, S.S., Zhang, Z.F., et al.: A dynamic memory allocation optimization mechanism based on spark. Comput. Mat. Continua **58**(02), 739–757 (2019)
11. Vengadeswaran, B.: Core–an optimal data placement strategy in hadoop for data intentive applications based on cohesion relation. Int. J. Comput. Syst. Sci. Eng. **34**(01), 47–60 (2019)
12. Huang, C.J.: Research on Data Balanced Distribution Algorithm in Spark. University of Electronic Science and Technology of China (2018)
13. Li, Q.Q.: Research on Spark task division and scheduling strategy for load balancing. Hunan University (2017)
14. Zhang, Li.: Research on Spark Load Balancing and Equivalent Join Optimization of Large Tables. Hebei University of Economics and Business (2019)

15. Xia, Z., Lu, L., Qin, T., et al.: A privacy-preserving image retrieval based on ac-coefficients and color histograms in cloud environment. Comput. Mat. Continua **58**(01), 27–44 (2019)
16. Yang, Y., Zhao, Q., Ruan, L., et al.: Oversampling methods combined clustering and data cleaning for imbalanced network data. Intell. Autom. Soft Comput. **26**(05), 1139–1155 (2020)

Research and Implementation of Dimension Reduction Algorithm in Big Data Analysis

Si Yuan He, Shan Li, and Chao Guo(⊠)

Department of Electronics and Communication Engineering,
Beijing Electronic Science and Technology Institute, Beijing 100070, P. R. China

Abstract. With the rapid development of computer and Internet technologies, these data are usually high-dimensional, and the huge amount of data information puts a burden on our calculation and information acquisition. Especially in the fields of data analysis and prediction, it is about that for us to obtain the target data efficiently. Big data analysis is a technique for quickly and efficiently extracting information from multiple types of data. The dimensionality reduction algorithm is an important part of it, which can help us quickly extract valuable parts from a huge amount of data and improve the efficiency of calculation. The core idea of the dimensionality reduction algorithm is to use a mapping method to map the data points in the original dimensional space to the low-dimensional space. This article mainly uses dimensionality reduction algorithms to deal with air quality data sets concept of data classification is introduced into the dimensionality reduction algorithm, which improves the accuracy of data dimensionality reduction. On this basis, a logistic regression algorithm is added, boulevard improving the effect of data visualization.

Keywords: Big data analysis · Dimensionality reduction · Air quality · Classification

1 Introduction

In recent years, with the rapid development of the Internet, people are confronted with the impact of a large amount of data and information on the Internet every day, and the concept of big data comes with it. Due to digitization, a huge volume of data is being generated across several sectors such as healthcare, production, sales, IoT devices, Web, organizations [1]. The industrial Internet of Things is the trend in factories, and it will also generate a lot of data [2]. IoT-generated data are differentiated as user-private data preserved locally in IoT devices, edge-private data isolated on the edge and public data uploaded to the cloud [3]. Air quality prediction is an important part of environmental governance, so it is of great significance to mining effective information from a large number of air pollution data [4]. Big data can be summarized into five V's, including volume, velocity, variety, value, and veracity [5]. As the core of the current IT industry, big data, data analysis, data mining, data security, and other industries around data generation has also come into people's vision. With the advent of the era of big data,

X. Sun et al. (Eds.): ICAIS 2021, LNCS 12737, pp. 14–26, 2021.
https://doi.org/10.1007/978-3-030-78612-0_2

big data analysis arises at the historic moment. Big data analysis refers to the analysis of large-scale data, including five basic aspects: Analytic Visualizations (AV), Data Mining Algorithms (DMA), Predictive Analytic Capabilities (PAC), Semantic Engines (SE), Data Quality and Master Data Management (MSM).

Dimensionality reduction algorithm is an indispensable part of big data analysis [6]. In this connection, dimensionality reduction plays a vital role in reducing the high-dimensional data into reduced dimensionality [7]. Because most data sets have dimensions in the tens, hundreds, or even thousands. But in the real applications, the use of effective information does not need so high dimension, and an additional dimension, the required number of samples grown exponentially, which might be at work and in daily use of difficulties [8], such as computer processing data time is too long, the data processing efficiency is low, etc., so I need through the use of different dimension reduction algorithm for data dimension reduction.

Dimensionality reduction in machine learning refers to the mapping of data points in the original high-dimensional space to the low-dimensional space [9]. Machine learning is used for processing high-dimensional data, mining data content for data analysis [10]. The essence of dimension reduction is to learn a mapping function $f : x \rightarrow y$, where x is the expression of the original data point, using vector expression form Y is the low-dimensional vector expression after data point mapping, and the dimension of y is usually less than the dimension of x.

2 Preliminary

2.1 Principal Component Analysis Algorithm PCA

Principal Components Analysis (PCA) is one of the most widely used data dimension reduction algorithms so far. In [11], Feature selection performed with PCA as a pre-processing stage in machine training has proven to be very effective in improving computational time and accuracy. In [12], the authors integrate PCA and K-means algorithms to predict diabetes. Dimensionality reduction is the process of reducing data from high dimension to low dimension, revealing the low-dimension structure of data, and visualizing unknown high-dimension data, which plays an important role in overcoming the "dimensionality disaster" [13]. The essence of PCA is a mapping method based on high-dimensional space mapping to low-dimensional space, and it is the most widely used and most basic unsupervised dimensionality reduction algorithm. The core idea of PCA is to map the feature of a N dimension to the dimensional space $(k < n)$. This K-dimension space is not simply a reduced dimension, but a new feature dimension, which is a reconstructed dimensional feature. Therefore, PCA can be defined as the orthogonal projection of data in a low-dimensional linear space.

PCA is from the original space, according to the order to find a set of orthogonal coordinate axes, the selection of the new coordinate axis and the original data of the intimate relationship, one of the first axis is variance in the direction of the largest in the raw data, and so on, the purpose of PCA is to extract the most valuable information, in other words, to extract the maximum variance of data. Principal component analysis is often used to reduce the dimension of data and maintain the feature with the greatest difference contribution [14]. The main method is to do Eigen decomposition of the covariance matrix to obtain the eigenvalue and eigenvector of the data, which represent the principal component of the data set. This means that PCA can extract the vital part, the principal component, from the redundant features, and can improve the processing speed of data without losing the original data model.

Since the mean value after projection is 0, the total variance after projection is:

$$\frac{1}{m}\sum_{i=1}^{m}\left(x^{(i)T}w\right)^2 = \frac{1}{m}\sum_{i=1}^{m}w^T x^{(i)}x^{(i)T}w = \sum_{i=1}^{m}w^T\left(\frac{1}{m}x^{(i)}x^{(i)T}\right)w_1 \tag{1}$$

In formula (1) is the covariance matrix of the original data $\frac{1}{m}x^{(i)}x^{(i)T}$

$$\lambda = \frac{1}{m}\sum_{i=1}^{m}(x^{(i)T}w)^2 \tag{2}$$

$$\sum = \frac{1}{m}x^{(i)}x^{(i)T} \tag{3}$$

It can be seen from the formula that:

$$\lambda = w^T\sum w \tag{4}$$

Multiply both sides of the formula by w to the left, then:

$$\lambda w = \sum w \tag{5}$$

So, $w\sum w$ it's the eigenvectors that correspond to the eigenvalues of the matrix.

The aim is to maximize the total variance after the projection, so the optimal projection vector w is the eigenvector corresponding to the eigenvalue at the maximum. Therefore, the variance is maximized when w is set to be equal to the eigenvector with the maximum eigenvalue, which is called the first principal component.

Therefore, the data covariance matrix can be decomposed by eigenvalues, and the obtained eigenvalues can be sorted from large to small to obtain the eigenvectors corresponding to the previous eigenvalues, and a new projection can be formed to process the original data.

PCA takes data variance as the criterion to measure information: the greater the variance, the more information it can include, and the less information it can include. It can be seen that PCA does not involve some knowledge of space, but simply processes data. However, PCA is used to reduce the dimension of the data, sort the newly obtained eigenvalues, and use them according to individual needs. The first k important parts are extracted and the later unimportant dimensions are omitted, to achieve the purpose of reducing dimensions and retain the information of the original data to the maximum extent.

PCA is an unsupervised dimensionality reduction algorithm with no restrictions on labels or parameters. During the process of calculation, PCA will not be disturbed by other parameters set artificially. The final result is completely related to the data and independent of human beings. CA each principal component is orthogonal, which can eliminate the influence between each principal component. The most important thing is that the calculation is simple and easy to implement, so PCA is now the most widely used dimension reduction algorithm.

However, PCA also has some shortcomings, such as the expected effect, because it is not affected by human parameters. If there is a certain knowledge reserve on the characteristics of the data in advance, it cannot be calculated by the human intervention model, and the data processed by PCA may not reach the expected effect and the efficiency will not be too high.

The most essential feature of PCA is that it belongs to a linear dimensionality reduction algorithm. If the high-dimensional data is a nonlinear structure, PCA cannot effectively extract the principal components of the data, failing to obtain ideal processing results. Moreover, PCA may not be the optimal solution when dealing with non-Gaussian distribution data, because the variance at this time cannot represent the degree of dispersion.

2.2 Linear Discriminant Analysis Algorithm LDA

Linear Discriminant Analysis (LDA) is a dimensionality reduction algorithm widely used in Discriminant Analysis (Discriminant Analysis) [15]. The difference between LDA and PCA is that, in order to find the most effective classification direction for data, it takes into account the classification information of data in the process of dimension reduction. There is no better or worse, but each has its advantages.

The basic idea of LDA is to project high-dimensional data samples to the optimal vector space in order to extract classification information and reduce characteristic dimensions. LDA is an effective feature extraction technique, which can find the feature subspace of optimal classification, improve the computational efficiency and accuracy in big data analysis, and reduce the over-fitting caused by "dimensional disaster".

LDA is a supervised dimensionality reduction algorithm that is different from a PCA unsupervised algorithm while maintaining the information that distinguishes different categories while completing the projection of original data in high-dimensional space to low-dimensional space.

Like PCA, LDA belongs to the linear dimension reduction algorithm, but LDA is supervised, so LDA mainly takes category as the main factor of dimension reduction. It makes the projected data samples as separable as possible. By creating a projected plane in the K-dimensional space, the projected distance of different categories of data in the plane is as close as possible, and the distance between projections of different categories is as far as possible, so as to achieve the classification of the original data. Take two-dimensional space ($k = 2$) as an example, when processing new original data samples, project them onto the same straight line, and then determine the new classification according to the location of projection points.

In Fig. 1, Y represents the direction of projection, " $+$ " and " $-$ " respectively represent the original data samples of two different categories, the dashed line represents the projection of the original samples on the new vector, and the two red solid circles represent the center points of the two categories on the projection direction respectively.

Suppose the existing D-dimensional space (D is the number of features), is the mean of all samples, m_i is the sample mean of the class, S_w is the intra-class divergence matrix, S_B is the inter-class divergence matrix.

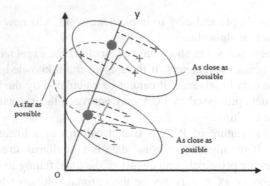

Fig. 1. LDA schematic diagram

Firstly, the mean value of samples in the category stored by mean vectors is calculated, and then:

$$m_i = \frac{1}{n_i} \sum_{x \in D_i}^{c} x_m \tag{6}$$

After the mean vectors of each class are calculated, the divergence matrix of each class is calculated by adding the divergence matrix of each class:

$$S_i = \sum_{x \in D_i}^{c} (x - m_i)(x - m_i)^T \tag{7}$$

$$S_W = \sum_{i=1}^{c} S_i \tag{8}$$

Calculate the divergence matrix between classes, where the global is mean, and use all samples in all categories in the calculation.

$$S_B = \sum_{i=1}^{c} N_i(m - m_i)(m - m_i)^T \tag{9}$$

Finally, the generalized eigenvalues of the matrix are solved $S_W^{-1} S_B$. The previous eigenvalues and their corresponding eigenvectors are obtained to obtain the projected matrix, and then the projection of the original data sample in the new low-dimensional space is calculated to output the new data sample set k.

In the process of data dimension reduction, LDA fully considers the key information of different categories of data compared with PCA, so the sample set of low-dimensional spatial data obtained is easier to distinguish and retains the distinction of the original sample. In addition, as a supervised dimensionality reduction algorithm, LDA measures the different data sample sets by labels or categories. Compared with the unsupervised dimensionality reduction algorithm, LDA has a clearer purpose of dimensionality reduction, and the data after dimensionality reduction can better reflect the differences and similarities between data samples.

However, LDA also has some shortcomings. It belongs to the same linear dimensionality reduction algorithm as PCA, which is unable to perform effective dimensionality reduction for data with nonlinear structure and also has unsatisfactory effects for data samples with the non-Gaussian distribution. And, everything has two sides, the advantages of a relative to other algorithms, it is also possible for the processing of data sets in trouble, the LDA proud classification processing, the data sample classification depends on the average, still need the artificial control of dimensions and data, the calculation and processing data, the trouble, and the mean and variance, the variance can retain the original data information, so the LDA in handling some data may not be the effect of PCA to dimension reduction.

3 Research and Implementation of the Dimension Reduction Algorithm

3.1 PCA Algorithm Flow and Implementation

In the implementation of the dimension reduction algorithm, the Iris data set is used in the initial research. It is a classic data set, which was organized by Fisher in 1936 and is often used as an example in the fields of statistics and machine learning. The dataset consists of three types of 150 records, each with 50 data. Each record has four characteristics: calyx length, calyx width, petal length, and petal width. The units of these four attributes are centimeters. According to the above four attributes, it can be predicted which category of iris belongs to mountain iris, variegated iris, and Virginia iris. In the algorithm implementations described in this chapter, Iris data sets are used.

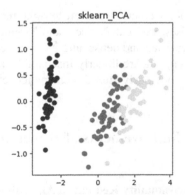

Fig. 2. PCA dimensionality reduction renderings (Color figure online)

Call Sklearn. Decomposition function to directly process the Iris data set. Finally, data visualization is carried out. PCA dimensionality reduction renderings are shown in Fig. 2. As shown in Fig. 2, the abscissa represents the first principal component and the ordinate represents the second principal component. Three colors, from left to right, represent the three different varieties of irises: mountain irises, variegated irises, and Virginia irises. It can be seen that because the two irises are linearly inseparable, the coincidence of data sample points of these two irises after dimension reduction is more obvious than that of the other one.

3.2 LDA Algorithm Flow and Implementation

The goal of LDA is to ensure that the post-projection data samples have the maximum inter-class distance and the minimum inter-class distance in the new low-dimensional space, in other words, the best separability in this space.

Call Sklearn. Decomposition function to directly process the Iris data set. Finally, data visualization is carried out. The LDA dimension reduction effect is shown in Fig. 3.

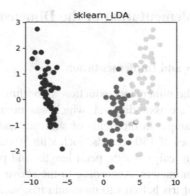

Fig. 3. LDA dimension reduction renderings (Color figure online)

As shown in Fig. 3, the three colors, from left to right, represent the three different types of irises: mountain irises, variegated irises, and Virginia irises. Light green and yellow data points are concentrated and dense, and it can be seen that because the irises of variegated and Irises of Virginia are linearly inseparable, the data sample points of these two irises overlap more obviously after dimension reduction than that of the other type.

4 Shortcomings and Improvements of Dimensionality Reduction Algorithm

4.1 Shortcomings of Dimensionality Reduction Algorithm in Data Processing

In the implementation of the dimensionality reduction algorithm, the classical data set, the Iris data set, is first used.

In the study, this paper uses all the data related to air quality in Tianjin from January to April 2020. The quality grades are divided into five categories, namely: excellent, good, light pollution, moderate pollution, and heavy pollution. The indices used to measure air quality are PM2.5, PM10, SO2, CO, NO2, and O3_8h. These data are frequently used in the research and improvement of the dimension reduction algorithm below.

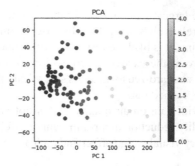

Fig. 4. PCA dimensionality reduction renderings

After applying the PCA dimensionality reduction algorithm to the air quality data set, the processing effect is shown in Fig. 4.

In the implementation of the algorithm, excellent, good, light pollution, moderate pollution and heavy pollution are successively defined as 0, 1, 2, 3 and 4.

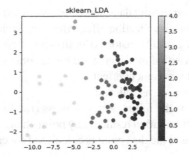

Fig. 5. LDA dimension reduction renderings

As shown in Fig. 4 and Fig. 5, the data sample points cannot be effectively classified after dimension reduction. The data points of different quality grades are concentrated, especially the three grades of excellent, good and mild pollution, and the coincidence phenomenon is serious, and the classification discrimination is very unclear.

After spending a lot of time observing the air quality data set and studying the dimensionality reduction algorithm, it is found that the data set has a great influence on the effect of dimensionality reduction. The different quality levels in the Air Quality data set are divided by Air Quality Index (AQI). Because in the relevant air quality data set, the proportion of days with a quality rating of excellent, good and mild pollution is far higher than the mean value, and there are more critical values in the data set. For example, AQI is 50, 51, 100, 101, etc. Therefore, in the visualization of data after data dimension reduction processing, the data sample points with the quality level of excellent, good and slight pollution will be relatively concentrated.

In the previous paper, in the implementation of the dimension reduction algorithm, if the value of a feature (a column of the matrix) in the data is particularly large, then it will account for a large proportion of the overall error calculation. The entire projection will try to approximate the largest feature, namely the first principal component while ignoring the feature with a relatively small value. Because the importance of each feature is not known before modeling, it is likely to result in a large amount of information loss. Therefore, in order to prevent the excessive acquisition of some features with large values, each feature is first standardized to make its size within the same range, and then dimensionality reduction is carried out.

But when combined with data on air quality, that's not all. Due to different data sets, the basic dimensionality reduction algorithm cannot effectively process the data, resulting in an unsatisfactory visualization effect and data accuracy after dimensionality reduction.

In view of the above problems, combining with relevant data, two improvement directions are proposed:

Step 1: Process data sets, reclassify them and improve accuracy.

Step 2: Set the training set and test set, and use the regression method to process the training set and test set, and divide the regions for the data to improve the visual effect.

4.2　Improvement Direction of Dimension Reduction Algorithm

Due to the concentration of air quality data, some data are relatively concentrated, resulting in low accuracy and poor visualization effect after dimension reduction. A new idea is proposed: at the beginning of dimension reduction and before standardizing the data set, the data should be reclassified to disperse the more concentrated part of the data, so as to achieve an effective improvement effect.

The implementation steps are as follows:

Step 1: Create k points as the initial center of mass (randomly selected).

Step 2: When the class distribution result of any point changes, the Euclidean distance between the center of mass and the data point is calculated for each point and each center of mass of the data set.

Step 3: Assign data points to the closest class.

Step 4: For each class, calculate the mean value of all points in the class and take its mean value as the new center of mass until the class no longer changes or reaches the maximum number of iterations.

On this basis, the quality levels of the original data set are classified into three categories: excellent, good, light pollution, moderate pollution and heavy pollution. The above problem is solved by dividing the more concentrated data into one category and dividing the data points that are originally estranged into different categories.

Logistic Regression (LR) is a classification model in traditional machine learning. Logistic Regression algorithm is widely applied due to its simple and efficient characteristics.

The implementation steps are as follows:

Step 1: Set the mark and color of data sample points, and draw the background color of the image.

Step 2: Use sample points to create a mesh grid. The mesh grid is the grid data needed to generate images and has a wide range of applications in graphics rendering.

Step 3: Use logistic regression combined with the mesh grid created in step 2 to predict the classification results.

Step 4: Draw the contour line of the predicted results and draw the overall image.

While improving the data visualization effect, logistic regression can also be used to process the training set and data set and calculate the accuracy rate of the dimensionality reduction algorithm.

5   Simulation and Analysis of Dimension Reduction Algorithm

In this paper, two simulation tools, Visual Studio Code and Jupyter Notebook were used to study and implement the algorithm, and the effect of the improved algorithm and the basic algorithm were compared.

The computer programming language Python, a cross-platform computer programming language, is mainly used in the development of the Web and Internet, scientific computing and statistics, artificial intelligence, and other fields. Python is easy to learn, fast, and open source for free. Python has a library of functions related to machine learning, which makes it easier and faster to study dimensionality reduction algorithms. Iris data set and air quality data set were selected for simulation.

In the above introduction of the PCA dimensionality reduction algorithm, it can be seen that the eigenvectors corresponding to the first two eigenvalues are taken to conduct dimensionality reduction processing on the data. As can be seen above, the data set has 6 features. To select different features as the main components, the proportion of features should be calculated (Fig. 6).

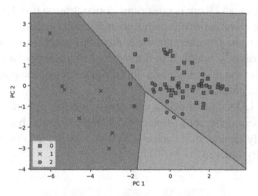

Fig. 6. PCA improvement renderings

In the rendering, the original single sample point is improved and various types of graphics are used. Among them, 0, 1, 2, 3, and 4 respectively represent different quality levels, excellent, good, light pollution, moderate pollution, and heavy pollution. After the improvement, the effect of data visualization is better. There is no serious problem of concentration of sample points of different categories, and no coincidence of data sample points of different categories is found. In the improved renderings, 0, 1, and 2 are redefined as excellent, medium, and poor to represent air quality levels.

Finally, there is the comparison of accuracy. PCA dimensionality reduction algorithm is designed to reduce redundant errors and retain the original maximum information of the data. If the accuracy cannot be guaranteed after dimensionality reduction, it cannot be done. The comparison of the accuracy before and after the improvement is shown in Fig. 8. The accuracy of the first behavior before improvement and the second behavior after improvement is shown in Fig. 7. After the improvement, the PCA dimensionality reduction algorithm's accuracy reaches about 85%, proving the feasibility and effectiveness of the improvement.

```
Accuracy of LR Classifier:0.259259
Accuracy of LR Classifier:0.851852
```

Fig. 7. Comparison of accuracy before and after improvement

In the above introduction to the basic principle of the LDA dimensionality reduction algorithm, it can be seen that the main purpose of LDA is to ensure that the data samples after projection have the minimum inter-class distance and the maximum inter-class distance in the new low-dimensional space. Therefore, after the matrix eigenvalues are decomposed, the proportion of the eigenvalues is calculated respectively to obtain the "differentiation degree" of different categories.

In the improved renderings of PCA, 0, 1 and 2 are redefined as excellent, medium and poor to represent the air quality level. The comparison of the renderings before and after the LDA improvement is shown in Fig. 8. The improved renderings have a better data visualization effect, and there is no serious concentration problem of sample points of different categories, and no overlapping phenomenon of sample points of different categories is found. The improvement of the continuous optimization is the visualization based on logistic regression, which is to draw the background color of the image, draw the grid matrix, predict the maximum and minimum values of the data points, and draw the contour line of the predicted results.

After processing LDA data, the data visualization effect is better than that of PCA. LD1 and LD2 represent different features respectively, and the background green, red and blue are obviously separated. It can be seen that only the red dots have a small error, which can be basically ignored.

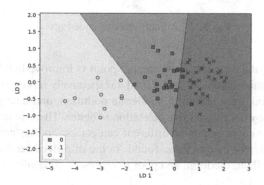

Fig. 8. LDA improvement renderings

6   Conclusion

In recent years, with the rapid development of computers and the Internet, dimensionality disaster, this once strange word, is gradually familiar to everyone. A dimensional disaster is usually a phenomenon in which the amount of computation involved in a problem increases exponentially as the number of dimensions increases. In modern hot IT fields, such as machine learning and data mining, the disaster of dimensionality hinders people's progress in research, so in order to overcome the disaster of dimensionality, data dimensionality reduction is created. Now, big data is a hot topic in today's era. In the near future, big data will also receive more and more attention and research.

The improvement direction proposed in this paper improves the accuracy of data dimension reduction, solves the problem of data set sample point concentration, and improves the effect of data visualization. However, there are still some shortcomings in the improvement and optimization of the dimensionality reduction algorithm. Because the center of mass is selected randomly, the classification effect is relatively random, which may not reach the expected effect. Moreover, this paper only conducts dimensionality reduction processing for the Iris data set and air quality data set. With the continuous development of society, data will be presented in different ways and in different forms to all people. The research on data dimension reduction algorithm is far from over, so we cannot stop the pace of further exploration.

Funding Statement.   This work is supported by Higher Education Department of the Ministry of Education Industry-university Cooperative Education Project.

References

1. Thippa, R.G., Praveen, K.R.M., Lakshmanna, K., et al.: Analysis of dimensionality reduction techniques on Big Data. IEEE Access **8**, 54776–54788 (2020)
2. Hui, H., Zhou, C., Xu, S., Lin, F.: A novel secure data transmission scheme in industrial internet of things. China Commun. **17**(1), 73–88 (2020)
3. Gong, C., Lin, F., Gong, X., Lu, Y.: Intelligent cooperative edge computing in Internet of Things. IEEE Internet Things J. **7**(10), 9372–9382 (2020)
4. Chen, G., Zhu, M., Ji, Y., Yu, Z., Yang, J., et al.: Air quality prediction based on Kohonen clustering and relief feature selection. Comput. Mater. Continua **64**(2), 1039–1049 (2020)
5. Mcafee, A., Brynjolfsson, E.: Big data: the management revolution. Harv. Bus. Rev. **90**(10), 60–66 (2012)
6. Dai, Y.X., Lu, D.D.: Multidimensional data dimension reduction method. Electron. Technol. Softw. Eng. **17**, 170–171 (2019)
7. Maaten, L.V.D., Postam, E., Herik, J.V.D.: Dimensionality reduction: a comparative review. Rev. Lit. Arts Am. **10**(1), (2019)
8. Zhao, G.R.: Research on key technologies of high-dimensional data dimensionality reduction processing. Comput. Knowl. Technol. **10**(08), 1835–1837 (2014)
9. Liu, J.H.: Research on deep model construction method for dimensionality reduction and classification of high-dimensional data. Chongqing University (2016)
10. Zhang, B., Li, W., Wang, S.W., Chen, W.: MII: a novel text classification model combining deep active learning with bert. Comput. Mater. Continua **63**(3), 1499–1514 (2020)

11. Zhang, Y., Zhao, Z.: Fetal state assessment based on cardiotocography parameters using PCA and AdaBoost. In: 10th International Congress on Image and Signal Processing, BioMedical Engineering and Informatics IEEE (2017)

12. Zhu, C., Idemudia, C.U., Feng, W.: Improved logistic regression model for diabetes prediction by integrating PCA and K-means techniques. Inf. Med. Unlocked. **17**, 100179 (2019)

13. Liu, J., Zhao, F.Y.: Dimensioning reduction technology and research progress of high-dimensional data. Electron. Sci. Technol. **31**(03), 36–38+43 (2018)

14. Peter, W., Marie, P.K., Haik, K., et al.: Feature selection and dimension reduction of social autism data. PubMed **25**, 707–718 (2020)

15. Weng, J., Young, D.S.: Some dimension reduction strategies for the analysis of survey data. J. Big Data **4**(1), 43 (2017)

Exploring the Informationization of Land Reserve Archives Management

YuXian Zhu[✉]

Tengzhou Land Reserve Center of Shandong Province, Zaozhuang, China

Abstract. Land Reserve is an innovation of land system reform in China, which plays an important role in promoting urban construction and economic development. The archives, as the historical records of the circulation of the Land tenure, have become an important part of the land reserve work and play an irreplaceable role in verifying it. It is a basic work in the whole land reserve undertaking, and also an important part of the National Archives System. Because the function of the Land Reserve Archives cannot be ignored, the corresponding archives management work needs to be raised to a new height. But in the actual work, there are many problems such as lack and lag, and the rapid development of information technology will also have a great impact on the traditional land reserve file management. The Land Reserve Archives Management Department has to take into account the present situation of its own archives management and actively explore corresponding strategies to meet the various challenges brought about by the information age in the light of the problems existing in the present reserve archives management work, only then can the information technology become the powerful power which promotes the file management to upgrade, promotes the land reserve work quickly and efficiently, realizes the land reserve file management informationization.

Keywords: Land reserve · File management · Information

1 Introduce

Since the implementation of the Land Reserve System, the land from the collection and storage to the reserve and then to the supply are carried out step by step, in these processes, produce a large number of preservation value of words, charts, drawings and other land reserve files. These traditional archives are based on paper materials, management is more difficult, not only need a lot of storage space, control temperature and humidity, but also consume a lot of manpower and material resources. At the same time find difficult, inefficient, to a certain extent affected the quality of work. Today, with the rapid development of information technology, the wide application of information technology has effectively broken down the drawbacks of the traditional file management work, and classified storage, management and sharing of files are carried out according to the needs

© Springer Nature Switzerland AG 2021
X. Sun et al. (Eds.): ICAIS 2021, LNCS 12737, pp. 27–40, 2021.
https://doi.org/10.1007/978-3-030-78612-0_3

of work, to a certain extent, the efficiency of file utilization has been improved. More in line with the needs of file management, file managers through the use of information technology to build a sound file management system, in the process of file collection and archiving, the realization of useful information retrieval, and encryption of important files. In the process of file inquiry, by setting the corresponding authority to facilitate users who meet the authority to consult the land reserve files, the file manager can also check the files regularly through the management system and know the situation of borrowing and returning the files, it can basically realize the informationization of land reserve file management.

2 The Importance of Information Management of Land Reserve Archives

The Land Reserve files are the primary source accumulated by the Land Reserve Center while undertaking a great deal of business work. They cover various policies, plans, drawings, agreements, contracts, etc. of the Land Reserve, it is an important achievement and wealth of land reserve management, and a powerful testimony of the regulation and control of the land market by the government, the improvement of land use efficiency and the standardization of the land market. It has important preservation value and can provide the land information basis for the work of land, planning, construction and other departments. Due to the decentralized nature of the land reserve work, the lack of effective links in the links of land acquisition, reserve and transfer, problems such as unclear sources of power, difficulty in linking up and difficulties in sorting out the archives have emerged, in particular, it is difficult to manage the drawings, because the drawings of the same plot in different coordinate systems will be biased, which requires the recording of important coordinate information of the drawings, because there are more plots, most of the traditional file management is simple manual management, which will undoubtedly increase the workload of file managers and reduce work efficiency. After the transfer of the archives, if the archivists only file the archives, they lack the understanding of the plot information and the awareness of the utilization and development of the archive resources, which underestimates the value of the archives to the management of the land reserves. Result in land archives in the long-term low-efficiency, low value-added use of the reserve. Cannot meet the present stage of Land Reserve Management Needs. Therefore, it is imperative to carry out the informationization of land collection and storage archives management. Once the management of Land Reserve files is informationalized, it will help to improve the management level of the files, better realize the value of the files, and also track the whole process of land reserve work, so as to improve the connection of various working links, to ensure the development of land reserve business and promote the development of land reserve information.

3 The Current Situation of Land Reserve File Management Informatization

3.1 The Importance Attached to the Information Management of the Reserve Archives Is Not Enough to Be Influenced

Influenced by the traditional archives management system, most people have a prejudice to the archives management, and think that the archives are only the work decoration of the unit. At present, the archives work is often hanging on the lips of leaders, posted on the wall, written on the unit summary, long-term in a dispensable embarrassing situation. It's only important when it's needed. The reluctance of many staff members to engage in archival work has resulted in a chronic shortage of professional personnel in archival management, let alone those who understand information technology. If the leaders do not pay enough attention to it, it will inevitably lead to the existing file management staff work enthusiasm is not high, low efficiency, the actual work process may appear the file disorderly, damaged, lost and so on. Not a good protection and use of the value of the file, file management there are many mistakes, cannot keep up with the pace of information development.

3.2 The Lack of Professional Personnel File Management Information

The file management itself is a very trivial, boring and professional work. At the same time, the nature and characteristics of the land reserve work require high quality of the file managers, in addition to having good professional qualities in the management of Land Reserve Archives, it is also necessary to have a good command of Basic Archives Management Knowledge, business knowledge of Land Reserve and professional qualities with high information technology processing ability, to adapt to the information requirements of file management. At present, most of the county and city land reserve file managers are still stuck in the traditional working mode of paper storage and have too little knowledge of the application of modern information technology, lack of Information System Planning, program design and database construction and management skills, it is difficult to truly achieve the construction of archives information.

3.3 The Information Level of File Management Is Not High

At present, the files of the land reserve departments of most counties and cities are still in paper state, manual retrieval is the main operation, search is difficult, time-consuming, low efficiency, archives to the archives of an idle. The information-based management of land archives is equal to the simple introduction of hardware equipment, and the lack of analysis of the value of archives and a complete and standard archives management system leads to the failure of land archives management to keep pace with the development of the Times, can Not satisfy the file management staff's basic operation, the file management informationization will become the land reserve file management the inevitable trend of development.

3.4 The Problem of Information Security in Archives Management Needs to Be Considered

To improve the level of archives management by using modern information technology. First, the construction of archives information processing to the original archives, some long-term paper files if not handled well, may cause damage; Third, the backup of the file management system cannot be ignored in case of the loss of files in the event of a computer or network failure. Fourth, network security is very important for the protection of information resources. Once there is a lack of protection, it is attacked by malicious software, the loss of archival information will be incalculable.

3.5 The Laws and Regulations Concerning the Management of Land Reserve Archives Are Not Perfect

With the increasing awareness of human rights protection and the implementation of government information disclosure regulations, there is an increasing demand for "land information disclosure", but this will also involve changes in the scope of archives disclosure, the objects of access, the ways of utilization, etc., how public? To whom? These problems have been perplexing the thinking of Land Reserve workers, and the laws and regulations of land reserve archives need to come out.

4 The Countermeasures of Improving the Informatization Level of Land Reserve Archives Management

4.1 Improve the Consciousness of Land Reserve Archives Management

Because the file management basically belongs to "behind the scenes work", therefore, in the actual management, the existence neglects the land reserve file value the phenomenon. In view of this problem, first of all, we should change our ideas and concepts, starting from the present situation of Land Reserve, and in view of the problems existing in the management of archives, we should realize that with the help of information technology, we can improve the efficiency of the management of Land Reserve archives, in order to speed up the construction of land reserve file information platform. Secondly, the establishment of a Special Land Reserve Archives Work Leading Group. To clarify the duties and responsibilities of Land Reserve archives work, and formulate the collection and filing standards of archives. Do a good job in the land right source and transfer the effective link, to ensure that the archives in line with the status of land reserves. Thirdly, we should strengthen the management of land reserve files. It is necessary to configure the necessary hardware facilities such as computer, scanner and dense cabinet for the management of the land reserve archives, especially to develop the professional archives information management software, which provides a good foundation for the construction of the archives information.

4.2 To Improve the Quality Level of File Management Personnel

File management is a very complex and highly professional work, which needs people's care, patience and peace of mind, information-based development trend, it puts forward higher request to the file management personnel's quality. This requires the archivists not only to establish a correct file management thinking, according to the characteristics of land reserve work to formulate a set of standardized file management system. Also, must have a strong learning ability, skilled in the land reserve business, but also need to have computer software development and information technology application learning ability. Through the skilled operation of computer software, file information analysis and classified summary, improve the level of file information management.

4.3 Improving the Basic Business of Reserve Archives

The development of the informationization of Land Reserve Archives Management should do a solid job in basic business construction, according to the development of land reserve various businesses, do a good job in collecting, arranging, classifying, summarizing and filing entity archives in a timely manner, to ensure the accuracy, integrity, timeliness and security of the first-hand source data. On this basis, we should make a good transition from physical archives to the information-based management of archives. In this process, we should accurately extract the information elements of each file, classify them according to land expropriation, land reserve and land supply, and form a system, at the same time, a practical retrieval method is worked out to facilitate the accurate inquiry of land reserve information and better serve the development of land reserve business. Finally, deal with the transfer of archives management and loan relationship, grasp the dynamics of archives, to ensure the safety of archives.

4.4 Improving the Construction Information of the Land

Information System has entered the lives of millions of households and ordinary citizens. The archives information management needs to keep pace with the times and keep up with the Times. The construction of Information System should run through the whole process of land reserve file management. Through the development of functional integration of the file management system, a variety of functional modules in a software, to achieve the file information management. Then, a user-oriented service platform is established to search the needed land information through professional archives retrieval.

According to the reality of Land Reserve, the file management system mainly includes three main functional modules: Land Storage, land reserve and land transfer, user management and administrator management. According to the land source, the collection and storage system is divided into several sub-modules, such as enterprise bankruptcy, court seal-up, land acquisition, urban relocation, etc. The reserve system collects, analyzes and arranges the information of the reserve plots, and generates the reasonable land reserve plan, which provides the reference for the land transfer. Transfer system can reflect the transaction of land block data. Three functional modules, through the establishment of separate database, to achieve accurate and rapid retrieval of land information.

5   Land Reserve File Management System

5.1   Development Background

With the gradual improvement of the Land Reserve System, the number of land reserve files has been increasing, and the contents involved have also been increasing. The traditional manual management file model has exposed some problems, such as finding the land ownership of a plot of land, if it involves a large time span or a change of land title, it is very difficult to locate. In order to improve the working efficiency of the land reserve file managers and realize the informationization of the land reserve file management, a land reserve file management system is developed.

5.2   Demand Analysis

Through the management of Land Reserve archives by computer, the informationization of Land Reserve Archives Management is realized, which not only injects new vitality into the archive management, and in the process of file management can save a lot of manpower, material resources, financial resources and time, improve the efficiency of file management, but also for the land reserve work toward information development to provide a good support. Combined with the current status of land reserve file management, the system has the following functions:

- The requirement function is comprehensive, operation is simple.
- The management of basic information is required.
- Requires the management of all query file users.
- It is required to achieve the collection of land, land reserve, land transfer classified summary.
- The fast land information retrieval function is required to ensure the flexibility of data query.
- The request realizes the synthesis condition inquiry, like by the time inquiry, by the place number inquiry and so on.
- The archivist who requests the records to be handed over, borrowed or returned for each job.
- The request realizes to the case hand over, to borrow, the return process entire process data information tracking.
- The function of reminder is required to enable the manager to know the information of the file which arrived the date of return in time.
- The request provides the flexible, the convenient permission setting function.
- The system is required to be easy to maintain and operate.

5.3   System Design

System Objective. Based on the above needs analysis and the understanding of the status of the Land Reserve Archives, the Land Reserve Archives Management System should achieve the following objectives:

- The system is fully functional and easy to operate.
- Realize the management of land basic information.
- Manage all query file users.
- To achieve the collection of land, land reserve, land transfer classified summary.
- To realize the function of quick land information retrieval.
- To Achieve Comprehensive Condition Query, such as query by time, query by land number, etc.
- An archivist who keeps records of every work done at the time of transfer, loan, or return.
- To achieve the transfer of the case, lending, return the process of the entire data information tracking.
- Realize the reminder function of the overdue return of files.
- The implementation of the operator to set different operation rights and modify the rights to set functions.
- The system is stable, safe and reliable.

System Functional Structure. According to the characteristics of Land Reserve file management system, it can be divided into 5 parts: User Management, Administrator Management, land storage, land reserve, land transfer, etc. The functional module structure of each part is shown in the following Fig. 1.

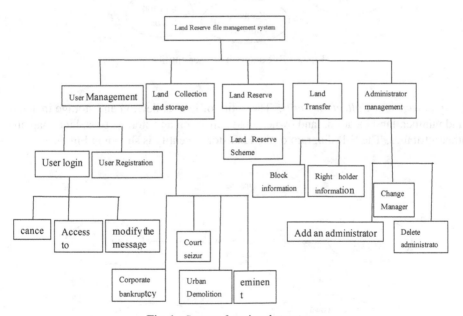

Fig. 1. System functional structure

5.4   Database Design

Conceptual Design of Database. According to the requirement analysis and the functional module diagram of the system, the database entities used in the system are planned as user entities, land storage entities, land reserve entities, land transfer entities and administrator entities. Considering the problem of cost and management requirement, we can use E-R graph to represent the conceptual model. Finally, E-R graph is transformed into database.

User Entity. User entities include attributes such as name, address, ID card number, contact number, registration date, query content, and so on. The E-R diagram of the user entity is shown in Fig. 2.

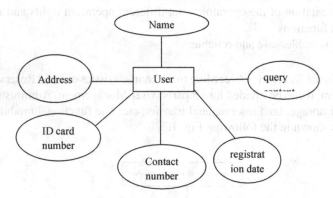

Fig. 2. E-R diagram of user entities

Land Storage and Collection Entity. The entity of land collection and storage includes land number, land location, land owner, land collection and storage type, land map and other attributes. The E-R diagram of the land storage entity is shown in Fig. 3.

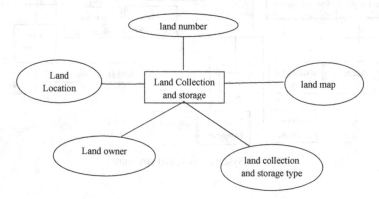

Fig. 3. E-R Map of land storage entity

Land Reserve Entity. The Land Reserve entity includes the attribute of land number, land location, land map, reserve plan and so on. The E-R map of the Land Reserve entity is shown in Fig. 4.

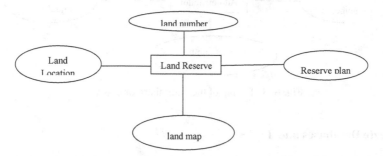

Fig. 4. E-R Map of the land reserve entity

Land Transfer Entity. The land transfer entity includes land number, land location, land map, assignee and other attributes. The E-R map of the Land Reserve entity is shown in Fig. 5.

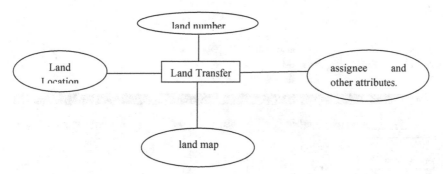

Fig. 5. E-R Map of the land transfer entity

Administrator Entity. The administrator entity includes attributes such as name, ID card number, contact number, and permission to modify. The E-R Diagram of the administrator entity is shown in Fig. 6.

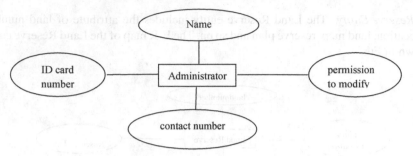

Fig. 6. E-R Map of the administrator entity

5.5 Create Databases and Tables

Land Reserve Archives Management System Database. Combined with the actual work and analysis of user needs, land reserve file management system mainly includes users, land storage, land reserve, land transfer and administrator 5 data tables.

User Data Table. The user data table is mainly used to store the user information of the query file, including the fields of name, address, ID card number, contact number, registration date, query content and so on. All users can search, borrow and return files only after registering and logging in. The table structure of the data table is shown in Fig. 7.

表名称	User		引擎	InnoDB
数据库	land		字符集	utf8
			校对	utf8_general_ci

列名	数据类型	长度	默认	主键?	非空?	Unsigned	自增?	Zerofill?	注释
ID	int	11		☑	☑	☐	☑	☐	唯一标识
Name	varchar	20		☐	☐	☐	☐	☐	姓名
Address	varchar	50		☐	☐	☐	☐	☐	地址
query content	varchar	100		☐	☐	☐	☐	☐	咨询内容
registration date	varchar	20		☐	☐	☐	☐	☐	注册日期
Contact number	int	11		☐	☐	☐	☐	☐	联系方式

Fig. 7. User data table

Land Collection and Storage Data Table. The land collection and storage data table is mainly used to store the information of each land collection and storage, including the fields of land number, land Location, land owner, land collection and storage type, land map and so on. Through this data table can be a comprehensive grasp of land storage information. The table structure of the data table is shown in Fig. 8.

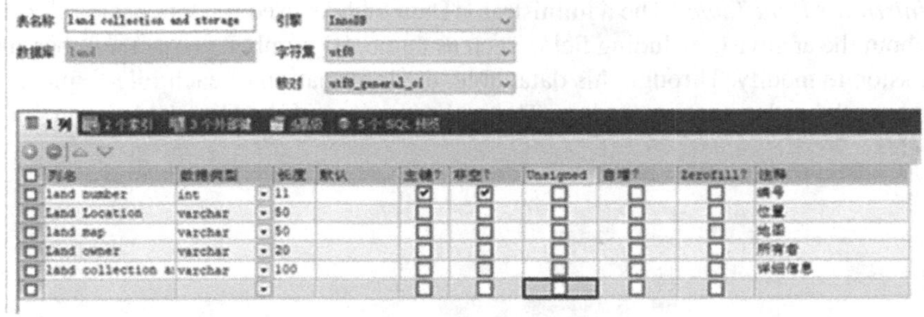

Fig. 8. Land Collection and storage data table

Land Reserve Data Table. The Land Reserve data table is used to store the information of each land in the land reserve, including the fields of land number, land location, land map, reserve plan, etc. Through this data table can be a comprehensive grasp of land reserve information. The table structure of the data table is shown in Fig. 9.

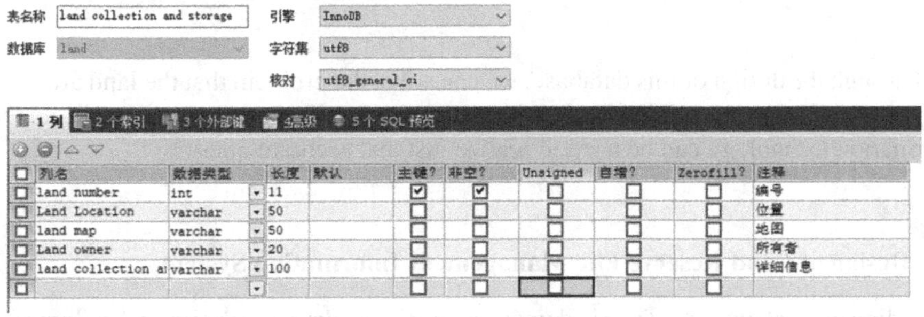

Fig. 9. Land Reserve data table

Land Transfer Data Table. The land transfer data table is used to store the data information of each land transfer, including the fields of land number, land location, land map, assignee and other attributes and so on. Through this data table can be a comprehensive grasp of land transfer information. The table structure of the Data table is shown in Fig. 10.

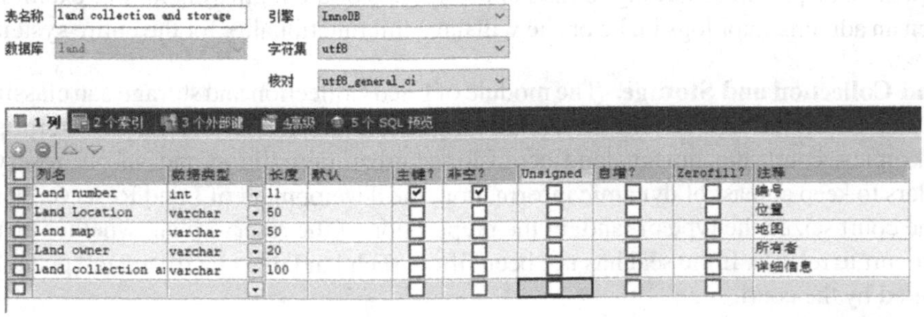

Fig. 10. Land Transfer Data table

Administrator Data Table. The administrator Data table is used to store basic information about the archivist, including fields such as name, ID number, contact number, and permission to modify. Through this data table, the information of each File Explorer is very clear, the authority is very clear. The table structure of the Data table is shown in Fig. 11.

Fig. 11. Administrator data table

Through the design of this database, we can solve the problem that the land archives filing system is not clear, all the land archives can be classified and summarized, and the information technology can be used to realize fast and accurate query.

5.6 Design of Land Reserve File Management Information System

According to the status quo of work, demand analysis and database design, a development software is selected to design the land reserve file management information system. The modules of the system are classified as follows.

Login System. No matter is the user or the administrator, only through the "login system" verification, to log on to the land reserve file management system home page.

Home Page Design. Home page design should be fully functional, can query the home page by clicking the corresponding button, land storage, land reserve, land transfer and other information query and switching functions. The function menu in the navigation bar will be displayed according to the People's rights of the login system. For example, when an administrator logs in, he or she will have full functionality for the entire system.

Land Collection and Storage. The module of Land Collection and storage can classify and summarize the land of collection and storage according to the situation of enterprise bankruptcy, court attachment, land acquisition, urban demolition and so on, reserve leaders to keep abreast of dynamic information, the development of Land Reserve Plan. If the court seized the type of land, in the preparation of the reserve plan, whether there is a court to release. If the seal has not been lifted, such land must be frozen or specially ordered by the court.

Land Reserve. Land Reserve Module, not only records the basic information of each land, but also through data collection, analysis of land reserve, to provide a reference for land transfer.

Land Transfer. The land transfer module needs to record in detail the information of each land transfer and the information of the bidders. The data analysis of land transfer fees is a very important work, which can provide data support for the work led by the Land Reserve, this is important work, and it needs to be kept secret.

File Transfer. In the process of transferring files, there should be accurate records of transferring, and the file-keeper and the file-receiver should transfer files according to the transfer letter.

Loan of File. File lending should be handled strictly in accordance with the file lending system, registration of lending time, lending content and return time, so that file managers grasp the whereabouts of files.

Return of Files. When returning the archives, in addition to writing off the records of borrowing the archives, the archivists should also check whether the archives are damaged or not and put the returned archives into storage in a timely manner.

Through the function design of the above module, we can change the file management from manual management to information management, improve the file management level, and promote the file management to information direction.

5.7 Focusing on Information Security Issues in Archives Management

Land frameworks involve state sovereignty and the property rights of citizens, the loss of sovereignty of countries with missing archives and the loss of property to citizens, therefore, it is very important to strengthen information security. In order to ensure the security of the information system effectively, it is necessary to improve the security awareness and security awareness of file managers. In addition to the file management system in the establishment of the corresponding query and management authority to protect land information security. Also, in the technical level, download good antivirus software, regular site virus detection and killing work, to avoid the platform because of attacks caused by a large number of information data leakage. Preventing the loss of important information through data backup. By installing more advanced firewalls to encrypt important data to prevent data loss.

5.8 Improve Relevant Rules and Regulations for the Management of Land Reserve Archives

At present, there are not many rules and regulations concerning the open use of Land Reserve Archives in China, which still need to be further explored and improved. Land Reserve management departments at all levels should constantly explore and formulate the applicable scope of open archives and information disclosure.

In Conclusion: To sum up, in the development of information technology today, land reserve file management is facing the challenges of information, into a transitional stage. To improve the quality of file management in an all-round way, the land reserve file managers need to change their working concepts, understand the value of file management, recognize the trend of information-based development of file management, give full play to their advantages, and improve their professional quality, keep learning the latest archives management methods, so that their professional skills are improved, so as to be more competent for this work, to lay a good foundation for the smooth running of this work. At the same time, the relevant departments should train the professional knowledge of the archivists, provide a platform for them to learn, so that the staff can update their ideas in time, use brand-new management technology to carry out their work, and effectively improve the efficiency of the archive management. To explore an efficient way of information management of archives and to explore the information management of reserve archives.

References

1. Jiang, F.: Construction practice **07** (2020)
2. Yiqi, X.: Urban construction **18** (2020)
3. Huanmin, C.: Current situation and countermeasures of Land Reserve Archives Management. In and Out of Lantai. **18**, 37–38 (2019)
4. Boggitten: On strengthening the management of Land Reserve Archives. Global Mark. **34**, 27 (2016)
5. Yanfang, G.: On information construction of archives management at the grass-roots level. Sci. Rep. (2018)

Research and Implementation of Anomaly Detection Algorithm in Data Mining

Yang Zhou, Fazhou Liu, Shan Li, and Chao Guo[✉]

Department of Electronics and Communication Engineering, Beijing Electronic Science and Technology Institute, Beijing 100070, People's Republic of China

Abstract. When data mining, there will be a lot of abnormal data, abnormal data refers to data in the data set that is inconsistent with most data or deviates from the normal behavior pattern. In this paper, the KNN (k-Nearest Neighbor) algorithm, the Local Outlier Factor algorithm, and the Isolation Forest algorithm will be used to process the MIT-BIH arrhythmia data set. The KNN algorithm is an Anomaly detection algorithm based on distance but may divide normal data into abnormal data due to the deviation of parameter selection. The improvement proposed in this paper is to add weight to the distance to reduce the probability of division error. The Isolation Forest algorithm divides the data according to the characteristics of the data and then predicts the data to be abnormal or normal data. The improvement proposed in this paper is to first select the features of the data, so that the algorithm can be more accurate when dividing the data, thereby improving the detection. Effect. In terms of visual display of test results, this article selects the Receiver Operating Characteristic Curve graph, which can intuitively show the detection effect of the algorithm.

Keywords: Anomaly detection algorithm · MIT-BIH arrhythmia dataset · Receiver operating characteristic curve

1 Introduction

As society enters the information age, the amount of data is also increasing rapidly. Under such circumstances, people have obtained the technology of data mining through research and thinking. Data mining is the process of extracting potentially useful information and knowledge hidden in it from a large amount of incomplete, noisy, fuzzy, and random data. In the process of data mining, the database may contain some data objects that are inconsistent with the general behavior or model of the data. These data objects are called abnormal points. The process of finding ab-normal points is called abnormal data mining, which is a data mining technology [1]. Through data mining, people can dig out valuable information, association rules, or higher-level knowledge from a huge set of related data, so that people can discover a certain specific pattern and law [2].

© Springer Nature Switzerland AG 2021
X. Sun et al. (Eds.): ICAIS 2021, LNCS 12737, pp. 41–53, 2021.
https://doi.org/10.1007/978-3-030-78612-0_4

2 Related Work

2.1 Data Mining

In the context of the information age, people will face the problem of increasing data. How to quickly and effectively use large amounts of data or discover valuable information contained in large amounts of data is a challenge we are now facing. Data mining is the intersection of artificial intelligence, pattern recognition, machine learning, statistics, and other disciplines. It is a new discipline developed in response to the development of information technology to find useful information from huge data. Data mining is a non-trivial process, whose purpose is to obtain useful, novel, potential, and ultimately understandable knowledge and information from huge data. Current data mining has been applied to many fields. Some scholars use data mining methods to analyze clinical pathology data (including prognosis) to predict the predictability of hepatocellular carcinoma (HCC) postoperative recurrence [3, 4].

2.2 Anomaly Detection

With the continuous study of anomaly detection, a large number of anomaly detection algorithms have been proposed by assuming different existing forms of anomaly data. People also introduce the connectivity principle in graph theory to calculate the distance between data, which improves efficiency and reduces the complexity of calculation time [5–7]. Other scholars have proposed that clustering by fast searching and finding density peak (CFSFDP) is a simple and clear density clustering algorithm. The original algorithm is not suitable to be directly applied to anomaly detection. Its clustering results have a high level of redundancy density information. If it is directly used as a behavior profile, the calculation and storage cost of anomaly detection is very high. Therefore, an improved algorithm based on CFSFDP is proposed for anomaly detection [8].

3 Sample and Key Algorithm Principles

3.1 MIT-BIH Arrhythmia Data Set

In this study of the anomaly detection algorithm, the MIT-BIH arrhythmia data set is used. Since 1975, Beth Israel Hospital in Boston (now Beth Israel Deaconess Medical Center) and the laboratory of MIT have been studying arrhythmia analysis and related topics, thus obtaining MIT-BIH arrhythmia database, which is the first widely used data set containing standard test materials for evaluating the performance of arrhythmia detectors. There are 48 and a half hours of two-channel dynamic electrocardiogram excerpts, which were obtained from 47 subjects studied by BIH Arrhythmia Laboratory from 1975 to 1979. The records are digitized at a rate of 360 samples per second per channel in a range of 10mV with an 11-bit resolution. Two or more cardiologists annotate each record separately; Disagreements were resolved to obtain computer-readable reference notes for each beat attached to the database (about 110,000 notes in total) [9].

3.2 The Basic Principle of the KNN Algorithm

KNN algorithm [10] (KNN) is a classification algorithm, which is one of the simpler algorithms in data mining technology. The main content is that if a data sample is in a certain data sample feature range, which is similar to most of its K nearest neighbor data samples, then it is considered that the data sample may have the characteristics of this data and the sample characteristics in this category. When the KNN algorithm is used for classification judgment, it is judged by data samples that are very close to it. It is a classification method based on statistics, which was first proposed by Cover and Hart, and the theoretical research is relatively mature at present. Finally, the classification result with the highest frequency among the k classified samples is the predicted classification result of the current unclassified samples. The algorithm flow is shown in Fig. 1.

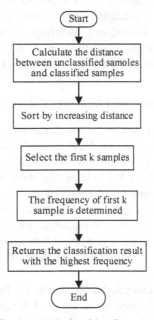

Fig. 1. KNN algorithm flow chart

Distance is the straight line distance between two points on the plane. In the KNN algorithm, distance measure describes the distance between two samples in feature space, that is, the similarity between two samples. As for the measurement methods of distance, Euclidean distance, cosine value, correlation degree, and Manhattan distance are commonly used, and their formulas are as follows:

Euclidean distance formula:

$$L(x, y) = \sqrt{\sum_{i=1}^{n} (x_i - y_i)^2} \tag{1}$$

Manhattan distance formula:

$$L(x, y) = \sum_{i=1}^{n} |x_i - y_i| \tag{2}$$

Minkowski distance formula:

$$L(x, y) = \sqrt[p]{\sum_{i=1}^{n} |x_i - y_i|^p} \tag{3}$$

For the classification decision rules in the KNN algorithm, majority voting is often adopted, that is, most classes in the K nearest neighbor training sets of the sample to be classified determine the classification of the sample. In this paper, the KNN algorithm uses Euclidean distance, which calculates the distance of samples, to compare each sample to see if the data are similar, thus avoiding the matching problem be-tween samples. The approximate error represents the training error of the existing training set. And that estimated error represents the terror of the test set.

3.3 The Basic Principle of the Local Anomaly Factor Algorithm

LOF algorithm is a classical algorithm among density-based local anomaly detection algorithms. This algorithm calculates the local anomaly factor of each data in the data set, and in this way, determines whether the data is abnormal. If the local anomaly factor is too large, the possibility of determining that the data is abnormal is greater, and vice versa. LOF algorithm determines whether a data object is abnormal data not only because of the distance between it and its neighbors but also because of the density of its neighboring data. The density-based local outlier factor algorithm mainly involves the calculation of k-distance and reachable density of data objects and local outlier factors. Then judge whether the data is abnormal by comparing the density [2]. The algorithm flow is shown in Fig. 2.

The neighborhood of k distance is defined as the kth field of point p, which means all points of point p within k distance, including the kth distance. It satisfies,

$$N_k(p) = \left\{ p^{'} \in D \backslash \{p\} | d(p, p^{'}) \leq d_k(p) \right\} \tag{4}$$

Therefore, the number of k-th domain points of p is $N_k(p) \geq k$.

The definition of reachable distance is related to k-adjacent distance. When the parameter K is selected, the reachable distance from data point P to data point O is obtained $reach - dis(p, o)$ is the maximum value of the k-nearest distance of data point o and the direct distance between data point p and point O, That is:

$$reach - dis_k(p, o) = \max\{k - dis(o), d(p, o)\} \tag{5}$$

It represents the average reachable distance from every point in the kth neighborhood of point O. If there is more than one point on the boundary of the kth neighborhood, the number of points in the range is still recorded as K. The adjacent points are in the same

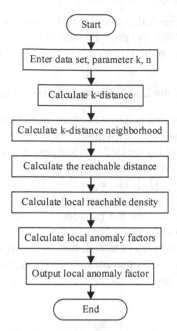

Fig. 2. LOF algorithm flow chart

cluster, the reachable distance is more likely to be relatively small $d_k(o)$. Therefore, the sum of reachable distances is relatively small, while the local reachable density is relatively large. If the distance between the O point and the nearby point is far, the reachable distance may be larger $d(o, p)$. In this way, the sum of reachable distances is too large, and the local reachable density is relatively small.

The local reachable density represents the reciprocal of the average reachable distance from point p in the kth neighborhood of point p, and the formula is:

$$lrd_k(p) = 1/\frac{\sum_{o \in N_k} reach-dis(p, o)}{|N_k(p)|} \tag{6}$$

Represents the neighborhood of point P average of the ratio of the local reachable density of other points in $N_k(p)$ to the local reachable density of point p. If the average value approaches 1, the density of points in the neighborhood of point P is not much different, so it is considered that point P may belong to the same class as the neighborhood; If the average value is greater than 1, it means that the density of point P is less than the density of neighboring points, so point P is called abnormal point. The local anomaly factor represents the average of the ratio between the local reachable density of the neighboring points of point P and the local reachable density of point P. The formula is:

$$LOF_k(p) = \frac{\sum_{o \in N_k(p)} \frac{lrd_k(o)}{lrd_k(p)}}{|N_k(p)|} = \frac{\sum_{o \in N_k(p)} lrd_k(o)}{|N_k(p)|}/lrd_k(p) \tag{7}$$

If the value obtained by the above formula approaches 1, it means that the density of point P and its neighborhood is not much different, and P may be of the same class as the neighborhood; If the average value is less than 1, it means that the density of point P is higher than that of its neighbors, so point P is called dense point; If the obtained value is greater than 1, it means that point P is more likely to be an abnormal point.

3.4   The Basic Principle of the Local Anomaly Factor Algorithm

IForest (isolated Forest) algorithm is a new anomaly detection algorithm, and it is a fast anomaly detection method based on Ensemble. Outliers generally account for a small part of the data and can be quickly divided into leaf nodes in the iTree. Then, an iForest isolated forest is formed by constructing t iTree, and finally, the data can be detected through the constructed iForest [11]. The algorithm flow is shown in Fig. 3.

The algorithm is divided into several steps during detection, in which the partition of data space is very important, but the partition is random. Therefore, through the Monte Carlo method, iForest is composed of t Isolation Tree, and each iTree is a binary tree structure. After the t iTrees are obtained, the iForest is constructed, and then the constructed iForest can be used to evaluate the data to be tested. According to a test data x, it is detected in each iTree, and then the layer of each tree where x finally falls (x is at

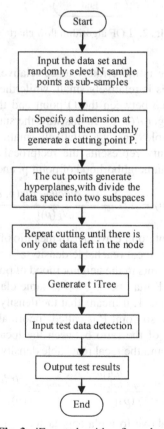

Fig. 3. iForest algorithm flow chart

the height of the tree) is calculated. Then get the average value of x in the height of each tree. When the height average of each test data is obtained, space is divided by setting a threshold and repeating it.

4 Problem Description and Algorithm Improvement

4.1 Problems of KNN Algorithm

KNN algorithm is a nonparametric and inert algorithm model, which is simple and easy to implement and does not need to add parameters. When there are new data to be added to the training set, there is no need to retrain. However, the time complexity and storage space of the KNN algorithm will increase rapidly with the increase of training set size and feature dimension. Because whenever new data appears, it needs to be compared with all the data in the training set to find out the nearest k known data. The time complexity of the algorithm is expressed by $O(m \times n)$, where m is the number of feature items in the data set and n is the number of training set data. Therefore, if the dimension of the selected data set is too high, the KNN algorithm will have dimension disaster, and the original two similar points will become farther and farther away [12].

4.2 Problems of iForest Algorithm

iForest algorithm is an unsupervised algorithm, and the data does not need to be labeled. When the proportion of abnormal data is too small, it is too small to have only a few abnormal data for testing and cannot be trained. If there are only normal samples to build iForest as a whole, the effect will be reduced, but the sampling size can be adjusted appropriately to improve the effect. Most of the traditional anomaly detection algorithms first build a portrait of a normal instance and then regard the instances that do not conform to this portrait as anomalies. However, based on the normal instance detection, it is easy to identify the normal instance as abnormal data, or only a few abnormal data will be detected. iForest has linear time complexity. Because it is a Monte Carlo method, it can be used in data sets with large amounts of data. Generally speaking, the more trees there are, the more stable the algorithm is. Because each tree is generated independently and has no influence on each other, it can speed up the operation in large-scale distributed systems. iForest is not suitable for particularly high-dimensional data. Because every time the data space is divided, a certain dimension is randomly selected. After the iTree is built, most of the dimension information is still unused, which reduces the reliability of the algorithm. And there are a lot of noise dimensions or irrelevant dimensions in the high-dimensional space, which is unfavorable to the tree construction [11].

4.3 Improvement of Two Algorithms

Dimension reduction methods mainly include feature selection and feature transformation, while feature transformation is divided into linear dimension reduction and nonlinear dimension reduction. The linear dimension reduction algorithm is simple and fast to implement, and it is still applied in today's scientific research and engineering practice [13]. When dividing data x, the original data x should be judged as normal data, but if the value of k is slightly larger, it is easy to divide it into abnormal data. To solve this problem, an improvement is proposed, which will add weight when calculating the distance at each point, so that the neighboring points can have a higher weight. There are two methods to choose from when weighting. Inverse function and Gaussian function are relatively simple, which is the reciprocal of the return distance. Assuming that the distance is d, the weight is 1/d. In some cases, the weight of identical or very close points will be very large. Avoid such a situation, when the distance is counted down, add a constant to the distance:

$$weight = \frac{1}{d + const} \tag{8}$$

In this paper, we choose the Gaussian function:

$$f(x) = e^{-\frac{d^2}{2}} \tag{9}$$

Therefore, the data x is weighted by distance, and the detection efficiency of the kNN algorithm is improved. At the same time, the operation time of the algorithm will be shortened.

5   Simulation and Results

5.1   Detection Effect of LOF Algorithm

In this paper, the ROC diagram is used to show the detection effect. The following Fig. 4 is the ROC diagram after LOF detects the MIT-BIH arrhythmia data set.

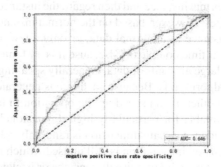

Fig. 4. Detection results of MIT-BIH by lof algorithm

At the same time, the accuracy, precision, precision, recall rate, and comprehensive evaluation index of the LOF algorithm are obtained.

As shown in Table 1 above. It can be seen from Fig. 4 and the Table 1 that the accuracy rate is 0.86, and the macro average of the accuracy rate is 0.57, but the value obtained by this algorithm is low, and the detection effect on data is not very good, which may of course be caused by the unbalanced distribution of samples.

Table 1. Evaluation index after LOF algorithm detection

	Precision	Recall	f1score	Support
0	0.93	0.91	0.92	1757
1	0.21	0.27	0.23	153
Accuracy			0.86	1910
Macroavg	0.57	0.59	0.58	1910
Weightedavg	0.88	0.86	0.87	1910

5.2 Detection Effect of KNN Algorithm

Figure 5 below is the ROC diagram after detecting the MIT-BIH arrhythmia data set by an improved KNN algorithm.

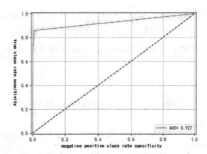

Fig. 5. Detection results of MIT-BIH by improved KNN algorithm

In Fig. 5, we can intuitively see the red ROC and the area AUC formed by it and the abscissa, which is 0.927, reflecting that the detection effect of the kNN algorithm before improvement is relatively good, because this algorithm has a supervised anomaly detection algorithm, and its performance is better than that of the unsupervised anomaly detection algorithm.

Table 2. Evaluation index of detection before improvement of KNN algorithm

	Precision	Recall	f1score	Support
0	0.98	1.00	0.99	7025
1	0.99	0.72	0.83	613
Accuracy			0.98	7638
Macroavg	0.98	0.86	0.91	7638
Weightedavg	0.98	0.98	0.97	7638

The detection results of the kNN algorithm before improvement can be known from Fig. 5 and Table 2 above. It can be seen that the effect of the algorithm in detecting normal data is relatively better than that in detecting abnormal data.

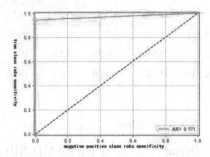

Fig. 6. Detection results of MIT-BIH by improved KNN algorithm

Compared with Fig. 5, we can intuitively see that the area under the curve has increased, and its AUC value is 0.971, reflecting that the detection performance of the improved algorithm has been improved. From the data in the table, we can get a detection accuracy of 0.99.

Table 3. Evaluation index of improved KNN algorithm

	Precision	Recall	f1score	Support
0	0.99	1.00	0.99	3518
1	0.99	0.93	0.96	310
Accuracy			0.99	3819
Macroavg	0.99	0.96	0.98	3819
Weightedavg	0.99	0.99	0.99	3819

Figure 6 and Table 3 shows the detection effect of the improved KNN algorithm. However, compared with other indicators, the accuracy rate, recall rate, and F1 values in the table are all very high, so we can know that the detection effect of the algorithm is already very good, and after the improvement, the running time of the algorithm has been shortened and the operation is faster.

5.3 Detection Effect of iForest Algorithm

The following Fig. 7 is the ROC diagram obtained by detecting the MIT-BIH arrhythmia data set with the improved iForest algorithm.

In the figure, we can see the ROC and the area under the curve, and its AUC value is 0.847, which is slightly worse than the KNN algorithm, but its detection performance is relatively good and meets the improvement requirements.

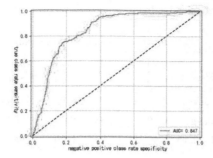

Fig. 7. Detection results of MIT-BIH by improved iForest algorithm

Table 4. Evaluation index of detection before improvement of iForest algorithm

	Precision	Recall	f1 score	Support
0	0.93	0.99	0.96	2654
1	0.17	0.02	0.04	211
Accuracy			0.92	2865
Macroavg	0.55	0.51	0.50	2865
Weightedavg	0.87	0.92	0.89	2865

Figure 7 and Table 4 show the detection effect of the improved iForest algorithm. Table 4 shows that its accuracy rate is 0.92, and its value is still very high. Secondly, its accuracy rate, recall rate, and F1 value can be obtained. The following Fig. 8 and Table 5 shows the detection results after the improved iForest algorithm.

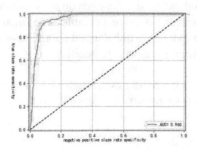

Fig. 8. Detection results of MIT-BIH by improved iForest algorithm

It can be seen from the figure that the AUC value is 0.960, which is greatly improved comparsed with 0.847 before improvement, and the detection effect is better.

It can be seen from Fig. 8 and Table 5 above that the improved algorithm is improved compared with that before improvement. It can be seen from Table 5 that the accuracy of the algorithm is 0.93, which is very high for the first time, and the accuracy rate,

Table 5. Evaluation Index of Improved iForest Algorithm

	Precision	Recall	f1score	Support
0	0.93	0.99	0.96	2654
1	0.46	0.06	0.10	211
Accuracy			0.93	2865
Macroavg	0.70	0.53	0.53	2865
Weightedavg	0.90	0.93	0.90	2865

recall rate, and F1 have been improved to some extent compared with those before the improvement, and the detection time of the algorithm has also been accelerated when the algorithm is running. According to the demonstration of these three algorithms, the detection effect of the KNN algorithm is the best.

6   Conclusion

In this paper, the KNN algorithm, LOF algorithm, and iForest algorithm are selected for the research and implementation of anomaly detection algorithms in data mining. The MIT-BIH arrhythmia data set is detected by implementing these three algorithms, in which the KNN algorithm is improved by distance weighting, and the iForest algorithm is improved by feature selection, which improves the reliability of detection. The detection results are displayed visually by the ROC graph, which can be compared intuitively. Therefore, the detection effect of the KNN algorithm is relatively good. Also, this paper puts forward the improvement direction, improves the effect of data anomaly detection, and solves the shortcomings of the algorithm in processing high latitude data, and needs to continue to learn and improve. At present, most data sets are labeled data, but the dynamic data, in reality, is unlabeled, so it depends on an unsupervised anomaly detection algorithm. Unsupervised learning is often unstable in anomaly detection, which is a classification problem with extremely unbalanced data. These are aspects that need to be further studied, and continuous efforts are needed.

Funding Statement.   This work is supported by the Higher Education Department of the Ministry of Education Industry-university Cooperative Education Project.

References

1. Gong, C., Lin, F., Gong, X., Lu, Y.: Intelligent cooperative edge computing in the internet of things. IEEE Internet Things J. **7**(10), 9372–9382 (2020)
2. Lu, W., Meng, F., Wang, S., Zhang, G., Zhang, X., et al.: Graph-based Chinese word sense disambiguation with multi-knowledge integration. Comput. Mater. Continua **61**(1), 197–212 (2019)
3. Zhang, C.K., Yin, A.: Anomaly detection algorithm based on subspace local density estimation. Int. J. Web Serv. Res. **16**(3), 1 (2019)

4. Shi, I., Ammar, G.A., et al.: Predictability of postoperative recurrence on hepatocellular carcinoma through data mining method. Mol. Clin. Oncol. **13**(5), 1 (2020)
5. Lu, Y., Wu, Z.W., Wang, Y., Yu, Y.: Research on abnormal behavior detection method based on KNN algorithm. Comput. Eng. **2007**(07), 133–134+138 (2007)
6. Shi, Y.G., Mei, Y.J., Shi, F.: Application of data mining technology in alarm analysis of communication network. Microcomput. Inf. **2008**(18), 159–160+232 (2008)
7. Zhou, Y.B., He, X.H., Zhang, S.J., Qing, L.B.: A new abnormal behavior detection algorithm. Comput. Eng. Appl. **48**(03), 192–194+220 (2012)
8. Ren, W.W., Zhang, J.F., Di, X.Q.: Anomaly detection algorithm based on CFSFDP. J. Adv. Comput. Intell. Intell. Inform. **24**(4), 453–460 (2020)
9. Song, X.G., Deng, Q.K.: Reading and application of MIT-BIH arrhythmia database. Chin. J. Med. Phys. **2004**(04), 230–232 (2004)
10. Hui, H., Zhou, C., Xu, S., Lin, F.: A novel secure data transmission scheme in the industrial internet of things. China Commun. **17**(1), 73–88 (2020)
11. Xu, D., Wang, Y.J., Meng, Y.L., Zhang, Z.Y.: Improved data anomaly detection method based on Isolation Forest. Comput. Sci. **45**(10), 155–159 (2018)
12. Feng, G.L., Zhou, W.G.: Parallel KNN anomaly detection algorithm based on the Spark platform. Comput. Sci. **45**(S2), 349–352+366 (2018)
13. Zhao, Y.J.: Analysis of common methods of data dimension reduction. Sci. Technol. Innov. Herald **16**(32), 118–119 (2019)

An Empirical Study on Data Sampling for Just-in-Time Defect Prediction

Haitao Xu[1], Ruifeng Duan[1], Shengsong Yang[1], and Lei Guo[2(⊠)]

[1] University of Science and Technology Beijing, Beijing 100083, China
[2] Systems Engineering Institute AMS, Beijing 100071, China

Abstract. In this paper, the impact of Data Sampling on Just-in-Time defect prediction is explored. We find that there is a significant negative relationship between the class imbalance ratio of the dataset and the performance of the instant software defect prediction model. Secondly although most software defect data are not as unbalanced as expected, a moderate degree of imbalance is sufficient to affect the performance of traditional learning. This means that if the training data for immediate software defects show moderate or more severe imbalances, one need not expect good defect prediction performance and the data sampling approach to balancing the training data can improve the performance of the model. Finally, the empirical approach shows that although the under-sampling method slightly improves model performance, the different sampling methods do not have a substantial impact on the evaluation of immediate software defect prediction models.

Keywords: Data sampling · Just-in-time defect · Empirical study

1 Introduction

To help ensure the reliability of software quality, developers have invested heavily in testing software modules, but the growth in size and complexity of software systems is posing an increasing challenge due to limited resources [1]. Effective defect prediction can help test managers locate defects and allocate test resources more effectively. The real-time software defect prediction technology proposed by Kamei et al. is a technology that uses historical change data to predict whether new changes contain defects [2]. A fine-grained defect software defect prediction technology with the advantages of instantaneity and easy traceability.

However, class imbalance is always an important issue that restricts the performance of real-time software defect prediction models and even machine learning domain models [3]. Most of the data extracted from the project software repository is clean data, that is, data that does not contain defects, which is also in line with the actual situation of programming field data, that is, software defects are a small number after all. For existing research, the use of various machine learning models to establish defect prediction models has become an important method for software defect research. Models trained with unbalanced data often fail to achieve the desired results, because most machine

© Springer Nature Switzerland AG 2021
X. Sun et al. (Eds.): ICAIS 2021, LNCS 12737, pp. 54–69, 2021.
https://doi.org/10.1007/978-3-030-78612-0_5

learning classifiers will predict the defective change data of some minority samples as clean change data. In addition, real-time software defect prediction models need to encourage generalization and simple models to avoid the possibility of over-fitting the underlying data.

At the data level of solving the problem of class imbalance, adjusting the imbalance of data through sampling technology is an important way to change the distribution of original data [4]. Data sampling techniques for raw data, such as oversampling and under-sampling, have been proposed by researchers to solve the problem of class imbalance. Over-sampling and under-sampling technologies are respectively for the minority and majority types of sampling in the data set. For the over-sampling technology, when sampling, some minority types of data will be randomly copied, that is, defect change data will be added. For under-sampling technology, when sampling, most types of data will be randomly deleted, that is, non-defect change data will be deleted. The purpose of the above two data sampling methods is to keep the data class balance of the training data set. Other sampling methods based on over-sampling and under-sampling also include the Smooth method, which is a comprehensive sample synthesis sampling method.

In summary, the uncertainties regarding the use of data sampling for immediate software defect prediction are reflected in, first, the commonly used performance measures are biased and do not explore the degree of imbalance in software defect data and its relationship to prediction performance. In addition, the interaction between the choice of unbalanced learning method and the choice of classifier is not well understood. Finally, different studies used different experimental procedures, selection of hyper-parameters, etc., which may not make the results strictly comparable.

Therefore, this paper hopes to address the following research questions:

RQ1: How unbalanced is the data set of real-time software defect prediction?
RQ2: What impact does class imbalance have on the performance of real-time software defect prediction models?
RQ3: What are the effects of different data sampling techniques on the evaluation of real-time software defect prediction models?

2   Related Works

Software defect prediction technology aims to predict the defect tendency, number of defects, or defect severity of software modules by using software measurement meta-data [8]. Code change defect prediction is an important fine-grained defect prediction technology. First of all, Mockus and Weiss from Bell Labs proposed defect prediction at the code change level in 2005 [3]. In their prediction technology, the predicted software entity is a code change combination composed of multiple code change submissions. Kim et al. in 2008 IEEE Transaction on Software Engineering (TSE) first proposed defect prediction for each code change [4]. Later, Kamei et al. summarized this defect prediction technology as Just-in-Time Defect Prediction at TSE in 2013 for the first time [2]. Instant defect prediction technology refers to the technology that predicts whether there are defects in each code change submitted by the developer. In the instant defect prediction technology, the software entity to be predicted is a code change [6]. Instant defect prediction technology is instantaneous, which is embodied in that this prediction technology can analyze the defects of the changed code after the developer submits a code change, and predict the possibility of defects. Yang et al. applied deep learning technology to JIT defect prediction for the first time at the 2015 Software Quality and Reliability Security Conference [5]. They found that using deep learning technology significantly improved the performance of instant defect prediction models. At the 2019 International Conference on Software Engineering, Cabral et al. [9] studied the impact of change concept evolution on instant software defect prediction technology based on the change data of 10 open source projects that Commit Guru advanced to different programming languages. Catolino [10] and others applied the real-time software defect prediction technology to 14 mobile software project change data sets at the 2019 Mobile Software Engineering and Systems Conference, and evaluated the practicality of the real-time software defect prediction technology in mobile software quality maintenance. McIntosh et al. [17] published two project change data sets extracted from the code review system on the 2018 TSE. Research on these two project change data found that the fluctuation of fixed induced change attributes will affect the performance and interpretation of the JIT model.

In all the above-mentioned research work, researchers have put forward a lot of valuable theories and techniques in model construction and model evaluation. This article hopes to study the real-time software defect data source and further evaluate the impact of data quality on real-time software defect prediction technology from the perspective of data sampling.

3　Experiment Setup

3.1　Studied Projects

In order to analyze the degree of imbalance of historical change data more comprehensively, this article first obtained a total of 32 data sets disclosed by previous instant software defect researchers. Specifically, Kamei et al. [2] published the change data set extracted from the version repositories of 6 open source projects, and Cabral et al. [9] published the change data of 10 open source projects based on different programming languages that Commit Guru arrived in advance. Catolino et al. [10] publicly extracted 14 mobile software project change data sets, and McIntosh et al. [17] publicly extracted 2 project change data sets extracted from the code review system.

The above open source software projects take a long time to maintain, and the data sets have different sizes, which fully meet the technical requirements of real-time software defect prediction. However, the above public JIT software defect data sets do not provide detailed descriptions of processing branches and mining algorithms [21] In order to ensure the experimental conclusions Robustness. This chapter uses 8 projects extracted from the Apache open source project as model training data and test data. At the same time, it comprehensively analyzes the imbalance of the above 40 project change data sets. A brief description of the research projects in this paper is given as follows (Table 1).

Table 1. Overview of studied projects.

Projects	#Changes
AcitiveMQ	8210
Camel	27729
Derby	9439
Geronimo	9146
HBase	14593
Hadoop-Common	27240
OpenJPA	6368
Pig	3103
Total	105828

We use the 14 basic features proposed by Kamei et al.to construct JIT models [2]. As shown in Table 2, they are concerned with five dimensions including diffusion (i.e., NS, ND, NF, and Entropy), size (i.e., LA, LD, and LT), purpose (i.e., FIX), history (i.e., NDEV, AGE, and NUC), and experience (i.e., EXP, REXP, and SEXP). In order to ensure the accuracy of defect change marking, this paper uses a variant of the data annotation algorithm SZZ, based on the Refactoring Aware SZZ (RA-SZZ)).

Table 2. Studied change metrics.

Dimension	Metric	Description
Size	LA	Lines of code added
	LD	Lines of code deleted
	LT	Lines of code in a file before the change
Diffusion	NF	The number of modified subsystems
	ND	The number of modified directories
	NS	The number of modified files
	Entropy	Distribution of modified code across each file
Purpose	FIX	Whether or not the change is a defect fix
History	NDEV	The number of developers that changed the modified files
	NUC	The average time interval between the last and the current change
	AGE	The number of unique changes to the modified files
Experience	EXP	Developer experience
	REXP	Recent developer experience
	SEXP	Developer experience on a subsystem

3.2 Data Preprocessing

The 14 features of the above five dimensions used in this article are highly correlated and inclined features. Algorithms directly using these features to build models may result in reduced model performance or inaccurate model interpretation [22]. Therefore, it is necessary to preprocess the extracted original data to alleviate the skewness between features and remove the features with relatively high correlation.

Logarithmic Normalization. Logarithmic normalization is a widely used technology to deal with alleviating highly inclined features. This article uses standard logarithmic normalization to normalize all the quantitative features of each research project except FIX, because FIX features It is a binary variable and does not have the conditions for normalization. Specifically, this paper adopts the standard logarithmic formula, where is the original eigenvalue.

Remove Related Features. Previous studies have proved that relevant features can affect the performance of defect prediction models. Therefore, before using features to construct a model in this article, the relevant features are removed by performing feature selection. Since the changed features in different projects may show different degrees of correlation, this article performs feature selection for each project separately. Please note that the feature selection in this article is performed after applying logarithmic transformation normalization to the features, because the model in this article is trained using transformed features.

3.3 Data Sampling

Although relatively little research has been done in the software engineering field related to the problem of learning from unbalanced data, the machine learning community, as well as the data mining community, has done a great deal of work on data processing. There are several classically widely used data sampling methods on the data level.

Under-Sampling. Under-sampling refers to deleting some data from the majority class of the dataset so that the remaining majority class is approximately equal in number to the minority class in the dataset, and finally the new dataset is used as training data for the model [24]. In the instant software defect prediction dataset, i.e., deleting some non-defective change data, a common method is to randomly delete the non-defective change data so that the number of non-defective changes in the deleted dataset is consistent with the number of defective changes.

Over-Sampling. Over-sampling is the process of increasing the number of classes in a dataset so that the increased number of classes is roughly equal to the number of classes in the dataset, and finally the new dataset is used as training data for the model [24]. In the instant software defect dataset, i.e., copying some defect change data, a common method is to randomly copy the defect change data so that the number of defect changes and the number of non-defect changes in the increased dataset are consistent.

Smote. Synthetic Minority Oversampling Technique (Smote) is a special kind of data oversampling method in terms of methodology [24]. To overcome the bias of random oversampling on model performance, the method randomly selects one sample from its nearest neighbors for each sample of the minority class, i.e., defect change, at a European distance, and then randomly selects a point on the line from the nearest neighbor as the new synthetic sample. Increasing the number of minority samples, i.e., the dataset after a defect change, in this way balances the number of majority and minority samples.

3.4 Case Study Design

Data imbalance is a challenge for software defect prediction, and in order to mitigate the bias that data imbalance brings to model training, many researchers have focused on addressing data imbalance at the data level. This paper builds on previous research to explore the evaluation of immediate software defect prediction models under different data sampling methods, and thus, there is a particular need to be able to comparatively analyze model performance under different levels of class imbalance. To assess the effects of imbalance learning and its complex interactions between classifier type, dataset sampling method and model evaluation metrics to improve software defect prediction practice. Also in order to answer the three research questions posed, it is expected that the analysis of the degree of class imbalance will explore how much the degree of data imbalance affects the evaluation of the model, and how the interaction between the data sampling method and the classifier and evaluation metrics will affect the evaluation of the model.

Based on these related requirements, the research in this paper follows the overall framework of the experimental design as shown in Fig. 1.

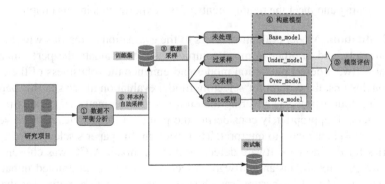

Fig. 1. Experimental framework.

Class imbalance is a very common phenomenon in real-time software defect prediction data sets. In order to measure the degree of imbalance in project change data, this paper chooses the imbalance ratio IR (Imbalance Ratio) as the measurement index. The specific class imbalance ratio is defined as:

$$IR = \frac{Major}{Minor} \tag{1}$$

Major indicates that the majority category in the data set is non-defective changes, and Minor indicates that the minority category in the data set is defect changes.

Out-of-Sample Bootstrap Sampling. Out-of-sample bootstrap sampling is a model validation technique by having a put-back sampling process that first randomly samples change data from the training data set equal to the total number of samples of the training data to train the model in each iteration, and then uses the remaining number of samples in the training data set that are not used as a test set to sample the training data. In this paper, the out-of-sample bootstrap sampling process is set to 1000 iterations.

Data Sampling. Data sampling is the sampling processing of the training set of the model, this paper uses three sampling methods namely under-sampling, oversampling, and synthetic sampling to process the model training data to obtain training samples, and also as a comparison experiment, also set the training data without sampling processing of the sample.

Build Model. The construction of the model is learned with a specific classifier on each type of sample data sampled, and models using different data sampling methods are defined as different models, where the model trained on sample data that has not been processed by sampling is used as the baseline model, called Base_model; the model trained on sample data that has been processed using the under-sampling method is called Under_model; the model trained using the over The model trained on the sample data processed by the sampling method is called Over_model; the model trained on the sample data processed by the Smote sampling method is called Smote_model. in the selection of classifiers, this paper first selects three representative and widely used underlying classifiers: random forest classifier (RF), logistic regression classifier (LR), plain Bayesian Classifiers (NB). The above three classifiers represent different ideas of machine learning and meet the requirements of the experiments in this chapter.

Model Evaluation. Model evaluation refers to the evaluation of metrics with machine learning models, and in order to more comprehensively evaluate the performance of the instant software defect prediction model and enhance the robustness of the experimental conclusions, the criteria for selecting model evaluation metrics in this paper set the following four aspects: 1) covering the entire confusion matrix; 2) evaluating specific classifiers; 3) appropriately considering the potential frequencies of positives and negatives; and 4) being easy to interpret. Therefore, in this paper's selection of evaluation metrics for the instant software defect prediction model, MCC was chosen as the evaluation metric for the instant software defect model in the unsampled unbalanced training dataset; AUC, F1-measure was chosen as the evaluation metric for the categorical regression instant software defect prediction model constructed in the balanced training dataset.

4 Result

In this section, we aim to display experimental results and address the following research questions.

(1) **RQ1: How unbalanced is the data set of real-time software defect prediction?**

Motivation: Instant software defect prediction is a technique that uses historical change data to train machine learning models to predict whether new changes contain defects, and is very dependent on the quality of the training data, however, in a real programming field software development practice environment, defective change data is very small and non-defective change data becomes the majority class in the dataset [20]. Machine learning models trained on such a highly skewed and unbalanced dataset will lack generalization capabilities. In previous instant software defect prediction studies, researchers have made their datasets public, but the size of the dataset's imbalance also varies for different software projects. Only by recognizing the data distribution and balance in the dataset can we efficiently adopt different data balancing methods to improve the practicality of instant software defect prediction techniques, and at present, little is known about the degree of imbalance in instant software defect prediction datasets, and this chapter aims to synthesize the datasets from previous studies to investigate the degree of imbalance in instant software defect prediction datasets.

Approach: A total of 32 datasets previously made public by instant software defect researchers were first obtained. Specifically, these included the change datasets extracted from the version repositories of six open source projects as published by Kamei et al., the change datasets of 10 open source projects in different programming languages based on the advance arrival of Commit Guru as published by Cabral et al., and the change datasets of 14 mobile software projects extracted as published by Catolino et al., McIntosh et al. publicly available datasets of two project changes extracted from the code review system. In addition, eight project datasets were extracted from the Apache open source project as described in Sects. 3 and 4 were used. In total, 40 publicly available datasets from projects in different domains were obtained. As mentioned in the previous research project subsection, a total of 40 public instant software defect prediction datasets were identified in this paper, and these datasets provided enough information to calculate the imbalance ratios (IRs) for the 40 datasets by the number of changes in the dataset, the number of defect change data, and the number of non-defect changes, respectively.

Result: Figure 2 is a histogram of the log-standardized imbalance ratios for the 40 project datasets, because the distribution of IR is highly skewed (skewness $= 5.50$, peak $= 30.75$), so the horizontal coordinate is the log of the IR obtained by solving the IR, and the vertical coordinate is the number of projects. The blue bars indicate the dataset of 8 projects extracted from the Apache open source project selected for this chapter, which is the dataset to be used in the next analysis in this chapter. The dashed line shows the median value of all datasets (IR $= 3.69$).

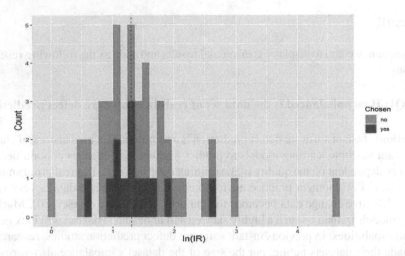

Fig. 2. Histogram of the unbalanced ratio of the data set (ln(IR))

(2) **RQ2: What impact does class imbalance have on the performance of real-time software defect prediction models?**

Motivation: immediate software defect prediction researchers are often actively looking for ways to predict the susceptibility of new software changes to defects, and most research has focused on the use of dichotomous classification methods in cases where the label of the change is defective or non-defective. However, class imbalance is easily seen in immediate software defect data and there is still a lack of awareness of the need for data imbalance. Furthermore, some of these experiments report results that lack robustness. Potential causes include different data sets, experimental designs and performance measurements, and different parametric approaches to classifiers. This makes it difficult to determine what conclusions to draw and what advice to give to practitioners trying to predict defect-prone software components. Although, as stated in RQ1, the vast majority of imbalances in instant software defect prediction data are of moderate and low levels, and previous research will train and evaluate models in the presence of data imbalances, little is known about whether data imbalances affect the performance of instant software defect prediction models or not. This chapter aims to illustrate in a more intuitive way the impact of data imbalance on the performance of an on-the-fly software defect prediction model.

Approach: In order to answer research question 2, this paper trains an on-the-fly software defect prediction model constructed from three classifiers on raw unbalanced data from eight projects, as shown in Fig. 3, by first training the model, called Base_model, on the raw unbalanced training set through out-of-sample self-service sampling, and then using the test set to evaluate the model performance. Random forest (RF), logistic regression (LR), and plain Bayesian classifier (NB) are used for the underlying classifiers of the model, respectively. In the choice of model performance metrics, this paper uses MCC ((Matthews correlation coefficient) i.e., Matthews correlation coefficient, this metric has been proven to be a metric that can integrate the positive and negative cases, especially in the case of unbalanced data, the MCC metric has been proven to cover the entire bicategorical prediction case, experiments Demonstrate that MCC is more sensitive to unbalanced distributions of data than measures derived from recall and accuracy, such as F1, which ignore pseudo-negative samples. MCC is incoherent compared to AUC, which is calculated based on different misclassification cost distributions as different thresholds involve different misclassification costs. AUC is not appropriate for the purpose of this research question. MCC is appropriate as a measure of the model's performance under unbalanced data.

In order to better visualize the relationship between data imbalance and model performance, this paper draws a graph of the relationship between the ratio of data imbalance (IR) and the change in model performance metrics (MCC).

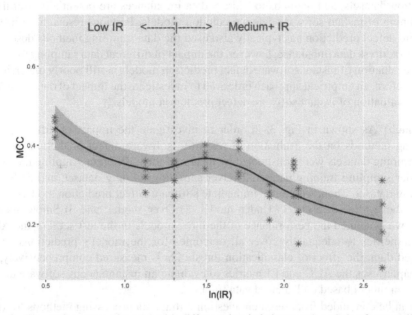

Fig. 3. The performance of model with different data imbalance ratios (Color figure online)

Result: Figure 3 shows a scatter plot of the MCC distribution of the data model performance metrics under different data imbalance ratios. Where MCC is obtained from the model Base_model trained on an unprocessed unbalanced dataset and ln (IR) is the unbalanced ratio using the eight research project datasets. The blue line is drawn by a nonparametric smoother (loess smoothing) with confidence intervals shown as grey areas. To correspond to Research Question 1 using the log-standardized IR, ln(IR) is plotted in the horizontal coordinates instead of IR, as shown in Fig. 3 similarly, in Fig. 3, the dashed line shows the median imbalance ratio (IR = 3.69), which is the line separating the low level imbalance levels from the moderate and above imbalance levels.

(3) **RQ 3: What are the effects of different data sampling techniques on the evaluation of real-time software defect prediction models?**

Motivation: In order to address the challenges posed by data imbalance to machine learning models, previous research has focused on mitigating data imbalance at the data level, and three classical data sampling methods have been proposed: under-sampling, oversampling, and synthetic sampling. Each of the three sampling methods has different advantages and disadvantages in order to meet the requirement of balanced sample distribution in datasets from different perspectives. Under-sampling, for example, seeks to balance the majority and minority classes in a new dataset by deleting some majority classes, but in doing so, the deleted samples will cause the new dataset to lose some information, making the final training model biased. In conjunction with Research question 1 and Research question 2, data imbalances can also occur in instant software defect prediction datasets, and methods to address data imbalances are potentially useful for the training of instant software defect prediction models. Previous research on instant software defect prediction has typically also used the data sampling methods described above to address data imbalance, however, the impact of different data sampling methods on the evaluation of instant software defect prediction models is still poorly understood, and therefore, an empirical approach is desired to investigate the impact of data sampling on the evaluation of instant software defect prediction models.

Approach: As shown in Fig. 3, in order to investigate the impact of different data sampling methods on the evaluation of real-time software defect prediction models, three training datasets were constructed by means of three different sampling methods: 1) Under sampling training dataset, 2) Over sampling training dataset, and 3) Smote sampling dataset. Then, we trained immediate software defect prediction models based on the above three datasets: 1) Under_model; 2) Over_model; and 3) Smote_model. finally, we evaluated the performance of the three models in the test set. For the AUC and F1 metrics to adequately cover all outcomes for the model's predictions under balanced data, the effect of classification thresholds is measured comprehensively, so this chapter uses the AUC and F1 metrics to evaluate an instantaneous software defect prediction model based on balanced data training.

It can be concluded from research question 2 that data processing methods for data imbalance, including data sampling, are useful for improving the performance of immediate software defect prediction models, and therefore, in this chapter model performance is compared for models constructed from three data sampling methods. The most used method in the previous study was the under-sampling method, so Under_model was used as the baseline model and the remaining two models, Over_model and Smote_model, were used as comparison models and the ratio of the absolute performance difference (i.e., the difference between their scores) between Over_model, Smote_model and Under_model to the Under_model model performance was computed in turn.

In order to test whether the model measures, i.e., AUC and F1, are statistically significant, the statistical differences in the model performance measures were compared by applying the Bonferroni-corrected Wilcoxon signed-rank [18]. In addition, Cliff's delta test was also used in this paper to measure the significance of the differences [19]. The value of Cliff's delta δ is in the range $(-1, 1)$, where there is no difference (N:0.000

$\leq |\delta| \leq 0.147$), small difference (S:$0.147 \leq |\delta| \leq 0.330$), medium difference (M:$0.330 \leq |\delta| \leq 0.474$), large difference (L:$0.474 \leq |\delta| \leq 1.000$).

Result: Tables 3 and 4 show the average AUC and F1 for the three models using different data sampling methods. Tables 3 and 4 also show the ratios of the absolute performance differences between Over_model, Smote_model, and Under_model versus Under_model for AUC and F1 versus the Under_model model performance. Tables 3 and 4 also show the P-values of Wilcoxon signed-rangk and the δ-values of Cliff's delta for Over_model, Smote_model vs. Under_model for AUC and F1 metrics.

Table 3. The average AUC scores of the Over_model, Smote_model and Under_model. The AUC scores of the Over_model, Smote_model that are higher than those of the Under_model are in bold.

Classifiers	Projects	AUC				
		Over_model		Smote_mode		Under_model
RF	ActiveMQ	0.83	1%	0.82	0%	0.82
	Camel	0.85	0%	0.85	0%	0.85
	Derby	0.81	1%	0.80	0%	0.80
	Geronimo	0.89	−1%	0.89	−1%	0.90
	HBase	0.86	0%	0.86	0%	0.86
	Hadoop C	0.88	2%	0.86	0%	0.86
	Openjpa	0.81	1%	0.80	0%	0.80
	Pig	0.85	1%	0.85	1%	0.84
LR	ActiveMQ	0.82	0%	0.81	−1%	0.82
	Camel	0.84	0%	0.83	−1%	0.84
	Derby	0.76	0%	0.75	−1%	0.76
	Geronimo	0.86	0%	0.85	−1%	0.86
	HBase	0.85	1%	0.84	0%	0.84
	Hadoop C	0.81	1%	0.79	−1%	0.80
	Openjpa	0.74	0%	0.73	−1%	0.74
	Pig	0.82	0%	0.81	−1%	0.82
NB	ActiveMQ	0.78	0%	0.77	−1%	0.78
	Camel	0.81	0%	0.81	0%	0.81
	Derby	0.75	0%	0.74	−1%	0.75
	Geronimo	0.85	1%	0.84	0%	0.84
	HBase	0.83	1%	0.82	0%	0.82
	Hadoop C	0.75	−1%	0.75	−1%	0.76
	Openjpa	0.74	0%	0.73	−1%	0.74
	Pig	0.80	0%	0.79	−1%	0.80
Avg		0.82	1%	0.81	0%	0.81
P-value		>0.01		>0.05		
Cliff's delta		0.06(N)		−0.06(N)		

From Tables 3 and 4, the following findings can be made: firstly for the Over_model, Smote_model and Under_model models, although the under-sampling-based technique Under_model is not inferior to other sampling techniques in most cases. In terms of the model evaluation metric AUC, the over-sampling technique outperforms the other

Table 4. The average F1 scores of the Over_model, Smote_model and Under_model. The F1 scores of the Over_model, Smote_model that are higher than those of the Under_model are in bold.

Classifiers	Projects	F1				
		Over_model		Smote_mode		Under_model
RF	ActiveMQ	0.65	−3%	0.65	−3%	0.67
	Camel	0.51	−7%	0.54	−2%	0.55
	Derby	0.35	−19%	0.44	2%	0.43
	Geronimo	0.40	−7%	0.48	12%	0.43
	HBase	0.40	−17%	0.48	0%	0.48
	Hadoop C	0.33	0%	0.40	21%	0.33
	Openjpa	0.34	−13%	0.41	5%	0.39
	Pig	0.49	0%	0.52	6%	0.49
LR	ActiveMQ	0.67	0%	0.64	−4%	0.67
	Camel	0.52	0%	0.53	2%	0.52
	Derby	0.38	0%	0.39	3%	0.38
	Geronimo	0.37	0%	0.39	5%	0.37
	HBase	0.40	−5%	0.42	0%	0.42
	Hadoop C	0.26	4%	0.28	12%	0.25
	Openjpa	0.32	0%	0.33	3%	0.32
	Pig	0.45	0%	0.41	−9%	0.45
NB	ActiveMQ	0.63	−2%	0.62	−3%	0.64
	Camel	0.51	0%	0.51	0%	0.51
	Derby	0.37	0%	0.37	0%	0.37
	Geronimo	0.36	−3%	0.36	−3%	0.37
	HBase	0.37	−8%	0.37	−8%	0.40
	Hadoop C	0.20	−5%	0.21	0%	0.21
	Openjpa	0.32	0%	0.31	−3%	0.32
	Pig	0.40	−2%	0.40	−2%	0.41
Avg		0.42	−2%	0.44	2%	0.43
P-value		>0.01		>0.01		
Cliff's delta		−0.12(N)		0.02(N)		

techniques, considering the average AUC score of the three classifiers. However, there was no statistically significant difference in the AUC of the oversampling, synthetic and undersampling techniques. In terms of the model's evaluation metric F1, the synthetic sampling technique outperformed the other sampling techniques in terms of using the random forest classifier and the logistic regression classifier as the underlying classifier. However, the under-sampling technique did not show a statistically significant difference in average F1 compared to the other sampling techniques, i.e., the over-sampling technique and the synthetic sampling technique.

5 Conclusions

Data imbalance is an important issue that constrains the performance of immediate software defect prediction models and even models in the field of machine learning. The data extracted from the project software repository is mostly clean data, i.e., data that does not contain defects, which is also in line with the actual situation of data in the programming field, i.e., software defects are ultimately a minority. Data sampling technique is an important way to bring the distribution of raw data into balance, this paper investigates the effect of data sampling technique on the instant software defect prediction technique, the experimental results show that firstly, there is a significant negative relationship between the class imbalance ratio of the dataset and the performance of the instant software defect prediction model. Secondly although most software defect data are not as unbalanced as expected, a moderate degree of imbalance is sufficient to affect the performance of traditional learning. This means that if the training data for immediate software defects show moderate or more severe imbalances, one need not expect good defect prediction performance and the data sampling approach to balancing the training data can improve the performance of the model. Finally, the empirical approach shows that although the under-sampling method slightly improves model performance, the different sampling methods do not have a substantial impact on the evaluation of immediate software defect prediction models.

Acknowledgement. This work is supported by the National Key R&D Program of China (No. 2018YFB1003905) and the National Natural Science Foundation of China under Grant (No. 61971032), Fundamental Research Funds for the Central Universities (No. FRF-TP-18-008A3).

Conflicts of Interest. The authors declare that they have no conflicts of interest to report regarding the present study. The authors declare that they have no conflicts of interest to report regarding the present study.

References

1. Atluri, S.N., Shen, S.: Global weak forms, weighted residuals, finite elements, boundary elements & local weak forms. In: The Meshless Local Petrov-Galerkin (MLPG) Method, 1st edn, vol. 1, pp. 15–64. Tech Science Press, Henderson (2004)
2. Kamei, Y., Shihab, E.: Defect prediction: accomplishments and future challenges. In: Proceedings of the 23rd International Conference on Software Analysis, Evolution, and Reengineering. IEEE, Washington (2016)

3. Kamei, Y., et al.: A large-scale empirical study of just-in-time quality assurance. IEEE Trans. Software Eng. **39**(6), 757–773 (2013)
4. Mockus, A., Weiss, D.M.: Predicting risk of software changes. Bell Labs Tech. J. **5**(2), 169–180 (2000)
5. Kim, S., Whitehead, E.J., Zhang, Y.: Classifying software changes: clean or buggy? IEEE Trans. Software Eng. **34**(2), 181–196 (2008)
6. Yang, Y., et al.: Effort-aware just-in-time defect prediction: simple unsupervised models could be better than supervised models. In: Proceedings of the 24th International Symposium on Foundations of Software Engineering. ACM Press, New York (2016)
7. Li, H., Zhou, C., Haitao, X., Lv, X., Han, Z.: Joint optimization strategy of computation offloading and resource allocation in multi-access edge computing environment. IEEE Trans. Veh. Technol. **69**(9), 10214–10226 (2020)
8. Jiang, T., Tan, L., Kim, S.: Personalized defect prediction. In: Proceedings of the 28th International Conference on Automated Software Engineering. IEEE, Washington (2013)
9. Shivaji, S., Whitehead, E.J., Akella, R., Kim, S.: Reducing features to improve code change-based bug prediction. IEEE Trans. Software Eng. **9**(4), 552–569 (2013)
10. Cabral, G.G., Minku, L.L., Shihab, E., Mujahid, S.: Class imbalance evolution and verification latency in just-in-time software defect prediction. In: 2019 IEEE/ACM 41st International Conference on Software Engineering (ICSE), Montreal, QC, Canada (2019)
11. Catolino, G., Di Nucci, D., Ferrucci, F.: Cross-project just-in-time bug prediction for mobile apps: an empirical assessment. In: 2019 IEEE/ACM 6th International Conference on Mobile Software Engineering and Systems (MOBILESoft), Montreal, QC, Canada (2019)
12. Fukushima, T., Kamei, Y., McIntosh, S., Yamashita, K., Ubayashi, N.: An empirical study of just-in-time defect prediction using cross-project models. In: Proceedings of the 11th Working Conference on Mining Software Repositories, New York (2014)
13. Tan, M., Tan, L., Dara, S., Mayeux, C.: Online defect prediction for imbalanced data. In: Proceedings of the 37th International Conference on Software Engineering. IEEE, Washington (2015)
14. Kamei, Y., Fukushima, T., McIntosh, S., Yamashita, K., Ubayashi, N., Hassan, A.E.: Studying just-in-time defect prediction using cross project models. Empir. Softw. Eng. **21**(5), 2072–2106 (2016)
15. Yang, X., Lo, D., Xia, X., Zhang, Y., Sun, J.: Deep learning for just-in-time defect prediction. In: Proceedings of the 15th International Conference on Software Quality, Reliability and Security. IEEE, Washington (2015)
16. Huang, Q., Xia, X., Lo, D.: Supervised vs unsupervised models: a holistic look at effort-aware just-in-time defect prediction. In: Proceedings of the 33rd International Conference on Software Maintenance and Evolution. IEEE, Washington (2017)
17. Fu, W., Menzies, T.: Revisiting unsupervised learning for defect prediction. In: Proceedings of the 25th International Symposium on Foundations of Software Engineering. ACM Press, New York (2017)
18. McIntosh, S., Kamei, Y.: Are fix-inducing changes a moving target? A longitudinal case study of just-in-time defect prediction. IEEE Trans. Software Eng. **44**(5), 412–428 (2018)
19. Wilcoxon, F.: Individual comparisons by ranking methods. Biometrics Bull. **1**, 80–83 (1945)
20. Cliff, N.: Ordinal Methods for Behavioral Data Analysis. Psychology Press, New York (1996)
21. Tantithamthavorn, C., Hassan, A.E., Matsumoto, K.: The impact of class rebalancing techniques on the performance and interpretation of defect prediction models. IEEE Trans. Software Eng. **46**(11), 1200–1219 (2018)
22. Galar, M., Fernandez, A., Tartas, E.B., Sola, H.B., Herrera, F.: A review on ensembles for the class imbalance problem: bagging-, boosting-, and hybrid-based approaches. IEEE Trans. Syst. Man Cybern. Part C **42**(4), 463–484 (2012)

23. Batista, G., Prati, R., Monard, M.: A study of the behavior of several methods for balancing machine learning training data. ACM SIGKDD Explor. Newsl. **6**, 20–29 (2004)
24. Chawla, N., Bowyer, K., Hall, L., Kegelmeyer, P.: Smote: synthetic minority over-sampling technique. J. Artif. Intell. Res. **16**, 321–357 (2002)
25. Song, Q., Guo, Y., Shepperd, M.: A comprehensive investigation of the role of imbalanced learning for software defect prediction. IEEE Trans. Software Eng. **45**, 1253–1269 (2019)

Design and Implementation of Data Adapter in SWIM

Yangfei Sun[✉] and Yuanchun Jiang

Civil Aviation University of China, Tianjin 300300, China
2019022090@cauc.edu.cn

Abstract. In the background of the globalized interaction needs of civil aviation information services, the definition of System Wide Information Management (SWIM) was proposed by International Civil Aviation Organization (ICAO). However, the issue of interaction between traditional business systems and heterogeneous systems still exists on the SWIM platform. The data adapter is an important functional component to solve this problem, which can not only solve the problems of high coupling among systems, poor compatibility, low sensitivity, non-standard syntax and poor semantics, but also realize the high sharing of information between systems. Based on the SWIM platform, this article redefines SWIM. First, this article analyzes the concept and architecture of SWIM as well as the role and logical architecture of adapters. Then, according to the requirements of the adapter, a design method of the adapter structure is proposed, and the process design methods of the two main functional modules, data transformation and service encapsulation, are proposed respectively, including data standard and service standard. Extensible Markup Language (XML) technology is a platform independent language, 90% of systems support XML, it is self-descriptive and extensible, suitable for storage and transport on the network, therefore it is the preferred language for software development and is important for the design of SWIM data adapter. Finally, the data adapter is designed and implemented.

Keywords: SWIM · Adapter · Data conversion · Service encapsulation

1 Introduction

With the continuous development of informatization in the civil aviation industry, aircraft operators, airports, air traffic control (ATC) units, etc. have designed, developed and maintained specific information business systems, as a result, more and more appear inconsistent data interface among systems, which increase the coupling in traditional point-to-point communication systems, the paralysis of one system may affect the normal operation of many systems. The differences in data structures and definitions between different business systems will make it necessary to develop different interface standards for different system interfaces due to the increasing in system access, which improves the cost and obstacles of system interaction, it will adversely affect the normal operation of aircraft especially during cross-country flight. As an information exchange platform for global air traffic management, SWIM changes the traditional data sharing architecture

X. Sun et al. (Eds.): ICAIS 2021, LNCS 12737, pp. 70–81, 2021.
https://doi.org/10.1007/978-3-030-78612-0_6

from a traditional point-to-point model to a SWIM sharing architecture centered on data transmission, exchange and management, as shown in Fig. 1. For example, for N different business systems, N (N-1) specific interfaces are needed to connect the systems. The number of development interfaces will increase geometrically with the increase of business systems, which not only increases development costs, but also leads to unnecessary waste of resources. For the model with SWIM as the shared architecture, you can access N different business systems only by developing common interfaces for new services or applications, which greatly improves the shielding ability of internal details and transparent services between different software and hardware systems.

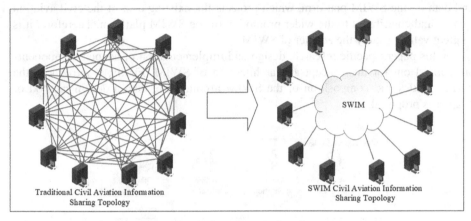

Traditional Civil Aviation Information
Sharing Topology

SWIM Civil Aviation Information
Sharing Topology

Fig. 1. SWIM can effectively reduce the interface among systems.

SWIM is a new, system-wide aeronautical information management method that integrates the air traffic management (ATM) network from the information level [1]. It is a platform based on this method that can provide airlines, airports, and ATC units access and interaction capabilities of different systems. According to ICAO's conceptual introduction to SWIM [2], the SWIM system adopts a service oriented architecture (SOA). Therefore, SWIM can improve the traditional point-to-point aeronautical information transmission mode into a centralized platform-based interaction method based on service management. It is based on this architecture that it can reduce the cost of system interaction, minimize the degree of tight coupling among different systems, and conveniently provide comprehensive management capabilities for aeronautical shared information, making information interaction more sensitive and economical. The SWIM interaction architecture is mainly divided into five layers, as shown in Fig. 2, which are SWIM application layer, information service exchange layer, information exchange model layer, SWIM infrastructure layer, and network interconnection layer.

As shown in Fig. 2, the SWIM coverage includes the middle three layers. The information service exchange layer defines appropriate services that the stakeholders reach a consensus for the corresponding information domain. The SWIM application layer will directly use the services provided by this layer for information exchange. The information exchange model layer provides the upper layer with a standard definition of the data model covering ATM shared information, including data content, structure and format.

The SWIM infrastructure layer provides infrastructure for sharing information, including interface management, message routing, security services, and enterprise service management.

An illustration is that SWIM is a "system of systems" [3], that is to say, SWIM is actually a platform for accessing the system, and actual services and data are distributed and provided by each access system, so ensuring the access capability of existing systems on the platform has become an issue that the SWIM must consider. To enable such systems to directly access the infrastructure layer of the SWIM core, the adapter architecture should include the second and third layer functions in the SWIM architecture. The adapter is an important component that guarantees the interaction of legacy services and data on the SWIM platform, which protects the existing cost of the civil aviation system and contributes to the wider promotion of the SWIM platform. Therefore, it is of great value to study the adapter of SWIM.

In this paper, specific research, design and implementation of adapter components are carried out for the concept and architecture of SWIM. Firstly, it introduces the characteristics and composition of the SWIM architecture, then a design method of adapter is proposed.

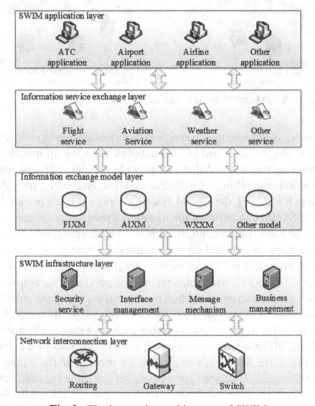

Fig. 2. The interactive architecture of SWIM.

2   The Analysis of Adapter Functional Requirement

Based on the analysis of SWIM's interactive architecture and the role played by the adapter, taking two access systems as examples, the logic architecture of the adapter in SWIM is designed, as shown in Fig. 3.

The logical architecture of the adapter describes its logical position and logical function on the SWIM platform. The two access systems in Fig. 3 are both legacy systems that need to access the SWIM platform infrastructure to complete the interaction process. Therefore, the data first undergoes data conversion and service encapsulation through the adapter before it can be successfully connected to the SWIM infrastructure. In addition, the infrastructure in the logical architecture needs to provide basic interface access functions, namely service dock and message routing functions. The service dock is a public interface provided by the infrastructure to access the service, while the message routing provides the ability to connect to each other in the case of multiparty interaction. The SWIM-based adapter needs to have the following two functions.

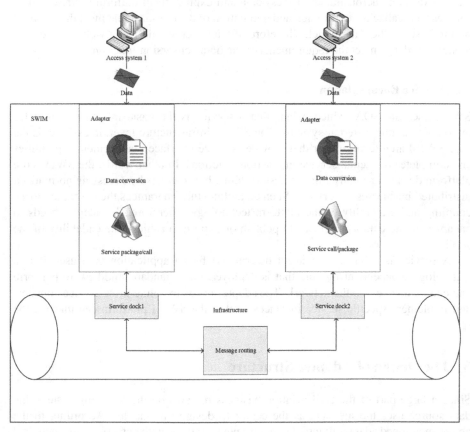

Fig. 3. The organization structure of adapter.

2.1 Data Conversion

Due to the differences in the format of the data sources of each access system, there are certain differences in data structure and semantics, which directly affect the accuracy and effectiveness of information interaction, resulting in obstacles in data exchange and management on the SWIM platform. Therefore, when each system is connected to SWIM respectively, the adapter should complete the data format conversion function, and the infrastructure should use a unified data format for information management. According to the recommendations of the ICAO and European and American countries in studying SWIM [4], XML, as a language that has nothing to do with the system platform environment, and is standardized, versatile, and extensible, is suitable to be a general-purpose language data format. Therefore, the adapter should support the data conversion function that converts the data format to the XML format.

In order to form a standardized XML data format, it is necessary to establish an appropriate data model to restrict the format and structure of the data source. The SWIM data model is a model formed by using certain modeling standards and technologies to classify different aeronautical business data and express them uniformly. Various data sources can realize the conversion and unification of data formats that meet the standard on the basis of the data model. Therefore, the adapter should use a well-defined data model in order to meet the requirements of the data conversion function.

2.2 Service Encapsulation

SWIM uses the SOA, which means that a service is the basic information unit for interaction among different systems. The SWIM infrastructure layer, in essence, is the core SWIM architecture layer that provides service interface management capabilities and completes the actual service interaction functions. In other words, the SWIM core platform does not actually run business systems, but interacts by accessing normalized distributed businesses as services. Such an architecture guarantees the neutrality, loose coupling and scalability of the platform technology. Therefore, the adapter needs to encapsulate the data as a service to publish or expose to achieve the callability of the service.

A service is a business concept determined by an application or a user. It is a technology-independent module that is deployed on a standard middleware platform and can be invoked on the network. The adapter needs to define these service concepts and implement specific service instances so that the SWIM platform can manage the services.

3 The Design of Adapter Structure

Since a large part of the civil aviation business remains on the reporting system, the data source uses the message as the center to design the adapter. According to the above-mentioned adapter functional requirement analysis, with corresponding technical support, the design of the specific structure of the adapter is shown in Fig. 4.

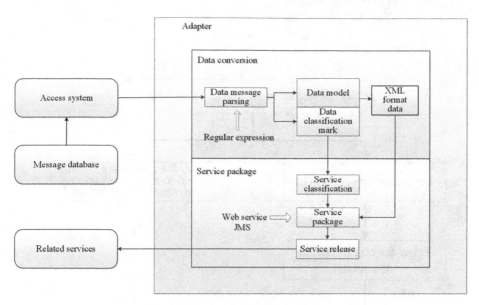

Fig. 4. The design of adapter structure.

3.1 The Design of Data Conversion Module

According to the requirement analysis of the adapter, the data passing through the data conversion module should be in a standard XML format. Therefore, the data conversion module needs to parse the message data source and use the standard data model to unify the data format. The data conversion module is composed of several sub-modules, namely the message parsing sub-module, the data model sub-module and the corresponding data classification and marking sub-module.

The main function of the data conversion module is to process the input message data source through each sub-module, and finally obtain the XML data that conforms to the data model. First, the data source message will be parsed by the message parsing submodule, which uses regular expressions to match the relevant content of the message. Regular expression is a method of extracting information using a specific type of character to match data. The analysis content includes judging the message type and mapping the aeronautical data related to the message. Then, the parsed message type will be handed over to the message type marking module for marking, and help the service encapsulation module to select different services. At the same time, the relevant aeronautical information data will be transferred into the data model corresponding to the mark for the conversion and unification of the data format, and finally the data in the standardized XML format will be obtained. The specific design method is shown in Fig. 5.

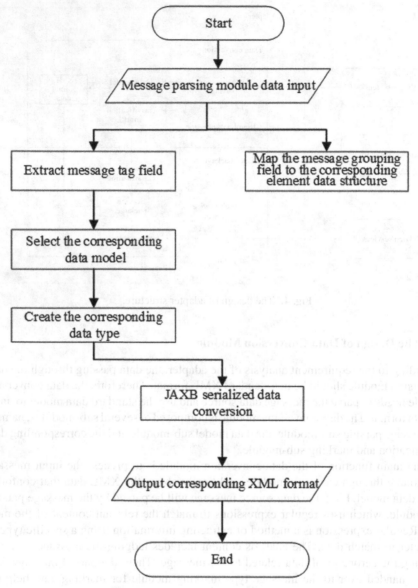

Fig. 5. The flowchart of data conversion.

3.2 The Design of Service Encapsulation Module

The service package module further encapsulates the data in the standard format into general services, in order to shield the heterogeneous interaction problems, and can more efficiently manage the interactive business on the SWIM platform. This module mainly provides several functional sub-modules of service classification, service encapsulation and service publishing. The design among modules is as follows.

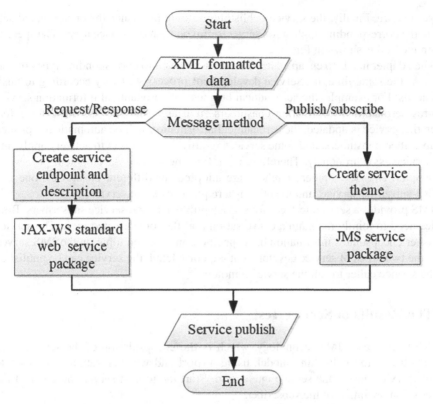

Fig. 6. Data conversion flowchart.

Firstly, the service classification module selects the corresponding service to be encapsulated according to the service mark in the upper data conversion module, and then loads the converted format data into the corresponding business class to encapsulate the service, which can realize business process by using Web Service or Java Message Service (JMS) technology. Web Service is a very commonly used technology in SOA, which is a network-based distributed modular component that can publish callable functions to the Web for application access (applications can use standard Web protocols and data formats to access it). Because Web Service follows certain technical specifications, it can have good compatibility with other components or systems [5]. Web Service provides a standard method for converting the functions of legacy applications into reusable, self-contained, and self-describing services, and a standard way for convenient and flexible application integration. Therefore, it is very suitable as a standard technology for service encapsulation modules. A development method that requires high real-time information services. JMS is an application program interface used to access asynchronous messaging systems, and publish-subscribe model can be used to implement publish-subscribe services. ICAO recommends using JMS as a viable implementation method before the Web Service standards for service subscription are not yet mature. Finally, the service publishing module publishes the encapsulated service to the corresponding application server for invocation by service users. The specific design method is shown in Fig. 6.

The adapter needs to encapsulate different services into corresponding types of services. At the same time, the service development process will vary according to business needs. For example, the aeronautical business of aeronautical information service requires aeronautical information consumers such as airlines to subscribe for a fee. When the service is updated, the aeronautical information will be automatically pushed to subscribed consumers, and some services require service users to actively apply and call services synchronously. Therefore, regarding the service development process of the adapter, two development methods are adopted for different businesses, one is a publish-subscribe service, and the other is a request-response service.

JMS provides a set of interfaces for service publishers and service subscribers. Both parties need to jointly maintain a conversation and the topic created by it. The service publisher encapsulates information on a specific conversation topic on the JMS server. After the two types of service development are completed, the service can be published for the service caller to call the service remotely.

4   The Results of Service Test

Service testing uses JMS technology, which is the encapsulation of the service used in the subscription publishing model, using airport and weather data as test cases to test the service during the service interaction. Start the tomcat server and conduct the subscription operation of the subscriber.

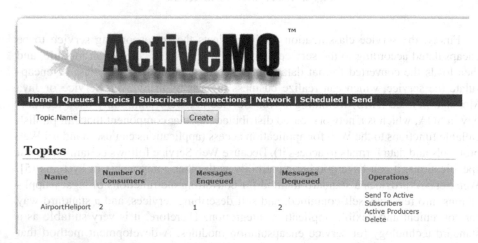

Fig. 7. Test results that airport heliport information service JMS releases.

The test results are displayed through the console and web port. In the test case, after two subscribers subscribe to the service whose subject is AiportHeliport, the service provider publishes the service, the two subscribers can obtain service information and log in to the server using a browser, namely can display test results and the displayed test results are shown in Fig. 7.

In Fig. 7, the JMS server shows the interactive test results of the subscriber and the publisher under the message topic about the airport service. There are two subscribers under the AirportHeliport topic. When the service message enters the topic, the two subscribers will get the message respectively. The console output of the two subscriber clients is shown in Fig. 8.

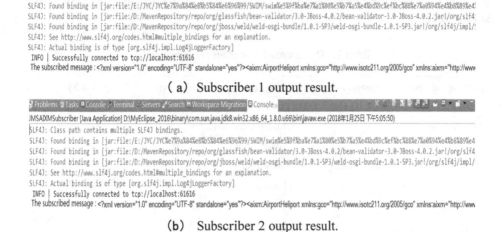

Fig. 8. The output results of airport heliport information service test subscriber.

Figure 8(a) and Fig. 8(b) respectively show the XML message output of the AirportHeliport service received by two subscribers.

5   The Results of Performance Test

Performance testing is to test the content of the adapter's performance requirements and give conclusions including the adapter's data conversion time efficiency, as well as the adapter user interface loading time, resource consumption, and operating conditions in different environments.

The time efficiency performance of the adapter's data conversion refers to the time consumption of its data conversion module. The average time-consuming test for different test case inputs uses four test cases, and the data conversion module is used to perform the time-consuming test of data conversion. After 30 tests, count the test time and calculate the average data conversion time of each test case. The test results are shown in Table 1.

Table 1. The test results (ms) of data conversion time efficiency.

Testing frequency	1	2	3	4	5	6	7	8	9	...	30	Average time
Test case 1	365	386	362	370	369	386	345	365	336	...	362	369.2
Test case 2	326	325	305	315	316	320	333	295	327	...	330	316.4
Test case 3	302	286	288	310	293	297	303	305	293	...	295	294.3

The test results of other performance indicators of the adapter, computing resource consumption, including page loading time, and operating environment feasibility are shown in Table 2.

Table 2. The test results of other performance.

Computing resource consumption	Program space occupation	19.4 M
	Server running memory usage	92.3 M
Page loading time	Login page load time	243 ms
	Main page loading time	295 ms
Operating environment feasibility	Windows	Feasible
	Linux	Feasible

In the performance test results in Table 2, the adapter's computing resource consumption, including the space occupied by the program and the memory occupied by the server, are all at the M level, and the page load time is at the ms level, and it can run on both Windows and Linux at the same time, conforming the adapter performance requirements.

Based on the introduction of the SWIM platform, this article designs and implements the adapter. As an important component to ensure the smooth interaction of legacy systems on SWIM, adapters need to implement data conversion and service encapsulation functions. At the same time, the design and implementation should meet the data model specifications and data format standards provided by ICAO. Realize with JAXB technology, and finally get data conforming to the data model and XML format. The service encapsulation module encapsulates and publishes services based on the service business. With the further deepening of civil aviation informatization, future adapters can expand the adaptation of more aeronautical systems on the basis of considering more services and processes.

References

1. Zhigang, L., Yanying, G.: Research on the survivability of system wide information management (SWIM). In: 2019 IEEE 5th International Conference on Computer and Communications (ICCC), Chengdu, China, pp. 1388–1392 (2019)

2. ICAO, Manual on System Wide Information Management (SWIM) Concept, Doc. 10039 (2014). https://www.icao.int/airnavigation/IMP/Documents/SWIM%20Concept%20V2% 20Draft%20with%20DISCLAIMER.pdf
3. Morioka, K., et al.: Field taxing experiments of aircraft access to SWIM over AeroMACS. In: 2018 IEEE Conference on Antenna Measurements & Applications (CAMA), Vasteras, pp. 1–4 (2018)
4. SESAR Joint Undertaking, SWIM-TI Yellow Profile Technical Specification 2.1, Edition 00.10.00 (2014). http://www.sesarju.eu/sites/default/files/solutions/07_TS_Solution_20_14. 01.04.D44-004-SWIM-TI_Yellow_Profile_Technical_Specification.pdf
5. Papazoglou, M.P.: Principle and Technology of Web Services. Machinery Industry Press (2010)

Cloud Computing and Security

Encrypted Medical Records Search with Supporting of Fuzzy Multi-keyword and Relevance Ranking

Xiehua Li[✉], Gang Long, and Sijie Li

Hunan University, Changsha 410082, Hunan, China
beverly@hnu.edu.cn

Abstract. Medical records are highly private and sensitive. To protect the information security of patients and medical institutes, medical records and data should be encrypted before outsourcing to the cloud storage. However, the retrieval of the encrypted data is currently a crucial issue of medical big data security. The existing searchable encryption methods can hardly satisfy the goals of fuzzy multi-keywords search, relevance ranking, access pattern protection and high retrieval efficiency simultaneously. Thus, in this paper, we propose an encrypted medical records searching scheme that can achieve those goals. A new spelling correction algorithm is proposed to support fuzzy multiple input keywords. A new relevance score encryption and calculation algorithm is introduced for ranking medical records with privacy preserving. In addition, a queue-based query procedure is also applied in this scheme to protect the access pattern from statistical attack and file-injection attack. Our proposed scheme achieves fuzzy matching without expending index table or sacrificing computational efficiency, and can support dynamic file updating. The theoretical analysis and experiment results show that our scheme is secure, accurate, error-tolerant and very efficient.

Keywords: Encrypted medical record · Fuzzy multi-keyword search · Relevance ranking · Searchable encryption

1 Introduction

As the healthcare industry is moving toward digitization, electronic medical record systems are becoming increasingly popular. A lot of hospitals adopt electronic health records, and start using the expert system for medical diagnosis. Due to the huge amount of electronic medical records and images, most hospitals and medical institutions outsource such data to the public cloud storage platform (CSP). However, medical records contain highly private personal information that should not be outsourced without any protection. One naive way to protect the information security is to encrypt data before outsourcing, which reduces the accuracy and efficiency of data searching and retrieval. Aim to solve this practical problem, the concept of searchable encryption was proposed by

© Springer Nature Switzerland AG 2021
X. Sun et al. (Eds.): ICAIS 2021, LNCS 12737, pp. 85–101, 2021.
https://doi.org/10.1007/978-3-030-78612-0_7

Song et al. [1]. After that searchable encryption becomes an important technology for ciphertext retrieval [3–5]. Most researches on searchable encryption are aiming at improving security and accuracy of data retrieval. Boneh et al. [2] proposed the first public key encryption scheme that support keyword search. Sun et al. [7] proposed a multi-keyword search scheme using a vector space model and a cosine measure with TF (word frequency) IDF (inverse text frequency index) to provide order preserved file retrieval. Kabir et al. [9] improved Sun's scheme by writing the plaintext TF values in the index tree orderly. However, the TF values may leak the keywords and documents information. Liu et al. [10]proposed a verifiable searchable encryption scheme that can verify the correctness of search results over dynamic data collection. Du et al. [11] proposed a searchable symmetric encryption scheme that adopt access control and boolean queries. Pappas et al. [12] proposed a scalable private DBMS, Blind Seer, based on a Bloom filter tree index to support rich query functionalities. Liu et al. [13] adopted attribute hierarchy with the comparison-based encryption to achieve dynamic access control over encrypted personal health record. Also, there are many researches on searchable encryption schemes with multiple keyword support [14–16] and are applied in many areas [17,18].

For the keyword-based ciphertext retrieval scheme, another issue that would effect the retrieval accuracy and efficiency is the correctness of the input keywords. That is because the search queries are based on users' input keywords and spelling errors may cause retrieval failure. The scheme proposed in [13] can partly solve this by involving vector space model, but the search accuracy is not desirable. Other traditional spelling correction approaches like Levenshtein distance can achieve a higher accuracy only if the spelling error is less than 2 letters and is not misalignment. Some studies have also proposed fuzzy keyword search schemes. Zhou used k-gram to construct fuzzy keyword sets and used Jaccard coefficients to calculate keyword similarity [19]. Gnanasekaran [20] converted keyword into a vector, and used LSH (local sensitive hash) to calculate the vector to support fuzzy keyword search. Yang [22] proposed a keyword fuzzy search scheme based on Simhash that combines Hamming distance and similarity score. Wang [24] used sensitive hash function to index keywords, and used Bloom filter to realize fuzzy search of multiple keywords. All those schemes did not consider the misalignment of letters in the keywords, which may lead to less accurate search results. In this paper, we proposed an encrypted medical record search scheme that can support fuzzy multiple keywords and relevance score ranking (EMR-SMR). We adopted our former proposed Probability-Levenshtein based Spelling Correction (PLSC) algorithm to support fuzzy multiple keywords input and provide a more accurate search query. Then, we use Paillier to encrypt the keywords relevance scores for each document, so that the sums of multi-keyword relevance can be calculated by the cloud server without leaking information. In addition, proxy is introduced in our scheme to support multiple DOs and multi-keyword relevance score ranking. Third, we queued the search results by the proxy to hide the connection between keywords and downloaded files, further improving the security of the search. Our contributions can be summarized as follows.

- To the best of our knowledge, we first proposed a spelling correction algorithm that uses both probability and Levenshtein to improve the correction accuracy of electronic medical records. In order to test the accuracy of our spelling correction algorithm, we use more than 3000 medical words to generate a library with 2000 medical records.
- We designed a relevance score encryption and ranking algorithm to support private-preserving ranking search. w that can calculate encrypted multi-keyword relevance scores and return top-k related search results.
- We built up a system that can support multiple DOs EMR outsourcing, user queries and data retrieval. Furthermore, a queue-based retrieval strategy is proposed and carried out in this system to resist file-injection and statistical attack. The experiment results demonstrate the accuracy and efficiency of our scheme.

The rest of the paper is organized as follow. Section 2 presents the constructions and definitions of our scheme. Section 3 describes the definition of basic functions used for supporting multi-keyword fuzzy search. Theoretical system performance is analyzed in Sect. 4. We give the scheme implementation results and comparison in Sect. 5. Section 7 is the conclusion of the whole paper.

2 Constructions and Definitions

2.1 System Model

Figure 1 shows the system structure of our scheme. Before outsourcing EMR to the CSP, the EMR owners build indexes and encrypt EMRs. Then they upload encrypted EMRs and their associated indexes to the Proxy. Proxy builds and uploads the secured indexes with the encrypted files to the Cloud Server. Meanwhile, EMR owners distributes file decryption keys to authorized users via secure channel.

2.2 Threat Model

In this scheme, the is assumed as "honest-but-curiou", the cloud server will honestly implement the program but is willing to get illegal profits if given the opportunity. In addition, the cloud server may analyze the stored data and search queries to learn more information. We assume that the principals who outsource EMR are honest because they have the original data. Proxy is a trusted entity who builds up secured indexes of outsourcing data for each EMR owners, and processes users' searching requests. Users here are untrusted entities, they may collude with CSP or other users to get more information about the encrypted data. The secure channel in this system is assumed to be credential. Information transferred via the secure channel is considered uncompromisable.

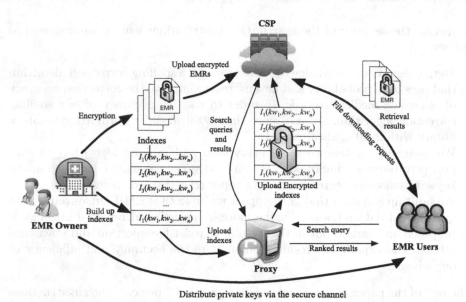

Fig. 1. System structure of EMR-SMR

2.3 System Goals

In this scheme, there are three mail goals need to be fulfilled to achieve multi-keyword fuzzy search and relevance ranking over encrypted EMRs:

- Security: keep the indexes secure and break the linkablility of index and files, so that the cloud server and other malicious entities won't get valuable information about the encrypted data;
- Fuzzy searchable: automatic and accurate spelling correction should be supported since misspelling may lead to search error or failure;
- Multi-keyword ranked search: the new scheme should support multi-keyword ranked search and be both time- and space-efficient because the cloud servers have massive data to process; Additionally, results relevance ranking should be supported to improve the search accuracy.

3 Multi-keyowrds Input Correction

When performing an online search, input keywords errors often occur, such as wrong letters, missing or redundant letters, messy letters. The misspelling keywords may cause imprecise research result or even failure. In this paper we adopt our previous proposed PLSC (Probability-Levenshtein based spelling correction) [26] algorithm to provide a more accurate spelling correction and support multiple keywords input. For more details of PLSC algorithm, please read our former published paper [26].

In this paper, we choose 3000 medical keywords and put them in EMR format to generate 2000 EMR documents. The EMR is organized as followed: the diseases, symptoms and tests will be put in one document to generate a formal EMR, a simple example of the EMR is shown in Fig. 2.

We use these 2000 EMRs as the library to implement our scheme. The PLSC rule set is organized as a 4-tuple (word, combination, frequency, P_i). P_i is the Derivative Possibility of correct keyword. The value of α, β can be defined by users. The average accuracy score $AAS(W_i)$ is calculated with Eq. (1).

$$AAS(W_i) = \frac{1}{k} \sum_{i=1}^{k} k - i \tag{1}$$

Where W_i is the correct word. We tested the PLSC algorithm with $k = 10$. Based on our observation, when $\alpha = 0.3, \beta = 0.7$ PLSC is more accurate. Table 1 shows the $AAS(W_i)$ value of correction with different α, β values.

Table 1. Grades of correction with different α, β values

α/β	0.1/0.9	0.2/0.8	0.3/0.7	0.4/0.6	0.5/0.5
$AAS(W_i)$	9.286	9.473	9.776	9.727	9.698

4   Encrypted EMR Searching with Relevance Ranking

4.1   Notations

- **R**: plaintext EMR set, $\mathbf{R} = \{R_1, R_2, ..., R_n\}$;
- **R′**: encrypted EMR set, $\mathbf{R}' = \{R'_1, R'_2, ..., R'_n\}$;
- ID: EMR identifier in plaintext $ID = \{id_1, id_2, ..., id_n\}$;
- ID': encrypted EMR identifier, $ID' = \{id'_1, id'_2, ..., id'_n\}$;
- **SW**: keywords set in plaintext, $\mathbf{SW} = \{W_1, W_2, ..., W_m\}$;
- **SW′**: keywords set in ciphertext, $\mathbf{SW}' = \{W'_1, W'_2, ..., W'_n\}$;
- $S_{i,j}$: plaintext relevance score of keyword W_i in R_j; S_j: sum of relevance score in R_j in plaintext;
- $S'_{i,j}$:encrypted relevance score of keyword W_i in document R_j; S'_j: sum of relevance score in R_j in ciphertext;
- $\mathbb{Z}^*_{y^2}$ is the set of integers range between 1 and y^2.

Our EMR-SMR scheme includes three major processes: EMR index building, encrypted EMR searching and queue-based ciphertext retrieval.

Medical Record

Name	Bob	Emergency Contact Name	Alice
Birth Date	26/01/1949	Address	529 Yuelu Road
Medical Plan	HPR	Phone	13812345678
Medical Plan ID	HPR 11	Record Date	03/07/2020

Medical History

Diabetes, ankle fracture 3 years ago, bone tuberculosis 15 years ago, abdominal surgery 20 years ago.

Description

Paroxysmal chest tightness, palpitation for more than one month, chest pain lasted more than 4 hours.

Physical Examination

Body temperature: 36.5°C, respiration: 18 beats/min, pulse: 85 beats/min, blood pressure: 120/80mmHg, normal development and nutrition, flat car pushed into the ward, self-position, physical examination cooperation. Conscious mind, normal skin and mucous membranes, no enlargement of superficial lymph nodes, facial features, no cyanosis of lips, no jugular vein enlargement, symmetry of thoracic gallery, clear breath sounds of both lungs, no dry and wet rales, no percussion Large, heart rate 85 beats/min, regular heart rhythm, no murmur heard in each valve auscultation area, flat abdomen, no tenderness and rebound pain, untouched liver and spleen, no edema in lower limbs. Physiological reflexes exist, and pathological reflexes are not elicited.

Diagonsis

Coronary atherosclerotic heart disease, Acute inferior myocardial infarction, pump function grade I

Tests Performed

Blood routine, ECG, Blood pressure

Tests Results

Blood pressure: 120/80mmHg, no positive signs were found on the other examinations.
ECG diagram II, III, aVF lead ST segment is raised about 0.2 -0.4m V, T wave is inverted.
Cardiac ultrasonography: left ventricular enlargement accompanied by weakened left ventricular overall contractile activity, and left ventricular EF decreased by 29%.

Fig. 2. EMR-SMR medical record template

4.2 Cryptographic Preliminaries

In our EMR-SMR scheme, symmetric key algorithm (SKA) is employed to encrypt keywords and document identifiers. Asymmetric key algorithm (AKA) is employed to encrypt relevance scores. Relevance score calculation algorithm (RSC) is employed to calculate encrypted relevance scores. The algorithms that are involved in the EMR-SMR are defined as followed.

- SKA = $(T, K, \text{ENC1}, \text{DEC1})$ is a symmetric key encryption algorithm, where T is the input data, K is the symmetric key, ENC1 is the encryption algorithm; DEC1 is the decryption algorithm.

- AKEA $= (RS, PK, SK,$ ENC2, DEC2$)$ is an asymmetric key algorithm, where RS is the input relevance score, PK is the public key used for relevance score encryption, SK is the secret key used for relevance score decryption. ENC2 and DEC2 are the encryption and decryption algorithms which will be defined in next section. PK and SK in AKEA algorithm are generated with the followed method: select two large prime numbers $p, q \in Z_n$, and $\gcd(pq, (p-1)(q-1)) = 1$, $\Phi(n) = (p-1)(q-1)$. Let $n = pq$, $\lambda = \mathrm{lcm}(p-1, q-1)$. The multiplicative subgroup $Z_n \times Z_n^* \rightarrow Z_{n^2}^*$. $|Z_{n^2}^*| = \Phi(n^2) = n\Phi(n)$. Suppose $g \in Z_{n^2}^*$ is a random integer, and $r \in (0, n)$ is a random integer, $\gcd(r, n) = 1$, $r^{(p-1)} \equiv 1 (\mathrm{mod}\ p)$ then $r^\lambda = 1$ mod n, $r^{n\lambda} = 1$ mod n^2. Defines $L(x) = \frac{x-1}{n}$ is the quotient of $(x-1)$ divided by n, the modular multiplicative inverse $\mu = (L(g^\lambda \bmod n^2))^{-1}$ mod n. The asymmetric key pair is $PK = (n, g)$ and $SK = \lambda$.
- RSC $= (S'_{i,j}, \prod_{i,j} S'_{i,j})$ is the calculation algorithm to get the sum of encrypted relevance scores. This algorithm is implemented by CSP, so that the heavy computation can be loaded to CSP without leaking any useful information about EMR. We use the Paillier-based encryption algorithm, the sum of relevance score is defined with Eq. (2).

$$\prod_{i,j} S'_{i,j} = g^{\sum S_{i,j}} \times \prod_i r_i^n \quad \mathrm{mod} \quad n^2 \tag{2}$$

4.3 EMR Index Building

In the index building process, EMR owners need to extract keywords from their EMRs, build up inverted plaintext index and encrypt original EMRs. Then, EMR owners will upload the plaintext index and encrypted EMRs to the Proxy and EMR storage sever respectively. Proxy is responsible for collecting indexes from all EMR owners, merging and building up the secure inverted index for all EMRs.

Index Building by EMR Owners. EMR owners extract keywords from their EMRS and calculate the relevance scores of each keyword with TF-IDF algorithm. EMR owners build up the plaintext index **I** for all EMRs, $\mathbf{I} = I_1, I_2, I_3 \ldots$ I_m, $I_i = (W_i, \bigcup_j < id''_j, S'_{i,j} >)$, I_i is the index of keyword W_i, id_j is the identifier of the EMR that contains W_i, $S_{i,j}$ denotes the relevance score of keyword W_i in R_j. EMR owner runs SKA(*, K_1, ENC1) to encrypt EMR records and their identifiers. The ciphertext generation process is defined with Eq. (3)

$$id'_n \leftarrow \mathrm{SKA}(id_n, K_1, \mathrm{ENC1})$$
$$R'_i \leftarrow (R_i, K_1, \mathrm{ENC1}) \tag{3}$$
$$C = \{(id'_1, R'_1), (id'_2, R'_2), \ldots, (id'_n, R'_n)\}$$

EMR owners then upload I and C to the Proxy and CSP respectively. ERM owners finally distribute decryption keys to authorized users.

Index Merging and Encryption. In the actual application scenario, there are usually multiple EMR owners uploading medical records. Since EMR owners use different encryption keys, this will cause difficulties in searching and relevance ranking. Thus, we introduce the Proxy to handle the indexes merging and encryption. Upon receiving multiple indexes from EMR owners, the Proxy merges the indexes with the respect of keywords and then generates the encrypted index I' with the following steps.

Step 1. Keywords and EMR identifier encryption. Proxy runs $SKA(*, K_2,$ ENC1) to get W_i' and id_j'' in **I'**.

$$W_i' \leftarrow SKA(W_i, K_2, ENC1) \quad id_j'' \leftarrow SKA(W_i, K_2, ENC1) \tag{4}$$

Where K_2 is the symmetric key generated by Proxy. The EMR identifiers are encrypted with different keys in index and C so that the CSP or attackers can?t get the connection between keywords and associated EMRs.

Step 2. Proxy encrypts the relevance score with $AKEA(RS, PK, ENC2)$. ENC2 uses Eq. (5) to encrypt relevance score $S_{i,j}'$.

$$S_{i,j}' = g^{S_{i,j}} \times r^n \mod n^2 \tag{5}$$

Finally, Proxy forms the secure index **I'** and upload it to the CSP.

$$\mathbf{I'} = \{I_1', I_2', I_3' \dots, I_i'\}, I_i' = \{W_i', \bigcup_j < id_j'', S_{i,j}' >\} \tag{6}$$

4.4   Encrypted EMR Searching

User starts searching process by inputting a set of search keywords, the PLSC algorithm corrects input errors and sends the keywords set $\mathbf{SW} = \{W_1, W_2, \dots, W_t\}$ to the Proxy. Proxy uses $SKA(SW, K_2, ENC1)$ to generate the trapdoor and submits $\mathbf{SW'} = \{W_1', W_2', \dots, W_t'\}$ to CSP for searching.

CSP Searching Algorithm. CSP performs a ciphertext searching algorithm based on $\mathbf{SW'}$ and **I'**. The search result is the conjunction of documents that contains all queried keywords in $\mathbf{SW'}$. After then, CSP implements $RSC(S_{i,j}', \prod_{i,j} S_{i,j}'))$ algorithm to get the sum of the keywords relevance score with Eq. (2). The searching algorithm is described in Algorithm 1.

$$S_j' = \prod_{i,j} S_{i,j}', \quad \text{for each} \quad D_j \quad \text{has} \quad W_i' \in \mathbf{SW} \tag{7}$$

After completing the calculation of the relevance scores, the CSP sends the search result which contains required keywords, EMR identifiers and summation of relevance scores to the Proxy.

Algorithm 1. Ciphertext searching by CSP

Input: input keywords $SW' = \{W'_1, W'_2, W'_t$ from users;
Output: search results
1: **function** CIPHERTEXT SEARCHING & SCORE CALCULATION
2:    $\mathbf{I}'_r = \mathbf{I}\,'$;
3:    **for** $i \leq t$ **do**
4:      Search I';
5:      **if** $W'_i = \mathbf{I}'_i.W'_i$ **then** $\mathbf{I}'_r = \mathbf{I}'_r \cap \mathbf{I}'_i$;
6:        **while** $\mathbf{I}'_r \neq \emptyset$ **do**
7:          **for** e doach $\mathbf{I}'_r.id_j$
8:            run RSC($S''_{i,j}, S'_j$) ;
9:            $S'_j = \prod_{i,j} S'_{i,j}$;
10:          **end for**
11:        **end while**
12:      **end if**
13:    **end for**
14:    return($\mathbf{I}'_r$)
15: **end function**

Relevance Ranking Algorithm. Aiming to give users the most relevant EMRs based on their input keywords, Proxy needs to rank the summation of relevance scores for each returned EMR. This function is performed with SKA() and SKEA() algorithms. Proxy implements SKA($*, K_2$, DEC1) to get the plaintext keywords W_i and EMR identifiers R_i. Furthermore, Proxy runs SKEA(S'_j, SK, DEC2) to get the plaintext relevance score summation. The SKEA($*, SK$, DEC2) decryption algorithm is defined with Eq. (8).

$$
\begin{aligned}
S_j &= L(S'^\lambda \mod n^2) \times \mu & \mod\ n \\
&= \frac{L(S'^\lambda \mod n^2)}{L(g'^\lambda \mod n^2)} & \mod\ n \\
&= \frac{L(g^{\lambda \Sigma S_{i,j}} \times \prod_i r_i^{\lambda n} \mod n^2)}{L(g^\lambda \mod n^2)} & \mod\ n \qquad (8) \\
&= \frac{L(g^{\lambda \Sigma S_{i,j}} \mod n^2)}{L(g^\lambda \mod n^2)} & \mod\ n \\
&= \sum S_{i,j}
\end{aligned}
$$

Where $\prod_i r_i^{\lambda n} \equiv 1$. After getting the plaintext EMR identifiers and summation of relevance scores, Proxy ranks the top-k EMR based on their $\Sigma S_{i,j}$ and send their identifiers back to the users. Upon receiving the EMR identifiers, users send downloading requests to the CSP directly.

Queuing-Based Ciphertext Retrieval. As an honest but curious principal, CSP tries to obtain information about the linkablity of keywords, indexes and documents by analyzing queries and search results. Current state-of-art searchable encryption schemes have two main information leakage threats: file-access pattern (which files are returned in response to each query) and keywords query pattern (when a query is repeated). In our scheme, we avoid these two threats in the following ways:

- EMR identifiers in the index and storage are encrypted with different keys, so that relationship between keywords, index and EMRs can be hidden.
- A queuing-based ciphtertext retrieval scheme is proposed to obfuscate the query pattern. A pseudo query method is also proposed to hide the query pattern in case there are no adequate queries in the queue. The queuing-based ciphertext retrieval scheme is performed by Proxy, the algorithm is defined in Algorithm 2.

Algorithm 2. Queue-based ciphertext searching

Input: W_i from users;
Output: Encrypted queries; search results
1: **function** QUEUE-BASED QUERIES(W_i)
2:      set time slot T_s, minimum queued queries Q_{min}
3:      define buffer Q_s
4:      $t \leftarrow 0, k \leftarrow 0$
5:      **while** $t < T_s$ **do**
6:          $W_i' = \text{SKA}(W_i, K_2, \text{ENC1})$
7:          $Q_s \leftarrow W_i'$
8:          $k++$
9:      **end while**
10:     **if** $k < Q_{min}$ **then**
11:         Proxy generates pseudo queries PW
12:         $Q_s \leftarrow PW$
13:     **end if**
14:     forward queries in Q_s to CSP
15: **end function**

In this scheme, after receiving research results from CSP, Proxy will wait a preset time slot T_r, then if the number of returned results are more than the required minimum number, Proxy will forward the query results to users simultaneously. Otherwise, Proxy will attach n random results to the query results and send them to users simultaneously. In this way, multiple users will ask for a number of documents downloading at the same time, and the connection between keywords and file identifiers can be hidden.

5   Security Analysis

In this section, the scheme security will be analyzed on two aspects: ciphertext retrieval security and possibility of EMR privacy leakage. In this scheme the ciphertext retrieval security is guaranteed by the queue-based searching policy implemented by Proxy, while private preserving is ensured by the encryption algorithms of SKA() and SKEA().

5.1   Possibility of Privacy Leakage

Users search for EMRs by sending keywords to the Proxy. Proxy then encrypts the keywords and forwards the queries to the CSP. So that, the CSP cannot get the keywords or user information, user privacy is guaranteed. Meanwhile, in order to hide the connection between keywords and documents, Proxy generates forge queries and queues the search results. So that in the time slot T, the number of queries N would be no less than the number of users M.

– for $M = N$, each user sends only one search query in a time slot. After the Proxy queuing, the possibility of CSP successfully guesses the correspondence between keywords and documents is shown in Eq. 9.

$$\frac{1}{A_M^M} = \frac{1}{M!} \tag{9}$$

– for $N > M$, the number of schemes that can separate N queries into M groups is:

$$S(N, M) = \frac{1}{M!} \sum_{k=0}^{M} (-1)^k \binom{M}{k} (M-k)^N \tag{10}$$

Then the probability of CSP successful guessing is:

$$P = \frac{M^k}{S(N, M) \times M!} \tag{11}$$

It is safe to conclude that with the increase of N, the probability P decreases significantly and continuously. If a user sends multiple search requests in a short period of time, the queuing query through the Proxy can greatly improve the guessing difficulty of the CSP. If the Proxy sends a forged search request, since the search request contains a forged search request, the CSP cannot guess the correspondence between the completely correct keyword and the file. Therefore, setting the proxy queuing query and forging the search request can effectively prevent the CSP statistical guessing attack and improve security.

5.2   Data Confidentiality

In our scheme, the plaintext documents are encrypted before outsourcing to the cloud and the decryption keys are distributed to users by EMR owners via secure channel. Hence, documents security can be achieved. Index is built by EMR owners and encrypted by the Proxy. In addition, we encrypt the file identifier of the index and documents with different keys (K_3 and K_1) so that the CSP cannot obtain the connection between the encrypted documents and the encrypted index. Keywords relevance scores for each document is encrypted and calculated with algorithm RSC(), even though the encrypted relevance scores are accumulated by the CSP, the CSP can not get any information about keywords or their relevance scores. Therefore, as long as the Proxy and users keep their respective keys properly, the confidentiality of data, index, keyword information and relevance scores can be guaranteed.

6   Performance Evaluation

Our performance experiment is implemented in C++ language on Windows 7 with Intel(R) Core(TM) i5 6500 3.2 GHz and 2 GB RAM. We use more than 3000 medical keywords to generate 2000 EMRs that contain various diseases. We evaluate the scheme performance in the following ways: (1) index generation efficiency (2) trapdoor generation efficiency (3) retrieval efficiency. We compare our scheme with the most relevant researches on searchable encryption: FMS [13] and TBMSM [12].

6.1   Index Building Efficiency

In this section, we compare the index building time and storage cost among our scheme, FMS, TBMSM and Zhong's scheme. Figure 3(a) shows the time overhead required to build an index with the number of keywords ranging from 1000 to 3000. TBMSM has a greater growth rate with the increase number of keywords. While the time cost on building index with other three schemes are stable and increase slowly. Figure 3(b) shows the time required for generating indexes with the number of EMRs ranging from 100 to 2000. It can be seen that as the number of EMRs grows, the index generation time of our EMR-SMR scheme increases slowly. When the number of EMRs is smaller than 500, the efficiencies of all schemes are almost the same. However, if the number of EMRs is more than 500, the index building time of FMS grows dramatically. Compared with other searchable encryption methods, our EMR-SMR is the most efficient scheme in index building.

Figure 4 shows the index storage space required for all schemes. Figure 4(a) and Fig. 4(b) show that when there are more than 300 EMRs or the number of keywords in the index is more than 1000, the index storage overhead of the EMR-SMR scheme is better than that of the FMS scheme, and the growth rate of EMR-SMR is slower than that of FMS. The index storage overhead of TBMSM is much larger than that of EMR-SMR. When the number of keywords in the index reaches 2000, the index storage space of TBMSM exceeds 100 MB. In the real-world applications, especially in the CMT (Cloud Medical Treatment) systems, there would be a massive number of encrypted medical records and keywords. The efficiency of index generation and storage size should be considered seriously. Our EMR-SMR scheme has a better performance both in index generation time and storage space than the other schemes.

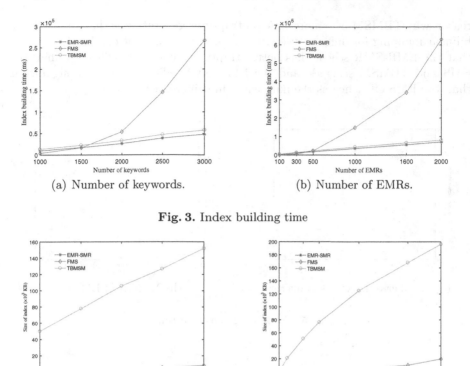

(a) Number of keywords.   (b) Number of EMRs.

Fig. 3. Index building time

(a) Number of keywords.   (b) Number of EMRs.

Fig. 4. Index storage space

6.2 Trapdoor Generation Time

This section compares the trapdoor generation efficiency of the three schemes discussed before. Figure 5(a) shows the trapdoor generation efficiency over 1000 EMRs with queried keywords ranging from 10 to 50. Figure 5(b) shows the trapdoor generation efficiency on 20 keywords with the number of files ranging from 100 to 2000. In Fig. 5(a) we can see that the trapdoor generation time in FMS is not affected by the number of search keywords. The trapdoor generation time in our EMR-SMR and the TBMSM scheme is only related to the number of queried keywords. With the growth of keywords, the trapdoor generation time in TBMSM grows linearly while EMR-SMR grows slowly regarding to the number of search keywords. In Fig. 5(b), the number of query keywords is set to be 20. The trapdoor generation time of FMS grows linearly with the increase of files number, while the TBMSM and our EMR-SMR schemes remain stable. The reason why FMS has a linear growth is that the trapdoor is generated with matrix operation $(M_1^{-1}qa, M_2^{-1}qb)$. Therefore, as the number of files and keywords in the index increases, the dimension of the encryption matrix increases accordingly, which causes the linear growth of trapdoor generation time. The reason why TBMSM uses more time on trapdoor generation is that they use the bilinear mapping for different users. From the two figures, it can be clearly seen that the EMR-SMR scheme has better trapdoor generation efficiency than the FMS and TBMSM schemes, and the EMR-SMR efficiency is more significant than the FMS efficiency as the number of files increases.

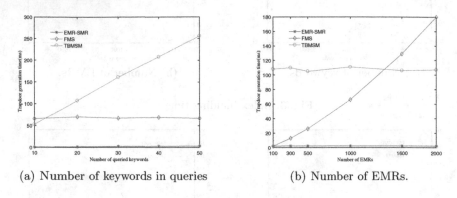

(a) Number of keywords in queries   (b) Number of EMRs.

Fig. 5. Trapdoor generation time

6.3 Search Efficiency

This section compares the search time overhead of SMR-EMR, FMS and TBMSM schemes. All schemes are tested with the number of files ranging from 100 to 2000, and the number of queried keywords is set to be 5 per query. As shown in Fig. 6, our EMR-SMR scheme has less search time than the FMS and TBMSM schemes. The search time of EMR-SMR is less than 1s even though

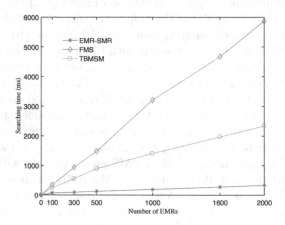

Fig. 6. Search efficiency with different number of EMRs

there are 1600 encrypted papers in the database. The search time in the FMS and TBMSM schemes increases as the number of files increases.

7   Conclusion

We proposed a privacy-preserving searchable encryption scheme to protect the security of EMRs. In this scheme, we use the PLSC algorithm to support multiple keywords input and fuzzy search. Furthermore, a homomorphic encryption algorithm is designed to keep the relevance scores secure and computable. Also, we proposed a queue-based query strategy that can hide the access pattern and query pattern to protect the highly sensitive medical records. Based on our theoretical security proof, our scheme can guarantee both data security and search security. Finally, we implement and compare our scheme with another two close relevant schemes, where the implementation results show that our EMR-SMR scheme is more efficient in many ways.

Acknowledgment. This work is supported by the National Natural Science Foundation of China under grant 61402160 and 61872134. Hunan Provincial Natural Science Foundation under grant 2016JJ3043. Open Funding for Universities in Hunan Province under grant 14K023.

References

1. Song, X.D., Wagner, D., Perrig, A.: Practical techniques for searches on encrypted data. In: Proceeding of 2000 IEEE Symposium on Security and Privacy, Berkeley, CA, USA, pp. 1–12 (2000)
2. Boneh, D., Di Crescenzo, G., Ostrovsky, R., Persiano, G.: Public key encryption with keyword search. In: Cachin, C., Camenisch, J.L. (eds.) EUROCRYPT 2004. LNCS, vol. 3027, pp. 506–522. Springer, Heidelberg (2004). https://doi.org/10.1007/978-3-540-24676-3_30
3. Li, H., Liu, D., Dai, Y.: Enabling efficient multi-keyword ranked search over encrypted mobile cloud data through blind storage. IEEE Trans. Emerg. Topics Comput. **3**(1), 127–138 (2015). https://doi.org/10.1109/TETC.2014.2371239
4. Li, R., Liu, A.X., Wang, A.L., Bruhadeshwar, B.: Fast and scalable range query processing with strong privacy protection for cloud computing. IEEE/ACM Trans. Netw. **24**(4), 2305–2318 (2015). https://doi.org/10.1109/TNET.2015.2457493
5. Kale, V.K.: A secure and dynamic multi-watchphrase ranked search scheme over encrypted cloud data. IJASRET **5**(10), 5933–5947 (2020). https://doi.org/10.1109/TCSVT.2014.2358031
6. Mollah, M.B., Azad, M.A.K., Vasilakos, A.: Security and privacy challenges in mobile cloud computing: survey and way ahead. J. Netw. Comput. Appl. **84**, 38–54 (2020)
7. Sun, W., Wang, B., Cao, N.: Verifiable privacy-preserving multi-keyword text search in the cloud supporting similarity-based ranking. IEEE Trans. Parallel Distrib. Syst. **25**(11), 2025–3035 (2014). https://doi.org/10.1109/TPDS.2013.282

8. Kabir, T., Adnan, M.A.: A dynamic searchable encryption scheme for secure cloud CSP operation reserving multi-keyword ranked search. In: Proceedings of 2017 the 4th International Conference on Networking, Systems and Security (NSysS), Dhaka, Bangladesh, pp. 1–9 (2017)

9. Liu, Q., Tian, Y., Wu, J., Peng, T., Wang, G.: Enabling verifiable and dynamic ranked search over outsourced data. In: Proceedings of the 18th IEEE International Conference on Trust, Security and Privacy in Computing and Communications, Rotorua, New Zealand, pp. 1–14, August 2019

10. Du, L., Li, K., Liu, Q., Wu, Z., Zhang, S.: Dynamic multi-client searchable symmetric encryption with support for boolean queries. Inf. Sci. **506**, 234–257 (2020). https://doi.org/10.1016/j.ins.2019.08.014

11. Pappas, V., et al.: Blind seer: a scalable private DBMS. In: 2014 IEEE Symposium on Security and Privacy, San Jose, CA, USA, pp. 359–374 (2014)

12. Peng, T., Lin, Y., Yao, X., Zhang, W.: An efficient ranked multi-keyword search for multiple data owners over encrypted cloud data. IEEE Access **6**, 21924–21933 (2018)

13. Li, H., Yang, Y., Luan, T.H.: Enabling fine-grained multi-keyword search supporting classified sub-dictionaries over encrypted cloud data. IEEE Trans. Dependable Secure Comput. **13**(3), 312–325 (2016). https://doi.org/10.1109/TDSC.2015.2406704

14. Pakiat, N., Shiraly, D., Eslami, Z.: Certificateless authenticated encryption with keyword search: enhanced security model and a concrete construction for industrial IoT. J. Inf. Secur. Appl. **53**, 1–10 (2020). https://doi.org/10.1016/j.jisa.2020.102525

15. Wang, C., Yuan, X., Cui, Y., Ren, K.: Toward secure outsourced middlebox services: practices, challenges, and beyond. IEEE Network **32**(1), 166–171 (2018). https://doi.org/10.1109/MNET.2017.1700060

16. Utsumi, A.: Refining pretrained word embeddings using layer-wise relevance propagation. In: Proceedings of the 2018 Conference on Empirical Methods in Natural Language Processing, Brussels, Belgium, pp. 4840–4846, October 2018

17. Hao, J., Huang, C., Ni, J., Rong, H., Xian, M.: Fine-grained data access control with attribute-hiding policy for cloud-based IoT. Comput. Netw. **153**, 1–10 (2019). https://doi.org/10.1016/j.comnet.2019.02.008

18. Zhang, L., Liang, P., Mu, Y.: Improving privacy-preserving and security for decentralized key-policy attributed-based encryption. IEEE Access **6**, 12736–12745 (2018)

19. Zhong, H., Li, Z., Cui, J., Sun, Y., Liu, L.: Efficient dynamic multi-keyword fuzzy search over encrypted cloud data. J. Netw. Comput. Appl. **149**, 1–10 (2020). https://doi.org/10.1016/j.jnca.2019.102469

20. Gnanasekaran, P., Mareswari, C.: A secure and dynamic multi-keyword ranked search scheme over encrypted cloud data. IRJAES **2**(3), 70–75 (2017)

21. Liu, Y., Peng, H., Wang, J.: Verifiable diversity ranking search over encrypted outsourced data. Comput. Mater. Continua **55**(1), 37–57 (2018)

22. Yang, Y., Yang, S., Ke, M.: Simhash based fuzzy ranked search scheme over encrypted cloud data. Chin. J. Comput. **40**(2), 431–444 (2017)

23. Zhang, Y., Katz, J., Papamanthou, C.: All your queries are belong to us: the power of file-injection attack on searchable encryption. In: Proceedings of the 25th USENIX Security Symposium 2016, USENIX, Austin, TX, USA, pp. 707–720 (2016)

24. Wang, K., Li, Y., Zhou, F.: Fuzzy ciphertext search scheme for multi-keywords. J. Comput. Res. Dev. **54**(2), 348–360 (2017). https://doi.org/10.7544/issn1000-1239. 2017.20151125
25. Wang, B., Yu, S., Lou, W., Hou, Y.H.: Privacy-preserving multi-keyword fuzzy search over encrypted data in the cloud. In: IEEE Conference on Computer Communications (IEEE INFOCOM 2014), Toronto, CAN, pp. 2112–2120 (2014)
26. Li, X., Li, F., Jiang, J., Mei, X.: Paillier-based fuzzy multi-keyword searchable encryption scheme with order-preserving. CMC-Comput. Mater. Contin. **65**(2), 1707–1721 (2020)
27. Chen, L., Liao, X., Mu, N., Wu, J., Qing, J.: Privacy-preserving fuzzy multi-keyword search for multiple data owners in cloud computing. In: IEEE Symposium Series on Computational Intelligence, Xiamen, China, pp. 2166–2171 (2019)

A Container-Oriented Virtual-Machine-Introspection-Based Security Monitor to Secure Containers in Cloud Computing

Zhaofeng Yu[1]([⊠]) [iD], Lin Ye[1], Hongli Zhang[1], Dongyang Zhan[1,2], Shen Su[3], and Zhihong Tian[3]

[1] Harbin Institute of Technology, Harbin 150001, China
20S003135@stu.hit.edu.cn
[2] The Ohio State University, Columbus 43202, USA
[3] Guangzhou University, Guangzhou 510006, P.R.China
{sushen,tianzhihong}@gzhu.edu.cn

Abstract. In recent years, container technology has been widely used in cloud computing, so the security monitoring technology for containers has also received widespread attention. To enhance the isolation of containers, cloud service providers usually run containers in different virtual machines. In this environment, in-container security tools can be detected or attacked by in-container attackers, and in-VM security tools face the risk of container escape attacks. This paper proposes a container-oriented virtual machine introspection technology to secure containers in cloud computing. It runs in cloud hypervisor and analyzes in-VM containers, so it is more secure and transparent. Even though there is container escaping to the operating system of VM, the security monitors are secure. Firstly, our approach automatically identifies the namespace and container processes in the virtual machine from outside by using virtual machine introspection technology. Secondly, security analysis is performed on processes belonging to different containers in the virtual machine, and our system can perform real-time abnormal response based on the analysis results. Finally, our system can monitor container escape behaviors from outside. Experimental results show that the approach proposed in this paper can automatically perform security analysis for different containers, and can monitor container escape behaviors with acceptable overhead.

Keywords: Container monitoring · Virtual machine introspection · External monitoring

1 Introduction

With the development of container technology, mainstream cloud computing vendors including Amazon and Google have provided container-based cloud computing services. Container is a lightweight operating system virtualization technology, which uses Linux namespace technology (Namespace) and control group technology (CGroup) to isolate

---

The original version of this chapter was revised: Shen Su and Zhihong Tian have been added as co-authors and their affiliation have been added. The correction to this chapter is available at https://doi.org/10.1007/978-3-030-78612-0_61

resources (such as file system, process number, network, etc.) in the operating system for different container processes. It makes the process in the container seem to be running in an independent operating system. However, because different containers share the same operating system kernel, the isolation and security of container is weaker than that of virtual machine. In recent years, multiple container escape vulnerabilities have been discovered. By exploiting these vulnerabilities, an attacker in the container can control the host. In order to improve the isolation of containers, virtual machines are widely used to isolate containers. For example, Kata Containers [3] and Firecracker [1] enable containers to run in independent lightweight virtual machines, and enhance the isolation of containers to the virtual-machine level.

There are several challenges of monitoring containers. In–container security tools can be detected or attacked by malicious processes in container. So, it is more secure to monitor containers from outside. But monitoring containers in host is still not secure. Since containers are able to perform privilege escalation attacks, managing and monitoring containers in the host faces security risks.

To address these security challenges, this paper proposes an external monitoring approach to monitor containers based on virtual machine introspection technology. In this architecture, target containers are running in virtual machines for stronger isolation. Security tools work in the hypervisor, which can obtain the execution information of target virtual machines. Since the hypervisor has the highest privilege, monitors running inside the hypervisor are more secure and transparent.

Based on virtual machine introspection, security monitor can obtain the binary execution information of target virtual machine, then it analyzes the memory and file system to extract the processes of different containers. Finally, the extracted information is analyzed to detect abnormal behaviors of containers. In addition, two approaches are proposed to detect container escape attack from hypervisor. The first one is to monitor the statues of Linux namespaces, the second one is to monitor the integrity of some critical files. In summary, the contributions of this paper are as follows.

- An external virtual-machine-introspection-based monitoring approach is proposed to monitor containers from hypervisor. In this architecture, containers are running inside virtual machines, and monitors are running in the VMM layer.
- An automatic namespace analysis method is proposed to extract container processes from virtual machine by analyzing the kernel memory of it.
- A namespace-based and a file-based monitoring approach are proposed to detect privilege escalation behaviors of containers.

The rest of this paper is organized as follows. Section 2 summaries the related work of container security analysis and virtual machine introspection. Section 3 describes the design of container-oriented security introspection. Section 4 evaluates the effectiveness and performance of the prototype. The conclusion is given in Sect. 5.

2 Related Work

When the lightweight virtualization technology brings convenience to users, the security issues of containers have always attracted wide attention. Literature [8] proposes to protect container security from four aspects: 1. Protect the program in the container;

2. Protect the attacks between containers; 3. Protect the host from container attacks; 4. Protect the container from host attacks. Literature [10] proposes that the vulnerabilities of containers originate from four aspects: 1. Vulnerabilities caused by container configuration; 2. Vulnerabilities in images; 3. Vulnerabilities in image configuration; 4. Vulnerabilities contained in software in unsafe image sources and containers. Literature [7] proposed a cloud computing-oriented container security detection method to detect the security of container images and the programs contained in the images.

Since the operating system kernel of the host is shared between the containers in the same host, the isolation between the container and the host is poor. Literature [7] found that 3 Linux kernel vulnerabilities can be exploited to realize container escape. Once the attacker achieves the escape of the container, the entire host will be threatened. For this reason, Kata Container and gVisor adopt full virtualization and para-virtualization methods to improve the isolation of containers; Nabla reduces the attack surface by reducing the number of system calls that the container can access, making it more difficult for the container to escape. Literature [10] proposes a dynamic detection method to detect container escape behavior. It summarizes the attack process after the container escapes and finds that after the container escapes, the commit_creds() function is often called to enhance the container's permissions and realize the escape. By intercepting the execution of this function, the escape behavior of the container can be detected. Because Linux's security mechanism cannot serve the container multi-tenant service model well. Literature [9] proposed a container-oriented Linux security mechanism (such as AppArmor), so that the security mechanism of Linux can be used in the container namespace.

Due to the easy escape characteristics of containers, security detection of containers in the host faces the threat of container escape. Once the container escapes, the monitoring program will not work properly. There are several containers proposed to enhance the isolation.

Kata Containers is based on full virtualization isolation. In 2017, Intel Clear Containers and Kata Containers were merged, using lightweight virtual machines to improve container isolation. In Kata Containers, each container runs in a separate virtual machine. The user configures and manages the container outside the virtual machine. A configuration client is running in the virtual machine, and an agent outside the virtual machine can remotely call functions in the client, thereby configuring and managing the container in the virtual machine. Kata Containers makes use of Intel Clear Containers technology to make the virtual machine kernel lighter, realizing fast startup of the virtual machine and minimizing resource usage. However, Kata Containers still faces several problems: First, each container runs in a virtual machine, which occupies more host resources; second, the management tool (configuration client) in the virtual machine faces the threat of container escape. Once the container escape occurs, the management tools in the virtual machine domain may be attacked. Finally, Kata Containers only speeds up virtual machine startup by reducing the size of the virtual machine operating system, and there is still room for improvement.

gVisor [2] is based on para-virtualization isolation. gVisor was developed by Google based on the go language, using para-virtualization to isolate containers, and is compatible with OCI standards like Kata Containers. The runtime of gVisor is called runsc, similar to Docker's runc, which can respond to OCI commands. Runsc is composed of two parts: Sentry and Gofer. Sentry is a virtual lightweight operating system kernel, which is responsible for handling all system calls for container access. Sentry can simulate most system calls, reducing the host's attack surface. However, some system calls still cannot be simulated and need to be completed by the host operating system. Gofer is the agent program of the container file system, which forwards all I/O requests of the container to the host. Since gVisor relies on the host operating system to a certain extent, its isolation is weaker than the isolation method of full virtualization. Moreover, gVisor cannot implement all system calls, and it is not as versatile as Kata Containers.

Virtual machine introspection technology solves this problem. Virtual machine introspection technology is a security monitoring technology for external virtual machines. In the virtual machine introspection architecture, the security monitoring program runs in the virtual machine management layer and the secure virtual machine. Because the virtual machine management layer has the highest authority and there is a strong isolation between virtual machines, the virtual machine introspection technology has high security and transparency. When the container runs in a virtual machine and the monitoring program runs outside the virtual machine domain, the monitoring program will have higher security.

Based on virtual machine introspection technology, a variety of security monitoring systems have been proposed. Literature [6] proposed a virtual machine extra-domain intrusion detection system based on virtual machine introspection, which can analyze multiple security states of virtual machines outside the domain to realize intrusion detection. Literature [11] proposed a file monitoring system based on virtual machine introspection technology. It performs target-based monitoring of files in virtual machines, and can realize lightweight realtime monitoring of important files in virtual machines. Literature [5] proposed an intrusion detection system based on virtual machine introspection technology. It first analyzes the security of the virtual machine's network packet. After discovering anomalies, it detects whether the virtual machine is attacked in a fine-grained manner outside the domain.

In addition to security monitoring, literature [4] can use virtual machine introspection technology to achieve automatic fine-grained virtual machine management outside the domain. It uses system call reuse technology and uses virtual machines outside the domain to automatically handle semantic gap issues. However, the monitoring system based on virtual machine introspection technology is not optimized and designed for containers, and cannot adapt to the multi-tenant scenarios that may appear in the same virtual machine. This paper studies the container-oriented virtual machine introspection technology. We use virtual machine introspection technology to automatically identify and analyze the containers running in the virtual machine, and at the same time detect the container escape behavior.

3   Container-Oriented Virtual Machine Introspection

3.1   Identification of Container Processes

Since Linux 2.6, the Linux kernel has introduced namespace technology (Namespace), and containers are implemented based on namespace technology. Linux has 6 different namespaces, including: UTS Namespace, used to isolate host names and domain names; IPC Namespace, used to isolate communication between processes; Mount Namespace, used to isolate file systems; PID Namespace, used to isolate process identifiers; Network Namespace, used to isolate the network; User Namespace, used to mark the owner and permissions of the namespace. Only processes with the same namespace are resource-sharing and mutually visible. For example: when two processes have the same IPC Namespace, they can communicate. however, they cannot communicate with processes that have different IPC Namespaces. When the container is created, these Namespaces are automatically created and assigned to the processes in the container. Processes in the same container have the same Namespace, so the processes in the same container are mutually visible and cannot access other containers.

In order to realize container-oriented out-of-domain analysis, we must first identify all namespaces in the virtual machine. Processes with the same namespace belong to the same container. Therefore, this article analyzes the namespaces of all processes in the virtual machine outside the virtual machine domain and classifies them. All process structures in the Linux operating system are linked together by a doubly linked list, and the first address of the linked list is recorded by the init_task identifier. Therefore, the system can obtain and analyze all the process structures by analyzing the doubly linked list formed by the process structures in the virtual machine memory.

After obtaining the process structure, we analyze the namespace corresponding to the structure. The relationship between the process structure and the namespace is shown in Fig. 1. After that, based on the namespace, all containers and corresponding processes in the virtual machine can be automatically identified.

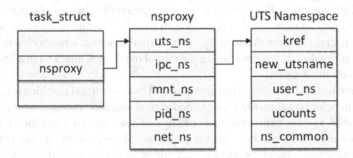

Fig. 1. Relationship diagram between process structure and namespace

3.2 Security Monitoring of Containers

The architecture of the monitoring system is shown in Fig. 2. The monitored container runs in the target virtual machine. The security analysis program runs in the virtual machine management layer and the secure virtual machine. The virtual machine management layer provides virtualization services for virtual machines and strictly isolates them. Since the monitoring program runs in a virtual machine management layer with higher authority and a security virtual machine, even if the container escapes, it cannot threaten the monitoring program. This article separately detects malicious processes and malicious files for containers.

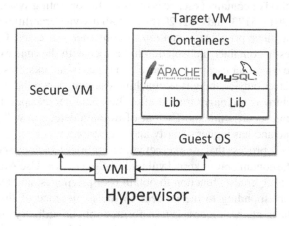

Fig. 2. The architecture of security monitor

This article monitors the creation of container processes to detect malicious processes in containers. In order to monitor the process creation in the container in real time, the system monitors the process creation system call (EXECVE) in the target virtual machine. When a virtual machine creates a new process, if the corresponding namespace belongs to a container, it means that a new process is created in the container. In order to obtain the namespace information of the newly created process, the system reads the memory of the virtual machine after the execution of the EXECVE system call ends and analyzes the structure of the newly created process. After that, the system analyzes the binary executable file corresponding to the new process to determine the safety of the new process.

This article analyzes the files in the container file system to determine the security of executable files and discover malicious files. The file system of the container is composed of multiple layers of image, namely: basic image and incremental image. The base image is a readable original file system, also known as the original layer. This layer holds the original files of the container. The incremental layer is readable and writable and records the modification of the container to the original layer. All files in the container can be read by analyzing the image of the container. In order to analyze the security of executable files, this article extracts the target files from the image and uses security analysis software (such as NOD 32, etc.) for detection.

When the basic image is not customized by the user, this article extracts all the newly added files from the incremental image and performs a security check on them. This effectively reduces the number of file scans and can efficiently find malicious files in the container.

3.3 Container Escape Attack Detection

Container escape is one of the most important threats to container security. At present, the most common method of container escape is to attack the operating system kernel. CVE-2017-7308, CVE-2017-5123, and CVE-2016-8655 all use vulnerabilities in the operating system kernel to achieve privilege escalation of container processes. CVE-2019-5736 uses vulnerabilities in container file isolation to tamper with the runc executable file in the host to achieve container escape. For these two types of attacks, this paper proposes two methods to detect outside the virtual machine domain. Since the operating system of the virtual machine is no longer trusted after the container escapes, the detection in the domain is facing security threats. The out-of-domain detection will not be affected by container escape and has higher security and transparency.

A common attack process that uses kernel vulnerabilities to achieve container escape is: the process in the container uses kernel vulnerabilities (such as Use After Free attacks) to execute the commit_creds() function to obtain root privileges, and then tamper with the namespace corresponding to the process to the namespace of the non-container process. So that the container process is transformed into an ordinary process with root privileges. In response to the above attack path, this article monitors the execution of commit_creds() in the virtual machine to monitor container escape. This article replaces the first instruction of the function with the INT3 interrupt instruction. When the function is executed, the VMExit event will be triggered, so the monitoring program running on the VMM layer can capture the event. When the function is executed, the system checks whether the process executing the function belongs to the container.

After that, this article monitors the integrity of the runc file to monitor container escape. Aiming at the situation of tampering with the runc executable file to achieve escape, this article polls the integrity of the file outside the virtual machine domain. In addition, when the runc file is executed, the integrity of the file is checked again to ensure that the attack cannot occur. This article monitors the execution behavior of runc files by monitoring the EXECVE system call.

4 Evaluation

4.1 Experimental Environment

The experiment uses Intel Core(TM) i7 CPU, 4-core 2.60 GHZ, 16G RAM. The operating system of the host is Ubuntu 16.04; the operating system of the virtual machine is Ubuntu 16.04. The virtual machine is configured with 1 VCPU and 1 GB RAM.

4.2 Effectiveness

To test the effectiveness of the system, first run multiple containers in a virtual machine and perform a container escape attack in the container. The monitoring system monitors the containers in the virtual machine at the virtual machine management layer and detects container escape attacks.

After running two containers in the virtual machine, the system obtains the list of processes in the virtual machine outside the virtual machine domain and obtains the corresponding namespace. After testing, the system can detect two container processes. After that, the malicious file is executed in the container. The monitoring system can capture the creation behavior of the process, and can obtain executable files. Using the method of [8] to inject the KILL system call into the virtual machine, the malicious process can be terminated.

After that, the container escape attack was performed in the two containers respectively. After running the PoC code corresponding to CVE-2017-7308 in the container, the system detects the execution of the commit_creds() function. Then, this article restores the test environment and performs CVE-2019-5736 attacks in the container. After the attack, the system detected that the runc file in the virtual machine was tampered with.

4.3 Performance

The monitoring overhead of this system mainly comes from the real-time monitoring of the commit_creds() function, the EXECVE system call and the system call return in the virtual machine. In order to test the overhead, this article monitors these three events separately and tests the performance. In this paper, lmbench is used for testing. Since the system call return is a high frequency event, continuous monitoring of it will cause high overhead. Therefore, this article first performs a load test on the commit_creds() function and EXECVE, and then tests the three events at the same time. For the accuracy of the experimental results, this paper selects the lmbench as the measurement toolkit.

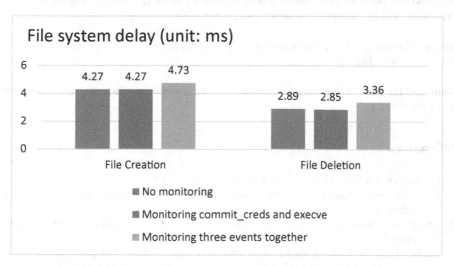

Fig. 3. The performance of the file system under different conditions.

We test the task processing delay under different monitoring conditions. When the monitoring is not turned on, it takes 0.34 microseconds for the processor to complete a system call. After monitoring the commit_creds() function and the EXECVE syscall, it takes 0.35 microseconds. When the monitoring of the three target events was turned on at the same time, the processing time reached 0.84 microseconds and the overhead reached 147%.

In addition, we also tested the file system reading and writing. When only the commit_creds() function and the EXECVE system call monitoring are enabled, there is no significant difference with the monitoring that is not enabled. When monitoring is enabled for three targets at the same time, the file system creation performance loss is 10.77%, the file system delete performance loss is 16.26%. The test result is shown in Fig. 3.

It can be seen from the results that when the system monitors commit_creds() and the EXECVE syscall at the same time, the system overhead is extremely low. When the three events are monitored at the same time, the system overhead is higher. Since monitoring the commit_creds() and the EXECVE syscall can detect container escape attacks and the third event does not require continuous monitoring, so the system overhead is acceptable.

5 Conclusion

This paper proposes a container-oriented virtual machine introspection technology. The monitoring program runs outside the virtual machine domain and can automatically identify the namespace and container process in the virtual machine, perform security analysis according to the process of different containers, and respond in real time according to the analysis results. In addition, it is possible to monitor container escape attacks outside the virtual machine domain. Experiments show that the method proposed in this paper can perform automated security analysis and exception handling for different containers, and can monitor container escape behavior.

Funding Statement.   This paper is supported by National Natural Science Foundation of China under grants No. 61872111.

Conflicts of Interest.   The authors declare that they have no conflicts of interest to report regarding the present study.

References

1. Firecracker container. https://firecracker-microvm.github.io/
2. gviosr: A container sandbox runtime focused on security, efficiency, and ease of use. https://gvisor.dev/
3. Intel clear containers. https://clearlinux.org/news-blogs/intel-clear-containersnow-part-kata-containers
4. Baohui, L., Kefu, X., Peng, Z., Li, G.: pTrace: a counter technology of DDoS attack source for controllable cloud computing. J. Comput. Res. Dev. **52**(10), 2212 (2015)
5. Fu, Y., Zeng, J., Lin, Z.: HYPERSHELL: a practical hypervisor layer guest OS shell for automated in-VM management. In: 2014 USENIX Annual Technical Conference (USENIX ATC 2014), pp. 85–96 (2014)
6. Garfinkel, T., Rosenblum, M., et al.: A virtual machine introspection based architecture for intrusion detection. In: NDSS, vol. 3, pp. 191–206. Citeseer (2003)
7. Lin, X., Lei, L., Wang, Y., Jing, J., Sun, K., Zhou, Q.: A measurement study on Linux container security: attacks and countermeasures. In: Proceedings of the 34th Annual Computer Security Applications Conference, pp. 418–429 (2018)

8. Sultan, S., Ahmad, I., Dimitriou, T.: Container security: issues, challenges, andthe road ahead. IEEE Access **7**, 52976–52996 (2019)
9. Sun, Y., Safford, D., Zohar, M., Pendarakis, D., Gu, Z., Jaeger, T.: Security namespace: making Linux security frameworks available to containers. In: 27th USENIX Security Symposium (USENIX Security 2018), pp. 1423–1439 (2018)
10. Torkura, K.A., Sukmana, M.I.H., Cheng, F., Meinel, C.: Cavas: neutralizing application and container security vulnerabilities in the cloud native era. In: Beyah, R., Chang, B., Li, Y., Zhu, S. (eds.) SecureComm 2018. LNICSSITE, vol. 254, pp. 471–490. Springer, Cham (2018). https://doi.org/10.1007/978-3-030-01701-9_26
11. Zhan, D., Ye, L., Fang, B., Du, X., Su, S.: CFWatcher: a novel target-based real-time approach to monitor critical files using VMI. In: 2016 IEEE InternationalConference on Communications (ICC), pp. 1–6. IEEE (2016)

A Computing Task Offloading Scheme for Mobile Edge Computing

Wang Ben[1(✉)], Li Tingrui[1], Han Xun[2], and Li Huahui[2]

[1] Beijing Fibrlink Communications Co. Ltd., Beijing 100085, China
[2] Department of Electronic and Communication Engineering, North China Electric Power University, Baoding 071003, China

Abstract. The mobile edge computing (MEC) technology sinks the computing and storage resources to the network edge and reaches the goal of improving user service quality by formulating reasonable task offloading strategies. As the number of edge users increases, the energy consumption and energy cost of the MEC are also increasing. Therefore, we investigated the task offloading problem in MEC, and proposed a computational task offloading scheme based on immune clone. Taking the minimization of energy cost as the objective and in consideration of the relationship between number of users unloaded in the computing and energy price. It can be solved by the immune clone algorithm and determined the optimal offloading scheme. Simulation results demonstrate the superiority of the proposed scheme over other the traditional task computing scheme. That this scheme can effectively reduce the system energy cost and improve the solving efficiency as compared to the traditional task computing scheme, in terms of the solving efficiency.

Keywords: Mobile edge computing · Energy cost · Computing task offloading · Hybrid energy supply · Immune algorithm

1 Introduction

As an emergent network architecture, mobile edge computing (MEC) can provide users equipment with computing and caching services, and it unloads the tasks to the MEC servers of user equipments, which can effectively reduce the power supply and computing pressure of user equipments and improve better QoS (Quality of Service) [1]. As the number of edge nodes increases, a reasonable task offloading strategy is formulated to realizing efficient collaboration between local user equipments and edge servers has become the key to application in MEC [2, 3]. Zhang W, Wen Y, Wu DO in [4] investigated the collaborative mode between mobile equipments and servers under random wireless channel, formulated a task offloading scheme by taking the energy consumption of mobile equipments as the objective under the latency constrain, and obtained the optimal solution by transforming this problem into the shortest path problem. With the application of new energy sources, the power supply with new energy sources has become a method of reducing the traditional energy consumption. Literature [5] solved

© Springer Nature Switzerland AG 2021
X. Sun et al. (Eds.): ICAIS 2021, LNCS 12737, pp. 112–123, 2021.
https://doi.org/10.1007/978-3-030-78612-0_9

the energy consumption problem by ways of multi-source power supply. In addition, Ye Y, Shi L, Sun H, et al. in [6] to address the computing energy efficiency problem in the non-orthogonal multiple access edge network system, we utilized the fractional programming theory and introduced auxiliary variables, and put forward an energy-saving resource allocation scheme based on the iterative algorithm of Dinkelbach to acquire the maximum system computing energy efficiency.

Most of the existing literatures have formulated the offloading schemes by taking the energy consumption and delay as the objective functions. Under the premise of ensuring the users' QoS, how to offloading the same computing tasks, pay the minimum energy cost and lower the energy cost of computing network has become one of problems needing high attention in the application of edge computing. Thus, Sun X, Ansari N in [7] combined the renewable energy sources with mobile edge computing system to establish a unified energy management framework, proposed a supply scheme of new energy sources, but did not formulate any concrete task computing scheme.

In this paper, we proposed a task offloading scheme based on immune clone with the immune algorithm to solved. The energy supply device of new energy sources was configured at edge node, the system energy cost was taken as the objective function to analyze the economic cost caused by the energy consumption.

2 System Model

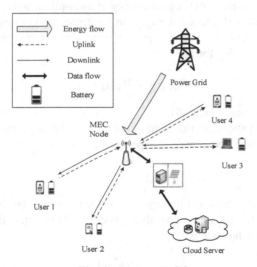

Fig. 1. System model

As shown in Fig. 1, which consists of one edge node and K user equipments, where the edge node is deployed in the BS of wireless cells, along with a renewable energy source supply device. The hybrid power supply mode which integrates traditional energy sources power supply and renewable energy sources power supply is adopted. The user gains the access to power grid using wired mode. The K user equipments are randomly distributed in the cells, and each user equipment is configured with one antenna. The offloading scheme corresponding to user equipments k is set as I_k, and then the offloading scheme under the whole system can be expressed as $\Gamma = \{I_1, I_2, ..., I_k\}$.

2.1 Computing Model

The computing task allocated by the user k is $Task(l_k, \tau_k)$, where l_k is the length of input data, in terms of bit; τ_k is delay constraint of task, Unit is ms. Within this time slot, the total number of Central Processing Unit (CPU) cycles required by the computing task of user k is expressed as:

$$W_k = C_k l_k \tag{1}$$

where C_k is number of CPU cycles needed by the per bit computing of user k The local computing delay of the corresponding task is:

$$D_{loc,k} = \frac{W_k}{f_k} = \frac{C_k l_k}{f_k} \tag{2}$$

where f_k is computing frequency of this task.

The computing energy consumption of user-end mobile equipments are mainly determined by CPU, storage devices and internal storage, where the energy consumption of CPU accounts for the majority of the total energy consumption, so the energy consumed by storage equipments and internal storage can be neglected in comparison with CPU energy consumption, and the local computing energy consumption of task k can be simplified into the following form:

$$E_{loc,k} = \alpha W_k (f_k)^2 \tag{3}$$

where α is capacitance coefficient [8].

When the user k offloading the computing task to the edge node, the computing energy consumption at the edge node is expressed as follow:

$$E_{ep,k} = \beta l_k \tag{4}$$

where β is the electric energy required by edge node server for per bit computing, and its value depends on the structure of the edge server [9]. At the time, the task computing time delay of user k at the node is:

$$D_{ep,k} = \frac{l_k C_{ep,k}}{f_{ep,k}} \tag{5}$$

where $C_{ep,k}$ is the number of CPU cycles needed by per bit computing when the edge node server is executing the task of user k; $f_{ep,k}$ is the computing frequency when the edge node is executing this task.

2.2 Communication Model

When the user k chooses computing its task by edge node, the task data can be transmitted to the edge server via the uplink. The time division multiple access mode is adopted in the communication, where the users are not mutual interference. According to the number of users K, each energy supply time slot is divided into blocks for each user to realize data transmission. The data computing result through the edge server is much smaller than the uploaded data size, and the transmission rate of downlink is far away more than the uplink. Therefore, the energy consumption and delay for the user to download the computing result are neglected. The uplink transmission rate for the user k to transmit the task to edge node is expressed as:

$$r_k = B \log(1 + \frac{p_k g_k}{\sigma^2}) \tag{6}$$

In (6), $g_k = (d_k)^{-\partial}$ is the channel gain between user k and edge node, where d_k is the distance from user k to node; ∂ is loss factor; B is channel bandwidth; p_k is the transmitted power of user k; σ^2 is mean square value of Gaussian white noise. At the time, the communication delay for the user k to transmit the task to the edge node can be showned as:

$$D_k = \frac{l_k}{r_k} \tag{7}$$

Hence, the energy consumed by the user k to offloading the task to the edge node is:

$$E_{tra,k,m} = P_{k,m} D_{k,m} = \frac{p_k l_k}{r_k} \tag{8}$$

2.3 Energy Supply Model

The edge node is supplied with energy by the power grid energy of traditional energy sources, and renewable energy sources. The user-end mobile equipments (smartphone, wearable equipment and PC) gain the access to the power grid under the wireless mode. According to [10, 11], the solar energy generation rate is approximate to normal distribution within one day, which can be expressed as:

$$e\_sun(t) = \exp(-\frac{(t-48)^2}{81}), t \in T \tag{9}$$

The energy generation rate of wind energy can be approximated as a constant as:

$$e\_wind(t) = \lambda_w, t \in T \tag{10}$$

The energy supply for the system is realized by integrating the traditional energy sources and new energy sources. The renewable energy source at the edge node can be expressed as $E_{harv}(0 \leq E_{har} \leq E_{max})$, where E_{max} is the maximum energy storage capacity of this edge node.

3 Computing Task Unloading Scheme

Through the analysis, each user has two task computing schemes: offloading computing to edge node or local computing, corresponding to 0 and 1, respectively. The formulation problem of task offloading scheme is transformed into the binary combination optimization. The conventional traversal solving algorithm is of high complexity and low solving efficiency. In order to improve efficiency, we formulate the offloading algorithm corresponding to the objective of system energy cost was the optimal offloading scheme as 0-1 programming problem. We then solved by the immune algorithm to the optimal offloading scheme was obtained by setting reasonable parameters and improving some functions of the algorithm.

Immune clone algorithm is a random swarm intelligence algorithm. Through self-iterative mechanism, it can effectively keep the swarm diversity, overcome the local convergence problem in the general optimizing process, and further solve the global optimal solution. It has been extensively applied by virtue of swarm diversity, parallelism and high convergence, etc. [12].

In the algorithm, antibodies are used to express the category of offloading schemes, and the coding rules suitable for the antibodies are designed according to the features of the problem needing optimization; the quality of offloading schemes are evaluated through the antibody density factor; the antigen denotes the energy cost of objective function, namely the system cost; immune behaviors include selection, cross, replication and inhibition of offloading scheme, and the solution space of offloading scheme is updated.

3.1 Algorithm Formulation

There are multi-user in the system model, and each user has idled computation offloading schemes. The offloading mode for the user k under offloading scheme i is recorded as $a_{i,k}$, and the offloading scheme i as follow:

$$A_i = \{a_{i,1}, \ldots, a_{i,k}\}, k \in K \tag{11}$$

The system energy cost under the offloading scheme is presented as:

$$price(A_i) = \sum_{i=1}^{K} \lambda(a_{i,k}E_{loc,k} + (1 - a_{i,k})E_{tra,k}) + \phi(1 - a_{i,k})E_{ep,k} \tag{12}$$

$E_{loc,k}$, $E_{tra,k}$ and $E_{ep,k}$ are energy consumed by the user in local computing, energy consumed by task transmission and computing energy consumption of edge node, respectively in (12); λ and ϕ are electricity prices of traditional energy sources and new energy sources, respectively.

We can formulate the system energy cost serves as the optimized objective function as:

$$\min_{A,l,f,p:} \quad price(A_i) \tag{13a}$$

$$\text{s.t.}\, a_{i,k} = \{0, 1\}, \; i \in NP, \; k \in K \tag{13b}$$

$$0 \le f_k \le f_k^{\max} \tag{13c}$$

$$0 \le f_{ep,k} \le f_{ep}^{\max} \tag{13d}$$

$$\{D_{loc,k}, \; D_{tra,k} + D_{ep,k}\} \le \tau_k \tag{13e}$$

$$p_k \le p^{\max} \tag{13f}$$

The objective function of (13a) and the category of offloading scheme in (13b). $a_{i,k}$ = 0 means that the user k decides to compute its task locally on own device under the offloading scheme in i. $a_{i,k}$ = 1 means that the user k chooses to offload the computation to the edge node. (13c) and (13d) represent the computing power limitations for local equipment and edge node, respectively; (13e) represents the delay limitation of the task; (13f) means the limitation of transmitted power when the unloading computing is executed. The energy cost is the algorithm optimization problem and corresponds to the objective function in the immune algorithm, namely the antigen.

For the two computation offloading modes, an initial solution matrix about the offloading schemes can be generated according to the system model analysis as:

$$A_{np} = \begin{pmatrix} a_{1,1} & \cdots & a_{1,k} \\ \vdots & \cdots & \vdots \\ a_{np,1} & \cdots & a_{np,k} \end{pmatrix}, \; k \in K \tag{14}$$

In the immune clone algorithm, the matrix corresponds to antibodies, i.e., feasible solutions of the offloading scheme, where NP is the number of initial populations, i.e., the number of offloading schemes. K is the number of users. For any $a_{i,k} (i \in NP, k \in K)$, they are generated by following the uniform random distribution as:

$$a_{i,k} = \begin{cases} 0 & rand() < 0.5 \\ 1 & else \end{cases} \tag{15}$$

When the optimal offloading scheme is solved, the initial schemes are sorted using the sort function according to the generated objective function (e.g., system energy cost), the offloading scheme matrix is updated while corresponding to the minimum energy cost is reserved. Then chooses the $NP/2$ groups of schemes and randomly crossed. The objective function values of these schemes and the corresponding offloading schemes are solved again. The optimal task offloading scheme is replicated for cg times to realize updating of the task offloading schemes, and the rest are the offloading schemes randomly generated when the limitations are satisfied, and the updated populations are merged with the random populations. In the algorithm, this updating operation of offloading schemes corresponds to the immune clone behavior.

It can be found through the updating operation of the offloading schemes that when they are randomly generated, many similar solutions appear, and they may be excessively concentrated in one area, which is not good for global searching. Therefore, a density evaluation function for the offloading schemes is proposed in this algorithm to repress the solutions with too high frequency of occurrence, thus guaranteeing the diversity of offloading schemes, and this corresponds to the antibody evaluation behavior of the immune algorithm.

In order to evaluate the frequency of occurrence of offloading schemes, the antibody density is expressed by the following formula:

$$den(a_i) = \frac{1}{K} \sum_{k=1}^{K} df(a_i, a_j) \tag{16}$$

K is user scale; $df(a_i, a_j)$ denotes the similarity degree between antibodies(e.g., the similarity degree between feasible solutions). It can be known from the analysis that the feasible solutions in this chapter are obtained based on the discrete coding algorithm. Therefore, Hamming distance is used to calculate the similarity degree between antibodies, and the calculation formula is as follow:

$$df(a_i, a_j) = \sum_{k=1}^{K} \delta_k \tag{17a}$$

$$\delta_k = \begin{cases} 0, \ a_{i,k} \neq a_{j,k} \\ 1, \ a_{i,k} = a_{j,k} \end{cases} \tag{17b}$$

$a_{i,k}$ and $a_{j,k}$ are the k (th) places of feasible solutions a_i and a_j, respectively. When the k (th) places of offloading schemes i and j appear at the same position, δ_k will be 1, otherwise it will be 0. In other words, δ_k is the frequency for the same elements to appear in the two unloading schemes.

The steps of the immune clone algorithm-based task offloading scheme are as follows:

Step 1: According to the mobile edge computing model generate prior parameters, construct the objective functions of the optimization problem, and formulate the constraint conditions;

Step 2: Initialization. Randomly generate the initial solution space $A_{NP \times K}$ of an offloading scheme in the solution space;

Step 3: Evaluate each feasible offloading scheme based on the utility function, sort the feasible solutions according to the ranking of objective functions, and update the initial solutions;

Step 4: Set and select the immune cycle index gen and i (1-X) offloading schemes, conduct clone operation for cg generations, and implement element crossing after the post-clone offloading schemes are randomly selected; inhibit the post-clone solution sets, evaluate the antibody concentration, and save the solution with the highest affinity and the corresponding offloading scheme; refresh $NP - X$ to randomly generate, update the offloading schemes with too high similarity according to the antibody density factor until the limitation of antibody density is satisfied, calculate the corresponding objective function value, and then merge the immune populations with new populations;

Step 5: Output the optimal result of each generation and the corresponding offloading scheme; $gen = gen + 1$. If $g < G$, skip to step 3; or otherwise end the cycle.

4 Numerical Results and Analysis

A system consisting of a single base station and multi-user are considered, where the base station is connected to the MEC server. The edge node is integrated with the renewable energy power generation units. 25 users are randomly distributed within the coverage (200 m) of the base station. The user needs to complete computing tasks with data size of 100 kB-200 kB following uniform distribution, and the transmitted power of the user equipment ranges from 50 mW to 100 mW. The energy dissipation coefficient β of the edge server is 2×10^{-5} J/bit [9]; the computing power of local user equipment is f_k, $f_k \in \{1, 2, 3\}$ GHz; the capacitance coefficient α is 10^{-28} [8]; the number of cloning generations is cg, $cg \in \{4, 5, 10, 15\}$; the electricity prices ($\lambda = 1.33$ and $\phi = 0.02$) within peak time lost are respectively used for traditional energy sources and new energy sources [5]. The other simulation parameters are seen in Table 1.

The task offloading algorithm based on immune cloning generates a total of:

$$G \times (\frac{NP}{2} \times cg + cg + \frac{NP}{2}) \tag{18}$$

The number of algorithm iterations G, clone algebra cg, and the solution to unmount NP are all constant and have a certain multiple relation with user K. Therefore, the above equation can be simplified as follows:

$$K^3(\frac{b_1 \times b_2 \times b_3}{2}) + K^2(b_1 \times (b_3 + \frac{b_2}{2})) \tag{19}$$

b_1, b_2 and b_3 are constants, so the time complexity of the algorithm is expressed as. The algorithm execution times generated by traversal are as follows:

$$(2^K + 1) \times (K + 1) \tag{20}$$

It can be seen that the time complexity of ergodic offloading can be expressed as that the computing frequency of ergodic algorithm increases exponentially. As can be seen from Fig. 2, with the gradual increase of the number of users k in the cell, the computational complexity of the task unloading scheme based on the immune clone algorithm is significantly lower than that of the traversal algorithm.

The influences of different parameters on the algorithm convergence among the immune clone-based task offloading schemes are discussed and shown in Fig. 3 and Fig. 4. First, no matter whether the clone factor cg or antibody density factor den is changed, the total system energy cost presents a declining trend with the increase of number of iterations, and finally tends to be stable. However, the convergence speed varies. The algorithm realizes the fastest convergence under $cg = 10$, which is obviously better than the results under $cg = 4$ and $cg = 15$. When $cg = 5$, the algorithm fails to

Table 1. Simulation parameters

Parameter	Value
Number of immunized individuals NP	300
Maximum immune generation G	50
User equipment k calculates the number of CPU cycles executed per bit C_k	$\{500, 1000, 1500\}\,cycles/bit$
The edge server m calculates the CPU cycles executed per bit C_m^{ep}	$200\ cycles/bit$
Task max delay τ_k	100 ms
Computing frequency of edge server m f_m^{ep}	10 GHZ
Antibody density factor den	$\{0.5, 0.75, 0,9\}$
System channel bandwidth B	10 MHz
Gaussian white noise variance σ^2	10^{-10} W

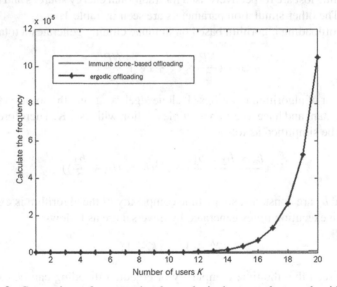

Fig. 2. Comparison of computational complexity between the two algorithms

find the minimum energy cost even within the limited number of iterations. Therefore, different antibody density factors exert different influences on the algorithm convergence speed. The premature convergence problem exists under $den = 0.5$ and $den = 0.9$ because of the probability for similar solutions to appear in the solution space of offloading schemes will be extremely similar when the density factor is too hight, which, if not inhibited, will result in premature convergence. Moreover, when the density factor is too low, the probability for random solutions to appear in the solution space of offloading

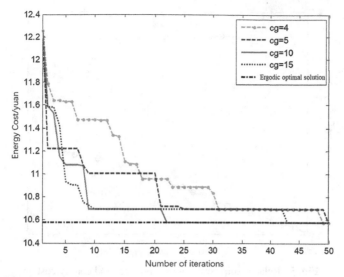

Fig. 3. Comparison of system energy cost with different clone factors

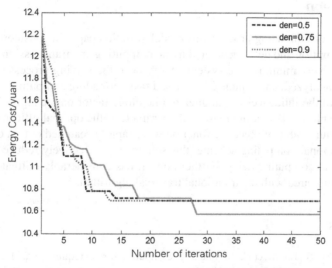

Fig. 4. Comparison of system energy cost with different antibody density factors

schemes will also be elevated, the algorithm will probably evolve towards a regular direction, thus degrading its optimization ability.

The relationships of number of users performing the computing task offloading with the system energy cost and time delay under task load of 100–200 kB are shown in Fig. 5. As the number of users increases, both the system energy cost and delay will be increased, but it can be observed that the growth speed of the task offloading algorithm based on immune clone is evidently lower than the traditional task computing scheme, and moreover, the system energy cost is remarkably reduced.

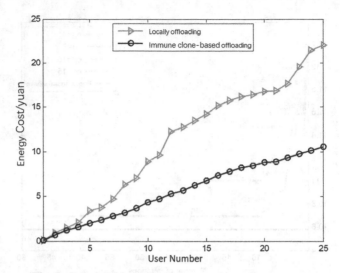

Fig. 5. Relationship between user number and energy cost

5   Conclusion

The computation offloading process was modeled in this paper in consideration of the energy consumption and delay generated in the computing and transmission process. In order to effectively minimize the system energy cost, the solving process of objective function was analyzed, an immune clone-based task offloading computing scheme was developed, and the influences of parameters like clone factor on the algorithm convergence were explored. By setting reasonable parameters, the optimal offloading scheme and the minimum value of objective function were rapidly searched out. In comparison with the traditional computing scheme, this scheme can effectively reduce the system energy cost and computing delay. Furthermore, it has considerably mitigated the time complexity compared with the traditional traversal algorithm.

References

1. Tian, H., Fan, S., Lü, X., et al.: Mobile edge computing for 5G requirements. J. Beijing Univ. Posts Telecommun. **40**(2), 1–10 (2017)
2. Yu, W., Liang, F., He, X., et al.: A survey on the edge computing for the internet of things. IEEE Access **6**, 6900–6919 (2017)
3. Zishu, L., Renchao, X., Li, S., et al.: A survey on edge computing. Telecommun. Sci. **34**(1), 87–101 (2018)
4. Zhang, W., Wen, Y., Wu, D.O.: Collaborative task execution in mobile cloud computing under a stochastic wireless channel. IEEE Trans. Wireless Commun. **14**(1), 81–93 (2015)
5. Han, D., Zheng, B., Chen, Z., et al.: Cost efficiency in coordinated multiple-point system based on multi-source power supply. IEEE Access **6**, 71994–72001 (2018)
6. Ye, Y., Shi, L., Sun, H., et al.: System-centric computation energy efficiency for distributed NOMA-based MEC networks. IEEE Trans. Veh. Technol. **69**(8), 8938–8948 (2020)

7. Sun, X., Ansari, N.: Green cloudlet network: a distributed green mobile cloud network. IEEE Network **31**(1), 64–70 (2017)
8. Mao, Y., Zhang, J., Letaief, K.B.: Dynamic computation offloading for mobile-edge computing with energy harvesting devices. IEEE J. Sel. Areas Commun. **34**(12), 3590–3605 (2017)
9. Li, W., Yang, T., Delicato, F.C., et al.: On enabling sustainable edge computing with renewable energy resources. IEEE Commun. Mag. **56**(5), 94–101 (2018)
10. Niyato, D., Lu, X., Wang, P.: Adaptive power management for wireless base station in smart grid environment. IEEE Wirel. Commun. **19**(6), 44–51 (2014)
11. Sudevalayam, S., Kulkarni, P.: Energy harvesting sensor nodes: survey and implications. IEEE Commun. Surv. Tutor. **13**(3), 443–461 (2011)
12. Jin, Z., Fan, H.: An improved immune genetic algorithm for multi-peak function optimization. In: Proceedings of the 2013 5th International Conference on Intelligent Human-Machine Systems and Cybernetics-Volume 01. IEEE, vol. 13, no. 3, pp. 443–461 (2013)

Security Transmission Scheme of Sensitive Data for Mobile Terminal

Jicheng He[1,2]($\boxtimes$), Minghui Gao[1,2], Zhijun Zhang[1,2], Li Ma[1,2], Zhiyan Ning[1,2], and Jingyi Cao[3]

[1] Nari Group Corporation State Grid Electric Power Research Institute, Nanjing 211106, China
[2] Beijing Kedong Electric Power Control System Co., Ltd., Beijing 100192, China
[3] China Electric Power Research Institute, Beijing 100192, China

Abstract. In response to mobile terminal threats, this work is innovative, and gives practical solutions and prototype systems. The work first analyzes in detail the entire process of the generation, transmission and use of user-sensitive data within the Android system. In order to achieve resource sharing and data transmission between different applications and processes, the Android system provides a mechanism for inter-process communication based on Binder. Sensitive data is transmitted through Binder as a channel in the system. But sensitive data is carried out in the form of clear text during Binder transmission, which allows malware to easily intercept and tamper with sensitive data based on Binder communication, such as SMS content and GPS location information. In response to this problem, based on the above research, this work innovatively proposes and implements an adaptive transparent encryption protection scheme for sensitive data in the Android system from generation to use throughout the life cycle, effectively preventing sensitive data from being. The threat of theft and tampering by malicious third parties guarantees the privacy and integrity of user sensitive data during the internal transmission of the system. In addition, the system provides users with a simple and flexible operating experience, allowing users to independently protect specific types of sensitive data in specified applications, enhancing the ease of use and practicality of the system.

Keywords: Sensitive data · Mobile terminal · Android · Security transmission

1 Introduction

With the rapid development of mobile Internet in recent years, mobile phones, tablets and other mobile terminals have become the most closely related electronic devices [1] in people's life and work. Compared with traditional personal user computers, mobile intelligent terminals contain more user privacy information and daily sensitive data due to their rich sensors and good portability [2, 3]. However, the research on the security of intelligent terminals and the protection of user privacy data in intelligent devices are still in the initial stage, so it is of great significance to study the protection of user privacy in intelligent devices [4, 5].

X. Sun et al. (Eds.): ICAIS 2021, LNCS 12737, pp. 124–134, 2021.
https://doi.org/10.1007/978-3-030-78612-0_10

Strategy analytics released the global distribution of smartphone operating systems in the second quarter of 2019. According to the report, the market share of Android operating system in the world has reached 84.6% (the highest proportion ever). It is no doubt that Android has become the most dominant smartphone system. According to the Report on Mobile Phone Security in China in the First Quarter of 2019 released by 360 Internet Security Center, privacy theft programs accounted for 81% of the newly added malicious programs in the Android system in the first quarter of 2019, far higher than other types such as service charges. To sum up, it is of great significance to study the ecological environment security of Android system and the whole Android system.

The Android system allocates and manages resources as a unit of process. When a process needs a certain service, it must apply for the service from the corresponding manager, who will respond to the request. Among them, the request and response to the service are conducted by Binder. In the process of issuing a service request, the program will first pass the requested data and the type of service to the Binder, which will then pass it to the corresponding service manager, who will then pass back the response through the Binder. Therefore, Binder as if is used for communication between the client and the server, the postman, however, the "postman" is not very safe, because the data in the transmission process of Binder is expressly transmission, is equivalent to the postman send letters is no envelope, as long as through the attack of Binder, carry to intercept "postman" letters. Data can then be sent out via Broadcast, Intent, Content Provider, etc. Binder packet contents are stored in the form of clear text during the whole communication process. This means that once the packet is intercepted by attackers, the privacy of users will be compromised, which will bring great harm to the security of users. As for Android system, due to the serious fragmentation of its ecosystem, many devices provide or can easily obtain Root permissions, so that an attacker or malicious software can easily steal and tamper with sensitive information in Binder communication data.

Therefore, for users with high security requirements and specific application scenarios, The Binder based IPC communication mechanism of Android has some shortcomings in security, and it is in urgent need of a flexible security enhancement method to ensure users' privacy and system security.

With the popularization of 5G networks and the wide application of Android system, the mobile phone protection software industry has developed rapidly in recent years [6–8]. Various security protection software mushroomed as The Times require, such as 360 security Guard, QQ security butler, including foreign AVG phone antivirus, Norton phone security software, etc., are very popular in the market security protection software. As a new type of application software, mobile phone protection software has the greatest advantage of being convenient to use and protecting the personal interests of mobile phone users.

According to the 2018 Annual Android Security Ecological Environment Study released by 360, according to the detection data, by January 2019, the proportion of Android phones with security vulnerabilities in the detected devices reached a staggering 99.99%, which means that only 0.01% of Android phones failed to be detected with vulnerabilities. Compared with 2017, the security of Android phones has shown a significant downward trend. On the phones that were found to be vulnerable, information leaks accounted for an additional 95.6% of all vulnerabilities. In short, information breaches are by far the most common way to attack Android users.

However, AV-Comparatives, a security testing agency, has been testing about 250 domestic and foreign security apps on Android, according to Techradar. It found that more than 30% of malware detected in 2018 was successfully detected with no false positives, just a third of the time. What's more, some inferior protection apps even mark normal software as a virus.

In addition, most of the security protection software is mainly aimed at the detection and protection of mobile malware, and its main direction is the analysis of software characteristic codes [9, 10]. At present, it has basically realized the reminder and interception of all kinds of harmful behaviors, such as the short message of fee deduction, the short message of fraud, the call of charge fraud, etc. However, Binder transmission mechanism of Android system is not protected by software. As a result, there are still huge hidden dangers in sensitive information transmission for Android users.

2 Preliminaries

2.1 Binder

By analyzing the data flow of Binder, vulnerability points of Binder were found out and vulnerability points were demonstrated. The details are as follows:

(1) Binder framework layer creates an IOCtl Syscall with file descriptions as parameters and related data passed into the kernel.
(2) Binder Driver looks for the corresponding service, copies the data to the space of the server, and creates a thread to wait for processing.
(3) The server responds to the service and submits the request to the relevant hardware.
(4) Hardware response request.
(5) Pass the reply to the driver.
(6) Pass the reply to the client process.

The above model is the flow of data to the Binder of the client. For example, in the case of short message writing with the short message APP, during (1) the short message APP process will create an IOCtl SYscall and pass the relevant data (sending address and short message information) into the Binder Driver. In this process, the data is transmitted in the original clear text, that is, the malware can obtain relevant information as long as it intercepts (1) the process. And the malicious behavior may be for almost all of the Binder communication data, because in the picture above you can see in the model, each process is through the ioctl with Binder Driver to communicate, as long as stopped ioctl, text messages, to get the contact information, access to the phone call records the purpose of stealing sensitive information such as can be easily achieved.

2.2 API Hook

Through API Hook, the behavior of the method can be changed, thus affecting the behavior of the process. Its essence is to redirect the target method to other methods, perform some additional operations, and then jump back to the target method. By using API Hook technology to intercept key function calls, so as to achieve the encryption and decryption of sensitive data. The intercepting methods of these two types of APIS are described next.

Xposed Framework. Xposed framework is an android environment auxiliary tool, it can be on the premise of not modified APK affect the operation of the program or modify the system, based on the xposed framework can produce a variety of functional modules, the core Android system permissions management, clear memory, battery control, interface display, and other functions, and can be peace do not conflict with each other to function properly. Once you install the Ximproving framework in an android environment, developers will be able to use the ximproving framework's interface by writing the Ximproving module. The flag bits of some special data are set up in the Ximproving module, so you need to configure them in the corresponding project of your application.

Ptrace. Figure 1 and Fig. 2 take the Ioctl() method as an example, compare the call flow of methods before and after hook, and demonstrate the basic principle of hook.

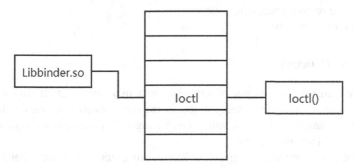

Fig. 1. Normal invocation flow of loctl

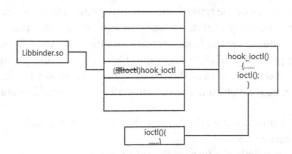

Fig. 2. Invocation flow of loctl after hook

As shown in Fig. 2, the normal invocation process is that libbinder. so calls the Ioctl method through the Ioctl address in its GOT table. After Hook, the GOT table enters the new Ioctl address, and libbinder. so will execute the hooked_IOCtl method before the Ioctl () execution.

As a shared library in Linux environment, SO library is used to provide a collection of various functional methods, and also provides a standard interface for dynamic loading. Similar to Windows system. DLL file.

(1) ShellCode is to use assembly language to write a program, the program can realize the SO library load, method search function, as well as the execution of SO library methods.
(2) ATTACH to the remote process via the remote process PID.
(3) Obtain and save the register value of the remote process, which can be used to restore the original state of the process after injection.
(4) Call dlopen, Mmap, DLSYm and other call addresses.
(5) Call process Mmap to allocate a section of storage space, and then write Shellcode and SO library path as well as other method call parameters in the space.
(6) Execute the code of process Shellcode, successfully load SO library, and implement SO library method to find and execute the method in SO library (in this method library can realize the desired method function).
(7) Restore the remote process register.
(8) Detach remote process.

3 Business Process

The security transmission system of sensitive data in Android environment aims to protect users' sensitive data from being stolen during transmission, and the whole process of protection is transparent to users, without requiring additional operations by users and without affecting their normal use.

This system does not need to register to log in, prevented as a result of database theft and lead to the disclosure of user basic information. This system encrypts where sensitive information is generated, only allows applications with decryption rights to decrypt, and allows users to freely choose the type of sensitive information to be protected and choose to grant permission to the application software, so as to ensure user privacy. This system is responsible for monitoring the basic security situation of Android phones, opening the corresponding protection module according to user input, and giving feedback and evaluation on the protection status of the whole system, as shown in Fig. 3.

The specific process involved in the system will be described in detail below:

(1) The program starts to obtain the basic status of the phone and display the current protection information.
(2) The user selects whether to turn on the safe mode.
(3) If the protection mode has been turned on, judge which functional module needs to be protected under the current situation.
(4) After determining the function module, determine the application program to be protected.
(5) After judging the success, implement the protection scheme for the corresponding program functions of the mobile phone and feedback the protection results.

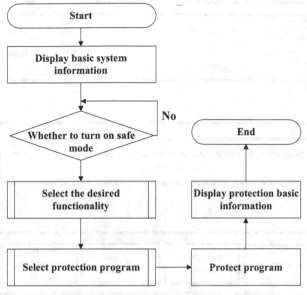

Fig. 3. Business process

4 System Architecture

The business process of the sensitive data security transmission system under the Android environment involves the client user and the server. The system adopts three-tier architecture, including the application layer, the business layer and the data layer. The system logic architecture is shown in Fig. 4.

(1) Data layer: Provides the data access interface for the business layer and accesses the service side through data access.
(2) Business layer: provide the logic realization of various functions of sensitive data security transmission system, and encapsulate four functions of application management, task planning, logging and security configuration;
(3) Application layer: the client user issues a request to the server; The server replies to the client after processing the request, in which the packets are encrypted through hash operation to generate the secret key before transmission.

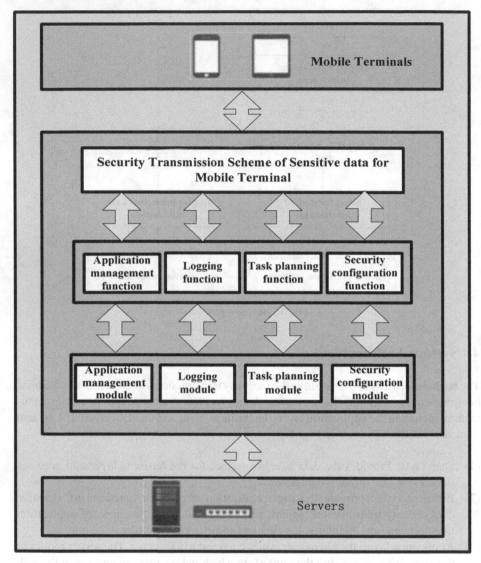

Fig. 4. System logic architecture

5 Key Technologies

Application management module is one of the core functions of the four modules of the sensitive data security transmission system under the whole Android environment. After the APP is authorized by the user, open the application management function, and you can see the list of sensitive software on the phone. Click one of the software at will, and the system can get the icon, name, version, software permission and so on of the software. Click on the CAMERA function, for example, after can see version

3.0, the APP permissions include android. Permission. CAMERA, android. Permission. RECORD_AUDIO permission, etc.

The main functions related to the above operations are information acquisition and data presentation. In addition, the most important role of application management module is to add protection to the application. Open the drop-down menu under this function, you can see that all the software is divided into GPS app and SMS app. Then click anyone, such as GPS app, and you can find that all the GPS-sensitive information involved in the operation of the app is in the GPS app. Then you can add protection to the GPS application and view details. After the corresponding application is used to add protection, the protection APP can protect the application without interruption for 24 h without affecting the normal use.

In this module, the protection of user data is implemented through the Xhook specific method operating, so the key can be passed into the method requiring hooks in the form of parameters, so as to achieve the key release and management.

In addition, for the selection of the key in the process of data protection, we carry out a hash operation on the data and take the operation result as the key, which can guarantee the randomness of the key and prevent attackers from using common statistical attack methods such as dictionary attack to decipher the ciphertext.

As shown in Fig. 5, taking SMS and GPS as examples, SMS and GPS services are protected service types. The encryption module intercepts the data sent by SMS and GPS services. After encryption, encrypted data is given to the binders, in which the encrypted data is delivered. When Binder data transmission is requested by application software with authority (such as official SMS and Baidu map in the figure above), it shall be decrypted to ensure that the application software with authority can obtain plaintext information. Applications without authority will obtain ciphertext even if the Binder is requested by them, or application software that attacks the Binder maliciously (such as stealing information locating APP). The following model can be applied to the process of applying the Binder to request sensitive data, for example, requesting memos, viewing call records, etc. SMS and GPS are just the tips of the iceberg.

During Binder transmission, another data flow is transmitted from the application software to the corresponding service manager, such as the process of editing and sending SMS messages with SMS application. In this information transmission model, the server is the application software and the client is the service manager. See Fig. 6.

Figure 7 describes the workflow of the data protection module, where function A and function B represent the services in the Android system, such as SMS service and GPS positioning service. The corresponding program, program represents the program that invokes the corresponding service, such as information APP, Baidu Map, etc.

The relevant steps of the system to protect the private data and feedback the results are as follows:

(1) Turn on the protection function and determine the functional modules to be protected.
(2) Determine the APP to be protected.
(3) Distribute the key for the Server side of the corresponding service and APP that needs to be protected.

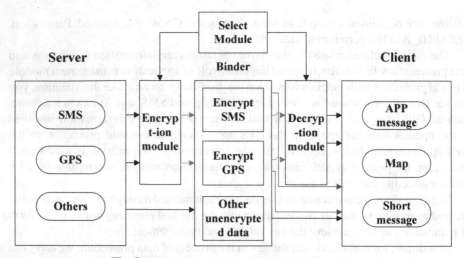

Fig. 5. Encryption process of sensitive information

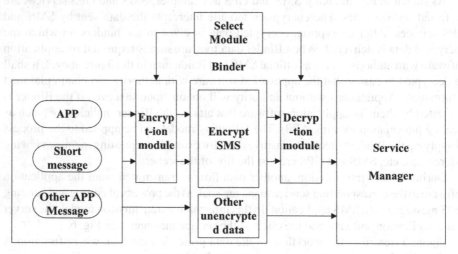

Fig. 6. SMS encryption process

(4) Select the corresponding Hook method to protect the sensitive data in Binder packet according to the functional module of protection.

(5) Call SM4 encryption and decryption module to process sensitive data.

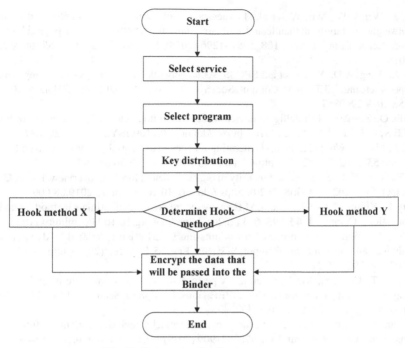

Fig. 7. Data protection business processes

6   Conclusion

From Android IPC communication mechanism, the innovation was put forward and implemented for the Android system sensitive data from production to use the entire life cycle of the adaptability of the transparent encryption protection scheme, effectively prevent the sensitive data by malicious third party to steal and tamper with the threat, guarantee the user sensitive data within the system the privacy and integrity in the process of transmission. Based on the realization of basic functions, the upper interface encapsulation provides users with simple and flexible operation experience, which enables users to protect the specific type of sensitive data in the specified application independently and enhances the usability and practicability of the system.

Acknowledgement. This research was funded by the Science and Technology Project Funding of State Grid Corporation of China (Research on Key Technologies of Energy Internet Mobile and Internet Security in 2019–2021, Contract no.: 5700-210955463A-0-0-00).

References

1. Choe, C., Chen, C.T., Nagao, S., et al.: Real-time acoustic emission monitoring of wear-out failure in SiC power electronic devices during power cycling tests. IEEE Trans. Power Electron. **36**, 4420–4428 (2021). https://doi.org/10.1109/TPEL.2020.3024986

2. Xu, J., Wei, L.W., Wu, W., et al.: Privacy-preserving data integrity verification by using lightweight streaming authenticated data structures for healthcare cyber-physical system. Future Gener. Comput. Syst. **108**, 1287–1296 (2018). https://doi.org/10.1016/j.future.2018.04.018

3. Xu, J., Wang, A.D., Wu, J., et al.: SPCSS: social network based privacy-preserving criminal suspects sensing. IEEE Trans. Comput. Soc. Syst. **7**, 261–274 (2020). https://doi.org/10.1109/TCSS.2019.2960857

4. Bello, O., Zeadally, S.: Intelligent device-to-device communication in the internet of things. IEEE Syst. J. **10**, 1172–1182 (2016). https://doi.org/10.1109/JSYST.2014.2298837

5. Xu, J., Liu, H., Wu, D.X., et al.: Generating universal adversarial perturbation with ResNet. Inf. Sci. **537**, 302–312 (2020). https://doi.org/10.1016/j.ins.2020.05.099

6. Al-Turjman, F.: Intelligence and security in big 5G-oriented IoNT: an overview. Future Gener. Comput. Syst. **102**, 357–368 (2020). https://doi.org/10.1016/j.future.2019.08.009

7. Rajy, L., Kiram, M.A., Ghazouani, M.E.: New security risk value estimate method for android applications. Comput. J. **63**, 593–603 (2020). https://doi.org/10.1093/comjnl/bxz109

8. Kelec, A., Djuric, Z.: A proposal for addressing security issues related to dynamic code loading on android platform. Comput. Syst. Sci. Eng. **35**, 271–282 (2020). https://doi.org/10.32604/csse.2020.35.271

9. Feng, R.T., Chen, S., Xie, X.F., et al.: A performance-sensitive malware detection system using deep learning on mobile devices. IEEE Trans. Inf. Forens. Secur. **16**, 1563–1578 (2021). https://doi.org/10.1109/TIFS.2020.3025436

10. Qamar, A., Karim, A., Chang, V.: Mobile malware attacks: review, taxonomy & future directions. Future Gener. Comput. Syst. **97**, 887–909 (2019). https://doi.org/10.1016/j.future.2019.03.007

Efficient Utilization of Cache Resources for Content Delivery Network Based on Blockchain

Hongyan Zhang[1], Bo Liu[1], Long Qin[2], Jing Zhang[2], and Weichao Gong[1,2(✉)]

[1] State Grid Henan Electric Power Company, Zhengzhou 450000, China
[2] State Grid Henan Electric Power Information and Communication Company, Zhengzhou 450000, China

Abstract. Content delivery network (CDN) has become an important means to alleviate network congestion and improve user service quality. However, with the emergence of new services such as short video and live streaming, traditional CDN has faced some challenges. In order to alleviate the lag problem of passive cache, we propose an active cache delivery scheme based on smart contract. In order to improve the utilization of storage resources in non-core locations of the network, we put forward the CDN-P2P network structure based on blockchain. Furthermore, the model predictive control (MPC) method is adopted to solve the joint optimization problem of bandwidth and delay in replica server selection. A large number of simulation experiments have been done to prove the effectiveness of our proposed scheme.

Keywords: Content delivery network · Cache · Blockchain

1 Introduction

With the explosion of mobile data traffic, network traffic congestion becomes more and more serious. Large-scale user requests tend to increase the centralized server load, significantly increase the delay of user acquisition of content, and seriously reduce the quality of user experience. In order to solve the above problems, content distribution networks are proposed [1]. CDN is made of the distribution in the network edge cache server layer smart virtual network, the main principle is to copy content caching to close to the client cache server, all nodes in real-time according to the network traffic and connection, load condition and the distance to the user and comprehensive information such as response time will the user's request to guide users closest service node [2]. It allows users to access the content they need nearby, effectively relieving backbone traffic congestion caused by extensive remote access.

However, with the emergence of new services such as short video and live streaming, traditional CDN is faced with the following challenges: 1) Large-scale deployment of cache servers is needed to guarantee the performance of CDN system, which brings great financial pressure to CDN operators [3]; 2) Passive content caching has lag, content lag

© Springer Nature Switzerland AG 2021
X. Sun et al. (Eds.): ICAIS 2021, LNCS 12737, pp. 135–146, 2021.
https://doi.org/10.1007/978-3-030-78612-0_11

and potential user demand [4]; 3) User-driven server cache space utilization is low, and cache nodes have a large amount of idle cache space [5].

To solve the above problems, there have been some relevant studies. In [6], the authors proposes a blockchain-based content distribution network (B-CDN) architecture, which provides a decentralized and secure platform to connect content providers and users to realize their win-win situation. In [7], a decentralized framework for active caching is proposed. The authors use smart contracts to build an autonomous content caching market. In the marketplace, the interaction between the cache helper and the content provider is modeled as a Chinese restaurant game. The authors proposed a solution for 5G content center mobile network privacy based on blockchain, which realized the mutual trust between content providers and users in [8]. In [9], the authors combined the provisioning framework with blockchain, i.e. blockchain assisted CDN, which utilizes distributed contracts to dynamically change virtual instances of proxy servers based on client requests and resource capacity. In [10], the authors propose blockchain-driven smart contracts and network services to support user-centered collaboration solutions. In [11], the authors propose a novel delivery proof mechanism to encourage peers to participate in peer-to-peer content delivery services in a safe and effective manner. A trusted peer will gain higher transmission performance, while a spoofing peer will be isolated from the network.

In this paper, we mine the storage resources of user servers in the CDN-P2P network. In the network, the federated blockchain is built to do authentication and audit for the cache nodes. The main contributions are summarized as follows:

1. The CDN-P2P network is constructed, which mines the bandwidth, computing and storage resources of common user devices in non-core locations of the network, and distributes computing tasks and data storage in the CDN system to common user nodes. The CDN-P architecture can reduce the delay and improve the service quality of users.
2. We designed an active caching scheme based on smart contract, in which the federated blockchain was built to authenticate and audit the nodes.
3. Design the replica server selection strategy based on model predictive control (MPC), which can balance the importance of the two optimization objectives, response time and bandwidth satisfaction, by adjusting the weight value according to the actual network demand.
4. A large number of simulation experiments have been done to prove the effectiveness of the scheme.

The rest of the organization is as follows: Sect. 2 is an overview of the system model. Section 3 introduces the consensus strategy applied in blockchain network. The caching content delivery process based on smart contract is described in Sect. 4. Section 5 solves the joint optimization of delay and bandwidth in the process of selecting replica server. The experimental results and analysis are given in Sect. 6. The conclusion is given in Sect. 7.

2 System Model

2.1 Network Model

As shown in Fig. 1 (a), we design a four-layer network architecture, which is composed of physical layer, edge layer, blockchain layer and distributed cloud from top to bottom. The details are as follows:

Physical layer: Suppose there are N content providers (red nodes: servers deployed by operators) in this layer, who provide content services $K = \{1, \ldots, k, \ldots K\}$ to normal users. There are M active users (blue nodes), who help cache CDN service content, contribute their spare bandwidth and storage resources to get Token reward, reduce the service pressure of CDN operators, and improve network efficiency.

Edge layer: The deployment in the edge layer definition support software is a network of distribution and exchange of equipment, on the one hand, closer to the user equipment, can provide a low latency, high reliability of service, on the other hand can sense the network state information, defined by the software of data forwarding plane forward path, the forward rate.

Blockchain layer: At this layer, the blockchain consortium is deployed to do the following three things: 1) provide trusted authentication services for content providers and users; 2) Encapsulate the service records of active users as blocks containing transactions and then add them to the blockchain as reward credentials. This part is described in detail in Sect. 2.2; 3) Complete the automatic cache content delivery process for active users through the deployed smart contract, and issue Token rewards to active users. This section is described in detail in Sect. 4.

Distributed cloud: Under the support of distributed storage technology, a large number of cloud servers are integrated into a supercomputer to provide a large number of data storage and processing services. Distributed file system allows access to common storage resources and IO sharing of application data files. Furthermore, distributed cloud can break through the limitation of a single physical machine, dynamically adjust resources, eliminate single point of failure of servers and storage devices, and achieve high availability.

2.2 Blockchain Model

We the consortium blockchain is constructed to ensure that credible content delivery services in our league chain model put forward by the operators of the server (content provider, CP) and active users (cache helper, CH) respectively, the whole node and all nodes involved in consensus process, through mutual consultation to add to the data on the blockchain agree; Light node does not participate in the process of consensus, encapsulation, only generated block asymmetric encryption is used to ensure the security of data, each node contains a pair of asymmetric keys, including the public key (pk_i) and a private key (sk_i). If consensus is reached, node i is added to the blockchain, business address $H(pk_i)$ will be as the only identification.

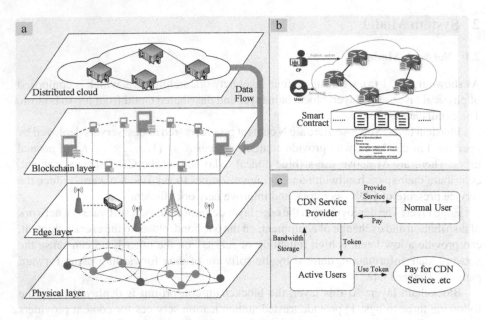

Fig. 1. Blockchain-based content delivery network model

We will describe transactions, block, and blockchain in detail as follows:

Transaction: The record of active user i's cache content successfully delivered to normal user j is described as transaction $tx_{i,j} = \langle H(pk_i), H(pk_j), d_{i,j}, \sigma_i \rangle$, where $d_{i,j}$ is the description information of the cache content and σ_i is the digital signature. The nodes encapsulate records over a period of time into transactions and broadcast them to the entire blockchain network via P2P protocol. The timestamp was added to ensure the reliability of the transaction and strict time ordering.

Block: We use the standardized block structure $B_t = \langle t, TX_t, (pk_m, \sigma_m), H(B_t), H(B_{t-1}) \rangle$, where t is the timestamp; $TX_t = \{tx_1, \ldots, tx_l\}$ is a set of transactions, which contains a set of transactions occurring over a period of time; (pk_m, σ_m) contains the private key and digital signature of the publishing block node; $H(B_t)$ is the head of the current block, which contains the version number, the root node of the "Merkel Tree" where the transaction data is stored.

Blockchain: $C(t) = \{B_0, \ldots, B_t\}$, a chained data structure in which blocks are added in strict chronological order. If a node wants to modify any transaction in the block of a local copy of the blockchain, it must iterate through all subsequent blocks, so the blockchain is tamper-proof. Furthermore, we reach an agreement on the local copy of the blockchain by adopting a reliable and efficient consensus mechanism. By querying transaction records on the blockchain, active users can dynamically adjust their caching strategies to get higher rewards. Moreover, blockchain will improve network security by authenticating node identity (Fig. 2).

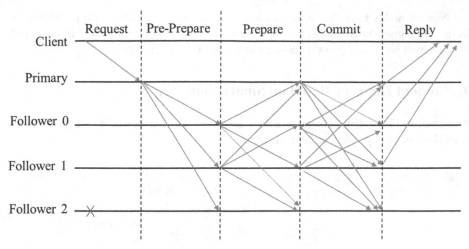

Fig. 2. PBFT consensus Policy process

3 Blockchain Consensus Mechanism

We use PBFT consensus algorithm to achieve the agreement between local replicas. The detailed consensus process is described as follows:

step1: The system selects a primary in turn according to the number, and the primary initializes to send a View-New message to synchronize the data of all nodes;
step2: The client initiates the request and forwards it to the primary. After the primary verification is passed, it will broadcast the request, launch a pre-prepare message to all follower nodes, and save the request itself.
step3: After receiving the pre-prepare message, all followers take the first step to verify it, including data sequence, transaction signature, etc. (to prevent client side fraud or primary node tampering fraud);
step4: After verifying correctly, followers write to their own disk, broadcast the Prepare message, and enter the Prepare stage.
step5: All nodes count the prepare message for a Request. When the statistical result exceeds 2f nodes, it indicates that most nodes have completed the persistence and enter the COMMIT stage.
step6: The node broadcasts the COMMIT message and counts the number of received COMMIT messages. When more than 2f nodes all issue the COMMIT message, the node completes the commit phase, writes data, and updates the controller table data.

It should be noted that the selected master node mainly has the following three functions: 1) During normal operation, receive the client's transaction request, set the number for the request after verifying the identity of the request, and broadcast the pre-prepare message; 2) When a new primary is elected, it will send View-news messages according to the View-change messages collected by itself to let other nodes synchronize the data; 3) Primary maintains heartbeat with other nodes.

Primary nodes have the same status as follower nodes and have no privileges. If the machine goes down and no message occurs, any incorrectly numbered or tampered message will be sensed by other nodes and triggered view-change.

4   Content Delivery Based on Smart Contract

As shown in Fig. 1 (b), content providers automate the delivery of cached content to normal users by deploying smart contracts.

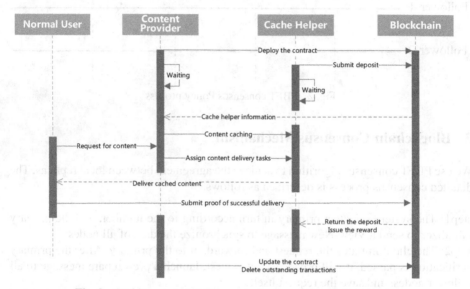

Fig. 3. Caching content delivery process based on smart contracts

The detailed flow of content delivery based on smart contracts is shown in Fig. 3. We designed the delivery process to be proactive, reducing back-trip congestion, reducing costs for content providers and improving the quality of the mobile user experience (QoE), while reducing heavy traffic while ensuring delivery under high volatility. For ease of understanding, the active delivery process is described in two parts: the cache helper prestores the content provider content and the cache helper delivers the content to normal users through an smart contract.

Pre-caching phase: 1) The content provider issues caching orders for content through deploying smart contracts that provide rewards for successful delivery of cached content in the future; 2) The cache helper accepts the contract, provides the cache for the content K, and sends the deposit(mortgage) to the smart contract; 3) An event response is triggered, notifying the content provider of the need to make a response about the cache helper; 4) Assuming that multiple cache helpers are willing to help content delivery, content providers select specific cache helpers by invoking smart contracts; 5) The content provider transfers a copy of content K to the cache helper for caching; 6) In order to get a refund, the cache helper needs to provide an interactive recyclable certificate to the blockchain platform to prove that the cached content K has been successfully delivered; 7) After confirmation of receipt of the certificate, the cache helper can get the returned deposit;8) At the end of each period, the existing contract will be destroyed by CP to avoid pending transactions, and a new contract of the same form will be deployed in the next period.

Cache delivery phase: 1) Content providers deploy smart contracts to publish content available for delivery, 2) Normal users make content requests to content providers, 3) After the content providers listen to the normal users' requests, the cache helper selected in the pre-cache phase will respond to the delivery function to deliver the cached content K to the users; 4) After successful delivery, the cache helper will send the proof of recycling to the blockchain platform to obtain the deposit and reward; 5) Finally, at the end of the period, the delivery contract is updated to delete the outstanding transactions.

5   The Selection Policy for Replica Server

This paper uses model predictive control (MPC) to solve the problem of simultaneous optimization of bandwidth and delay. Define the system state at time t as Z_t, N_t is the total number of requests in the system at time t, the system input of MPC is $p_{l,s}(t)$, CDN proxy server set $S = \{1, 2, \ldots s, \ldots\}$, and path set $L = \{1, 2, \ldots, l, \ldots\}$. Optimization goal: the user's average response time is the smallest; the user's bandwidth satisfaction conversion is the smallest.

The average user response time is the round-trip delay of the user, including the round-trip link delay and the processing delay of the server. Regarding the server as an M/M/1 queuing model, the processing time of the server can be expressed as

$$d_s(t) = \sum_{s \in S} \frac{v_t p_s(t)}{v_s - v_t p_s(t)} \tag{1}$$

v_t represent the rate at which requests arrive at time t, v_s is the processing speed of the server, and $p_s(t)$ is the probability of the task being processed by the proxy server s. In the SDN network, the controller can obtain the global status information of the network, including the link delay. The link delay detected by the controller is expressed by d_l, then the average round-trip delay requested by the user is:

$$d(t) = \sum_{s \in S} d_s(t) p_s(t) + \sum_{l \in L} d_l p_{l,s}(t) \tag{2}$$

Among them $p_{l,s}(t)$ is the probability that the task will be processed by the proxy server through the path. Therefore, the delay optimization function J_a is defined as:

$$J_a = \sum_{k=t+1}^{t+T} d(k) \tag{3}$$

Then consider the user's bandwidth satisfaction, the ratio of the bandwidth that the network can actually provide to the bandwidth requested by the user, so the user bandwidth satisfaction offset on the link l is represented by $B_l(t)$, which is defined as follows:

$$B_l(t) = \left[\frac{\sum\limits_{l \in L} p_{l,s}(t) - C_l}{\sum\limits_{l \in L} p_{l,s}(t)RN_t} \right]^+ \tag{4}$$

R is the average size of user requests, $[x]^+$ represents when $x > 0$, the value is itself, when $x \leq 0$, the value is 0, therefore, the optimization function J_b that defines the bandwidth satisfaction offset is:

$$J_b = \sum_{k=t+1}^{t+T} p_{l,s}(t)B_l(t) \tag{5}$$

Finally, consider reducing the change value of the system input $P_{l,s}(t)$ to maintain the stability of the system, and define the third optimization function J_c as:

$$J_c = \sum_{k=t+1}^{t+T} \sum_{s \in S} \sum_{l \in L} |p_{l,s}(k) - p_{l,s}(k-1)| \tag{6}$$

In order to consider three optimization functions at the same time, define the joint optimization function as $J_a + \omega_b J_b + \omega_c J_c$, where ω_b and ω_c are the weight values of and respectively relative to J_a. By solving the following nonlinear programming problem, all the values in each time slot $t+1 \leq k \leq t+T$ can be calculated:

$$\min J_a + \omega_b J_b + \omega_c J_c$$

$$s.t. \begin{cases} p_s(t) = \sum\limits_{l \in L} p_{l,s}(t) \\ \sum\limits_{l \in L} \sum\limits_{s \in S} p_{l,s}(t) = 1 \\ 0 \leq p_{l,s}(t) \leq 1, \forall l, \forall s \end{cases} \tag{7}$$

The importance of the two optimization goals of response time and bandwidth satisfaction is balanced by adjusting the weight value according to the actual network demand.

6   Experiment and Analysis

We evaluated the cache hit rate, the benefit of the cache helper, and the delivery delay of the proposed scheme.

1) Cache hit ratio: When a normal user makes a content request, it is a hit if the cache helper caches the data to be accessed. If not, you need to go to the original server to fetch, which is a miss. Cache hit ratio is an important factor to evaluate CDN acceleration effect.

$$R_{hit} = \frac{number_{hit}}{number_{hit} + number_{nohit}} \tag{8}$$

Where, R_{hit} is the cache hit ratio, $number_{hit}$ is the number of hit requests, and $number_{nohit}$ is the number of missed requests.

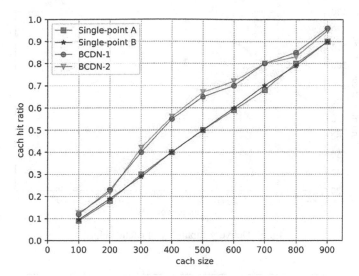

Fig. 4. Comparison of the cache hit ratio

The comparison of the cache hit ratio is given in Fig. 4. It is obvious that our proposed scheme has a higher cache hit ratio with the same cache capacity. It is important to note that the cache hit ratio generally increases as the cache capacity of the helper increases.

2) Cache helper benefit: This section evaluates cache helper's ability to deliver cached content and how much it can be rewarded based on incentive strategies.

Figure 5 shows the ability of the cache helper to deliver, and our solution can deliver first. It is obvious that for the same number of cache helpers, our solution delivers more content. The expected reward for the cache helper is depicted in Fig. 6. If the cache helper successfully delivers the requested content, it is rewarded with incentives to better participate in task collaboration. Our scheme has a better incentive effect, since the cache helper is expected to get a higher reward.

3) Delay: We evaluate the delay of the scheme according to the standardized delivery time. For a normal user's request, we calculate its delivery time as follows:

$$\tau_t = \begin{cases} \tau_{ch}, & \text{if cached} \\ \tau_{ch} + \tau_{cp}, & \text{if not cached} \end{cases} \tag{9}$$

τ_t is the standardized delivery time, τ_{ch} is the delay when delivering content requests directly for the cache helper, and τ_{cp} is the interactive delay when actively caching from the content provider for the cache helper.

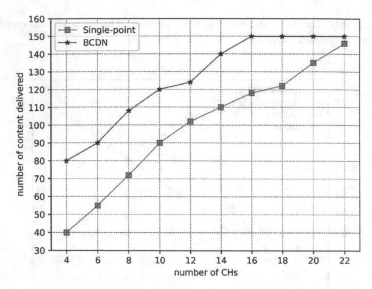

Fig. 5. Delivery capability of cache helper

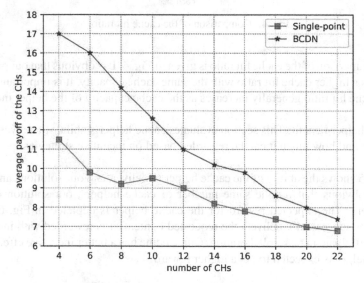

Fig. 6. Cache helper's expected reward

The comparison of standardized content delivery delay is given in Fig. 7. When the number of normal user requests is lower than the threshold, the proposed scheme is not much different from the traditional CDN. However, when the user demands are large, the proposed scheme can reduce the delay to some extent.

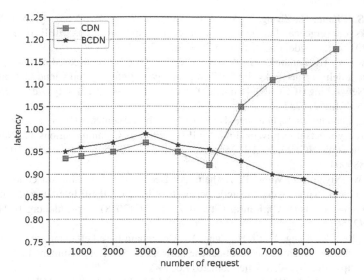

Fig. 7. Standardized content delivery delay

7 Conclusion

We have designed a blockchain-based CDN-P2P network where cache utilization is improved by mining storage resources in non-core locations of the network. The consortium blockchain is built to provide authentication and audit services to the cache nodes to ensure that the cache helpers can deliver content reliably. We have described in detail the active cache delivery process based on smart contracts in this paper. The model predictive control is used to jointly optimize the bandwidth and delay during the replica server selection process. A number of simulations have been done to support the theory.

Acknowledgement. This work was supported by research of unified trusted data Management of government administration and enterprise "One Netcom" (State Grid science and technology program 5217Q020002Q).

Conflicts of Interest. The authors declare that they have no conflicts of interest to report regarding the present study."

References

1. Vakali, A., Pallis, G.: Content delivery networks: status and trends. IEEE Internet Comput. 7(6), 68–74 (2003). https://doi.org/10.1109/MIC.2003.1250586
2. Sung, J., Kim, M., Lim, K., Rhee, J.K.: Efficient cache placement strategy in two-tier wireless content delivery network. IEEE Trans. Multimedia 18(6), 1163–1174 (2016). https://doi.org/10.1109/TMM.2016.2543658
3. Lu, Z., et al.: Machine learning empowered content delivery: status, challenges and opportunities. IEEE Netw. https://doi.org/10.1109/MNET.011.2000141

4. Wang, S., Zhang, X., Zhang, Y., Wang, L., Yang, J., Wang, W.: A survey on mobile edge networks: convergence of computing, caching and communications. IEEE Access **5**, 6757–6779 (2017). https://doi.org/10.1109/ACCESS.2017.2685434

5. Haribowo, Y., Kistijantoro, A.I.: Performance analysis of content-based mobile application on content delivery networks. In: 2012 International Conference on Cloud Computing and Social Networking (ICCCSN), Bandung, West Java, pp. 1–4 (2012). https://doi.org/10.1109/ICCCSN.2012.6215747

6. Vu, T.X., Chatzinotas, S., Ottersten, B.: Blockchain-based content delivery networks: content transparency meets user privacy. In: 2019 IEEE Wireless Communications and Networking Conference (WCNC), Marrakesh, Morocco, pp. 1–6 (2019). https://doi.org/10.1109/WCNC.2019.8885904

7. Wang, W., Niyato, D., Wang, P., Leshem, A.: Decentralized caching for content delivery based on blockchain: a game theoretic perspective. In: 2018 IEEE International Conference on Communications (ICC), Kansas City, MO, pp. 1–6 (2018). https://doi.org/10.1109/ICC.2018.8422547

8. Fan, K., Ren, Y., Wang, Y., Li, H., Yang, Y.: Blockchain-based efficient privacy preserving and data sharing scheme of content-centric network in 5G. IET Commun. **12**(5), 527–532 (2018). https://doi.org/10.1049/iet-com.2017.0619

9. Ak, E., Canberk, B.: BCDN: a proof of concept model for blockchain-aided CDN orchestration and routing. Comput. Netw. **161**, 162–171 (2019)

10. Herbaut, N., Negru, N.: A model for collaborative blockchain-based video delivery relying on advanced network services chains. IEEE Commun. Mag. **55**(9), 70–76 (2017)

11. Park, K., Cho, K., Han, D., Kwon, T., Pack, S.: Proof of delivery in a trustless network. In: 2019 IEEE International Conference on Blockchain and Cryptocurrency (ICBC), Seoul, Korea (South), pp. 196–200 (2019). https://doi.org/10.1109/BLOC.2019.8751417

A Dynamic Processing Algorithm for Variable Data in Intranet Security Monitoring

Chunru Zhou[1] (iD), Guo Wu[1], Junhao Li[1], and Chunrui Zhang[1,2](✉)

[1] Institute of Computer Application, China Academy of Engineering Physics,
Mianyang 621900, China
[2] Department of Computer Science and Technology, Harbin Institute
of Technology, Harbin 150001, China

Abstract. Nowadays corporate Intranet Security Monitoring generally relies on SIEM products or SOC platforms. The data comes from a large number of system logs, application running logs and business data, which are generated by network device, security protection device and application systems, etc., is finally stored as normalized data after word segmentation, field parsing and data type mapping. The Intranet Security Monitoring are extremely sensitive to data quality because of the efficiency and accuracy requirements, but the continuous business changes and system upgrades in the intranet environment make both of the data structure and content variable. The existing automated log parsing algorithms are mainly aimed at system logs with a fixed structure, cannot handle variable data with multiple types and structures, besides, the parsing work only completes word segmentation and field parsing. As for data type identification and mapping, there should be several security experts to wait to write static templates, in case the data is changed. In response to the above problems, an ontology model of data knowledge for Intranet Security Monitoring is constructed, and using the computing power of cloud computing, a dynamic processing algorithm for variable data (DPAVD) based on structural information entropy is proposed, in which the correlation between data fields is used as the core factor, can reduce the interference caused by the difference in character expression and meet the requirements of high-quality data for Intranet Security Monitoring.

Keywords: Intranet security monitoring · Variable data · Dynamic processing · Structural information · Ontology model

1 Introduction

In response to the increasingly severe network security situation, various enterprises and institutions have deployed SIEM (Security Information and Event Management) products or SOC (Security Operation Center) platforms based on Cloud Computing and Big Data technology for Intranet Security Monitoring [1]. Intranet Security Monitoring pursues precise positioning and rapid discovery, so it is extremely sensitive to the quality of the data input from the network device, security protection device and application systems, etc. There are big differences in the structure and content of the original data

X. Sun et al. (Eds.): ICAIS 2021, LNCS 12737, pp. 147–156, 2021.
https://doi.org/10.1007/978-3-030-78612-0_12

from different sources. In the actual work of enterprises and institutions, business changes and system upgrades are frequent, which makes the data in a state of change, that means the data is variable data. However, most of the existing automated methods for data processing of SOCs can only achieve good results for specific situations, the data sources or devices are from the same vender, with the same data standard. When facing different security vendor and different data standard, the usual method is to adopt manual configuration, the static parsing template and single mapping method of fixed target data types is used for data processing. Although the basic functional requirement for data processing is completed, it cannot deal with unpredictable changes in data and cannot meet the accuracy and efficiency requirements of security monitoring.

This paper builds an ontology model of data knowledge for Intranet Security Monitoring, and on this basis, proposes a **D**ynamic **P**rocessing **A**lgorithm for **V**ariable **D**ata (DPAVD) that introduces structural information entropy into the decision tree, and uses the correlation between data fields as the core factor. According to the basis, it avoids the interference of character matching caused by the difference in text expression, can accurately and effectively complete the data parsing task, and continue to maintain high-quality data input. Finally, the simulation data results and algorithm analysis are given.

2   Raw Messages to be Processed

The normalized data required for Intranet Security Monitoring is mainly collected by various security devices and application systems through data acquisition probes in an active or passive way to collect raw messages, and obtain it through word segmentation, field parsing and data type mapping. The data processing flow is shown in the Fig. 1 below.

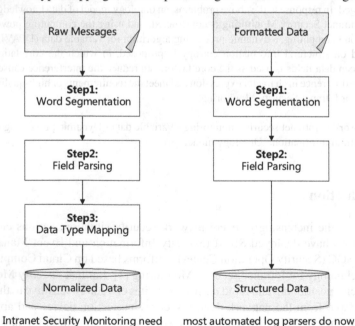

Fig. 1. Data processing steps

Unfortunately, what Intranet Security Monitoring need is well normalized data that not only has clear structure but also contains useful security information, that work need we to do the step 1, 2, 3 shown in Fig. 1, but what most of the automated log parsers do is step1 and 2, which aim at building up structured data from different original formatted data.

The raw messages can generally be divided into two categories, namely formatted data with a fixed structure and variable data with uncertain format.

2.1 Formatted Data

The formatted data is generated in a fixed format, usually composed of fixed keywords, specified variables and wildcards [2]. Take the first message in Table 1 as an example, it has a fixed keyword "INFO", some specified variables like DATE, TIME and IP, and a detailed description. Since the format is fixed, the keywords, the separator for word segmentation(usually are Space) and the parsing template can be fixed, both manually written and automatically generated parsing templates can achieve relatively ideal results.

Table 1. Examples of formatted data and parsing template.

Formatted Data		Parsing Template
INFO 2020-01-01 10:11:23 sip:10.1.1.2 dip:10.2.2.3 a hello is sent by the src user	→	INFO DATE TIME sip:IP dip:IP *
081109 204655 Received block blk_3587 of size 67108864 from /10.251.42.84	→	NUM NUM Received block blk_NUM of size NUM from /IP
<180> 2020-01-01 10:11:23 src:Alice dst:Bob type:Mail attachment:True att_num:2 att_size:17892 status:1	→	<180> DATE TIME src:* dst:* type:* attachment:BOOL att_num:NUM att_size:NUM status:NUM

To deal with the formatted data, there are some representative log parsers or open-source tools such as LenMa [3], LogMine [4], Spell [5] (with longest common subsequence computation), Drain [6] (with parsing tree) and MoLFI [7]. With these tools, automated log parsing lately becomes an appealing selling point in some trending log management solutions. But in the environment of Intranet Security Monitoring, the target of data processing is not only to manage the system log, but also to extract effective information from the network that can provide any clue about inner threat. So the information we need is not just come from the formatted system log, the variable data of business and application is more important.

2.2 Variable Data

Besides the formatted system logs, the other important data collected for Intranet Security Monitoring is variable data, which come from different network devices, security products, business and application systems, etc. The data types are diverse due to differences in monitoring scope, device types, manufacturers, and collecting methods. In addition, it changes dynamically with the actual security status during operation, which makes the received raw data unstructured in different degrees. There are some common variable data shown in Table 2, including the fixed separator, the mixed use of multiple separators, Key-Value format, JSON format, multiple combinations of forms, and even irregular data formats. The length of the data field and its meaning may also change with the intranet security status.

Table 2. Examples of raw messages of variable data.

Formatted with	Examples
fixed single delimiter	WARNING 2020-01-01 10:11:23 10.1.1.2 "a problem is found"
multiple delimiter	<190>May 6 16:42:56 13044(root) 4424361f Traffic@FLOW: SESSION: 192.168.1.2:5404->192.168.1.3 (UDP), interface xe-thernet1/7, vr trust-vr, policy 1, user -@-, host -, policy deny
Key-Value Pattern	id=tos time="2019-05-20 09:18:30" fw=TopsecOS pri=6 type=conn src=192.168.1.2 dst=192.168.1.3 proto=tcp sport=54294 dport=1521 inpkt=25 outpkt=21 sent=3774 rcvd=5151 duration=53 connid=50606618 msg="null"
JSON Pattern	{"alarm_time":"2019-04-19 20:34:45","subtype":"AppProtection", "name":"Instant Msg", "detail":"Alice sent a message to Bob", "user_name":"Admin", "sip":"192.168.1.2"}
Hybrid Structural Pattern	<188>2019/02/24 07:24:29 IPS %%01IPS/4/DETECT(l): An intrusion was detected. {SyslogId=3875999744, VSys="public", Policy="ips_capture_policy", SrcIp=192.168.1.2, DstIp=192.168.1.3}
Blur Pattern	Feb 1 06:16:37 asm processor_server: classid:202, level:3, devid:1242, devip:10.1.1.2, Admin on switch [100.1.1.2:gei_1/9]find[2]set of MAC[00:aa:bb:cc:dd:ee-/00:aa:bb:cc:dd:ff-100.100.70.80/]

In order to meet both of the business attribute and security attribute requirements of data for Intranet Security Monitoring, the structured data obtained after word segmentation and parsing needs to be mapped to data types. The data is firstly divided into categories depended on different data source, and then according to the specific information content: alarms, operation logs, business logs, etc., the data will be divided into different data type. Data type under the same category contains some common fields, like IP, DATE, TIME, USERNAME etc., and each specific data type contains its own unique fields.

3 Ontology Model for Data in Intranet Security Monitoring

The original data can be processed by word segmentation and parsing to obtain several original data fields. Due to the diversity of expression methods, it is difficult to unify them in a vector with fixed characteristics. If all different expressions are regarded as a new characteristic value, then the unified vector will far exceed the actual calculation capacity in terms of dimensions. In fact, it is impossible and meaningless to store every unique expression characteristics of data, because the vector space is infinite. Therefore, commonly used machine learning-based data classification or clustering algorithms [9] will be difficult to deal with when facing these dynamically changing data, and it is necessary to use more appropriate expressions to describe the data knowledge for Intranet Security Monitoring.

Ontology theory is an excellent formal model for the description of a certain domain knowledge, which can express the relationship between concepts and entities [10, 11]. The core concept to be processed by the ontology model of data knowledge for Intranet Security Monitoring is the original data. Starting from the original data, in the ontology model, the upstream relationship mainly includes data source devices, the stage of the cyber kill chain [12] to which the data source belongs, and the triggering of security protection alarms or specific attack methods to leave traces, etc., and the downstream relationship mainly includes specific data types, fields, and basic format features of the data. Therefore, it is suitable to adopt ontology model to describe the data knowledge for Intranet Security Monitoring.

An example of the ontology model of data knowledge for Intranet Security Monitoring is shown in Fig. 2. In this ontology model, the data field is not subordinate to a specific data type, so the subordination relationship between the field and the data type may overlap; the attributes of the field can be divided into the word order of the field in the data and the feature format. The word order refers to the specific position of the field in the data, the feature format can be constrained by regular expressions or template data. Fields with the same meaning may also have different format constraints, and the same feature constraint format may have different data fields conforming to it.

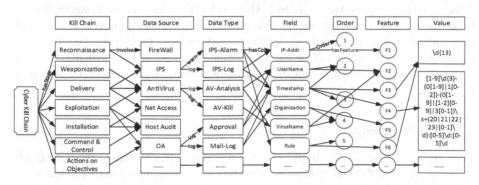

Fig. 2. Ontology model of data knowledge for intranet security monitoring

The original data after word segmentation is introduced into the ontology model through the matching with the defined feature constraint formats, and the matching can be achieved by a similarity pattern matching method combining multiple strategies, which will not be repeated in this article.

4 Data Type Mapping Based on Structural Information Entropy

4.1 Question Description

For a piece of original data, after the completed word segmentation, parsing, and feature constraint format matching, it is introduced into the ontology model and the irrelevant attributes and fields are eliminated, a subgraph of the relationship between the piece of data in the data knowledge can be obtained. Due to the different degrees of overlap between feature constraints and the relationships between fields and data types, after all the fields of this piece of data are taken into consideration, there may be multiple data types have the close relationship.

In response to the need for data accuracy in Intranet Security Monitoring, on one hand, if this piece of data is closely related to multiple data types, we need to consider how to classify this piece of data when generating processing rules, that is, what type of specification should be selected to output and storage; On the other hand, if the degree of association is weak, the piece of data may be invalid and need to be cleaned up, or is a useless piece with a small amount of information, or even a brand new type of data that cannot be resolved by the current data knowledg. In addition, how to calculate the final oriented data type and quickly generate processing rules is an inevitable problem to meet the real-time data requirements of Intranet Security Monitoring. In view of the above-mentioned scientific problems and difficulties, this paper adopts the introduction of structural information entropy into the decision tree algorithm as a key of decision-making to achieve rapid and accurate automatic generation of processing rules.

Previously, the Shannon entropy method was mainly used to measure information, which measured the uncertainty of the probability distribution, but in doing so, the information of the data in the structure was lost. The structural information measurement theory was researched and proposed by [13] on the basis of Shannon's information theory. It can measure the high-dimensional information embedded in a graph (i.e, structural information). Taking structural information measurement as the core of the processing algorithm can effectively avoid the interference caused by the difference in the character representation of the original data, and pay more attention to the inner relationship of the data fields.

4.2 Algorithm Design

The structural information entropy is based on graph. Given a simple connected graph $G = (V, E)$, and the coding tree T of graph G, the structural information entropy determined by G is defined as:

$$H^T(G) = -\sum_{\substack{\alpha \in T \\ \alpha \neq \lambda}} \frac{g_\alpha}{2m} \log \frac{V_\alpha}{V_{\alpha^-}} \tag{1}$$

For a simple connected graph G, the structural information entropy of G is defined as:

$$H(G) = \min_T \{H^T(G)\} \tag{2}$$

When the data collector obtains a brand new piece of original data, the existing processing template cannot be matched, it enters the variable data dynamic processing flow, that is, it needs to generate a new processing rule for this unknown original data. We take the entropy gain idea in decision tree algorithm [14] as a basic method, and create a relationship subgraph about the data types on the basis of the ontology model above, every time when we do a decision, the structural information entropy for this relationship subgraph is used as the key decision basis. We name the specific method DPAVD.

Assuming that a piece of variable data after word segmentation and parsing, it has been divided into n fields. The original data can be expressed as $D = \{d_1, d_2, \ldots, d_n\}$, for the i field, there is $d_i = \{i, F_i\}$, in which i is the word order, F_i is the feature constraint of this field, and d_i is the field that satisfy the feature constraint in the ontology model. If there are m_i estimated fields D'_i, recorded as $D'_i = \{d'_{i1}, d'_{i2}, \ldots, d'_{im_i}\}$, and the mapping relationship is expressed as $d_i \rightarrow D'_i$, then all the fields in the model that meet the characteristics can be recorded as $D' = \{D'_1, D'_2, \ldots, D'_m\}$, there are m that fields and $m = m_1 + m_2 + \ldots + m_n$. D' can be correspond to the data types $L = \{l_1, l_2, \ldots, l_k\}$, there are k of L, the mapping relationship is expressed as $D' \rightarrow L$.

As long as the original log data is determined, the corresponding estimated field and the data type can also be determined, that is, the scope of data knowledge is determined. Therefore, a directed connected graph about the original data fields, the estimated fields in the ontology model, and the data type can be constructed. As shown below in Fig. 3.

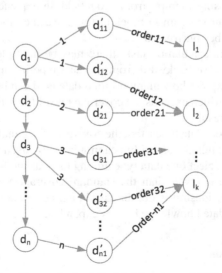

Fig. 3. Relationship graph of original field, estimated field and data type

In the relationship subgraph, the distance from node d to node d' is equal to the order of the field d in the original data, and the distance from node d' to node l is the order of the estimated field in the data type. Selecting a certain field d of the original data as the starting point, walking through only a branch path to the data type node will be regarded as a processing attempt (decision branch selection), after all the original fields have been selected, that is, after the complete n processing attempts, a relationship subgraph of the aforementioned data knowledge relationship graph can be formed, which is the final processing results, and the decision tree that guides the execution of each processing attempt is the processing rule. The decision tree generation steps are as follows:

1) Calculate the structural information entropy of the relationship graph after $i - 1$ original field has been selected, recorded as $H(G_{i-1})$.
2) Perform processing attempts of each field to calculate the structural information entropy gain of the relationship subgraph under different selection paths. For example, we have had $H(G_{i-1})$, and then start from the i-th field of D, that is d_i, when the j-th estimated field d'_{ij} is selected, the structural information gain of d'_{ij} is:

$$Gain(d'_{ij}) = H_{d'_{ij}}(G_i) - H(G_{i-1}) \tag{3}$$

According to the corresponding relationship $d_i \rightarrow D'_i$, in order to complete the selection started from d_i, a total of m_i times of structural information entropy need to be calculated. The estimated field corresponding to the relationship subgraph with the largest structural information entropy gain will be selected as the new leaf node of the decision tree, so $H(G_i)$ is:

$$H(G_i) = \max\{Gain(d_{ij})\} + H(G_{i-1}) \tag{4}$$

3) Complete the processing attempts from 1 to n fields in sequence, calculate the structural information entropy gain m times in total, and then the decision tree of the processing rule can be constructed.
4) After completing the calculation task, there may be multiple target data types to be matched. Then move backward from the data type in turn, and set a standard coverage rate λ to express how many original data field can be reached from a data type. The data type which exceeds the coverage rate of the original data mostly will be selected as final result.
5) If there are two or more data types, that the coverage of original fields are the same or the coverage rate is high, the algorithm cannot judge by itself, and then the security personnel manually select one data type among them as the final result.
6) If the coverage rate is lower than the standard coverage rate λ, the current corresponding field relationship is output as a brand new data type, and the existing ontology model of data knowledge base is expanded.

4.3 Algorithm Analysis

Taking firewall data as an example, we conducted data processing experiments on a total of 9 data types in different formats generated by three firewalls (Huawei, TopSec,

HillStone). Under the condition that the ontology model is relatively complete, more than 85% of the data is correctly parsed and mapped to the correct log type. Using typical algorithms Drain, Spell, and IPLoM as a reference, the three algorithms have higher parsing accuracy when the data format is fixed and the target data type is definite, but when the data format changes, the parsing accuracy rate shows a cliff-style drop, sometimes even cannot parse at all. The results are shown in Table 3:

Table 3. Accuracy of data processing experiments on firewall data

Algorithms/Accuracy (%)	Huawei			TopSec			HillStone		
	Deny	Warn	Fault	Deny	Warn	Fault	Deny	Warn	Fault
Drain	96	72	9	95	75	10	96	69	8
Spell	94	69	8	93	69	7	95	62	7
IPLoM	93	60	5	92	66	7	93	59	8
DPAVD	91	88	85	90	87	86	92	90	87

According to the previous experience in data processing, in a relatively stable intranet security monitoring environment, a piece of variable data that needs to be processed generally contains fields less than 30. Assuming that each original field has 2–3 estimated fields to satisfy its characteristic constraints, a brand new processing rule generation requires 60–90 calculations of structural information entropy. Considering the actual situation, the frequency of data change, which caused by business upgrade, device change or the occurrence of security threats, is generally above the minute level, or even the hour level. And in most cases, the data processing module is mainly to complete the tasks with existing processing rules, and do not face large-scale data change in a very short time. Therefore, the existing server performance using the DPAVD can fully meet the performance requirements.

5   Conclusion

In view of the dynamic characteristics of the data source of Intranet Security Monitoring and the problems that conventional data parsing methods are difficult to deal with the variable data, this paper builds up an ontology model of data knowledge for Intranet Security Monitoring, and makes an explicit formal representation of the data knowledge in the form of graphs. The decision tree method based on structural information entropy is proposed to quickly and accurately construct processing rules, which can effectively use the associated information between data fields and solve the inefficiency of the current processing methods using static parsing templates. The problem provides a feasible solution for Intranet Security Monitoring to continuously maintain high-quality data input.

However, the good result in this paper is based on the good ontology model of data knowledge, the establishment of the model itself requires security personnel to have long-term experience in the industry, and a deeper understanding of the internal network structure, security monitoring items, events, and business scenarios, which is one of the main bottlenecks restricting the development of Intranet Security Monitoring techniques to be more universal.

Acknowledgement. This work is supported by Defense Industrial Technology Development Program (JCKY2018603B006).

Funding Statement. This work is supported by CAEP Foundation (PY2019132 C. R. Zhou, CX2019040 C. R. Zhang).

References

1. Yao, D., Chen, Y.: Design and implementation of log data analysis management system based on hadoop. J. Inf. Hiding Privacy Protect. **2**(2), 1–7 (2020)
2. Zhu, J., et al.: Tools and benchmarks for automated log parsing. In: Proceedings ICSE-SEIP, pp. 121–130 (2019)
3. Shima, K.: Length matters: clustering system log messages using length of words (2016). arXiv:1611.03213
4. Hamooni, H., Debnath, B.K., Xu, J.W., Zhang, H.G., Jiang, F., Mueen, A.: LogMine: fast pattern recognition for log analytics. In: Proceedings of CIKM, pp. 1573–1582 (2016)
5. Du, M., Li, F.F.: Spell: streaming parsing of system event logs. In: Proceedings of ICDM, pp. 859–864 (2016)
6. He, P., Zhu, J., Zheng, Z., Lyu, M.R.: Drain: an online log parsing approach with fixed depth tree. In: Proceedings of ICWS, pp. 33–40 (2017)
7. Messaoudi, S., Panichella, A., Bianculli, D., Briand, L., Sasnauskas, R.: A search-based approach for accurate identification of log message formats. In: Proceedings of ICPC (2018)
8. Wu, Q., Huang, X.H., Ma, Y., Cong, Q.: A template extraction method for composite log. J. Zhejiang Univ. (Eng. Sci.), **54**(8), 1557–1561 (2020)
9. Harrington, P.: Machine Learning in Action. Post & Telecom Press, Beijing (2017)
10. Kotenko, I., Saenko, I., Polubelova, O., et al.: The ontology of metrics for security evaluation and decision support in SIEM system. In: Proceedings of ICARS, Regensburg, pp. 638–645 (2013)
11. Si, C., Zhang, H.Q., Wang, Y.W., Yang, Y.J.: Research on network security situational elements knowledge base model based on ontology. Comput. Sci. **42**(5), 173–177 (2015)
12. Yadav, T., Rao, A.M.: Technical Aspects of cyber Kill Chain. Secur. Comput. Commun. **536**, 438–452 (2015)
13. Li, A.S.: Structural information theory. Commun. CCF **9**, 24–30 (2018)
14. Uma, K.V., Alias, A.: C5.0 decision tree model using tsallis entropy and association function for general and medical dataset. Intell. Autom. Soft Comput. **26**(1), 61–70 (2020)

Personalized Recommendation of English Learning Based on Knowledge Graph and Graph Convolutional Network

Yuan Sun[1,2]([✉]) [iD], Jiaya Liang[1,2] [iD], and Pengchao Niu[1,2]

[1] Minzu University of China, Beijing 100081, China
[2] Minority Languages Branch, National Language Resource and Monitoring Research Center, Beijing, China

Abstract. With the rapid development of education, a large number of the online learning platforms have emerged. Although they provide the convenience to the students, they cannot provide students with in-depth personalized services. To solve this problem, in this paper, we propose a method to personalize the recommendation of English learning based on knowledge graph and graph convolutional network. Firstly, we construct a knowledge graph containing a large number of Junior High School English exercises, which are classified by the knowledge points. Secondly, a graph convolutional neural network is used to generate a personalized knowledge graph for each student. Finally, it provides students with in-depth personalized services by generating personalized learning path. The experimental results prove the effectiveness of our method.

Keywords: Knowledge graph · Graph convolutional network · Personalized learning path

1 Introduction

The idea of personalized education has been widely advocated since ancient times, but in traditional classroom teaching, personalized teaching is difficult to achieve, because lacking teacher resources and messy teaching resources. Moreover, there are differences among students, and different students have different requirements on the speed of classroom teaching. In traditional classes, teachers often choose contents which they think is appropriate to apply to the classroom teaching based on subjective experience. For different students, their personalized requirements for learning speed and learning strategies cannot be satisfied, which will reduce students' learning efficiency. The lack of personalized education has become a pain point in the current field of education, and the development of personalized adaptive education have become one of the hot topics in education at the moment.

Supported by National Nature Science Foundation (No. 61972436).

X. Sun et al. (Eds.): ICAIS 2021, LNCS 12737, pp. 157–166, 2021.
https://doi.org/10.1007/978-3-030-78612-0_13

In recent years, with the rapid development of computer technology, it has been widely used in the education industry. The teaching method has changed from a single traditional method in the past to a diversified modern teaching method. Nowadays, online education resources are very rich, and students do the questions efficiently. It is particularly important that how to choose the most suitable personalized learning path from these questions according to the different situations of students. After comparing several domestic and foreign applications commonly used by students for personalized learning, such as Xueersi Online School, Homework-Help and BYJU'S etc. It is found that these methods carry out layered education for students. Although personalized education is realized to a certain extent, there is no deep personalized education for students. Based on this, this paper proposes to use knowledge graphs and Graph Convolutional Network (GCN) to achieve deep personalized education for students. This paper does the following research:

(1) Construct knowledge graph based on NEO4J [1]. This paper uses web crawler to obtain data of Junior High School English (JHSE) exercises. The cosine similarity between exercises is used to determine the relationship between exercises, and NEO4J is used to form knowledge graph.
(2) Generate personalized knowledge graph based on GCN. After constructing the JHSE knowledge graph, a small number of nodes in the knowledge graph are labeled, and personalized knowledge graph is generated by GCN.
(3) Generate personalized learning path based on Prim algorithm [2] and Kruskal algorithm [3]. Based on the previously generated personalized knowledge graph, Prim algorithm and Kruskal algorithm can be used to generate a personalized learning path.

2 Related Work

Personalized learning refers to the self-adjusting system according to external input information. Scholars at home and abroad have conducted in-depth research on personalized learning. Li and Jiang [4] interpreted personalized learning from a theoretical level. Yang and Hao [5] analyzed the realization of personalized learning and resource acquisition in the light of the current information technology. Cao and Zhu [6] built a personalized learning platform based on learning analysis. Shi et al. [7] studied the recommendation of personalized learning resources based on knowledge status, using knowledge graph and similarity iterative algorithm, and Li [8] studied personalized mathematics teaching in primary school based on big data. Bernacki and Walkington [9] discussed the influence of situational interest on students' personalized learning by adding situational teaching to students' learning process. Martinez [10] explored personalized learning by studying how individuals learn in an adaptive Web learning environment, and finally generated a guide for personalized learning in a Web environment. Lin et al. [11] developed a personalized learning system using data mining technology based on decision tree to promote the development of personalized learning and conduct personalized learning research. Wu et al. [12]

recommended learning path for students based on the knowledge graph in the MOOC platform, and Wang [13] used collaborative filtering to recommend personalized learning resources based on the knowledge graph.

Rotmensch et al. [14] applied knowledge graph to medical diagnosis. Sang et al. [15] combined knowledge graph with drug development. Graph data here refers not to traditional graphs and images, but to graphs composed of nodes and edges. Because of its excellent effect, it has made great progress and many variants have appeared. Marcheggiani and Titov [16] proposed a variant of GCN to label sentences with semantic roles, Song et al. [17] proposed dynamic graph convolution neural network to classify EEG (electroencephalogram) with emotion. Ryu et al. [18] proposed Bayesian graph convolution neural network to predict the properties of chemical molecules. Graph convolutional neural network refers to a neural network that performs convolution operations on graphs. It can be seen that with the emergence of new technologies, some problems in education will be solved slowly.

3 Model

When generating personalized learning path, firstly we generate a JHSE knowledge graph, then use a GCN to generate a personalized knowledge graph, and finally use a path generation algorithm to generate a personalized learning path, as shown in Fig. 1.

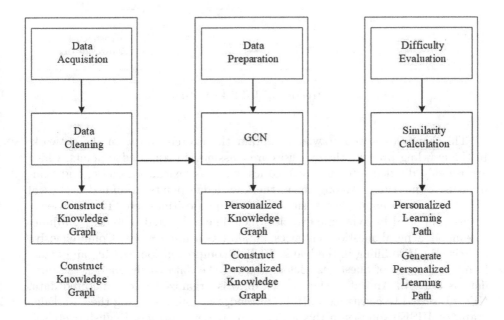

Fig. 1. Construction process of the knowledge graph.

3.1   Construction of JHSE Knowledge Graph Based on NEO4J

The construction method of knowledge graph can be summarized as top-down construction method and bottom-up construction method. According to the characteristics of the data, this paper uses a top-down approach when constructing knowledge graph. The construction of the knowledge graph can be divided into three parts: data acquisition, data cleaning, and the construction of the knowledge graph, as shown in Fig. 2.

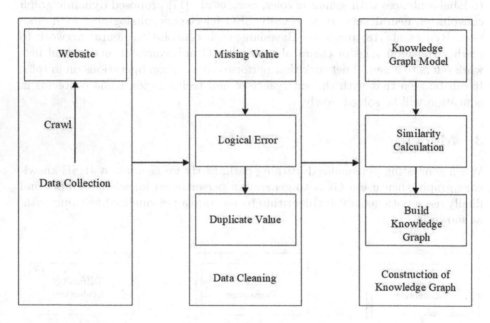

Fig. 2. Construction of JHSE knowledge graph.

This paper uses web crawler to obtain the exercise data on the network. In the crawling process, the exercises are classified by knowledge points, which are roughly divided into three categories, such as lexical, syntactic, and comprehensive questions. Among them, the knowledge points examined by lexical exercises include nouns, verbs, similar words, prepositions, etc. The knowledge points examined by syntactic exercises include emphasized sentences, subjunctive mood, general question sentences, imperative sentences, etc. Comprehensive exercises include filling in the blank, reading comprehension, writing and translating four types of questions. Before sending the data to the model, the dirty data is cleaned. And after the cleaned data is organized into structured data, NEO4J is used to construct a JHSE knowledge graph. Designing the knowledge graph of JHSE exercises in this article, this paper abstracts English exercises, knowledge points examined by the exercises, answer to the exercises and analysis the exercises into individual nodes. The interrelationships among exercises, knowledge points, explanations are used as edges connecting these nodes to form knowledge graph about JHSE exercises.

3.2 Generation of Personalized Knowledge Graph Based on GCN

When generating a personalized knowledge graph firstly, based on the original knowledge graph, the same set of exercises are generated for each student. The number of exercises are 100 and covers all details. The topic that the students do right is marked as mastered, and the label is set to 1. On the contrary, the topic is marked as not mastered, and the label is set to 0. After that, word2vec is used to generate word vectors for the stem and analysis of exercises. We add the stem of the exercise and the word vector of the analysis and divide it by the number of words contained in each exercise to obtain the corresponding sentence vector. We take this approach to generate feature vectors with a dimension of 512 for each exercise.

In this paper, the application of graph convolution neural network in node classification can be used to generate personalized knowledge graph. This is a semi-supervised learning process which only the categories of a small number of nodes need to be marked out and the categories of most nodes are unknown when training the network model. In the process of convolution, the features of the nodes around the nodes of the exercise will affect the representation of the current exercise nodes. The essence of the process is feature extraction. With the continuous increase of model training times, deeper features will be extracted.

The convolution mode of graph convolution neural network can be divided into spectral convolution and spatial convolution. Considering that spectral convolution can transfer the filters and graph signals in graph convolution network to Fourier Transformation for calculation, which can simplify the calculation, reduce the calculation amount and speed up the calculation of the model. In order to make the model have better results, in the process of convolution, the characteristic matrix can be converted into a Laplacian matrix which is a positive semi-definite symmetric matrix with n linearly independent eigenvectors. Such matrix could completely eigen-decomposed, so that the graph convolution operation can be carried out smoothly.

Graph convolution neural network can stack multiple convolution layers. With the increase of convolution layers, the parameters in the model also increase, which leads to the problems of slow calculation speed and over-fitting of the model. In order to prevent the above problems, the number of convolution layers are set at 2 in this paper. Through the forward propagation model, the class probability of each node will be obtained. If the probability value is large, it will be labeled as mastered, otherwise it will be labeled as not mastered. The probability value output by the model is converted into the label of the exercise, and the mapping file of the exercise number in the label is established to link the exercise label with the exercise number, so as to generate a personalized JHSE knowledge graph.

3.3 Generation of Personalized Learning Path Based on Personalized Knowledge Graph

According to the classification of exercise nodes, the difficulty of exercises and the similarity among exercises in the personalized knowledge graph, the personalized learning path is generated by using the graph path generation algorithm in the data structure for reference, and then the personalized learning path is modified continuously according to the changes of students learning situation.

Taking the actual situation of the students into account, the number of exercises in the generated personalized learning path is 35. The number of exercises that the students made wrong in the previous set of exercises is counted, if the number is greater than 35, finding 35 problem nodes with the highest similarity to these problems in the personalized knowledge graph.

Conversely, for each exercise that students make mistakes, this research selects n nodes that are connected to it and have the greatest similarity in the personalized knowledge graph, and then selects 35 nodes from it. The calculation method of n is as in Eq. 1.

$$n = ceil \left(\frac{Number\ of\ Exercises\ in\ the\ Set}{Number\ of\ Wrong\ Exercises} \right) \tag{1}$$

In the above Equation, ceil means rounding up the decimal. This paper examines the difficulty of the exercises from three aspects: the existence of beyond the teaching syllabus's words in the exercises, the similarity of the answers, the number of knowledge points in the exercises to make the personalized learning path generated more reasonable.

4 Experimental Results

4.1 Dataset

This paper finally got 24,092 exercises, which became 9,449 after data cleaning. Among them, there are 4,892 lexical exercises, 4,325 grammatical exercises, and 232 comprehensive questions. Examples of exercises are shown in Table 1.

In the experiment of personalized knowledge graph based on GCN, we divide the dataset to the train dataset and the test dataset, which are 70% and 30%, 6,614 and 2,835 respectively.

4.2 Experiment on Knowledge Graph Generation

This paper chooses to use the NEO4J graph database to build JHSE knowledge graph. The English exercises, the knowledge points examined in the exercises, the answers to the exercises, and the explanations will be abstracted into separate nodes.

Node hierarchy information consists of five layers, the central node is the subject of English. The second level nodes are the various knowledge points

Table 1. Exercise example

Tag	Content
Question	We need some pork to make dumplings. Would you please help me_____ ? A. eat it up B. eat up it C. cut it up D.cut up it
Answer	C. cut it up
Analysis	Test question analysis: sentence meaning: we need some pork to make dumplings, can you help me chop? cut up is a phrase composed of verb + adverb. The object uses the pronoun in the middle, combining the meaning of the sentence, so choose C

covered in middle school English. The third level node is made up of exercises, reading comprehension and translation. The fourth level node consists of answers to lexical, syntactic exercises and comprehensive questions. The last level consists of the answers and explanations corresponding to the comprehensive questions.

Based on the node hierarchy of the knowledge graph, the structure of this knowledge graph can be obtained. The JHSE structure of the knowledge graph in this paper is shown in Fig. 3.

4.3 Experiment on Personalized Knowledge Graph Generation Based on GCN

To generate a personalized knowledge graph for each student, an identical set of exercises are generated for each student based on the original knowledge graph, covering all the knowledge points and the number of exercises are 100. Then, marking the part of exercises according to the result of student's training. Questions that the student gets right are recorded as mastered and the label is set to 1, otherwise the label is set to 0. The corresponding adjacency matrix is then generated for the entire knowledge graph. The personalized knowledge graph in this paper is shown in Fig. 4.

4.4 Generation of Personalized Learning Path

The number of exercises generated for the students for the first time are 100, and 24 exercises are marked as unmastered by means of artificial annotation. Next, this paper takes one of the questions as an example to introduce how to choose the exercises in the personalized learning path according to the wrong exercises made by the students. First of all, all exercises connected to this question in the knowledge graph is found.

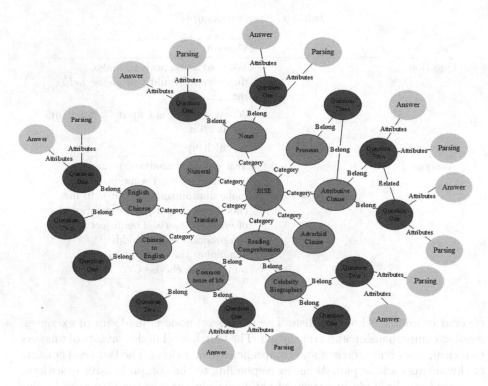

Fig. 3. The structure of knowledge graph.

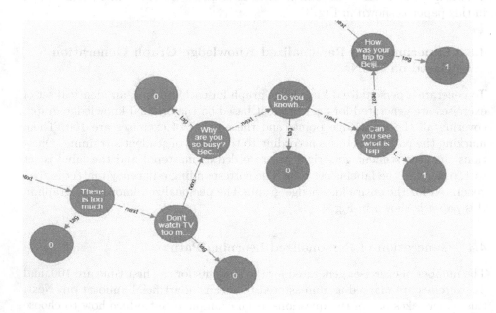

Fig. 4. Personalized knowledge graph.

This paper finds the two exercises with the highest similarity to the 24 exercises of the above middle school students, so that the number of exercises finally selected are 48, and then choose the 35 exercises with the largest similarity value among these 48 exercises. The 35 exercises are the exercise nodes that make up the personalized learning path.

Selecting the exercise nodes that make up the personalized learning path, these exercise nodes are organized into personalized learning path according to the difficulty of the exercises. The difficulty of the exercises in the personalized learning path is gradually increasing, which is in line with the general students' learning habits. The personalized learning path generated in this paper is shown in Fig. 5.

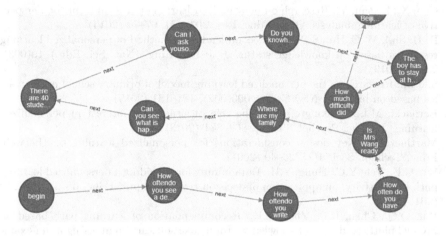

Fig. 5. The personalized learning path.

After the students have finished learning the exercises in the personalized learning path, according to the current situation of the students, the exercises in the JHSE knowledge graph are marked with new marks, and they are put into the convolutional neural network for training. The latest personalized knowledge graph is obtained, and then a new personalized learning path is generated according to the method for generating the personalized learning path described above.

5   Conclusion

This paper constructs JHSE exercises into JHSE knowledge graph and then generates a personalized learning path based on the knowledge graph, which has a very positive effect on the application of artificial intelligence technology in the education industry. At the same time, there are some areas in this paper that can be optimized. Firstly, there are insufficient exercises when it comes to some knowledge points in this paper. Secondly, the evaluation of difficulty degree of exercises may not be accurate. Finally, the architecture of the GCN model can be modified or replaced with a better model to improve the accuracy.

References

1. Vukotic, A., Partner, J., Watt, N.: Neo4j in Action, 2nd edn. Manning Publishing, New York (2013)
2. Surhone, L.M., Tennoe, M.T., Henssonow, S.F.: Prim's Algorithm. 2nd edn. Betascript Publishing, Beau Bassin (2004)
3. Broutin, N., Devroye, L., McLeish, E.: Note on the structure of Kruskal's algorithm. Algorithmica **56**(2), 141–159 (2010)
4. Li, G., Jiang, Y.J.: The theoretical construction and characteristic analysis of personalized learning. Northeast Normal Univ. News **25**(3), 152–156 (2005)
5. Yang, J., Hao, Y.Y.: Personalized learning in the context of information technology. Inf. Technol. Educ. China 000(011), 98–99 (2019)
6. Cao, X.M., Zhu, Y.: Research on personalized learning platform from the perspective of learning analysis. Open Educ. Res. **2014**(5), 67–74 (2014)
7. R. H. Shi., M, C. Hu., S. X. Li.: Recommendation method of personalized learning resources based on knowledge status. J. Jishou Univ. (Nat. Sci. Edn.) **40**(003), 23–27 (2019)
8. S. J Li.: Research on the personalized learning model of primary school mathematics based on big data. New Course 000(002), 181–181 (2019)
9. Bernacki, M.L., Walkington, C.: The role of situational interest in personalized learning. J. Educ. Psychol. **110**(6), 864–881 (2018)
10. Martinez, M.: Key design considerations for personalized learning on the web. Educ. Technol. Soci. **4**(1), 26–40 (2001)
11. Lin, C.F., Yeh, Y.C., Hung, Y.H.: Data mining for providing a personalized learning path in creativity: an application of decision trees. Comput. Educ. **68**(9), 199–210 (2013)
12. Wu, Q.Q., Chen, H.P., Zhao, Z.H.: Recommendation of learning path based on MOOC platform data and knowledge graph-take software engineering as an example. Softw. Eng. **21**(10), 27–30 (2017)
13. Wang, F., Zhang, L.L., Chen, X.C.: Research on personalized learning resource recommendation based on knowledge graph. Softw. Eng. **21**(10), 27–30 (2018)
14. Rotmensch, M., Halpern, Y., Tlimat, A.: Learning a health knowledge graph from electronic medical records. Sci. Rep. **7**(1), 5994–5994 (2017)
15. Sang, S.T., Yang, Z.H., Wang, L.: A knowledge graph based literature mining method for drug discovery. BMC Bioinform. **19**(1), 193–204 (2018)
16. Marcheggiani, D., Titov, I.: Encoding sentences with graph convolutional networks for semantic role labeling. ACL **2**(5), 1506–1515 (2017)
17. Song, T.F., Zheng, W.M., Song, P.: EEG emotion recognition using dynamical graph convolutional neural networks. IEEE Trans. Affect. Comput. **11**(03), 532–541 (2020)
18. Ryu, S., Kwon, C., Kim, W.Y.: A Bayesian graph convolutional network for reliable prediction of molecular properties with uncertainty quantification. Chem. Sci. **10**(36), 8438–8449 (2017)

Optimizing Data Placement in Multi-cloud Environments Considering Data Temperature

Pengwei Wang[✉], Yi Wei, and Zhaohui Zhang

School of Computer Science and Technology, Donghua University, Shanghai 201600, China
wangpengwei@dhu.edu.cn

Abstract. Most data in the real world have spatial and temporal attributes, and some other essential data attributes also have temporal and spatial variability. In the research field of cloud and edge computing, these features always have great impact on data placement and task scheduling. However, these critical spatiotemporal features have been largely ignored by existing studies. To this end, this work firstly synthesizes data popularity, geographical location distribution and other spatiotemporal features to abstract the definition of data temperature, and a temperature calculation model is proposed to reflect the spatiotemporal correlation and variation trend. Then, we put forward a multi-cloud dynamic storage strategy considering data temperature to improve service quality and reflect the value of data temperature. Experiments are performed to evaluate the proposed strategy, which can effectively reduce the total cost and improve data availability.

Keywords: Multi-cloud · Data temperature · Data placement · Spatiotemporal features · Multi-objective optimization

1 Introduction

Driven by global informatization, the development and diversity of human society and the progress of information technologies, the data generated and acquired by people has increased substantially. Furthermore, with the improvement of computing power and algorithm breakthroughs in data processing, cutting-edge technologies, cloud computing has become an indispensable new generation of internet infrastructure, enabling devices to obtain rich computing and storage resources through the cloud data center. In recent years, the number of intelligent terminal devices increases rapidly, and the scale of sensory data shows an explosive growth trend. These real-time data usually have geographical location tags, and their characteristics change significantly over time.

Most data in the real world have temporal and spatial information, and some other properties of data also have spatiotemporal variability. In the life cycle of data, this process of change has a huge impact on the subsequent data research. Take the impact of spatial change as an example, to obtain lower latency services, it's more reasonable to store data dynamically in data centers or edge nodes closer to users or in regions where data is used more frequently. For such spatiotemporal data, the public usually only has a vague definition of cold or hot. Since data have diversified properties, it is important

© Springer Nature Switzerland AG 2021
X. Sun et al. (Eds.): ICAIS 2021, LNCS 12737, pp. 167–179, 2021.
https://doi.org/10.1007/978-3-030-78612-0_14

to abstract the concept, define the spatiotemporal data temperature, and observe its change for subsequent optimization processes under the cloud environment. As the data temperature generalizes the above three characteristics, when the data temperature changes, the temperature change mode can be analyzed to adjust the existing scheduling scheme dynamically, and the temperature change trend can be predicted to achieve optimization in the whole life cycle. Nonetheless, the difference in time and space often results in a strong demand for multi-cloud storage. In the multi-cloud environment, most existing research only relies on the current or historical data access frequency to optimize storage and lack careful consideration of various spatiotemporal characteristics. Therefore, it is innovative and challenging to carry out dynamic storage and calculation based on spatiotemporal data temperature changes.

Therefore, given massive spatiotemporal data, combining the ideas of geographic science and the "hot" calculation methods of popularity data of social networking, we propose a method for calculating the temperature of spatiotemporal data, and use this method to adjust the storage strategy in the cloud data center dynamically. The main contributions of this work are as follows:

First of all, existing related research has developed a large number of theories, methods and technologies about data storage and task scheduling in cloud environments. However, most solutions ignore spatiotemporal attributes and also the spatiotemporal variability of related data attributes. Our work aims to improve the quality and coverage of the research area from a novel perspective, thereby the concept and definition of "data temperature" is proposed to consider this issue. Then, under each time slice, we use the density clustering method to explore the irregular distribution features of spatial geographic locations, and draw on the experience of popularity calculation methods to define the distribution of users' preferences. As the basis for subsequent research work, we propose a temperature calculation model for spatiotemporal data, reflecting the spatiotemporal correlation and variation trend. Finally, due to the correlation between temperature changes and subsequent data storage schemes, we propose a data temperature-based strategy for optimizing data placement in multi-cloud environments, which can be dynamically adjusted according to the temporal and spatial variability.

2 Related Work

There are numerous researches on cloud storage. Aiming at the defects of single cloud storage in data security and service elasticity, multi-cloud storage achieves unified storage, performance tuning, data security, and privacy protection by integrating online storage services from multiple cloud providers. In this context, various cloud service providers have launched cloud storage services, and there are differences among them in price strategy, availability, persistence. Therefore, selecting suitable cloud services or their combination from such a complex cloud market has been a hot research direction. Existing data optimization storage can be classified from two different perspectives, static data storage and dynamic data storage. This study focuses on the latter.

Unlike the static data storage strategy that determines the data redundancy scheme and storage location in advance, in dynamic data storage, the data storage scheme can adjust according to changes in its attributes such as access frequency and popularity.

Zhang et al. [2] proposed a storage mode replacement algorithm based on user access frequency, but this algorithm did not carry out a global optimization, only proposed a condition satisfying data migration. In addition to the consideration of data access frequency, Gill and Singh [3] proposed a dynamic data placement strategy based on the data file's popularity. The more popular the file, the more likely it was to be copied. However, this scheme needed to repeat its strategy at every time point, so it couldn't achieve the optimization of the whole cycle. In our previous works, there were abundant researches on data placement in the multi-cloud environment, including the selection of cloud instances [19, 20], and some optimization methods for cost effectiveness and high availability [4, 5, 21] throughout the entire data life-cycle. However, these methods neglected the spatial and temporal characteristics of data. For the consideration of spatial attributes, Oh et al. [6] proposed the Wiera model, a multi-layer geographically distributed cloud storage system driven by strategy. It could determine optimal data placement, deal with the uncertain network or access dynamics, and achieve minimizing costs while meeting SLA minimization requirements. Nevertheless, it did not adequately consider migration cost. Because of the many factors that influence the storage solution, the tradeoff between different costs remains an important issue.

Given the information above, within researches on data storage in the cloud environment, some of them focus on the multi-cloud environment, however, there is still has a lack of consideration of the tradeoff between optimization objectives and conditions. As for the dynamic data storage strategy in the multi-cloud environment, most existing research only relies on the current or historical data access frequency to optimize the storage and lacks the careful consideration of various data spatiotemporal characteristics. It is difficult to achieve the optimal placement of data throughout the life cycle.

3 Motivation

There is no standard definition of data temperature. In traditional database research, it has always been a research hotspot to store data in different media according to the degree of hot or cold of data, and reduce the storage cost to the maximum extent under the premise of ensuring system performance. At present, in the research of database cache replacement and migration strategy, the identification of data temperature mostly depends on specific data structures and the relative position of data to determine temperature.

However, with the development of mobile Internet and location service technology, and the popularization of mobile devices, in the operation process of location-based social networks, streaming media platforms and crowdsourcing platforms, massive spatiotemporal data are generated, which are more sensitive to heat. In terms of social networks, the comments, thumb up, times, and frequency of forwarding generated by users on news websites, Weibo, forums, and other social platforms can indirectly reflect the heat of a message spread on the corresponding social platforms. Furthermore, in recent years, streaming media platforms have flourished globally, both online video users and market scale have a growing trend. For example, Netflix, providing different content based on the current IP address of users. Due to the influence of humanities, policies, and other factors, the popularity of the same video varies in different regions, and the average charge in different regions varies. However, in recent years, user growth rates in Europe, the Middle East, and Africa have far outpaced those in the rest of the world, inevitably leading to changes in service strategies. Therefore, the spatiotemporal data of social networks and streaming media platforms have obvious differences in individual users and regions. There is a heat fluctuation of data in time and space, which has a strong demand for multi-cloud storage.

Furthermore, with the development of the sharing economy and mobile payment, crowdsourced applications have gradually come into our daily life. The data generated by applications during operation usually has the starting to end time, the starting to end geographical location, and other attributes. This type of spatiotemporal data containing movement trajectories has precise characteristics of time distribution and geographic distribution. Compared with the previous discussions on social networks and online video platforms, these crowdsourcing data still has obvious temporal and spatial differences.

Above all, most studies on data temperature do not consider the spatiotemporal data, especially the heat distribution under different time sections. Moreover, considering the diversity of the cloud market, few storage researches mention the temporal and spatial differences. Based on that, the data placement scheme in multi-cloud environment have to improve in both innovation and optimization.

4 Problem Formulation

The main purpose of our research is to solve the problem of data placement in the multi-cloud environment. Therefore, we first define the problem in detail.

Definition 1 (Data Center): Suppose there are N data centers $DC = \{d_1, d_2, \ldots, d_N\}$, and each data center has a tuple $\{P_d^s, P_d^b, P_d^o, a_d, L_d\}$. P_d^s represents the storage price of data center; P_d^b means that the bandwidth operation price of data center; P_d^o is the Get operation price of data center; a_d refers to the availability of data center; L_d indicates the location of data center, including longitude and latitude.

Definition 2 (Data Object): Data object covers photos, videos, web pages, and other multimedia files. Assume that the size of a data object the user needs to store is S, the data temperature is $T_P(t)$, where $t \in [1, T]$, the minimum availability to be obtained is A_{req}, and the maximum delay required for data access is L_{req}.

Definition 3 (Availability): To cost optimization, Erasure Coding [7] is one of the most commonly used data redundancy strategies for improving data availability in both static and dynamic storage. Since users can accept no more than $(n - m)$ data centers that are down at the same time, the availability of data is equal to the sum of possibilities for all cases when k data centers are available simultaneously, where $k \in [m, n]$. Suppose $D(t) = \{d_1, d_2, \ldots, d_N\}$ represents the data center selected for data storage at time t, using $\Theta = (\frac{|D(t)|}{k})$ to refer to the total number of cases when k cloud providers are workable in the meantime, D_j^Θ is the j of all Θ cases. The calculation formula of data availability $A(t)$ at time t is shown in Formula 1:

$$A(t) = \sum_{k=m}^{n} \sum_{j=1}^{\Theta} \left[a_d \prod_{d \in D_j^\Theta} \prod_{d \in D(t) \backslash D_j^\Theta} (1 - a_d) \right] \tag{1}$$

$D(t) \backslash D_j^\Theta$ means that the data centers in $D(t)$ that is not in D_j^Θ.

Definition 4 (Base Cost): The base cost includes storage cost, bandwidth cost, and operation cost. Storage cost is the sum of storage costs of N data blocks at time t, $\frac{S}{m}$ indicates the size of data blocks stored in each data center. In the stored procedure of data objects, accepting outbound requests of the data requires paying bandwidth cost to the corresponding cloud service provider. In Erasure Coding, users only need to access any m data blocks to restore the original data. Therefore, in order to reduce the bandwidth cost, m cloud service providers with the cheapest bandwidth are selected for data access. Operation cost mainly considers Get operation cost when users access their own data. The calculation method is shown in Formula 2:

$$C_B(t) = \sum_{d \in D(t)} \frac{S}{m} P_d^S + min_{j \in [1, \Theta]} \sum_{d \in D_j^d(t)} r(t)(\frac{S}{m} P_d^b + P_d^o) \tag{2}$$

Definition 5 (Migration Cost): Different data have various data access frequency. If users continue to use the previous scheme to store their data, it may incur high bandwidth or storage costs. Therefore, adjusting the storage scheme dynamically according to the change of data temperature can save users' costs. However, changes in data storage solutions bring about data migration, which also incur a certain cost. Using $D(t-1)\backslash D(t)$ to indicate the data centers that need to be migrated. The calculation method of migration cost is shown in Formula 3:

$$C_M(t) = \sum_{d \in D(t-1)\backslash D(t)} (\frac{S}{m} P_d^b + P_d^o) \tag{3}$$

Definition 6 (Retrieval Latency): We define the data center for data access at time t as $D_r(t)$. Since a user needs m data blocks to recover the data, the retrieval latency is the maximum value of that in $D_r(t)$. The delay of the data access process is mainly caused by network bandwidth, RTT (round-trip time) [1, 15, 16] is used to calculate the retrieval latency. The calculation method is shown in Formula 4:

$$l(t) = max_{d \in D_r(t)}\{5 + 0.02Distance(d)\} \tag{4}$$

Where $Distance(d)$ represents the distance between users and data centers.

In this chapter, the goal of the proposed method is to figure out the data storage scheme $D(t)$ at each moment so that achieving the minimized total cost of storage and the excellent data availability within the life cycle. Therefore, the entire optimization problem can be defined as follows:

$$min_{D(t)} \sum_{t \in [1,T]} (C_B(t) + C_M(t)) \tag{5}$$

$$max_{D(t)} \sum_{t \in [1,T]} A(t) \tag{6}$$

Simultaneously, the problem has some constraints. The first constraint is that each data center can only store one data block. The second and third constraint respectively require that the data storage scheme obtained at each moment must meet the user's availability A_{req} and latency demands L_{req}.

5 The Model and Calculation of Data Temperature

In this paper, our method defines spatiotemporal data temperature and places data blocks according to the different temperatures in different regions. Therefore, as the basis for solving data placement problem in multi-cloud environments, this chapter starts from explaining the concept of classic spatiotemporal data and will introduce the temperature calculation method in detail. Spatiotemporal data is the geographical entities whose spatial elements or attributes change over time. In this essay, we use the vector describing the geographic data model and consider its order relationship. Furthermore, time is also one of the critical elements to describe the dynamic changes of spatiotemporal objects. In most geographic information system applications, we believe that time is a one-dimensional attribute of spatiotemporal data. This axis has no endpoints and extends infinitely to the past and the future; it is irreversible.

This section normalizes the representation of spatiotemporal data. Assume that spatiotemporal objects are unique and invariant [10], we define the space-time o as:

$$o = \{u_{ID}, S(t), P(t), T(t), A\} \tag{7}$$

In this section, u_{ID} represents the object identifier of spatiotemporal data object o, which is its unique identifier in the collection. $S(t)$ refers to the set of spatial characteristics that change with time in a specific spatial coordinate system. $P(t)$ is a set of attribute features, and this study focuses on the popularity of data. $T(t)$ means the temporality of changes in the state of spatiotemporal objects (here T is only applicable in this chapter), and the data set includes the time of data generation. A represents the behavioral operation of a spatiotemporal object (the meaning of A is limited to this chapter), i.e., the operation of the object's time, space, and properties. The following formulas are detailed definitions in the space-time collection:

$$S(t) = \{(p_1, t_1), (p_2, t_2), \ldots, (p_n, t_n)\} \tag{8}$$

$$p_i = \{(x_1, y_1), (x_2, y_2), \ldots, (x_m, y_m)\}, i \in [1, m] \tag{9}$$

$$P(t) = \{(A_1, S(t_1)), (A_2, S(t_2)), \ldots, (A_n, S(t_n))\} \tag{10}$$

$$T(t) = \{(l_1, t_1), (l_2, t_2), \ldots, (l_n, t_n)\} \tag{11}$$

$$l_i = \{d_1, d_2, \ldots, d_m\} \tag{12}$$

Among them, m says the number of time-space data blocks, n is the nth time point in the spatiotemporal data (the meaning of n is only applicable to this chapter), t represents the time, p_i refers to the position of m data blocks in the spatial coordinate system, A_n means the popularity of data at time n, l indicates the set of data generation time, d is the generation time.

Space and time are an order between things. Space describes the configuration of objects; time describes the sequence of events, and some of other properties are often associated with time and space [8]. Therefore, through spatiotemporal relations, we introduce the temperature calculation method from three parts.

Location Popularity. When using latitude and longitude coordinates as the basis for calculation, location and density play a vital role in determining the epidemic distribution of data. To measure it as the heat value in our calculation method, we first use the geographic location data at the time of access through an improved DBSCAN algorithm based on the neighbor similarity and fast nearest neighbor query [9] for dynamic geographic location clustering. DBSCAN is a typical density-based clustering algorithm that does not need to specify the number of clusters, divides regions with sufficiently high density into clusters, and discover clusters of any shape. It is suitable for the temperature calculation of spatiotemporal data with moving characteristics. Due to its limitations, in the second step, the Euclidean distance formula is used to calculate the distance between each point in the cluster and the virtual center point. We also consider the density around each point involved in the above clustering process. According to the coordinates on the two-dimensional plane, the method normalizes the calculation results to the range of 0–1 and obtains the popularity value of each point. Importantly, in the first step of clustering, the location popularity of noise points is 0.

Data Popularity. Popularity signifies how much users like the data. In previous research, there are two ways to compute the popularity of data, one is the times of data access based on the statistical time, the other one is the frequency of data access based on the statistical time. Notably, the popularity may remain stationary for a period, but it may change in spatial distribution. In addition, the content located in the cloud data center is changing due to the constant emergence of new data. Hence, the popularity cannot be measured only by uniform distribution, it should be considered changes in space-time and tracked it in time to ensure the model's accuracy.

Then, we introduce the calculation method of regional data popularity in the cloud environment at time t [11]. Our method defines the number of popular regions, the concentration of regional requests, and the average number of users' requests in popular regions. It is stipulated that $\{p_1, p_2, \ldots, p_J\}$ refers to the areas that requests the same data simultaneously, and J is the serial number of the areas. Intuitively, the number of requests for data in a period of time can be used as one of the popular metrics, so we define the area where the number of data requests exceeds a given threshold as the popular area of the data. Specifically, given the threshold number of requests N, N_m indicates the number of regions in which data m receives at least one request. We define the quantity of popular regions of data m to be represented by $POP_m(N)$, as shown in Formula 13:

$$POP_m(N) = \sum\nolimits_{j=1}^{J} I(R_{m,j} - N) \tag{13}$$

Where $R_{m,j}$ is the number of requests for data m in region j. In addition, if $x \geq 0$, then $I(x) = 1$, otherwise $I(x) = 0$. According to the above formula, the higher the value of $POP_m(N)$, the wider the popular range of data m.

If most requests are concentrated in popular areas, that means the high concentration. To further research the spatial characteristics of data popularity, we study the degree of request concentration in popular areas. The calculation method of request concentration degree in hot regions for data m is shown in Formula 14:

$$CON_m^{POP}(N) = \frac{1}{R_m} \sum\nolimits_{j=1}^{POP_m(N)} R_{m,j} \tag{14}$$

In the formula, $R_m = \sum_{j=1}^{J} R_{m,j}$, represents the total number of requests for data m. The higher $CON_m^{POP}(N)$ indicates the higher request concentration.

To eliminate the influence of the number of users on the number of requests, we define the average number of user request in popular areas of data m, as shown in Formula 15:

$$AVG_m(N) = \frac{1}{POP_m(N)} \sum_{j=1}^{POP_m(N)} \frac{R_{m,j}}{U_{m,j}} \quad (15)$$

$U_{m,j}$ is the number of users who request data m in region j. The higher $AVG_m(N)$ value results in the greater number of centralized requests within each region.

In this paper, data popularity lifetime [12] represents the time range in which data has valid requests by users in sufficient numbers. If the data has not received enough daily requests for consecutive t days after generation, we thought that the lifetime ends on the t day, so its epidemic lifetime is $t - 1$ days.

Data Temperature. According to the content of the above parts, the spatiotemporal data temperature of p at time t is set as $T_P(t)$, as shown in Formula 16:

$$T_p(t) = a^{Popularity_m} \times b^{10L_p} \quad (16)$$

a and b are exponentials greater than 1 and $a \neq b$, $Popularity_m$ refers to the calculation result of popularity, L_p means the temperature of the place. The calculated results can be expressed as a two-dimensional array such as $[coordinate, temperature]$.

6 Data Temperature-Based Placement Strategy

This section mainly includes storage strategy considering regional data temperature and data optimization storage method based on ant colony algorithm.

At this area, we refer to the calculation method of data cache hit ratio [13] in part of edge computing to find the optimal allocation of data blocks to cloud servers when requesting data. According to the different temperatures in different regions in this study, the data should be placed as far as possible in a place where the data temperature is relatively high to give full play to its data utilization value. There are two definitions of the metrics, namely the cache hit indicator and the storage scheme score function.

Definition 11 (Cache hit indicator): Given cloud data center d and data block n, we use two cache hit indicators to indicate that the data block is stored locally or within a range of "neighbor data centers". The first indicator $Indi_0(d, n)$ indicates whether n data blocks are redundant to the data stored in the data center d. The second indicator $Indi_1(d_{neighbor}, n)$ indicates whether n blocks of redundant data are stored in the "neighbor" data centers within a certain range. The definitions of $Indi_0(d, n)$ and $Indi_1(d_{neighbor}, n)$ are shown in Formula 17 and 18:

$$Indi_0(d, n) = \begin{cases} 1 \ n \in D(t) \\ 0 \ otherwise \end{cases} \quad (17)$$

$$Indi_1(d_{neighbor}, n) = \begin{cases} 1 \ n \in D(t) \\ 0 \ otherwise \end{cases} \quad (18)$$

Definition 12 (Storage scheme score): The first is defining a scoring function for each data center's storage performance, which is based on the cache hit indicator. When the algorithm gets the server combination, each server in the data storage scheme is rated for maximum advantage in the distributed storage area. The specific operation is as follows: when request a data block, the method at initial views for its local storage and looks for the storage of its "neighbor" server. A single data center's score is defined as the linear combination of the weight of local storage and the weight of the block stored in the "neighbor" data center, which is expressed as:

$$Score = \sum_{d \in D(t)} [(1 - \lambda) \times T_d(t) \times Indi_0(d, n) + \lambda$$

$$\times \sum_{d_{neighbor} \in D(t)} T_{d_{neighbor}}(t) \times Indi_1(d_{neighbor}, n) \times \frac{1}{\left(\sum_{d \in D(t)} \frac{1}{l_i}\right) \times l_{neighbor}}$$

$$(19)$$

Where $T_d(t)$ is the data temperature around the data center, we use parameter λ to combine the weight of locally stored block with that of remotely stored blocks. Intuitively, the cost of acquiring a remote block is higher than acquiring of local blocks, this is the reason we recommend setting λ to $0 \leq \lambda \leq 0.5$. A higher storage scheme score indicates the data temperature around the server which stored data is higher. The higher data temperature means that the data has a higher data access frequency and popularity in this area. Therefore, a data placement with a higher score may result in a more significant cache to reach ratio by placing the data where it is needed more.

Ant colony algorithm [18] is a parallel algorithm that starts an independent solution search at multiple points in the problem space concurrently, which increases the reliability of the algorithm and makes the algorithm stronger in the global search. In this research, an ant chooses the path among the data centers that store n data blocks. In this paper, the multi-objective optimization problem uses the weight method to determine how importance the cost and availability. Since the optimization goal is to maximize availability and minimize cost, the max-min method is first used to normalize the values of different units.

Next, the probability that an ant chooses the next data center is determined by the cost and availability. We use roulette to select the cloud service provider. Assuming that all data is stored in a cloud server, its total cost and availability are considered to evaluate quality. The evaluation $Score_{QoS}$ is shown in formula 20:

$$\begin{cases} Score_{QoS} = \omega_1 f_1(C_i) + \omega_2 f_2(A_i) \\ \omega_1 + \omega_2 = 1 \end{cases} \tag{20}$$

Algorithm RT is a server selection algorithm based on data temperature, and its pseudo-code is shown in **Algorithm RT**. In this algorithm, three strategies are used to find the best cloud server combination according to the regional data temperature to realize distributed data storage in areas with various data temperatures. Also, in areas with higher data temperature, the server selection greatly influences the result.

Algorithm RT: Getting the best result for data placement based on regional temperature
Input: Continents' server set CSD, continents' temperature CTL, hot continent temperature threshold Hot_Thres, continents' countries set CCD, data size S, primary server num m, redundant server num n, the number of ants $antNum$, and the parameters of ant colony algorithm, MAX_GEN;   **Output:** The best data placement solution $BestCombination$;   1: Set $BestCombination$ as a list;   2: **foreach** $this\_continent\_temperature$ in CTL **do**   3:   **if** $this\_continent\_temperature$ is better than Hot_Thres **then**   4:   Disappoint this continent's server number by its temperature;   5:   Get continent servers' combinations $Combinations\_Matrix$ by $Score$;   6:   Get this continent servers' transfer cost $TransferCost\_Matrix$;   7:   Calculate $Score_{Qos}$ of every server;   8:   Get the best server combination in $Score_{Qos}$ by Ant Colony Algorithm;   9:   Add the best server combination to $BestCombination$;   10:   **else**   11:   Choose the cheapest server in this continent as $Best\_InContinent$;   12:   Add $Best\_InContinent$ to $BestCombination$;   13:   **end if**   14: **end for**   15: **return** $BestCombination$;

7 Experiments and Discussions

This section mainly displays the experimental part. For one thing, we introduce the spatiotemporal dataset we used, the cloud data center information, and experimental parameter settings.

Spatiotemporal Dataset. These experiments use the Gowalla check-in data set [14]. Gowalla is a location-based social networking site that allows users to share their location by checking in. We have collected 6,442,890 check-ins of these users throughout Feb. 2009 - Oct. 2010. Stanford University provided the download address for this data.

Data Center. This study collects real cloud service information from Cloud Harmony [17], including the storage prices, bandwidth prices, get operation prices, and the longitude and latitude of data centers.

For another, to prove the performance of the strategy we proposed, cost and data availability are compared with the DP algorithm and genetic algorithm under the same experimental data in the same period. We design three controlled experiments with different independent variables. In experiments, (m, n)-Erasure Coding is selected as the data segmentation method.

In the first experimental scenario, the performance of the proposed algorithm is evaluated by increasing the data size from 100 GB to 1000 GB. Figure 1 describes the corresponding cost of the scheme obtained by three algorithms, and the scheme's availability obtained by three algorithms. Suppose *LifeTime* = 10, *m* and *n* are 15 and

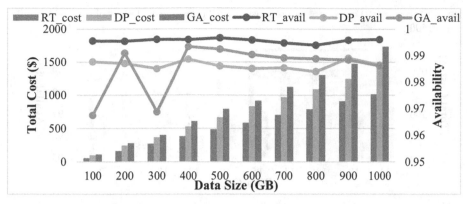

Fig. 1. Total cost and data availability of the three algorithms under different data sizes.

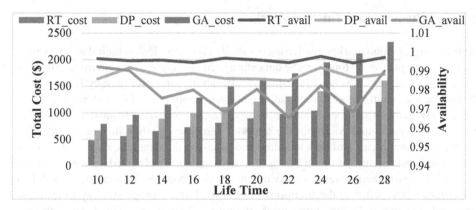

Fig. 2. Total cost and data availability of the three algorithms under different time cycles.

20 respectively in the Erasure Coding policy. For areas with high regional temperatures, data access delays are limited to 20 ms and availability limits are between 0.96 and 0.99. In the case that data temperature is not considered, the DP algorithm can obtain the optimal solution. However, the spatial and temporal distribution characteristics of data are rarely considered in the traditional research field, the result may not be suitable for users. According to the spatiotemporal data temperature, the total cost is reduced by about 20% and availability is correspondingly improved.

In the second experiment scenario, the influence of the lifetime on the algorithm results is analyzed. Set the data size as 500GB, and other experimental parameters are consistent with scenario 1. Figure 2 shows the cost of optimal schemes obtained by the three algorithms when T increases from 10 to 28, and the comparison of data availability among the three methods. In the third experiment scenario, the performance of the strategy we proposed is further compared by changing the number of data copies. Assume that $DataSize = 500$, $LifeTime = 10$, the remaining parameters are consistent with the above experiments (Fig. 3).

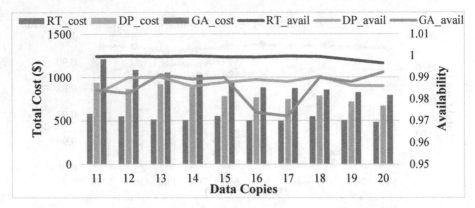

Fig. 3. Total cost and data availability of the three algorithms under different data copies.

8 Conclusions and Future Work

At the complex cloud market, novice users usually choose to deploy their data to a single cloud service provider. However, the data storage in the single cloud environment faces numerous risks such as vendor lock-in, low availability, and user privacy leakage, etc. In case of that, multi-cloud storage has become a commonly used data storage method. This study quotes the related definition of spatiotemporal data from the geographic information system and combines the temporal attributes, spatial attributes, and other attributes of spatiotemporal data to define and calculate the data temperature. Based on the regional temperature, we optimize the cost and availability of such data in multi-cloud storage. The experimental results show that the method considering spatiotemporal data temperature is superior to the traditional multi-cloud data storage strategy in terms of cost and availability. In our future work, we will still study the data storage strategy combining cloud and edge.

References

1. Wu, Z., Butkiewicz, M., Perkins, D., et al.: Spanstore: cost-effective geo-replicated storage spanning multiple cloud services. In: 24th ACM Symposium on Operating Systems Principles, pp. 292–308. ACM, New York (2013)
2. Zhang, Q., Li, S., Li, Z., et al.: CHARM: A cost-efficient multi-cloud data hosting scheme with high availability. IEEE Trans. Cloud Comput. **3**(3), 372–386 (2015)
3. Gill, N.K., Singh, S.: A dynamic, cost-aware, optimized data replication strategy for heterogeneous cloud data centers. Future Gener. Comput. Syst. **65**, 10–32 (2016)
4. Wang, P., Zhao, C., Zhang, Z.: An ant colony algorithm-based approach for cost-effective data hosting with high availability in multi-cloud environments. In: 2018 IEEE 15th International Conference on Networking, Sensing and Control (ICNSC). IEEE, NJ (2018)
5. Wang, P., Zhao, C., Wei, Y., et al.: An adaptive data placement architecture in multi-cloud environments. Sci. Program. **2020**(1), 1–12 (2020)
6. Oh, K., Qin, N., Chandra, A., Weissman, J.: Wiera: Policy-driven multi-tiered geo-distributed cloud storage system. IEEE Trans. Parallel Distrib. Syst. **31**(2), 294–305 (2020)

7. Mu, S., Chen, K., Gao, P., et al.: μlibcloud: providing high available and uniform accessing to multiple cloud storages. In: the 2012 ACM/IEEE 13th International Conference on Grid Computing, pp. 201–208. IEEE, NJ (2012)

8. Chen, S., Li, Y.: Visual modeling and representations of spatiotemporal transportation data: An object-oriented approach. In: 2011 International Symposium on Computer Science and Society, pp. 218–222. IEEE, NJ (2011)

9. Li, S.: An improved DBSCAN algorithm based on the neighbor similarity and fast nearest neighbor query. IEEE Access 8, 47468–47476 (2020)

10. Viswanathan, G., Schneider, M.: The objects interaction graticule for cardinal direction querying in moving objects data warehouses. In: Catania, B., Ivanović, M., Thalheim, B. (eds.) ADBIS 2010. LNCS, vol. 6295, pp. 520–532. Springer, Heidelberg (2010). https://doi.org/10.1007/978-3-642-15576-5_39

11. Yan, H., Liu, J., Li, Y., et al.: Spatial popularity and similarity of watching videos in large-scale urban environment. IEEE Trans. Netw. Serv. Manage. 15(2), 797–810 (2018)

12. Li, C., Liu, J., Ouyang, S.: Characterizing and predicting the popularity of online videos. IEEE Access 4, 1630–1641 (2016)

13. Li, Y., Luo, J., Jin, J., et al.: An effective model for edge-side collaborative storage in data-intensive edge computing. In: 2018 IEEE 22nd International Conference on Computer Supported Cooperative Work in Design (CSCWD), pp. 92–97. IEEE, NJ (2018)

14. SNAP: Network datasets Gowalla. http://snap.stanford.edu/data/loc-gowalla.html. Accessed 21 July 2020

15. Mansouri, Y., Buyya, R.: To move or not to move: Cost optimization in a dual cloud-based storage architecture. J. Netw. Comput. Appl. 75, 223–235 (2016)

16. Wu, Y., Wu, C., Li, B., et al.: Scaling social media applications into geo-distributed clouds. IEEE/ACM Trans. Netw. (TON) 23(3), 689–702 (2015)

17. CloudHarmony. http://www.cloudharmony.com. Accessed 21 July 2020

18. Dorigo, M., Maniezzo, V., Colorni, A.: Ant system: optimization by a colony of cooperating agents. IEEE Trans. Syst. Man. Cybern. Part B (Cybern.) 26(1), 29–41 (1996)

19. Liu, W., Wang, P., Meng, Y., et al.: A novel algorithm for optimizing selection of cloud instance types in Multi-cloud Environment. In 2019 IEEE 25th International Conference on Parallel and Distributed Systems (ICPADS), pp. 167–170. IEEE, NJ (2019)

20. Liu, W., Wang, P., Meng, Y., et al.: A novel model for optimizing selection of cloud instance types. IEEE Access 7, 120508–120521 (2019)

21. Wang, P., Zhao, C., Liu, W., et al.: Optimizing data placement for cost effective and high available multi-cloud storage. Comput. Inform. 39(1–2), 51–89 (2020)

Detection of Virtual Machines Based on Thread Scheduling

Zhi Lin[1]([✉]), Yubo Song[2,3], and Junbo Wang[1,4]

[1] School of Information Science and Engineering, Southeast University,
Nanjing 211111, China
[2] Key Laboratory of Computer Network Technology of Jiangsu Province, School
of Cyber Science and Engineering, Southeast University, Nanjing 211111, China
[3] Purple Mountain Laboratories, Nanjing 211111, China
[4] National Mobile Communications Research Laboratory, Southeast University,
Nanjing 211111, China

Abstract. With the rapid development of cloud computing, virtual
machines are now attracting more and more attention. Virtual machines
used at malicious motivation cause enormous threats to the security of
computer systems. Virtual machine detection is crucial for honeypot systems and software that provide free trials. Various strategies based on
local register values affected by virtualization have been proposed. However, these strategies have a limited scope of application since they can
only run natively. What's more, the values they depend on can be modified with ease. In this paper, we propose a new remote virtual machine
detection strategy applying to different types of virtual machines and different operating systems based on time difference in thread scheduling.
Our main contribution is to set up a probability-based thread scheduling
analysis model to describe the time difference between physical machines
and virtual machines. This paper shows that the probability distribution
of execution time of a piece of CPU-bound code in virtual machines has
higher variance along with lower kurtosis and skewness, which make up
our index system for detection. Results of Numeric simulation and real
test show good agreement and provide a clear criterion for detection. In
the real test all the virtual machines and 97.2% of the physical machines
were identified correctly.

Keywords: Virtual machine · Remote detection · Probability ·
Thread scheduling

1 Introduction

Since virtual machines have been widely used not only by professionals but also
by normal people, it is significant for software or a website to detect a virtual
machine in order to escape unfriendly acts. Some software needs to change their
activities in honeypot systems to evade analysis [4]. Commercial software wants
to prevent the overuse of free trial. A virtual-machine based rootkit (VMBR) is

© Springer Nature Switzerland AG 2021
X. Sun et al. (Eds.): ICAIS 2021, LNCS 12737, pp. 180–190, 2021.
https://doi.org/10.1007/978-3-030-78612-0_15

a virtual machine monitor (VMM) installed underneath an existing OS, which controls the victim OS as a virtual machine [9]. The detection of virtual machines is crucial for finding a VMBR. Some special attacks are targeted at virtual machines on cloud infrastructures, and the detection of virtual machines is their first step [13]. Asvija listed three types of attacks in cloud computing including attacks on I/O channels, side-channel/covert channel attacks, and attacks on trusted execution and secured boot technologies [2]. Studies in virtualization detection strategies could help improve the security of computers, mobile devices, and cloud infrastructures.

Code segments that can detect a virtual machine environment is also named as a red pill, on the contrary with a blue pill. There have been many kinds of red pills, mostly run natively because of the dependency on some local fingerprints like Windows registry and CPU registers, or local operations like executing special instructions and reading from special ports. Klein implemented a tool ScoopyNG which detects VMM by SIDT, SGDT instruction, reading value in the Interrupt Descriptor Table Register (IDTR) and Global Descriptor Table Register (GDTR) [10]. Keith proposed a method using Translation Lookaside Buffer (TLB) capacity to detect VMM by revealing the fact that the TLB size will be affected by executing some particular instructions including CPUID in the virtual machine [8]. These methods cause little false positive but usually can be prevented by virtual machine providers or VMBR producers. Sierra-Arriaga listed three types of avoiding detection strategies including the use of thin hypervisors, Timestamp Counter offset manipulation, and the "Blue Chicken" Technique [12]. Moreover, they cannot handle each type of virtual machine with a single standard. For example, virtual machines from different companies may have different SDTR values, and VMBR developers can even modify them at will.

Some researchers proposed detection strategies based on the time difference of some special instructions. These strategies are usually aimed at detecting hardware-assisted virtualization, which is believed to be stealthier to attackers. Brengel used instructions that can provoke a VM Exit and measured the CPU cycles used by the operating system [3]. These instructions cost physical machines less time because they don't need to perform VM Exit on physical machines. Zhang used Last-Level Cache (LLC) and Level-1 Data (L1D) Cache to detect hardware-assisted virtualization [14]. These strategies are effective most of the time regardless of the types of virtual machines, but they also need to run natively.

Some related works focused on remotely detecting the existence of VMM. Jämthagen used information in IP packets and HTTP requests to infer the source of an Internet connection [7]. But it only works when the virtual machine works under NAT and the host and guest OS should be completely different. Franklin provides a fuzzy benchmarking strategy by calculating the execution time of a piece of code on the remote system [5]. However, the result may be affected by the efficiency of hardware. Ho applied redpill to browsers and combined four types of operations to distinguish virtual machines, hardware-assisted virtual machines with different OS versions, which is also based on the time difference [6].

It also reveals that less running time in physical machines is not a certainty. In this paper, we talk about a remote detection strategy based on the time difference. However, we do not use the absolute value of time difference, which is highly correlated with hardware performance. Instead, this paper cares about the distribution characteristics. In section two we explain some assumptions and definitions involved, and proposes the thread scheduling model. Then in section three numeric simulations and real tests are performed and their results are analyzed. In section four we put brief conclusions and future outlook. Our contributions mainly include:

- We set up a new probability-based thread scheduling model to analyze the difference between virtual machines and physical machines.
- We propose a new remote virtual machine detection strategy based on characteristics of probability distributions instead of the absolute values. It depends slightly on hardware efficiency.
- We design and implement the remote detection system on websites, making it functional on browsers.
- We do numeric simulations and real tests to prove the validity of theories and provide a clear index system in practical use.

2 Probability Model of Thread Scheduling

2.1 Assumptions and Definitions

MLFQ to RR. Thread scheduling is a base activity of an OS. There are many types of scheduling algorithms like First Come First Service (FCFS), Shortest Job First (SJF), Round Robin (RR), etc. But the most frequently used algorithm on PC operating systems is Multi-Level Feedback Queue (MLFQ), the base for Windows and some Linux scheduling algorithms. Different OS also applies their own priority models to achieve more refined control on processes or threads, which makes it difficult to set up a unified model for most of the OS.

However, in some cases, MLFQ in various forms can be simplified to RR. Take Windows for example, if we run a piece of CPU-bound code in thread A with expected execution time T_A, and suppose that all the CPU-bound threads share the priority range (normal priority), some characteristics of MLFQ will become similar to RR after a limited period of time. That's because inserted thread, mostly system call with real-time priority, cost far less time. And the scheduler, in most time slices, concentrates on the priority queues where A and other CPU-bound threads appear. In a single queue, threads are scheduled as RR. In Linux, the case is similar. Real time processes and I/O-bound processes cost little CPU time compared to CPU-bound normal processes. Therefore, the following analysis is based on RR.

Probability Model. At the macro level, a RR operating system is a probability system with thread inserting probability p_1 and thread releasing probability p_2.

p_2 can also be denoted by the average expected execution time of threads T_A because $p_2 = \frac{1}{T_A}$. In other words, the probability that the current time slice is the last one is p_2. Figure 1 shows the timeline of the execution of a thread.

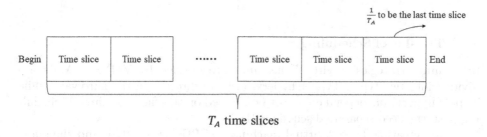

Fig. 1. Thread execution timeline

From the position of operating systems or schedulers, in a certain time slice, there's a p_2 chance that the current thread ends and $1 - p_2$ chance it goes to the back of the queue, as Fig. 2 shows. The time interval between two runs of thread A on the CPU is a random variable decided by the number of existing threads to be scheduled and we call this time interval a **round**.

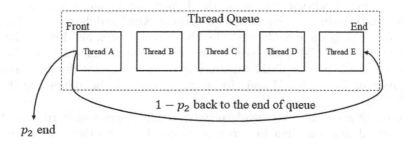

Fig. 2. Scheduling activity from OS position

Assume at the start of the k_{th} round, the number of threads in the queue is n_k, so we have:

$$n_{k+1} = n_k + B(1, p_1) - B(n_k, p_2) \qquad (1)$$

$B(n, p)$ is the Binomial distribution with total number of experiments n and success probability of each experiment p. This equation shows a simple recurrence relation of thread numbers in a stable OS: some new threads are inserted and some old threads end. Therefore, given the initial number of threads in the system, the total needed time of thread A could be calculated by adding the numbers of threads in all the rounds together, as Eq. 2 shows:

$$T = \sum_{i=1}^{T_A} n_i \tag{2}$$

2.2   Two-Level Scheduling

Scheduling strategies of virtual machines are decided by VMMs. VMMs are divided into two types. Type 1 hypervisors run directly on the hardware while Type 2 hypervisors depend on a host OS. Based on this fact, the thread scheduling patterns need separate discussions [1].

When creating Type 2 virtual machines, vCPUs are created, and the guest OS schedules tasks on the vCPUs. However, threads are executed on physical CPUs in real. For example, in KVM, each vCPU is a thread in the host machine. Host OS can schedule each vCPU independently. Although some advanced virtual machine scheduling strategies have been proposed [11], generally applied algorithms are similar to the thread scheduling in the OS. This pattern can also be seen as a superposition of two thread scheduling activities, the thread scheduling of guest OS, and the thread scheduling of host OS. Note that only CPU tasks are considered here, other devices, like I/O devices and GPU are not included.

As to Type 1 virtual machines, the hypervisor manages several virtual machines and schedules the resource among them. Xen has different VMM schedulers, and credit is the default one. The changing credit value decides the real CPU time that the VM could gain. If we see the virtual machines on Xen as processes/threads and the VMM scheduler as the host machine thread scheduler, any activity of Type 1 VMM and virtual machines could be mapped to that of Type 2 VMM.

Intuitively speaking, this two-level scheduling means longer running time in the virtual machine than in a real machine, because other threads in the virtual machine cost extra time. But it is not always the truth especially when running I/O operations [6]. Anyway, we are focusing on CPU-bound operations which have a small relationship to virtualized I/O devices. Assuming a piece of CPU-bound code requires N CPU time units and a virtual machine could run M CPU time units. Threads in the same queue of the host machine cost L CPU time units in total. Therefore, this piece of code needs about $N\frac{L}{M}$ CPU time units in the virtual machine. It is in line with some researches or virtual machine detection methods that virtual machines usually cost more time, but it is too ideal. Firstly, there doesn't exist a standard of the length of time. It is only a relative relationship on the same hardware. On an old computer, the running time may be very long so that the computer will be identified as a virtual machine. Secondly, even on the same machine, it could be affected much by inserted high-priority threads.

2.3 Probability-Based Two-Level Scheduling

As is explained above, the probability model can reflect the start and end of threads in the operating system, and now we care about combining the probability model with two-level scheduling to analyze the behavior of virtual machines.

If we run a CPU-bound thread A for enough times and get the set of time it costs $T_1, T_2, \ldots, T_n$, we can say they observe a probability distribution $D(p_1, p_2, T_A, n_1)$ where n_1 is the initial number of threads in the queue. Note that $D(p_1, p_2, T_A, n_1)$ is decided by the state of an OS, whether it's a host OS or a guest OS. Therefore, for a guest machine with average thread insert probability p_1', average thread end probability p_2' and initial thread number n_1', there exists a distribution $D(p_1', p_2', T_A', n_1')$.

If we run the test code in the virtual machine, $D(p_1', p_2', T_A', n_1')$ means the expected vCPU time between the start and end of the test thread. However, vCPU should join the scheduling of threads in the host OS to share CPU resources. In that case, A in the host OS is the vCPU thread, and the real running time is:

$$Z = X \cdot Y, X \sim D(p_1, p_2, T_A, n_1), Y \sim \frac{D(p_1', p_2', T_A', n_1')}{T_A'} \tag{3}$$

Y is called Expand Factor, which refers to the ratio of used CPU time unit by VM and used CPU time unit by thread A'. The PDF of Z could be calculated if X and Y could be expressed mathematically. However, they are virtual distributions and we cannot find their real mathematical representations. A Monte Carlo Simulation method is used to simulate the probability density function (PDF) of Z.

3   Numeric Simulations and Real Tests

Based on Eq. 3, we could run a numerical simulation for a host machine and a virtual machine to discover features that could be used to identify them. p_1, p_2 and n_1 are specified manually. In our simulation, $p_1 = 0.002$, $p_2 = 0.01$, $n_1 = 3$, and $T_A = 1000$. We also use kernel density estimation (KDE) to get the PDF curve. The result is shown in Fig. 3.

For virtual machines, as Eq. 3 shows, it is a product distribution of two distributions that belong to the host OS and guest OS respectively. Here we assume that $p_1 = p_1'$, $p_2 = p_2'$ and $n_1 = n_1'$ to make it simpler to reveal the key relationships. We use a Monte Carlo Simulation to calculate the product distribution. The result is shown in Fig. 4.

Put the KDE curve together, as Fig. 5 shows, and the two curves show huge differences. The curve of the virtual machine situation has a lower peak at the higher time unit number, which is in line with our preliminary analysis. It is obvious that two-level scheduling will enlarge the range of possible running time. We apply Variance, Kurtosis, and Skewness to express this difference.

Table 1 shows the variance, kurtosis and skewness of simulated data for physical machines and virtual machines. All the running time data has been divided

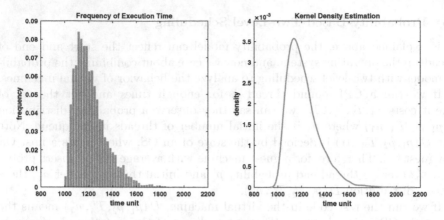

Fig. 3. Frequency and KDE of numerical simulation: physical machine

by T_A to eliminate the difference of test code. The virtual machine has a higher variance, as its distribution curve is flatter. It also has lower kurtosis and skewness because its tail is short. Based on the fact above, we propose a composite index, which describes how likely is an operating system running under a VMM: Virtual Machine Index.

Table 1. Key Statistics of Distribution.

Type	Variance	Kurtosis	Skewness
Physical machine	0.018	5.60	1.30
Virtual Machine	0.052	5.09	1.15

The Virtual Machine Index (VMI) is defined as:

$$VMI(X) = \lg \frac{\text{Var}(x)}{\text{Kurtosis}(X) \cdot \text{Skewness}(X)} \qquad (4)$$

Since VMI is usually negative, in this paper we use it's opposite, which is named as Physical Machine Index (PMI):

$$PMI(X) = \lg \frac{\text{Kurtosis}(X) \cdot \text{Skewness}(X)}{\text{Var}(X)} \qquad (5)$$

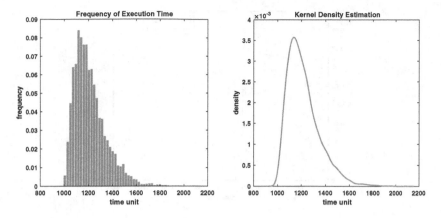

Fig. 4. Frequency and KDE of numerical simulation: virtual machine

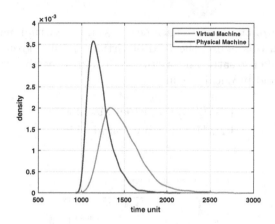

Fig. 5. KDE curve of virtual machine and physical machine

To verify the findings and get a reference value, we perform actual testing on physical machines and virtual machines. Physical machines have different operating systems (Windows and Linux), processor types, and running status (Controlled by opening different kinds of other applications). Virtual machines are running under different types of VMMs, mainly VMware WorkStation and KVM. Virtual machines on the cloud are also included.

The test code was written in JavaScript, mainly for two reasons: Firstly, JavaScript codes run in a single thread, it can eliminate the effect of parallel optimization and multi-core to the most extent. Secondly, JavaScript code embedded in a web page can run on the browser, which means it can be applied to detect virtual machines remotely. One of the test result groups on a physical machine and a virtual machine run on it is shown in Fig. 6. The results in the real test show similar patterns as simulation results.

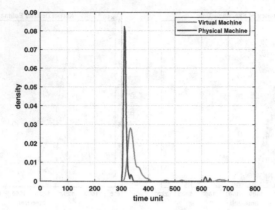

Fig. 6. KDE curve of virtual machine and physical machine: real test

The test results of 36 physical machine cases and 28 virtual machine cases are shown in Fig. 7. In this figure, the PMI of virtual machine groups and physical machine groups differ greatly, and a criterion could be easily set up to identify virtual machines and physical machines.

$$\begin{cases} PMI < 4 & \text{Virtual Machine} \\ PMI > 4 & \text{Physical Machine} \end{cases} \tag{6}$$

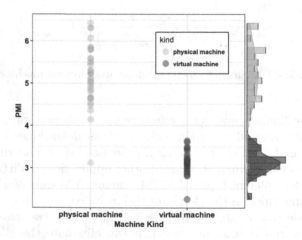

Fig. 7. Results of all the cases

Under this standard, the identification results are shown in Table 2, where the accuracy of identifying physical machines is 0.9722 and for virtual machines it is 1, which means all the virtual machines are successfully identified.

A physical machine was identified as a virtual machine maybe because it was an old computer or it was running some applications that change the environment of the OS fast.

Table 2. Identification Results.

Real Type	Identified as a PM	Identified as a VM	Accuracy
Physical Machine	35	1	0.9722
Virtual Machine	0	28	1

4   Conclution and Future Work

The former studies on virtual machine detection strategies mainly focus on some variables in CPU registers or in the guest OS. However, these strategies can only be applied natively, and these variables can be modified by VMM easily. Some research care about remote detection methods, mainly through Network packages. This method demands many preliminary requirements, which make it less practical. Benchmark test is a new direction that is practical in remote scenarios, but it has more randomness, and how to reduce the effect of hardware difference is a problem.

We noticed the time difference between running the same program in physical machines and virtual machines, and explain that by introducing a probability-based thread scheduling model. This model focuses on MLFQ and RR scheduling algorithms, and includes a recurrence formula to calculate the number of threads any round. We also set a clear index system called physical machine index to identify virtual machines in practical scenarios. Results of the numeric simulation and the real tests show that this model can explain the main points of the existing difference, and gain a high accuracy in identifying virtual machines.

Some other factors that are not taken into consideration, however, may also affect the test accuracy. For example, a MITM attack. Any test data was collected on the user's computer and sent back to the server, which is of a high risk of being modified in this process. Moreover, the user could view the test code fragments in the browser and make some disruption. The test efficiency is also a point to consider in practical application since we use some CPU-bound logic, which may occupy the processor for a long period of time and impact the user's experience. On balance, we hope the testing strategy mentioned in this paper will be a prototype for more practical red pill schemes in the future.

References

1. Alnaim, A.K., Alwakeel, A.M., Fernandez, E.B.: A pattern for an NFV virtual machine environment. In: 2019 IEEE International Systems Conference (SysCon), pp. 1–6. IEEE (2019)

2. Asvija, B., Eswari, R., Bijoy, M.: Security in hardware assisted virtualization for cloud computing-state of the art issues and challenges. Comput. Netw. **151**, 68–92 (2019)
3. Brengel, M., Backes, M., Rossow, C.: Detecting hardware-assisted virtualization. In: Caballero, J., Zurutuza, U., Rodríguez, R.J. (eds.) DIMVA 2016. LNCS, vol. 9721, pp. 207–227. Springer, Cham (2016). https://doi.org/10.1007/978-3-319-40667-1_11
4. Favre, O., Tellenbach, B., Asenz, J.: Honey-copy: a concept and prototype of a generic honeypot system. In: ICIMP 2017 the Twelfth International Conference on Internet Monitoring and Protection, Venice, Italy, 25–29 July 2017, pp. 7–11. IARIA (2017)
5. Franklin, J., Luk, M., McCune, J.M., Seshadri, A., Perrig, A., Van Doorn, L.: Remote detection of virtual machine monitors with fuzzy benchmarking. ACM SIGOPS Oper. Syst. Rev. **42**(3), 83–92 (2008)
6. Ho, G., Boneh, D., Ballard, L., Provos, N.: Tick tock: building browser red pills from timing side channels. In: 8th {USENIX} Workshop on Offensive Technologies ({WOOT} 14) (2014)
7. Jämthagen, C., Hell, M., Smeets, B.: A technique for remote detection of certain virtual machine monitors. In: Chen, L., Yung, M., Zhu, L. (eds.) INTRUST 2011. LNCS, vol. 7222, pp. 129–137. Springer, Heidelberg (2012). https://doi.org/10.1007/978-3-642-32298-3_9
8. Keith, A.: Detection in two easy steps. http://x86vmm.blogspot.mx/2007/07/bluepill-detection-in-two-easy-steps.html
9. King, S.T., Chen, P.M.: Subvirt: Implementing malware with virtual machines. In: 2006 IEEE Symposium on Security and Privacy (S&P 2006), pp. 14-pp. IEEE (2006)
10. Klein, T.: Scoopyng-the vmware detection tool. http://www.trapkit.de/research/vmm/scoopyng/index.html
11. Ma, T., Pang, S., Zhang, W., Hao, S.: Virtual machine based on genetic algorithm used in time and power oriented cloud computing task scheduling. Intell. Autom. Soft Comput. **25**(3), 605–613 (2019)
12. Sierra-Arriaga, F., Branco, R., Lee, B.: Security issues and challenges for virtualization technologies. ACM Comput. Surv. (CSUR) **53**(2), 1–37 (2020)
13. Wang, Q., Zhu, F., Leng, Y., Ren, Y., Xia, J.: Ensuring readability of electronic records based on virtualization technology in cloud storage. J. Internet Things **1**(1), 33 (2019)
14. Zhang, Z., Cheng, Y., Gao, Y., Nepal, S., Liu, D., Zou, Y.: Detecting hardware-assisted virtualization with inconspicuous features. IEEE Trans. Inf. Forensics Secur. **16**, 16–27 (2020)

Graph Attention Network for Word Embeddings

Yunfei Long[1], Huosheng Xu[2], Pengyuan Qi[1], Liguo Zhang[1], and Jun Li[3(✉)]

[1] College of Computer Science and Technology,
Harbin Engineering University, Harbin 150001, China
zhangliguo@hrbeu.edu.cn
[2] Wuhan Digital Engineering Institute, Wuhan 430000, China
[3] China Industrial Control Systems Cyber Emergency Research Team, Beijing 100000, China

Abstract. The word embeddings approaches have attracted extensive attention and widely used in many natural language processing (NLP) tasks. Relatedness between words can be reflected in vector space by word embeddings. However, the current word embeddings approaches commonly do not explore the context-specific information of word deeply in the overall corpus. In this paper, we propose to use graph attention network for word embeddings. We build a large single word graph for a corpus based on word order, then learn a word embeddings graph attention network (WEGAT) for the corpus. Our WEGAT is initialized with one-hot representation for word. We propose to use masked language model (MLM) as supervised task. In addition, through the text classification experiment, it is showed that accuracy of the word embeddings represented by WEGAT is higher than the current method for the same classification method.

Keywords: Word embeddings · Word graph · Graph attention network

1 Introduction

For natural language processing (NLP), the most important step is to convert word into word embeddings. The representational basis for downstream NLP tasks, such as text classification, knowledge mining, question-answering, smart Internet of Things systems and so on, is word embeddings Many tasks conventionally take one-hot word representation method early, where each word is represented as a vocabulary-size vector with only one non-zero entry. However, this method does not reflect semantic relatedness between words because of discretization encoding, and faces the data-sparse problem 0.

According to the word distribution hypothesis [2, 3], the contextually similar words have similar semantics. Distributed representation can convert words into dense vectors. In the subsequent development, word representation methods based on the distribution hypothesis are mainly divided into three types: matrix-based distributed representation [4–6], also known as distributional representation, and neural network-based distributed representation, also known as word embeddings [7–10]. The critical ideology of matrix-based methods is to count co-occurrence between word for a corpus. Vector Space Model [11] is the earliest matrix-based method. It uses term frequency and inverse

© Springer Nature Switzerland AG 2021
X. Sun et al. (Eds.): ICAIS 2021, LNCS 12737, pp. 191–201, 2021.
https://doi.org/10.1007/978-3-030-78612-0_16

document frequency as relevance between word and documents and element of the co-occurrence matrix. The critical flaw of this method is that the dimension of distributed representation is the same as vocabulary. Latent Semantic Analysis [12] use Singular Value Decomposition for dimension reduction of co-occurrence matrix and discovery latent semantic. In addition, the Non-negative Matrix Factorization is also used for dimension reduction of co-occurrence matrix [12].

With the improvement of hardware performance, the neural network-based word embeddings have become a widely used methods of word distributed representation because it can better model the word and its context. The earliest neural network-based method is NNLM proposed by Bengio et al. [13]. It obtains word embeddings as the product while training language model and uses the previous $n-1$ words to predict nth word as its overall structure. NNLM bases on a neural network to modeling rather than predicting the occurrence probability of nth word with counting between it and traditional language. Word2vec [15, 16] is an efficient and effective neural network-based method for learning word representations from corpus, which implements two models: CBOW and Skip-gram. These two models can effectively capture the semantics of words and easily transferred into other downstream tasks. As shown in Fig. 1 left, CBOW contains three parts. the training objective of CBOW is to find word representations that are useful to predict the target word by its context. As shown in Fig. 1 right, Skip-gram use a single word to predict its context, which is as opposed to CBOW. The word embeddings trained from Word2vec can better capture the semantics of words and exploit the relatedness of words. However, Word2vec only focus on the information obtained from local context window while the global statistic information is not used well. Glove [17] is a popular model based on the global co-occurrence matrix, each element in the matrix represents the frequency of the word and the word co-occur in a particular context window. The commonality of the two methods above is that they use the same objective function in pre-training, and both use a one-way language model. However, they do not make good use of contextual information. BERT (Bidirectional Encoder Representations from Transformers) [18] uses the bi-Transformer technique which can effectively exploit the deep semantic information of a sentence, as shown in Fig. 2. The advantage of this is that the learned characterization can fuse the context in both directions. In terms of the input of the model, BERT also did more details. They use WordPiece embedding as a word embedding and added a position embedding and a sentence segmentation embedding. In the language model pre-training, they do not use the standard to predict the next word from left to right as the target task but propose two new tasks. The first task is Masked Language Model (MLM), that is, in the input word sequence, randomly mask 15% of the words, and then the task is to predict the words which is masked.

All above neural network-based models take a document from corpus as input. Graph-based text representation model is proposed which represents the text as data in non-Euclidean space, uses text feature items as the nodes of the graph, and uses the correlation between the feature items as the edges of the graph to build the graph. Take into semantic concepts, words, phrases [19], sentences, etc. can be used as feature items. Higher semantic units such as text concepts [20] and topics can be used as feature items from semantic processing methods. For edges in text graph, there are three main

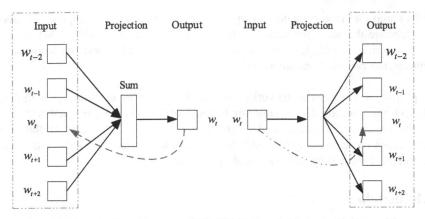

Fig. 1. The overall architecture of CBOW (left) and skip-gram (right) model.

ways to construct edges: co-occurrence relationship, syntactic relationship and semantic relationship.

Recently, a new research direction called graph neural networks or graph embeddings has attracted wide attention. Graph neural networks have been effective at tasks thought to have rich relational structure and can preserve global structure information of a graph in graph embeddings. Text Classification Graph Convolution Network [21] is proposed for text classification with Graph Convolution Network (GCN) [22], which build a single text graph for a corpus based on word co-occurrence and document word relations and learn a Text Graph Convolutional Network (Text GCN) for the corpus. Text GCN is initialized with one-hot representation for word and document, it then jointly learns the embeddings for both words and documents, as supervised by the known class labels for documents.

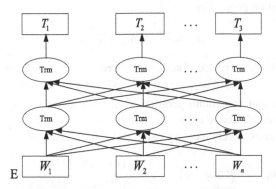

Fig. 2. The overall architecture of BERT.

In this paper, we proposed a new neural network-based method for word embeddings. We build a single word graph based on word order from entire corpus, whose edges between words are bidirectional. We learn the graph with graph attention network (GAT) [23], which leverages masked self-attentional layers to address the shortcomings of prior methods based on graph convolutions or their approximations. We propose a 3 layers GAT to encode the word graph, and a masked word node model (MWNM) in word graph as decoding layer. The output of encoding layer is word embedding we want. To summarize, our contributions are as follows.

- We propose a novel neural network-based method for word embeddings with GAT. WEGAT has a encode-decode structure because of 3 layers GAT and MWNM.
- Results on several benchmark datasets demonstrate that accuracy of the word embeddings represented by WEGAT higher than the current method for the same classification method by text classification experiment.

2 Methodology

2.1 Graph Attention Network

A GAT23 is a multilayer neural network that applicates self-attention in the GCN22. The input to graph attention layer is a set of node features, $h = \left\{ \vec{h}_1, \vec{h}_2, ..., \vec{h}_N \right\}, \vec{h}_i \in R^F$, where N is the number of nodes, and F is the number of features in each node. The layer produces a new set of node features, $h = \left\{ \vec{h}_1', \vec{h}_2', ..., \vec{h}_N' \right\}, \vec{h}_i' \in R^{F'}$ as its output. At least one learnable linear transformation is used to transform the input features into higher-level features for obtaining the sufficient expressive power. To that end, as an initial step, a shared linear transformation, parametrized by a weight matrix, $W \in R^{F'} \times R^F$, is applied to every node. GAT implicitly assigns different attention weights to neighboring nodes, which avoids costly matrix operations and do not need to know the structure of the topological graph in advance. GAT is suitable for inductive and direct inference problems, and has obtained the most advanced results on three benchmark data sets. The renewal process of node features is as follow:

Computes attention coefficients

$$ e_{ij} = \vec{a}^T \left[W\vec{h}_i \| W\vec{h}_j \right] \tag{1} $$

Where e_{ij} indicates the importance of node j's features to node i. The attention mechanism a is a single-layer feedforward neural network, which parametrized by a weight vector $\vec{a}^T \in R^{2F'}$. $\|$ is the concatenation operation. GAT only computes e_{ij} for nodes $j \in N_i$ where N_i is some neighborhood of node i in the graph.

Normalize e_{ij} across all choices of j using the softmax function:

$$ a_{ij} = soft \max\left(e_{ij} \right) = \frac{\exp\left(LeakyReLU\left(e_{ij} \right) \right)}{\sum\limits_{k \in N_i} \exp(LeakyReLU\left(e_{ik} \right))} \tag{2} $$

Where activative e_{ij} with LeakyReLU nonlinearity (with negative input slope $\alpha = 0.2$).

The aggregated features from each head areconcatenated or averaged to obtain $\vec{h}_i'$

$$ \vec{h}_i' = \sigma\left(\sum\limits_{j \in N_i} a_{ij} W\vec{h}_j \right) \tag{3} $$

Where σ is a nonlinearity function.

The multi-attention machanism is applicated for comprehensive feature acquisition of neiberhood node, Specifically, K independent attention mechanisms execute the transformation of Eq. 4, and then their features are concatenated, resulting in the following output feature representation:

$$\vec{h}_i' = \overset{K}{\underset{k=1}{\Big\|}}\ \sigma\left(\sum_{j \in N_i} a_{ij}^k W^k \vec{h}_j\right) \tag{4}$$

The critical advantage of attention machanism is that weight parameters used for the effected by neighbor node features are different, so as to extract node features more accurately. The attention mechanism also has a stronger interpretation ability, and the graph attention neural network has the ability to process directed graphs.

2.2 Word Embeddings Graph Attention Network

We build a single bidirectional word graph so that the global context-specific can be modeled easily and take into fully. For example, there are two document $d_1 : w_1 \rightarrow w_2 \rightarrow w_4 \rightarrow w_6 \rightarrow w_7 \rightarrow w_5$ and $d_2 : w_2 \rightarrow w_3 \rightarrow w_4 \rightarrow w_5 \rightarrow w_8 \rightarrow w_1$, the word graph is shown in Fig. 3. The number of nodes in the word graph is the number of vocabulary and edges between word is bidirectional so that renewal of word nodes features can be effected by its context. We simply set feature matrix h $= I$ as an identity matrix. It means every word is represented as a one-hot vector and dimensionality equal vocabulary.

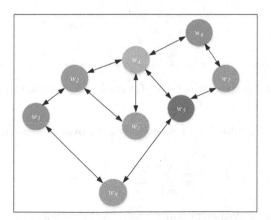

Fig. 3. Demonstrate of word graph.

After building the word graph, we feed the graph into a four-layer GAT. The features of multi-attention mechanism are averaged instead of concatenation, which results in the following output feature representation:

$$\vec{h}_i' = \sigma\left(\frac{1}{k}\sum_{k=1}^{k}\sum_{j\in N_i} a_{ij}^k W^k \vec{h}_j\right) \tag{5}$$

First third-layer GAT can allow message passing among nodes that are at maximum three steps away. It means the length of context that target word node can be effected is three. The one-hot word representation will be encodered to low-dimensional and dense vetor which is word embeddings we want. We propose a masked word node model (MWNM) at last layer GAT (weight matrix $W \in R^{F'} \times R^F$) as supervised task and decoder layer. It will mask some word nodes at random and use neiborhood word nodes to predict one-hot representation of these nodes, as shown in Fig. 4. We think MWNM as Masked Language Model in graph.

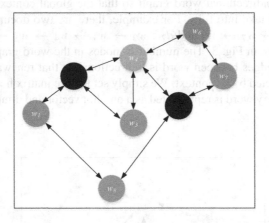

Fig. 4. Demonstrate of MLM. The black node is masked node.

The loss function is defined as cross-entropy error over all masked node:

$$L = -\frac{1}{m}\sum_{m\in Y_M}\sum_{f=1}^{F} y_{mf}\log(h_{mf}) \tag{6}$$

Where Y_M is a set of masked node, and F is dismension of the output features which is equal to one-hot representation and vocabulary. The weight parameters of encoder layer and decoder layer can be trained via gradient descent. We found that a three-layer GAT performs better than a two-layer GAT, and rate of masked word nodes is 20% performs best. The overall structure of WEGAT model is as shown in Fig. 5.

3 Experiments

In this section, we evaluate our WEGAT on two experimental tasks. We want to determine:

- Are the semantically similar word approached in vector space?
- Will word embeddings by WEGAT improve ability of downstream model for processing tasks?

3.1 Dataset and Experiment Platform

We ran our experiments on five widely used benchmark corpora including English dataset 20-Newsgroups (20NG), and Chinese dataset sougou chinese news (SogouCS). The 20NG dataset (bydate version) contains 18,846 documents evenly categorized into 20 different categories. In total, 11,314 documents are in the training set and 7,532 documents are in the test set. The SogouCS contains 3,000 documents evenly categorized into 10 different categories. We use stop-words list and jieba word segmentation technology for SogouCS preprocessing. We train our model on the NVDIA TITAN Xp by CUDA 9.0 and Tensorflow.

3.2 Implementation Details

Baselines. We compare our WEGAT with multiple state of-the-art text classification and word embedding methods as follows:

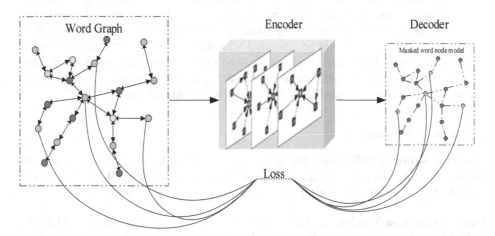

Fig. 5. The overall architecture of WEGAT.

- **Word2vec + CNN**: Pre-trained word embeddings by Word2vec as input to Convolution Neural Network.

- **Word2vec + LSTM**: Pre-trained word embeddings by Word2vec as input to Long and Short-Term Memory network.
- **GloVe + CNN**: Pre-trained word embeddings by Glove as input to Convolution Neural Network.
- **GloVe + LSTM**: Pre-trained word embeddings by Glove as input to Long and Short-Term Memory network.
- **WEGAT + CNN**: Pre-trained word embeddings by WEGAT as input to Convolution Neural Network.
- **WEGAT + CNN**: Pre-trained word embeddings by WEGAT as input to Long and Short-Term Memory network.

Settings. For WEGAT, we set the embedding size of the first attention layer as 200, the second as 400, and the third as 300. We set the learning rate as 0.01, dropout rate as 0.25, we trained WEGAT for a maximum of 200 epochs with Adam. For baseline models, we used default parameter settings as in their original papers or implementations. For baseline models using pre-trained word embeddings, we use 300-dimensional GloVe word embeddings and 300-dimensional Word2vec word embeddings.

Assessment Method

- The higher the positive correlation between the cosine similarity of word embeddings and the semantic similarity of word, the better the effect of the word embedding.
- Word embedding can quantify the semantics of words. However, its meaning is in actual tasks. Such as, for text classification task, it is first step to translate word into word embeddings which is used as input to the classification methods. The role of word embeddings is ultimately to improve the classification accuracy of the text classification task. Therefore, influence degree for the downstream task should be considered as the assessment method. Assuming that word embedding is used in text classification tasks, it should be compared with different word embedding methods on the accuracy of text classification tasks with the same classification method. The higher the accuracy, the better the word embedding. It is necessary to combined with a specific scenario for evaluating the quality of word embeddings.

3.3 Test Performance

Word Embeddings Validation. We select four word which include Chinese and English, and find five word which is approached to them by cosine similarity. As shown in Table 1, the semantically similar word is also approached in vector space.

Downstream Task Validation. Table 2 presents test accuracy of each model. **WEGAT + LSTM** performs the best and significantly outperforms all baseline models on two datasets, which showcases the effectiveness of the proposed method.

Table 1. The word1–word5 are approached to selected word in vector space, and word in second row and third row are from 20NG, while word in third row and fourth row is from SoGouCS.

Word	Word1	Word2	Word3	Word4	Word5
Chief	Chief	Staff	Officer	Lieutenant	Whilst
Asia	Asia	Asian	Southwest	India	China
Yixue	*Yixue*	*Zhongyi*	*Linchuang*	*Zhenduan*	*Bingxue*
Suanfa	*Suanfa*	*Tulun*	*Jihe*	*Jiwang*	*Tuopu*

Table 2. Test Accuracy on document classification task. We run all models 5 times and report mean. WEGAT + LSTM significantly outperforms baselines on 20NG, SogouCS.

Model	20NG	SogouCS
Word2vec + CNN	0.731	0.825
GloVe + CNN	0.737	0.831
WEGAT + CNN	0.796	0.865
Word2vec + LSTM	0.752	0.831
GloVe + LSTM	0.754	0.837
WEGAT + LSTM	0.805	0.876

4   Conclusion and Future Work

In this study, we propose a novel word embeddings method, which essentially belongs to neural networks-based method. There is a different between WEGAT and existing method that we build a word graph with word nodes and bidirectional edges based on word order and learning word graph with GAT23 so that the feature renewal of node can be effected by its neighborhood nodes. We draw on the Transform and MLM of the BERT18 model, and proposes the downstream task of predicting randomly masked word nodes through its neighborhood nodes. A simple four-layer WEGAT demonstrates promising results by outperforming numerous state-of-the art methods on benchmark datasets.

In addition, there are some interesting work values to do, such as improving the way of building word graph and how to make the GAT layer can be deeper.

Acknowledgement. We express our heartfelt thanks to Velickovic P, Cucurull G, Casanova A, et al. for providing the open source.

Funding Statement. Our research fund is funded by Fundamental Research Funds for the Central Universities (3072020CFQ0602, 3072020CF0604, 3072020CFP0601) and 2019 Industrial Internet Innovation and Development Engineering (KY1060020002, KY10600200008).

Conflicts of Interest. The authors declare that they have no conflicts of interest to report regarding the present study.

References

1. Zhang, Y., Jin, R., Zhou, Z.-H.: Understanding bag-of-words model: a statistical framework. Int. J. Mach. Learn. Cybern. **1**(1–4), 43–52 (2010)
2. Firth. J.R.: A synopsis of linguistic theory, 1930–1955. In: Studies in linguistic analysis, Philological Society, Oxford (1957)
3. Harris, Z.S.: Distributional structure. Word **10**(2–3), 146–162 (1954)
4. Pennington, J., Socher, R., Manning, C.D.: Glove: global vectors for word representation. In Empirical Methods in Natural Language Processing (EMNLP), pp 1532–1543 (2014)
5. Baroni, M., Dinu, G., Kruszewski, G.: Don't count, predict! A systematic comparison of context counting vs. context-predicting semantic vectors. In: Proceedings of the 52nd Annual Meeting of the Association for Computational Linguistics, vol. 1, pp. 238–247 (2014)
6. Dhillon, P.S., Foster, D.P., Ungar, L.H.: Eigen words: spectral word embeddings. J. Mach. Learn. Res. **16**, 3035–3078 (2015)
7. Bengio, Y., Ducharme, R., Vincent, P., Jauvin, C.: A neural probabilistic language model. J. Mach. Learn. Res. **3**, 1137–1155 (2003)
8. Turian, J., Ratinov, L., Bengio, Y.: Word representations: a simple and general method for semi-supervised learning. In: Proceedings of the 48th Annual Meeting of the Association for Computational Linguistics (ACL), pp 384–394 (2010)
9. Xu, W., Rudnicky, A.: Can artificial neural networks learn language models? In: Sixth International Conference on Spoken Language Processing (2000)
10. Mnih, A., Hinton, G.: Three new graphical models for statistical language modelling. In: Proceedings of the 24th International Conference on Machine Learning, pp. 641–648 (2007)
11. Salton, G., Wong, A., Yang, C.S.: A vector space model for automatic indexing. Commun. ACM **18**(11), 613–620 (1975)
12. Deerwester, S., Dumais, S.T., Furnas, G.W., et al.: Indexing by latent semantic analysis. J. Am. Soc. Inf. Sci. **41**(6), 391–407 (1990)
13. Lee, D., Seung, H.S.: Learning the parts of objects by non-negative matrix factorization. Nature **401**(6755), 788–791 (1999)
14. Bengio, Y., Ducharme, R., Vincent, P., et al.: A neural probabilistic language model. J. Mach. Learn. Res. **3**(6), 1137–1155 (2003)
15. Mikolov, T., Chen, K., Corrado, G., Dean, J.: Efficient estimation of word representations in vector space. In: International Conference on Learning Representations Workshop Track (2013)
16. Mikolov, T., Sutskever, I., Chen, K., Corrado, G.S., Dean, J.: Distributed representations of words and phrases and their compositionality. In: Advances in Neural Information Processing Systems, pp. 3111–3119 (2013)
17. Pennington, J., Socher, R., Manning, C.D.: Glove: global vectors for word representation. In: Empirical Methods in Natural Language Processing (EMNLP), pp. 1532–1543 (2014)
18. Devlin, J., Chang, M.W., Lee, K., Toutanova, K.: Bert: pre-training of deep bidirectional transformers for language understanding. arXiv preprint arXiv:1810.04805 (2018)
19. Jin, W., Srihari, R.K. :Graph - based text representation and knowledge discover. In: 2007 ACM Symposium on Applied Computing, pp. 807–811 (2007)
20. Chay, R., Tsoi, A.C., Hagenbuchner, M., et al.: A concept link graph for text structure mining. In: 32nd Australasian Computer Science Conference (2009)
21. Yao, L., Mao, C., Luo, Y.: Graph convolutional networks for text classification (2018)

22. Kipf, T.N., Welling, M.: Semi-supervised classification with graph convolutional networks. In: ICLR (2017))
23. Velickovic, P., Cucurull, G., Casanova, A., et al.: Graph attention networks (2017)

Firewall Filtering Technology and Application Based on Decision Tree

Yujie Jin and Qun Wang[✉]

Jiangsu Police Institute, Nanjing 210000, China
wangqun@jspi.edu.cn

Abstract. In recent years, with the development of computer technology and communication technology, computer networks have developed rapidly to become an indispensable part of people's lives. In the same time, network attacks have been increasing exponentially. Countries around the world have raised network security issues to the height of their national strategies, which shows the importance of network security. Firewall is an important technology for network security at present, and it is a barrier to protect the internal network. However, in the era of information explosion, the data flow of network communication is very large, due to the limitations of memory, CPU, etc., firewalls will become a communication bottleneck. Therefore, this paper introduces the idea of machine learning into the filtering rules of the decision tree, and uses the optimized decision tree C4.5 algorithm to predict the optimal ranking of the firewall filtering rule table attributes, which improves the efficiency of the firewall and thus the throughputs of the firewall.

Keywords: Firewall · Decision tree · Packet Filtering · Information gain ratio

1 Introduction

Following the huge wave of the third industrial revolution, the rapid development and integration of computer technology and communication technology has promoted the rapid development of computer network technology and the rapid expansion of its application fields. From the "Arpanet" in the 1950s to the ubiquitous Internet now, the Internet is closely related to all aspects of people's lives, and its applications have also expanded from the early education, politics, and military fields to business, entertainment, and personal In terms of application, it has brought huge benefits to the progress of human society and has played an important role in the current information society.

While computer networks penetrate into people's lives and affect people's work, they also bring many threats and risks. Network security mainly has the following five major threats: physical threats, system vulnerability threats, identity authentication threats, cable connection threats, and harmful program threats [1]. At present, in response to the above threats, the mainstream security control measures include: firewall technology, encryption technology, identity authentication technology, vulnerability scanning technology, intrusion detection technology, etc. Among them, firewall technology began in

© Springer Nature Switzerland AG 2021
X. Sun et al. (Eds.): ICAIS 2021, LNCS 12737, pp. 202–215, 2021.
https://doi.org/10.1007/978-3-030-78612-0_17

the 1980s, and it can be said to be one of the earliest and fastest-developing security products in computer network security management. The traditional firewall is generally located at the boundary between the internal network and the internet, and is the only channel for data exchange between the internal and external networks. In the current information society, when the network data flow is too large, the firewall will become the bottleneck of the data flow in the internal and external networks, and the firewall filtering rules are the core of the firewall. Therefore, the firewall filtering rules should be optimized to increase the firewall throughputs (The maximum data frame forwarding rate that the firewall can achieve without losing data frames) [2] is an important content in the field of firewall research. Based on the characteristics of network traffic, some literature proposes a firewall rule optimization method that dynamically adjusts firewall rules according to network traffic changes, so that the more rules that match network packets, the first to match the packets, thereby minimizing the packet filtering time [3]. A firewall optimization method based on default rules is proposed in some literature. Starting from the matching probability of rules, simple rules are separated from the default rules according to the firewall log. After analyzing the relationship between these rules and the original rules, these rules are merged into new rules to evaluate the impact of these rules on the Firewall Performance, and the new rules are selectively added to the firewall rule base, Realize the firewall linear matching optimization [4]. In this paper, the idea of machine learning is introduced into the filtering rules of the firewall, and the optimal ranking of the attributes of the filtering rule table is predicted by the decision tree to achieve the purpose of improving the efficiency of the firewall. The firewall filtering technology based on the decision tree is proposed to make the firewall more intelligent.

2 Firewall Filtering Technology

A firewall is a widely used network security product. When building a secure network environment, the firewall is often the first line of defense. From a functional point of view, a firewall is a barrier between the protected internal network and the external network, and is the only entry and exit of information between different networks or network security domains. Logically speaking, the firewall is an isolator, a filter, and an analyzer. In terms of physical composition, a firewall is an application gateway located between the internal and external networks, including a series of hardware and software components [5]. Firewalls generally have the following functions: monitoring and restricting access, controlling protocols and services, protecting internal networks, network address translation, virtual private networks, and logging and review [6]. From the principle of firewall implementation, we can divide firewalls into Static Packet Filtering Firewall, Stateful Inspection Firewall and Application Proxy Firewall. This article focuses on the optimization of static packet filtering firewalls.

The Static Packet Filtering Firewall acts on the network layer and the transport layer, according to the "IP header" information (source IP address, destination IP address, protocol and port) of the data packet (IP packet). According to the filtering rules set by the network administrator in advance, it decides whether the packets pass or not. Filtering rules are the core of static packet filtering technology, which is specifically represented as an access control list (ACL) [7]. ACL is composed of filter rules arranged in sequence, and each filter rule is composed of three parts: rule number, matching rule and firewall operation. The rule number is the order of the filtering rules in the ACL and determines the order of IP packet matching. The matching rule is based on the IP header information. It can only use the source IP address as the rule, or it can integrate the address, protocol, port, and identification bits to construct a compound rule. Generally, there are only two kinds of firewall operations in static packet filtering: permit and deny. If the permission operation is performed, the IP packets can enter and exit the firewall normally without being affected. If the deny operation is performed, the IP packets will be discarded and cannot pass through the firewall to reach the destination host [8].

Figure 1 shows the basic flow of static packet filtering processing IP packets. The IP packets arriving at the firewall are matched with the filtering rules in the ACL according to the rule sequence number, and the filtering rules that first match the IP packets determine whether to allow or deny the IP packets. If an IP packet does not match any filtering rules, the IP packet will be rejected.

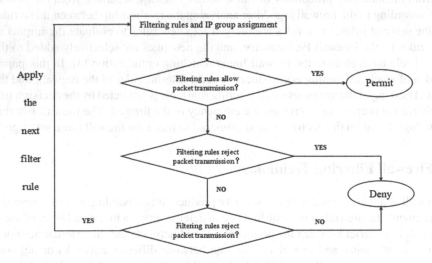

Fig. 1. The basic process of static packet filtering processing IP packets

Table 1 is an example of ACL in static packet filtering:

Table 1. Static packet filtering rules for SMTP service cases

Rule number	Packet flow	Source address	Destination address	Protocol	Source port	Destination port	Firewall operation
1	In	172.17.200.210	Any	Any	Any	Any	Deny
2	In	Any	10.5.201.29	TCP	>1023	25	Permit
3	Out	10.5.201.29	Any	TCP	25	>1023	Permit

The function of this filtering rule is that all data packets originating from the IP address 172.17.200.210 are not allowed to enter the intranet, while all other hosts can access the SMTP service of host 10.5.201.29.

3   Firewall Filtering Technology Based on Decision Tree

Firewall packet filtering technology is actually a classification technology for data packets, and throughputs is an important criterion for evaluating firewalls. Therefore, starting from the theory of data mining, we use the classification method of the decision tree in machine learning to optimize the firewall filtering rules to improve the throughputs of the firewall.

3.1   Introduction to Basic Knowledge of Decision Tree

Data Mining. In the 1990s, with the rapid development of database technology and the wide application of database management systems, people accumulated more and more data. However, due to the lack of effective tools and reasonable algorithms, people could not learn from the massive amounts of data stored in the database. Knowledge is found in the data. As a result, these data have become "data graves", leading to the phenomenon of data explosion but poor knowledge. So data mining technology came into being, and it has received extensive attention and rapid development.

Data mining is the process of extracting knowledge that is hidden in it that people do not know in advance but has potential useful value from massive, incomplete, noisy, fuzzy, and random practical application data [9]. Decision tree is a common technology in data mining, which realizes the role of data classification and data prediction in data mining [10].

Decision Tree Concept. As the name suggests, a decision tree is a tree structure in machine learning, mainly to classify instances. This article quotes a picture to introduce the concept of decision tree more intuitively.

The entire Fig. 2 can be intuitively understood as a tree model, which is mainly composed of two parts: "black box" and "arrow". The part of the black box is called node, the top node looks like the root of the entire tree, we call it the root. The node in the third row is the end point of the whole tree growth, which is similar to the leaf of the tree. We call it leaf. Each leaf corresponds to a subset of the original sample space that is disjoint and merged to form a complete original sample space[11]. The characters on each box represent the feature value of each leaf, that is, the category label. The arrow in the figure represents the growth direction of the tree. We generally say that the starting point of the arrow is the parent node of the ending point, and the end of the arrow is the child node of the starting point.

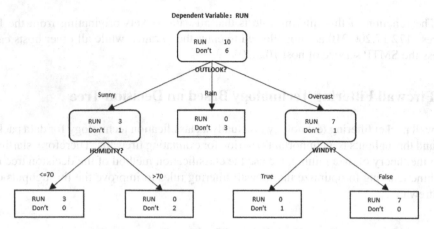

Fig. 2. Schematic diagram of decision tree model

Information Gain Ratio. When you keep hitting the "if else" code, you are already applying the idea of a decision tree. The key is to choose what criteria to sort the if conditions. In the 1970s, the ID3 algorithm proposed by Quinlan selected entropy as the measure of selected features. Entropy measures the uncertainty of things, and the size of the entropy value is proportional to its uncertainty. The formula is:

$$H(Y) = -\sum_{k=1}^{K} pk \log pk \qquad (1)$$

After defining the uncertainty metric, we can look at what is meant by "obtaining information", that is, information gain. Intuitively speaking, the information gain is defined for the random variable y and the characteristics describing the variable. At this time, the data set $D = \{(x_1,y_1), ..., (x_N, y_N)\}$, where $x_i = (x_i(1), ..., x_i(n))$ is the feature vector describing y_t, and n is the number of features. You can first study the case of a single feature (n = 1): Let's set the feature as A, and the data set $D = \{(A_1, y_1), ..., (A_N, y_N)\}$. At this time, the so-called information gain reflects the amount of information about y that feature A can bring to us.

Here, we introduce the concept of conditional entropy H(y|A) to define information gain. It also has a better intuition: Conditional entropy is a measure of the uncertainty of the random variable y under the restriction of conditional feature A. The mathematical calculation method is to first calculate the conditional entropy of random variable y under the different value $\{a_1, ..., a_m\}$ of conditional characteristic a, and then sum these information entropy according to the probability of corresponding conditional characteristic value itself [12].

Therefore, the smaller the conditional entropy H(y|A), the smaller the total uncertainty after y is restricted by A, which means that A can help us make decisions.

The mathematical definition of conditional entropy is:

$$H(Y) = -\sum_{k=1}^{K} pk \log pk \qquad (2)$$

When we use another variable to classify the original variables, the uncertainty of the original variables will be reduced, because the information of Y is added. How much the degree of uncertainty is reduced is the information gain. Therefore, the formula for information gain is very intuitive:

$$g(y, A) = H(y) - H(y|A) \qquad (3)$$

The g(y,A) here is often called Mutual Information, and the ID3 algorithm in the decision tree uses it as a feature selection criterion.

The information gain ratio is the ratio of the information gain to the entropy of y with respect to A. The specific formula is:

$$gR(y, A) = g(y, A)/HA(y) \qquad (4)$$

Decision Tree Generation. Using decision trees to classify data is mainly divided into two steps: the first step is to input the training set into the decision tree algorithm to generate a decision tree and build a decision tree model. This is actually a machine learning process [13]; The second step is to use the determined decision tree model to classify the data set. Among them, the generation of decision tree is a key step.

The intuitive generation process of the decision tree is:

(1) Input data to the root node.
(2) According to the measurement of information gain, select a certain characteristic of the data to divide the data into several (disjoint) pieces and input them to the new node respectively.
(3) If the uncertainty of a certain data is small and is close to a certain threshold, that is, a certain category of samples account for the majority, then this data is no longer divided, and its corresponding node is converted into Leaf node.
(4) If the uncertainty of a certain piece of data is still large, then this piece of data must continue to be divided (repeat step (2)).

There are currently three main decision tree generation algorithms: ID3 algorithm, C4.5 algorithm and CART algorithm. The difference between these three algorithms is only reflected in the method of measuring information gain and dividing data.

3.2 Optimization of Firewall Filtering Domain Attribute Sorting Based on Decision Tree

In terms of function, a firewall is a packet classification system [14]. When the data packet passes through the firewall, it is matched with the filtering rules in the ACL according to the rule number. If the data packet cannot completely match any of the rules, it means that the data packet and these rules are not the same type.If the data packet and a certain rule can exactly match, then the data packet and this rule are of the same type, which is the principle of static packet filtering technology to accept or reject data packets [15]. Therefore, we can intuitively regard the matching process between the data packet and the ACL as the classification process of the data packet. Therefore, we can apply decision tree theory to the firewall rule matching technology to reduce the total number of tuple comparisons between packets and rules by optimizing the sorting of ACL filtering domain attributes, thereby improving the efficiency of the firewall.

The Impact of Firewall ACL Filtering Domain Attribute Sorting on the Total Number of Packet Matches. From a vertical point of view, changing the rule number of the filtering rules in the ACL will cause errors in the function of the entire firewall. Then this section will give an example of what results will be caused by changing the order of the attributes in the filtering domains in the horizontal direction.

(1) Assume that the data packet P (D = {1, A, a}) enters the filter domain as shown in Fig. 3 and matches its ACL1.

SID	R1	R2	R3
1	1	B	a
2	1	A	a

Fig. 3. ACL1 of the example firewall

Then the total number of matches D = {1, A, a} with ACL1 is $(1 + 1) + (1 + 1 + 1) = 5$.

(2) Now we change the sorting of the attributes in the first column and the second column, swap the position of the RI attribute and the R2 attribute, and get ACL2 as shown in Fig. 4.

SID	R1	R2	R3
1	B	1	a
2	A	1	a

Fig. 4. ACL2 of the example firewall

Then the total number of times D = {A, 1, a} matches ACL2 is $(1) + (1 + 1 + 1) = 4$.

(3) Now we change the sorting of the attributes in the second column and the third column, swap the R2 attributes and R3 attributes, and get ACL3 as shown in Fig. 5

SID	R1	R2	R3
1	1	a	B
2	1	a	A

Fig. 5. ACL3 of the example firewall

Then, the total number of matches between D = {1, a, A} and ACL3 at this time is $(1 + 1 + 1) + (1 + 1 + 1) = 6$.

To sum up, the example shows that adjusting the filter domain attributes has a direct impact on the number of packet matching. Therefore, we can use the decision tree theory in data classification to predict and optimize the ranking of filtering domain attributes, so as to reduce the time complexity of firewall filtering algorithm and improve the throughputs of firewall.

Use the Improved C4.5 Algorithm to Generate a Decision Tree. We obtain the ACL training set of the firewall, and generate the decision tree by calculating the probability that the data packet entering the firewall matches the filtering rule successfully. Since this article is mainly optimized for static packet filtering firewalls, we only consider the five most common attributes of source port, destination port, source IP address, destination IP address, and protocol in the static packet filtering firewall ACL. This paper aims to find the optimal ranking of these five attributes through the decision tree algorithm to increase firewall throughputs. Since the filtering rules of the static packet filtering firewall are determined, they will not be changed unless they are operated by the firewall administrator, and each column in the ACL is the same attribute, so the algorithm for generating a decision tree with ID3 and C4.5 is not applicable to the filtering domain in this article. Sorting problem. Therefore, this paper adopts the improved C4.5 algorithm and uses the information gain ratio to construct the decision tree.

The following is the algorithm of using information gain ratio to generate decision tree proposed in this paper:

(1) Calculate the information gain ratio of the five attributes of the firewall ACL filtering domain, and use the attribute R with the highest information gain ratio as the root node.
(2) The rules with the same attribute value as R in the firewall filtering rules are classified into the same subset Ri, and each subset is a branch.
(3) Calculate the weight Wi of the number of rules in the subset Ri to the total number of rules.

(4) Calculate the information gain ratio Pi for the remaining attributes, and use Wi as the weight to weight the sum of $\sum Wi$.
(5) Take the largest attribute of $\sum Wi$ as the split attribute F of the next layer and the attributes of the second layer are all F.
(6) If the filter domain attributes have been tested, it ends; otherwise, repeat (2)–(6).

The Improvement of the C4.5 Algorithm by Using the Information Gain Ratio to Generate the Decision Tree Algorithm. The algorithm of using information gain ratio to generate decision tree proposed in this paper draws on the recursive idea of C4.5 algorithm and the measurement method of information gain ratio, and has made adaptive improvements to the characteristics of firewall ACL. It is different from using the C4.5 algorithm to generate a decision tree:

(1) Due to the limitation of the characteristics of the firewall ACL filtering rule table, the attributes of each layer of the decision tree constructed by the improved C4.5 algorithm proposed in this paper are consistent. This is different from the attribute of the decision tree generated by the C4.5 algorithm.
(2) In this paper, the information gain ratio is used as a measure of attribute selection, which effectively avoids the problem of selecting features with more values as the basis for division.
(3) In the C4.5 improved algorithm proposed in this paper, a step of calculating the weight of the number of rules in each subset in the total number of cabinets is added, that is, Wi in the third step. This is because when determining node attributes other than the root node, there may be more than one attribute. At this time, due to the difference in the number of rules in each subset, we can take the weight into account, and the information gain ratio of the attribute is weighted and summed with the number of rules in each subset to the total number of rules. The maximum value is the attribute of the next layer.

4   Simulation Experiment and Result Analysis

In this paper, a simulation experiment was carried out, using a database to store the firewall's ACL and other related data, and using python language to implement related algorithms on the Windows 10 operating system to verify the effectiveness of the optimization algorithm.

4.1   Introduction to Sample Data Sources

Since the firewall ACL publicly available on the Internet are rarely difficult to find, we selected Win10's Windows Defender firewall's stacking rule table as the experimental object and made appropriate modifications (select the five most common filter domain attributes: source port, destination port, Source IP address, destination IP address) to construct the rule table for simulation experiments in this article.

4.2 Data Preprocessing

In order to reduce the complexity of the experiment and ensure that the experiment does not lose its rationality, we first perform preprocessing such as non-numerical attribute digitization and class label digitization on the experimental data. Since the source IP address and destination IP address are a binary number and are 32 bits, we can convert them to an integer corresponding to the interval (0,255). Similar to the ip address, the source port and destination port can also correspond to an integer in the interval (0, 65535). And any represents the entire interval. Since the protocol types of static packet filtering firewalls generally only include TCP and UDP, we replace them with integers 0 and 1, respectively. Finally, we store the preprocessed data in the R table in the database for data matching.

4.3 Experimental Process

The process of the experiment is to simulate a certain number of data packets entering the firewall, that is, the data packets are matched with the ACL, and the total number of matches is calculated. This experiment uses python to write a data packet generator to obtain the data stream, and stores the randomly generated data stream in the D table of the database, and uses python to write a small program to compare the number of tuple comparisons, and the input is the database R table and D table, the output is the total number of matching between the two.

First, calculate the total number of comparisons between data packets and firewall ACL filtering domains under the optimal order constructed by the decision tree algorithm in Sect. 3.2.2 and denoted as X*. Then calculate the total comparison times X under the other A_5^5-1 types of firewall filtering domain attributes sorting. If X* is the smallest value among all X, it indicates the effectiveness of the algorithm in Sect. 3.2.2.

4.4 Experimental Results and Analysis

In order to ensure the rigor of the experiment, this experiment constructed three ACL with rules of 30, 60, and 90 respectively, and used the data packet generator program to randomly generate three data sets consisting of 50 data packets.

We record the data obtained by comparing the total number of matches when the number of ACL filtering rules are 30, 60, and 90 respectively in Table 2, Table 3 and Table 4. Among these data, the data with a hash pound (#) is the result X* of the optimized filter domain attribute sorting obtained by the improved C4.5 algorithm to form a decision tree.

Table 2. When the number of rules is 30, the total number of comparisons between the data set and the rule matching the A_5^5 types of attributes

4990	5060	4439	5381	5868
5979	5086	5130	4410	4509
5972	4199	5900	4509	6039

(continued)

Table 2. (*continued*)

4672	5249	4478	4639	6203
4690	5843	5881	5894	4019
5116	4879	4116	4313	4326
5021	5796	4830	5952	5437
4079	4843	4084	6047	6377
6009	6014	5699	6304	4873
4621	5875	5619	4558	5625
5493	4793	4128	6370	4665
4532	5597	6398	4510	5370
4360	4014	5515	6196	4260
4825	5054	5891	5838	4356
5852	4944	4024	5782	4395
4490	4684	5884	5764	6336
6187	4089	4408	5596	4603
6116	5043	5424	6067	6254
4161	5306	4193	4137	5243
4396	5753	5783	5714	5484
5259	5860	4779	4777	5363
5305	4676	3994	4997	4460
4298	4680	5256	5156	6325
4462	5376	4679	5380	4175

Table 3. When the number of rules is 60, the total number of comparisons between the data set and the rule under the order of A_5^5 attributes

7766	9102	8730	10655	11663
9305	10099	11046	11356	10931
7766	8152	8641	10309	11499
8233	8471	9233	11408	10920
10720	10192	10977	9280	7658
9748	7586	10377	8007	8944
11293	7322	10329	11125	9035
9473	8058	8538	9511	9686
10924	10003	7673	9150	7855

(continued)

Table 3. (*continued*)

7259	9725	8613	9967	9631
7872	7175	9353	11381	8182
10946	7815	9211	7449	8060
8280	8576	7108	10743	11436
10798	11328	7872	10505	7743
9555	10906	11191	7261	8249
8394	9761	9031	10196	10143
10490	11568	10962	7510	10354
7803	7630	9485	7066	10158
9102	8488	10085	11073	8445
8579	7999	9997	10890	8344
10557	9596	10360	9333	10230
7603	9918	#7049	10746	10476
7223	8283	8667	9296	11606
11331	11361	9098	11375	8349

Table 4. When the number of rules is 90, the total number of comparisons between the data set and the rule under the order of A_5^5 attributes

10686	15875	14801	15661	13073
11166	12602	14127	13017	15445
13158	14391	12915	12461	14334
13777	14192	11423	16419	16267
10939	14247	15722	13093	13583
12039	11836	13564	10930	13055
11682	15154	16442	14008	10888
12269	11197	15203	12853	11329
14226	11161	14071	10960	15936
11677	15654	14130	15876	10661
12571	14525	10987	15243	13593
15516	13798	12210	12760	15855
10493	11774	10895	11149	15113
15766	16220	13847	11666	14244
11314	14423	13255	12762	14803

(*continued*)

Table 4. (*continued*)

13104	10683	13045	14049	10327
12145	13341	11933	15153	13724
13439	12267	15218	16460	14548
15276	16455	10623	13501	12810
11540	15565	14323	16498	10464
14789	10804	11795	11981	10853
12292	11191	#10256	16357	13762
13802	13470	15895	15686	10703
15455	16321	11301	15987	14973

The data in the above three tables all show that under the optimal ranking of the filter domain attributes determined by the improved C4.5 algorithm to construct the decision tree, the total number of times the experimental data set matches ACL of different sizes is the smallest, which means that effectiveness of the 3.2.2 algorithm.

5 Summary

As one of the earliest and most mature network security measures, firewalls have been researched on issues such as their security and utility. In the current information age of information explosion, traditional firewalls often become a bottleneck for data exchange between internal and external networks. Based on the decision tree theory in machine learning, this article proposes an improved C4.5 algorithm to optimize the sorting of firewall ACL filtering domain attributes, thereby improving the efficiency of firewalls.

The simulation experiment designed in this paper also proves that the algorithm proposed in this paper can obviously shorten the matching time between data flow and ACL. However, in reality, the scale of fireproof ACL is often very large, and it is very complicated to use the algorithm of this paper to build a decision tree. Therefore, improving the efficiency of the algorithm has become the content of this paper to continue research in the future. And this article is mainly aimed at optimizing the filtering rules of static packet filtering firewalls. Once the ACL of static packet filtering firewalls is determined, it will generally not change. How the algorithm adapts to dynamically changing ACL such as state inspection firewalls is also the direction of this article.

References

1. Xiren, X.: Computer Network. Electronic Industry Press, Beijing (2009)
2. Noonan, W., Dubrawsky, I.: Firewall Foundation. People's Posts and Telecommunications Press, Beijing (2007)
3. Xiangbin, H., Cong, Z.: Research on dynamic optimization of firewall rules based on Huffman tree. Comput. Moderniz. **8**, 207–215 (2010)

4. Li, Z.: Research on Firewall Optimization Based on Statistical Analysis Method. Chongqing University, Chongqing (2011)

5. Anxi, R., Shoubao, Y., Hongwei, L.: A firewall rule matching optimization method based on statistical analysis. Comput. Eng. Appl. **42**(4), 162–164 (2006)

6. Qingwei, Z., Aiying, F.: Firewall Technical Standard Course. Beijing Institute of Technology Press, Beijing (2010)

7. Malik, S.: CCIE#4955.2 Principles and Practice of Network Security. Beijing: People's Posts and Telecommunications Press (2008)

8. Qun, W.: Extraordinary Network Management-Network Foundation. People's Posts and Telecommunications Press, Beijing (2006)

9. Jiawei, H.: Data Mining: Concept and Technology. Mechanical Industry Press, Beijing (2012)

10. Jing, Y., Nannan, Z., Jian, L., Yanming, L., Meihong, L.: Research and application of decision tree algorithm. Comput. Technol. Dev. **20**(02), 114–116+120 (2010)

11. Shaorong, F.: Research and improvement of decision tree algorithm. J. Xiamen Univ. (Nat. Sci. Ed.) **04**, 496–500 (2007)

12. Sun Lin, X., Jiucheng, M.Y.: Decision tree rule extraction method based on new conditional entropy. Comput. Appl. **04**, 884–887 (2007)

13. Jingqiong, Z.: Research on Firewall Technology Based on Learning. Nanjing University of Science and Technology, Nanjing (2004)

14. Weiping, W., Wenhui, C., Zupeng, L., Huaping, C.: Firewall policy inconsistency detection algorithm. J. Graduate Univ. Chin. Acad. Sci. **24**(3), 378 (2007)

15. Jiaye, W., Jiwu, J., Sencun, Z. Security research of packet filtering firewall. Comput. Sci. 1999(08): 34–36+42 (1999)

Encryption and Cybersecurity

A DAPP Business Data Storage Model Based on Blockchain and IPFS

Xiangyan Tang[1,2], Hao Guo[1,2(✉)], Hui Li[3], Yuming Yuan[3], Jianghao Wang[1,2], and Jieren Cheng[1,2]

[1] School of Computer Science and Cyberspace Security, Hainan University, Haikou 570228, China
[2] Hainan Blockchain Technology Engineering Research Center, Haikou 570228, China
[3] Hainan Huochain Tech Company Limited, Haikou 570100, China

Abstract. Blockchain technology has been applied in various fields, providing strong support for the medical field, supply chain and other industries, followed by the emergence of DApp based on blockchain smart contract technology. DApp as a distributed application model, implements part of the background business functions by the smart contract of blockchain to ensure the transparency, openness and traceability of key businesses, and can effectively resist DDoS attacks. However, blockchain data storage is expensive and not suitable for storing large amounts of data. This is a key barrier to the large amount of user data generated by DApp, and the risk of data loss, tampering and so on if the data is stored in a centralized service organization. In addition, smart contracts cannot be modified once deployed, and DApp often need frequent iterative updates in the later maintenance process, which will be faced with the need to modify the business logic of smart contracts. To solve the above problems, this paper proposes a user's data storage model of DApp based on IPFS to reduce the storage cost of data, and designs a set of hot-swapping smart contract architecture based on contract address to manage DApp user data, so as to meet the functional business replacement in the later stage of smart contract. In addition, for the privacy security of data, this paper introduces the Diffie-Hellman key exchange technology as the encryption scheme to protect user data.

Keywords: Blockchain · Distributed file system · Diffie-Hellman · DApp

1 Introduction

With the rapid development of smart phones in recent years, the types and quantity of APPs in the current application market have increased sharply in recent years, providing people with more convenient and intelligent services, enriching People's Daily life and greatly improving people's quality of life. With the emergence and development of blockchain technology, a kind of APP which uses smart contract technology as the service background begins to appear, which is called distributed application program (DApp). Compared with the traditional App, DApp transfers the main functions undertaken by the centralized server to the blockchain and implements the relevant functions with smart

© Springer Nature Switzerland AG 2021
X. Sun et al. (Eds.): ICAIS 2021, LNCS 12737, pp. 219–230, 2021.
https://doi.org/10.1007/978-3-030-78612-0_18

contracts. The data generated by the user is stored on the blockchain [1–4]. At present, compared with the traditional APP application market, the number and scale of DApp is much smaller. According to the statistics of the website DappTotal in 2020, the total number of DApp on Ethereum is more than 3,000, and the number of DAPP-related smart contracts is more than 16,000 [5]. It can be seen that the number and type of DApp are less than traditional ones, and the development of DApp is still in the early stage compared with traditional ones.

As for the traditional centralized server as the background of App, it faces two prominent problems. (1) The background business logic of APP is realized by the Web background. All front-end requests are sent to the Web background, and the results are returned to the front-end after being processed by the Web. This centralized service mode is vulnerable to malicious attack, typically DDoS leads to service paralysis [6]. (2) Users' data is often stored in the database on the server, and such centralized database data may face the risk of being tampered with and lost [7].

For DAPPs based on blockchain technology, the on-chain data of the blockchain is characterized by traceability, immutability, transparency, etc. and the storage of the business data of the DAPP on the blockchain can effectively maintain data security [8, 9]. In addition, due to the distributed architecture of blockchain itself, such smart contract through blockchain replaces the traditional centralized back-end service, and the model of front-end access to smart contract to meet business needs can effectively resist the influence brought by DDoS [10].

However, DApp also face the following three problems: (1) the cost of on-chain data storage; (2) Security and privacy of on-chain data; (3) Iterative updating of functions of smart contract as a background service [2, 11, 12]. With Ethereum, for example, storing 1KB of data on the blockchain in a smart contract costs about $5, which is expensive to run for DApp that are likely to produce and store large amounts of user data. As a public chain, the data on the chain of Ethereum is open to the outside world, and anyone can view the data in the blockchain. If the data on the chain of DApp users are not protected, they will face the risk of privacy leakage [13, 14]. In addition, smart contracts in Ethereum can no longer modify their code content after they are deployed, only allowed to be destroyed. If the back-end functions need to be changed during the update iteration of the later DApp, the new smart contract can only be redeployed and the old smart contract destroyed, which is extremely tedious for the developers and maintenance personnel.

To solve the problems mentioned above, this paper designs and implements a DAPP user data storage model based on distributed storage system. The system uses IPFS, a distributed storage system, to store user data to reduce the data storage cost of blockchain, and a smart contract system is designed to manage each user's stored data. In order to solve the problem of iterative update of smart contract, this paper divides the background service function into several sub-functions, and realizes the sub-functions through the smart contract respectively. Smart contracts call each other through the contract address, so as to build the hot swapping architecture of the background service function to reduce the iterative update and maintenance cost of the background. To solve the privacy problem of user data, this paper uses Diffie-Hellman key exchange technology to generate corresponding keys for different data to encrypt the data.

2 Background Knowledge

2.1 Blockchain

Blockchain is a peer-to-peer distributed ledger. Each node in the system will back up a copy of all the transaction data. When a new transaction occurs, each node verifies the transaction through a consensus mechanism, and if it passes the verification, the validity of its transaction is recognized and recorded in the ledger. This process does not require the participation of a third party, so it has the characteristics of decentralization. Blockchain can be divided into public chain, alliance chain and private chain. Public chain is a kind of block chain open to everyone. Anyone can participate in transaction and verification and obtain all transaction data in the public chain. Public chain is the most widely used block chain at present. Alliance chain is a group of bookkeepers who are elected in some way within a group. These bookkeepers maintain the ledger of transactions, while other common nodes only participate in the generation of transactions and are not responsible for the verification of transactions. A private chain is a block chain that is not open to the outside world. The block chain is only owned by an organization or individual, and outsiders cannot access the data within the block chain.

The structure of the data in the blockchain is chain-like. Each data block is related to the hash value of the data in the previous block. Changing the data in any block will change the hash value of the data in that block. Each block stores the data hash value of the previous block, so if there is data tampering in the blockchain ledger data, illegal data can be easily verified according to the hash value of the data [15–17] (see Fig. 1).

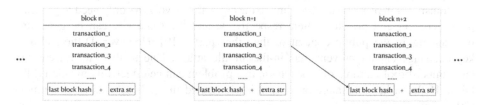

Fig. 1. Block structure

2.2 Distribute File System

Distributed storage system consists of peer-to-peer nodes, which is a content-addressable file system. Currently, such as IPFS, Swarm, etc. adopt this model. The distributed system is open to the outside world and any device can be added as a storage node. There is no need for trust between nodes, and nodes can store and download data with the help of clients. For each stored data in the distributed storage system will be cut into smaller blocks of data, from different nodes are stored, when a node to request a copy of data to the other nodes through P2P networks when they initiate the request, will send the data to request the rest of the node, it will effectively improve data throughput and save broadband [7, 12]. Since each piece of data is stored in various nodes in a distributed way, this can effectively avoid the network attacks faced by traditional centralized mode, such as DDoS (see Fig. 2).

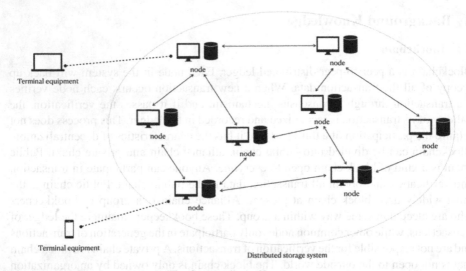

Fig. 2. Distribute file system

2.3 Diffie-Hellman Key Exchange

Diffie-Hellman key exchange is a key exchange algorithm, which was proposed by Whitfield Diffie and Martin Hellman in 1976. This algorithm can generate the same encryption key for two roles in a fully public environment. It is widely used in various data transmission protocols. According to the algorithm, two users only need to generate public content and private content respectively, and the same key can be generated by exchanging the public content of the other party [19]. However, Diffie-Hellman key exchange cannot prevent man-in-the-middle attack. Due to the data traceability and tamper-proof features of blockchain, this problem can be effectively avoided if the Diffie-Hellman key exchange process is implemented in the blockchain environment [20].

3 System Architecture Design

3.1 The Overall Architecture

The system model proposed in this paper includes the following four roles: (1) DApp front-end; (2) Blockchain smart contract system; (3) Distributed storage system; (4) Management Organization. Its detailed introduction is as follows:

- The front end of DApp is the program used by users, which provides corresponding services for users. The front-end processes user data by interacting with smart contracts and distributed storage systems.
- Blockchain smart contracts provide back-end services for DApp, which manage users' data hashes and generate data encryption keys.

- Distributed storage systems divide data into several small data blocks and store them on multiple devices, which will synchronize relevant data between devices. After users upload data to the system, they will get the encrypted hash value of the data, through which they can query data in the system.
- The management body is responsible for the late iteration and update of the DApp, which is responsible for the iteration of the front end of the DApp and the management and update of the smart contract.

3.2 Smart Contract System Design

By default, each DApp user has a separate set of public and private keys as an Ethereum account, and each user interacts with the smart contract through the Ethereum account. Smart contract is divided into user data storage contract, data management contract, key contract and directory contract. The following sections describe the content and functionality of each of these contracts.

DataStorage Contract. DataStorage contract are responsible for storing two types of data. One is to store relevant data of users, which maintains a user data table, and its structure is shown in the following table. Each user is uniquely identified by the account address. Data with a large amount of data is first uploaded to IPFS and then the hash value is stored in the smart contract. Data with a small amount of data can be directly stored in the smart contract. This contract only accepts the data in the DataManage contract to modify the data inside the contract. When the DApp requests to update the data of the user in the DataStorage contract, it will send a request to the DataManage contract first. The DataManage contract verifies the account permissions of the requestor, and after the permissions are approved, the DataManage contract modifies the hash value in the DataStore contract. The other is the system data that can be obtained by all users, which is publicly available without encryption. For the data with a large amount of data, it is stored in IPFS, and only the hash value is stored in the contract, while for the data with a small amount, it can be stored directly in the contract. This type of data can also only be manipulated by a DataManage contract, and only the specified account address (usually the service manager) has the right to modify the data (Tables 1 and 2).

Table 1. The structure of user data stored in the DataStorage contract.

User	Data1 hash	Data2 hash	...
User1	mbsPceqURmvYefhH jo4PfmGbRgEcbBVc6BonjSHF4Rru	QmeqYYxh6HbfwhSKwaB5DzZ77A yPV9VfKm1pNNvwuyrhyF	...
User2	QmbTqKdRi7H7CkvyghuB6eilztdlh 8HhnwytADf1gox9Xd	QmdgmHHitPahhd2k85bXZ5VtrwtCL8my VYZUgwXv1CTTNP	...
User3	QmUAT8T24ESpMvvkTkRYYep bPdu9tmGFcWtHhBiJLfXDyi	QmdmJW3XCcbTDQCZQTGB5Bu W7ZfXmN1L89mB39N3pJrxKe	...
...	...	...	...

Table 2. The structure of public data stored in the DataStorage contract.

Data1	Data2	Data3	...
QmVd8EbQYj9zA	QmXJv98swdb	QmejkAXfh32SZWn	...
8Ya67mzboPYR1	WHJ9JwmWCA28Tgqc	QJp9BRP2R7yaft	
KPb9kwP6BiLVrgdDRZrE	9JgGXvkBy2eDYPw35oP	EMXQKI2dgX8YhUNHD	

DataStorage contract should have the following functions to manage the internal data.

- *initUserData()*: This method is used to initialize the data information of a user account, which usually occurs during the DApp user registration phase.
- *updateUserData()*. This method is used to modify or add data to the specified user.
- *addPublicData()*. This method is used to add new public system data.
- *updatePublicData()*. This method is used to modify or add information that specifies the name of the exposed system data.
- *deleteContract()*. This method is used to delete this contract, after which the contract cannot be called again.

DataManage Contract. The DataManage contract is used to manage the contents of the DataStorage contract. Its internal functions need to design corresponding functions according to the specific DApp type, and call the functions of the DataStorage contract through these functions. The DataManage contract should contain the following functions.

- *userAuthorityVerification()*. This method is used to determine whether the caller has the right to modify the data in the data storage contract. If the caller has the right (for example, the data that the caller applies to modify belongs to the user address itself), he or she can choose to conduct subsequent related operations; if not, he or she will refuse other subsequent requests.
- *manageUserData()*. This method is used to manage user data. For example, to modify or add account data, this method calls functions in the data management contract for user data.
- *managePublickData()*. This method is used to manage system exposed data, such as adding new data or modifying existing data. This method calls functions in the data management contract for system data.
- *deleteContract()*. This method is used to delete this contract, after which the contract cannot be called again. This function can only be called by the operator.

SecretKey Contract. From the perspective of data privacy security, this paper divides data into the following two types.

- *Public data.* This type of data is visible to everyone, and its data itself or hash values are stored directly in smart contracts, so encryption is not required.

- *Data visible only to the user and operator*. This type of data is generated by DApp users, and its information is visible to both the operators and the users themselves. In order to generate encryption key of data, Diffie-Hellman key exchange technology is adopted in this paper. The manager and the user respectively generate public content and secret content for the corresponding stored data. The secret content is not public as private data, while the public content can be obtained by anyone. Users and managers respectively drop their public content and store it in the SecretKey contract, through which both parties can obtain the other party's public content and calculate the same data encryption and decryption key by mathematical formula.

The SecretKey contract maintains a Diffie-Hellman disclosure table internally, as shown in the following table. The contract provides the corresponding public key for different types of data, and the front-end user obtains the public key by accessing the SecretKey contract to encrypt the data. The Diffie-Hellman Open Information Table maintains multiple data tables for different types of data. Each data table is provided by the operator with one public information. DApp users who want to store such data must also provide one public information and store it in the data table. Operator and user can respectively generate the same key to encrypt and decrypt data through the public information provided by the other party (Table 3).

Table 3. A Diffie-Hellman public information table for a class of data.

Manager public content	User1 public content	User2 public content	...
QmNU32urwsz VZULo4tBoczwiqjk 41TyBxWc1hwVcAUuaBt	QmVjdMtgPE4bpalck PrmJs4xi1aob DkJoS59Emg8J7dHQQ	Qmbzr59EzXAos xBqTgo4o3Vshsrgj VQE97cwTQitUi1kHr	...

The SecretKey contract contains the following functions internally.

- *changePublicContent ()*. This function modifies the public key of a piece of data in a key contract. This function can only be called by an operator.
- *createPublicContent ()*. This function creates a new Diffie-Hellman disclosure table for a new piece of data in the key contract, along with the operator's key disclosure information. This function can only be called by the operator.
- *addUserPublicContent ()*. This function is called by the DApp user to add the user's public key information to a certain piece of data in the key contract.
- *deleteContract ()*. This method is used to delete this contract, after which the contract cannot be called again. This function can only be called by the operator.

Directory Contract. The directory contract is used as a smart contract system subdirectory, which contains the address index of other sub-function modules and the ABI of other contracts stored in IPFS. DAPP can access the directory contract to search for other sub-function contracts. The catalog contract maintains a table of data about the subfunction contract internally, as shown below.

The directory contract implements the following functions.

- *addChildContract ().* This function adds a new subcontract information inside the directory contract, including the contract name, the contract address, and the contract ABI.
- *changeChildContract ().* This function modifies the information of one of the subcontracts in the catalog contract, such as the contract address and the contract ABI.
- *deleteChildContract ().* This function invalidates a contract information in a directory contract.
- *deleteContract ().* This function is used to delete this contract.

Note that the call authority of the directory contract should be strictly controlled. Generally, it can only be operated by the account address of the manager, and ordinary DApp users have no right to call (Table 4).

Table 4. Subfunction contract data table.

Contract name	Contract address	Contract ABI hash
Data storage contract	0x26AAA1C996354a56Gi 755726cAC15FEaA618FD21	QmYyKJUJiFiZLSgAKXAg7F63 PWeoaxEfVimmTo88HfRe5B
Secret key contract	0xCA0D34C770835go8340 CC7731b484c0Ae1e9A2d6	QmPjuKrBWQHDQJSygjmXUNKa E3GV1QNshzD8u23wZGxFuq
Data manage contract	0x52B49a8DFoF9A048ka35 BC5c8Db3e7888B60E400	QmcbvD7y5uyF8HRdzpJ459s2 AqNspvr6Meue8xtaHnSsT5
…	…	…

3.3 The Front End Designs

The front end of the DApp uses Android system as the platform to develop the corresponding App to interact with the Ethereum smart contract. For convenience of testing, the front-end program is responsible for two parts: (1) uploading data to IPFS and calling the corresponding smart contract. (2) Call the smart contract to obtain the corresponding data and hash value, and access the IPFS system to download the data to the local area according to the hash value.

Upload Data. The front-end user data is uploaded using HTTPS protocol to interact with the smart contract with the help of Infura. The front-end device needs to access the directory contract to get the address of the data management contract to call the smart contract. For the data to be encrypted, the SecretKey contract is called to get the public key of the manager of the corresponding data to generate the key, and its hash value will be used as the key of AES encryption. User data is encrypted by the AES of the key and then uploaded to IPFS. IPFS will return the hash value of the data. Similarly, the hash value also needs to be encrypted by the AES of the key to ensure privacy. Finally, DataManage Contract is called to store the encrypted hash value in the blockchain. For the public data without encryption, you can directly store the data hash returned by uploading to the IPFS system in DataStorage Contract (see Fig. 3).

Download Data. Data downloading is similar to uploading. The front-end device first accesses the directory contract to get the address of the data management contract and then accesses the function of the data management contract to get the hash of the data. For the unencrypted hash value, the user data of the hash value can be obtained directly by accessing the IPFS system. For the encrypted hash value, the front-end device needs to access the SecretKey Contract to obtain the Manager Publick Key of the data, and then generate the corresponding Key according to the Private Keys stored by the front-end device itself to decrypt the encrypted hash value. Finally, the decrypted hash value is submitted to the IPFS system to obtain the data, and the obtained data is decrypted.

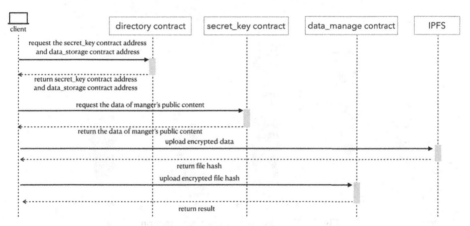

Fig. 3. Upload encrypted data

4   Experimental Evaluation

In this paper, related experiments are carried out to evaluate the system. Smart contracts are deployed in the Ethereum test chain. The DApp manager uses the Python-based Web3 library to interact with the smart contract, while the DApp client uses the Java-based Web3 library to interact with the smart contract. An Intel Core i5 quad-core 2.3 GHz desktop is used as the IPFS client.

The deployment cost of each sub-function smart contract is as follows (Fig. 4):

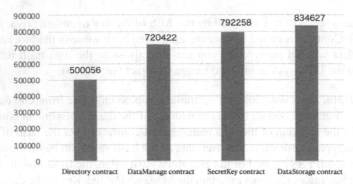

Fig. 4. The gas used of contract deploy

Gas consumption of function call related to operation data in the contract is as follows (Fig. 5):

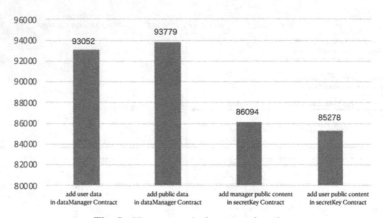

Fig. 5. The gas used of contract function

IPFS client local data upload efficiency is as follows (Fig. 6):

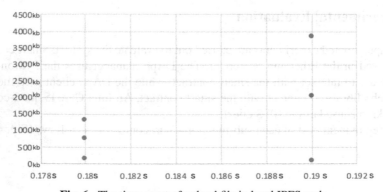

Fig. 6. The time coast of upload file in local IPFS node

5 Conclusion

This paper designs a business data storage model for DApp, which stores business data with distributed storage system, maintains the hash value of business data with blockchain smart contract, and implements the data encryption key with Diffie-Hellman key exchange technology. This model can guarantee the high throughput of data storage, and has the characteristics of traceability and tamper-proof. And this kind of distributed architecture can resist DDoS well.

Acknowledgement. This work was supported by the Hainan Provincial Natural Science Foundation of China (Grant No. 2019RC041 and 2019RC098), Research and Application Project of Key Technologies for Blockchain Cross-chain Collaborative Monitoring and Traceability for Large-scale Distributed Denial of Service Attacks, National Natural Science Foundation of China (Grant No. 61762033), Opening Project of Shanghai Trusted Industrial Control Platform (Grant No. TICPSH202003005-ZC), and Education and Teaching Reform Research Project of Hainan University (Grant No. hdjy1970).

References

1. Tsung-Ting, K., Hyeon-Eui, K., Lucila, O.M.: Blockchain distributed ledger technologies for biomedical and health care applications. J. Am. Med. Inform. Assoc. **24**(6), 1211–1220
2. Dwivedi, A., Srivastava, G., Dhar, S., et al.: A decentralized privacy-preserving healthcare blockchain for IoT. Sensors **19**(2), 326 (2019)
3. Li, M., Weng, J., Yang, A., et al.: CrowdBC: a blockchain-based decentralized framework for crowdsourcing. IEEE Trans. Parall. Distrib. Syst. **30**(6), 1251–1266 (2018)
4. Decentralized Applications – dApps. https://blockchainhub.net/decentralized-applications-dapps/. Accessed 20 Sept 2020
5. dapptotal Homepage. https://dapptotal.com/. Accessed 12 Oct 2020
6. Peng, T., Leckie, C., Ramamohanarao, K.: Survey of network-based defense mechanisms countering the DoS and DDoS problems. ACM Comput. Surv. **39**(1), 31–342 (2007)
7. IPFS-Content Addressed, Versioned, P2P File System. https://arxiv.org/pdf/1407.3561.pdf. Accessed 21 Nov 2020
8. Wang, S., Ouyang, L., Yuan, Y., et al.: Blockchain-enabled smart contracts: architecture, applications, and future trends. IEEE Trans. Syst. Man Cybernet. Syst. **49**(11), 2266–2277 (2019)
9. Treiblmaier H.: The impact of the blockchain on the supply chain: a theory-based research framework and a call for action. Supply Chain Manage. (2018)
10. Dai, H.N., Zheng, Z., Zhang, Y.: Blockchain for Internet of Things: a survey. IEEE Internet Things J. **6**(5), 8076–8094 (2019)
11. Nizamuddin, N., Salah, K., Ajmal Azad, M., et al.: Decentralized document version control using Ethereum blockchain and IPFS. Comput. Electr. Eng. **76**, 183–197 (2019)
12. Patsakis, C., Casino, F.: Hydras and IPFS: a decentralised playground for malware. Int. J. Inf. Secur. **18**(6), 787–799 (2019)
13. Zhumabekuly Aitzhan, N., Svetinovic, D.: Security and privacy in decentralized energy trading through multi-signatures, blockchain and anonymous messaging streams. IEEE Trans. Dependable Secure Comput. **5**, 840–852 (2016)
14. Shi, P., Wang, H., Yang S., et al.: Blockchain-based trusted data sharing among trusted stakeholders in IoT. Software Pract. Exper. (15) (2019)

15. Li, Y., Yang, W., He, P., et al.: Design and management of a distributed hybrid energy system through smart contract and blockchain. Appl. Energy **248**, 390–405 (2019)
16. Treiblmaier H. The impact of the blockchain on the supply chain: a theory-based research framework and a call for action. SSRN Electron. J. (2018)
17. Blockchain-for-beginners-what-is-blockchain-just-7-step. https://ethfans.org/posts/blockc hain-for-beginners-what-is-blockchain-just-7-step. Accessed 12 Sept 2020
18. Ali, M.S., Dolui, K., Antonelli, F.: IoT data privacy via blockchains and IPFS. In: International Conference on the Internet of Things, pp. 1–7. ACM (2017)
19. Joux, A.: A one round protocol for tripartite Diffie–Hellman. J. Cryptol. **17**(4), 263–276 (2004)
20. Kocher, P.C.: Timing Attacks on Implementations of Diffie-Hellman, RSA, DSS, and Other Systems. In: Koblitz, N. (ed.) CRYPTO 1996. LNCS, vol. 1109, pp. 104–113. Springer, Heidelberg (1996). https://doi.org/10.1007/3-540-68697-5_9

IPv6-Darknet Network Traffic Detection

ChenHuan Liu, QianKun Liu, ShanShan Hao, CongXiao Bao, and Xing Li[(⊠)]

Department of Electronic Engineering, Tsinghua University, Tsinghua National Laboratory for Information Science and Technology, Beiging 10084, China
xing@cernet.edu.cn

Abstract. The state of the network can be reflected by the background traffic. Negative network measurements can be a very important way to understand the Internet. I would like to express appreciation to CERNET, who provided us with an IPv6 address space allocated but not a fully used network. By announcing a large /20 covering prefixes on this address, we have published routing information on China's domestic education network, business network, and foreign education network. Based on the honeypot method, we collect relative traffic at the last hop router of the experiment network. Thus, we make our experiment environment a network telescope. We discover that background radiation traffic grew more rapidly than it was years ago under the current ipv6 network situation. Moreover, suspicious IPv6 address scanning traffic shows up. We classify and analyze the traffic and classify all the source addresses and destination addresses. We found that the source addresses are mainly from Asian countries. In particular, we conduct further detection and monitor on the suspicious source addresses. We analyze the time when it appears and what it scans, including the destination address and the port type. The most interesting destination ports to the outside world are mainly 80, 8080, 443, 53, 21, 22, 23, and 25, which are related to web services and host system applications. We explain most of the data and highlight the significant attributes of the data. We found several special addresses scanning our address segment periodically. Our work reveals the situation and the problem under the current IPv6 network situation.

Keywords: Honeypot · Darknet · IPv6 · Background radiation

1 Introduction

Darknet exists in the Internet address space but doesn't offer any network services. However, it can be a useful environment to monitor the impact. Now Darknet is used to help to confirm the type and source of malicious traffic [1]. In history, Darknet was used to capture background traffic in the IPv4 network and was also used to capture malicious applications and events on the Internet [2, 3]. For example, Darknet can be used to detect net worms, DoS attacks, malicious scanning, and configuration errors, etc. There are two purposes for monitoring background radiation traffic. One is to figure out the regularity of these appearances, the other is to explain the reason why they occur. Furthermore, a Darknet that occupies a few address spaces can monitor a huge amount of traffic. For

© Springer Nature Switzerland AG 2021
X. Sun et al. (Eds.): ICAIS 2021, LNCS 12737, pp. 231–241, 2021.
https://doi.org/10.1007/978-3-030-78612-0_19

instance, the average amount of network traffic in a single /24 IPv4 network can be up to 541.8 kbps [4].

Surveillance in the inner environment is needed to learn Darknet. To realize the surveillance, honeypot [23] can be a useful method. There are always possibilities to be attacked by hackers in a network linked to the Internet. A defense system means it can capture suspicious attacks and record the information of the attackers. A huge advantage of honeypot is that it will not generate wrong alarms, because every traffic watch is suspicious. Nowadays, honeypot is widely used in IPv6 networks [5]. As the IPv6 network develops, honeypot systems have been gradually used to collect traffic and confirm cyber security.

As time went on, we came to a turning point where IP protocol transformed from IPv4 to IPv6. The main address pool of IANA was used up on Feb 3, 2011, after the last five address blocks were assigned to five Regional Internet Registrations (RIRs). The growth rate of the IPv4 network slows down from the exponential rate to nearly linear speed. On the contrary, the growth rate of the IPv6 network speeds up from the linear rate to an exponential rate. With the popularization of IPv6 applications and services, system configuration differences and software and hardware errors may lead to background radiation. However, we lack experience of IPv6 background radiation. By collecting and identifying the background radiation, we may effectively provide a better experimental model for future IPv6 carriers and users.

The IPv6 address space is massive, while background traffic in the IPv6 network is comparatively thin. A single IPv6 address can hardly be visited or scanned. In this way, a general method of research is based on IPv6 Darknet [6–9]. It means we conduct experiments on several IPv6 prefix networks and monitor the Darknet. I would like to express appreciation to CERNET, who provided us a 240c:c000::/20 address space, which is allocated but not a fully used network. We have published routing information on China's domestic education network, business network, and foreign education network. We collected traffic data for over 4 months by setting a honeypot server at the last-hop router of the address block mentioned before. On this scale of time and address number, we get data samples in higher quality and larger scale, which helps to understand the temporal and spatial characteristics of background radiation traffic in the IPv6 network.

Under the network configuration environment described in 3.1, our contributions include:

Characteristic description of IPv6 background radiation traffic:

- We observe the growth ratio of background radiation traffic is stable at 20 kb/min, which is much smaller than the IPv4 traffic of a same network segment size [4].
- We find the initial background traffic from address configuration is increasing gradually and become stable in a week.
- We find that there is always regular traffic and sometimes a burst of traffic that is malicious. This is similar to IPv4 network background radiation [2, 10, 11].
- We conclude the source of active IPv6 addresses. These addresses are mainly from Asian countries such as India, Malaysia, Thailand, and Vietnam.

The type of IPv6 background radiation traffic:

- Most of the scanning destination ports are concentrated in port 80. This is similar to IPv4 network background radiation [2, 10, 11].
- More than 87% of the traffic uses TCP protocol. UDP and ICMPv6 traffic is generated randomly.
- The main types of ICMPv6 traffic are Echo Request, ICMP Node Information Query, and Destination Unreachable.

2 Related Work

2.1 The Early Stage of IPv6 Darknet Measurement

The earliest known research on IPv6 Darknet took place in 2006. Researchers conducted experiments in a comparatively small network. They captured a month of background traffic in /48 IPv6 darknet. During this time, they only collected 12 ICMP packets which were generated by IPv6 users network configuration errors in their analysis [6]. In 2012, Deccio et al. did short-term research on a /12 IPv6 address. They collected two weeks of traffic data. The average traffic on the network was 74 packets/s. It indicated that users had begun to use the IPv6 network on a large scale [7]. Huston et al. conducted experiments on the address segment of /12. Most of the addresses in this address segment have been configured and used. Their research shows that during the research period, the background average traffic of the network did not increase. The research also focused on generating traffic. A detailed analysis has been performed on the addresses, and most of the traffic (95%) is generated from addresses that have been configured to use [8]. Czyz et al. conducted experiments on the five-segment/12 address segment, and 86% of the addresses have been configured and used. Their research analyzed the IPv6 network routing configuration of these addresses through traffic analysis, and concluded that most of the IPv6 network background traffic is caused by incorrect network configuration.

IPv6 network has developed rapidly in recent years. The governments and industries around the world have carried out IPv6 transformation on the infrastructure. We did further work based on earlier approaches. We conducted a network experiment for more than four months on a /20 unassigned IPv6 network that did not offer any web service. An unassigned network can prevent the configured address from disturbing the background traffic. We collected the clearest traffic by this means and analyzed the type of traffic and related address in detail and comprehensively. Our results have strong universality for the whole network of IPv6.

2.2 The Feature of Honeypot and IPv6 Applications

Sindhu s Pandya et al. summarized the development process of Honeypot in an article in 2015. The article first introduced the types, uses, and characteristics of honeypot, and then predicted the future of honeypot and large-scale honeypot network systems [23]. According to the type of service, it can be divided into high interaction honeypot and low interaction honeypot. High interaction honeypot can capture large-scale black pot attack information, while low interaction honeypot only provides limited service functions to detect unauthorized network activities. According to the usage, it can be divided into research honeypot and production honeypot. As a method for researchers to obtain network environment security information, the research honeypot can help researchers understand the attack types and attack sources in the network, while the production honeypot is mainly deployed in the network system as a network security measure. Before the network is about to be attacked, the information will be sent to the management personnel. Production network helps to protect the network environment.

The Honeypot system has been widely used in the IPv4 network, and the IPv6 network can also use the honeypot system to collect network traffic. Kazuya Kishimoto et al. proposed a strategy to detect the external IPv6 scanning by using a honeypot system [24].

S Schindler et al. designed a low interaction honeypot, which can simulate the whole IPv6 network on a single host. Because of the huge IPv6 address space, it needs a new method to induce attackers to use IPv6 honeypot. S Schindler et al. solved this problem through a dynamic instantiation mechanism, which increased the possibility of attackers finding target hosts in our IPv6 Honeynets [25, 26].

2.3 IPv4 Background Radiation Analysis

The early work of Darknet mainly focused on the IPv4 network environment. Wustrow et al. collected a five-year sample of data in an unallocated and several allocated but unused IPv4 address blocks with a prefix of /8 [3]. The results showed that the pollution flow was four times the normal flow, and the pollution flow is mainly caused by the wrong configuration. In the work of Pang et al., Yegneswaran et al., and Cooke et al., their research mainly focused on the source of pollution flow [2, 10, 11]. Bailey et al. mainly studied and discussed the method of active measurement to study network background traffic [12].

In our approach, we do not adopt active measurements to ensure that there is no effect on effective IPv6 background traffic. Furthermore, given that we have published a /20 address segment, this active measurement may also interfere with normal host traffic.

Glatz et al. and Brownlee et al. mainly detected the source of Internet pollution traffic, and created a classification scheme for this traffic according to the parameters of network traffic (such as source address, protocol, and arrival interval). The data they provide can quantify the number and attributes of such traffic given [13, 14].

After the background traffic of the Internet is analyzed, it can be used to review large-scale scanning activities [15], Internet censorship [16], and even large-scale events such as earthquakes or hurricanes [17, 18]. Barford et al. used similar data to find the location of malicious hosts [19].

2.4 Factors Influencing Network Background Radiation

Compared with the previous work, Bailey's work has similar methods and techniques to ours. Their work used honeypot as a passive measurement method to monitor the network background traffic in the Darknet [20]. They analyzed a distributed Darknet with more than 60 small address blocks containing 17 million routable addresses to determine the difficulty of implementing such a hybrid monitoring system.

The size and spatial location of the Darknet are also important factors related to background traffic. Moore et al. studied the influence of Darknet size on network security event types, such as worm propagation, scanning, and distributed denial of service (DDoS) attacks. Similarly, Cook et al. studied how location affects the collected data through data on ten distributed monitors [21, 22]. These different studies have concluded that location, visibility, and routing announcements can all affect observed traffic. Based on these conclusions, we pay special attention to these data collection details when designing the experiment, and analyze the scanning situation of different subnets in /20.

3   Proposed Method

In this section, we will describe our experimental design methods and classification methods for data collection. Huston et al. have shown that it is possible to carry out a secure experiment of IPv6 covering a prefix [8]. We hope to replicate and refine the results and depth of the experiment through our work.

3.1   BGP Announcement and Experimental Design

At the end of April 2019, CERNET provided us a 240c: c000::/20 address space. After much deliberation, we configured the next hop of the address 2001: da8: fa00::/48 to one of our data collection server addresses. After a series of tests, we configured the next hop of 240C: C000::/20 to our data collection server address on May 1, 2019. Then, we published the route through the NOC of BGP 23910. We have published routing information on China's domestic education network, business network, and foreign education network. The relevant international backbone network confirmed that the route had been received. BGP 23910 belongs to the CNGI-BJIX-AS-AP autonomous system, and the address of 240C: C000::/20 belongs to the China education network. In the four months from May 1, 2019, we grabbed all the traffic passing through 240C: C000::/20 through the data collection server and stored it.

3.2   Data Set Description and Data Classification

The dataset we captured contains all the traffic data of 240c: c000::/20 communications. We mainly analyze the data of three common protocols: TCP, UDP, and ICMPv6. The data of the dataset spans over four months from May 1 to September 1, 2019. We captured the five-tuple information (including five-tuple, timestamp, and packet length) of the TCP/IP packets and the three-tuple information (triple, timestamp, packet length) of the ICMP packets on the data collection server. We had no packets on May 26 due to an electrical failure early in the morning of that day (Fig. 1).

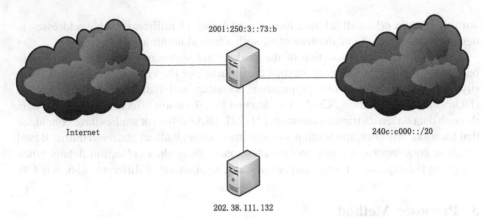

2001:250:3::73:b

Internet

240c:c000::/20

202. 38. 111. 132

Fig. 1. Schematic of the experimental configuration environment

4 Background Radiation Result

For IPv6 Darknet background radiation results, we mainly analyze and discuss the space and time distribution of background radiation traffic. At the same time, we process and analyze the background traffic related to the active source addresses to count the country distribution of the addresses and study the protocol and port distribution.

4.1 Time Analysis

We observed the time distribution of TCP, UDP, and ICMPv6 traffic of 240c: c000::/20 over a period of 4 months. The background traffic is sparse from 22:00 on May 1 to 12:00 on May 3 in the configuration environment. A steady and large amount of background traffic has appeared since 12:00 on May 3. We can see from the time series diagram that there is some special periodic traffic in TCP traffic. We will discuss this special traffic in Sect. 4.4. And there is some random traffic like white noise in UDP and ICMPv6. During the experimental period, due to the failure of the experimental environment or the power failure of the experimental environment, we miss some time data, but we can still analyze the regularity of these data from the existing data.

As shown in Table 1, before we delve into the background traffic data, we made some basic statistics on the overall data collection, and we collected about 5 million packets from more than 1 million data streams. The number of packets and flows included in the traffic is counted, and the average rate of packets and flows is calculated. At the same time, we also make basic statistics about the main protocol distribution proportion of the collected background traffic. It shows most of the protocols are concentrated in the TCP protocol, which accounts for 87.6% of the total packet.

Table 1. Packet and Flow counts, Packet and Flow rates, and protocol breakdown in the complete datasets

Protocol	kPackets	Average		% Protocol Type	
		pkts/m	kbits/m	pkts	bits
Total	5613.41	31.69	19.91	100	100
TCP	4917.49	27.76	17.40	87.60	87.37
UDP	12.55	0.07	0.14	0.22	0.71
ICMPv6	683.37	3.86	2.38	12.17	11.92

4.2 Spatial Analysis

Figure 3 shows the cumulative distribution function (CDF) of source addresses sorted by the number of packets captured in external data and 240c: c000::/20 communication data. We can see that some source addresses account for a large part of the traffic, especially 240e:f7:c000::23, which contributes 37.87% of the packets. The top 10 addresses accounted for 99% of the total traffic. Only two packets communicate between addresses, which account for 97% of the source addresses, in a large part of the traffic.

Figure 3 shows the cumulative distribution function (CDF) of destination addresses sorted by the number of packets captured. It can be seen from the graph that more than 50% of the destination addresses have only two packets of traffic, but less than 50% of the destination addresses are accessed extensively. From the CDF diagram of the source and destination addresses, we can see that a small number of destination addresses access to the addresses in Sect. 240c: c000::/20 of IPv6.The RESULTS of the CDF show that there is an interest in specific address segments of the IPv6 network that will be scanned on a large scale. This indicates that the outside world may scan the whole network segment of IPv6 regularly with a certain IPv6 scanning algorithm (Fig. 2).

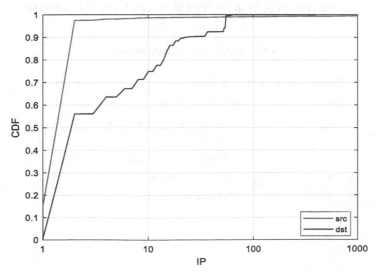

Fig. 2. Cumulative distribution of source and destination IP addresses sorted by the number of collected packets

Table 2. Top 10 Dest Port by Packet

TCP			UDP		
Dest Port	Pockets	%	Dest Port	Pockets	%
80	2947741	59.90	443	2121	16.9
22	308945	6.27	53	1152	9.17
443	288305	5.86	11211	592	4.71
21	287190	5.83	5683	306	2.44
23	283860	5.81	5060	198	1.58
25	283116	5.75	0	185	1.47
53	210262	4.27	6881	140	1.11
8443	76448	1.55	500	128	1.02
8080	72238	1.47	389	116	0.92
554	71628	1.45	3283	114	0.91

Table 2 shows the ten destination ports with the largest number of TCP/UDP traffic packets. TCP-related destination port which ranks first in the list is port 80, accounting for nearly 60% of the total traffic packets. Port 8080 and port 80 in the top 10 list are HTTP ports, port 8443 and port 443 are HTTPS ports, indicating that most of the traffic is mainly to access the destination's web services. The corresponding ports of FTP, SSH, Telnet, SMTP, and DNS services are port 21, port 22, port 23, port 25, and port 53. These services are common types of system services. UDP-related destination ports are port 443 and port 53, while the rest are uncommon ports. The above results show that the outside world is interested in the destination party's web services and common services. As can be seen from our experimental results, the scanning rule of ports in the IPv6 network is similar to that of ports in the IPv4 network [2, 10, 11] (Table 3).

Table 3. Top 5 ICMPv6 type by packets

ICMPv6_Type_num	ICMPv6_Type	Packets
128	Echo Request	679037
139	ICMP Node Information Query	3356
1	Destination Unreachable	1606
4	Parameter Problem	64
3	Time Exceeded	51

4.3 IP Analysis

As shown in Table 4, we list the number of source and destination addresses of TCP, UDP, and ICMP. For the source address, we statistically analyze the proportion of its country of origin. As shown in Fig. 3, we found that these source addresses are mainly from Asian countries such as India, Malaysia, Thailand, Vietnam, and China, while only a small part are from European and American countries. We found that the source addresses related to the three protocols, TCP, UDP and ICMP, were mainly from India, Malaysia and Thailand.

Table 4. IP counts

IP count	TCP	UDP	ICMP
src	5352	4478	1845
dst	517512	5669	27864

We observed TCP has periodic traffic appearing every day, and sudden surges in traffic occur at some point in the node. These are all suspicious traffic in our observations.

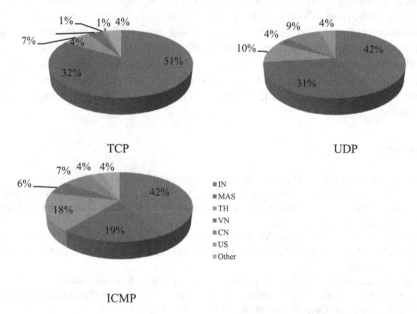

Fig. 3. Country Distribution of Source IP for TCP, UDP and ICMP

We studied this shunt specifically and found that 2607: fca8:16::, 2605: fe00:0:17::1, 2a02:29e0:1:140:: these three addresses access port 80 different addresses in the experimental network segment from 12:00 to 24:00 each day, and the traffic rate remains stable.2607: fca8:16::, 2605: fe00:0:17::1 are from the US and 2a02:29e0:1:140:: is from Italy. At about 6:00 a.m. every day, different addresses of port 80 in the experimental network segment were accessed at 6:00:2001:4ca0:108:42:0:80:6:9, and the access time was fixed at 139 s. This address is from the Technical University of Munich in Germany. Starting from May 3, every other week, 2A06: e881:5101:: 666 accesses port 80 and port 22 of 240C: Cxxx:: 1 for several seconds. We think that the purpose of this traffic is to find the possible gateway hosts and obtain gateway information. This address is from Pascal Mathis trading as snapserv Mathis, Switzerland. In the three days of July 4, 5, and 11, 2019, 240E:F7:C000::23 generated a large number of data packets, and accessed different ports of the address of the experimental network segment. This address is from China Telecom IDC, Wenzhou City, Zhejiang Province, China.

5 Conclusion

In this paper, we present our observations on background traffic of IPv6 Internet. In our experimental environment, we found specific network traffic. Our results show that with the development of the IPv6 network, network communication over IPv6 is very common. TCP protocol accounts for the majority of traffic, while UDP and ICMPv6 traffic are basically generated in real-time. Less than 10% of addresses generate more than 90% of traffic data. From the source of these addresses, we found that these source addresses are mainly from Asian countries such as India, Malaysia, Thailand, Vietnam, and China. Traffic over ICMPv6 are basically echo requests or replies. From the ranking of destination ports, we find that there is a particular interest in the host's web services and common services. Our work demonstrates the current security environment of IPv6 networks. Hosts requiring IPv6 services can make corresponding protective measures based on these conclusions. We will continue our work in order to understand the latest IPv6 network background radiation trends and broader regularities in our experimental environment.

References

1. The Team Cymru Darknet Project. http://www.cymru.com/Darknet/
2. Pang, R., Yegneswaran, V., Barford, P., Paxson, V., Peterson, L.: Characteristics of internet background radiation. In: Proceedings of the 4th ACM SIGCOMM Conference on Internet Measurement, pp. 27–40 (2004)
3. Wustrow, E., Karir, M., Bailey, M., Jahanian, F., Huston, G.: Internet background radiation revisited. In: Proceedings of the 10th ACM SIGCOMM Conference on Internet Measurement, pp. 62–74 (2010)
4. Darknet Incoming Traffic Stats. http://www.cymru.com/Reach/darknet.html
5. Zhang, G., Quoitin, B., Zhou, S.: Phase changes in the evolution of the IPv4 and IPv6 AS-Level Internet topologies. Comput. Commun. 34(5), 649–657 (2011)
6. Ronan, J., Ford, M., Stevens, J.: Initial results from an IPv6 Darknet. (2006)
7. Deccio, C.T.: Turning Down the Lights: Darknet Deployment Lessons Learned. No. SAND2012–3966P. Sandia National Lab. (SNL-CA), Livermore, CA (United States) (2012)
8. Huston, G.: IPv6 Background Radiation. Technical report, Slides of a talk given at DUST 2012–The 1st International Workshop on Darkspace and UnSolicited Traffic Analysis, San Diego, California (2012)

9. Czyz, J., Lady, K., Miller, S. G., Bailey, M., Kallitsis, M., Karir, M.: Understanding IPv6 internet background radiation. In: Proceedings of the 2013 Conference on Internet Measurement Conference, pp. 105–118. (2013)

10. Cooke, E., Bailey, M., Watson, D., Jahanian, F., Nazario, J.: The Internet motion sensor: a distributed global scoped Internet threat monitoring system. Technical Report CSE-TR-491–04 (2004)

11. Yegneswaran, V., Barford, P., Plonka, D.: On the design and use of Internet sinks for network abuse monitoring. In: Jonsson, E., Valdes, A., Almgren, M. (eds.) RAID 2004. LNCS, vol. 3224, pp. 146–165. Springer, Heidelberg (2004). https://doi.org/10.1007/978-3-540-301 43-1_8

12. Bailey, M., Cooke, E., Jahanian, F., Myrick, A., Sinha, S.: Practical darknet measurement. In: 2006 40th Annual Conference on Information Sciences and System, pp. 1496–1501. IEEE (2006)

13. Brownlee, N.: One-way traffic monitoring with iatmon. In: Taft, N., Ricciato, F. (eds.) PAM 2012. LNCS, vol. 7192, pp. 179–188. Springer, Heidelberg (2012). https://doi.org/10.1007/978-3-642-28537-0_18

14. Glatz, E., Dimitropoulos, X.: Classifying internet one-way traffic. In: Proceedings of the 2012 Internet Measurement Conference, pp. 37–50 (2012)

15. Dainotti, A., King, A., Claffy, K., Papale, F., Pescapé, A.: Analysis of a "/0" stealth scan from a botnet. IEEE/ACM Trans. Networking 23(2), 341–354 (2014)

16. King, A.: Syria disappears from the Internet (2012)

17. Aben, E., King, A., Benson, K., Hyun, Y., Dainotti, A., Claffy, K.: Lessons learned by "measuring" the Internet during/after the Sandy storm. In: Proceedings of FCC Workshop on Network Resiliency (2013)

18. Dainotti, A., et al.: Analysis of country-wide internet outages caused by censorship. In: Proceedings of the 2011 ACM SIGCOMM Conference on Internet Measurement Conference, pp. 1–18 (2011)

19. Barford, P., Nowak, R., Willett, R., Yegneswaran, V.: Toward a model for source addresses of internet background radiation. In: Proceedings of the Passive and Active Measurement Conference (2006)

20. Bailey, M., Cooke, E., Jahanian, F., Provos, N., Rosaen, K., Watson, D.: Data reduction for the scalable automated analysis of distributed darknet traffic. In: Proceedings of the 5th ACM SIGCOMM Conference on Internet Measurement, p. 21 (2005)

21. Cooke, E., Bailey, M., Mao, Z. M., Watson, D., Jahanian, F., McPherson, D.: Toward understanding distributed blackhole placement. In: Proceedings of the 2004 ACM Workshop on Rapid Malcode, pp. 54–64 (2004)

22. Moore, D., Shannon, C., Voelker, G., Savage, S.: Network telescopes: technical report. In: Cooperative Association for Internet Data Analysis (CAIDA) (2004)

23. Pandya, S.S.: Active defence system for network security – honeypot. Adv. Comput. Sci. Inf. Technol. (ACSIT) 2(4), 383–386 (2015)

24. Kishimoto, K., Ohira, K., Yamaguchi, Y., Yamaki, H., Takakura, H.: An adaptive honeypot system to capture ipv6 address scans. In: 2012 International Conference on Cyber Security, pp. 165–172. IEEE (2012)

25. Schindler, S., Schnor, B., Kiertscher, S., Scheffler, T., Zack, E.: HoneydV6: A low-interaction IPv6 honeypot. In: 2013 International Conference on Security and Cryptography (SECRYPT), pp. 1–12. IEEE (2013)

26. Schindler, S., Schnor, B., Kiertscher, S., Scheffler, T., Zack, E.: IPv6 network attack detection with HoneydV6. In: Obaidat, M.S., Filipe, J. (eds.) ICETE 2013. CCIS, vol. 456, pp. 252–269. Springer, Heidelberg (2014). https://doi.org/10.1007/978-3-662-44788-8_15

Neural Control Based Research of Endogenous Security Model

Tao Li[1,2], Xu Hu[1(✉)] (iD), and Aiqun Hu[1,2]

[1] School of Cyber Science and Engineering, Southeast University, Nanjing 211189, China
huxu@seu.edu.cn
[2] Purple Mountain Laboratories, Nanjing 211111, China

Abstract. With the development of information technology, the architecture of information system has become increasingly complex, and the performance of terminal equipment has become stronger. The existing centralized defense and passive defense methods will cause problems such as low service efficiency and insufficient defense capabilities in future networks. This paper proposes an endogenous security protection mechanism based on neural control of the human body. The main purpose of this paper is to learn from neural control mechanism, and build an autonomous active defense mechanism, so that the security elements and functional elements of the system can be highly integrated. This paper firstly mapped the human nerve control to the information system through the study of the human nerve control system. Then the nervous system-like control architecture was constructed, and a task-oriented execution architecture was rebuilt. In proposed system, security elements and functional elements are highly integrated into one model. The verification based on the prototype system construction framework shows that this endogenous security model based on neural control can maintain the security of the information system.

Keywords: Endogenous security · Neural control · Information security · System security model · Active defense

1 Introduction

With the development of information systems in the direction of huge traffic and rich text, the shortcomings to protect the security of information systems through the deployment of firewalls, antivirus software, intrusion detection systems and other methods for network routers and terminal increasingly apparent. In order to solve the above problems, the defense method must be changed from passive to active method.

For building a credible relatively controlled environment by using the security system in conditions of limited trust, Feng Deng Guo [1] designed a defense mechanism from malicious code attacks on architecture. This framework can promptly identify the "self" and "non-self" component. In order to build a dynamic chain of trust, Zheng Yan [2, 3] proposed a method which can maintain the credibility of application operation through real-time evaluation and dynamic management. Shen Chang Xiang [4] designed a trusted

© Springer Nature Switzerland AG 2021
X. Sun et al. (Eds.): ICAIS 2021, LNCS 12737, pp. 242–252, 2021.
https://doi.org/10.1007/978-3-030-78612-0_20

immune architecture through the principle of active immunity. However, dynamic trust management and trust immunity are both trust mechanisms proposed for the system operation process. Consequently, there is still a lack of application support during the process of implementation.

Intelligent security uses artificial intelligence to analyze threats and has the advantage of discovering unknown threats. Buczak [5] discussed the challenges of using machine learning and data mining for network security. Hanzhong Zheng [6] used boolean networks and reinforcement learning for monitoring. However, artificial intelligence did not build an active defense architecture from the foundation.

Automatic computing was first proposed by IBM to build a system with self-awareness, self-optimization, self-repair, and self-defense [7, 8]. At present, the idea of automatic computing is only applied in cloud computing [9] and In the Internet of Things [10]. It is mainly used to optimize and dynamically adapt computing resources, and does not own effective active defense capabilities.

Computer immunology applies the human immune architecture to computer systems, and proposes a security architecture inspired by immunity, including distributed multi-agent detectors similar to antigens and antibodies, as well as detector generation and distribution mechanisms [11–15]. However, the constructed immune defense mechanism lacks the support of the application environment because of the limitations of the existing architecture of the information system.

In order to closely integrate the various parts of information system and highly integrate security and system native functions, we start with the overall architecture, fully analyze and learn from the principles of the human neural control system, and propose a new endogenous security architecture. Then we rebuild the information system architecture based on a task-oriented mechanism, and incorporated security elements into functional modules. Finally, the prototype system is verified through experiments.

2   Neural Control Mechanism of Human Being

In the defense process of human being, human body not only effectively avoids threats, but also avoids affecting normal daily life. At the same time, it can also continuously adjust and improve the ability to respond to threats. When encountering unknown threats, the human body will gradually acquire the ability to guard against such threats through self-learning. It's a kind of "endogenous" security mechanism, which is highly similar to the information system security defense in terms of system goals, structure and the working mode.

The control system of human being mainly includes two parts: the control unit and the controlled object [16], from the perspective of the composition of the neural control system. The control unit is mainly composed of a controller, a sensor and an effect/actuator. The core is the controller. The controlled object is a living body or its different physiological and metabolic processes.

The nervous system is mainly controlled and adjusted by the internal feedback [16]. As shown in Fig. 1, the controller firstly receives the information sensed by the "Sensory Receptor", then the controller outputs the information to the effector, so that the controlled object to make a reaction. The actual status of its implementation will also be reported to the controller through the feedback device, and the controller will perform comparative analysis and judgment processing on the transmitted information. Then, the effector is instructed to take further adjustment measures to give a correct response to the external interference according to the deviation between the actual effect and the expected target. This is a process of negative feedback control adjustment.

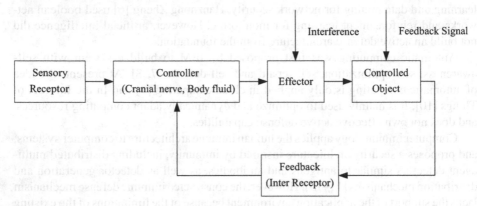

Fig. 1. Principles of neurofeedback control

Based on the above research, the main elements of the realization of the human nerve control system are:

- There are a large number of security neurons all over the system. Additional neurons are highly integrated with functional organs.
- After clarifying a specific task, a series of basic actions are used as the elements to spontaneously combine actions to perform the task.
- It has a feedback system that provides real-time feedback on performance of the task, responds through system linkage, and calibrates deviation actions to ensure that tasks are completed as expected.
- A comprehensive analysis of processing centers of the brain. Analysis and decision-making, with their own ability to learn.

3   Control Architecture Like Nervous System

Through the imitation of the human being's neural control system, a task-oriented fine-grained monitoring mechanism of implementation actions can be constructed in the information system.

The control process is divided into two parts: static analysis and dynamic defense. The former is the basis of control, which can analyze the normal implementation features of tasks and generate behavior libraries.

The process of dynamic defense is shown as Fig. 2. After the analysis is completed, the dynamic defense stage is reached. The system senses actions through a large number of security neurons and compares them with the behavior library to feedback the effect. If a deviation is found after the comparison, calibration is performed, and the upper layer generates and issues a calibration strategy. The calibration strategy is issued based on the existing calibration library.

If there is an implementation deviation caused by an unknown attack, the machine learning algorithm will formulate an optimal strategy based on the monitoring parameters and system expectations, and continuously optimize the strategy based on the effect of the calibration to realize the function of autonomous evolution.

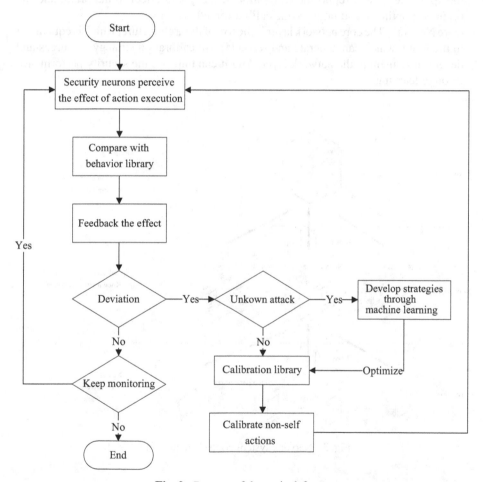

Fig. 2. Process of dynamic defense

Based on the above control process, an endogenous security system architecture that connects the terminal, network, and core network layer of the information system is constructed, as shown in Fig. 3. The function of each layer is described as follows:

- Terminal. The terminal is mainly responsible for perception, feedback and calibration. Security neurons throughout the terminal devices sense and control the activities of each terminal system. During the implementation process, various operating parameters are sensed and fed back to the spinal nerves. If there is a deviation, the terminal neuron will command the effector to calibrate according to the calibration strategy, such as: replacing the module, reducing the load.
- Network Layer. The network layer contains terminal nodes that have interaction requirements at a higher level. The spinal nerve is mainly responsible for receiving implementation information from the terminal neuron. If there is a deviation, spinal nerve will find out whether there is a corresponding calibration strategy, and the spinal nerve will report the calibration strategy and effect to the brain, and the brain will optimize and improve the calibration efficiency.
- Core Network. The core network layer is the top of the architecture, which is equivalent to the brain, which can generate and self-adaptive calibration strategy resources and decentralize them to the network layer. And it can improve the security performance through learning.

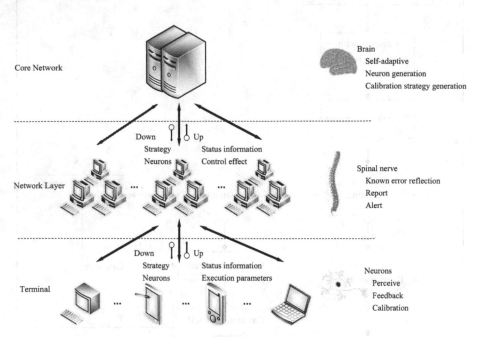

Fig. 3. Nervous system control architecture

4   Rebuild the System Architecture

An important feature of human nerve control is task-oriented. To imitate this principle of autonomous neural control, an information system with endogenous security attributes also needs to clarify the tasks to be performed, divide functional modules, and call functional modules to perform operations based on task implementation conditions.

The system can perceive the path of implementation, find errors through feedback, and calibrate according to the strategy. In order to achieve the above operations, the information system architecture should be rebuilt.

As shown in Fig. 4, in the process of designing the system, each basic function module corresponds to a basic action. In addition, the execution effect of the module is reflected by the output of the action.

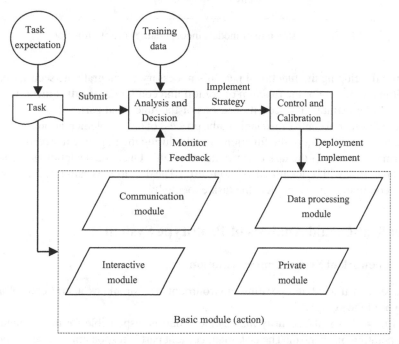

Fig. 4. Task-oriented execution architecture

When a task is submitted, the system analyzes it to determine the modules and execution order required to complete the task. Subsequently, the basic structure of the module is constructed, and the security part is integrated into the functional module. Then it will realize perception and calibration like neurons, thus completing monitoring and adjustment functions. Finally the system feeds back to the upper layer in real time and calibrates the execution deviation.

In order to construct the above neural control mechanism, as shown in Fig. 5, we incorporate the security part into the divided functional modules to achieve the function of perception and calibration similar to neurons.

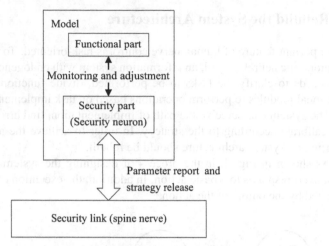

Fig. 5. Basic structure of models incorporating security functions

While developing the functional part, it's necessary to integrate the security part to realize the monitoring of the function operation and configuration adjustment, which is equivalent to integrating the security neurons of the functional part.

Under this neural control mechanism, the process of task implementation is identified by monitoring the output of the function module during the implementation of the task. The normal situation of the task corresponds to "self". Once the deviation is found, the execution of task will be identified as "non-self". The deviation is calibrated through the strategy configuration to complete the task expectedly.

5　Realization and Analysis of Prototype System

5.1　Framework of System Implementation

This paper constructed an operating environment that simulates neural control at the core layer of the system.

As Fig. 6 shows, the security management part is responsible for the management of the operating mechanism. The task management part is responsible for decomposing the tasks of the system and selecting modules and parameter settings according to the expectations of the task. The operation monitoring part perceives the operation process of the module, and then reconfigures the strategy according to the feedback parameters. In addition, the resource management part conducts unified management of the underlying resources of the system, and the connections with the upper layer for security communication.

This article used Erlang language to write a module to rewrite a communication application that encrypts and transmits data in Linux (Ubuntu 16.04). The modularity of Erlang language and the feature of supporting hot update can make the module be adjusted in real time. Two modules were implemented in the application: communication module and the encryption-decryption module.

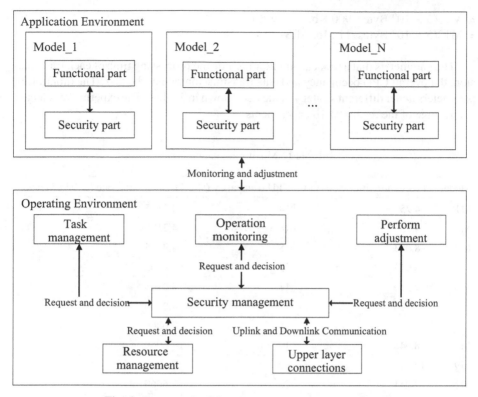

Fig. 6. Framework of the prototype system construction

5.2 Experiment and Analysis

The task used the communication module and the encryption module to complete data encryption and transmission. Configurable options included block size, transmission bandwidth and encryption form of data. The block size of data in each transmission can be set to 1×10^6 Bytes or 5×10^6 Bytes. The transmission bandwidth can be set to 900 Kb or 11 Mb. In addition, the encryption module can be set to no encryption, AES-128 encryption or AES-256 encryption.

There were 12 modes that constructed based on configurable parameters:

- M1 (1×10^6 Bytes, 900 Kb, no encryption)
- M2 (1×10^6 Bytes, 11 Mb, no encryption)
- M3 (1×10^6 Bytes, 900 Kb, AES-128)
- M4 (1×10^6 Bytes, 11 Mb, AES-128)
- M5 (1×10^6 Bytes, 900 Kb, AES-256)
- M6 (1×10^6 Bytes, 11 Mb, AES-256)
- M7 (5×10^6 Bytes, 900Kb, no encryption)
- M8 (5×10^6 Bytes, 11Mb, no encryption)
- M9 (5×10^6 Bytes, 900 Kb, AES-128)
- M10(5×10^6 Bytes, 11 Mb, AES-128)

- M11(5 × 10^6 Bytes, 900 Kb, AES-256)
- M12(5 × 10^6 Bytes, 11 Mb, AES-256)

The parameters that a task can monitor include the processing time of each transmission, the overall CPU occupancy and data transmission rate of the task. The monitoring parameters under different strategy modes are shown in Table 1. The experiment selected the average of the results of 10 experiments.

Table 1. Monitoring parameters

Model	Processing time ($*10^{-1}$s)	CPU occupancy (%)	transmission rate ($*10^6$ Bytes/s)
M1	4.75	4	4.2105
M2	4.75	18	4.2105
M3	8.013	8	4.2105
M4	8.013	22	4.2105
M5	12.226	11	4.2105
M6	12.226	25	4.2105
M7	8.948	5	7.6069
M8	8.948	19	7.6069
M9	12.211	9	7.6069
M10	12.211	23	7.6069
M11	16.424	12	7.6069
M12	16.424	26	7.6069

Table 1 is revealing in several ways. Firstly, with the increase of block size, the processing time increased apparently, the increase of CPU occupancy was not obvious, but the data transmission rate increased significantly. Secondly, since the transmission rates of the two data blocks set were lower than the two bandwidths set, the increase in bandwidth did not bring about the improvement of the transmission effect, but increased the CPU occupancy. Finally, the increase of encryption strength resulted in raising the processing time and CPU occupancy of task, which was the cost of implementing high security.

According to the above analysis, the communication task module has completed the integration of the security part and the function part. It can perform neuron-like monitoring and adjustment.

6 Conclusion

In view of the fact that the existing "SHELL" defense system cannot cope with the security challenges brought by the huge traffic and rich applications of information systems, this paper studies and summarizes the basic principles of the human neural control system, and proposes an endogenous security model based on the neural control mechanism.

This paper introduces elements of neurons, spinal nerves, and human brains into the information system network. The security system and system functions are highly integrated. On the basis of modularization based on the basic functional elements of the system, task-oriented fine-grained security control is carried out. Analysis of the constructed model shows that the control mechanism proposed in this paper can maintain the security of the system under the conditions of action output verification, result isolation properties and observation equivalence. Through the verification of the prototype system, the basic module proposed in this paper can complete the role of neuron-like. The endogenous security model proposed in this paper is a new active security framework. In the follow-up research work, researchers can build more modules and more complex tasks for the system implementation, so as to observe the effects of tasks and face complex attacks.

Further, researchers need to combine and adjust basic functional modules, introduce artificial intelligence methods to improve the functions of autonomous judgment and strategy configuration, and realize configuration and optimization by using adaptive security strategy.

Acknowledgments. This research was supported by Zhishan Youth Scholar Program Of SEU, Purple Mountain Laboratories for Network and Communication Security, National Science Foundation (No. 61601113).

References

1. Feng, D.G., Qin, Y., Wang, D., Chu, X.B.: Research on trusted computing technology. J. Comput. Res. Dev. **48**(8), 1332–1349 (2011). (in Chinese)
2. Yan, Z., Govindaraju, V., Zheng, Q., Wang, Y.: IEEE access special section editorial: trusted computing. IEEE Access. **8**, 25722–25726 (2020). https://doi.org/10.1109/ACCESS.2020. 2969768
3. Wu, Y., Yan, Z., Choo, K.R., Yang, L.T.: IEEE access special section editorial: Internet-of-Things big data trust management. IEEE Access. **7**, 65223–65227 (2019). https://doi.org/10. 1109/ACCESS.2019.2915489
4. Hu, J., Shen, C.X., Gong, B.: Trusted Computing 3.0 Engineering Fundamentals. Posts and Telecom Press, Beijing (2017). (in Chinese)
5. Buczak, A.L., Guven, E.: A survey of data mining and machine learning methods for cyber security intrusion detection. IEEE Commun. Surv. Tutor. **18**(2), 1153–1176 (2016). https:// doi.org/10.1109/COMST.2015.2494502
6. Zheng, H., Shi, D.: A multi-agent system for environmental monitoring using boolean networks and reinforcement learning. J. Cyber Secur. **2**(2), 85–96 (2020). https://www.techsc ience.com/JCS/v2n2/39508
7. Horn, P.: Autonomic Computing: IBM's Perspective on the State of Information Technology. International Business Machines Corporation, New York (2001)
8. Kapoor, V.: Services and autonomic computing a practical approach for designing manageability. In: 2005 IEEE International Conference on Services Computing (SCC 2005), Orlando, FL, USA, vol. 1, pp. 41–48. IEEE (2005). https://doi.org/10.1109/SCC.2005.88

9. Coutinho, E.F., Gomes, D.G., de Souza, J.N.: An Autonomic Computing-based architecture for cloud computing elasticity. In: 2015 Latin American Network Operations and Management Symposium (LANOMS), Joao Pessoa, Brazil, pp. 111–112. IEEE (2015). https://doi.org/10.1109/LANOMS.2015.7332681

10. Tahir, M., Mamoon Ashraf, Q., Dabbagh, M.: Towards enabling autonomic computing in IoT ecosystem. In Proceedings of the 2019 IEEE International Conference on Dependable, Autonomic and Secure Computing, Intl Conf on Pervasive Intelligence and Computing, International Conference on Cloud and Big Data Computing, International Conference on Cyber Science and Technology Congress (DASC/PiCom/CBDCom/CyberSciTech), Fukuoka, Japan, pp. 646–651. IEEE (2019). https://doi.org/10.1109/DASC/PiCom/CBDCom/CyberSciTech.2019.00122

11. Mohamed, Y.A., Abdullah, A.B.: Immune inspired framework for ad hoc network security. In: Proceedings of the 2009 IEEE International Conference on Control and Automation, Christchurch, New Zealand, pp. 297–302. IEEE (2009). https://doi.org/10.1109/ICCA.2009.5410147

12. Li, T.: Dynamic detection for computer virus based on immune system. Sci. China Ser. F: Inf. Sci. **51**(10), 1475–1486 (2008)

13. Hou, C.Z., Zhang, Y.J.: Biologically inspired immunity based on multi-agent: a new idea of research on computer anti-virus measures. J. Beijing Inst. Technol. **22**(3), 270–274 (2002). (in Chinese)

14. Li, T.: An immune based dynamic intrusion detection model. Sci. Bull. **50**(17), 1912–1919 (2005). (in Chinese)

15. Song, J., Meng, Q., Luo, C., Naik, N., Xu, J.: An immunization scheme for ransomware. Comput. Mat. Continua **64**(2), 1051–1061 (2020). https://www.techscience.com/cmc/v64n2/39345

16. Nicholls, J.G., Martin, A.R., Fuchs, P.A., Brown, D.A., Diamond, M.E., et al.: From neuron to brain. Sinauer Associates, Cary, NC, USA (2012)

Keyword Guessing Attacks on Some Proxy Re-Encryption with Keyword Search Schemes

Xuanang Yu, Yang Lu$^{(\boxtimes)}$, Jinmei Tian, and Fen Wang

School of Computer and Electronic Information,
Nanjing Normal University, Nanjing 210046, China

Abstract. Public key encryption with keyword search (PEKS) is a practical cryptographic paradigm that enables one to search for the encrypted data without compromising the security of the original data. It provides a promising solution to the encrypted data retrieval issue in public key cryptosystems. As a combination of PEKS and proxy re-encryption (PRE), proxy re-encryption with keyword search (PRES) allows a semi-trusted proxy to simultaneously re-encrypt and search a delegator's encrypted data. So far, several PRES schemes have been proposed in the literature. However, most of these schemes did not consider the keyword guessing attack. In this paper, we analyze the security of some PRES schemes and demonstrate that they are vulnerable to the keyword guessing attack. The presented attacks show that a malicious proxy can reveal the keyword encoded in any keyword trapdoor generated by these PRES schemes.

Keywords: Public key encryption · Keyword search · Proxy Re-Encryption · Keyword guessing attack · Malicious proxy

1 Introduction

In recent years, cloud computing has gained increasing attention because it provides a more convenient and cost-efficient solution for users to manage the data [1]. By migrating the local data to the cloud in large numbers, the users can reduce the heavy task of local data management and access the data anywhere through an authorized Internet-connected device [2–4]. As a service platform with strong computing power, cloud computing technology provides an economical, flexible and convenient solution for the growing storage and computing needs of enterprises and individuals. However, with the popularization of Internet and cloud computing, more and more information leakage events also make information security issue widely concerned.

Traditional data encryption technology effectively guarantees the confidentiality of user data, but it also creates new problems. It is hard for a server to selectively retrieve the encrypted data in the cloud storage system when a user needs to search for the data containing some specified keywords. In order to solve the problem, searchable encryption (SE) was introduced by Song *et al.* [5]. With SE, a user is able to authorize an untrusted server to test whether the encrypted data sent to him/her contain some specified keywords without leaking the privacy of the data contents and the search queries. Because SE

© Springer Nature Switzerland AG 2021
X. Sun et al. (Eds.): ICAIS 2021, LNCS 12737, pp. 253–264, 2021.
https://doi.org/10.1007/978-3-030-78612-0_21

provides a promising solution for the encrypted data retrieval, it is widely concerned by cryptographers since its introduction. SE can be broadly categorized into searchable symmetric encryption (SSE) and searchable public key encryption (SPKE). SSE [6–11] has the merit of high execution efficiency, but its application is limited because it suffers from the key management and distribution problems. To address the problem of searching on data that is encrypted using a public key cryptosystem, Boneh *et al.* [12] proposed the notion of public key encryption with keyword search (PEKS) in 2004. Following Boneh *et al.*'s pioneering work, Baek *et al.* [13] proposed the framework of secure channel free PEKS (SCF-PEKS) to eliminate the requirement of a secure channel for sending the keyword trapdoor in PEKS. In SCF-PEKS, a storage server is designated as a tester. Therefore, this framework is also called PEKS with a designated server (dPEKS) [14]. So far, a lot of PEKS and dPEKS schemes have been presented in the literature, e.g. [15–23].

Proxy re-encryption (PRE), introduced by Blaze *et al.* in Eurocrypt'98 [24], offers us an effective solution to share encrypted data. The main goal of PRE is to solve the problem of secure delegation for the decryption right from a delegator to a delegate. In a PRE system, a semi-trusted third party called proxy is employed by the delegator so that it can convert a ciphertext encrypted under the delegator's public key into a new ciphertext of the same message encrypted under the delegate's public key without decrypting the ciphertext. In [25], Shao *et al.* proposed the notion of proxy re-encryption with keyword search (PRES) which is a combination of PEKS and PRE. This primitive allows a semi-trusted proxy to simultaneously re-encrypt and search a delegator's encrypted data. Since its introduction, PRES has attracted great attention from the research community and many PRES schemes have been proposed in the literature, *e.g.* [26–35].

In [36], Byun *et al.* first presented the keyword guessing attack in the context of PEKS. The keyword guessing attack exploits the low-entropy property of the commonly-used keywords. By performing this attack, an attacker (an outside attacker or a malicious storage server) may correctly guess the keyword encoded in a keyword trapdoor and even the keyword encrypted in a keyword ciphertext in an offline/online manner. In practice, users often choose some keywords from a small keyword space (such as an English dictionary) to generate the searchable encrypted data and the keyword trapdoor. The keyword guessing attack has become the most devastating attack on the SPKE schemes, since it leads to the leakage of the information pertaining to the encrypted data. Till now, many PEKS and dPEKS schemes have been shown to be insecure under the keyword guessing attack [37–42].

In this paper, we analyze the security of some PRES schemes. Most of the previous constructions of PRES did not consider the keyword guessing attack. Our cryptanalysis demonstrates that the PRES schemes proposed in [25, 33–35] are insecure under the keyword guessing attack. The presented attacks show that an attacker (an outside attacker or a malicious server) is able to execute the keyword guessing attack to successfully expose the keyword encoded in any keyword trapdoor generated by these PRES schemes.

Paper Organization: In Sect. 2, we briefly review some notations and the definition of bilinear pairing. In Sect. 3–6, we overview four existing PRES schemes and execute the keyword guessing attacks on them, respectively. Finally, we conclude our paper in Sect. 7.

2 Notations and Bilinear Pairing

Throughout the paper, k denotes a security parameter, q denotes a big prime number (G_1, G_2) are two cyclic group of same order q, g is a random generator of the group G_1 and Z_q^* is a set $\{1, 2, \cdots, q-1\}$.

A bilinear pairing is a map $e\colon G_1 \times G_1 \to G_2$ that satisfies the following three attributes:

- Bilinearity: $e(g^x, g^y) = e(g, g)^{xy}$ for all $x, y \in Z_q^*$.
- Non-degeneracy: $e(g, g) \neq 1$.
- Computability: There is an efficient algorithm to compute $e(g^x, g^y)$ for all $x, y \in Z_q^*$.

3 Keyword Guessing Attack on Shao *et al.*'s PRES Scheme

In this section, we present an offline keyword guessing attack on the first PRES scheme proposed by Shao et al. [25].

3.1 Review of Shao *et al.*'s PRES Scheme

Shao *et al.* PRES scheme consists of the following algorithms:

- **Setup**: Assume that h is a random number in the group G_1, $sig = (G, S, V)$ is a strongly unforgeable one-time signature scheme. Furthermore, $H_1\colon \{0, 1\}^* \to G_1, H_2\colon \{0, 1\}^{\leq l} \to G_1, H_3\colon \{0, 1\}^{\leq l} \to G_1$ and $H_4\colon G_2 \to \{0, 1\}^k$ are four hash functions, where l is the length of the verification keys output by $G(1^k)$. This algorithm outputs the global parameters $gp = \{q, G_1, G_2, e, g, h, sig, H_1, H_2, H_3, H_4\}$.
- **KeyGen**: On input gp, this algorithm selects $x \in Z_q^*$ randomly and outputs a public key $pk = g^x$ and a secret key $sk = x$.
- **Trapdoor**: On input a user's secret key sk and a keyword w, this algorithm outputs a trapdoor $T_w = H_1(w)^{1/sk}$ of the keyword w corresponding to the public key $pk = g^{sk}$.
- **ReKeyGen**: On input user i and user j's secret keys (sk_i, sk_j), this algorithm produces a bidirectional re-encryption key $rk_{i \to j} = sk_j/sk_i$ in the following way:

  • User i selects a random $r \in Z_q^*$ and sends $(sk_i \cdot r \bmod q)$ to user j and r to the proxy.
  • User j sends $(sk_j \, r/sk_i \bmod q)$ to the proxy.
  • The proxy computes $(sk_j/sk_i \bmod q)$.

- **Enc**: On input a user's public key pk, a keyword w and a message $m \in G_2$, this algorithm does the following:

  • Select a one-time signature key pair as $G(1^k) \to (svk, ssk)$. Set $A = svk$.
  • Select a random $r \in Z_q^*$ and computes $B = pk^r, C = e(g, H_2(A))^r \cdot m, D = H_3(A)^r$, $E = h^r, t = e(g, H_1(w))^r$ and $F = H_4(t)$.
  • Run the signing algorithm $S(ssk \, (C, D, E, F))$ to produce a signature σ, where the message to sign is the tuple (C, D, E, F).

- Output the ciphertext $(A, B, C, D, E, F, \sigma)$.

- **ReEnc**: On input a re-encryption key $rk_{i \to j} = sk_j/sk_i$ and a ciphertext $(A, B, C, D, E, F, \sigma)$ under the public key $pk_i = (g^{sk_i})$, this algorithm re-encrypts the ciphertext to be a new ciphertext under the public key $pk_j = (g^{sk_j})$ as follows:

- Run the signature verification algorithm $V(A\,(C, D, E, F), \sigma)$ to verify signature σ on message (C, D, E, F) with respect to the verification key A.
- Check that $e(B, H_3(A)) = e(pk, D)$ and $e(B, h) = e(pk, E)$.
- If the above checks pass, compute $B' = B^{rk_{i \to j}} = (g^{sk_i \cdot r})^{sk_j/sk_i} = g^{sk_j \cdot r} = (pk_j)^r$, output the new ciphertext $(A, B', C, D, E, F, \sigma)$; else, output 0.

- **Test**: On input a user's public key $pk = g^{sk}$, a trapdoor $T_w = H_1(w)^{1/sk}$ and a ciphertext $(A, B, C, D, E, F, \sigma)$, this algorithm checks if $F = H_4(e(B, T_w))$. If it does, output "yes"; otherwise, output "no".
- **Dec**: On input a user's secret key sk and a ciphertext $(A, B, C, D, E, F, \sigma)$, this algorithm outputs a message $C/e(B, H_2(A))^{1/sk}$ if the ciphertext passes the check procedure or $\perp$ otherwise.

3.2 Keyword Guessing Attack on Shao *et al.*'s PRES Scheme

An attacker can perform an offline keyword guessing attack on Shao *et al.*'s scheme through the following steps:

- **Step 1**: It selects any user as a target and then captures a valid trapdoor $T_w = H_1(w)^{1/sk}$ from this user.
- **Step 2**: It guesses an appropriate keyword w' and computes $H_1(w')$.
- **Step 3**: It takes the user's public key pk and the hash of the guessed keyword $H_1(w')$, and checks if $e(T_w, pk) = e(H_1(w'), g)$ holds. It is easy to deduce that $e(T_w, pk) = e(H_1(w)^{1/sk}, pk) = e(H_1(w), g)$. Therefore, if $w = w'$, then the attacker's guess is correct.
- **Step 4**: If the equation holds, then w' is a correct guess and the attacker succeeds. Otherwise, it goes to Step 2 and continues its guessing.

The above attack can be performed by either an outside attacker or a malicious server. Although the attack by the outside attacker can be avoided if the keyword trapdoors are sent via secure channel. But, the scheme is still vulnerable to the malicious server. What's worse, after correctly guessing a keyword, the malicious server can further determine which encrypted data contains the keyword by running the test algorithm. Therefore, Shao *et al.*'s scheme fails in protecting the privacy of both the user's data and the search queries.

4 Keyword Guessing Attack on Fang *et al.*'s PRES Scheme

In this section, we present an offline keyword guessing attack on Fang *et al.*'s PRES scheme [33].

4.1 Review of Fang *et al.*'s PRES Scheme

Fang *et al.* PRES scheme consists of the following algorithms:

- **Global Setup**: Let $sig = (G, S, V)$ be a strongly unforgeable one-time signature scheme. Let the message space be $M = \{0, 1\}^k$ and the condition space be $W = Z_q^*$. Let $H_1: \{0, 1\}^* \to Z_q^*$, $H_2: G_2 \to \{0, 1\}^k$, $H_3: \{0, 1\}^* \to Z_q^*$, $H_4: \{0, 1\}^* \to Z_q^*$ be hash functions. This algorithm outputs the global parameters $gp = (q, g, G_1, G_2, e, k, H_1, H_2, H_3, H_4, sig)$.
- **KeyGen**: On input gp, this algorithm selects $x_i, y_{i,1}, y_{i,2}, y_{i,3}, y_{i,4} \in Z_q^*$ randomly, computes $X_i = g^{x_i}$, $Y_{i,1} = g^{y_{i,1}}$, $Y_{i,2} = g^{y_{i,2}}$, $Y_{i,3} = g^{y_{i,3}}$ and $Y_{i,4} = g^{y_{i,4}}$, sets user i's public key as $pk_i = (X_i, Y_{i,1}, Y_{i,2}, Y_{i,3}, Y_{i,4})$ and the secret key $sk_i = (x_i, y_{i,1}, y_{i,2}, y_{i,3}, y_{i,4})$.
- **RKeyGen**: On input user i's pubic key pk_i and secret key $sk_i = (x_i, y_{i,1}, y_{i,2}, y_{i,3}, y_{i,4})$, a condition w, and user j's public key $pk_j = (X_j, Y_{j,1}, Y_{j,2}, Y_{j,3}, Y_{j,4})$, this algorithm selects $s_1, s_2 \in Z_q^*$ randomly, computes $d_k = (Y_{j,k} Y_{i,k}^{-1} g^{-S_k})^{1/(x_i - w)}$ and sets the re-encryption key $rk_{i \to j} = (d_k, s_k)_{k \in \{1,2\}}$.
- **Trapdoor**: On input user i's pubic key pk_i and private key sk_i and a condition w, this algorithm selects $s_3, s_4 \in Z_q^*$ randomly, computes $d_k = (Y_{i,k} g^{-s_k})^{1/(x_i - w)}$ and set the trapdoor $T_{i,w} = (d_k, s_k)_{k \in \{3,4\}}$.
- **Enc1**: On input user i's pubic key pk_i and a message $m \in M$, this algorithm picks $R \in G_2$ and $svk \in \{0, 1\}^{k_1}$ randomly, sets $C_0 = svk$ and $r = H_1(m, R)$, computes $C_2 = e(g, g)^r$, $C_4 = m \oplus H_2(R)$, $\varphi' = H_0(C_0, C_2, C_4)$ and $C_3 = e(g, Y_{i,1})^{r\varphi'} e(g, Y_{i,2})^r R$, outputs the first level ciphertext $CT_i = (C_0, C_2, C_3, C_4)$.
- **Enc2**: On input a user's public key pk_i, a keyword w and a message $m \in M$, this algorithm does the following:

- Select a one-time signature key pair $(ssk, svk) \leftarrow G(k)$ and set $C_0 = svk$.
- Pick $R \in G_2$, compute $C_1 = (X_i \cdot g^{-w})^r$, $C_2 = e(g, g)^r$, $C_3 = e(g, Y_{i,1})^{r\varphi'} e(g, Y_{i,2})^r R$, $C_4 = m \oplus H_2(R)$ and $C_5 = e(g, Y_{i,3})^{r\varphi'} e(g, Y_{i,4})^r$, where $r = H_1(m, R)$, $\varphi' = H_0(C_0, C_2, C_4)$ and $\varphi = H_3(C_0, C_1, C_2, C_3, C_4)$.
- Generate a one-time signature $\sigma = S(ssk\ (C_1, C_2, C_3, C_4, C_5))$ on the pair $(C_1, C_2, C_3, C_4, C_5)$.
- Output the second level ciphertext $CT_i = (C_0, C_1, C_2, C_3, C_4, C_5, \sigma)$.

- **Test**: On input a trapdoor $T_{i,w} = (d_k, s_k)_{k \in \{3,4\}}$ and a second level ciphertext $CT_i = (C_0, C_1, C_2, C_3, C_4, C_5, \sigma)$, this algorithm does the following:

- Compute $\varphi = H_3(C_0, C_1, C_2, C_3, C_4)$.
- Test if $V(C_0, \sigma\ (C_1, C_2, C_3, C_4, C_5)) = 1$, $C_5 = e(C_1, d_3^\varphi d_4) C_2^{s_3\varphi + s_4}$.
- If one of the checks fails, outputs "0", otherwise it outputs "1".

- **ReEnc**: On input a re-encryption key $rk_{i \to j} = (d_k, s_k)_{k \in \{1,2\}}$ and a second level ciphertext $CT_i = (C_0, C_1, C_2, C_3, C_4, C_5, \sigma)$, this algorithm tests if $V(C_0, \sigma\ (C_1, C_2, C_3, C_4, C_5)) = 1$. If so, it re-encrypts CT_i by computing $C_3' = e(C_1, d_1^{\varphi'} d_2) C_2^{s_1\varphi' + s_2} \cdot C_3$ where $\varphi' = H_0(C_0, C_2, C_4)$. The re-encrypted ciphertext is $CT_j = (C_0, C_2, C_3', C_4)$.

– **Dec1**: On input a secret key sk_j and a first level ciphertext (re-encrypted ciphertext) $CT_j = (C_0, C_2, C_3, C_4)$, this algorithm does the following:

- Compute $\varphi' = H_0(C_0, C_2, C_4)$ and $R = C_3/(C_2)^{y_{j,1}\varphi'+y_{j,2}}$, $m = C_4 \oplus H_2(R)$, $r = H_1(m, R)$.
- Check whether $C_2 = e(g, g)^r$ holds, if yes, it returns m; else it returns $\perp$.

– **Dec2**: On input a secret key sk_i and a second level ciphertext (re-encrypted ciphertext) $CT_i = (C_0, C_1, C_2, C_3, C_4, C_5)$, this algorithm does the following:

- Computes $\varphi = H_3(C_0, C_1, C_2, C_3, C_4)$, $\varphi' = H_0(C_0, C_2, C_4)$
- Test if $V(C_0, \sigma\ (C_1, C_2, C_3, C_4, C_5)) = 1$, $C_5 = (C_2)^{y_{i,3}\varphi+y_{i,4}}$, if one of the checks fails, outputs $\perp$.
- Otherwise, compute $R = C_3/(C_2)^{y_{i,1}\varphi'+y_{i,2}}$, $m = C_4 \oplus H_2(R)$, $r = H_1(m, R)$ and check whether $C_2 = e(g, g)^r$ holds. If yes, it returns m; else it returns $\perp$.

4.2 Keyword Guessing Attack on Fang et al.'s PRES Scheme

An attacker can perform an offline keyword guessing attack on Fang *et al.*'s PRES scheme through the following steps:

– **Step 1**: The attacker receives a valid trapdoor $T_{i,w}$ from any receiver R.
– **Step 2**: The attacker guesses a candidate keyword w' and tests whether the equality $e(X_i g^{-w'}, d_k) = e(g, Y_{i,k}g^{-s_k})$ holds. It is easy to deduce that $e(X_i g^{-w}, d_k) = e(g^{x_i} \cdot g^{-w}, Y_{i,k}g^{-s_k}) = e(g, Y_{i,k}g^{-s_k})$. Therefore, if $w = w'$, then the attacker's guess is correct.
– **Step 3**: If the equality holds, then w' is a correct keyword and the attacker succeeds. Otherwise, it repeats Step 2 and continues its guessing.

Clearly, a malicious server can perform the above attack to reveal the keyword in any keyword trapdoor. In addition, the malicious server can proceed to run the Test algorithm to find out which ciphertext contains the keyword. Therefore, Fang *et al.*'s PRES scheme is insecure under the keyword guessing attack.

5 Keyword Guessing Attack on Chen *et al.*'s PRES Scheme

In this section, we show that the PRES scheme proposed by Chen *et al.* [34] is insecure under the offline keyword guessing attack.

5.1 Review of Chen *et al.*'s PRES Scheme

Chen *et al.* PRES scheme consists of the following algorithms:

- **Setup**: Choose a random generator $g \in G_1$ and compute $Z = e(g, g)$. Select two hash functions $H_1: \{0, 1\}^* \rightarrow G_1$ and $H_2 : G_2 \rightarrow \{0, 1\}^{\log_2 q}$. The public parameters are $gp = (q, G_1, G_2, e, g, Z, H_1, H_2)$.
- **KeyGen**: On input gp, for user i and user j, the key pairs are of the form $(sk_i = a,\ pk_i = g^a)$ and $(sk_j = b,\ pk_j = g^b)$, respectively, where a and b are chosen from Z_q^* randomly.
- **ReKeyGen**: On input user i and user j's secret keys $(sk_i = a,\ sk_j = b)$, this algorithm produces a re-encryption key $rk_{i \rightarrow j} = b/a\ (mod\ q)$.
- **Publish**: For proxy P, the key pair is of the form $(sk_p = p,\ pk_p = g^p)$, where p is chosen from Z_q^* randomly. Proxy P randomly and uniformly chooses n values $a_1, \ldots, a_n$ from Z_q^* and constructs a polynomial $f(x) = p + a_1 x + a_2 x^2 + \ldots + a_n x^n (mod\ q)$ of degree n. Later, it publishes $params = (g^{a_1}, \ldots, g^{a_n})$.
- **Verify**: This algorithm does the following:

- User i chooses a random number $u \in Z_q^*$ and sends it to proxy P.
- Proxy P evaluates $f(x)$ at u and sends $f(u)$ to user i.
- User i checks whether $g^{f(u)} = g^p g^{a_1 u} \ldots g^{a_n u^n}$. If it holds, that means proxy P has faithfully committed to n.

- **Enc**: On input $m \in G_2$ and keyword $w \in \{0, 1\}^*$, user i randomly chooses $k \in Z_q^*$ and computes $C_1 = mZ^k$, $C_2 = (g^a)^k$, $t = e(H_1(w), g)^k$ and outputs the ciphertext $C_i = (C_1, C_2, t, H_2(t))$.
- **ReEnc**: On input the ciphertext $C_i = (C_1, C_2, t, H_2(t))$ (the ciphertext of user i) and a re-encryption key $rk_{i \rightarrow j}$, this algorithm outputs the ciphertext C_j for user j using the re-encryption key $rk_{i \rightarrow j} = b/a\ (mod\ q)$ as follows:

$$C_1' = C_1, \quad C_2' = C_2^{b/af(C')} = g^{akb/af(C_1')} = g^{bkf(C_1')}, \quad C_3' = f(C_1'), \quad t' = t$$

Consequently, $C_j = (C_1', C_2', C_3', t', H_2(t'))$.

- **Trapdoor**: On input user j's secret key $sk_j = b$ corresponding to the public key $pk_j = g^b$ and a keyword w', outputs a trapdoor $T_{w'}' = H_1(w')^{1/b}$.
- **Test**: On input the trapdoor $T_{w'}'$ and the ciphertext $(C_1', C_2', C_3', t', H_2(t'))$, this algorithm checks whether $H_2(e(C_2', T_{w'}')) = H_2(t')$. If it holds, proxy P releases the re-encrypted ciphertext (C_1', C_2', C_3'), otherwise abort.
- **Dec**: On input user j's secret key sk_j and a ciphertext (C_1', C_2', C_3'), this algorithm outputs a message $m = C_1'/e(g, C_2')^{1/bC_3'}$ if the ciphertext passes the **Verify** procedure or $\perp$ otherwise.

5.2 Offline Keyword Guessing Attacks on Chen *et al.*'s PRES Scheme

An attacker can perform an offline keyword attack on Chen *et al.*'s scheme through the following steps:

- **Step 1**: It selects any user as a target and then captures a valid trapdoor $T_w = H_1(w)^{1/sk}$ from this user.
- **Step 2**: It guesses an appropriate keyword w' and computes $H_1(w')$.
- **Step 3**: It takes the user's public key pk and the hash of the guessed keyword $H_1(w')$, and checks if $e(T_w, pk) = e(H_1(w'), g)$ holds. It is easy to deduce that $e(T_w, pk) = e(H_1(w)^{1/sk}, pk) = e(H_1(w), g)$. Therefore, if $w = w'$, then the attacker's guess is correct.
- **Step 4**: If the equation holds, then w' is a correct guess and the attacker succeeds. Otherwise, it goes to Step 2 and continues its guessing.

According to the above attack, we can conclude that Chen *et al.*'s PRES scheme is insecure under the keyword guessing attack.

6 Keyword Guessing Attack on Wu *et al.*'s PRES Scheme

In [35], Wu *et al.* presented a secure channel free PRES scheme. In this section, we show that the scheme is insecure under the offline keyword guessing attack.

6.1 Review of Wu *et al.*'s PRES Scheme

Wu *et al.*'s PRES scheme consists of the following algorithms:

- **GlobalSetup**: The cloud server initializes a bilinear map $e: G_1 \times G_1 \to G_2$ and chooses a hash function $H: \{0, 1\}^* \to Z_q^*$. In addition, the cloud server selects a random value sk_C from Z_q^* as the secret key, and computes the corresponding public key $pk_C = g^{sk_C}$. Thus, the global parameter can be denoted as $gp = \{q, G_1, G_2, e, g, H, pk_C\}$.
- **KenGen**: On input gp, then the sender randomly chooses a secret value sk_S from Z_q^* as the secret key and computes its public key $pk_S = g^{1/sk_S}$. Similarly, each receiver $R_i \in R$, where R is the receiver set, can generate his secret key $sk_{R_i} \in Z_q^*$ and public key $pk_{R_i} = g^{1/sk_{R_i}}$, respectively.
- **Enc**: On input gp, an EMR plaintext M and the sender S's private key sk_S, the sender S chooses a random value k from Z_q^*, and then computes $C_1 = M \oplus e(g^{sk_S}, g^k), C_2 = g^k$. The encrypted record is denoted as $C = \{C_1, C_2\}$.
- **IndexGen**: On input gp, the sender's private key sk_S and a keyword set W, the sender runs this algorithm to generate a secure index. Specifically, for each keywor $w \in W$, the sender computes $\tau_w = pk_C^{sk_S \cdot H(w)}$. Thus, the index can be denoted as $I = \{\tau_w\}_{w \in W}$.
- **ReKeyGen**: On input gp, the sender S's private key sk_S and each receiver R's public key pk_{R_i}, the sender S computes $rk_{S \to R_i} = pk_{R_i}^{sk_S}$ as the re-encryption key. The re-encryption key and the keyword index compose the keyword ciphertext.

- **Trapdoor**: On input gp, the receiver R's private key sk_{R_i} and a keyword w', the receiver chooses a random value $r \in Z_q^*$, and computes $T_1 = pk_C^r$ and $T_2 = pk_C^{H(w') \cdot r \cdot sk_{R_i}}$, sets $T_{w'} = (T_1, T_2)$ as the trapdoor of the keyword w'.
- **Search**: On input gp, an index I, a trapdoor $T_{w'} = (T_1, T_2)$, a re-encryption key $rk_{S \to R_i}$ and the cloud storage server sk_C, the cloud server checks whether $e(\tau_w, T_1) = e(T_2, rk_{S \to R_i})^{sk_C}$ for each $\tau_w \in I_W$. It outputs 1 if the above equation holds, which implies $w = w'$. In that case, the cloud server sends$\{C, rk_{S \to R_i}\}$ back to the receiver R_i; otherwise, sends $\perp$.
- **Dec**: On input gp, an EMR ciphertext C, a re-encryption key $rk_{S \to R_i}$ and the receiver R's private key sk_R, the receiver R computes $M = C_1 \oplus e(rk_{S \to R_i}, C_2)^{sk_{R_i}}$.

6.2   Keyword Guessing Attacks on Wu *et al.*'s PRES Scheme

An attacker can perform an offline keyword guessing attack on Wu *et al.*'s scheme through the following steps:

- **Step 1**: It obtains a valid trapdoor $T_{w'} = (T_1, T_2)$ from a target receiver R.
- **Step 2**: It guesses an appropriate keyword w'', and computes $H(w'')$.
- **Step 3**: It takes the public key pk_R and the hash of the guessed keyword $H(w'')$ and checks if $e(T_2, pk_R) = e(T_1, g^{H(w'')})$. It is easy to deduce that $e(T_2, pk_R) = e((pk_C)^{H(w') \cdot r \cdot sk_R}, g^{1/sk_R}) = e(pk_C^r, g^{H(w')}) = e(T_1, g^{H(w')})$. Therefore, if $w' = w''$, then the server's guess is correct.
- **Step 4**: If the equation holds, then w'' is a correct guess and the cloud storage server succeeds. Otherwise, it goes to Step 2 and continues its guessing.

Because the keyword trapdoor is sent via public channel in Wu *et al.*'s PRES scheme, the above attack can be performed by either an outside attacker or a malicious cloud server. Therefore, Wu *et al.*'s PRES scheme is insecure under the offline keyword guessing attack by either the outside attacker or the malicious cloud server.

7   Conclusion

In this paper, four existing PRES schemes are shown to be insecure under the keyword guessing attack. The security vulnerability of these schemes is due to the fact that the keyword trapdoors are produced by combining the keyword with the user's private key simply. As a result, an attacker can easily guess the keyword encoded in the trapdoor using the receiver's public key. So, to fight against the keyword guessing attack, we should place particular emphasis on the generation of the keyword trapdoor when devising a PRES scheme. In addition, none of the previous works has considered the definition of the keyword guessing attack in the security model of PRES. Therefore, it is necessary and important for us to setup a formal security model for PRES schemes that captures the keyword guessing attack.

Acknowledgments. This work was supported in part by the National Natural Science Foundation of China under Grant Nos. 61772009, 61972095, 62072104 and U1736112, the Natural Science Foundation of Jiangsu Province under Grant No. BK20181304.

References

1. Armbrust, M., et al.: A view of cloud computing. Commun. ACM **53**(4), 50–58 (2010)
2. Liu, Q., Cai, W.D., Shen, J., Fu, Z.J., Liu, X.D., Linge, N.: A speculative approach to spatial-temporal efficiency with multi-Objective optimization in a heterogeneous cloud environment. Secur. Commun. Netw. **9**(17), 4002–4012 (2016)
3. Xia, Z.H., Wang, X.H., Zhang, L.G., Qin, Z., Sun, X.M., Ren, K.: A privacy-preserving and copy-deterrence content-based image retrieval scheme in cloud computing. IEEE Trans. Inf. Forensics Secur. **11**(11), 2594–2608 (2016)
4. Fu, Z., Huang, F., Sun, X., Vasilakos, A.V., Yang, C.: Enabling semantic search based on conceptual graphs over encrypted outsourced data. IEEE Trans. Serv. Comput. **12**(5), 813–823 (2019)
5. Song, D.X., Wagner, D., Perrig, A.: Practical techniques for searches on encrypted data. In: IEEE Symposium Security Privacy, pp. 44–55. IEEE, USA (2000)
6. Zuo, C., Macindoe, J., Yang, S., Steinfeld, R., Liu, J.K.: Trusted boolean search on cloud using searchable symmetric encryption. In: 2016 IEEE Trustcom/BigDataSE/ISPA, pp. 113–120. IEEE, USA (2016)
7. Xia, Z., Wang, X., Sun, X., Wang, Q.: A secure and dynamic multi-keyword ranked search scheme over encrypted cloud data. IEEE Trans. Parallel Distrib. Syst. **27**(2), 340–352 (2015)
8. Fu, Z., Wu, X., Guan, C., Sun, X., Ren, K.: Toward efficient multi-keyword fuzzy search over encrypted outsourced data with accuracy improvement. IEEE Trans. Inf. Forensics Secur. **11**(12), 2706–2716 (2016)
9. Fu, Z.J., Sun, X.M., Liu, Q., Zhou, L., Shu, J.G.: Achieving efficient cloud search services: multi-keyword ranked search over encrypted cloud data supporting parallel computing. IEICE Trans. Commun. **98**.B(1), 190–200 (2015)
10. Yang, X., Lee, T., Liu, J.K., Huang, X.: Trust enhancement over range search for encrypted data. In: 2016 IEEE Trustcom/BigDataSE/ISPA, pp. 66–73. IEEE, USA (2016)
11. Curtmola, R., Garay, J., Kamara, S., Ostrovsky, R.: Searchable symmetric encryption: improved definitions and efficient constructions. In: 13th ACM Conference on Computer and Communications Security, pp. 79–88. ACM, USA (2006)
12. Boneh, D., Di Crescenzo, G., Ostrovsky, R., Persiano, G.: Public key encryption with keyword search. In: Cachin, C., Camenisch J. (eds.) International Conference on Theory and Applications of Cryptographic Techniques, LNCS, vol. 3027, pp. 506–522. Springer, Heidelberg (2004)
13. Baek, J., Safavi-Naini, R., Susilo, W.: Public key encryption with keyword search revisited. In: Gervasi, O., Murgante, B., Laganà, A., Taniar, D., Mun, Y., Gavrilova, M.L. (eds.) ICCSA 2008. LNCS, vol. 5072, pp. 1249–1259. Springer, Heidelberg (2008). https://doi.org/10.1007/978-3-540-69839-5_96
14. Rhee, H.S., Park, J.H., Susilo, W., Lee, D.H.: Improved searchable public key encryption with designated tester. In: 4th International Symposium Information, Computer and Communications Security (ASIACCS), pp. 376–379. ACM USA (2009)
15. Islam, S.K.H., Obaidat, M.S., Rajeev, V., Amin, R.: Design of a certificateless designated server based searchable public key encryption scheme. In: Giri, D., Mohapatra, R.N., Begehr, H., Obaidat, M.S. (eds.) ICMC 2017. CCIS, vol. 655, pp. 3–15. Springer, Singapore (2017). https://doi.org/10.1007/978-981-10-4642-1_1
16. Hu, C., Liu, P.: A secure searchable public key encryption scheme with a designated tester against keyword guessing attacks and its extension. In: Lin, S., Huang, X. (eds.) CSEE 2011. CCIS, vol. 215, pp. 131–136. Springer, Heidelberg (2011). https://doi.org/10.1007/978-3-642-23324-1_23

17. Lu, Y., Wang, G., Li, J., Shen, J.: Efficient designated server identity-based encryption with conjunctive keywords search. Ann. Telecommun. **72**(5–6), 359–370 (2017)

18. Guo, L.F., Yau, W.C.: Efficient secure-channel free public key encryption with keyword search for EMRs in cloud storage. J. Med. Syst. **39**(2), 11 (2015)

19. Zhou, Y., Xu, G., Wang, Y.: Chaotic map-based time-aware multi-keyword search scheme with designated server. Wireless Commun. Mob. Comput. **16**(3), 1851–1858 (2016)

20. Wang, H.J., Dong, X., Cao, Z.: Secure and efficient encrypted keyword search for multi-user setting in cloud computing. Peer-to-Peer Netw. Appl. **12**(1), 32–42 (2019)

21. Hamlin, A., Shelat, A., Weiss, M., Wichs, D.: Multi-key searchable encryption, revisited. In: Abdalla, M., Dahab, R. (eds.) PKC 2018. LNCS, vol. 10769, pp. 95–124. Springer, Cham (2018). https://doi.org/10.1007/978-3-319-76578-5_4

22. Abdalla, M., et al.: Searchable encryption revisited: consistency properties, relation to anonymous IBE, and extensions. In: Shoup, V. (ed.) CRYPTO 2005. LNCS, vol. 3621, pp. 205–222. Springer, Heidelberg (2005). https://doi.org/10.1007/11535218_13

23. Rhee, H.S., Park, J.H., Susilo, W., Lee, D.H.: Trapdoor security in a searchable public-key encryption scheme with a designated tester. J. Syst. Softw. **83**(5), 763–771 (2010)

24. Blaze, M., Bleumer, G., Strauss, M.: Divertible protocols and atomic proxy cryptography. In: Nyberg, K. (ed.) EUROCRYPT 1998. LNCS, vol. 1403, pp. 127–144. Springer, Heidelberg (1998). https://doi.org/10.1007/BFb0054122

25. Shao, Z., Yang, B.: On security against the server in designated tester public key encryption with keyword search. Inf. Process. Lett. **115**(12), 957–961 (2015)

26. Hong, H., Sun, Z.: Towards secure data sharing in cloud computing using attribute based proxy re-encryption with keyword search. In: ICCCBDA 2017, pp. 218–223. IEEE, USA (2017)

27. Yang, Y., Ma, M.: Conjunctive keyword search with designated tester and timing enabled proxy re-encryption function for e-health clouds. IEEE Trans. Inf. Forensics Secur. **11**(4), 746–759 (2017)

28. Yang, Y., Zheng, X.H., Chang, V., Tang, C.M.: Semantic keyword searchable proxy re-encryption for postquantum secure cloud storage. Concurrency Comput. Pract. Experience **29**(19), e4211 (2017)

29. Lee, S.H., Lee, I.Y.: A study of practical proxy re-encryption with a keyword search scheme considering cloud storage structure. Scientific World Journal 2014, Article ID 615679 (2014)

30. Guo, L., Lu, B., Li, X., Xu, H.: A verifiable proxy re-encryption with keyword search without random oracle. In: 2013 Ninth International Conference on Computational Intelligence and Security, pp. 474–478. IEEE, USA (2013)

31. Chen, X., Li, Y.: Efficient proxy re-encryption with private keyword searching in untrusted storage. Int. J. Comput. Netw. Inform. Secur. **3**(2), 50–56 (2011)

32. Wang, X.A., Huang, X., Yang, X.Y., Liu, L.F., Wu, X.G.: Further observation on proxy re-encryption with keyword search. J. Syst. Softw. **85**(3), 643–654 (2012)

33. Fang, L.M., Susilo, W., Ge, C.P., Wang, J.D.: Chosen-ciphertext secure anonymous conditional proxy re-encryption with keyword search. Theoret. Comput. Sci. **462**(1), 39–58 (2012)

34. Chen, Z.H., Li, S.D., Huang, Q., Wang, Y.L., Zhou. S.F.: A restricted proxy re-encryption with keyword search for fine-grained data access control in cloud storage. Concurrency Comput. Pract. Exper. **28**(10), 2858–2876 (2016)

35. Wu, Y., Lu, X., Su, J., Chen, P.: An efficient searchable encryption against keyword guessing attacks for sharable electronic medical records in cloud-based system. J. Med. Syst. **40**(12), 258 (2016)

36. Byun, J.W., Rhee, H.S., Park, H.-A., Lee, D.H.: Off-line keyword guessing attacks on recent keyword search schemes over encrypted data. In: Jonker, W., Petković, M. (eds.) SDM 2006. LNCS, vol. 4165, pp. 75–83. Springer, Heidelberg (2006). https://doi.org/10.1007/118446 62_6

37. Yau, W.C., Phan, R.C., Heng, S.H., Goi, B.M.: Keyword guessing attacks on secure searchable public key encryption schemes with a designated tester. Int. J. Comput. Math. **90**(12), 2581–2587 (2013)

38. Yau, W.-C., Heng, S.-H., Goi, B.-M.: Off-line keyword guessing attacks on recent public key encryption with keyword search schemes. In: Rong, C., Jaatun, M.G., Sandnes, F.E., Yang, L.T., Ma, J. (eds.) ATC 2008. LNCS, vol. 5060, pp. 100–105. Springer, Heidelberg (2008). https://doi.org/10.1007/978-3-540-69295-9_10

39. Sun, L.X., Xu, C.X., Zhang, M.W., Chen, K.F., Li, H.W.: Secure searchable public key encryption against insider keyword guessing attacks from indistinguishability obfuscation. Sci. Chin. Inform. Sci. **61**(3), 228–230 (2018)

40. Ni, J.B., Yu, Y., Xia, Q., Niu, L.: Cryptanalysis of two searchable public key encryption schemes with a designated tester. J Inform. Comput. Sci. **9**(16), 4819–4825 (2012)

41. Shao, Z., Yang, B.: On security against the server in designated tester public key encryption with keyword search. Inform. Process. Lett. **115**(12), 957–961 (2015)

42. Lu, Y., Wang, G., Li, J.G.: On security of a secure channel free public key encryption with conjunctive field keyword search scheme. J. Inform. Technol. Control **47**(1), 56–62 (2018)

A Post-quantum Certificateless Ring Signature Scheme for Privacy-Preserving of Blockchain Sharing Economy

Mengwei Zhang and Xiubo Chen[✉]

Beijing University of Posts and Telecommunications, Beijing 100876, China

Abstract. Classical cryptography is no longer secure under quantum computing background. In traditional sharing economy, the centralized management mode leads to data tampering and privacy leakage problems. Targeting at these problems, in our paper, a novel privacy protection scheme is designed for sharing economy based on blockchain. Firstly, we propose a post-quantum certificateless ring signature algorithm over lattice, which can hide the signer's identity information and resist quantum computing attacks. Moreover, our proposed scheme can effectively avoid certificate management problem and third-party central key escrow problem. Secondly, we use the principle of bimodal Gaussian rejection sampling to generate signature. It can reduce the sampling times in signature phase and greatly improves the signature efficiency. Notably, the signature distribution is independent of signer's private key, which can better avoid the disclosure of signer's private key information. Thirdly, we construct a blockchain sharing economy transaction scheme based on the proposed signature algorithm that can protect the privacy of user. Finally, security and efficiency of our scheme are analyzed that have lower storage cost and time cost than other related schemes under the random oracle model.

Keywords: Lattice · Certificateless ring signature · Blockchain · Privacy protection

1 Introduction

The rapid development of 5G and Internet of Things (IoT) technologies have injected new vitality into sharing economy. In the near future, shared driverless cars are expected to become the mainstream, all idle resources can be shared, which greatly improves the utilization rate of resources. However, in the development mode of the sharing economy, data information is stored in a centralized manner that can lead to data leakage and data tampering. What's more, in the complex network environment, the issue of trust between nodes is also a major obstacle to the development of the sharing economy.

Blockchain is a distributed data storage ledger with the characteristics of decentralization, transparency, and tamper-proof which was proposed by Nakamoto firstly in paper "Bitcoin: A Peer-to-Peer Electronic Cash System" [1]. Transaction participants can reach trust and cooperation without trusted third party that can greatly promote

© Springer Nature Switzerland AG 2021
X. Sun et al. (Eds.): ICAIS 2021, LNCS 12737, pp. 265–278, 2021.
https://doi.org/10.1007/978-3-030-78612-0_22

the development of the sharing economy. Bitcoin is an application of blockchain technology. The researches [2, 3] have found that Bitcoin transaction address is strongly correlated with user's identity, the attacker can infer user's real identity information via data analysis.

In 2001, ring signature (RS) was first put forward by Rivest, et al. [4]. From then, it plays an important role in privacy protection. The signer generates signature by using the ring members' public key and his private key that is difficult for verifier to identify the real signer in ring. The certificateless cryptosystem was advanced by AI-Riyami et al. [5]. In this cryptosystem, on one hand, KGC cannot steal the user's complete private key, consisting of partial private key generated by KGC and a random value selected by user. On the other hand, introducing certificateless mechanism makes sure that the issue of key escrow in identity-based cryptosystem [6] and certificate management in traditional Public Key Infrastructure (PKI) cryptosystem disappear for good.

The development of quantum computing makes classical cryptography no longer secure. Lattice cryptography that can resist quantum computing attacks has gradually attract the attention of scholars. So far, there have been massive research achievements in lattice cryptography field. However, little research has been done in post-quantum blockchain based on lattice cryptography. How to improve the security of anti-quantum computing and privacy protection of user on blockchain is the problem we need to solve.

The following are our main contributions:

- We propose a lattice-based certificateless ring signature algorithm. It can be safely applied to blockchain to protect the identity information of signer effectively and resist quantum computing attacks.
- Based on the proposed signature algorithm, we construct a blockchain sharing economy scheme, which can effectively protect user's privacy and solve the centralization problem of traditional sharing economy.
- Through our analysis, the scheme satisfies the correctness and security. Notably, the signature distribution generated by the Bimodal Gaussian Rejection Sampling (BGRS) algorithm is independent of private key, avoiding disclosure of private key information and having higher signature efficiency due to the fewer sampling times.

2 Related Work

The post-quantum cryptosystem has gradually become a research hotspot in the field of cryptography [7, 8]. In 2010, Cash et al. [9] designed a lattice basis delegation algorithm called bonsai tree, and realized security under the standard model. In 2012, Micciancio et al. [10] implemented a novel lattice generation algorithm to simplify the extraction of private key in the signature scheme. In order to achieve privacy protection, many RS methods [11, 12] have been raised. In 2004, Dodis et al. [13] used Fiat-Shamir [14] transformation and achieved a RS scheme, and proved that his scheme satisfied security under the random oracle model. Chow et al. designed a certificateless RS scheme in [15] in 2005. The bad news is that it requires many pairing operations and exponential operations. One year later, Chow et al. [16] discovered a bilinear pair-based RS scheme. In 2014, Liu et al. [17] found a linkable RS method and further improved the security.

In 2018, Gao et al. [18] presented anti-quantum blockchain and prevented transaction process from the quantum computing attack.

Some scholars consider combining the characteristics of lattice cryptography and RS, researching lattice-based RS algorithms to further improve the security. In 2010, Wang et al. [19] used the bonsai tree model to propose an identity-based RS. In 2012, Li et al. [20] raised an attribute-based lattice cryptographic RS scheme which improved signature efficiency. In 2013, Ducas et al. [21] improved the rejection sampling algorithm in the literature [22], and proposed a signature scheme based on BGRS, which can effectively reduce the mean of sample times. In 2016, Gao et al. [23] proposed an extended split minimum integer solution concept, which effectively made the signature size shorter. In 2017, Jia et al. [24] designed an identity-based RS scheme using rejection sampling algorithm. However, due to using the lattice basis delegation algorithm, the efficiency of private key extraction is low. Subsequently, some other lattice-based RS schemes have been put forward [25, 26].

Although some achievements have been made in the field of lattice-based RS, most of them are on the basis of classical PKI cryptography or identity-based cryptography, the research on lattice-based certificateless RS is few. Therefore, we design a certificateless RS algorithm based on lattice, which can further improve security and efficiency of RS algorithm.

3 Preliminaries

Before constructing the signature algorithm, we introduce the definition of lattice and related theorems.

3.1 Lattice

In this paper, we agree that R denotes the real numbers collection, Z denotes the collection of positive integers, and R^m represents the Euclidean vector space with m-dimensional. $\Lambda^{\perp}$ is the orthogonal lattice of Λ. $\|A\|$ denotes the Euclidean norm of matrix A.

There are m linearly independent vectors $b_1, b_2, \cdots, b_n \in R^m$, a lattice Λ is generated by the set of all linear combinations of the integral coefficients of these vectors $b_1, b_2, \cdots, b_n$:

$$\Lambda = \mathcal{L}(B) = \{\sum\nolimits_{i=1}^{n} z_i \cdot b_i | z_i \in Z\} \tag{1}$$

and the matrix $B = (b_1, b_2, \cdots, b_n) \in R^{m \times n}$ is one base of Λ. Normally, n and m are the rank and dimension of the lattice respectively.

Besides, the definition of q module lattice is:

$$\Lambda_q(A) = \{e \in Z^m | \exists s \in Z^n, A^T s = e \bmod q\} \tag{2}$$

$$\Lambda_q^{\perp}(A) = \{e \in Z^m | A^T e = 0 \bmod q\} \tag{3}$$

and $\Lambda_q(A)$ is the coset of $\Lambda_q^{\perp}(A)$.

3.2 Sampling Algorithm

- **Trapdoor Generation.** Select prime $q \geq 3$, $m \geq 5n \log q$, the polynomial-time algorithm $TrapGen(q, n)$ can output (A, S) with $A \in Z_q^{n \times m}$, $S \in Z^{m \times m}$. S is a base of the lattice $\Lambda_q^{\perp}(A)$ and $\|S\| \leq O(\sqrt{n \log q})$.
- **Matrix Preimage Sampling.** The polynomial-time algorithm $SampleMat$ (A, T_A, σ, u) can output a matrix $S \in Z_q^{m \times k}$ that satisfies $AS = V$. The distribution of matrix V is closing to $D_{\Lambda^V(A), \sigma}$, and $\|V\| < \sigma \sqrt{m}$.

3.3 Small Integer Solution (SIS) Problem

Given m uniform random vectors $a_i \in Z_q^n$ to form a matrix $A \in Z_q^{n \times m}$ according to column vectors, try to find a vector $z \in Z_q^m$ of non-zero integers which satisfies $Az = 0 \mod q$, where $\|z\| \leq \beta$.

3.4 Gaussian Distribution

For arbitrary $x \in \Lambda$, $\rho_{s,c}(x) = \exp(-\pi \|x - c\|^2 / s^2)$ is defined as the continuous Gaussian distribution, the center is $c \in R^n$ and the standard deviation is $s > 0$. Besides, the discrete Gaussian distribution over lattice Λ is defined as

$$D_{\Lambda, s, c}(x) = \frac{\rho_{s,c}(x)}{\rho_{s,c}(\Lambda)} \tag{4}$$

3.5 Rejection Sampling

Given a positive integer m and arbitrary set $V \subseteq Z^m$, $h : V \to R$ is a distribution whose preimage is V. There is a constant M making the distribution of (1), (2) is less than $2^{-\omega(\log m)}/M$ at statistical distance:

(1) $v \leftarrow h, z \leftarrow D_{v,\sigma}^m$, there is a probability $min(D_{\sigma}^m/MD_{v,\sigma}^m, 1)$ to output (z, v).
(2) $v \leftarrow h, z \leftarrow D_{\sigma}^m$, there is a probability $1/M$ to output (z, v).

3.6 Bimodal Gaussian Rejection Sampling (BGRS)

In [22], signature is changed from $z = Sc + y$ in Gaussian rejection sampling to $z = bSc + y$, where $b \in \{-1, 1\}$. The probability distribution of z is $\frac{1}{2}D_{Sc,\sigma}^m + \frac{1}{2}D_{-Sc,\sigma}^m$, and we have

$$D_{\sigma}^m(x) / \left(\frac{1}{2}D_{Sc,\sigma}^m(x) + \frac{1}{2}D_{-Sc,\sigma}^m(x) \right) = \exp(\frac{\|Sc\|^2}{2\sigma^2}) / \cosh(\frac{\langle x, Sc \rangle}{\sigma^2}) \leq \exp(\frac{\|Sc\|^2}{2\sigma^2}) \tag{5}$$

Then, we can get $M = \exp(1)$ by making the smaller standard deviation $\sigma = \|Sc\|/\sqrt{2}$ instead of $\sigma = \tau \|Sc\|$.

4 Lattice-Based Certificateless Ring Signature (LCRS)

As shown in Fig. 1, LRCS can be divided into the following stages:

1. **Setup:** Given a security parameter n, a prime number $q \geq 3$, $m > 5n \log q$, $L \geq O(\sqrt{n \log q})$, $\sigma \geq L \cdot \omega(\sqrt{\log m})$, KGC performs the following steps:

(1) Execute the algorithm $TrapGen(1^n)$. The algorithm outputs an approximately randomly distributed matrix $A \in Z_q^{n \times m}$ and a base $T_A \in Z_q^{m \times m}$ of the lattice $\Lambda^\perp(A)$, where $\|T_A\| \leq L$.

(2) Select hash functions. $H_1 : \{0, 1\}^* \rightarrow Z_q^{n \times k}$, $H_2 : \{0, 1\}^* \rightarrow \{v : v \in \{-1, 0, -1\}^n, \|v\|_1 \leq n\}$, $H_3 : Z_q^{m \times n} \rightarrow \{0, 1\}^*$, $n = m - k$.

(3) Output public parameters. Output $PP = \{A, H_1, H_2\}$ and keep $MSK = T_A$ as system master private key.

2. **Key Generation:** For the signer whose identity is ID, the key pair generation steps are as follows:

(1) Partial private key generation. KGC calculates $R = H_1(ID)$ and executes $SampleMat(A, T_A, \sigma, R) \rightarrow S'_{ID}$, where $R \in Z_q^{n \times k}$, $S'_{ID} \in Z_q^{m \times k}$ and $AS'_{ID} = R$. Among them, S'_{ID} is treated as partial private key of signer. After that, KGC selects $A' \in Z_q^{n \times k}$ randomly, and sends (S'_{ID}, A') to signer safely.

(2) Select secret value. The signer randomly selects the secret matrix $P \in Z_q^{k \times n}$ and saves it.

(3) Public-private key pair generation. Owing to $m > n$, signer randomly selects the n rows of S'_{ID} and transposes to obtain the matrix $S' \in Z_q^{k \times n}$. Next, signer calculates $A'' = A'S' + A'P(\mathrm{mod}\, q)$, $A_{ID} = [2A'|2A'' + qI]$, $S_{ID} = [S' + PI| - I]^T$, where $A_{ID} \in Z_q^{n \times m}$, $S_{ID} \in Z_q^{m \times n}$, $A'' \in Z_q^{n \times n}$ and I are the identity matrix. In fact, $Q = A_{ID}S_{ID}(\mathrm{mod}\, 2q) = qI$, where $Q \in Z_q^{n \times n}$. Then, the signer's public key is (Q, A_{ID}) and private key is S_{ID}.

3. **Ring Signature:** Signer selects ring members $U = \{ID_1, ID_2, \cdots, ID_l\}$, and the ring public key is $rpk = \{A_{ID_1}, A_{ID_2}, \cdots, A_{ID_l}\}$, l is the maximum number of ring members. The message to be signed is μ, the identity of the signer is $ID_i(i \in [l])$, and the corresponding signature private key is S_{ID_i}. The process of ring signature is as follows:

(1) For all $j \in [l]$, select a uniform random vector $y_j \leftarrow D_\sigma^m$.

(2) Calculate $c = H_2\left(\sum_{j=1}^l A_{ID_j} y_j (\mathrm{mod}\, 2q), rpk, \mu\right)$.

(3) If $j \neq i$, let $z_j = y_j$; if $j = i$, let $z_j = bS_{ID_j}c + y_j$ with probability p, where $b \in \{-1, 1\}$, $p = 1 / \left(M \exp(-\frac{\|S_{ID_j}c\|}{2\sigma^2}) \cos h(\frac{\langle z_j, S_{ID_j}c \rangle}{\sigma^2}))\right)$.

(4) If there is no output vector z_i in step (3), reselect the random vector $y_i \leftarrow D_\sigma^m$ and repeat steps (2) and (3).

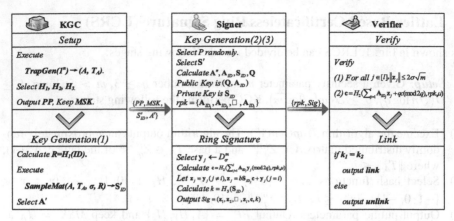

Fig. 1. Lattice-based certificateless ring signature.

(5) Generate a key image $k = H_3(S_{ID})$ of the signer.

(6) Output ring signature $Sig = (z_1, z_2, \cdots, z_l, c, k)$.

4. **Verify:** Input ring $U = \{ID_1, ID_2, \cdots, ID_l\}$, ring public key $rpk = \{A_{ID_1}, A_{ID_2}, \cdots, A_{ID_l}\}$, message μ and signature Sig. Verify that:

(1) For all $j \in [l]$, $\|z_j\| \le 2\sigma\sqrt{m}$.

(2) $c = H_2\left(\sum_{j=1}^{l} A_{ID_j}z_j + qc(\mathrm{mod}2q), rpk, \mu\right)$.

If the above two conditions are satisfied, then output "accept", otherwise output "reject".

5. **Link:** Input two message-signature pairs $(\mu_1, Sig_1(\mathbf{Z}_1, c_1, k_1))$ and $(\mu_2, Sig_2(\mathbf{Z}_2, c_2, k_2))$, in which, $\mathbf{Z}$ is a matrix composed of vectors $z_1, z_2, \cdots, z_l$. If $k_1 = k_2$, then output "link", otherwise, output "unlink".

5 Security Proof and Efficiency Analysis

5.1 Correctness

During the ring signature process, due to

$$\sum_{j=1}^{l} A_{ID_j}\mathbf{z}_j + q\mathbf{c}(mod\,2q) = \sum_{j \in [l]\backslash\{i\}} A_{ID_j}\mathbf{z}_j + A_{ID_i}\mathbf{z}_i + q\mathbf{c}(mod\,2q)$$

$$= \sum_{j \in [l]\backslash\{i\}} A_{ID_j}\mathbf{z}_j + A_{ID_i}(bS_{ID_j}\mathbf{c} + \mathbf{y}_j) + q\mathbf{c}(mod\,2q)$$

$$= \sum_{j \in [l]} A_{ID_j}\mathbf{z}_j + bA_{ID_i}S_{ID_j}\mathbf{c} + q\mathbf{c}(mod\,2q)$$

$$= \sum_{j \in [l]} \mathbf{A}_{ID_j} \mathbf{z}_j + bq\mathbf{c} + q\mathbf{c}(mod\,2q)$$

$$= \sum_{j \in [l]} \mathbf{A}_{ID_j} \mathbf{z}_j (mod\,2q) \tag{6}$$

we have $c = H_2\left(\sum_{j=1}^{l} \mathbf{A}_{ID_j} \mathbf{z}_j + q\mathbf{c}(mod\,2q), rpk, \mu\right)$. Therefore, the algorithm satisfies correctness.

5.2 Unforgeability

In certificateless RS security model, there are two types of adversaries. Adversary A_1 simulates a malicious user and can substitute someone's public key, but he cannot know MSK. The adversary A_2 simulates a malicious KGC, which is aware of the detailed information of MSK, but he cannot perform a replacement query on the signer's public key.

Next, we will prove our LCRS is unforgeable and completely anonymous.

Theorem 1: Assuming that there is an adversary A_1 who can create a forged signature with non-negligible advantage ε in polynomial-time, then challenger C must be able to find a solution for SIS problem with non-negligible probability.

Theorem 2: Assuming that there is an adversary A_2 who can create a forged signature with non-negligible advantage ε in polynomial-time, then challenger C must be able to find a solution for SIS problem with non-negligible probability.

Proof: Since the proofs of Theorem 1 and Theorem 2 are similar, here we only prove Theorem 1. Challenger C is responsible for maintaining the table $\{L_1, L_2, L_3, L_S, L_R, L_E\}$. Before querying, it is necessary to check in the tables whether it has been queried. If yes, it will return the same result as the last time, otherwise, perform other operations. The interaction between C and A_1 is as follows:

1. **Setup Phase:**

(1) Determine ring $U = \{ID_1, ID_2, \cdots, ID_l\}$, challenge user ID_{i*}, where $1 \leq i^* \leq l$.
(2) Generate $PP = \{A, H_1, H_2\}$. C sends (PP, U) to A_1.

2. **Query Phase:**

(1) H_1 inquiry: A_1 submits user $ID_i (i \in N)$ to C, C calculates $H_1(ID_i) = \mathbf{R}_i$ and returns it to A_1, then, C records it in table L_1.
(2) H_2 inquiry: A_1 submits message μ and ring $U = \{ID_1, ID_2, \cdots, ID_l\}$ to C, randomly selects l vectors $y_i \leftarrow D_\sigma^m (i \in [l])$. C randomly selects a vector v and returns it to A_1, then records it in table L_2.
(3) Public key query: A_1 queries public key of user ID_i from C, C selects random matrices $\mathbf{A}'_i \in Z_q^{n \times m}$ and $A_1 \mathbf{A}''_i \in Z_q^{n \times n}$, $\mathbf{S}'_{ID_i}$ returns $\mathbf{A}_{ID_i} = [2\mathbf{A}'_i | 2\mathbf{A}'' + q\mathbf{I}]$ to A_1, and records it in table L_3.

(4) Partial private key query: A_1 queries partial private key of user ID_i, if $ID_i = ID_{i*}$, then stop interaction. C executes $SampleMat(A_i, T_{A_i}, \sigma, R_i) \rightarrow S'_{ID_i}$ and returns to, then records it in table L_S.

(5) Public key replacement: A_1 selects a replacement public key A'_{ID_i} of user ID_i and sends it to C. C substitutes the public key A_{ID_i} of user ID_i with A'_{ID_i} in the system, then records it in table L_R.

(6) Secret value query: A_1 queries a secret val A_1 ue of user ID_i. C selects a random matrix $P_i \in Z_q^{k \times n}$, returns it to A_1 as the secret value, and records it in table L_E.

(7) Ring signature query: A_1 submits message μ and ring $U = \{ID_1, ID_2, \cdots, ID_l\}$, selects a member ID_i in the ring to C. C returns the signature $Sig = (z_1, z_2, \cdots, z_l, c)$ of user ID_i on message μ and ring U to.

3. **Forgery Phase:** A_1 submits a message μ^*, ring $U^* = \{ID_1^*, ID_2^*, \cdots, ID_l^*\}$, signer identity ID_i^* and forged ring signature $Sig^* = (z_1^*, z_2^*, \cdots, z_l^*, c^*)$ to C, and satisfies the following conditions:

(1) The target user ID_i^* has not appeared in the partial private key query, and A_1 doesn't know partial private key of user ID_i^*.

(2) μ^* doesn't appear in the ring signature query.

If Sig^* is a legal certificateless ring signature, the private key $S_{ID_i}^*$ of ID_i^* is obtained by C through (4)(6) in Query phase. If $i \neq j$, let $z'_j = y_j^*$; else $z'_j = bS_{ID_j}^* c^* + y_j^*$. It's obvious that $Sig' = (z'_1, z'_2, \cdots, z'_l)$ is also legal. Then there must be $H_2\left(A_{ID_i}^* z_i^* + qc^*, \mu\right) = H_2\left(A_{ID_i}^* z'_i + qc^*, \mu'\right)$, and $\mu = \mu'$, $A_{ID_i}^* z_i^* + qc^* = A_{ID_i}^* z'_i + qc^*$. If these equations are not satisfied, we can tell that hash collision phenomenon happened. Under these circumstances, we are able to obtain $A_{ID_i}^* (z_i^* - z'_i) = 0 (\mod 2q)$, where $\|z_i^* - z'_i\| \leq \|z_i^*\| + \|z'_i\| \leq 2\sigma\sqrt{m} + 2\sigma\sqrt{m} = 4\sigma\sqrt{m}$ is one solution of SIS problem. However, SIS is recognized as a difficult problem over lattice. Thus, it can be concluded that our signature algorithm is unforgeable.

5.3 Complete Anonymity

Theorem 3: Under the random oracle model, the signature algorithm proposed in this paper satisfies complete anonymity.

Proof:

Here, the adversary can be A_1 or A_2, we assume it is A_1.

1. **Setup Phase:**

(1) Determine the ring $U = \{ID_1, ID_2, \cdots, ID_l\}$.

(2) Challenger C generates public parameter $PP = \{A, H_1, H_2\}$, $MSK = T_A$, and the private key S_{ID_i} with each user respectively. Then, C sends public parameter PP to A_1 and retains (T_A, S_{ID_i}).

2. **Query Phase:** A variety of queries with an upper limit of the polynomial time are adaptively made to C.

3. **Challenge Phase:** A_1 submits a message μ, ring $U = \{ID_1, ID_2, \cdots, ID_l\}$ and two different users' identities (ID_0, ID_1) to C. C selects $s \in \{0, 1\}$, $y_j \leftarrow D_\sigma^m (j \in [l])$ randomly, calculates $z_j^* = y_j (j \neq i_s), z_{i_s}^* = bS_{ID_{i_s}} c + y_{i_s} (j = i_s)$, and performs a ring signature $Sig^* = (z_1^*, z_2^*, \cdots, z_l^*, c^*)$, then sends it to $A_1 (z_1^*, z_2^*, \cdots, z_l^*, c^*)$.

4. **Guess Phase:** A_1 outputs the guess result s'.

For the signature Sig^*, it is known from the bimodal Gaussian rejection sampling theorem that $z_{i_s}^*$ and the bimodal Gaussian distribution $\frac{1}{2}D_{S_{ID^c,\sigma}}^m + \frac{1}{2}D_{-S_{ID^c,\sigma}}^m$ are statistically indistinguishable. Thus, is statistically indistinguishable with $(\frac{1}{2}D_{S_{ID^c,\sigma}}^m + \frac{1}{2}D_{-S_{ID^c,\sigma}}^m)^{l+1}$. Similarly, let $z'_j \leftarrow D_m^\sigma$ when $j \neq i_{1-s}$; $z'_{i_s} = bS_{ID_{i_s}} c' + y_{i_s}$ when $j = i_{1-s}$. z'_{i_s} and the bimodal Gaussian distribution $\frac{1}{2}D_{S_{ID^c,\sigma}}^m + \frac{1}{2}D_{-S_{ID^c,\sigma}}^m$ are statistically indistinguishable. Therefore, $(z'_1, z'_2, \cdots, z'_l, c')$ and $(\frac{1}{2}D_{S_{ID^c,\sigma}}^m + \frac{1}{2}D_{-S_{ID^c,\sigma}}^m)^{l+1}$ are statistically indistinguishable.

So, the Sig^* and Sig' are statistically indistinguishable, and the proposed signature scheme is completely anonymous.

5.4 Efficiency Analysis

Compared with Wang et al. [20], Gao et al. [24] and Jia et al. [25], our scheme has better performance in time cost and storage cost.

Table 1. Comparison of storage cost.

Schemes	Public key size	Signature size	Security model
Wang et al. [20]	$mn \log q$	$(l+1)m \log q + l\| ID\|$	ROM
Gao et al. [24]	$(2k+3)mn \log q$	$(lm+k) \log q$	SM
Jia et al. [25]	$(k+m)n \log q$	$(lm+k) \log q$	ROM
Our scheme	$mn \log q$	$(lm+n) \log q$	ROM

Most calculations in lattice cryptography are matrix and vector operations, and storage cost determines the practicability of scheme mostly. Generally, we mainly take the size of public key and signature into consideration, because they are both important in storage performance evaluation. In Table 1, the size of public key in our scheme is equivalent to that in [20], but it is shorter than [24, 25]. In addition, the signature size is similar with [24, 25], but it is shorter than [20]. All in all, our signature algorithm has lower storage cost and better practicability.

Table 2. Comparison of time cost.

Schemes	System key generation	User key generation	Signature generation
Wang et al. [20]	T_T	$mT_E + T_R$	$(l+1)mT_S + lmnT_M$
Gao et al. [24]	T_T	$mT_M + mT_E + kT_S$	$m(l+1)T_M$
Jia et al. [25]	T_T	$mT_M + T_I + mT_B + kT_S$	$m(l+1)T_M$
Our scheme	T_T	$nT_M + kT_S$	$m(l+1)T_M$

As shown in Table 2, we mainly consider the comparison of three phases in the time cost: system key generation, user key generation and signature generation. We ignore less time-consuming operations such as matrix addition and hash algorithm. We agree that T_M represents matrix multiplication, T_I represents matrix inversion, and T_B, T_R, T_E, T_S, T_T represent *BasisDel*, *RandBasis*, *ExtBasis*, *SamplePre* and *TrapGen* algorithms respectively. Compared with [20, 24, 25], our signature algorithm does not use *BasisDel*, *RandBasis*, *ExtBasis* and other complex operations such as matrix inversion, which have a tremendous time cost. Actually, we only use the matrix preimage sampling algorithm and matrix multiplication in user key generation phase, so our signature algorithm has higher efficiency. It is worth mentioning that the generation of signature is based on the BGRS algorithm. Compared with general Gaussian rejection sampling algorithm in [24], it can effectively reduce the sampling times required to create a valid signature. In other words, our scheme has higher signature efficiency. On the other hand, in our scheme, compared with the preimage sampling algorithm used in [20], the distribution of output signature is independent of private key, which can further protect the signer's private information.

6 Secure Blockchain Sharing Economy Scheme Based on LCRS

Based on the lattice certificateless ring signature (LCRS) proposed above, we construct a sharing economy scheme on the blockchain. There are four roles in our scheme: Consumer, Provider, KGC and Miner.

Consumer. The consumer sends a transaction request to the provider, and trades with the provider. What's more, the consumer is responsible for selecting some ring members and performing ring signature on the transaction that would be recorded to the blockchain.

Provider. The provider registers the commodity information on the blockchain. And the provider can generate a new one-time temporary Bitcoin address controlled by itself to receive fees in each transaction.

KGC. In the blockchain sharing economy scheme, KGC is a generator of system public parameters and the partial public-private key of users.

Miner. The miner is responsible for collecting and verifying transactions, and packs the legal transaction into a new block. In addition, miner prevents user from double spending. After the block is verified as legal by the consensus mechanism, it will be added to the blockchain.

For simplicity, we denote Consumer, Provider as C, P respectively. As shown in Fig. 2, the transaction process of C and P is described as follows:

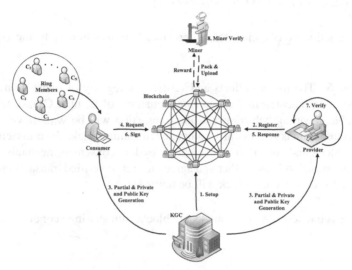

Fig. 2. Blockchain sharing economy scheme based on LCRS.

1. **Setup:** KGC selects the security parameter, prime number $q \geq 3$, $m > 5n \log q$, then outputs public parameter $PP = \{A, H_1, H_2\}$ and $MSK = T_A$.
2. **Register:** In this step, P registers the commodity information on the blockchain, and generates $reg = (inf, sn)$, where inf includes the type of commodity, the price of commodity and other information. sn is used to uniquely identify the commodity.
3. **Key Gen:** KGC generates the partial keys for ring members and P. Then, the ring members and P select secret values to gain their public-private key pairs respectively. In which, the public-private key pairs for C and P are (A_{ID_C}, S_{ID_C}), (A_{ID_P}, S_{ID_P}) respectively, and $rpk = \{A_{ID_1}, A_{ID_2}, \cdots, A_{ID_l}\}$ is the ring public key.
4. **Request:** Suppose that C intends to obtain the right to use the commodity from P, then C sends a transaction request to P.
5. **Response:** P uses its own public key and random numbers to generate a one-time temporary address P_{addr}, and signs the temporary address to generate $Sig(P_{addr})$, then sends it to C.
6. **Sign:** C receives the temporary address P_{addr} and signature $Sig(P_{addr})$, verifys the legality of the signature. Then, C pays v bitcoins to the temporary address P_{addr} through an anonymous address. C selects the ring members to form a ring, performs a ring signature on $tx = (v, P_{addr}, tag)$ and generates a key image

$k = H_3(S_{ID_C})$, tag represents the type of transaction. Then, C sends the ring signature $Sig = (z_1, z_2, \cdots, z_l, c, k)$ to P.

7. **Verify:** In this step, P verifies the ring signature, if it satisfies (1), (2), accept it; otherwise, reject it.

(1) For all $j \in [l]$, $z_j \leq 2\sigma\sqrt{m}$

(2) $c = H_2\left(\sum_{j=1}^{l} A_{ID_j}z_j + qc(\mathrm{mod}2q), rpk, tx\right)$

After transaction tx is completed, C broadcasts transaction tx to the entire P2P network.

8. **Miner Verify:** The miner collects and verifies the legality of transaction tx. If the key image k is repeated in the two ring signatures of C, then C is considered to have double spending behavior, and the transaction will be withdrawn. After the verified transaction is successfully completed, the miner packs the transaction into a bran-new block and adds it to blockchain. Based on consensus mechanism, miners can communicate with each other and agree on a set of verified transactions, and the miners who produce a new block will be rewarded.

The above is the description of our secure blockchain sharing economy scheme.

7   Conclusion

In this paper, a secure and efficient post-quantum certificateless ring signature scheme is constructed based on lattice, which can be applied to protect the private identity information of user and resist quantum computing attacks in blockchain sharing economy. Our proposed scheme can effectively avoid the certificate management and the third-party central key escrow problem. Besides, our scheme is proved much safer under the random oracle model. In addition, by use of BGRS algorithm, our scheme can effectively reduce sampling times required to create a valid signature and the distribution of signature is independent of the signer's private key, which has greatly improved the efficiency and security of signature.

In next step, we will continue to study lattice-based ring signature and other signature algorithms, such as blind signature and aggregate signature, to further improve the security and efficiency of transactions on the blockchain.

References

1. Nakamoto, S.: Bitcoin: A peer-to-peer electronic cash system (2008). http://bitcoin.org/bit coin.pdf
2. Ron, D., Shamir, A.: Quantitative analysis of the full bitcoin transaction graph. In: Sadeghi, A.-R. (ed.) FC 2013. LNCS, vol. 7859, pp. 6–24. Springer, Heidelberg (2013). https://doi. org/10.1007/978-3-642-39884-1_2

3. Meiklejohn, S., Orlandi, C.: Privacy-enhancing overlays in bitcoin. In: Brenner, M., Christin, N., Johnson, B., Rohloff, K. (eds.) FC 2015. LNCS, vol. 8976, pp. 127–141. Springer, Heidelberg (2015). https://doi.org/10.1007/978-3-662-48051-9_10

4. Rivest, R.L., Shamir, A., Tauman, Y.: How to leak a secret. In: Boyd, C. (ed.) ASIACRYPT 2001. LNCS, vol. 2248, pp. 552–565. Springer, Heidelberg (2001). https://doi.org/10.1007/3-540-45682-1_32

5. Al-Riyami, S.S., Paterson, K.G.: Certificateless public key cryptography. In: Laih, C.-S. (ed.) ASIACRYPT 2003. LNCS, vol. 2894, pp. 452–473. Springer, Heidelberg (2003). https://doi.org/10.1007/978-3-540-40061-5_29

6. Shamir, A.: Identity-based cryptosystems and signature schemes. In: Blakley, G.R., Chaum, D. (eds.) CRYPTO 1984. LNCS, vol. 196, pp. 47–53. Springer, Heidelberg (1985). https://doi.org/10.1007/3-540-39568-7_5

7. Gentry, C., Peikert, C., Vaikuntanathan, V.: Trapdoors for hard lattices and new cryptographic constructions. In: STOC, pp. 197–206 (2008)

8. Lyubashevsky, V.: Fiat-shamir with aborts: applications to lattice and factoring-based signatures. In: Matsui, M. (ed.) ASIACRYPT 2009. LNCS, vol. 5912, pp. 598–616. Springer, Heidelberg (2009). https://doi.org/10.1007/978-3-642-10366-7_35

9. Cash, D., Hofheinz, D., Kiltz, E., Peikert, C.: Bonsai trees, or how to delegate a lattice basis. In: Gilbert, H. (ed.) EUROCRYPT 2010. LNCS, vol. 6110, pp. 523–552. Springer, Heidelberg (2010). https://doi.org/10.1007/978-3-642-13190-5_27

10. Micciancio, D., Peikert, C.: Trapdoors for lattices: simpler, tighter, faster, smaller. In: Pointcheval, D., Johansson, T. (eds.) EUROCRYPT 2012. LNCS, vol. 7237, pp. 700–718. Springer, Heidelberg (2012). https://doi.org/10.1007/978-3-642-29011-4_41

11. Shacham, H., Waters, B.: Efficient ring signatures without random oracles. In: Okamoto, T., Wang, X. (eds.) PKC 2007. LNCS, vol. 4450, pp. 166–180. Springer, Heidelberg (2007). https://doi.org/10.1007/978-3-540-71677-8_12

12. Herranz, J., Sáez, G.: New identity-based ring signature schemes. In: Lopez, J., Qing, S., Okamoto, E. (eds.) ICICS 2004. LNCS, vol. 3269, pp. 27–39. Springer, Heidelberg (2004). https://doi.org/10.1007/978-3-540-30191-2_3

13. Dodis, Y., Kiayias, A., Nicolosi, A., Shoup, V.: Anonymous identification in ad hoc groups. In: Cachin, C., Camenisch, J.L. (eds.) EUROCRYPT 2004. LNCS, vol. 3027, pp. 609–626. Springer, Heidelberg (2004). https://doi.org/10.1007/978-3-540-24676-3_36

14. Fiat, A., Shamir, A.: How to prove yourself: practical solutions to identification and signature problems. In: Odlyzko, A.M. (ed.) CRYPTO 1986. LNCS, vol. 263, pp. 186–194. Springer, Heidelberg (1987). https://doi.org/10.1007/3-540-47721-7_12

15. Chow, S.S.M., Yiu, S.-M., Hui, L.C.K.: Efficient identity based ring signature. In: Ioannidis, J., Keromytis, A., Yung, M. (eds.) ACNS 2005. LNCS, vol. 3531, pp. 499–512. Springer, Heidelberg (2005). https://doi.org/10.1007/11496137_34

16. Chow, S., Liu, J., Wei, V., Yuen, T.H.: Ring signatures without random oracles. In: Shieh, S., Jajodia, S. (eds.) Proceedings of ASIACCS 2006, March 2006, pp. 297–302. ACM Press, New York (2006)

17. Liu, J.K., Au, M.H., Susilo, W., Zhou, J.: Linkable ring signature with unconditional anonymity. IEEE Trans. Knowl. Data Eng. 26(1), 157–165 (2014)

18. Gao, Y.L., Chen, X.B., Chen, Y.L., Sun, Y., Niu, X.X., Yang, Y.X.: A secure cryptocurrency scheme based on post-quantum blockchain. IEEE Access 6, 27205–27213 (2018)

19. Wang, J.: Identity-Based Ring Signature From Lattice Basis Delegation. Tsinghua University, Beijing (2008)

20. Li, W., Fan, M., Jia, Z.: An attribute-based ring signature scheme in lattice. Wuhan Univ. J. Nat. Sci. 4(17), 297–301 (2012)

21. Ducas, L., Durmus, A., Lepoint, T., Lyubashevsky, V.: Lattice signatures and bimodal gaussians. In: Canetti, R., Garay, J.A. (eds.) CRYPTO 2013. LNCS, vol. 8042, pp. 40–56. Springer, Heidelberg (2013). https://doi.org/10.1007/978-3-642-40041-4_3
22. Lyubashevsky, V.: Lattice signatures without trapdoors. In: Pointcheval, D., Johansson, T. (eds.) EUROCRYPT 2012. LNCS, vol. 7237, pp. 738–755. Springer, Heidelberg (2012). https://doi.org/10.1007/978-3-642-29011-4_43
23. Gao, W., Hu, Y., Wang, B., Xie, J.: Improved lattice-based ring signature schemes from basis delegation. J. Chin. Univ. Posts Telecommun. **23**(3), 11–17 (2016)
24. Jia, X., He, D., Xu, Z.: An efficient identity-based ring signature scheme over a lattice. J. Cryptologic Res. **4**(4), 392–404 (2017)
25. Agrawal, S., Boneh, D., Boyen, X.: Lattice basis delegation in fixed dimension and shorter-ciphertext hierarchical IBE. In: Rabin, T. (ed.) CRYPTO 2010. LNCS, vol. 6223, pp. 98–115. Springer, Heidelberg (2010). https://doi.org/10.1007/978-3-642-14623-7_6
26. Li, C., Dong, M., Li, J.: Healthchain: secure EMRs management and trading in distributed healthcare service system. IEEE Internet of Things Journal (2020)

A Transaction Model of Bill Service Based on Blockchain

Xinyan Wang[1], Jianxun Guo[2], Dong Li[1], Xin Chen[1], and Kailin Wang[3(✉)]

[1] State Grid Henan Electric Power Company Information Communication Company, Zheng Zhou, China
[2] State Grid Henan Electric Power Company, Zheng Zhou, China
[3] Beijing University of Posts and Telecommunications, Beijing, China

Abstract. In recent years, the bill business has developed rapidly, but it can not be ignored that there are also great risks in the bill business. In 2016, an Agricultural Bank of China (ABC) Bill case involving 3.9 billion yuan of paper swap with newspapers has aroused widespread social concern. At present, there are many problems in the traditional bill trading platform: Firstly, the transaction process is not transparent, and there are trust problems, which makes the bill circulation complicated and the cooperation efficiency low. Secondly, the paper-based bill is easy to be damaged and replaced in the process of delivery and storage, and there is a high operational risk. What's more, paper bills are often unable to be handed over in time, providing loopholes for illegal activities such as empty-shell commercial bills and excessive sales of one bill. In order to deal with these problems, we need a new type of bill trading model without trust problems. As a new database technology, blockchain technology has the characteristics of distributed storage, consistent algorithm, intelligent contract, asymmetric encryption and so on, which can effectively solve the trust and security problems existing in the bill trading service platform. In view of the above research, firstly we briefly introduce the bill business process. After the demand analysis, the bill service transaction model based on blockchain is designed. Finally, by building the fabric blockchain platform and coding the smart contract, the model of the electronic bill transaction service based on the blockchain is realized. This model realizes bill issuance, endorsement transfer, discounting services on the blockchain platform.

Keywords: Bill transaction · Blockchain · Smart contract

1 Introduction

Bill business refers to the daily business activities carried out by credit institutions in accordance with certain methods and requirements of the establishment, transfer and repayment of bills, which mainly include bill issuance, ownership transfer and discounting. The bill business has developed rapidly in recent years. However, it should not be ignored that the bill business also has great risks. For example, a number of major bill cases that were exposed in the first half of 2016 have aroused widespread public concern. Among them, the Agricultural Bank of China bill case involving a value of

© Springer Nature Switzerland AG 2021
X. Sun et al. (Eds.): ICAIS 2021, LNCS 12737, pp. 279–288, 2021.
https://doi.org/10.1007/978-3-030-78612-0_23

3.9 billion yuan is particularly eye-catching. In this case, some bills were exchanged with newspapers. It can be seen that there are many defects in the current traditional bill service transactions:

- Operation is not transparent: only internal personnel of banks, bill intermediaries, and related institutions know the process of transaction operations. There is no authentication process which involves multiple parties to confirm. It not only brings a crisis of trust, but also greatly reduces the efficiency of cooperation.
- Transaction records cannot be traced: The transaction records of traditional bill services are mainly paper-based. They are not only easy to lose, but also difficult to trace back, which lead to the problem of bill fraud.
- Manual operation error: More than 80% of bill transactions are conducted offline. In practice, it is often impossible to complete the transfer of bills in time. This loophole, along with the need for high bill turnover, huge benefits and other circumstances have prompted banks to collude with bill intermediaries to conduct illegal operations.

In summary, the bill business urgently needs a traceable and transparent multi-party trust technology to standardize business operations. And as a trusted technology, blockchain has attracted widespread attention [1].

The blockchain uses distributed ledgers and hash encryption algorithms to store data, which guarantees the integrity and authenticity of the data while being traceable and non-tamperable. It uses a consensus algorithm to synchronize the ledgers of each node so that the data is consistent and unified. It solves trust issues and ensures data sharing and information transparency at the same time. Also, the blockchain system uses smart contracts to implement business logic and triggers the transfer of assets through certain conditions, minimizing the interference of manual operations [2].

The main research contents of this paper are as follows:

(1) Analyze the problems of traditional bill trading platforms and propose to use blockchain technology to solve them.
(2) Analyze the bill business requirements and design a bill transaction model based on the blockchain.
(3) By designing the data structure and coding smart contracts, realize and test the blockchain-based bill transaction model.

2 Related Work

2.1 Introduction of Bill Business

Acceptance bill is widely used in actual financial activities. It is a kind of long-term payment method for the holder when the capital turnover is not ideal and the enterprise can not pay the full amount at one time. It includes Bill Issuing, Endorsement and Discount, etc.

- Bill Issuing: it refers to the behavior that an enterprise issues and delivers bills to the payee when the capital flow is poor and cannot be paid in one time.

- Endorsement: it refers to the behavior that the holder transfers the ownership of the bill to the endorsee (the new holder) by taking the bill as a means of payment.
- Discount: it refers to the behavior of the bill holder demanding the face value of the bill from the bill issuer.

2.2 Introduction of Fabric and Smart Contract

Hyperledger fabric is an open source blockchain project led by IBM [3], mainly for enterprise customers. Unlike Ethereum, bitcoin and other public blockchains, fabric belongs to the alliance chain. In fabric network, nodes must be authorized and authenticated before they can join the blockchain network, which avoids the large amount of computing resources cost caused by proof of work [4], and greatly improves the efficiency of transaction processing [5].

Smart contract is the blockchain application business logic written in the form of computer code [6], and it's implemented by compilation and deployment. It automatically executes by triggering the conditions of established rules, which can minimize the impact of human intervention.

Blockchain is a distributed database, which uses "key value" pairs to save data. For smart contracts, the core is to add, delete, update and query the state database according to the business logic. The main API provided by Hyperledger Fabric is as follows [7]. The format is Function-Parameter-Return Value.

- Query data: GetState (key string) ([] byte, error)
- Update data: PutState (key string, value [] byte) error
- Delete data: DelState (key string) ([] byte, error)

3 Demand Analysis and Design

3.1 Role Analysis

In the traditional bill business platform, there are usually three types of roles: acceptance enterprise, bill holder, and bank. The acceptance enterprise is the drawer and transfers the bill to the holder as a means of payment. The holder can discount the bill or transfer it to the next holder as a means of payment. And the bank acts as the manager of the bill. We use the blockchain transaction model to replace the bank, aiming to realize trustless bill transactions and automated bill management.

(1) Acceptance enterprise (Drawer)

In the commercial transaction, the drawer is the issuer of the bill and the final destination after repeated circulation. When the enterprise is unable to make one-time payment due to capital turnover problems, it will use the acceptance bill as a means of payment to deliver the bill to the holder. At the same time, the acceptance enterprise shall pay the holder the corresponding amount when receiving the discount apply. Therefore, the acceptance enterprise is involved two businesses: Bill issuing and discount.

(2) Holder

The holder can be subdivided into several roles, such as endorser, endorsee and discount applicant. The endorser refers to the current bill holder who transfers the bill to others as a means of payment, and the endorsee is the new holder. The discount applicant is the person who applies to the acceptance enterprise for money. As every holder may participate in these activities, the three roles are merged into one and are involved in three businesses: Bill issuing, endorsement and discount.

(3) Blockchain trading model

In the traditional bill transaction platform, the bank, as the management institution of bill information, has multiple loopholes such as opaque transactions and manual illegal operations [8]. We use blockchain technology to encrypt and store bills in a distributed manner, and call smart contracts to achieve automated transaction. So this role is the most important part of the model. The blockchain model needs to judge the legality of the transaction and update the bill data (such as the bill holder, the bill transaction status, etc.) after the transaction. It's involved in three businesses of bill issuing, endorsement, and discount.

The use case diagram is as follows (Fig. 1).

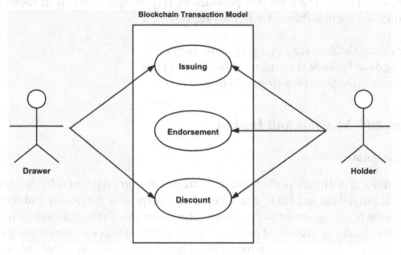

Fig. 1. Use case diagram

3.2 System Data Flow Diagram

Based on the use case diagram, we integrate the interaction process between different roles and the model into a system data flow diagram, as follows (Fig. 2).

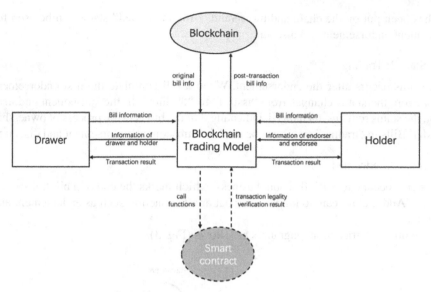

Fig. 2. System data flow diagram

The data flow of the model is as follows:

(1) When a role initiates a business request, it is necessary to send the identity information and bill information of both parties to the blockchain bill transaction model.

(2) The trading platform obtains all the information of corresponding bills from the blockchain by calling fabric API, including ownership, denomination, transaction status, etc.

(3) Use smart contract to verify the transaction legitimacy according to the identity information and bill information of both parties [9].

(4) If the transaction is legal, the blockchain bill transaction model will write the updated bill data back to the blockchain. Whether the transaction is successful or not, the transaction result will be returned to both parties.

3.3 Transaction Logic Design

Design of Bill Transaction State. The completion of each of the three business will be accompanied by the change of bill status. And the legality test of the transaction is also inseparable from the judgment of the current transaction status of the bill. For example, a discounted bill should not be transferred or discounted again.

We designed three bill transaction states, which are explained as follows.

(1) State 1: issued

This state occurs when bill issuing is completed. When a new set of bill information is written into the blockchain, the status of the bill is set to issued, indicating that a new bill has been put on the chain and turns valid. Bills in "issued" status can be used for subsequent endorsement and discount.

(2) State 2: Trading

This status occurs after the endorsement. When a bill complete the first endorsement transaction, the status changes from "issued" to "trading". In the subsequent endorsement, the status remains unchanged, indicating that the bill is in the process of ownership transfer. Bills in "trading" status can be used for subsequent endorsement and discount.

(3) State 3: redeemed

This status occurs after the discount business, which marks the end of a bill transaction process. And the bill can no longer carry out any transaction such as endorsement and discount.

The bill state transition diagram is as follows (Fig. 3).

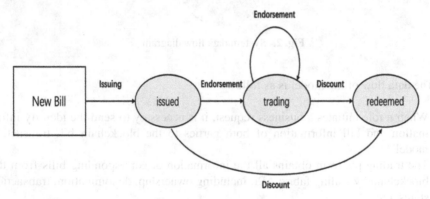

Fig. 3. Bill state transition diagram

Transaction Legality Verification

(1) Verification on the legality of ticket issuing

The blockchain bill transaction model uses the GetState API of Fabric to query the ledger based on the bill unique id. If the query result is not empty, it means the bill with this id already exists, so the transaction is illegal. Otherwise, the transaction is legal.

(2) Verification on the legality of endorsement

Use GetState API to query the complete information of the bill by the bill id. If the transaction status of the bill is "redeemed", it means that the ticket has been invalidated and the transaction is illegal. If the owner information is inconsistent with the current holder, it means that the ticket does not belong to the current endorsement applicant and the transaction is illegal. Otherwise, the transaction is legal.

(3) Verification on the legality of discount

It is necessary to judge not only the transaction status of the bill, but also whether the owner of the bill and the current discount applicant are the same. It is similar to the judgment of endorsement legality, and will not be repeated.

4 System Implementation

4.1 Software Environment

We use virtualization technology based on Docker to build the model. Based on fabric image, multiple docker containers are started on a computer to realize the interconnection between nodes to form a blockchain network. In addition, other software environments are required as follows (Table 1).

Table 1. Software environment

Software	Version
Go	1.9
Node.js	8.15.1
Docker	18.09.2
Docker-compose	1.19

4.2 Implementation of Smart Contracts

The data structure of the bill stores the bill information, including the drawer, holder, face value, issue date, due date and transaction status.

```
type paperInfo struct {
    Issuer     string  `json:"Issuer"`      //Drawer of the bill
    Owner      string  `json:"Owner"`       //The bill holder
    FaceValue  string  `json:"FaceValue"`   //The bill face value
    IssueDate  string  `json:"IssueDate"`   //Issue date of the bill
    DueDate    string  `json:"DueDate"`     //Due date of the bill
    State      string  `json:"State"`       //The bill transaction state
}
```

Smart contract implements the business logic of bill issuing, endorsement and discount, and realizes the storage, update and query of bill data on the blockchain.

The implementation part of the smart contract is summarized, and the function name and parameter table are as follows (Table 2):

Table 2. Smart contract function table

Function	Name and Parameters
Account register	{"Function": "register", "Args": ["owner", "password"]}
Issuing	{"Function": "issue", "Args": ["paperID", "issuer", "owner", "faceValue", "issueDate", "dueDate"]}
Endorsement	{"Function": "buy", "Args": ["paperID", "currentOwner", "newOwner"]}
Discount	{"Function": "redeem", "Args": ["paperID", "redeemOwner"]}
Bill query	{"Function": "queryPaper", "Args": ["paperID"]}

5 Simulation Transaction Test

5.1 Legal Transaction Test

Test process: acceptance enterprise Apple issues the bill to Steve, and then Steve endorses the bill to Craig, another holder. Finally Craig discount the bill to the drawer apple. The bill data changes as follows, so that the legal transaction is correct (Table 3).

Table 3. Changes of bill data during transaction

Attributes	After issuing	After endorsement	After discount
Id	"PAPER1"	"PAPER1"	"PAPER1"
Issuer	"Apple"	"Apple"	"Apple"
Owner	"Steve"	"Craig"	"Apple"
FaceValue	"5000"	"5000"	"5000"
IssueDate	"2020-10-1"	"2020-10-1"	"2020-10-1"
DueDate	"2021-10-1"	"2021-10-1"	"2021-10-1"
State	"issued"	"trading"	"redeemed"

5.2 Illegal Transaction Test

(1) Illegal endorsement:

After Steve endorsed the bill to Craig, he tried to "sell one bill more than once" to Scott

The parameters are as follows:

```
var request = {
    chaincodeId: 'paper',
    fcn: 'buy',
    args: ['1', 'Steve', 'Scott'],
    chainId: 'mychannel',
    txId: tx_id
};
```

However, since Steve has transferred the bill to Craig before, the ownership of the bill no longer belongs to him. Therefore, the transaction failed with an error of "the paper is not owned by Steve. The owner is Craig".

(2) Illegal discounting:

After Criag discounted the bills to Apple, he tried to "cash out an empty ticket" and applied for the discount again.

The parameters are as follows:

```
var request = {
    chaincodeId: 'paper',
    fcn: 'redeem',
    args: ['1', 'Craig'],
    chainId: 'mychannel',
    txId: tx_id
};
```

But because Craig had previously discounted the bill back to Apple, and the bill has expired. So the transaction failed and the error "The paper has been REDEEMED, it cannot be redeemed again" was reported.

6 Summary

In order to solve the problems of low efficiency, poor security and illegal operation of traditional bill trading platform, this paper designs and implements a model of bill transaction based on blockchain. The distributed storage, consensus algorithm and other features of the blockchain are conducive to solving the trust problem of traditional bill transactions. And we use smart contract to implement business logic, which greatly reduces the risks caused by illegal operations.

However, this system is not perfect. It did not realized more complicated business such as buy-back reselling and needs further improvement.

With the rise of mobile payment, we believe blockchain technology can have better applications and development in the transaction field.

Acknowledgement. This work was supported by State Grid science and technology program 5217Q020002Q. The program name is "Research and application of unified and credible data management of government enterprise one network all in one office".

References

1. Lee, Y.-T., Lin, J.-J., Hsu, J.Y.-J., Wu, J.-L.: A time bank system design on the basis of hyperledger fabric framework. In: 2020 IEEE International Conference on Blockchain and Cryptocurrency (ICBC), Toronto, ON, Canada, pp. 1–3 (2020)
2. Montes, J.M., Ramirez, C.E., Gutierrez, M.C., Larios, V.M.: Smart contracts for supply chain applicable to smart cities daily operations. In: 2019 IEEE International Smart Cities Conference (ISC2), Casablanca, Morocco, pp. 565–570 (2019)
3. Hyperledger. Hyperledger Fabric Documentation. https://hyperledger-fabric.readthedocs.io/en/release-1.4/
4. Yang, X., Chen, Y., Chen, X.: Effective scheme against 51% attack on proof-of-work blockchain with history weighted information. In: 2019 IEEE International Conference on Blockchain (Blockchain), Atlanta, GA, USA, pp. 261–265 (2019)
5. Sukhwani, H., Martínez, J.M., Chang, X., Trivedi, K.S., Rindos, A.: Performance modeling of PBFT consensus process for permissioned blockchain network (Hyperledger Fabric). In: 2017 IEEE 36th Symposium on Reliable Distributed Systems (SRDS), Hong Kong, pp. 253–255 (2017)
6. Christidis, K., Devetsiokiotis, M.: Blockchains and smart contracts for the IoT. IEEE Access **4**, 2292–2303 (2016)
7. Hyperledger. Hyperledger Fabric Documentation: Transaction Flow. https://hyperledger-fabric.readthedocs.io/en/latest/txflow.html
8. Zheng, W., Zheng, Z., Chen, X., Dai, K., Li, P., Chen, R.: NutBaaS: a blockchain-as-a-service platform. IEEE Access **7**, 134422–134433 (2019)
9. Malik, N., Puthal, D., Mohanty, S.P., et al.: The Blockchain as a decentralized security framework [Future Directions]. IEEE Consum. Electron. Mag. **7**(2), 18–21 (2018)
10. Liu, Q., Li, K.: Decentration transaction method based on blockchain technology. In: 2018 International Conference on Intelligent Transportation, Big Data & Smart City (ICITBS), Xiamen, pp. 416–419 (2018)

An N-gram Based Deep Learning Method for Network Traffic Classification

Wang Xiaojuan$^{(\boxtimes)}$ ⓘ, Kaiwenlv Kacuila ⓘ, and He Mingshu ⓘ

Beijing University of Posts and Telecommunications, Beijing 100876, China

Abstract. Various attacks have become the main threat in the Internet world. Traffic classification is the first step in network exception detection or network-based intrusion detection systems, and plays an important role in the field of network security. With the development of Internet technology, the source and complexity of network attacks are getting higher and higher, making it difficult for traditional anomaly detection systems to effectively analyze and identify malicious traffic. In recent years, the method of deep learning has been widely used in the field of traffic recognition, and the characteristics of traffic data can be automatically identified. Because of the size limit of the input data of the neural network, the flow data needs to be trimmed to feed into the network for learning, so the neural network cannot learn the characteristics of the traffic data well. In this paper, we propose an N-gram-based data processing method to convert the raw traffic data into N-gram features to represent more information. Then our method uses a detector based on convolutional neural network (CNN) to classify and detect data. Our experiments show that the detection accuracy of using N-gram feature data is better than the method using raw traffic. This method can more effectively detect malicious traffic data.

Keywords: Network security · Anomaly detection · Traffic classification · N-gram · Convolutional neural network

1 Introduction

Cyber security is a hot issue in recent years. Due to the rapid development of the Internet, cyberattack has become one of the biggest challenges facing today. With the deployment of the Internet of Things, security threats to the network are expected to increase further, with billions of devices connecting to the Internet and providing more opportunities for attackers. Therefore, cybersecurity has become more important than ever.

Traffic in a network is the data generated on the network by devices that can access the network. Traffic classification is a task that associates network traffic with applications, which has become a crucial task in network management, especially in the field of network security. In the field of network security, traffic classification is the first step in an intrusion detection system, that is, an anomaly detector, which is responsible for identifying malicious traffic so that the system can respond to network attacks in time.

So far, many papers have discussed and studied many different types of network traffic recognition methods. We can roughly divide these methods into three different

© Springer Nature Switzerland AG 2021
X. Sun et al. (Eds.): ICAIS 2021, LNCS 12737, pp. 289–304, 2021.
https://doi.org/10.1007/978-3-030-78612-0_24

types, 1) The most traditional traffic classification methods based on rules and port numbers [1] and Deep Packet Inspection (DPI) technology [2], 2) statistical-based and behavioral-based traditional machine learning traffic classification methods [3], 3) and automatic traffic classification methods based on deep learning, which have been widely used in recent years [4].

In many recent studies based on deep learning, they trim the flow data larger than the input size in data processing, and trim it into the size of the network input layer, because the input data size of the neural network is relatively small. This will have the effect of reducing the amount of information, and it is possible to trim the data containing important information and reduce the classification performance of the model. We propose a new traffic data processing method, which convert the raw data into frequency feature data. In order to achieve this method, we adopted the N-gram model to characterize the frequency feature of the traffic data. Our method uses CNN to learn and classify the traffic data. The main contributions of this work are as follows:

- In this work, a new method for processing traffic data is proposed. This method extracts N-gram fragments of raw traffic data, and then selects a gram set using feature selection technology to calculate the frequency of each gram to generate N-gram feature data for learning.
- We use CNN, which is a classic network in deep learning, to model and predict the traffic data. A set of experiments were conducted to demonstrate the classification ability of the proposed. The result proved that our method can effectively detect malicious traffic.

The rest of the sections of this paper are arranged as follows: Existing research works related to traffic classification is presented in Sect. 2. In Sect. 3 we present and provide details on our proposed approach. In Sect. 4 we discuss the classification performance achieved by our method. Finally, conclusions are presented in Sect. 5.

2 Related Work

Today's cyber attacks are becoming more serious and have become a serious threat to modern network security. In order to protect the network environment, it is important to identify malicious network traffic.

2.1 Traditional Methods

Both port-based and DPI-based methods are traditional rule-based methods. Port-based method is a classification method used in the early stages of network development. The port number of the transport layer is used to directly identify traffic. The DPI-based method not only checks the information of the port number of the transport layer, but the DPI technology also uses the information in the deeper layers, such as the information of the seventh application layer in the OSI model. Finsterbusch et al. [5] summarized current main DPI-based traffic classification methods. These are all using existing rules to match malicious traffic. When malicious traffic changes behavior, these methods will fail.

2.2 Machine Learning Methods

For the shortcomings of traditional traffic classification methods, many studies have tried statistical and behavior-based machine learning methods. Horng et al. [6] proposed an intrusion detection system based on SVM, which combines hierarchical clustering algorithm, a simple feature selection process and SVM technology. Syarif et al. [7] applies three ensemble algorithms, which are bagging, boosting and stacking, to intrusion detection problems to improve accuracy and reduce false alarm rates. The basic classifiers of these ensemble methods are Naive Bayes, decision tree, conventional induction and k-NN.

2.3 Deep Learning Methods

The related algorithms of deep learning and its application have been developed rapidly in recent years. The deep learning method has made good achievements in computer vision and other fields, and this method can save the cumbersome steps of feature engineering. Li et al. [8] proposed a CNN based method, which converts raw packets into an image, and then uses a CNN to learn the features from that graphics. ResNet50 and GoogLeNet were used as the network architectures, and they took NSL-KDD dataset [9] for evaluation. Result showed accuracies ranging from 79% to 82% in detecting attacks. Wang et al. [10] propose a hierarchical learning approach to construct spatio-temporal features, combining spatial feature learning through CNNs and temporal feature learning through long short-term memory(LSTM) networks. J. Cui et al. [11] propose an improved Network Intrusion Detection System(NIDS) using word embedding-based deep learning (WEDL-NIDS), which has the ability of dimension reduction and learning features from data with sophisticated structure and it can pre-analyze the raw traffic data for network intrusion detection.

Motivated by those studies, we propose to use the N-gram model in natural language processing to preprocess the traffic data, and use the CNN model to model and classify the N-gram feature data. Compared with the use of raw data, the data we have processed has better performance.

3 Proposed Method

The proposed N-gram-based malicious traffic detector consists of the preprocessing module, the training module, and the testing module, as shown in Fig. 1.

The preprocessing module is used to process the raw traffic data into N-gram feature data. It mainly comprises of three modules, which are Pcap files processing, N-gram feature extraction and N-gram feature data generator. The data generated by the preprocessing module is divided proportionally into training data and testing data. The training data is fed into the training module, and the designed CNN is used for training. Finally, the test module will utilize the testing data and the trained model to verify the proposed method.

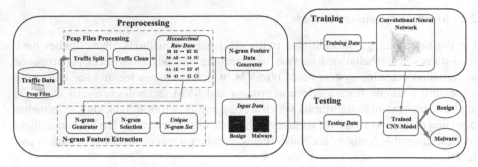

Fig. 1. The framework of the proposed method

3.1 Pcap Files Processing

Traffic Data. The granularity of network traffic splitting includes: TCP connection, flow, session, service and host [12]. According to different granularities, traffic data can be divided into different units of data. In recent years of research, flow and session are the most used split granularities. A flow is defined as all packets with the same 5-tuple, namely source IP, source port, destination IP, destination port and transport-level protocol. And a session is defined as bidirectional flows, both directions of traffic are included. Flow is used in the proposed method. The description of the different forms of traffic are depicted in Fig. 2.

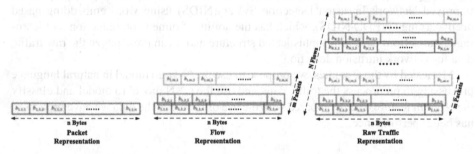

Fig. 2. The representations of different forms of traffic

Data Preprocessing. The processing procedure mainly includes two parts: flow generation and traffic clean. Figure 3 shows the whole process of Pcap files.

Step 1 (Flow Generation). The purpose of this step is to divide the continuous traffic data into discrete traffic data, namely flow data, based on the five-tuple. Output data format is also Pcap.

Step 2 (Traffic Clean). The IP address or MAC address information may damage the feature extraction process in training. And we need to eliminate this negative impact by removing the information through randomization, which is called traffic anonymization or sanitization [13]. So, first we need to randomly assign MAC ad-dresses and IP

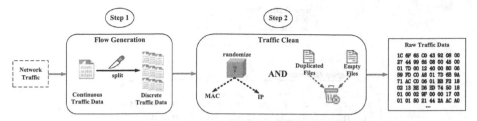

Fig. 3. Data preprocess procedure of Pcap files

addresses in the data link layer and the IP layer respectively. The second thing we need to do is to delete redundant data, namely duplicate files and empty files, because these redundant data can not benefit the training of the neural network.

3.2 N-gram Feature Extraction

N-gram Generator. N-gram is a language model, which is widely used as a text processing method in the fields of natural language processing and speech recognition. And N-gram model is also widely used in the cyber security field [14, 15]. N-gram is a sequence composed of 'N' consecutive bytes from a byte sequence, where 'N' represents the number of predefined bytes, and this sequence of consecutive bytes is called a gram fragment. In the proposed work, the first task of data processing is to generate N-grams. The whole processing procedure of the N-gram generator is depicted in Fig. 4.

The raw traffic data input to the generator in the figure is the hexadecimal data sequence generated by the Pcap file processing. For the raw data sequence, a sliding window with a size of two bytes is applied in the figure to process it, which generates a 2-g sequence, as shown in Fig. 4. Each data through the N-gram generator will generate an N-gram sequence, and a gram fragment is regarded as a feature, so we extract all the unique gram fragments in all the generated N-gram sequences to form an N-gram feature set.

N-gram Selection. Feature selection aims to find a small number of features that can describe the dataset as well as the original feature set, or even better than the original feature set. Feature selection speeds up the learning algorithm and sometimes improves its performance by eliminating irrelevant and/or redundant features [16]. In this work, we use the frequency of each gram fragment as the input data, so we can only use n gram fragments (n is the size of the input data, in this work n = 784, namely 1*784). Therefore, we need to utilize feature selection technology to select more important grams.

Chi-Square. The Chi-square is applied to examine the independence of two variables [17]. In this paper, it examine the independence between sample features and its class. If they are not independent, it means that the feature is strongly related to the class, so the feature can benefit the classification. The chi-square score is calculated as the Eq. (1) and higher Chi-Square scores indicate the close relationship between feature and class.

$$\tilde{X}^2(f, c) = \frac{N[AD - BC]^2}{(A + C)(B + D)(A + B)(C + D)} \tag{1}$$

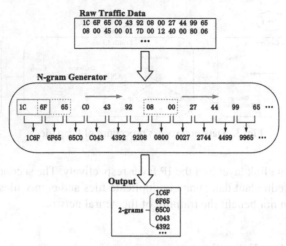

Fig. 4. The procedure of N-gram generator

Where, N represents the total files in the dataset, A denotes the total files containing the feature f in class c, C indicates the total files present in class c in which feature f does not exist, B represents the total files containing the feature f that does not exist in class c and D denotes files not present in class c and also does not have the feature f.

Information Gain. In Information Gain [18], the measure of importance is to see how much information a feature can bring to the classification system. The more information it brings, the more important the feature is. For a feature t, we calculate the amount of information when the system has it and when it does not and the difference between the two is the amount of information this feature brings to the system, namely the gain. The information gain of the feature is calculated as the Eq. (2).

$$IG(f) = P(f) \sum_{i=1}^{n} P(C_i|f) log_2 P(C_i|f) + P(\bar{f}) \sum_{i=1}^{n} P(C_i|\bar{f}) log_2 P(C_i|\bar{f}) \quad (2)$$

Where f represents the feature F appears, $\bar{f}$ represents the feature F does not appear. C_i denotes the i-th class.

Mutual Information. Mutual Information [19] estimates the lack of uncertainty about one random variable as a function of the other. When the mutual information score is zero, these two variables are considered independent. And a higher mutual information score means a higher correlation between the two variables. The calculation formula of Mutual Information is shown in Eq. (3).

$$MI(f, c) = \sum_{v_f \in \{0,1\}} \sum_{v_c \in \{0,1\}} P(f = v_f, c = v_c) ln \frac{P(f = v_f, c = v_c)}{P(c = v_c)P(f = v_f)} \quad (3)$$

f is a feature that takes the value $v_f = \{0, 1\}$. The value of $v_f = 0$ indicates that the feature f is not present in the file and $v_f = 0$ implies that the feature f is present in the file. c denotes class, and the value of the class $v_c = 1$ means the existence of a file in class c, otherwise $v_c = 0$.

ReliefF. This feature selection algorithm is an extension of the Relief algorithm. Relief uses feature relevance criteria to rank features. It is very efficient in estimating the features [20]. It quantifies the feature by the degree of difference between the instances where the feature value is close to each other. But its limitation is that it can only handle two classes of data. So there is an improved ReliefF algorithm, which can handle multiclass problems. When the ReliefF algorithm deals with multiple classes of problems, it randomly takes out a sample R from the training sample set each time, and then finds the k nearest neighbor samples (near Hits) of R from the sample set of the same class as R. Then we find k nearest neighbor samples (near Misses) from the sample sets of different classes of each R, and then update the weight of each feature, as shown in the Eq. (4):

$$W(A) = W(A) - \frac{\sum_{j=1}^{k} diff(A, R, H_j)}{mk} + \sum_{C \notin class(R)} \left[\frac{p(C)}{1 - p(Class(R))} \sum_{j=1}^{k} diff(A, R, M_j(C)) \right] / (mk) \tag{4}$$

In the above formula, $M_j(C)$ represents the j-th nearest neighbor sample in class C. $diff(A, R_1, R_2)$ represents the difference of sample R_1 and sample R_2 on feature A, and its calculation formula is shown in the Eq. (5):

$$diff(A, R_1, R_2) = \begin{cases} \frac{|R_1[A] - R_2[A]|}{\max(A) - \min(A)}, & \text{if } A \text{ is continuous} \\ 0, & \text{if } A \text{ is discrete and } R_1[A] = R_2[A] \\ 1, & \text{if } A \text{ is discrete and } R_1[A] \neq R_2[A] \end{cases} \tag{5}$$

3.3 N-gram Feature Data Generator

The last step of data processing is to generate N-gram feature data as the input data of CNN. The first is to feed each hexadecimal raw traffic data into the N-gram generator and convert it into an N-gram feature sequence. Then we calculate the number of appearances of the final N-gram feature set's each gram in the N-gram feature sequence to get the sum of the number of appearances of all gram in this data. Then divide the number of appearances of each gram by the total number of appearances to get the frequency of each gram. This frequency is the final input data of the data point where the gram is located.

Finally, we selected one of the datasets used in this work, namely ISCXIDS2012, to visually display and analyze the generated N-gram feature data, as shown in Fig. 5. The images in the leftmost column in Fig. 5 represent each class of data. Obviously, each image class has some characteristics that can be distinguished from other classes. The five images on the right of each row in Fig. 5 are the five visualized data we randomly selected in each class, which show the consistency of each class. It can be seen that these five data of each class have considerable similarities. Through visual analysis, we can see that the differences between classes and similarities within classes have good performance, so it is reasonable to infer that the data processing method we proposed is feasible.

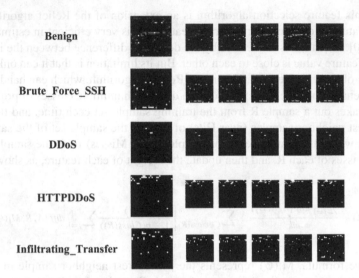

Fig. 5. Visualization of the generated data

3.4 Convolutional Neural Network

Training the classification model with the generated data is another important task. So far, CNN has been mainly used in the field of computer vision, such as image classification [21]. In addition, there are many successful cases of CNN in the field of natural language processing [22, 23]. CNN is most suitable for data in multiple array forms, and it can skillfully use multiple abstraction levels [24] to learn the representation of input data. In most recent research on malicious traffic detection, the use of CNN has a very good performance, so in the proposed method, we also adopted CNN.

1D-CNN is good for data like sequential data or language. And traffic data is also similar to the textual sequence data, it does not have the two-dimensional spatial features like images. Therefore, in this work we utilized 1D-CNN. Our CNN structure is depicted in Fig. 6. The previously generated N-gram feature data will first be normalized to [0, 1], and then flattened into one-dimensional data before being input to CNN. And the size of each layer of the network model is shown in Fig. 6. The output of the last fully connected layer is a one-dimensional array of the number of classes. Finally, the softmax function is used to output the probability of each class.

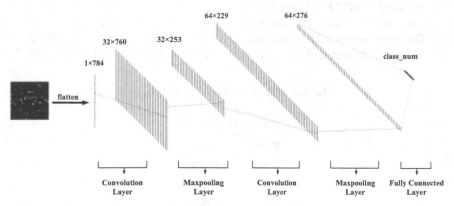

Fig. 6. Overview of the proposed CNN structure

4 Experimental Results and Discussion

4.1 Datasets Description

In this work, we used two public datasets to evaluate our proposed method. Both of these two datasets include normal traffic and multiple classes of malicious traffic, which are very suitable for our needs. These datasets are described as follows:

Dataset 1. The first dataset is ISCXIDS2012 [25]. This dataset contains 7 days of raw data, a total of 84.42GB, stored in Pcap format. In addition to benign traffic, it also includes 4 types of malicious traffic, namely BruteForce SSH, DDoS, HttpDoS and Infiltrating. Compared with the previously popular KDD99 data set, IDS2012's data is closer to the actual situation and more in line with the development trend of network behavior and intrusion. Table 1 shows the detailed distribution of ISCXIDS2012.

Table 1. The distribution of ISCXIDS2012

Flow types	Number
Benign	1433293
Brute Force SSH	14056
DDoS	45016
HttpDoS	6533
Infiltrating	19156

Dataset 2. The second dataset is CIC-IDS2017 [26]. They used their proposed B-Profile system [27] to describe the abstract behavior of human interaction and generate natural benign background traffic. For CIC-IDS2017 dataset, they built an abstract behavior of

25 users based on HTTP, HTTPS, FTP, SSH and email protocols. This dataset contains benign and the most up-to-date common attacks, which resembles the true real-world data. This work selected 11 attacks and its benign traffic in this dataset as the training and test data of the model. Table 2 shows the detailed distribution of CIC-IDS2017.

Table 2. The distribution of CIC-IDS2017

Flow types	Number
Benign	496922
Botnet	83865
DDoS	119293
FTP	98192
GoldenEye	30379
HeartBleed	42026
Hulk	48734
PortScan	410470
SlowHttp	37958
SlowLoris	37357
SqlInjection	4129
SSH	80441

4.2 Experimental Results

Evaluation Metrics. In this work, we used four evaluation metrics Precision, Recall, Macro-f1 and Weighted-f1 to evaluate the classification ability of our proposed method. These metrics are explained as follows:

$$Precision = \frac{1}{N} \sum_{i=1}^{N} \frac{TP}{TP + FP} \tag{6}$$

$$Recall = \frac{1}{N} \sum_{i=1}^{N} \frac{TP}{TP + FN} \tag{7}$$

$$Macro - f1 = \frac{1}{N} \sum_{i=1}^{N} \frac{2 \times Precision \times Recall}{Precision + Recall} \tag{8}$$

$$Weighted - f1 = \sum_{i=1}^{N} \omega \times \frac{2 \times Precision \times Recall}{Precision + Recall} \tag{9}$$

Where TP (true positive) is the number of positive samples which identified to be correct, TN (true negative) is the number of negative samples which identified to be correct, FP (false positive) is the number of positive samples which identified to be wrong, and FN (false negative) is the number of negative samples which identified to be wrong. And N is the number of classes of data, ω is the weight of the number of data samples of each class in the number of all data samples.

Results and Analysis. We use the same network structure to classify the raw traffic data for comparison. For the raw flow data, we first trim the hexadecimal flow data generated by the Pcap file processing into a one-dimensional matrix with a size of 784 bytes, which is the size of the CNN input data. Then we convert the hexadecimal data into decimal data and normalize it to [0,1]. At the same time, we also designed some comparative experiments using traditional machine learning methods. This work mainly involves five different machine learning algorithms, namely K-Nearest Neighbor (KNN), Logistic Regression (LR), Decision Tree (DT), Random Forests (RF) and Xgboost. The comparison results on the two datasets are shown in Table 3 and Table 4.

Table 3. Experimental results of ISCXIDS2012

Data types	Precision	Recall	Macro-f1	Weighted-f1
KNN	0.9582	0.9593	0.9586	0.9593
LR	0.6089	0.7483	0.5419	0.4697
RF	0.9775	0.9762	0.9768	0.9766
DT	0.9504	0.9498	0.9496	0.9504
Xgboost	0.9749	0.9781	0.9764	0.9759
CNN using Raw data	0.9907	0.9904	0.9905	0.9910
CNN using N-gram feature data	**0.9988**	**0.9988**	**0.9988**	**0.9989**

Table 4. Experimental results of CIC-IDS2017

Data types	Precision	Recall	Macro-f1	Weighted-f1
KNN	0.6220	0.5668	0.5868	0.6760
LR	0.0396	0.0926	0.0422	0.0885
RF	0.8954	0.8471	0.8639	0.8955
DT	0.8811	0.8791	0.8801	0.9067
Xgboost	0.9063	0.8273	0.8473	0.8869
CNN using Raw data	0.9575	0.9572	0.9572	0.9576
CNN using N-gram feature data	**0.9922**	**0.9922**	**0.9922**	**0.9924**

As can be seen from the tables, the classification results using the CNN based approach are better than 5 traditional machine learning based classifiers. Compared with the CNN model using raw traffic data, our proposed method achieved better performance.

For ISCXIDS2012 dataset, our method gained highest Precision of 0.9988 with 0.9988, 0.9988, and 0.9989 of Recall, Macro-f1, and Weighted-f1, respectively. And for CIC-IDS2017 dataset, our method also reached highest Precision of 0.9922 with 0.9922, 0.9922, and 0.9924 of Recall, Macro-f1, and Weighted-f1, respectively.

In this work, we adopted four feature selection techniques to select the most important 784 fragments from all N-gram fragments, and used these fragments to generate different N-gram feature data. Because N in the N-gram feature represents the size of the sliding window, namely the size of the gram fragment, we select a different N to process the raw traffic data, and obtain different N-gram feature data. In this work, we chose N as 2, 3, 4 for comparative experiments. For each N-gram, we use four feature selection techniques to filter gram fragments respectively. The experimental results on different data are shown in Table 5 and Table 6. It can be seen that the applications of the four feature selection techniques are effective. The CNN model achieved excellent performance on the four N-gram feature data generated by feature selection techniques. For ISCXIDS2012 dataset, ReliefF and Chi-Square performed better, and the data generated by ReliefF reached the highest classification results. For CIC-IDS2017 dataset, Chi-Square and Information Gain can achieve a better performance. And the data generated by Chi-Square gained the highest classification results. Among them, 4-g feature data performed best. The reason for this result can be explained as the gram fragment composed of 4 bytes in the 4-g feature data is more meaningful. The strings converted from these gram fragments may be specific or frequently appearing in a certain class of traffic. Therefore, the frequency of these gram fragments can benefit classification.

Table 5. Comparison of performance achieved by different feature selection techniques on ISCXIDS2012

Feature selection techniques	Metrics	N-gram feature data		
		2-g	3-g	4-g
Chi-Square	Precision	0.9980	0.9970	0.9981
	Recall	0.9979	0.9970	0.9980
	Macro-f1	0.9979	0.9970	0.9981
	Weighted-f1	0.9980	0.9971	0.9981
Information gain	Precision	0.9970	0.9960	0.9972
	Recall	0.9969	0.9959	0.9970
	Macro-f1	0.9969	0.9959	0.9971
	Weighted-f1	0.9971	0.9959	0.9972
Mutual information	Precision	0.9965	0.9953	0.9969
	Recall	0.9964	0.9953	0.9969
	Macro-f1	0.9965	0.9953	0.9969
	Weighted-f1	0.9966	0.9954	0.9970

(continued)

Table 5. (*continued*)

Feature selection techniques	Metrics	N-gram feature data		
		2-g	3-g	4-g
ReliefF	Precision	0.9986	0.9980	0.9988
	Recall	0.9986	0.9979	0.9988
	Macro-f1	0.9986	0.9979	0.9988
	Weighted-f1	0.9987	0.9980	0.9989

Table 6. Comparison of performance achieved by different feature selection techniques on CIC-IDS2017

Feature selection techniques	Metrics	N-gram feature data		
		2-g	3-g	4-g
Chi-Square	Precision	0.9800	0.9887	0.9922
	Recall	0.9799	0.9886	0.9922
	Macro-f1	0.9799	0.9886	0.9922
	Weighted-f1	0.9800	0.9888	0.9924
Information gain	Precision	0.9731	0.9834	0.9859
	Recall	0.9729	0.9833	0.9858
	Macro-f1	0.9730	0.9833	0.9858
	Weighted-f1	0.9731	0.9834	0.9858
Mutual information	Precision	0.9578	0.9669	0.9705
	Recall	0.9577	0.9666	0.9696
	Macro-f1	0.9577	0.9667	0.9696
	Weighted-f1	0.9577	0.9668	0.9695
ReliefF	Precision	0.9689	0.9734	0.9844
	Recall	0.9687	0.9732	0.9841
	Macro-f1	0.9688	0.9732	0.9842
	Weighted-f1	0.9690	0.9732	0.9841

In order to prove our proposed method, we generated a confusion matrix to show the classification of each class of data, as shown in Fig. 7 and Fig. 8. As can be seen from Fig. 7, in the classification of the raw data of the ISCXIDS2012 dataset, only 97.65% of the first class is correctly classified, and less than 99% of the second and third classes are correctly classified. In the results of classification using N-gram feature data, more than 99% of each class is correctly classified. In Fig. 8, it can be seen that the method of using raw traffic data are prone to confusion in different classes of CIC-IDS2017 dataset, but the proposed method improves the detection of many classes.

In summary, the proposed traffic data processing method based on the N-gram model is effective, and classification by the CNN proposed in our method has good performance. Compared with most recent methods that use raw traffic data for classification, the N-gram feature data processed by our proposed method is more distinctive and can better help classify network traffic data.

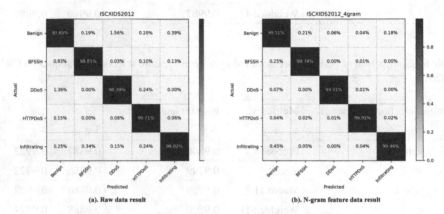

Fig. 7. Confusion matrixes of the results on ISCXIDS2012

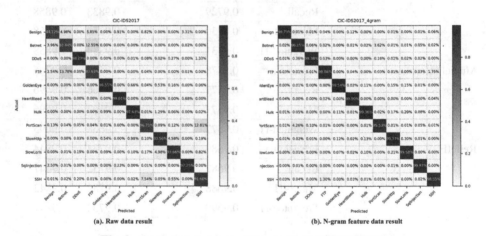

Fig. 8. Confusion matrixes of the results on CIC-IDS2017

5 Conclusion

In this paper, we propose a new traffic data processing method to detect malicious traffic. We use the N-gram model to extract gram fragments from the raw traffic data, and use feature selection techniques to pick out the most important 784 g fragments to form a gram set. Afterwards, the frequency each gram fragment in each data is calculated as input data to form the N-gram feature data. Then we use the CNN model proposed in our work to classify both N-gram feature data and raw traffic data. For the raw traffic data, we trim the hexadecimal data to the input size of the network and feed it directly into the network. The experimental results reveals that using N-gram feature data for classification can effectively improve the classification results of network traffic data and achieve high performance.

In the future, we will use other network models to design new classification models combined with our proposed data processing methods to classify traffic. For example, a deep unsupervised model such as an auto encoder can be used to cluster traffic data to solve the identification of unknown network malicious traffic. At the application level, we intend to further use our proposed method in actual flow data and actual production.

Acknowledgement. Thanks for the experimental environment provided by laboratory ICN&CAD of School of Electronic Engineering, Beijing University of Posts and Telecommunications. And thanks to He Mingshu, Jin Lei and Zhang Yu for their contributions to this work.

Funding Statement. This work was supported by the National Natural Science Foundation of China (62071056).

Conflicts of Interest. We declare that we do not have any commercial or associative interest that represents a conflict of interest in connection with the work submitted.

References

1. Biersack, E., Christian, C., Maja, M.: Data Traffic Monitoring and Analysis. Springer, Berlin (2013)
2. Dharmapurikar, S., et al.: Deep packet inspection using parallel Bloom filters. IEEE Micro **24**(1), 52–61 (2004)
3. Nguyen, T.T.T., Grenville, A.: A survey of techniques for internet traffic classification using machine learning. IEEE Commun. Surv. Tutorials **10**(4), 56–76 (2008)
4. Wang, W., et al.: Malware traffic classification using convolutional neural network for representation learning. In: 2017 International Conference on Information Networking (ICOIN). IEEE (2017)
5. Finsterbusch, M., et al.: A survey of payload-based traffic classification approaches. IEEE Commun. Surv. Tutorials **16**(2), 1135–1156 (2013)
6. Horng, S.J., et al.: A novel intrusion detection system based on hierarchical clustering and support vector machines. Expert Syst. Appl. Int. J. **38**(1), 306–313 (2011)
7. Syarif, I., Zaluska, E., Prugel-Bennett, A., Wills, G.: Application of bagging, boosting and stacking to intrusion detection. In: Perner, P. (ed.) MLDM 2012. LNCS (LNAI), vol. 7376, pp. 593–602. Springer, Heidelberg (2012). https://doi.org/10.1007/978-3-642-31537-4_46
8. Li, Z., et al.: Intrusion detection using convolutional neural networks for representation learning. In: International Conference on Neural Information Processing. Springer, Cham (2014)

9. Aggarwal, P., Sharma, S.K.: Analysis of KDD dataset attributes - class wise for intrusion detection. Procedia Comput. Sci. **57**, 842–851 (2015)
10. Wang, W., et al.: HAST-IDS: learning hierarchical spatial-temporal features using deep neural networks to improve intrusion detection. IEEE Access **6**(99), 1792–1806 (2018)
11. Cui, J., Long, J., Min, E., Mao, Y.: WEDL-NIDS: improving network intrusion detection using word embedding-based deep learning method. In: Torra, V., Narukawa, Y., Aguiló, I., González-Hidalgo, M. (eds.) MDAI 2018. LNCS (LNAI), vol. 11144, pp. 283–295. Springer, Cham (2018). https://doi.org/10.1007/978-3-030-00202-2_23
12. Dainotti, A., Pescape, A., Claffy, K.C.: Issues and future directions in traffic classification. IEEE Netw. **26**(1), 35–40 (2012)
13. Koukis, D., et al.: A generic anonymization framework for network traffic. In: 2006 IEEE International Conference on Communications, vol. 5. IEEE (2006)
14. Wang, K., Parekh, J.J., Stolfo, S.J.: Anagram: a content anomaly detector resistant to mimicry attack. In: Zamboni, D., Kruegel, C. (eds.) RAID 2006. LNCS, vol. 4219, pp. 226–248. Springer, Heidelberg (2006). https://doi.org/10.1007/11856214_12
15. Santos, I., et al.: N-grams-based file signatures for malware detection. ICEIS **2**(9), 317–320 (2009)
16. Zhao, Z., et al.: Advancing feature selection research. ASU Feature Selection Repository, pp. 1–28 (2010)
17. Ajay Kumara, M.A., Jaidhar, C.D.: Leveraging virtual machine introspection with memory forensics to detect and characterize unknown malware using machine learning techniques at hypervisor. Digital Invest. **23**, 99–123 (2017)
18. Kolter, J.Z., Maloof, M.A.: Learning to detect and classify malicious executables in the wild. J. Mach. Learn. Res. **7**, 2721–2744 (2006)
19. Singh, B., Kushwaha, N., Vyas, O.P., et al.: A feature subset selection technique for high dimensional data using symmetric uncertainty. J. Data Anal. Inform. Process. **2**(04), 95–105 (2014)
20. Coronado-De-Alba, L.D., Rodríguez-Mota, A., Escamilla-Ambrosio, P.J.: Feature selection and ensemble of classifiers for android malware detection. In: Proceedings of the 8th IEEE Latin-American Conference on Communications (LATINCOM), pp. 1–6. IEEE (2016)
21. Albawi, S., Mohammed, T.A., Al-Zawi, S.: Understanding of a convolutional neural network. In: Proceedings of the International Conference on Engineering and Technology (ICET), pp. 1–6 (2017)
22. Buczak, A.L., Guven, E.: A survey of data mining and machine learning methods for cyber security intrusion detection. IEEE Commun. Surv. Tuts. **18**(2), 1153–1176 (2016)
23. Berman, D., Buczak, A., Chavis, J., Corbett, C.: A survey of deep learning methods for cyber security. Information **10**(4), 122 (2019)
24. Albelwi, S., Mahmood, A.: A framework for designing the architectures of deep convolutional neural networks. Entropy **19**(6), 242 (2017)
25. Shiravi, A., Shiravi, H., Tavallaee, M., Ghorbani, A.A.: Toward developing a systematic approach to generate benchmark datasets for intrusion detection. Comput. Secur. **31**(3), 357–374 (2012)
26. Sharafaldin, I., Lashkari, A.H., Ghorbani, A.A.: Toward generating a new intrusion detection dataset and intrusion traffic characterization. In: ICISSP, pp. 108–116 (2018)
27. Sharafaldin, I., et al.: Towards a reliable intrusion detection benchmark dataset. Softw. Netw. **2017**(9), 177–200 (2017)

Interpretability Framework of Network Security Traffic Classification Based on Machine Learning

Mingshu He, Lei Jin(✉), and Mei Song

Beijing University of Posts and Telecommunications, Beijing 100876, China
jinlei@bupt.edu.cn

Abstract. With the increasing number of people accessing the Internet, attacks against users or web servers have become a serious threat to network security. Network traffic can record network behavior, which is an important data source for analyzing network behavior. Using machine learning algorithm to analyze network behavior is one of the effective methods. However, these methods always put the data into black boxes, which is not enough for business understanding and result reliability display. In this paper, we propose an interpretability framework of network security traffic classification and apply it on a network traffic dataset. In this work, we apply some interpretable models, including model structure-based and feature importance-based. We verify that the methods can help researchers better explain the business features of network security traffic and optimize the classification model in algorithm selection and feature selection. We also study the interpretability of network traffic on neural network and make some progress.

Keywords: Interpretability · Network security · Traffic · Machine learning

1 Introduction

With the continuous development of the Internet, the number and frequency of people accessing network are increasing rapidly in their life, study and work. Users are more likely to be affected by network attacks and malicious behaviors. Consequently, it is necessary to identify and analyze malicious and aggressive network behaviors, which is of great help to the security of network environment [1]. Using machine learning algorithm to analyze network traffic is a commonly used method in traffic classification [2]. Some methods, such as decision tree (DT), K-Nearest Neighbor (KNN), support vector machine (SVM)-based models, are designed to identify network traffic [3]. Methods based on deep learning (DL) can collect features automatically in the training process, thereby facilitating the process of acquiring typical features and important information [4–6].

Although in the field of traffic classification, the above methods based on machine learning has achieved good results. Most of these cutting-edge machine learning models are still black boxes, which can hardly perceive their internal working state. This brings

© Springer Nature Switzerland AG 2021
X. Sun et al. (Eds.): ICAIS 2021, LNCS 12737, pp. 305–320, 2021.
https://doi.org/10.1007/978-3-030-78612-0_25

us the question of credibility: should we believe that one of the predictions of that model is correct or should we believe that the prediction results of the model are generally reasonable?

To make our results more reliable, the interpretability of black box model has become a research focus in various fields. The interpretation technology of the model plays an important role in creating safer and more reliable products for the company. Similarly, the application of machine learning model in medicine, biology, image, natural language processing and other research needs not only to explain the trust and acceptance of results, but also to explain the openness of scientific discovery and the progress of research. The research on interpretable machine learning is favored by researchers, especially in specific application fields. Kang tec. proposed a machine learning interpretability on extreme Multi-label Learning [7]. Doshi-Velez et al. proposed a taxonomy for rigorous evaluation and expose open questions towards a more rigorous science of interpretable machine learning [8]. Tolomei et al. proposed a interpretable predictions model of tree-based ensembles via actionable feature tweaking [9]. Tan et al. proposed a tree ensembles interpretable model based on tree space prototypes [10]. Jung proposed an information-theoretic approach to personalized explainable machine learning, which could quantify the effect of an explanation by the conditional mutual information between the explanation and prediction [11]. At the same time, there are also a few applications of interpretable methods in the field of network security [12]. Kim analyzed the feature importance and interpretation for malware classification [13]. In this paper, we try to complete the feature interpretability and service interpretability of network traffic identification and propose the analysis method.

There are some commonly used interpretable models and methods, such as some model-based methods and feature-based methods including Shapley additive explanations (SHAP)-based interpretability method [14], local interpretable model agnostic explanations (LIME)-based interpretability method [15] and Partial Dependence Plot (PDP) [16]. In this research, we try to use these methods on network traffic data and verify the interpretability of these methods on traffic data.

The contributions of this paper can be summarized as follows:

1) Proposing an interpretable model of the structure and principle of different machine learning algorithms based on the network traffic abnormal behavior classification experiment.
2) Building a feature analysis model of interpretable machine learning algorithm based on network traffic classification results.
3) The business features of network traffic can be explained more intuitively, and some suggestions of algorithm selection and feature selection are proposed.

The remainder of this paper is arranged as follows. Section 2 explain the interpretability framework and process of classification experiments. In Sect. 3, we introduce the interpretability methods based on algorithm structure and analyze experiment results. In Sect. 4, we analyze results from the interpretability method of network traffic based on feature importance. Section 5 summarizes the paper and outlines directions for future research.

2   Interpretability Framework Overview and Experiment Process

2.1   Framework Description

Figure 1 shows the interpretability framework of network security traffic classification. It consists of data processing module, machine learning classification module, interpretability module and verification module. In classification model, we use logistic regression (LR), KNN, DT, random forest (RF) and generalized additive model with pairwise interaction (GA2M) [3]. The interpretability model consists of structure-based and feature-based methods. Some important information will output from interpretability model. It can help us understand the characteristics and models of network traffic data from a business perspective and give necessary advice to improve model reliability and promote classification results.

In the experiments, we chose a dataset of network traffic and train some classification models to verify interpretability methods. The processing process of the dataset and the results of the classification model are detailed in this section.

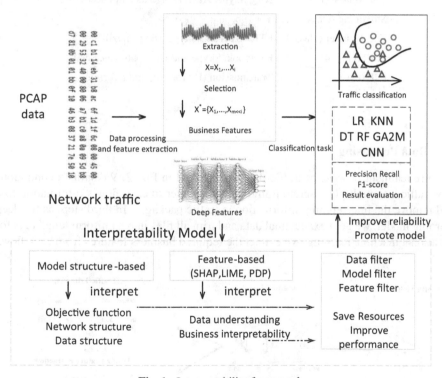

Fig. 1. Interpretability framework

2.2 Data Description

In this paper, we apply the proposed framework on the public dataset ISCX-VPN-NONVPN-2016, which include some different network traffic. The dataset will be described in this subsection.

Dataset ISCX-VPN-NONVPN-2016 is collected from the real network environment, which is the most original data flow package. It contains 14 traffic categories (SMPTS, Facebook, AIM, ICQ et al.) and 12 application protocol types (Email, VPN-Email, Chat, VPN-Chat). And we chose six VPN application protocol types as the training dataset. The details of each category shows in Table 1.

Table 1. Details of each category in dataset ISCX-VPN-NONVPN-2016

Traffic categories	Description (*Types of traffic*)
Email (class 0)	POP3, SMPT and IMAP
Chat (class 1)	ICQ, Skype, AIM, Hangouts and Facebook
Streaming (class 2)	YouTube and Vimeo
File Transfer (class 3)	FTP, FTPS and Skype using Filezilla
VoIP (class 4)	Facebook, Skype and Hangouts voice calls
P2P (class 5)	Transmission (BitTorrent) and uTorrent

2.3 Data Processing

The pretreatment process of traffic data is described in Fig. 2. We splits a continuous raw traffic into multiple discrete traffic units that refer to each flow's information first and remove the interferential information in traffic packages. In third step, as for deep learning model, we get hexadecimal data and trim all files into a uniform length. As for traditional machine learning, we extract the required business features from each flow.

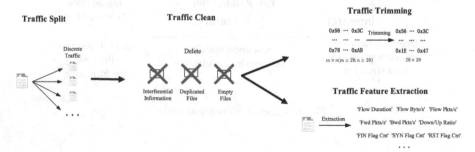

Fig. 2. Data processing

Table 2. Feature type details on dataset ISCX-VPN-NONVPN-2016

Feature		Type-No.	Feature		Type-No..	Feature		Type-No.
Feduration		2–1	Bwd IAT	Tot	1–29	Fwd Avg	ByteB	2–57
Flow Feduration		2–2		Std	1–30		PktsB	2–58
Tot	Bwd Pkt	1–3	Fwd Psh flag		1–31		Brate	2–59
	Fwd Pkt	1–4	Bwd psh flag		1–32	Bwd Avg	Size	2–60
Tot Len	Fwd Pkt	3–5	Fwd Urg flag		1–33		ByteB	2–61
	bwd Pkt	3–6	Bwd urg Flag		1–34		Pkts	2–62
Fwd Pkt Len	Min	3–7	Fwd head len		1–35		Brate	2–63
	Max	3–8	Bwd head len		1–36	S Flow BByte	FPkt	1–64
	Mean	3–9	FWD Pkts/s		1–37		FByte	1–65
	Std	3–10	Bwd Pkts/s		1–38		BPkt	1–66
Bwd Pkt Len	Min	3–11	Pkt Len	Min	3–39		BByte	1–67
	Max	3–12		Max	Act	Act	Min	1–68
	Mean	3–13		Mean	3–41		Max	1–69
	Std	3–14		Std	3–42		Mean	1–70
Flow Byte/s		2–15	Pkt Len Var		3–43		Std	2–71
Flow Pkt/s		2–16	FIN Flag	FIN	2–44	Idle	Min	2–72
Flow IAT	Mean	2–17		SYN	2–45		Mean	2–73
	Std	2–18		RST	2–46		Max	2–74
	Max	2–19		PSH	2–47		Std	2–75
	Min	2–20		ACK	2–48	I_W_byt fwd		3–76
Fwd IAT	Min	1–21		URG	2–49	I_W_byt bwd		3–77
	Max	1–22		CWR	2–50	A Da pkt fwd		1–78
	Mean	1–23		ECE	2–51	Min size fwd		1–79
	Std	1–24	down/Up Rat		2–52	fAvg byt PB		2–80
	Tot	1–25	Avg Pkt Size		3–53	fAvg Pkts PB		2–81
Bwd IAT	Min	1–26	Avgfwd segsize		3–54	fAvgBulkRat		2–82
	Max	1–27	Avgbwdsegsize		3–55	bAvg S Size		2–83
	Mean	1–28	Fwd Avg size		2–56			

Table 2 shows some features calculated from original network traffic. There are 83 features applied in this paper. For the convenience of description in the experiment, we number features from 1 to 83 and classify them into three classes. Type 1 denotes those features which describe packet statistical and packet header information. Type 2 is flow information and type 3 can be regarded as data related features. In experiments, we will use type-number to represent a feature. These features describe the length, size, duration and other basic characteristics of traffic, as well as the average access speed, packet length difference and many other statistical characteristics.

3   Interpretability Methods Based on Algorithms Structure

3.1   Classification Model Results

Table 3 shows the classification results on different algorithms. It will be described in the following analysis. From the table, we can find that there are some differences in the classification results of different algorithms and we will follow with interest in interpretable study.

Table 3. Classification results on each algorithm

Results of algorithm LR				Results of algorithm KNN			
Category	Precision	Recall	f1-score	Category	Precision	Recall	f1-score
0	0.33	0.01	0.02	0	0.60	0.49	0.54
1	0.45	0.03	0.05	1	0.89	0.88	0.89
2	0.12	0.71	0.21	2	0.70	0.77	0.73
3	0.44	0.19	0.26	3	0.62	0.54	0.58
4	0.80	0.67	0.73	4	0.90	0.93	0.91
5	0.12	0.14	0.13	5	0.66	0.62	0.64
Weight average	0.57	0.41	0.41	Weight average	0.83	0.83	0.83
Results of algorithm DT				Results of algorithm RF			
Category	Precision	Recall	f1-score	Category	Precision	Recall	f1-score
0	0.84	0.78	0.81	0	0.87	0.88	0.87
1	0.89	0.93	0.91	1	0.95	0.96	0.95
2	0.85	0.83	0.84	2	0.93	0.92	0.93
3	0.75	0.71	0.73	3	0.88	0.84	0.86
4	0.96	0.96	0.96	4	0.97	0.98	0.97
5	0.84	0.85	0.84	5	0.92	0.92	0.92
Weight average	0.90	0.90	0.90	Weight average	0.95	0.95	0.95
Results of algorithm EBM				Results of convolutional neural networks (CNN)			
Category	Precision	Recall	f1-score	Category	Precision	Recall	f1-score
0	0.87	0.83	0.85	0	0.94	0.98	0.96
1	0.95	0.95	0.95	1	0.92	0.96	0.94
2	0.92	0.93	0.93	2	0.98	0.99	0.99
3	0.89	0.85	0.87	3	0.96	0.98	0.97
4	0.97	0.98	0.97	4	0.98	0.89	0.93
5	0.97	0.93	0.95	5	0.99	0.99	0.99
Weight average	0.95	0.95	0.95	Weight average	0.96	0.96	0.96

3.2 Calculation Process of Algorithm Structure-based Methods

This subsection will introduce the interpretability method based on algorithm structure used in the experiment. They are LR, KNN, GA2M, DT and RF. Structurally, both RF and DT belong to tree structure algorithm and their interpretability methods are consistent. Their Characteristics are described in Table 4.

Table 4. Characteristics of each algorithm

Algorithm	Characteristic
LR	Good interpretability, Feature-based, Objective function-based, Small memory consumption
GA2M	Good interpretability, Feature-based, Consider the cross influence of features, Nonlinear
DT	Tree structure, No parameter assumption required, No domain knowledge
RF	required, Feature path-based
KNN	Data distance-based, Not sensitive to outliers, Complex feature interpretability

The interpretability of LR is easy to understand. Take the classification of two categories as an example, the objective function of LR is:

$$\log \frac{p}{1-p} = \beta_0 + \beta_1 x_1 + \beta_2 x_2 + \cdots + \beta_m x_m \tag{1}$$

where p is the probability that the sample belongs to class 1, x_i denotes the value of feature x_i and β_i denotes the weight of feature x_i. And we can regard the weight β_i as the interpretability of model.

The interpretability of GA2M is a little similar with LR. The objective function of GA2M is:

$$g(E[y]) = \beta_0 + \sum_j f_j(x_j) + \sum_{i \neq j} f_{ij}(x_i, x_j), \tag{2}$$

where $E[y]$ is an aggregate of dataset behavior or the probability of an event, g is a link function, f_j is a term for each dataset instance feature x_j and f_{ij} denotes the relationship of influence between different features. Therefore, the interpretability of this model can be considered as a nonlinear interpretation considering the influence of different features.

Interpretability of tree structure algorithms are relatively intuitive, such as DT and RF. We can regard tree decision as every feature decision. The prediction of an individual instance is the mean of the target outcome plus the sum of all contributions of each split that occur between the root node and the terminal node where the instance ends up. It can be regarded as restoring the path of the instance and accumulate the contribution of the node (feature). As for RF, it uses multiple decision trees to improve the generalization ability of the model.

As for the interpretability of KNN, it is a learning algorithm based on sample data without objective function. This means that the model has no parameters to learn, which makes it has no interpretability in structure. In this paper, we try to explain the model visually on the premise of a few features. The specific results can be seen in the experimental results.

3.3 Results of Algorithm Structure-based Methods

LR. The objective function of LR can explain its structure clearly. Figure 3 can be understood as the weight of different features in LR. Without more complex calculation, we can get the feature importance of LR from the calculation process of its objective function, which is also the expression of the algorithm structure.

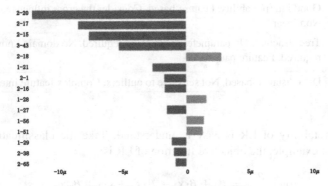

Fig. 3. Interpretable results in LR

DT and RF. Both DT and RF are tree structure models. Its structure can be understood as the decision of different features paths. Figure 4 shows some decision nodes in the model. We can see the weight relationship between different nodes in the Fig. 4 clearly. The role of different business features in the model will also be obvious.

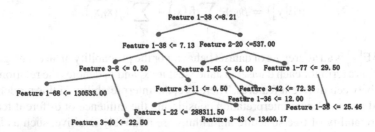

Fig. 4. Interpretable results in DT and RF

GA2M. Similar to LR, the interpretable method of GA2M can explain its objective function easily. The sorting results in the Fig. 5 analyze the influence of different business features on the model from the perspective of model structure.

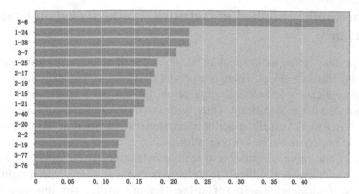

Fig. 5. Interpretable results in GA2M

KNN. Different from the above algorithm in principle, KNN is an algorithm based on instance data. Its prediction ability has a great relationship with the distance between data. When the K value is determined, the sample type to be predicted will be set to the category with the largest number of k neighboring samples. In other words, if in the feature space composed of two selected features, the numerical distribution of the same kind and other types is relatively clustered, then the two features have a better effect on distinguishing data.

Figure 6 is the feature plane that we generate. Although the black data points of the fourth category are generally scattered, there are basically similar data points around each data point, so the classification effect is better. However, red data points like 0 are very scattered in general and in individuals, so the classification effect is relatively poor.

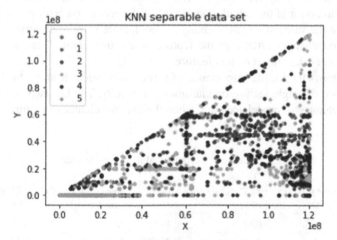

Fig. 6. Interpretable results in KNN

4 Interpretability Method of Network Traffic Based on Feature Importance

Generally speaking, some indicators like accuracy, recall and f1-score are used to evaluate a machine learning model. There is no doubt that these outcome indicators are very important in application. In practical application, the business significance of machine learning algorithm is also significant. Thus, we focus on the importance of features in this part. Features in a model usually describe characteristics of different aspects in datasets, which include important business implications.

As for network traffic, the process of feature extraction needs professional business knowledge, which makes it difficult to judge whether a feature is meaningful or not. Although we can calculate the weight of business features in the algorithm, we can't judge if it is reliable in many cases. Thus, we choose some feature-based interpretability method to describe the classification model of network traffic, which can help people understand the meaning of network traffic data representation. The methods to be discussed include direct calculation method of feature importance, Shapley additive explanations (SHAP)-based interpretability method, local interpretable model agnostic explanations (LIME)-based interpretability method and Partial Dependence Plot (PDP)-based interpretability method.

4.1 Direct Calculation Method of Feature Importance (FI)

Feature importance is a basic concept in machine learning model, which can play an important role in the prediction results of the model. Good features can improve the prediction results. On the contrary, bad features will take up more resources and reduce the prediction accuracy of the model. Direct calculation method of feature importance means to calculate directly according to the definition. It can be measured by the increase of the prediction error of the calculation model. If the prediction error of the model will increase when the value of a feature changes, this feature is more important. And if the prediction error changes little, then the feature is less important. This also means that the model ignores the impact of this feature.

Table 5 shows the feature importance of direct calculation. It mainly calculates the direct influence of single feature on classification results. The last two columns of the table are the changes of model accuracy when the average change of feature value is one unit.

Table 5. Feature importance value on top 10 features

Feature	Mean value of ACC change (%)	ACC change error (%)	Feature	Mean value of ACC change (%)	ACC change error (%)
3–76	0.81	0.17	1–36	0.09	0.06
3–77	0.44	0.08	3–53	0.08	0.14
2–56	0.30	0.13	1–68	0.06	0.07
2–49	0.25	0.02	1–69	0.05	0.07
1–35	0.10	0.11	3–9	0.05	0.07

4.2 SHAP-Based Interpretability Method

This section will introduce the theory of model interpretation based on the value of SHAP. In terms of basic principles, the target of SHAP is to explain the prediction of the sample x by calculating the contribution of each feature to the prediction, which is the same as most methods.

In this model, all features are considered as contributors. As for each prediction sample, the model generates a prediction value. SHAP value is the value assigned to each feature in the sample. Assuming that x_i is the sample i and x_{ij} is the feature j of sample i. The baseline of the whole model is y_{base}, which is usually the mean value of the target variables of all samples. Then, SHAP value is subject to the following equation:

$$y_i = y_{base} + f(x_{i1}) + f(x_{i2}) + \ldots + f(x_{ij}),   \quad (3)$$

where $f(x_{ij})$ sis the SHAP value of x_{ij}. $f(x_{i1})$ is the contribution value of the first feature in sample i to the final predicted value y_i. If $f(x_{i1}) > 1$, it means that the feature improves the predicted value which has a positive effect. Otherwise, it means that the feature reduces the predicted value which has a negative effect.

The traditional feature import only tells which feature is important, but we don't know how the feature affects the prediction results. The biggest advantage of SHAP value is that it can influence the characteristics of each sample, and it also shows the positive and negative effects.

SHAP-based results are described in Fig. 7. The points in the figure respectively represent the influence on the prediction results when a single sample changes. From the perspective of the average value of SHAP, there is a huge difference between the sorting of feature weight and the direct calculation.

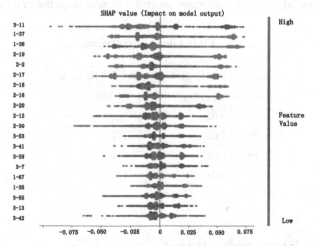

Fig. 7. Interpretable results in SHAP

4.3   LIME-Based Interpretability Method

The main idea of LIME is to use the local approximation of the model to explain the individual behavior of the predicted samples. This method does not go deep into the interior of the model. It detects the output change of the black box model by slightly disturbing the input, and trains an interpretable model based on the original input according to the change.

The process of LIME can be recognized as that we only use the model without training data. Test data can be put into the model and get the predicted results. LIME tries to understand what happens to the prediction results when we input different data into the machine learning model. And then, these samples will be used to train a new linear model to identify the local data.

The decision function of the original model is nonlinear. We assume that X denotes the interpreted sample. We take samples around x, and we calculate them according to their distance from X (weight here means size). We use the original model to predict these disturbed samples, and then learn a linear model to approximate the model well near X. This explanation only holds near X and is invalid for the whole. It can be recognized as the following formula:

$$E(x) = \arg \min_{g \in G} L(f, g, \pi_x) + \Omega(g) \tag{4}$$

where x denotes a samples and g denotes the linear model got before. We can compare the approximation of model g with the original classification model f by minimizing the loss function. $\Omega(g)$ is the complexity of g and G denotes all possible interpretability models. π_x defines the neighborhood of x. In the experiment, the model f will be interpretable by minimizing L.

Table 6 shows the results of LIME-based methods. Because LIME mainly consider the local influence of the data, the results are still different from the first two methods.

Table 6. LIME value on top 10 features

Feature	LIME value	Feature	LIME value
1–38	0.02	3–19	0.01
1–37	0.02	3–76	0.01
1–79	0.02	3–77	0.01
2–19	0.01	3–7	0.01
1–35	0.01	2–19	0.01

4.4   PDP-Based Interpretability Method

PDP can mainly express the marginal effect of one or two features on the prediction results of machine learning model. It can show whether the relationship between target and feature is linear, monotonous or more complex.

In this work, we used four evaluation metrics Precision, Recall, Macro-f1 and Weighted-f1 to evaluate the classification ability of our proposed method. These metrics are explained as follows:

$$\hat{f}_{x_s}(x_s) = \frac{1}{n} \sum\nolimits_{i=1}^{n} \hat{f}_{x_s}\left(x_s, x_c^{(i)}\right) \tag{5}$$

where x_s donates the features for which the partial dependence function should be plotted and x_c denotes actual feature values from the dataset for the features in which we are not interested in the machine learning model $\hat{f}$. n is the number of samples. PDP considers all instances and gives a statement about the global relationship of a feature with the predicted outcome.

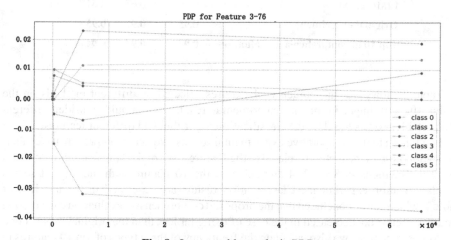

Fig. 8. Interpretable results in PDP

Figure 8 shows the PDP result, it is more directly to describe the impact of a single feature which shows the impact of the change of a single feature value on different prediction classes. Figure 8 describe forecast trends of six categories in traffic data when the feature Init Fwd Win Byts changes. The y-axis represents the value change of the feature. From Fig. 8, when the feature value reaches a certain point, its influence on each category will be significantly reduced.

It is obvious that Table 5, Fig. 7 and Table 6 rank the feature importance of network traffic according to different calculation principle which is described in Sect. 3. The advantage of SHAP is that it can reflect the influence of the characteristics in each sample, and also show the positive and negative effects. LIME focuses on the local influence of features. And to compare the differences between them, we also do comparative experiments on the top 5 feature importance of different methods, and the results can be seen in the last part of this subsection.

4.5 Comparison and Effectiveness Analysis

As for feature-based methods, we use top 5 important features output from SHAP-based, LIME-based and feature important interpretability models and feed them in RF classification again and get the follow results in Table 7.

Table 7. Comparison experiment results

Method	Precision	Recall	f1-score
Direct calculation of feature importance	0.90	0.90	0.90
SHAP-based	0.85	0.85	0.85
LIME-based	0.69	0.65	0.67
Original experiment	**0.95**	**0.95**	**0.95**
Top 10 in comprehensive evaluation	**0.93**	**0.94**	**0.94**

Table 7 shows that the influence of features selected by different methods on the model effect is huge. From the experimental results, we should consider different interpretable models to select the classification algorithm and different features.

In addition to the comparative experimental results, we get a comprehensive evaluation method for all the methods related to the features. We ranked the features calculated by all the methods in Sect. 3, 4 and selected the 10 feature with the highest scores for classification experiments. Classification results are described in the last line of Table 7, which can be concluded that the proposed comprehensive evaluation can keep the accuracy almost not decreased in the case of using far less than the original experiment.

At the same time, we also calculate the frequency of three types of top 10 features in different algorithms or interpretable methods. Table 8 shows the results. It can be found that different algorithms pay attention to different feature types, which also explains the difference of classification results caused by different methods from the perspective of characteristics and business and also shows that the proposed feature comprehensive evaluation method is effective.

Table 8. Frequency of three types of top 10 features in each algorithm

Type	LR	DT	GA2M	FI	SHAP	LIME	Total
1	3	5	4	4	2	4	22
2	6	1	3	2	7	2	21
3	1	4	3	4	1	4	17

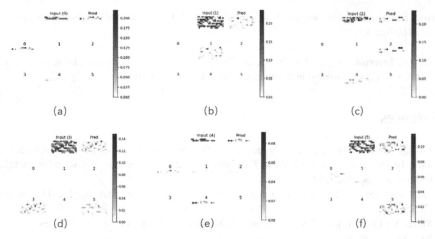

Fig. 9. Interpretable results of CNN

5 Conclusion and Future Work

In this paper, we proposed an Interpretability analysis framework of network security traffic classification based on machine learning and analyzed different interpretability methods on the dataset ISCX-VPN-NONVPN-2016. We find that these method can help us better explain the business features of network security traffic and optimize the classification model in algorithm selection and feature selection. Actually, we also apply these models on other network traffic datasets, such as CIC-IDS-2017, CIC-IDS-2012 et al., to verify the interpretability of data at the business level and try to get an overall interpretable framework for network traffic. We also try to explain the neural network model on network traffic.

We use CNN to achieve classification experiments on the same dataset and explain its structure. We find out the important data points (pixel points) of different types of data in the prediction process. The result shows in Fig. 9. The darker dots in the picture mean that they are more essential. As for class 2–5, source port is more important but not for class 0–1. And target port is more important for class 1–4 but not for class 0 and 5. The serial number of the data that receivers want to receive is necessary for each class. There are more relevant conclusions can be acquired, which also proves that the network security traffic can be further explained in the neural network.

In the future, we will further study the interpretability of neural network, and compare the difference between neural network and traditional machine learning method in the application of network traffic classification. At the same time, different network traffic datasets will be used to verify the interpretability methods.

Acknowledgement. Thanks for the experimental environment provided by laboratory ICN&CAD of School of Electronic Engineering, Beijing University of Posts and Telecommunications.

Funding Statement. This work was supported by the National Natural Science Foundation of China (61601053).

Conflicts of Interest. We declare that we do not have any commercial or associative interest that represents a conflict of interest in connection with the work submitted.

References

1. Lin, Q., Zhang, H., Lou, J.: Log clustering based problem identification for online service systems. In: Proceedings of IEEE/ACM 38th International Conference on Software Engineering Companion, pp. 102–111 (2016)
2. Salakhutdinov, R.: Learning deep generative models. Ann. Rev. Stat. Appl. **2**(1), 361–385 (2015)
3. Yang, X.: Optimization Techniques and Applications with Examples. John Wiley & Sons, New Jersey (2018)
4. Wang, P., Ye, F., Chen, X., Qian, Y.: Datanet: deep learning based encrypted network traffic classification in sdn home gateway. IEEE Access **6**, 55380–55391 (2018)
5. Du, C., Liu, S., Si, L., Guo, Y., Jin, T.: Using object detection network for malware detection and identification in network traffic packets. Comput. Mater. Continua **64**(3), 1785–1796 (2020)
6. Mo, C., Xiaojuan, W., Mingshu, H., Lei, J., Javeed, K.: A network traffic classification model based on metric learning. Comput. Mater. Continua **64**(2), 941–959 (2020)
7. Kang, Y., Cheng, I.L., Mao, W.: Towards interpretable deep extreme multi-label learning. In: Proceedings of IEEE 20th International Conference on Information Reuse and Integration for Data Science, pp. 69–74 (2019)
8. Doshi-Velez, F., Kim, B.: Towards a rigorous science of interpretable machine learning (2017). https://arxiv.org/abs/1702.08608
9. Tolomei, G., Silvestri, F., Haines, A.: Interpretable predictions of tree-based ensembles via actionable feature tweaking. In: Proceedings of the 23rd ACM SIGKDD International Conference on Knowledge Discovery and Data Mining, pp. 465–474 (2017)
10. Tan, S., et al.: Tree Space Prototypes: Another Look at Making Tree Ensembles Interpretable (2016). https://arxiv.org/abs/1611.07115
11. Jung, A.: An Information-Theoretic Approach to Explainable Machine Learning (2020). https://arxiv.org/abs/2003.00484
12. Guerra-Manzanares, A., Nmm, S., Bahsi, H.: Towards the integration of a Post-Hoc interpretation step into the machine learning workflow for IoT Botnet detection. In: Proceedings of International Conference on Machine Learning and Applications (ICMLA), pp. 1162–1169 (2019)
13. Kim, D., Shin, G., Han, M.: Analysis of feature importance and interpretation for malware classification. Comput. Mater. Continua **65**(3), 1891–1904 (2020)
14. Rathi, S.: Generating counterfactual and contrastive explanations using SHAP (2019). https://arxiv.org/abs/1906.09293?context=stat.ML
15. Ribeiro, M., Singh, S., Guestrin, C.: Local Interpretable Model-Agnostic Explanations (LIME): An Introduction (2016)
16. Greenwell, B.M.: pdp: an R package for constructing partial dependence plots. R J. **9**(1), 421 (2017)

Random Parameter Normalization Technique for Mimic Defense Based on Multi-queue Architecture

Shunbin Li, Kun Zhang, Ruyun Zhang(✉), MingXing Zhu,
Hanguang Luo, and Shaoyong Wu

Zhejiang Lab, Hangzhou 310012, China
zhangry@zhejianglab.com

Abstract. As a revolutionary and subversive theory and technology, the mimic defense system based on dynamic heterogeneous redundancy has played an essential role in cyberspace security. Processing equivalent tasks with heterogeneous executors and arbitrating a final output is the basis of the mimic defense theory. It is necessary to guarantee a normalized result under non-disturbing conditions in external communication sessions with random parameter requirements. Otherwise, it is difficult to distinguish whether the system is under attack. This paper proposes a normalized scheme to deal with the random parameter requests from heterogeneous executors based on the multi-queue architecture in response to this problem. Simulation and experimental results show that the proposed random parameter normalization module based on multi-queue architecture can provide uniform random parameters for the mimic defense system's heterogeneous executors, effectively synchronizing the random parameter requests in disorder.

Keywords: Mimic defense · Random parameter · Multi-queue · Normalization

1 Introduction

At present, network system based on the traditional protection concepts and technologies is no longer safe, due to their static, similarity and certainty of the target structure and operating mechanism. Once attackers find a loophole or preset a backdoor, they can play internal and external cooperation, forming one-way transparent action advantages to make the defender passive everywhere, trapped in constant fixing the loopholes, or even unable to defend [1].

The mimic defense theory characterized by dynamic, heterogeneous, and redundant architecture makes the security and credibility of network information systems no longer based on the premise of "non-toxic and aseptic" software and hardware construction. As a result, it can fully adapt to the economic and technological globalization ecosystem [2]. At present, mimic defense technology is already verified in the routers [3] and Web servers [4] in terms of principle verification and practice. Related industrialization work and other principle verification studies are also being carried out [5]. The essential operation of the mimic defense system is to perform majority voting on the output results

© Springer Nature Switzerland AG 2021
X. Sun et al. (Eds.): ICAIS 2021, LNCS 12737, pp. 321–331, 2021.
https://doi.org/10.1007/978-3-030-78612-0_26

of multiple equivalent heterogeneous executors, detect the attacked object in time and perform the cleaning operation [6]. The premise for the above voting to become effective is that equivalent heterogeneous executors have the same output response to the regular operation input. When an attacker attacks it, the executor's output shows differences related to the operating environment. The above model is also called the IPO model [7].

However, in many critical communication session scenarios, equivalent heterogeneous executors' output will also show randomness even though they are not under attack. The example scenario details are as follows. First, to ensure the communication session's freshness and the strength of security encryption, random numbers are required, and executors usually generate them by themselves. Second, random numbers also make great sense in distinguishing different communication sessions. Third, to carry the communication message's time information, timestamps are needed, which is usually strongly correlated with the executor's system clock. Fourth, all these random parameters required by the executor may be more than one simultaneously, and the requests to random parameters may also be out of order. As the mimic defense system implements a strict one-way communication mechanism to avoid additional attack paths between different executors, the software solution by negotiating normalized random parameters through an inter-communication channel is no allowed. To the end, the normalization of random parameter requests among different executors has become a common critical problem for mimic defense systems.

To cope with the above problems, we propose a multi-queue-based random parameters normalization method to provide an efficient solution for the random parameter requests and synchronization of heterogeneous executors in the mimic defense system.

2 System Structure

Figure 1 shows the function of the random parameters normalization module and its location in the mimic defense system Fig. 1. It is mainly responsible for receiving random parameter requests initiated from different executors, buffering and marking them, and then feeding back the normalized random parameter requests to the corresponding executors. Such a module can ensure that random parameter requests initiated by different executors with the same function session at other times can get the same normalized random value.

The overall architecture of the random parameter normalization module proposed in this paper is shown in Fig. 2. It contains five parts: service control interface, random parameter generator, MD5 calculator, cache queue, and queue searching engine. The primary function of each part is as follows.

Service control interface: responsible for receiving random parameter requests from an executor, identifying the executor that issued the random parameter request, extracting the requested random parameter type and specific information, and feeding back the obtained random parameter to the corresponding executor.

Random parameter generator: according to the requested random parameter type, the corresponding random number is generated under the queue searching engine's control and written into the cache queue.

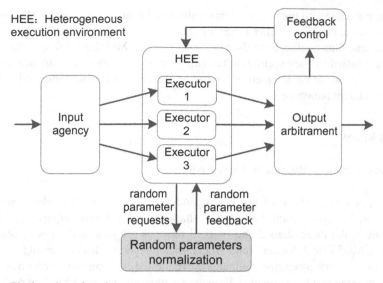

Fig. 1. The location of random parameter normalization module in a mimic defense system

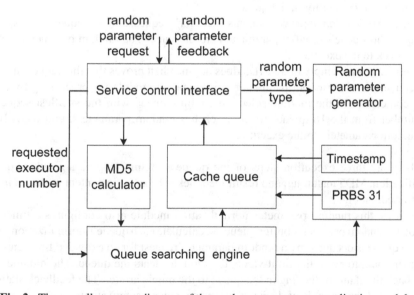

Fig. 2. The overall structure diagram of the random parameters normalization module

MD5 calculator: calculate the 512-bit MD5 hash value of the requested random parameter information according to the MD5 specification, and input the hash value into the queue searching engine after truncation.

Cache queue: record the access identification of different executors, MD5 hash data truncation value, random number/timer timestamp.

Queue searching engine: according to the number and MD5 hash value of the random parameter initiated by the executor, the engine searches for random parameter results in the random parameter cache queue to complete the generation, marking, and feedback control of random parameters.

3 Workflow

The details of the workflow are described below.

1) After any one or more of the heterogeneous executors send random parameter requests, the service control interface reshapes and encodes the requests of different executors. All these shaped and marked requests are sent to the queue searching engine, MD5 calculator, and random parameter generator for processing.
2) The queue searching engine compares the requested executor number with that in 16 random parameter cache queues. If other executors already mark random parameters in the queue, the MD5 calculation result of such a request is taken out and matched with the MD5 identity in the queue.
3) If their MD5 match, it proves that this executor's request and the request corresponding to this queue's random parameters are the same. The random parameter is then fed back to the executors.
4) If all queues are empty or all MD5 does not match, it proves that this request has not been sent to the random parameter normalization module for processing by other executors. Then the module selects the empty queue with the smallest sequence number from the 16 queues to mark, caches random parameters, and feeds back random parameters to the executor.

There are three execution steps of the queue searching engine algorithm: queue identification, MD5 matching, and result feedback. The specific content is shown in the pseudo-code in Fig. 3.

Besides, this random parameter normalization module also configures a timer for each of 16 random parameter buffer queues to calculate each queue's normalization time. When a queue is occupied by a random parameter request for an extended time, causing the timer count to reach the limit value, the module clears the queue. The module also feeds back the status of the flag in the queue to the mimic arbiter. The feedback status is used as one of the grounds of decision for the executor's safety status.

```
 1   i = 0;
 2   STEP1:       //queue identification
 3       while(i < 16){
 4           if(request_data[31:29]&queue_buffer[i][63:61] = request_data[31:29])
 5               Jump to STEP3
 6           else{
 7               if(queue_buffer[i] = 0){
 8                   queue_empty_flag = i
 9                   Jump to STEP3
10               }
11               else
12                   Jump to STEP2
13           }
14       }
15   STEP2:       //MD5 matching
16       wait(md5_data_valid = 1){
17           if(md5_match = 1){
18               executive_system = queue_buffer[i]
19               queue_buffer[i][63:61] = 001 or 010 or 100
20           }
21           else
22               Jump to STEP3
23       }
24   STEP3:       //result feedback
25       if(!queue_query_finish){
26           i = i + 1
27           Jump to STEP1
28       }
29       else{
30           i = 0
31           if(queue_empty_flag = 1){
32               Jump to empty queue j
33               queue_buffer[j] = random_number
34               executive_system = random_number
35           }
36           else{
37               executive_system = queue_overflow
38               queue_buffer[0~15] = 0
39               Jump to STEP1
40           }
41       }
```

Fig. 3. The pseudo-code of queue searching and matching engine algorithm

4 Hardware Implementation

The random parameter normalization module is designed using Verilog, a hardware description language, divided into five parts according to the main functions. The following is a separate introduction to the implementation of each module:

Service control interface: It uses a task storage queue to receive random parameter requests from different CPUs out of order. It uses a state machine to poll the corresponding flag bit and distribute the requested data to the MD5 calculator, queue searching engine, and random number generator for subsequent processing based on the polling result.

Random parameter generator: It contains a high-speed parallel PRBS31 random number generator [8] and a timestamp generator, which output the random number according to the type of random parameter specified by the flag bit in the request.

MD5 calculator: A hardware-implemented MD5 calculator [9] is integrated. As the 128-bit standard hash value will occupy an extensive hardware register resource, it is truncated to the first 29 bits to characterize the corresponding executive request.

Cache queue: To efficiently buffer the requested data from different executors, 16 buffer registers are adopted to implement this queue. As shown in Fig. 4, each register is divided into executor number valid bits, MD5 identify, random parameters, and timers.

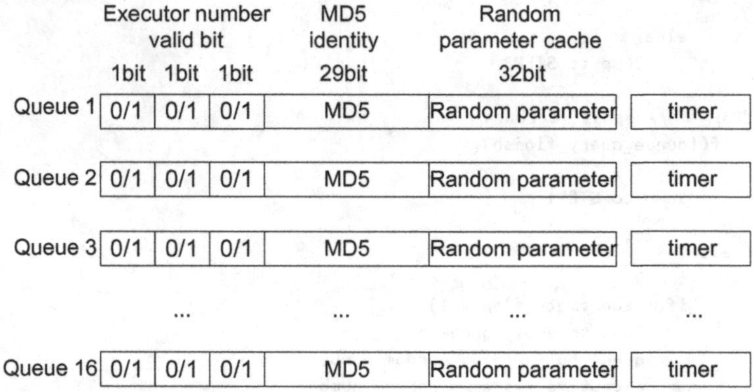

	Executor number valid bit			MD5 identity	Random parameter cache	
	1bit	1bit	1bit	29bit	32bit	
Queue 1	0/1	0/1	0/1	MD5	Random parameter	timer
Queue 2	0/1	0/1	0/1	MD5	Random parameter	timer
Queue 3	0/1	0/1	0/1	MD5	Random parameter	timer
	...			...	...	...
Queue 16	0/1	0/1	0/1	MD5	Random parameter	timer

Fig. 4. The schematic diagram of random parameter cache queue structure

Queue searching engine: As shown in Fig. 5, a finite state machine is proposed to complete the queue searching. The system starts by detecting whether the timer's time of each queue overflows, searches each queue one by one for a match, and finally ends with updating the queue and feeding back the corresponding random number to the executor. The above process is repeatedly run.

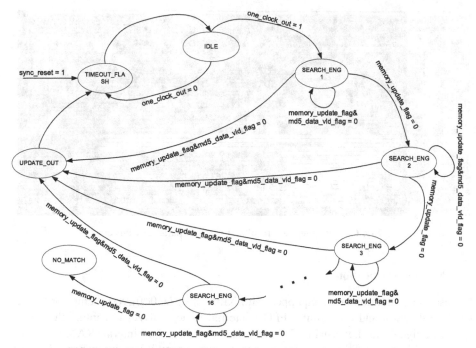

Fig. 5. The state machine of the queue searching and matching engine

5 Evaluation

The random parameter normalization scheme proposed in this paper synchronizes the out-of-order input requests of different executors to meet the requirement of outputting normalized random numbers stably and efficiently under various complex request combinations. Therefore, the entire verification process is divided into two steps: simulation verification and system verification, to thoroughly verify its feedback status under various complex input excitations.

5.1 Simulation Verification

We first perform behavioral simulation and verify the random parameter normalization module's function and timing through different excitations. Simulations are divided into regular case verification and abnormal case verification. The regular cases mainly verify the feedback results' consistency by simulating three executors to output many complex requests. The abnormal cases include timer overflow, random parameter cache queue overflow to verify the module's response and feedback under abnormal or error conditions.

Figure 6 describes the random parameter normalization module's partial simulation results, including input and output data, parameter access switching in 16 buffer queues, and the corresponding timer counting status. It can be seen from Fig. 6 that 16 parameter cache queues continuously update the corresponding flags, MD5 calculation value, and timer count values for the input of three executors.

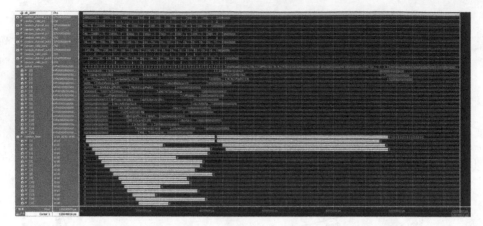

Fig. 6. The simulation results of random parameter buffer

5.2 System Verification

We use the evaluation board equipped with Xilinx's xc7z100ffg900-2 chip for board-level verification and use Xilinx's FPGA internal logic analyzer to capture the corresponding signals, as shown in Fig. 7. Due to the constraints of the internal RAM resources of the FPGA, the virtual logic analyzer cannot capture a sufficient number and depth of signals. However, by setting different capture conditions, we can still observe the consistency between timing details and output of each signal's behavior simulation, verifying the random parameter normalization module's implementation correctness.

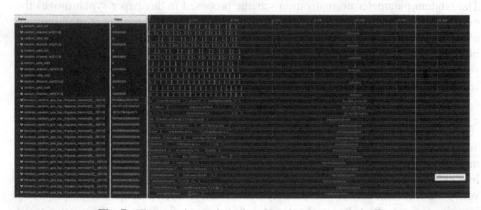

Fig. 7. The experimental results of random parameter buffer

In what follows, we provide a statistical analysis of performance metrics.

1) Because the MD5 calculator has high timing requirements, its timing is difficult to converge when the clock frequency rises above 100 MHz. Thus, 100 MHz is the highest clock frequency under this FPGA device type.

2) When three executors launch requests simultaneously, the module's MD5 calculator and queue searching engine needs to queue up to process the request. At this time, the normalized random number feedback delay reaches the maximum 1870 ns, i.e., a total of 187 clock cycles.

3) When three executors issue requests in a time-sharing way, the module can perform corresponding processing immediately. At this time, the feedback delay of the normalized random number is the minimum 780 ns, i.e., a total of 78 clock cycles.

4) In terms of power consumption, Xilinx's Vivado tool estimates that the total power consumption is about 0.389 W, of which static power consumption is 0.218 W and dynamic power consumption is 0.171 W. Because fewer logic resources are used in the algorithm implementation process, the dynamic power consumption is lower. The overall performance statistics are shown in Table 1.

Table 1. Overall performance statistics.

Maximum clock frequency	Maximum feedback latency	Minimum feedback latency	Static power consumption	Dynamic power consumption
100 MHz	1870 ns (187 cycles)	780 ns (78 cycles)	0.218 W	0.171 W

The resource consumption is shown in Table 2. The table separately counts the resource usage of each sub-module for Slice, LUT, Flip-Flop, and Block RAM of Xilinx FPGA device xc7z100ffg900-2. It calculates the overall resource consumption and the percentage of total device resources occupied.

Table 2. FPGA resource consumption statistics.

Device resource (total)	Slice (69350)	LUT (277400)	Flip-Flop (554800)	Block RAM (755)
Total consumption	2273	6645	3697	7.5
(percentage)	(3.28%)	(2.40%)	(0.67%)	(1.00%)
Queue searching engine	1097	2806	1710	0
MD5 calculator	1152	3817	1917	7.5
PRBS generator	24	22	70	0

The above statistical results show that implementing the multi-queue random parameter normalization algorithm proposed in this paper occupies less FPGA resource and achieves higher performance.

5.3 Extended Analysis

The experiment is set to use 16 random parameter cache queues to store out-of-order requests issued by three heterogeneous executors, which can meet most usage scenarios in the existing mimic defense system. However, there will be more heterogeneous executors in a few particular applications that require more cache queues. Users can pre-evaluate system performance and FPGA resource usages based on the relevant data listed in Table 1 and Table 2.

Although our proposed solution can efficiently and stably complete the random parameter normalization task of multiple heterogeneous executors and achieve good results in actual environment verification, some optimization spaces can further improve the module's performance. The specific ideas are as follows.

1) As described in [10], using a full pipeline architecture algorithm to implement an MD5 calculator can increase the clock frequency of the MD5 calculator and calculate the MD5 output value in parallel when multiple executors request simultaneously, thereby shortening the feedback latency in random parameters normalization.
2) In some particular applications that require multiple queues to cache random numbers (such as 64, 128, 256, or more), the queue searching and matching engine can be changed to a parallel matching and searching algorithm.
3) We can use a higher nanometer-level FPGA device to implement our algorithm. The advantage is that it can increase the system's maximum clock frequency and shorten random parameters' feedback latency.

Although the above methods can shorten the feedback latency of random numbers normalization and increase system clock frequency, it should be noted that these two metrics are not the only criteria for measuring the pros and cons of our proposed algorithm. In an actual case, it is also necessary to comprehensively consider many metrics such as occupied resources, energy efficiency ratio, device price, etc. We need to choose a suitable implementation plan based on actual needs to achieve an optimal balance.

6 Conclusions

In this paper, we propose a multi-queue random parameters normalization module suitable for mimic defense systems. The designed module adopted a multi-queue hardware structure. It uses the MD5 hash algorithm to normalize different random parameter requirements from different executors into a unified 32-bit address expression, which can efficiently and stably process the random parameters normalization request of the mimic defense systems. A large number of simulation and board verification experiments show that the random parameters normalization module can ensure the matching accuracy of parameters, meet the random parameters normalization requirements of the mimic defense systems, and improve random parameter generation and synchronization efficiency.

Acknowledgment. This work is supported by the national key R & D project (No. 2020YFB1804604), Zhejiang laboratory open project (No. 2018FD0ZX01), and "Digital Economy Standardization Pilot Project from Zhejiang market supervision and Administration Bureau" (No. ZJCT5-2019063).

References

1. Wu, J.: Robust control and endogenous safety. Civ.-Mil. Integr. Cyberspace **10**(3), 23–27 (2018)
2. Wu, J.: Mimic defense technology to build endogenous security in national information cyberspace. Inf. Commun. Technol. **6**(2), 1–6 (2019)
3. Ma, H., Yi, P., Jiang, Y., He, L.: Dynamic heterogeneous redundancy based router architecture with mimic defenses. J. Inf. Secur. **2**(1), 29–42 (2017)
4. Tong, Q., Zhang, Z., Zhang, W., Wu, J.: Design and implementation of mimic defense web server. J. Softw. **28**(4), 883–897 (2017)
5. Wu, Z., Zhang, F., Guo, W., Wei, J., Xie, G.: A mimic arbitration optimization method based on heterogeneous degree of executors. Comput. Eng. **46**(5), 12–18 (2020)
6. Gao, M., Luo, J., Zhou, H., Jiao, H., Ying, L.: A differential feedback scheduling decision algorithm based on mimic defense. Telecommun. Sci. **36**(5), 73–82 (2020)
7. Wu, J.: Research on cyber mimic defense. J. Cyber Secur. **1**(4), 1–10 (2016)
8. Liu, Y.: Design of collateral PRBS serial based on FPGA. Foreign Electron. Meas. Technol. **27**(5), 6–8 (2008)
9. Wang, B., Han, G., Zhang, X.: Design and implementation of MD5 algorithm based on FPGA. Commun. Technol. **1**(1), 69–71 (2010)
10. Tan, J., Zhou, Q., Si, X., Li, B.: Implementation and improvement of full-pipeline MD5 algorithm based on mimic computer. J. Chin. Comput. Syst. **38**(6), 1216–1220 (2017)

Secure and Efficient Key Hierarchical Management and Collaborative Signature Schemes of Blockchain

Rui Zhang[1,2], Zhaoxuan Li[1,2], and Lijuan Zheng[3(✉)]

[1] State Key Laboratory of Information Security, Institute of Information Engineering, Chinese Academy of Sciences, Beijing 100093, China
[2] School of Cyber Security, University of Chinese Academy of Sciences, Beijing 100049, China
[3] School of Information Science and Technology, Shijiazhuang Tiedao University, Shijiazhuang 050043, China
zhenglijuan@stdu.edu.cn

Abstract. As the core of the blockchain, reliable key management is the necessary guarantee for the security of the blockchain business. However, existing key management methods of blockchain mainly include local storage, offline storage, and wallet storage, and cannot meet the requirements of security, ease of use, and cost at the same time. Moreover, the key management scheme of the blockchain itself lacks a secure and efficient solution to manage the user's key. In addition, the situation of collaborative signatures should be considered in the blockchain to meet the needs of users. To this end, secure multi-party computation (SMPC) is the most used technology, and the security of these schemes can be further improved. In order to improve the security and efficiency of blockchain key management and meet the needs of collaborative work, key hierarchical management and collaborative signature schemes incorporating SMPC and feature encryption are proposed. In this scheme, the keys are divided into three layers, and the keys of the upper layer are used to encrypt the keys of the lower layer, thus ensuring the security of all keys. Moreover, the processes of key generation, recovery, revocation and update, and multi-party signature are designed in detail. Compared with other schemes through theory analysis and experiment, our schemes can reduce the file-sharing time and the storage overhead of the user. This can improve the utilization of system resources and system efficiency, while ensuring a high level of security.

Keywords: Blockchain · Key hierarchical management · Multi-party signature · Data sharing

1 Introduction

Blockchain, as a development technique, involves the operation of more transactions with the increasing of the number of application scenarios. This makes the current application structure of blockchain complex and huge, and makes it

© Springer Nature Switzerland AG 2021
X. Sun et al. (Eds.): ICAIS 2021, LNCS 12737, pp. 332–345, 2021.
https://doi.org/10.1007/978-3-030-78612-0_27

face more problems, such as key security issues. The user's keys which include private keys, etc., are the core of the blockchain, whose security directly determines the security of users' private data. The core of this problem is how to establish a feasible key management scheme for the blockchain. Besides, there are many scenarios of collaborative work in practice. Therefore, in the blockchain, the situation of collaborative signatures should be considered, and manage the collaborative signature keys in key management.

The existing key management methods of blockchain mainly include local storage, offline storage, and wallet storage. In local storage, the keys can be easily read and tampered with by attackers and cannot be recovered when the physical device is damaged. The network is still needed in offline storage, so malware intrusion cannot be completely avoided. In wallet storage, although a complicated process improves security, it increases the corresponding cost and reduces the ease of use [8]. Moreover, the current common wallet vulnerabilities were summarized in [5]. The corresponding schemes for key management are proposed in [9], etc. However, there are shortcomings in these schemes, such as security loopholes and imperfect solutions. In the current research on multi-party signatures in blockchain, secure multi-party computation (SMPC) is the most used technology, and the security of these schemes can be further improved.

In order to solve the above issues, this paper makes the following work:

- A key hierarchical management scheme is designed to solve the key security problem in the current blockchain (cf. Sect. 3). The scheme divides the key into three layers, and the encryption relationship is the upper layer encrypts the lower layer, thereby ensuring the security of all keys. Users are very convenient when using the system. Moreover, the combination of ECC and AES improves the efficiency of file operations and makes users' privacy secure.
- A storage architecture of on-chain and off-chain collaborative is proposed to reduce the storage pressure on the blockchain and improve the efficiency of operations on-chain (cf. Sect. 3.2). Contents such as data ciphertext are stored in the off-chain distributed database, and the storage ledger on-chain uses red-black trees to store the information such as off-chain storage addresses.
- Secure and efficient password recovery and multi-party signature mechanisms are described (cf. Sect. 3.4–3.5). These mechanisms combine SMPC and feature encryption to store and recover the user's password, and distribute multi-party signature keys, so as to meet the needs of users and avoid the loss of the user caused by the user forgetting the password.
- Proved by theory and experiment, our mechanisms consider the possibility of various aspects of key operations and make users' keys secure (cf. Sect. 4).

2 Related Work

As the core technique of the blockchain, key management has attracted a lot of attention. Fan et al. [7] proposed a key hierarchical management method to protect key security in the big data network cloud. But in their scheme, the user cannot use the system when he forgets the password, and the attacker can easily tamper with users' keys. Lou et al. [12] proposed a key management scheme for named data networks using blockchain to solve the problem of mutual trust between sites. But this scheme ignores the security of the private key. Ma et al. [14] proposed a blockchain-based distributed key management scheme for the Internet of Things, but this scheme requires higher costs. Lei et al. [9] proposed a dynamic key management scheme based on blockchain for heterogeneous intelligent transportation systems. However, in this scheme, the key can only be used in specific environments. There are similar schemes [1,11,18,19]. These schemes all use blockchain to solve the key problem in specific scenarios, and there is no research on the key problem of blockchain itself. Moreover, despite the schemes in [1,7,9,11,12,14,18–20] can improve the security of keys in specific fields under certain circumstances. However, these schemes ignore the mechanisms of key recovery, revocation and update. Therefore, these schemes are incomplete, which may cause irreparable harm to users.

In order to recover the key safely in the blockchain, a method for storing and recovering the private key of the blockchain using the threshold algorithm is proposed in [13]. However, once the user's mobile device certificate and password are lost, the user's key will be leaked and cannot be recovered. Xia et al. [16] hide the private key of the energy blockchain in the watermark information. The scheme is inefficient due to the complexity of it. Zhao et al. [20] designed a key recovery scheme for healthy blockchain using a human sensor network. In this scheme, there is no verification of actual efficiency. Thus, how to recover the keys effectively in the blockchain needs to be further studied.

In addition, in order to achieve collaborative work in the blockchain, multiple signatures need to implement different smart contracts for different chains. Due to the variety of chains, it will cost a lot of capital and labor. Moreover, it is inconvenient to modify the contract when the number of signers is temporarily changed. In 1979, Shamir [15] proposed a threshold secret sharing scheme. Subsequently, Yao et al. [17] proposed the concept of SMPC for the first time. Recently, PlatON and Ali respectively adopted SMPC to implement key management in the blockchain, so as to solve the problem of multi-party signatures matching with different chains. But in these schemes, the secret is simply decomposed. For example, the secret Q is split into a, b, c and $Q = a + b + c$, so the secret features are easily leaked. To this end, we will further use SMPC to achieve secure and efficient multi-party signatures.

3   Key Management and Signature Schemes of Blockchain

3.1   Overview

In the actual operation of the blockchain, data privacy must be ensured, and scenarios such as collaborative signatures must be considered. Thus, in this section, the design of key hierarchical management and collaborative signature schemes of blockchain will be introduced, which can ensure the privacy of data, improve the efficiency of key management and meet the needs of users in all aspects.

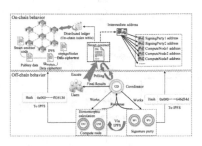

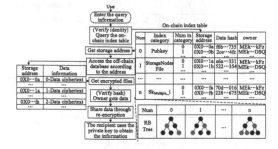

Fig. 1. Model architecture of scheme.

Fig. 2. The structure of index ledger on-chain. (Color figure online)

Figure 1 describes the main architecture of the scheme, which consists of two parts: on-chain and off-chain. Due to the basic properties of the public chain, the chain includes: on-chain index ledger, transaction, and smart contract. The IPFS distributed storage system [2] is used as a chain component because of its feasibility. The execution of contracts and currency settlement are mainly completed on-chain. Moreover, a lot of work is done off-chain, such as data encryption and decryption. Our schemes incorporate SMPC to provide password recovery, multi-party signature and other services. In these schemes, each node of the blockchain needs to vote for a reliable coordinator (called Coordinator) according to the consensus, which is used to connect on-chain and off-chain message exchange, manage and supervise the key process. In fact, the Coordinator does not participate in the core calculation, maintains zero-knowledge during the process, and mainly plays the role of verification and notification. Thus, the existence of the Coordinator does not affect the security of the key. On the contrary, the Coordinator completes a lot of work of the user, which simplifies the operation process of the user. It should be noted that Coordinator can also be replaced with smart contracts. In addition, in order to reduce the pressure on-chain and improve the efficiency of operations, the index ledger on-chain uses red-black trees to store data such as off-chain storage addresses.

3.2 On-chain and Off-chain Collaborative Architecture

In the process of blockchain key management, file information needs to be classified and published on the blockchain network, such as public-key pk and storage nodes information $storageNodes$ files. As we all know, blockchain has strict requirements on memory and time cost, and most operations on-chain are search and addition. In order to improve the efficiency of these operations, the ledger is stored in the form of the red-black tree called RBTree. Figure 2 shows the structure of the index ledger on-chain and part of the data sharing process. There are two parts in the ledger: 1) The file index class is a hash map, which uses the partitioning method to locate the file storage tree. 2) The file storage tree is a red-black tree that contains many file storage nodes. It provides efficient

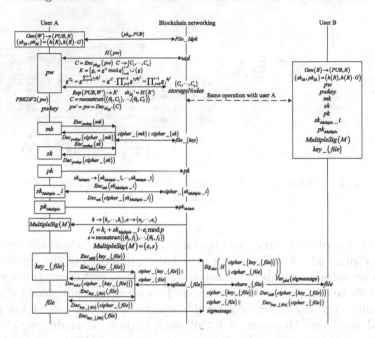

Fig. 3. Key management protocol.

insertion and other operations for managing file storage information (off-chain storage address, data hash and owner). After the data ciphertext is stored in the off-chain database, the related information is stored in the file storage node. The data owner is read from the file storage node to verify the identity of the accessor. The data creator can add other trusted accessors, which improves the security of the data. The accessor reads the storage address, accesses the off-chain database to read the file ciphertext, and then reads the data hash to verify whether the downloaded file from the off-chain database has been tampered with.

3.3   Process of Key Management Protocol

The key management protocol proposed in this paper is shown in Fig. 3. In the figure, the scheme divides the key into three layers according to the encryption relationship. The first layer is the password key, the second layer is the master key and the user's public-private key pair, and the third layer is the file encryption key and the multi-party signature key pair. In the daily operation process, the key management process includes the following four phases.

Initialization. 1) When users use the system of this scheme for the first time, they need to enter password pw and other information to generate identity file $File\_Idpk$ and login credentials $uid = H(pw)$ (where $H()$ is the SHA256 operation), and publish them to the blockchain network. The next time the user logs into the system, the contract is used to verify whether the password

$pw1$ is correct $uid = H(pw1)$. 2) After the registration, the password key $pwkey = \text{PBKDF2}(pw)$ is generated by PBKDF2 algorithm. The user's master key mk is generated by using a random number generator. 3) The ciphertext $cipher\_\{mk\} = Enc_{pwkey}(mk)$ is generated by encrypting mk with $pwkey$.

Remaining Keys Generation. 4) The sk and pk of users are generated by the elliptic curve algorithm, and pk is published to the blockchain network. 5) Then the ciphertext $cipher\_\{sk\} = Enc_{pwkey}(sk)$ can be obtained. 6) Because the user's mk and sk are at the same layer of encryption. Therefore, the key file $file\_\{key\} = cipher\{mk\} \parallel cipher\{sk\}$ can be spliced together during storage and stored in the blockchain network. 7) Conversely, users can get $file\_\{key\}$ from the blockchain network, and then use $pwkey$ to decrypt the split content to get $mk = Dec_{pwkey}(cipher\_\{mk\})$ and $sk = Dec_{pwkey}(cipher\_\{sk\})$.

Key Hierarchical Management. 8) When the user uploads $file$, the local client will use the random number generator to generate the file encryption key $key\_\{file\}$, then generate the file ciphertext $cipher\_\{file\} = Enc_{key\_\{file\}}(file)$, and use mk to encrypt $key\_\{file\}$ to generate the ciphertext $cipher\_\{key\_\{file\}\} = Enc_{mk}(key\_\{file\})$. 9) Since $key\_\{file\}$ and $file$ are one-to-one correspondence, they should be spliced together to generate an upload file $upload\_\{file\} = cipher\_\{key\_\{file\}\} \parallel cipher\_\{file\}$ and uploaded to the blockchain network. 10) Conversely, users can download $upload\_\{file\}$, and use mk to get $key\_\{file\} = Dec_{mk}(cipher\_\{key\_\{file\}\})$ and $file = Dec_{key\_\{file\}}(cipher\_\{file\})$.

File Sharing. There are two situations when user A wants to share a file with user B. 11) If the shared file is in the blockchain network, the operation in 10) should be performed first to get $key\_\{file\}$ and $cipher\_\{file\}$. 12) Obtain the pkB of user B from the blockchain network, encrypt $key\_\{file\}$ and splice with $cipher\_\{file\}$. Moreover, the skA of user A is used to sign the spliced content to generate a signature summary $sigmessage$. 13) Finally, it is sent to user B to share file $share\_\{file\} = sigmessage \parallel cipher\_\{key\_\{file\}\} \parallel cipher\_\{file\}$. 14) If the shared file is in local client, the random number generator is used to randomly generate $key\_\{file\}$ for $file$, and user A gets ciphertext $cipher\_\{file\} = Enc_{key\_\{file\}}(file)$. Then 12) and 13) operations. 15) When user B receives $share\_\{file\}$, it first splits to $sigmessage$, $cipher\_\{key\_\{file\}\}$ and $cipher\_\{file\}$. 16) Then $sigmessage$ is verified $Ver_{pkA}(sigmessage)$. Finally, user B can obtain $key\_\{file\} = Dec_{skB}(cipher\_\{key\_\{file\}\})$ and $file = Dec_{key\_\{file\}}(cipher\_\{file\})$.

3.4 Password Recovery

In the key hierarchical management scheme, when the user forgets the pw, they cannot use the system. In order to solve this problem, a password recovery method is designed. In SMPC, no node can independently recover the password based on its own fragment. But if at least t fragments are obtained at the same time, the shared secret can be reconstructed. In order to prevent password leakage, this scheme takes two measures: 1) the password will be re-sharded in a certain period, it makes attackers obtain t fragments hardly; 2) Users use their biometrics to encrypt before the segmentation password. In other words, even if the attacker can reconstruct the fragments, he cannot get the password.

When the user registers for the first time, the password will be stored separately, the specific process is as follows: 1) If the user does not complete the identity registration, the user needs to extract the biometric W (including fingerprints, irises, etc.) by using the feature extraction device, and then generates the public parameter PUB and secret parameter R by using the existing fuzzy extractor $Gen(W) \rightarrow (PUB, R)$. The hash value $sk_{Id} = H(R)$ of the secret parameter R is calculated, and then the identity public-private key pair $(sk_{Id}, pk_{Id}) = (H(R), H(R) \cdot G)$ is generated, and the identity file $File\_Idpk = (pk_{Id}, PUB)$ is published to the blockchain network. If the identity registration has been completed, $File\_Idpk$ can be downloaded directly from the blockchain network. 2) The standard challenge-response protocol is used to authenticate users. The verifier Coordinator sends a challenge to the user, who uses the private key to sign the challenge and sends the response to the Coordinator. The Coordinator uses the user's public key to authenticate the received response, thus authenticating the user's identity. 3) The Coordinator collects trusted storage nodes. Due to the (t, n) threshold secret sharing method, the number of collected nodes m should satisfy $m \geq n \geq t$. Coordinator stores the information of the nodes in the file (named "trustednodes") in the storage area. 4) The Coordinator connects to the "trustednodes" file and starts the daemons of n computing nodes. Moreover, the value $t = \lfloor (2 \cdot n)/3 \rfloor$ is calculated and the refresh period $T_{refresh}$ is set. 5) Use the identity public key pk_{Id} to encrypt pw to get the password ciphertext $C = Enc_{pk_{Id}}(pw)$. 6) The user client generates n shared values $C \rightarrow \{C_1, \cdots, C_n\}$ according to C, where $n \geq 1$. The generation process is: set $r_0 = C$, and randomly select $t - 1$ random numbers $(r_1, \cdots, r_{t-1})$ in F_p to construct the polynomial equation $f_C(x) = \sum_{i=0}^{t-1} r_i x^i$. The sub-secret obtained for the signer P_i with the identification θ_i (where $i \in [1, n]$) is (θ_i, C_i), where $C_i = f_C(\theta_i)$. 7) A verifiable secret sharing mechanism is further introduced to verify the correctness of the secret. Taking a p-order generator of the multiplicative group $\mathbb{Z}_q^*$ as g $(p|(q-1), g > 1)$ to obtain the cyclic subgroup $\langle g \rangle$, and then obtain the set $K = \{g_i = g^{r_i} \bmod q\}_{i=0}^{t-1} \cup \{g\}$. Moreover, the set K needs to be sent to the trusted nodes. 8) Each node P_i $(i \in [1, n])$ verifies the sub-secret by equation $g^{C_i} = g^{\sum_{j=0}^{t-1} r_j \theta_i^j} = \prod_{j=0}^{t-1} g_j^{\theta_i^j}$. Coordinator stores the information of nodes that successfully received the secret in $storageNodes$ file, uses the user's pk_{Id} to encrypt the file, and stores it in the blockchain network (the file owner is set to the user). 9) When the refresh period $T_{refresh}$ is reached, the client performs the above process again to refresh the fragments.

The process of the user recovers the password is as follows: 1) The user downloads $File\_Idpk$ from the blockchain network, and then uses the feature extraction device to extract its biological feature W' and restores the secret parameter R' with the public parameter PUB, the formula is $Rep(PUB, W') \rightarrow R'$ (W' must satisfy $distance(W, W') < t$). Then the identity private key $sk_{Id}' = H(R')$ can be calculated. 2) Since the user does not have the elliptic curve private key at this time, it is necessary to authenticate the identity public-private key pair based on the authentication method mentioned above. 3) The user downloads the *storageNodes* file from the blockchain network and decrypts it with the sk_{Id}. 4) The user selects at least t nodes information from the previously trusted nodes, encrypts and sends it to the Coordinator. Then the Coordinator downloads the fragment (θ_i, C_i) on the corresponding node. 5) The Coordinator uses *Lagrange* interpolation to recover the result $C = \text{reconstruct}((\theta_1, C_1), \cdots, (\theta_t, C_t))$ from t fragments and sends the encrypted result to the user. The recovery process is: the polynomial equation $f_C(x) = \sum_{j=1}^{t} y_j L_j(x) = \sum_{j=1}^{t} (C_j \cdot \prod_{i=1, i \neq j}^{t} \frac{x - \theta_i}{\theta_j - \theta_i})$ is recovered first, and then the secret $C = f_C(0)$ is recovered. 6) The user decrypts C with his own sk_{Id}' to get $pw' = Dec_{sk_{Id}'}(C)$. Since W' and W satisfy $distance(W, W') < t$, then $R' = R$, $sk_{Id}' = sk_{Id}$, $pw' = pw$.

3.5 Multi-party Signature

The threshold signature based on SMPC in this scheme can adapt to different chains and contracts. It only distinguishes signature algorithms, such as Schnorr. In order to cope with the situation of multi-party signatures, the scheme improves the stored password mentioned above, that is, the number of fragments depends on the number of signers. In the process of signature, the private key of the signature will not be recovered, which greatly improves the security of the signature. In addition, this method also refreshes the "fragmented" private key in a certain period. The generation process of multi-party signature key following:

1) The t participants inform the Coordinator to create a real public-private key pair $Gen \rightarrow (sk_{Multiple}, pk_{Multiple})$, where $pk_{Multiple}$ is published to the blockchain. 2) The Coordinator authenticates each signer's identity through the process is the same as that in step 2) of password storage. 3) The Coordinator generates t shared values $sk_{Multiple} \rightarrow \{sk_{Multiple\_1}, \cdots, sk_{Multiple\_t}\}$ and the set $K = \{g_i = g^{r_i} \bmod q\}_{i=0}^{t-1} \cup \{g\}$. The shared values generation process is similar to the method of steps 6) and 7) in the password storage. Subsequently, the Coordinator encrypts the corresponding subkey, and sends it and set K to the signer. 4) Each sigher uses his private key to obtain the sub-secret $(\theta_i, sk_{Multiple\_i})$. Then, the formula $g^{sk_{Multiple\_i}} = \prod_{j=0}^{t-1} g_j^{\theta_i^j}$ is used to verify the correctness of the reception. If the Coordinator receives error feedback, it will re-share the corresponding secret.

In a certain period of time, the Coordinator will repeat the above process to refresh the $sk_{Multiple\_i}$ of each signer. When signers need to perform multiple signatures, the following process is performed:

1) The signers send the secret k to the Coordinator. 2) The Coordinator generates t shared values $k \rightarrow \{k_1, \cdots, k_t\}$. The difference from the above process is that the random variable in the formula is r_i'. Then the shared sub-secrets (θ_i, k_i) (where $i \in [1, n]$) and set $P = \{p_i = g^{r_i'} \bmod q\}_{i=0}^{t-1} \cup \{g\}$ are sent to signers. 3) Each signer verifies the correctness by the equation $g^{k_i} = \prod_{j=0}^{t-1} p_j^{\theta_i^j}$ and performs a calculation $f_i = k_i + sk_{Multiple\_i} \bmod p$. Then the node sends the result (θ_i, f_i) to the Coordinator. 4) The Coordinator uses *Lagrange* interpo-

lation method to recover the result $s = \text{reconstruct}\,((\theta_1, f_1), \cdots, (\theta_t, f_t))$. Since the Shamir sharing scheme has the restricted multiplication homomorphism, multiplication operations can be performed. Furthermore, the mixed operation of addition and subtraction can be performed to complete the signature and decryption. For example, taking the signature method Schnorr as an example to calculate $Sig\,(M) = (e, s)$, where $e = H\,(r\|M)$ can be calculated directly, and $s = k + xe \bmod p$ can be calculated using SMPC. In the multi-party decryption operation, the calculation is similar to the above operation. Therefore, this scheme can meet the needs of users and provide accurate services.

3.6 The Supplement of the Scheme

The scheme also provides key update and revocation mechanisms. When updating the key, not only the current key needs to be replaced, but also the relevant content of the lower layer needs to be reset. Thus, the higher level of the key, the more complex update process. Besides, when the user logs out of the system, the local client will clean up all the plaintext to ensure security, and the ciphertext of the key forms the key sets. When the user needs the key, first access the key sets. If there is no such key in the key sets, download it from the blockchain.

4 Analysis and Evaluation

4.1 Analysis of Correctness and Security

Lemma 1. *The Shamir secret sharing scheme has additive and restricted multiplication homomorphism. Specifically, if multiple (t, n) sharing schemes share multiple secrets, then the fragmented sum of different secret values is the fragment to the sum of corresponding secret values. If $d\,(t, n)$ sharing schemes share multiple secrets, if and only if $d\,(t - 1) \leq n - 1$, the fragmented product of these secret values is still the fragment to the product of corresponding secret values.*

Proof. The proof process of the lemma is detailed in [3, 4].

Lemma 2. *If the biological feature W' and the original biometric W extracted by the fuzzy extractor satisfy distance $(W, W') < t$, the secret parameter $R' = R$ generated before and after. Where distance() is the similarity distance function and t is the error limit specified by the fuzzy extractor.*

Proof. The proof of the lemma is detailed in [6].

Correctness of the Scheme. Lemmas 1, 2 and verifiable Shamir secret sharing guarantee the correctness of the schemes.

Security Under Data Tampering Attacks. In our schemes, keys and files are verified by verifiable secret sharing, hash values in the index table on-chain, and signature mechanism. Moreover, the accessor's identity can be authenticated in each process. The consensus mechanism and distributed data storage in the blockchain can be used to ensure that data is tracked and not easily tampered with by the attackers. Thus, our scheme can resist data tampering attacks.

Security Under Key Stealing Attacks. Due to the encryption relationship in this scheme is that the upper key encrypts the lower key, the security of all keys is guaranteed. Moreover, the master key and file encryption key are random numbers of sufficient length generated by a secure random number generator, and one file corresponds to one file encryption key, which can prevent malicious users from cracking the file encryption key through known-plaintext attacks. So the plaintext of keys is hard to be stolen. In addition, password recovery, key update and revocation can reduce the loss of uses when they are damaged.

Security Under "Fragments" Leak Attacks. During password recovery and multi-party signatures, timing refresh and early encryption mechanisms are adopted. In the following scenario: set $n = 3$, $t = 2$, the refresh time as $T_{refresh}$, and the sk is divided into $C_{sk_1}, C_{sk_2}, C_{sk_3}$ after encryption and stored on three nodes. After $T_{refresh}$, the sk is divided into $C_{sk_1'}, C_{sk_2'}, C_{sk_3'}$, and the values on the three nodes are refreshed. If the attacker obtains C_{sk_1} within $T_{refresh}$, and obtains $C_{sk_2'}$ after $T_{refresh}$. The sk cannot be reconstructed correctly. In addition, even if the attacker obtains C_{sk_1} and C_{sk_2} in time $T_{refresh}$, only the ciphertext of sk is obtained, so the sk is still safe.

Security Under Plaintext Stealing Attacks. In our schemes, the attacker can only obtain file ciphertext data and cannot get any valuable information during data transmission and storage. Moreover, when the user logs out of the system, the local client will clean up all plaintext content. So the probability of the attacker offline attacking the user's local client to obtain the plaintext can be reduced. In addition, the Coordinator maintains zero-knowledge throughout the process of this scheme, mainly plays the role of verification and notification. We can replace the Coordinator with smart contracts to build scenarios without trusted third parties. Thus, our schemes can protect the data of users well.

4.2   Analysis of Efficiency

First of all, most keys and files in this scheme are encrypted by the symmetric encryption algorithm. Compared with the asymmetric encryption algorithm in the current blockchain, this method is more efficient and consumes fewer resources. Second, Ertaul et al. [10] proved that PBKDF2 used in this scheme is more efficient than Bcrypt and Scrypt algorithms. Third, the scheme adopts on-chain and off-chain collaboration methods, and makes full use of computing resources to improve operational efficiency. Moreover, the PBFT consensus enables chains to process thousands of transactions per second. Fourth, the index table on-chain uses red-black trees to perform query and other operations with time complexity of $O(\log_2(N))$, and any imbalance will be resolved within three rotations, so it is better than balanced binary trees in terms of efficiency. In summary, the scheme maintains high efficiency in both key management and file sharing.

4.3   Comparative Analysis of Scheme Performance

We use python to implement our schemes on Windows 10, Intel (R) Core (TM) i5-4200H 2.80 GHz and 12 GB RAM. In order to unify the variables in the comparative experiment, the storage rate to the off-chain database is 5 M/S (5 KB/ms), the download rate from the off-chain database is 10 M/S (10 KB/ms), the size of the stored file is 10 KB, and the message transmission time between nodes in the blockchain is 1 ms. Figures 4, 5 and 6 show the key generation time, file sharing time, and space overhead in the schemes of original blockchain, [7,12], and this paper. In order to improve the efficiency of file sharing, the symmetric encryption key is considered in the schemes of this paper and [7], so the key generation time and the number of files in Fig. 4 have a linear relationship. Moreover, under normal circumstances, the user's keys are generated only once. Thus, the key generation in this scheme is acceptable and has little effect on the system. It can be seen from Fig. 5 that the scheme can reduce the file-sharing time, so the efficiency of the system can be improved, as well as guarantee a superior security level. In order to accurately analyze the storage overhead, this paper unifies the security strength of the elliptic curve encryption key, symmetric encryption key and RSA encryption key with different lengths. It can be seen from Fig. 6 that this scheme can reduce the storage overhead, thereby improving the system utilization of resources and the efficiency of the system. In summary, compared with other schemes, our schemes achieve higher performance.

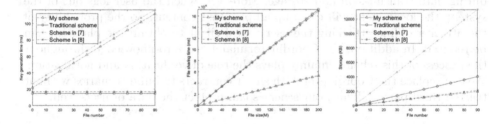

Fig. 4. Key generation time.   **Fig. 5.** File sharing time.   **Fig. 6.** Storage overhead.

Figure 7 shows the average time of each file uploaded and downloaded in this scheme and the scheme without RBTree. The graph can be divided into two parts, one is the time overhead in the index table on-chain, and the other is the total time. It can be seen from Fig. 7 that the addition and query time of this scheme in the index table on-chain are relatively stable and are less than 0.25 ms and 0.1 ms respectively (almost negligible). Moreover, the corresponding total upload and download time are also relatively stable and lower than the scheme without RBTree, and basically depend on the storage and download time of files in the database. As the number of files in the chain increases, the addition and query time overheads in the scheme without RBTree increase. It should be noted that this scheme is also optimal in terms of file deletion and modification.

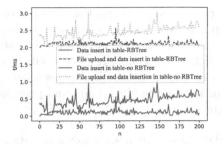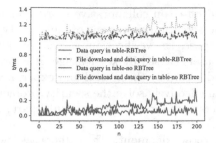

Fig. 7. The upload and download time of one file varies with files number on-chain.

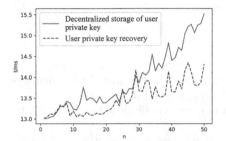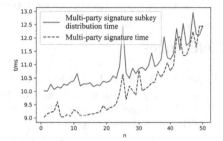

Fig. 8. Key storage and recovery time.   **Fig. 9.** Multi-party signature time.

Figure 8 shows the storage and recovery time of the private key changes with the number of storage nodes. It can be seen from Fig. 8 that the storage and recovery time of the private key increases with the number of decentralized nodes increases, which is in line with theory. In practice, the number of decentralized nodes is generally 10 to 30, so the scheme consumes little time (can even be ignored), and the corresponding security is sufficient. Figure 9 shows the signature key distribution and signature time changes with the number of participants. It can be seen from Fig. 9 that the time of signature key distribution and signature increases with the number of participants. In practice, the number of participants is generally about 10, so the time is basically negligible, and it can provide sufficient security and meet the needs of multi-party signatures. In summary, the performance of the scheme is excellent in terms of security, time overhead, and storage overhead, and it can provide users with more high-quality services.

5 Conclusion

In this paper, we design key hierarchical management and collaborative signature schemes of blockchain with high security and efficiency. In our schemes, the key is divided into three layers, and the upper-layer key encrypts the lower-layer key, thus ensuring the security of all keys. Moreover, the schemes combine SMPC and feature encryption to store and recover passwords on the on-chain and off-chain collaborative storage architecture, and complete the distribution and signature operations of multi-party signature keys. Besides, the scheme also proposes key verification, revocation, and update mechanisms to reduce the loss to users caused by key leakage. It is proved that the scheme is correct, efficient and secure by theoretical and experimental results. In other words, this scheme can effectively solve the security problem of keys in the blockchain, and provide users with services such as multi-party signatures.

Acknowledgement. The authors acknowledge the support from National Key R&D Program of China under Grant No. 2017YFB1400700, National Natural Science Foundation of China under Grant No. 61772514 and Beijing Municipal Science & Technology Commission (Project Number: Z191100007119006).

References

1. Albakri, A., Harn, L., Maddumala, M.: Polynomial-based lightweight key management in a permissioned blockchain. In: CNS, pp. 1–9. IEEE (2019)
2. Ali, M.S., Dolui, K., Antonelli, F.: IoT data privacy via blockchains and IPFS. In: IOT, pp. 14:1–14:7. ACM (2017)
3. Barkol, O., Ishai, Y., Weinreb, E.: On d-multiplicative secret sharing. J. Cryptol. **23**(4), 580–593 (2010)
4. Benaloh, J.C.: Secret sharing homomorphisms: keeping shares of a secret secret (extended abstract). In: Odlyzko, A.M. (ed.) CRYPTO 1986. LNCS, vol. 263, pp. 251–260. Springer, Heidelberg (1987). https://doi.org/10.1007/3-540-47721-7_19
5. Department, I.S.: Digital money wallet security white paper. https://www.anquanke.com/post/id/146233. Accessed 17 Sep 2020
6. Dodis, Y., Reyzin, L., Smith, A.: Fuzzy extractors: how to generate strong keys from biometrics and other noisy data. In: Cachin, C., Camenisch, J.L. (eds.) EUROCRYPT 2004. LNCS, vol. 3027, pp. 523–540. Springer, Heidelberg (2004). https://doi.org/10.1007/978-3-540-24676-3_31
7. Fan, K., Lou, S., Su, R., Li, H., Yang, Y.: Secure and private key management scheme in big data networking. Peer Peer Netw. Appl. **11**(5), 992–999 (2018)
8. Kingo: Classification and comparative analysis of bitcoin wallets. https://www.8btc.com/article/30431. Accessed 17 Sep 2020
9. Lei, A., Cruickshank, H.S., Cao, Y., Asuquo, P.M., Ogah, C.P.A., Sun, Z.: Blockchain-based dynamic key management for heterogeneous intelligent transportation systems. IEEE Internet Things J. **4**(6), 1832–1843 (2017)
10. Levent, E., Manpreet, K., Gudise, V.A.K.R.: Implementation and performance analysis of PBKDF2, Bcrypt, Scrypt algorithms. In: Proceedings of the ICWN, p. 66. The Steering Committee of WorldComp (2016)
11. Liu, J., Ping, J., Fu, X.: Research on a distributed public key system based on blockchain. Netinfo Secur. **18**(8), 25–33 (2018)
12. Lou, J., Zhang, Q., Qi, Z., Lei, K.: A blockchain-based key management scheme for named data networking. In: 2018 1st IEEE International Conference on HotICN, pp. 141–146. IEEE (2018)
13. Ma, C.: Method and system for implementing blockchain private key protection based on key segmentation. China Patent CN106548345A (March 2017)

14. Ma, M., Shi, G., Li, F.: Privacy-oriented blockchain-based distributed key management architecture for hierarchical access control in the IoT scenario. IEEE Access **7**, 34045–34059 (2019)
15. Shamir, A.: How to share a secret. Commun. ACM **22**(11), 612–613 (1979)
16. Xia, D., Wei, Z., Xu, K., Xu, J., Liu, X., Bi, W.: Energy blockchain private key storage algorithm based on image information hiding. Power Syst. Autom. **31**(1), 7–11 (2019)
17. Yao, A.C.: Protocols for secure computations (extended abstract). In: FOCS, pp. 160–164. IEEE Computer Society (1982)
18. Zhang, H., Wang, J., Ding, Y.: Blockchain-based decentralized and secure keyless signature scheme for smart grid. Energy **180**, 955–967 (2019)
19. Zhao, H., Bai, P., Peng, Y., Xu, R.: Efficient key management scheme for health blockchain. CAAI Trans. Intell. Technol. **3**(2), 114–118 (2018)
20. Zhao, H., Zhang, Y., Peng, Y., Xu, R.: Lightweight backup and efficient recovery scheme for health blockchain keys. In: ISADS, pp. 229–234. IEEE Computer Society (2017)

Information Hiding

Covert Communication via Modulating Soft Label of Neural Network

Gen Liu[1], Hanzhou Wu[1(✉)], and Xinpeng Zhang[1,2]

[1] School of Communication and Information Engineering, Shanghai University,
Shanghai 200444, People's Republic of China
h.wu.phd@ieee.org
[2] School of Computer Science, Fudan University,
Shanghai 200433, People's Republic of China

Abstract. In this paper, we present a novel method to covert communication based on a host deep neural network (DNN) itself, which is totally different from many traditional works that embed secret data into a digital image since: 1) there has no direct image transmission between the data hider and the data receiver, 2) there has no modification to the image content, and 3) the presence of the covert communication can be concealed by the large number of ordinary queries. The main idea is embedding secret data into the soft output of the host DNN by modifying the soft label according to the secret data and further fine-tuning the host DNN with the modified soft label together with its input. When the fine-tuned DNN is put into use, the data receiver can fully retrieve the secret data from the soft output of the DNN by uploading the corresponding image to the DNN. Experimental results have shown that, the secret data can be successfully embedded and extracted. And, it does not impair the performance of the original task, which has demonstrated the superiority and applicability. Moreover, the Kullback-Leibler divergence between the soft output produced by the embedded DNN and that produced by the original DNN is quite low, which can ensure the security.

Keywords: Covert communication · Steganography · Information hiding · Deep learning · Fine-tuning · Deep neural networks

1 Introduction

Information hiding [1,2], as a very important means to covert communication, allows us to embed a secret message into a seemingly-innocent digital object (also called *cover object*) such as digital image and video sequences by slightly modifying the object without impairing the value of the object. The resultant object containing hidden information (also called *stego object*) should be sent to the desired receiver who can use the secret key to drive the data extraction procedure to retrieve the embedded data from the object containing hidden information. The general framework of information hiding can be described as Fig. 1. A straightforward idea to categorize information hiding approaches is the

© Springer Nature Switzerland AG 2021
X. Sun et al. (Eds.): ICAIS 2021, LNCS 12737, pp. 349–359, 2021.
https://doi.org/10.1007/978-3-030-78612-0_28

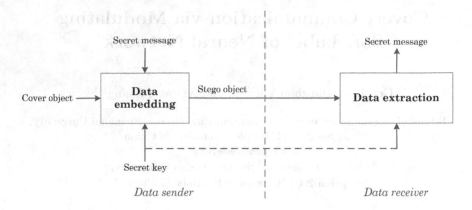

Fig. 1. General framework for information hiding.

used cover. For example, digital image [3,4] is the most popular cover type due to the ease of handling and its wide distribution over social networks. Other cover sources such as text [5,6] and video [7,8] are also attracting increasing interest to the research community due to the rapid development of network transmission and multimedia technologies. Recently, exploiting social behaviors for information hiding has also been studied in the literature, e.g., [9,10].

Early information hiding algorithms focus on minimizing the amount of modifications to the cover as they roughly assume that the costs of modifying different cover elements are equal to each other such as [11,12]. Advanced algorithms are thereafter proposed to enhance the security by first assigning an embedding cost to each of the cover elements and then minimizing the total embedding cost for a given payload, e.g., [13–15]. Regardless of the technical details, these conventional information hiding technologies rely heavily on the empirical knowledge of the system designer. Recently, deep learning has led to great success in many fields such as computer vision and pattern recognition [16,17]. It has promoted many attempts moving deep learning to information hiding, e.g., [18–20]. Most works combine deep neural networks (DNNs) to learn the near-optimal embedding strategy in a cover object [21]. They are still based on traditional multimedia covers, namely, in the real-world, one has to still transmit the media object containing hidden information to the receiver. Imagine that, if we could avoid the direct object transmission, the identity of the data receiver may be well concealed. The direct communication bandwidth between the data sender and the receiver can be reduced as well. It inspires us to propose to embed secret data into a DNN itself such that: 1) there has no direct communication between the data hider and the data receiver, 2) if the data receiver has the ability to retrieve secret data without taking suspicious action, his real role can be concealed, and 3) When the DNN is put into use, the covert communication can be concealed by the large number of ordinary queries.

We describe an application scenario as follows. The data hider wants to send a secret message to the data receiver via a classification based DNN. He has to fine-tune the host DNN with a pre-shared input sample and its soft label carrying the secret data in advance. Then, the fine-tuned DNN is released in the cloud. Any user can upload a sample to the DNN, and receive the classification result outputted by the DNN. The classification result corresponds to a vector, in which each element indicates the probability of belonging to the corresponding class. In order to extract the secret data, the data receiver can upload the pre-shared sample to collect the classification result, i.e., the soft output, from which the secret data can be further reconstructed, leading to successful communication.

The technical feasibility is that, most DNNs are redundant, which means that the undeveloped representation ability can be further exploited to realize other activity, which can make the DNN output desired result when it was activated. And, the DNN performs normally when fed with normal samples. Obviously, in this paper, the other activity is equivalent to information hiding. Recalling the aforementioned application scenario, as long as the soft output of the DNN matches the secret data, the data receiver can feed any sample to the DNN, which, however, may degrade the performance on the original task of the DNN that can arouse suspicious. Therefore, the DNN should be trained to produce the desired output containing secret information and its performance on its original task should not decline. To this end, we propose a reliable information coding technique such that the secret data can be embedded into the soft label and the embedded soft label does not impair the performance of the original task.

The rest of this paper is organized as follows. First of all, we show the details of the proposed method in Sect. 2. Then, the experimental results and analysis are provided in Sect. 3. Finally, we conclude this paper in Sect. 4.

2   Proposed Method

Figure 2 shows the sketch for the proposed framework, which follows the above-mentioned scenario. Without the loss of generalization, we focus on image classification based DNN. We propose to fine-tune a host DNN F_θ by an image $\mathbf{X}$ and the secret data $\mathbf{m}$ to produce a new DNN $F'_\theta \neq F_\theta$. It is easy to use more inputs when we want to send more secret bits. There are two features for the proposed method: 1) $\mathbf{X}$ does not arouse suspicion since its content will be unchanged, and; 2) the hard outputs of F'_θ and F_θ equal each other. For example, assuming that, we want to identify the digit number of an image, F_θ returns the soft output as {0.1, 0.6, 0.2, 0.01, 0.01, 0.01, 0.01, 0.01, 0.04, 0.01} and F'_θ returns the soft output as {0.15, 0.5, 0.25, 0.01, 0.01, 0.01, 0.01, 0.01, 0.04, 0.01}. Then, their hard outputs are identical, i.e., both classify the digit as "1" since "1" has the largest probability. In the following, we will show the details of the data hiding and data extraction procedure. Notice that, F_θ and F'_θ correspond to the trained DNN and the embedded DNN in Fig. 2. Moreover, $\mathbf{X}$ is the trigger sample.

2.1   Data Hiding

Let $H(F_\theta(\mathbf{X}))$ and $S(F_\theta(\mathbf{X}))$ respectively return the hard output and the soft output by feeding $\mathbf{X}$ to F_θ. The data hider uses $\mathbf{X}$ and $\mathbf{m}$ to train such F'_θ that

$$\|H(F_\theta(\mathbf{X})) - H(F'_\theta(\mathbf{X}))\| < \varepsilon \tag{1}$$

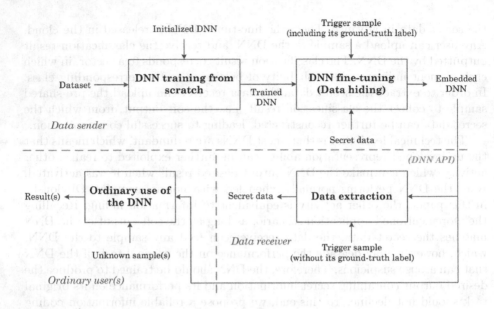

Fig. 2. Sketch for the proposed framework.

and

$$\text{Ext}(S(F'_\theta(\mathbf{X}))) = \mathbf{m}, \tag{2}$$

where ε is a small controllable threshold and $\text{Ext}(\cdot)$ means to extract $\mathbf{m}$ from $S(F'_\theta(\mathbf{X}))$. In this way, the data hider will perform the following steps.

Step 1. For the input $\mathbf{X}$, the data hider collects $\mathbf{y} = S(F_\theta(\mathbf{X}))$.

Step 2. The data hider embeds $\mathbf{m}$ into $\mathbf{y}$, i.e., $\mathbf{z} = \text{Emb}(\mathbf{y}, \mathbf{m})$. The details of $\text{Emb}(\cdot, \cdot)$ will be given latter.

Step 3. The data hider uses $\{\mathbf{X}, \mathbf{z}\}$ to fine-tune F_θ to produce F'_θ such that $\|H(F'_\theta(\mathbf{X})) - H(F_\theta(\mathbf{X}))\| < \varepsilon$ and $\text{Ext}(S(F'_\theta(\mathbf{X}))) = \mathbf{m}$. It is done by minimizing the soft loss $\|S(F'_\theta(\mathbf{X})) - \mathbf{z}\|$ during fine-tuning.

Step 4. Once F'_θ is generated, the data hider releases F'_θ to the cloud.

We write $\mathbf{y} = (y_0, y_1, ..., y_{n-1})$, $\mathbf{z} = (z_0, z_1, ..., z_{n-1})$, $\sum_{i=0}^{n-1} y_i = \sum_{i=0}^{n-1} z_i = 1$. We now introduce $\text{Emb}(\cdot, \cdot)$. We first scale $\mathbf{y}$ as follows:

$$\mathbf{y}' = \alpha\mathbf{y} = (\alpha y_0, \alpha y_1, ..., \alpha y_{n-1}), 0 < \alpha \leq 1, \tag{3}$$

for which we also write $y'_i = \alpha y_i$ for simplicity. Obviously, $\sum_{i=0}^{n-1} y'_i = \alpha$.

Given a threshold $T \geq 0$, we divide $\mathbf{y}'$ into two sets, denoted by:

$$S_0 = \{y'_i \mid y'_i < T, i \in [0, n)\}, S_1 = \{y'_i \mid y'_i \geq T, i \in [0, n)\}. \tag{4}$$

Only elements in S_1 are used for carrying $\mathbf{m}$. Each element carries one bit. Therefore, T can control the payload size. Let l_m be the size of $\mathbf{m}$. We then have $l_m = |S_1|$. The data embedding operation for $y'_i \in S_1$ is as follows:

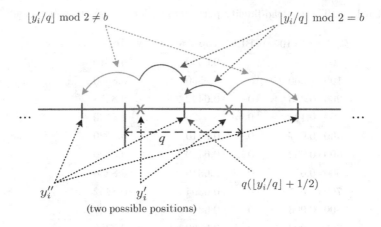

$\lfloor y_i'/q \rfloor \bmod 2 \neq b$ $\lfloor y_i'/q \rfloor \bmod 2 = b$

q

y_i'' y_i' $q(\lfloor y_i'/q \rfloor + 1/2)$

(two possible positions)

Fig. 3. Explanation for determining y_i'' from y_i' based on Eq. (5).

$$y_i'' = \begin{cases} q(\lfloor y_i'/q \rfloor + \dfrac{1}{2}), & \text{if } \lfloor y_i'/q \rfloor \bmod 2 = b, \\[2mm] \underset{t=q(\lfloor y_i'/q \rfloor + \frac{1}{2}) \pm q,\ t \in [0,1]}{\arg\min} |y_i' - t|, & \text{otherwise.} \end{cases} \tag{5}$$

where $b \in \{0,1\}$ is the present secret bit to be embedded and $q \in (0,1)$ is the predetermined quantization step. Figure 3 shows the intuitive understanding for Eq. (5), in which two possible values of y_i' are used as examples.

For each $y_i' \in S_0$, we perform:

$$y_i'' = \beta y_i', \tag{6}$$

where $\beta < 0.5$ scales the elements in S_0 so that the secret data can be fully recovered by the receiver without ambiguity. Finally, we adjust each y_i'' to z_i by adding e_i such that $z_i = y_i'' + e_i$ and $\sum_{i=0}^{n-1} z_i = 1$. We can write:

$$\begin{aligned} \Delta &= \sum_{i=0}^{n-1} e_i \\ &= 1 - \sum_{i=0}^{n-1} y_i'' \\ &= 1 - \alpha + \sum_{i=0}^{n-1} y_i' - \sum_{i=0}^{n-1} y_i'' \\ &= 1 - \alpha + \sum_{i=0}^{n-1} (y_i' - y_i'') \\ &= 1 - \alpha + (1-\beta) \sum_{y_i' \in S_0} y_i' + \sum_{y_i' \in S_1} (y_i' - y_i''). \end{aligned} \tag{7}$$

Table 1. The payload-fidelity performance for a single trigger image.

l_m	q ($\times 10^{-3}$)	BER	Top-1 accuracy	Top-5 accuracy
0	-	-	0.6560	0.8610
100	1.060	0	0.6550	0.8590
200	0.333	0	0.6442	0.8558
300	0.124	0	0.6430	0.8560
400	0.057	0	0.6410	0.8520
500	0.032	0	0.6420	0.8520
600	0.019	0	0.6319	0.8438
700	0.011	0	0.6394	0.8452
800	0.006	0	0.6310	0.8387
900	0.003	0	0.6300	0.8380
1000	0.001	0	0.6390	0.8440

Table 2. The payload-fidelity performance for multiple trigger images.

N	k	l_m	BER	Top-1 accuracy	Top-5 accuracy
10	100	1000	0	0.6170	0.8390
20	100	2000	0	0.6170	0.8350
30	100	3000	0	0.6100	0.8320
40	100	4000	0	0.6030	0.8221
50	100	5000	0	0.5764	0.7953

It can be inferred from Eq. (5) that, when the size of S_1, i.e., $|S_1|$, is large enough, we have $\sum_{y'_i \in S_1} (y'_i - y''_i) \approx 0$. Since we can use a very small T, $(1 - \beta) \sum_{y'_i \in S_0} y'_i$ can be considered as a quite small positive number. Thus, we can always keep Δ as a small positive number by well adjusting α and β. In general, α is close to 1, and β is close to 0. Moreover, since it is free for us to choose $\mathbf{X}$, Δ can be well controlled in practice. Accordingly, we write:

$$e_1 = e_2 = ... = e_{n-1} = \Delta/n, \tag{8}$$

which means that, when we find the sum of $\{y''_1, y''_2, ..., y''_{n-1}\}$ is not equal to 1, we determine its distance to 1 and divide the distance to n pieces to be added to $\{y''_1, y''_2, ..., y''_{n-1}\}$ so that the sum is equal to 1. It is mentioned that, Δ/n can be very much smaller than $q/2$ so that the data receiver can always identify the elements carrying the secret bits in practice.

2.2 Data Extraction

For the data receiver, he will upload $\mathbf{X}$ to the cloud and obtain $S(F'_\theta(\mathbf{X}))$, from which he can reconstruct $\mathbf{m}$. The steps can be briefly summarized as follows:

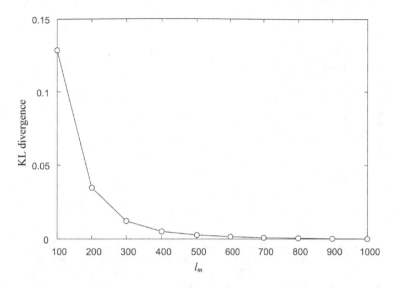

Fig. 4. The KL divergence due to different l_m in case $N = 1$.

Step 1. By feeding $\mathbf{X}$, the data receiver collects $\mathbf{z}' = S(F'_\theta(\mathbf{X}))$.
Step 2. The data receiver reconstructs $\mathbf{m}$ from $\mathbf{z}'$, i.e., $\mathbf{m} = \mathrm{Ext}(\mathbf{z}')$.
The details of $\mathrm{Ext}(\cdot)$ are as follows. First, the receiver collects two sets:

$$S'_0 = \{z'_i \mid z'_i < \frac{q}{2} - \xi, i \in [0, n)\}, S'_1 = \{z'_i \mid z'_i \geq \frac{q}{2} - \xi, i \in [0, n)\}, \quad (9)$$

where ξ is a quite small positive number, e.g., 10^{-8}, so as to keep the calculating precision as computers use float numbers. Then, for each $z'_i \in S'_1$, a secret bit $b \in \{0, 1\}$ can be recovered by:

$$b = \lfloor z'_i/q \rfloor \bmod 2. \quad (10)$$

By extracting all required bits, the secret message $\mathbf{m}$ can be fully retrieved.

3   Performance Evaluation and Analysis

We adopt the well-known VGG16 [22] pre-trained on the ImageNet dataset [23] as F_θ for experiments. The data split follows the default setting[1]. The images are sized $224 \times 224 \times 3$, belonging to one of 1000 classes. The DNN is optimized by stochastic gradient descent (SGD) with learning rate $l_r = 0.0001$. If only one image is used, then $l_m \leq 1000$. Moreover, since T can control the payload size, given l_m and a single image, for simplicity, we set T as the l_m-th largest value in $\mathbf{y}'$ so that $\mathbf{m}$ can be fully carried. We also empirically use $q = T, \alpha = 1 - q/10^5, \beta = 0.01$ in default. It is admitted that, it is free to tune the parameters.

---

[1] http://image-net.org/challenges/LSVRC/2012/.

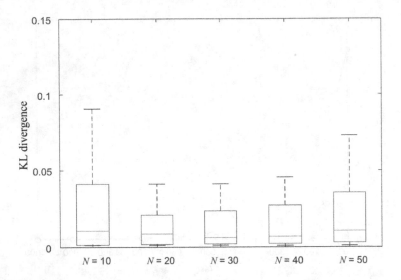

Fig. 5. The KL divergence due to different N in case $l_m = 100N$.

We first show the payload-fidelity performance, where only one trigger image was used. Table 1 shows the bit error rates (BERs), Top-1 and Top-5 accuracy. The BER is determined as the percentage of different bits between the extracted message and the original message. The Top-k accuracy means the percentage of testing samples that are correctly predicted in the Top-k list. It can be observed from Table 1 that, the fine-tuned DNN can perfectly convey the secret data in all the cases. It can be also seen that, the Top-1 and Top-5 accuracy values are respectively close to each other, meaning that, fine-tuning the DNN for covert communication does not impair the performance. More images can be used to transmit $\mathbf{m}$, where $l_m = kN$ if each one of the N images carries k bits. Table 2 shows the results for $k = 100$. It can be seen from Table 2 that, the performance on the original task declines as the number of used images increases, which is reasonable as fine-tuning the DNN means to force the DNN to fit the *stego* label. It can be also seen that, the secret data can be all perfectly reconstructed, which has shown the feasibility and applicability of the proposed work. In addition, by comparing Table 1 (in case $l_m = 1000$) with Table 2 (in case $N = 10, k = 100$), it is suggested that, to maintain the performance of the original task, it is suitable to distribute $\mathbf{m}$ into as few images as possible.

In terms of security, there has no modification to the input image(s). This indicates that, any steganalysis system directly applied to the input image(s) will not work. Moreover, our work does not expect to alter the hard prediction of a given image, which will not arouse attention from the monitor. Though the proposed work modify the soft label, the soft output of the fine-tuned DNN is quite close to that of the original one. To verify this, we determine the Kullback-Leibler (KL) divergence between $S(F'_\theta(\mathbf{X}))$ and $S(F_\theta(\mathbf{X}))$. The KL divergence measures how a probability distribution is different from another one. A smaller

KL divergence means that the two distributions are more close to each other. For two identical probability distributions, their KL divergence is zero. Figure 4 shows the KL divergence due to different l_m in case $N = 1$ (based on Table 1). It can be observed that, as l_m increases, the KL divergence decreases. That is because, for a smaller l_m, $q = T$ will be larger (which accelerates convergence). Thus, the modification degree will be higher, leading to the higher KL divergence. Figure 5 shows the KL divergence due to different N in case $l_m = 100N$ (based on Table 2). It can be seen from Fig. 4 and Fig. 5 that, all KL divergence values are kept low, indicating that, our work will not introduce significant degradation of the soft output vector, which has verified the aforementioned analysis. Furthermore, the presence of the covert communication can be concealed by the large number of ordinary queries, which can further ensure the security.

4   Conclusion and Discussion

In this paper, we present a novel DNN based method to covert communication. In the method, the soft output is fine-tuned to carry secret data without altering the hard output of the DNN. Experiments have shown that the proposed method can reliably transmit secret bits and do not impair the performance of the original task, which has shown the superiority and the applicability. Additionally, in the proposed work, there has no modification to the input data, meaning that, any steganalysis method directly analyzing the input content will not work. Moreover, we modify the soft output without changing the hard output, which will not cause alert. Though we focus on classification based DNNs, by adjusting accordingly, more sophisticated DNNs may be accommodated by the proposed framework. It is also worth mentioning that, though the proposed work uses the soft prediction to carry the secret data, one may also use the hard prediction to carry secret data. For example, for a classification task with n classes, when we use Top-k accuracy, the maximum embeddable payload size is $\log_2 \frac{n!}{(n-k)!k!}$ bits.

Recently, increasing attention has also been paid to embedding information into neural networks to protect the ownership of these neural networks, which is typically referred to as *watermarking DNNs* [24]. Though the major purpose of this paper is to securely transmit secret information, the proposed work can be also extended to watermarking DNNs. However, since watermarking DNNs may face various attacks such as model compression and fine-tuning. How to enhance the robustness of the proposed work is a core problem to be addressed, for which adversarial training strategy [25] may be necessary. We will extend the proposed work along this line and hope this work can inspire more advanced works.

Acknowledgement. It was supported by National Natural Science Foundation of China under grant Nos. 61902235, U1636206, U1936214, 61525203. It was also supported by "Chen Guang" project under grant No. 19CG46, which is co-funded by Shanghai Municipal Education Commission and Shanghai Education Development Foundation.

References

1. Petitcolas, F.A.P., Anderson, R.J., Kuhn, M.G.: Information hiding - a survey. Proc. IEEE **87**(7), 1062–1078 (1999)
2. Cox, I.J., Miller, M.L., Bloom, J.A., Fridrich, J., Kalker, T.: Digital Watermarking and Steganography, 2nd edn. Morgan Kaufmann, Burlington (2007)
3. Fridrich, J.: Steganography in Digital Media: Principles, Algorithms, and Applications. Cambridge University Press, Cambridge (2009)
4. Wu, H.-Z., Shi, Y.-Q., Wang, H.-X., Zhou, L.-N.: Separable reversible data hiding for encrypted palette images with color partitioning and flipping verification. IEEE Trans. Circuits Syst. Video Technol. **27**(8), 1620–1631 (2017)
5. Yang, Z.-L., Guo, X.-Q., Chen, Z.-M., Huang, Y.-F., Zhang, Y.-J.: RNN-Stega: linguistic steganography based on recurrent neural networks. IEEE Trans. Inf. Forensics Secur. **14**(5), 1280–1295 (2019)
6. Kang, H., Wu, H., Zhang, X.: Generative text steganography based on LSTM network and attention mechanism with keywords. In: Proceedings of IS&T Electronic Imaging, Media Watermarking, Security, and Forensics, pp. 291-1-291-8(8) (2020)
7. Chen, Y., Wang, H., Wu, H., Wu, Z., Li, T., Malik, A.: Adaptive video data hiding through cost assignment and STCs. IEEE Trans. Dependable Secur. Comput. **18**, 1320–1335 (2019). https://doi.org/10.1109/TDSC.2019.2932983
8. Liu, Y., Liu, S., Wang, Y., Zhao, H., Liu, S.: Video steganography: a review. Neurocomputing **335**, 238–250 (2019)
9. Wu, H., Zhou, L., Li, J., Zhang, X.: Securing graph steganography over social networks via interaction remapping. In: Sun, X., Wang, J., Bertino, E. (eds.) ICAIS 2020. CCIS, vol. 1254, pp. 303–312. Springer, Singapore (2020). https://doi.org/10.1007/978-981-15-8101-4_28
10. Wu, H., Wang, W., Dong, J., Wang, H.: New graph-theoretic approach to social steganography. In: Proceedings of IS&T Electronic Imaging, Media Watermarking, Security, and Forensics, pp. 539-1-539-7(7) (2020)
11. Westfeld, A.: F5—a steganographic algorithm. In: Moskowitz, I.S. (ed.) IH 2001. LNCS, vol. 2137, pp. 289–302. Springer, Heidelberg (2001). https://doi.org/10.1007/3-540-45496-9_21
12. Zhang, X., Wang, S.: Efficient steganographic embedding by exploiting modification direction. IEEE Commun. Lett. **10**(11), 781–783 (2006)
13. Filler, T., Judas, J., Fridrich, J.: Minimizing additive distortion in steganography using syndrome-trellis codes. IEEE Trans. Inf. Forensics Secur. **6**(3), 920–935 (2011)
14. Holub, V., Fridrich, J.: Designing steganographic distortion using directional filters. In: Proceedings of IEEE International Workshop on Information Forensics and Security, pp. 234–239 (2012)
15. Liu, Q., Wu, H., Zhang, X.: Adaptive video data hiding with low bit-rate growth based on texture selection and ternary syndrome-trellis coding. Multimed. Tools Appl. **79**(43), 32935–32955 (2020)
16. Ronneberger, O., Fischer, P., Brox, T.: U-Net: convolutional networks for biomedical image segmentation. In: Navab, N., Hornegger, J., Wells, W.M., Frangi, A.F. (eds.) MICCAI 2015. LNCS, vol. 9351, pp. 234–241. Springer, Cham (2015). https://doi.org/10.1007/978-3-319-24574-4_28
17. He, K., Zhang, X., Ren, S., Sun, J.: Deep residual learning for image recognition. In: Proceedings of IEEE Conference on Computer Vision and Pattern Recognition, pp. 770–778 (2016)

18. Zhu, J., Kaplan, R., Johnson, J., Fei-Fei, L.: HiDDeN: hiding data with deep networks. In: Ferrari, V., Hebert, M., Sminchisescu, C., Weiss, Y. (eds.) ECCV 2018. LNCS, vol. 11219, pp. 682–697. Springer, Cham (2018). https://doi.org/10.1007/978-3-030-01267-0_40
19. Guo, Y., Wu, H., Zhang, X.: Steganographic visual story with mutual-perceived joint attention. EURASIP J. Image Video Process. **2021**(1), 1–14 (2021). https://doi.org/10.1186/s13640-020-00543-1
20. Yang, J., Ruan, D., Huang, J., Kang, X., Shi, Y.-Q.: An embedding cost learning framework using GAN. IEEE Trans. Inf. Forensics Secur. **15**, 839–851 (2019)
21. Chaumont, M.: Deep learning in steganography and steganalysis from 2015 to 2018, 46 p. arXiv Preprint arXiv:1904.01444 (2019)
22. Simonyan, K., Zisserman, A.: Very deep convolutional networks for large-scale image recognition, 14 p. arXiv Preprint arXiv:1409.1556 (2014)
23. Deng, J., Dong, W., Socher, R., Li, L.-J., Li, K., Li, F.-F.: ImageNet: a large-scale hierarchical image database. In: Proceedings of IEEE Conference on Computer Vision and Pattern Recognition, pp. 248–255 (2009)
24. Uchida, Y., Nagai, Y., Sakazawa, S., Satoh, S.: Embedding watermarks into deep neural networks. In: Proceedings of ACM on International Conference on Multimedia Retrieval, pp. 269–277 (2017)
25. Wu, H., Liu, G., Yao, Y., Zhang, X.: Watermarking neural networks with watermarked images. IEEE Trans. Circuits Syst. Video Technol. (2020). https://doi.org/10.1109/TCSVT.2020.3030671

DCDC-LSB: Double Cover Dark Channel Least Significant Bit Steganography

Xin Zheng[1,3,4], Chunjie Cao[1,2,3,4(✉)], and Jiaxian Deng[3,4]

[1] Key Laboratory of Internet Information Retrieval of Hainan Province, Hainan University, Haikou 570228, China
[2] State Key Laboratory of Marine Resource Utilization in the South China Sea, Hainan University, Haikou 570228, China
[3] College of Computer and Cyberspace Security, Hainan University, Haikou 570228, China
[4] College of Information and Communication Engineering, Hainan University, Haikou 570228, China

Abstract. In this paper, we mainly discuss how to promote the robustness and invisibility of steganography. State-of-the-art steganography techniques have gained pretty good results on capacity, invisibility, and robustness. However, it is difficult to extract secret messages undamaged under lossy compression for these schemes, and no effective architectures have been proposed to implement a high capacity and invisibility steganography at the same time. In this work, we filled the gap and proposed the Double Cover Dark Channel Least Significant Bit (DCDC-LSB) steganography. Extensive experimental results demonstrate that the robustness of our method outperforms recent approaches in the Bit Error Ratio (BER), the invisibility of our method is better due to dark channel, and the capacity, as well as security, has good performance because we apply compression and encryption technology to our work.

Keywords: Dark channel · Double cover · Information hiding · LSB · Steganography

1 Introduction

Information hiding is a way of hiding information into a carrier such that an intruder will not be able to notice the existence of the hidden information. Carrier is a container to hide secret information. It can be any digital medium like images, audio files, video files, and text files. Generally, Information hiding is divided into steganography and watermarking. In this paper, we focus on steganography technology. When it comes to image steganography, the standard terminologies associated with Steganography are secret message, cover image, cover document, stego document, stego image [1], stego key, embedding algorithm, and extraction algorithm [2]. The cover image is an original image that is used as a carrier of a secret message. The output of the embedding algorithm is a stego document containing stego images that contains a secret message inside. The secret message is a plain message that you want to send secretly with the stego image.

© Springer Nature Switzerland AG 2021
X. Sun et al. (Eds.): ICAIS 2021, LNCS 12737, pp. 360–375, 2021.
https://doi.org/10.1007/978-3-030-78612-0_29

The stego key is a key that is used to embed or extract the secret message from the cover image and stego image. The embedding algorithm is used to embed a secret message into the cover image, and the extraction algorithm is used to extract the secret message from the stego image.

In our solution, a Microsoft Word document containing multiple 24-bit true-color images was selected as the cover document. The secret message will be compressed and then encrypted before embedding. LZ77 compression algorithm and SM4 encryption algorithm are adopted in DCDC-LSB. LZ77 is a lossless algorithm for sequential data compression [3]. SM4 is a block cipher algorithm adopted by the Chinese government. The dark channel is the result of the dark channel prior. The dark channel originates from the massive observation on haze-free outdoor images [4]. Kaiming He et al. observed that in most of the non-sky patches of haze-free outdoor images at least have one color channel have a very low intensity of pixels [4]. Formally, for an ordinary image P, we define

$$P^{dark}(x) = \min_{c \in \{r,g,b\}} (P^C(x)) \tag{1}$$

Where $P^c(x)$ is the color channel of image P at pixel x. We redefined the dark channel mentioned in [4] and we call P^{dark} the dark channel of P. Figure 1 shows a 24-bit true-color image and the corresponding dark channel image.

Fig. 1. Left: an original image. Right: the corresponding dark channel image.

The directions of image steganography are mainly in increasing the capacity of embedded secret message, imperceptibility and robustness, without visible difference of the cover image [5]. The secret messages usually are encrypted by symmetric or asymmetric cryptography before embedding the secret message into the cover image. Secure image steganography using AES cryptography was proposed to ensure double-layer security of the secret message in [6]. In our proposed technique we also adopted asymmetric cryptography called SM4 which is a block cipher algorithm whose block length and cipher key length are both of 128 bits. An unbalanced Feistel structure is adopted by SM4, and SM4 iterates the round functions for 32 times in both key expansion and encryption algorithm. The decryption structure is the same as the encryption but the decryption round keys. The SM4 decryption algorithm's round keys are in reverse order of the SM4 encryption algorithm's round keys.

Our main contributions are listed in the following:

(1) We propose a double cover dark channel method for document embedding, and this method has a good performance on robustness and invisibility.
(2) We implement a high capacity and secure image steganography method to hide secret messages by adopting compression and cryptography technology.
(3) Experimental results show that our solution has a lower Bit Error Rate, and a secret message can be extracted with 100% accuracy.

The remainder of the paper is organized as follows. In Sect. 2, we will review related work about the steganography scheme, followed by a detailed description of how our solution works in Sect. 3. In Sect. 4, we will discuss the results, limitations, and future improvements. Finally, we make a conclusion of our work about image steganography in Sect. 5.

2 Related Work

There are lots of practical steganography scheme which are capable of embedding secret messages into digital carriers. Currently, academic research on image steganography primarily focuses on Spatial Domain Techniques and Transform Domain Techniques. Spatial domain-based image steganography embeds the secret message into pixel gray level along with its color values. In the spatial domain, the best-known image steganography technique is least-significant-bit (LSB) which embeds a secret message by manipulating the LSB of an image's pixels. In [7], Chi-Kwong Chan, L.M. Cheng proposed a data hiding scheme by simple substitution of LSB. LSB natural reserves a high embedding capacity but bad robustness. Jun Tian [8] proposed to hide secret information using a difference expansion, which achieves a very high embedding capacity of image steganography and keeps the distortion low. In [9], Lee, Y. K., and Chen, L. H. provided a high capacity image steganographic model that is based on variable-LSB inserting. Their model embedded at least 4 bits in each pixel without deteriorating the perceptibility.

Takai, Nobukatsu, and Mifune, Yuto [10] proposed a holographic technique applied for digital watermarking, which increases the robustness compared to spatial domain techniques. In [11], Chang, Hsuan T., and Tsan, Chung L. proposed an image watermarking by embedding in the discrete-cosine-transform (DCT) domain. Their solution can reduce the degradation of the image and their method is robust under some kind of attack. Another robust image steganography was studied in [12] which can extract the secret data from the stego image with higher accuracy when the coefficients of the intermediate image are not changed under JPEG attack. Enhanced adaptive image steganography with multiple robustness was proposed in [13] showing that the scheme can extract the hidden messages with higher accuracy after different attacks.

Recently, Darshan M. Mehta and Dharmendra G. Bhatti [14] proposed a new image steganographic scheme that combines LSB embedding with Octa-PVD embedding. Comparing with existing LSB or multi-directional PVD embedding methods, their proposal has a better embedding capacity and PSNR. In [15], Liu, Hong Chao, and Chen, Wen proposed an optical ghost cryptography and steganography method based on ghost imaging (GI), which introduces a new ideal of steganography in GI. Tang, Weixuan and Li, Bin and Tan, Shunquan and Barni, Mauro and Huang, Jiwu [16], proposed a convolutional neural network (CNN) based adversarial steganographic embedding scheme, which embeds secret messages while fools a CNN steganalyzer at the same time. Cost-based steganography was studied in [17] and [18] showing that steganographers can design a crafted distortion function to minimize the detectability when hiding required messages. A statistical model based steganography was firstly studied in [19] which performs highly undetectable effect by using high-dimensional image models. Another statistical model-based steganography is proposed in [20] which models the stego messages by multivariate Gaussian random variables.

Most of the steganography cover media are images, audios, and videos. Also, the document used in daily life can be used to hide a secret message. A new data hiding in Microsoft Word Document was studied in [21] which embeds the data into the degeneration stage of Microsoft Word document transformation. A new system of covert communication within Microsoft Word documents via JPEG images was proposed in [22] which provides better results of the amount of the data.

The differences between our work and the related work are as follows: (1) we embed the message into a dark channel, (2) adopt double carriers to hide the secret message, and (3) use compression and cryptographic technology to improve confidentiality while increasing capacity of embedding messages.

3 DCDC-LSB Steganography Scheme

In this section, a robust high-capacity and secure image steganography in a dark channel are described, and then we will explain how our solution works. More details of the embedding algorithm and extraction algorithm will also be explained. In DCDC-LSB, a Microsoft Word document containing multiple 24-bit true-color images is used as a cover document, and 24-bit true-color images contained by Microsoft Word are used as cover images. 24-bits true-color image is divided into B, G, R three color channels and each of the color channels has 8-bits memory to store the value of the pixel. Therefore, a pixel is described by 24 bits in total. In our proposed technique, the dark channel which has minimum intensity among the color channels is used to hide secret data. SM4 cryptographic algorithm is used to encrypt the secret message compressed by the LZ77 compression algorithm.

The proposed method has five main parts:

- Stego image extraction: getting the stego images out from the stego document.
- Data compression: compressing the secret message to increasing the capacity of embedding data.
- Data encryption: encrypting the compressed data to strengthen secret message security.
- Data embedding: embedding the cipher into a dark channel of image covers.
- Document reconstruction: reconstructing the document after embedding secret data.

3.1 Embedding Algorithm

In a bitmap image, the color channel is managed by a certain order such as B, G, R, or R, G, B in one pixel of the image. In the DCDC-LSB method, the secret message bit is embedded into the LSB of the dark channel. There will be two things we need to do before embedding the secret messages into the dark channel. First, extract the image covers from the cover document. Second, compress the secret message with LZ77 and encrypt the compressed data with SM4. The process of embedding a secret message into cover images contained by the cover document is depicted in Fig. 2. The last thing we need to do in the end is to reconstruct the cover document.

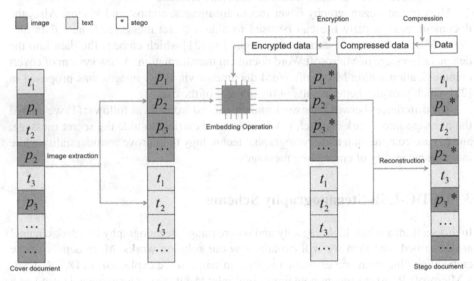

Fig. 2. Embedding algorithm framework of DCDC-LSB

In the proposed steganographic scheme, the secret message S is embedded into a cover document D to get a stego document D^*. The cover document D consists of text segments $d_1, d_2, d_3, ..., d_n$ and picture segments $p_1, p_2, p_3, ..., p_n$. Each segment d_i is kept unchanged, and each segment p_i contains secret messages or not, will depend on the size of secret messages. In essence, the secret messages is embedded into the cover image p_i within a cover document. For cover image P, we define P^* the stego image shown in Eq. (2).

$$P^* = H_{dcdc-lsb}(E_{enc}(C_{com}(S), K), P) \tag{2}$$

where S is original secret messages we need to hide, K is the encryption key, and P is the cover image used to hide information. $C_{com}(S)$ is the compression operation on S, and we define S' as the output of $C_{com}(S)$. $E_{enc}(S', K)$ is the encryption operation on S' with key K, and we define S'' as the output of $E_{enc}(S', K)$. $H_{dcdc-lsb}(S'', P)$ is the process of hiding S'' into cover image P.

For example, we embed 'D' whose ASCII Code is "01000100" in binary into the image covers. An example of a local area of image cover for embedding 'D' into the

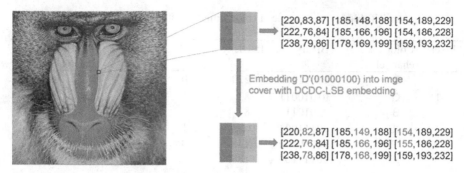

[220,83,87] [185,148,188] [154,189,229]
[222,76,84] [185,166,196] [154,186,228]
[238,79,86] [178,169,199] [159,193,232]

Embedding 'D'(01000100) into imge
cover with DCDC-LSB embedding

[220,82,87] [185,149,188] [154,189,229]
[222,76,84] [185,166,196] [155,186,228]
[238,78,86] [178,168,199] [159,193,232]

Fig. 3. An insight of Baboon's local window and its pixels

selected window is depicted in Fig. 3. The steps of hiding secret messages into a document are shown in Algorithm 1. The details of embedding 'D' into the dark channel are described in Table 1.

Algorithm 1: DCDC-LSB Embedding Algorithm

Input:

Cover document D, secret messages S, and secret key K

Output:

Stego document D^*

Step 1: Extract image covers.

1: **while** not at the end of D **do**

2:     Find a cover image p_i.

3:     Append p_i to a file.

4: **end while**

Step 2: Prepare encrypted data S''.

5: Compress S, $S' = C_{com}(S)$.

6: Encrypt S', $S'' = E_{enc}(S', K)$.

Step 3: Embed data into image covers.

7: **loop**

8:     Get a dark channel $D_{p_i}(x, y)$.

9:     Embed a bit of S'' into $D_{p_i}(x, y)$.

10:    Move to the next pixel.

11:    **if** at the end of S'' **then**

12:        **Goto** Step 4:

13:    **end if**

14: **end loop**

Step 4: Put stego images back to document

15: Output stego document D^*.

Table 1. An example of embedding 'D' into dark channel

Pixel	Color channel	Binary	Intensity	LSB	Embeing data	Embedded results
	R	11011100	220	0	- -	11011100
1st	G	01010011	83	1	0	10000010
	B	01010111	87	1	- -	10000111
	R	10111001	185	1	- -	10111001
2st	G	10010100	148	0	1	10010101
	B	10111100	188	0	- -	10111100
	R	10011010	154	0	0	10011010
3st	G	10111101	189	1	- -	10111101
	B	11100101	229	1	- -	11100101
	R	11011110	222	0	- -	11011110
4st	G	01001100	76	0	0	01001100
	B	01010100	84	0	- -	01010100
	R	10111001	185	1	- -	10111001
	G	10100110	166	0	0	10100110
5st	B	11000100	196	0	- -	11000100
	R	10011010	154	0	1	10011011
6st	G	10111010	186	0	- -	10111010
	B	11100100	228	0	- -	11100100
	R	11101110	238	0	- -	11101110
7st	G	01001111	79	1	0	01001110
	B	01010110	86	0	- -	01010110
	R	10110010	178	0	- -	10110010
8st	G	10101001	169	1	0	10101000
	B	11000111	199	1	- -	11000111
	R	10011111	159	1	- -	10011111
9st	G	11000001	193	1	- -	11000001
	B	11101000	232	0	- -	11101000

3.2 Extraction Algorithm

The extraction algorithm of DCDC-LSB is an inverse process of the embedding algo-rithm. For a stego image P^*, there are three steps we need to extract the secret message. At first, extract the encrypted data S'' from the dark channel. Second, decrypt the encrypted data S'' to get compressed data S'. At Last, decompress S' to get a secret message S. Formally, for a given stego image P^*, secret message S is shown as Eq. 3:

$$S = C_{com}^r(E_{enc}^r(H_{dcdc-lsb}^r(P^*), K)) \tag{3}$$

where $H^r_{dcdc-lsb}(P^*)$ is the reverse process of $H_{dcdc-lsb}(P^*)$, $E^r_{enc}(S'', K)$ is the reverse process of $E_{enc}(S'', K)$, and $C^r_{com}(S')$ is the reverse process of $C_{com}(S)$. The process of extracting secret messages from cover document is depicted in Fig. 4 and Algorithm 2.

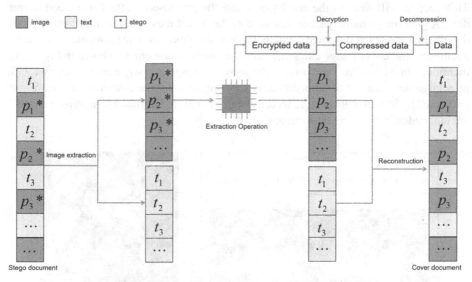

Fig. 4. Extraction algorithm framework of DCDC-LSB

Algorithm 2: DCDC-LSB Extraction Algorithm

Input:

Stego document D^*, and secret key K.

Output:

Secret messages S.

Step 1: Get image stegoes.

1: **while** not at the end of document **do**

2:      Find a stego image p^*_i.

3:      Append p^*_i to a file.

4: **end while**

Step 2: Extract the secret message.

5: Get the LSB of stego channel $D^*_{p_i}(x, y)$.

6: Decrypt the S'', $S' = E^r_{enc}(S'', K)$.

7: Decompress S', $S = C^r_{com}(S')$.

8: Get secret messages S.

---

4 Discussion

4.1 Results

This section will discuss the results of using the proposed method to embed secret data. A gray image namely Lena was used as the secret message and a Microsoft Word document was used as the cover document to hide information. The secret message, cover document, and cover image extracted from the cover document are shown in Fig. 5. As mentioned in Algorithm 1 previously, the secret message is firstly compressed by LZ77 to enlarge the capacity of embedding. After compression, the compressed data S' are encrypted by SM4 to enhance the security of information. Ultimately, encrypted data S'' are embedded into the cover document.

(a) Screenshot of Microsoft Word

(b) Extracted image

(c) Secret message

Fig. 5. Cover document, cover image, and secret message.

As depicted in Fig. 6, it is obvious that the stego image embedded secret message has less possibility to call attention to an attacker than single encryption protection.

Fig. 6. Left: single encryption protection. Right: stego image embedded encrypted secret message.

The histogram of the cover image and the corresponding histogram of the stego image is shown in Fig. 7. The changes in the histogram shown in Fig. 7 are negligible. Histogram, Mean-Squared Error (MSE), Peak Signal-to-Noise Ratio (PSNR), and Bit Error Rate (BER) are commonly used for evaluating the performance of embedding. The MSE is a simple method to quantify the difference between the cover image and the stego image. The evaluation of MSE between cover image $A(x, y)$ and stego image $B(x, y)$ is:

$$MSE = \sum_{i=1}^{x} \sum_{j=1}^{y} \frac{(|A_{ij} - B_{ij}|)^2}{x * y} \tag{4}$$

where x is the width of the image, and y is the height of the image. The PSNR used to measure image distortion is defined as:

$$PSNR = 10 \log_{10} \left(\frac{C_{max}^2}{MSE} \right) \tag{5}$$

where C_{max}^2 is the maximum pixel value of the image. In most cases, the $C_{max}^2 = 255$. The commonly used BER is used to evaluate the result of the extracted secret message. The BER between embedded secret message $\hat{w}$ and extracted data w is as follow:

$$BER(w, \hat{w}) = \frac{\sum_{i=1}^{M_w} \sum_{j=1}^{N_w} XOR(w_{i,j}, \hat{w}_{i,j})}{M_w \times N_w} \times 100\% \tag{6}$$

For more experiments, eight images whose size is 512×512 shown in Fig. 8 were used as a cover image. The secret message used in eight cover images is the same cipher in [6], and images shown in Fig. 9 is the corresponding stego cover.

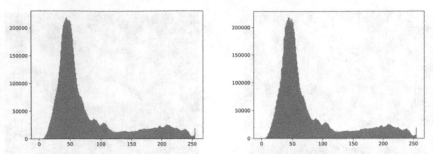

Fig. 7. Left: histogram of cover image. Right: histogram of stego image.

(a)Baboon   (b) Fishingboat   (c) House   (d) Jetplane

(e) Lake   (f) Lena   (g) Peppers   (h) Walkbridge

Fig. 8. Eight cover images

As shown in Fig. 8 and Fig. 9, the cover images, and stego images are pretty much the same. For further analysis, we have calculated the histograms of the cover image and stego image. Figure 10 and Fig. 11 show histograms of cover image and stego image respectively. Empirical results have shown that there is little difference between cover images and stego images. To further verify the performance of the proposed method, the MSE and PSNR values of eight different cover images have been calculated. Table 2 shows that the proposed DCDC-LSB method has a good performance on MSE and PSNR. For comparison, two different cover images were used to test the performance of PSNR. The results shown in Fig. 12 clearly state that the proposed method has a better performance.

(a)Baboon   (b) Fishingboat   (c) House   (d) Jetplane

(e) Lake   (f) Lena   (g) Peppers   (h) Walkbridge

Fig. 9. Eight stego images

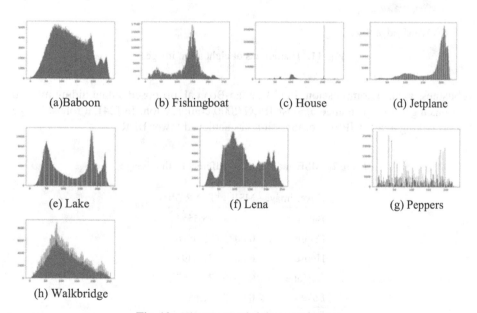

(a)Baboon   (b) Fishingboat   (c) House   (d) Jetplane

(e) Lake   (f) Lena   (g) Peppers

(h) Walkbridge

Fig. 10. Histograms of eight cover images

One of the difficulties of steganography is how to resist compression attack, such as JPEG compression, JPEG 2000 compression. In the field of steganography, the BER is an important evaluating index, and the lower, the better. So it is very important to test the

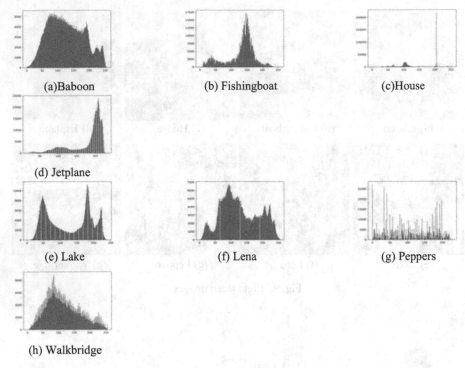

(a)Baboon   (b) Fishingboat   (c)House

(d) Jetplane

(e) Lake   (f) Lena   (g) Peppers

(h) Walkbridge

Fig. 11. Histograms of eight stego images

robustness against compression. In [23], Xiao-Bo et al. proposed a data hiding method that has a good performance against JPEG 2000 compression. In [24], a robust image watermarking against JPEG compression has achieved lower BER.

Table 2. MSE and PSNR of different testing images

Cover image	MSE	PSNR (dB)
Baboon	0.0018	75.5554
Fishingboat	0.0035	72.6548
House	0.0035	72.6392
Jetplane	0.0036	72.6267
Lake	0.0035	72.6564
Lena	0.0018	75.5370
Peppers	0.0018	75.4947
Walkbridge	0.0034	72.8386

However, there is no existing solution that can reduce the BER to zero, for lossy compression reason. To solve the problem of the lossy compression attack, the proposed double cover method provides a secure shell to protect the secret message from a lossy compression attack. Figure 13 shows that the proposed DCDC-LSB is robust to JPEG and JPEG 2000 compression.

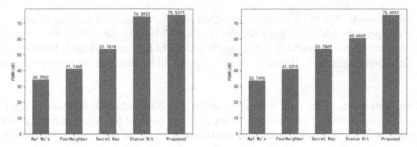

Fig. 12. Left: PSNR comparison of Lena. Right: PSNR comparison of Pepper

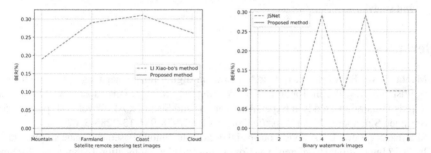

Fig. 13. Left: BER values of JPEG 2000 compression. Right: BER values of JPEG compression

4.2 Limitations and Future Improvements

A cover document that does not contain any picture inside is invalid in DCDC-LSB. Besides, DCDC-LSB works well on Microsoft Word, but it has a poor performance on WPS Word (a Word Processor similar to Microsoft Word). Our future work will focus on how to eliminate limitations of the proposed DCDC-LSB, and how to apply our technique to other file types, such as PowerPoint documents.

5 Conclusion

In this paper, we proposed a new scheme of Steganography, DCDC-LSB, to hide secret data in the dark channel with the double cover technique. In DCDC-LSB, the secret message is embedded into a more covert channel, dark channel, of image cover (first cover), and the second cover (cover document) provides a secure shell against a lossy compression attack. We tested enough experiments on invisibility and robustness. Experimental results show that the superiority of the invisibility of the proposed technique over the comparison scheme, as well as the robustness of the proposed method. Furthermore, Compression and Encryption algorithm were adopted in the DCDC-LSB scheme, to improve the security of data transmission in public networks, and the capacity of the message embedding.

Acknowledgement. We thank Fangjian Tao, Qian Wu, Yang Sun, and Jingjing Bian from the College of Computer and Cyberspace Security, Hainan University, for guiding academic article submission. We are also thankful to Shuaiqing Zhi and Na Li from the College of Information and Communication Engineering, Hainan University, for providing advice on improving this article.

Funding Statement. This work was supported by the National Natural Science Foundation of China (No. 61661019, C. J. Cao, http://www.nsfc.gov.cn/) and the National Natural Science Foundation of China Enterprise Innovation and Development Joint Fund (No. U19B2044, B. Li, http://www.nsfc.gov.cn/).

Conflicts of Interest. The authors declare that they have no conflicts of interest to report regarding the present study.

References

1. Mehta, D.M., Bhatti, D.G.: Research review on digital image steganography which resists against compression. In: Rathore, V.S., Worring, M., Mishra, D.K., Joshi, A., Maheshwari, S. (eds.) Emerging Trends in Expert Applications and Security. AISC, vol. 841, pp. 529–534. Springer, Singapore (2019). https://doi.org/10.1007/978-981-13-2285-3_62
2. Sharma, N., Batra, U.: A review on spatial domain technique based on image steganography. In: 2017 International Conference on Computing and Communication Technologies for Smart Nation (IC3TSN), pp. 24–27 (2017)
3. Ziv, J., Lempel, A.: A universal algorithm for sequential data compression. IEEE Trans. Inf. Theory **23**(3), 337–343 (1977)
4. He, K., Sun, J., Tang, X.: Single image haze removal using dark channel prior. IEEE Trans. Pattern Anal. Mach. Intell. **33**(12), 2341–2353 (2011)
5. Hernandez, H.C., Jimenez, V.M., Ramos-Corchado, M.A., Morales-Reyes, A., Romero-Huertas, M.: A review of steganography techniques for digital information transmission for secure channels with digital images. IEEE Lat. Am. Trans. **17**(11), 1831–1842 (2019)
6. Islam, M.R., Siddiqa, A., Uddin, M.P., Mandal, A.K., Hossain, M.D.: An efficient filtering based approach improving LSB image steganography using status bit along with AES cryptography. In: 2014 International Conference on Informatics, Electronics & Vision (ICIEV), pp. 1–6 (2014)
7. Chan, C., Cheng, L.M.: Hiding data in images by simple LSB substitution. Pattern Recogn. **37**(3), 469–474 (2004)
8. Tian, J.: Reversible data embedding using a difference expansion. IEEE Trans. Circuits Syst. Video Technol. **13**(8), 890–896 (2003)
9. Lee, Y.K., Chen, L.H.: High capacity image steganographic model. IEE Proc. - Vis. Image Signal Process. **147**(3), 288–294 (2000)
10. Takai, N., Mifune, Y.: Digital watermarking by a holographic technique. Appl. Opt. **41**(5), 865–873 (2002)
11. Chang, H.T., Tsan, C.L.: Image watermarking by use of digital holography embedded in the discrete-cosine-transform domain. Appl. Opt. **44**(29), 6211–6219 (2005)

12. Tao, J., Li, S., Zhang, X., Wang, Z.: Towards robust image steganography. IEEE Trans. Circuits Syst. Video Technol. **29**(2), 594–600 (2019)
13. Zhang, Y., Luo, X., Guo, Y., Qin, C., Liu, F.: Multiple robustness enhancements for image adaptive steganography in lossy channels. IEEE Trans. Circuits Syst. Video Technol. **30**(8), 2750–2764 (2020)
14. Kang, S., Park, H., Park, J.-I.: Combining LSB embedding with modified Octa-PVD embedding. Multimed. Tools Appl. **79**(29–30), 21155–21175 (2020). https://doi.org/10.1007/s11 042-020-08925-3
15. Liu, H.C., Chen, W.: Optical ghost cryptography and steganography. Opt. Lasers Eng. **130**, 106094 (2020)
16. Tang, W., Li, B., Tan, S., Barni, M., Huang, J.: CNN-based adversarial embedding for image steganography. IEEE Trans. Inf. Forensics Secur. **14**(8), 2074–2087 (2019)
17. Holub, V., Fridrich, J., Denemark, T.: Universal distortion function for steganography in an arbitrary domain. EURASIP J. Inf. Secur. **2014**(1), 1–13 (2014). https://doi.org/10.1186/ 1687-417X-2014-1
18. Li, B., Wang, M., Huang, J., Li, X.: A new cost function for spatial image steganography. In: 2014 IEEE International Conference on Image Processing (ICIP), pp. 4206–4210 (2014)
19. Pevný, T., Filler, T., Bas, P.: Using high-dimensional image models to perform highly unde-tectable steganography. In: Böhme, R., Fong, P.W.L., Safavi-Naini, R. (eds.) IH 2010. LNCS, vol. 6387, pp. 161–177. Springer, Heidelberg (2010). https://doi.org/10.1007/978-3-642-16435-4_13
20. Sharifzadeh, M., Aloraini, M., Schonfeld, D.: Adaptive batch size image merging steganog-raphy and quantized Gaussian image steganography. IEEE Trans. Inf. Forensics Secur. **15**, 867–879 (2020)
21. Liu, T.Y., Tsai, W.H.: A new steganographic method for data hiding in Microsoft Word documents by a change tracking technique. IEEE Trans. Inf. Forensics Secur. **2**(1), 24–30 (2007)
22. Uljarević, D., Veinović, M., Kunjadić, G., Tepšić, D.: A new way of covert communication by steganography via JPEG images within a Microsoft Word document. Multimed. Syst. **23**(3), 333–341 (2015). https://doi.org/10.1007/s00530-015-0492-3
23. Li, X., Zhou, Q.: Data hiding transmission method against compression for satellite image based on chaos and slant transform. Comput. Eng. Des. **34**(7), 2301–2305 (2013)
24. Chen, B., Wu, Y., Coatrieux, G., Chen, X., Zheng, Y.: JSNet: a simulation network of JPEG lossy compression and restoration for robust image watermarking against JPEG attack. Comput. Vis. Image Underst. **197–198**, 103015 (2020)

Halftone Image Steganography Based on Reassigned Distortion Measurement

Wenbo Xu[1], Wanteng Liu[1], Cong Lin[2], Ke Wang[1], Wenbin Wang[3], and Wei Lu[1(✉)] ⓘ

[1] School of Computer Science and Engineering, Guangdong Key Laboratory of Information Security Technology, Ministry of Education Key Laboratory of Machine Intelligence and Advanced Computing, Sun Yat-sen University, Guangzhou 510006, China
{xuwb25,liuwt25}@mail2.sysu.edu.cn, luwei3@mail.sysu.edu.cn
[2] School of Statistics and Mathematics, Guangdong University of Finance and Economics, Guangzhou 510320, China
[3] Guangdong Science and Technology Innovation Monitoring and Research Center, Guangzhou 510033, China

Abstract. Most state-of-the-art halftone image data hiding methods aim to preserve good visual quality when embedding messages, while ignoring the statistical security. This paper proposed a halftone steganographic scheme that improves the visual quality and the statistical security of the anti-steganalysis. First, a general distortion measurement for halftone images based on human visual system (HVS) model is proposed. Utilizing the Least-Mean-Square (LMS) method, halftone images can be converted to grayscale images and the objective image quality assessment is applied to evaluate the distortion caused by flipping pixels. Different distortion measurements can be derived from different image quality assessments. Then, to further measure the embedding distortions, we combine these distortion measurements to construct a reassigned distortion measurement based on the controversial pixels prior (CPP) rule. Finally, syndrome-trellis code (STC) is employed to minimize the number of flipping pixels. Experimental results have shown that the proposed steganographic scheme achieves strong statistical security with high capacity and visual quality.

Keywords: Halftone image steganography · Reassigned distortion measurement · Syndrome-trellis code

1 Introduction

Steganography is one of the branches of information hiding, which is the science and art of embedding secret messages into digital media. With the development of digital multimedia technology, the security of information content has received more attention [5,17,18,20–22,27]. As a type of host media, halftone image can

© Springer Nature Switzerland AG 2021
X. Sun et al. (Eds.): ICAIS 2021, LNCS 12737, pp. 376–387, 2021.
https://doi.org/10.1007/978-3-030-78612-0_30

be perceived as continuous-tone image when viewed from a distance with the low-pass nature of the human visual system (HVS). However, halftone image requires only 1 bit per pixel compared with 8 bits per gray pixel or 24 bits per color pixel. Many halftoning methods have been proposed and there are several classical methods such as ordered dithering [2], error diffusion [7,13] and dot diffusion [14,24]. The significant visual effect and the small storage requirement make the halftone image a practical format for digitizing, printing and transmitting. Many data hiding schemes [8,10,11,15,16,26] have been developed for halftone images in recent years. There are two kinds of data hiding schemes on halftone image according to whether the embedding operation is in the halftoning process or not. The first kind of scheme requires the original multi-tone images and can embed numerous secret messages during the process of halftoning [11,16]. The second kind of scheme can embed secret messages directly into the halftone images with no need for the original images [8,10,15,26]. The first scheme has the advantage of large embedding capacity and good image quality, while the second scheme has the advantage of only requiring halftone images. In general cases, the original grayscale images are not available. Considering the versatility of steganography, our work focuses on the second kind of scheme.

To achieve good visual quality, many state-of-the-art data hiding methods on halftone image [8–10,12,26] have been proposed. Fu and Au [9] proposed a data-hiding method named Data Hiding Pair Toggling (DHPT) which toggles a pair of pixels to preserve the local intensity when embedding secret messages. To improve the visual quality, they modified DHPT to a method called Data Hiding Smart Pair Toggling (DHSPT) [8] which selects the minimum connection pixels after data embedding. Since pair toggling strategy can preserve the local average intensity, Guo [10] also proposed a method named Pair Toggling with Human Visual System (PTHVS) based on pair toggling strategy. He designed a visual distortion measurement to evaluate the candidate slave pixels and the slave pixel with smallest distortion is selected as the optimal candidate pixel. In [12], Guo and Zhang employed the Grouping Index Matrix (GIM) to embed secret messages by toggling pixel pairs to improve the embedding capacity. It should be noticed that these data-hiding methods focus on improving the visual imperceptibility and embedding capacity. With the rapid development of the steganalysis techniques, the statistical security plays an increasingly important role in information hiding. Therefore, the statistical security against steganalyzers also needs to be guaranteed to reduce the suspicion from attackers. To this end, Xue et al. [26] focused on improving both the visual imperceptibility and the statistical security and proposed a halftone image steganographic method. They introduced the concept of dispersion degree (DD) and minimized the distortion of texture structure when embedding messages.

In this paper, we proposed a secure halftone image steganographic scheme focusing on both visual quality and the statistical security of anti-steganalysis. We first introduce a general distortion measurement for halftone image based on HVS model. Halftone image takes advantage of the low-pass nature of the HVS and can be resembled as a grayscale image when viewed from a distance.

Therefore, the distortion caused by embedding messages should be evaluated in inverse halftoning domain. Utilizing the Least-Mean-Square (LMS) method [10,11], halftone image can be converted to grayscale image. Then, the objective image quality assessment is applied to evaluate the distortion caused by flipping pixels and a general distortion measurement for halftone image based on HVS is proposed. Different distortion measurements can be derived from different image quality assessments. Structural Similarity Index Measure (SSIM) and Gradient Similarity (GSM) are employed in our work. To select more flippable pixels, we combine these distortion measurements to construct a reassigned distortion measurement based on the controversial pixels prior (CPP) rule. Furthermore, syndrome-trellis code (STC) [6] is employed to play the advantage of the distortion measurement. The experimental results have shown that the proposed steganographic scheme achieves a significant performance compared with the state-of-art methods.

The rest of this paper is organized as follows. Section 2 develops the proposed steganographic scheme in detail. In Sect. 3, the general framework of embedding and extraction is presented. In Sect. 4, experimental results about visual quality and the statistical security of anti-steganalysis are conducted. Section 5 concludes the whole paper.

2   The Proposed Method

In this section, we will introduce the proposed steganographic scheme in details. First, a general distortion measurement for halftone image based on HVS model is developed to evaluate the distortion caused by flipping pixels. With different objective image quality assessments, different distortion measurements can be designed. Then, a reassigned distortion measurement based on the controversial pixels prior (CPP) rule is proposed to better measure the distortions. Finally, syndrome-trellis code (STC) is employed to minimize the total distortions in embedding process.

2.1   General Distortion Measurement Based on HVS

Halftone image expresses the content information by simulating the grayscale image through the human low-pass filtered visual system. In halftone images, the average intensity of a local region is more important than the value of a single pixel. Therefore, to evaluate the visual quality of halftone images, we can convert them to the corresponding grayscale images and apply objective image quality assessments to the grayscale images.

For a cover halftone image C and a stego halftone image S with size $P \times Q$, we can obtain the corresponding grayscale images X and Y through the human visual filter ω:

$$x_{i,j} = \sum_{m=-M/2}^{M/2} \sum_{n=-N/2}^{N/2} \omega_{m,n} c_{i+m,j+n} \tag{1}$$

$$y_{i,j} = \sum_{m=-M/2}^{M/2} \sum_{n=-N/2}^{N/2} \omega_{m,n} s_{i+m,j+n} \tag{2}$$

where the variables $c_{i,j} \in C$ and $s_{i,j} \in S$ denote the pixel values of the cover halftone image and the stego halftone image, the variables $x_{i,j} \in X$ and $y_{i,j} \in Y$ denote the pixel values of the corresponding grayscale images and $\omega_{m,n}$ denotes the coefficient of the human visual filter with size $M \times N$.

There are two ways to obtain the suitable human visual filter ω, including conducting psychophysical experiments [23] and using training set of both pairs of grayscale images and good halftone results of them. In our work, we employ the Least-Mean-Square (LMS) method, which is proposed by Guo et al. [10,11]. The details of LMS method are described as follows:

$$\hat{g}_{i,j} = \sum_{m=-M/2}^{M/2} \sum_{n=-N/2}^{N/2} \omega_{m,n} h_{i+m,j+n} \tag{3}$$

$$e_{i,j}^2 = (g_{i,j} - \hat{g}_{i,j})^2 \tag{4}$$

$$\frac{\partial e_{i,j}^2}{\partial \omega_{m,n}} = -2e_{i,j} h_{i+m,j+n} \tag{5}$$

$$\omega_{m,n}^{(k+1)} = \omega_{m,n}^k + \begin{cases} \mu e_{i+m,j+n} h_{i+m,j+n}, & \text{if } \frac{\partial e_{i,j}^2}{\partial \omega_{m,n}} < 0 \\ -\mu e_{i+m,j+n} h_{i+m,j+n}, & \text{if } \frac{\partial e_{i,j}^2}{\partial \omega_{m,n}} > 0 \end{cases} \tag{6}$$

where $g_{i,j}$, $h_{i,j}$, and $e_{i,j}$ are the values of the grayscale image, the values of the corresponding halftone image, and the MSE between $g_{i,j}$ and $\hat{g}_{i,j}$, respectively; μ is the adjusting parameter used to control the convergent speed of the procedure, which is set to 10^{-5} in our experiments.

After performing inverse halftoning operation, halftone images can be converted from the binary domain to the grayscale domain. In this way, objective image quality assessments in grayscale domain are suitable for evaluating the image quality of halftone images. The more similar the stego image is to the cover image, the less the embedding distortion is. Therefore, we proposed a general distortion measurement for halftone image based on HVS. Different distortion measurements can be derived from different image quality assessments. In this paper, Structural Similarity Index Measure (SSIM) [25] and Gradient Similarity (GSM) [19] are selected as assessments for their superior performance. To this end, we can define Halftone Structural Similarity Index Measure (HSSIM) and Halftone Gradient Similarity (HGSM) based on the original SSIM and GSM. For the cover halftone image C and the stego halftone image S, the HSSIM is defined as follows:

$$HSSIM(C,S) = SSIM(X,Y) = (l(X,Y))^\alpha (c(X,Y))^\beta (s(X,Y))^\gamma \tag{7}$$

where $l(X,Y)$, $c(X,Y)$ and $s(X,Y)$ denote the luminance similarity, contrast similarity and structural similarity between inverse halftone image X and Y, respectively, which are defined as follows:

$$l(X,Y) = \frac{2\mu_x \mu_y + C_1}{\mu_x^2 + \mu_y^2 + C_1} \tag{8}$$

$$c(X,Y) = \frac{2\sigma_x\sigma_y + C_2}{\sigma_x^2 + \sigma_y^2 + C_2} \tag{9}$$

$$s(X,Y) = \frac{\sigma_{xy} + C_3}{\sigma_x\sigma_y + C_3} \tag{10}$$

where μ_x, μ_y, μ_x^2, μ_y^2, and σ_{xy} are the mean of X, the mean of Y, the variance of X, the variance of Y, and the covariance of X and Y, respectively; C_1, C_2, and C_3 are claimed as small constants to avoid the denominator being zero.

In the same way, the HGSM can be defined as follows:

$$HGSM(C,S) = GSM(X,Y) = \frac{2g_xg_y + C_4}{g_x^2 + g_y^2 + C_4} \tag{11}$$

where g_x and g_y are the gradient values for the central pixel of image blocks in X and Y, respectively, and C_4 is the small constant to avoid the denominator being zero.

It should be noticed that the value in HSSIM or HGSM lies in $[0, 1]$ and the higher the value of HSSIM or HGSM is, the more similar the halftone images C and S are. Considering embedding one bit message into the cover halftone image C, we can flip one pixel (denoted as pixel k) in C and obtain the stego halftone image S. Based on different image quality assessments, the distortion caused by flipping pixel k can be measured in different ways. Let D_{HSSIM} and D_{HGSM} denote the distortion measured by HSSIM and HGSM, respectively, i.e.,

$$D_{HSSIM}(k) = 1 - HSSIM(C,S) \tag{12}$$

$$D_{HGSM}(k) = 1 - HGSM(C,S) \tag{13}$$

It is obvious that pixel k is flippable when the distortion $D_{HSSIM}(k)$ or $D_{HGSM}(k)$ is small.

2.2 Reassigned Distortion Measurement

In Sect. 2.1, a general distortion measurement for halftone image based on HVS is proposed. With HSSIM and HGSM, we can obtain the distortion measurements D_{HSSIM} and D_{HGSM}. These measurements rank the flipping priorities for pixels by measuring the distortions caused by flipping them. To better measure the embedding distortions, we combine these distortion measurements to construct a reassigned distortion measurement. Zhou et al. [28] proposed the controversial pixels prior (CPP) rule to fuse several distortion measurements on grayscale images. They found that some minimal-distortion steganographic methods show comparable statistical security performances, while these methods define distortion measurements in different manners. Thus, different distortion measurements may assign very different costs to the same pixel and such pixels are called controversial pixels. To improve statistical security, Zhou et al. gave priority of modifications to such controversial pixels. Inspired by this, we modify the CPP rule and apply it to our scheme.

To generate an advanced distortion measurement from D_{HSSIM} and D_{HGSM}, we first calculate the mean of the distortion values for each pixel as their initial distortion value with D_{HSSIM} and D_{HGSM}:

$$\bar{D}(k) = \frac{1}{2}[D_{HSSIM}(k) + D_{HGSM}(k)] \tag{14}$$

To select the controversial pixels, the variance of distortion values is calculated:

$$v(k) = \frac{1}{2}[(D_{HSSIM}(k) - \bar{D}(k))^2 + (D_{HGSM}(k) - \bar{D}(k))^2] \tag{15}$$

It is obvious that a large $v(k)$ reflects that the changing scope of distortion values is dramatic, which demonstrates that the priorities of pixel k are controversial in different distortion measurements, and this pixel should be given higher priority of flipping in the CPP rule.

Utilizing the CPP rule, the reassigned distortion measurement is designed as follows:

$$D(k) = \begin{cases} \bar{D}_{min}, & \text{if } v(k) > T \\ \bar{D}(k), & \text{otherwise} \end{cases} \tag{16}$$

where $\bar{D}_{min}$ is the minimum distortion of $\bar{D}$ and T is the threshold determined by the payload. The pixels with variances larger than T are selected as the controversial pixels, which are the most suitable pixels for flipping. Eventually, we obtain a new adjusted distortion measurement D from D_{HSSIM} and D_{HGSM}. With the given payload and the adjusted distortion measurement, Syndrome-trellis code (STC) [6] is employed in our scheme to minimize the number of the flipping pixles.

3   General Framework of Embedding and Extraction

Based on the reassigned distortion measurement and STC-based embedding, the steganographic scheme is constructed in this section. The detailed embedding and extraction procedures are described in Sect. 3.1 and Sect. 3.2, respectively.

3.1   Embedding Procedure

1. Calculate the distortions D_{HSSIM} and D_{HGSM} for each pixel in cover image, respectively;
2. Reassign a new distortion for each pixel in cover image with the distortions D_{HSSIM} and D_{HGSM};
3. Shuffle cover image and distortions with the same random seed to keep corresponding order;
4. Employ the STC encoder with cover image, distortions and secret messages for embedding;
5. Rearrange the result with the same random seed to obtain the stego image.

3.2   Extraction Procedure

1. Rearrange the stego image with a scrambling via the same seed using in embedding;
2. Apply the STC decoder to extract the secret messages.

4   Experiments and Results

Since there is no commonly used halftone image dataset, we employ the Floyd error diffusion method [7] to convert the grayscale images in BossBase-1.01 [1] to halftone images. The constructed dataset contains different types of halftone images including natural scenery, building and people. Some grayscale images and the corresponding halftone images are shown in Fig. 1.

(a)

(b)

Fig. 1. (a) Examples of different grayscale images in BossBase-1.01 [1]. (b) The corresponding halftone images converted by Floyd error diffusion method [7].

The state-of-the-art data hiding schemes employed in our experiment for comparison are proposed in [8] (denoted as DHSPT), [10] (denoted as PTHVS), [12] (denoted as GIM) and [26] (denoted as DD). DHSPT selects the minimum connection slave pixels when embedding secret messages for better visual quality.

PTHVS modifies DHSPT by selecting the slave pixels with minimum visual distortion based on a human visual system model. GIM employs the group index matrix to enlarge the embedding capacity. DD toggles the pixels in complex region to improve the statistical security. Besides these existing schemes, to demonstrate the superiority of the reassigned distortion measurement, we also compare the steganographic schemes based on distortion measurements D_{HSSIM} and D_{HGSM} (denoted as HSSIM and HGSM), individually.

4.1 Comparison of Image Quality

It should be noticed that many visual quality assessment methods including Peak Signal-to-Noise Ratio (PSNR) and Structural Similarity Index Measure (SSIM) cannot be applied to halftone image. A halftone image with high visual quality may have equal PSNR and SSIM as a halftone image with poor visual quality. Fu and Au [8] proposed a suitable visual quality assessment method for halftone image which is widely employed in halftone image data hiding [8,12,15]. They introduced the following five scores:

$$S_1 = \sum_{i=0}^{4} N_i \tag{17}$$

$$S_2 = \sum_{i=0}^{4} (i+1)N_i \tag{18}$$

$$S_3 = \frac{S_2}{S_1} \tag{19}$$

$$S_4 = \sum_{i=2}^{4} N_i \tag{20}$$

$$S_5 = \sum_{i=0}^{4} iN_i = S_2 - S_1 \tag{21}$$

where the N_i is the sum of the modified pixels having i neighbors with same pixel values in the 4-neighborhood. The S_1 is the sum of the modified pixels which are the black pixels in bright region and the white pixels in dark region. The S_2 is the total area of the clusters formed by the black pixels in bright region and the white pixels in dark region. The S_3 is the average area per cluster. The S_4 is the number of modified pixels connected with clusters of size 3 or more. The S_5 gives a zero penalty score to isolated black or white pixels which look visually pleasing.

The smaller scores of S_1, S_2, S_3, S_4, S_5 are, the better visual quality of the halftone image is. As shown in Table 1, the average scores of HSSIM and HGSM are obviously smaller than the existing schemes except for S_3. Since STC-based embedding is employed with the distortion measurement in our scheme, the number of flipping pixels is smaller than the schemes without STC-based

Table 1. Average scores (S_1 to S_5) of various schemes on the halftone images dataset with 1024 bits embedded.

	S_1	S_2	S_3	S_4	S_5
Reassigned	**85.1**	**286.6**	3.368	**79.8**	**206.8**
HSSIM	122.6	405.2	3.305	105.6	240.6
HGSM	101.2	350.1	3.454	97.1	218.8
DD [26]	385.3	1160.9	**3.013**	269.6	803.2
PTHVS [10]	676.5	2371.5	3.441	533.7	1695.0
DHSPT [8]	786.9	2432.8	3.107	468.2	1645.9
GIM [12]	683.6	2198.5	3.216	398.3	1514.9

embedding. It should be noticed that the proposed scheme based on reassigned distortion measurement achieves the better performance on visual quality than HSSIM and HGSM.

4.2   Comparison of Statistical Security

The statistical security plays an important role in steganography scheme with the rapid development of steganalysis. Many binary image steganalysis methods [4] have been proposed. The PMMTM-320D features [4] capture the dependence on texture structures, which has good performance on halftone images. The RLCM-100D features [3] obtain the high-order difference images and extract the run length and co-occurrence matrices to detect stego images. With these features, the soft-margin SVMs with an optimized Gaussian kernel can be constructed as the steganalyzers. The steganalysis performance is measured by the decision error rate P_E defined as follow:

$$P_E = \frac{1}{2}(P_{F_p} + P_{F_n}) \tag{22}$$

where P_{F_p} is the probability of false positive (detecting cover as stego) and P_{F_n} is the probability of false negative (detecting stego as cover).

Figure 2 shows our experiment results about statistical security of anti-steganalysis. The results show that the performance of HSSIM and HGSM is higher than the existing schemes and the reassigned scheme has higher performance than the basic schemes HSSIM and HGSM, which proves the superiority of the reassigned distortion measurement. It can be observed that the STC-based schemes can better preserve the correlations between patterns in different shapes and sizes and can better preserve the changes of run-length and co-occurrence in local regions. The experiment results also demonstrate that the reassigned distortion measurement can better measure the embedding distortions and thus improves the statistical security.

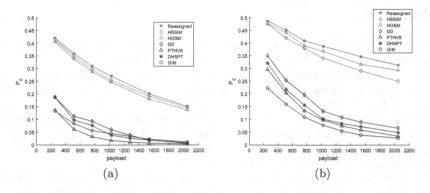

Fig. 2. The statistical security comparison of different steganographic schemes. The utilized steganalyzers are (a) PMMTM-320D [4], (b) RLCM-100D [3].

5 Conclusions

In this paper, we first review and analyze some state-of-the-art halftone image data hiding schemes. We find that visual quality plays an important role in halftone images, while the statistical security of anti-steganalysis also becomes more significant with the development of the steganalysis technique. To this end, we proposed a general distortion measurement for halftone image based on HVS. To better evaluate the distortion caused by flipping pixels in halftone image, halftone image is first converted to grayscale image with the LMS method. Then, the objective image quality assessment is applied to evaluate the similarity between cover image and stego image. The more similar they are, the less distortion caused by embedding messages. Different distortion measurements can be derived from different image quality assessments. SSIM and GSM are employed in our scheme for their superior performance. To further measure the embedding distortions, we combine these distortion measurements to construct a reassigned distortion measurement based on the CPP rule. The pixels have very different distortion values in different distortion measurements are regarded as the controversial pixels. To improve statistical security, the controversial pixels are given priority of flipping and we reassign distortion values for each pixel in halftone images. Experimental results have shown that the proposed steganographic scheme achieves strong statistical security with high capacity and visual quality.

In our future work, we will further reveal the relationship between the visual quality and statistical security in halftone image. We aim to design a better distortion measurement and improve the steganographic performance.

Acknowledgements. This work is supported by the Key Areas R&D Program of Guangdong (No. 2019B010136002), the National Natural Science Foundation of China (No. U2001202, No. 62072480, No. U1736118), the National Key R&D Program of China (No. 2019QY2202, No. 2019QY(Y)0207), the Key Scientific Research Program of Guangzhou (No. 201804020068).

References

1. Bas, P., Filler, T., Pevn, Y.T.: Break our steganographic system: the ins and outs of organizing boss. J. Am. Stat. Assoc. **6958**(454), 59–70 (2011)
2. Bayers, B.: An optimum method for two-level rendition of continuous-tone pictures. In: Proceedings of IEEE International Communication Conference, vol. 1, pp. 2611–2615 (1973)
3. Chiew, K.L., Pieprzyk, J.: Binary image steganographic techniques classification based on multi-class steganalysis. In: Kwak, J., Deng, R.H., Won, Y., Wang, G. (eds.) ISPEC 2010. LNCS, vol. 6047, pp. 341–358. Springer, Heidelberg (2010). https://doi.org/10.1007/978-3-642-12827-1_25
4. Feng, B., Lu, W., Sun, W.: Binary image steganalysis based on pixel mesh Markov transition matrix. J. Vis. Commun. Image Represent. **26**(C), 284–295 (2015)
5. Feng, B., Lu, W., Sun, W.: Secure binary image steganography based on minimizing the distortion on the texture. IEEE Trans. Inf. Forensics Secur. **10**(2), 243–255 (2015)
6. Filler, T., Judas, J., Fridrich, J.: Minimizing additive distortion in steganography using syndrome-trellis codes. IEEE Trans. Inf. Forensics Secur. **6**(3), 920–935 (2011)
7. Floyd, R.W., Steinberg, L.: Adaptive algorithm for spatial greyscale. In: Proceedings of SID, pp. 75–77 (1976)
8. Fu, M.S., Au, O.C.: Halftone image data hiding with intensity selection and connection selection. Sig. Process. Image Commun. **16**(10), 909–930 (2001)
9. Fu, M.S., Au, O.C.: Data hiding watermarking for halftone images. IEEE Trans. Image Process. **11**(4), 477–484 (2002)
10. Guo, J.M.: Improved data hiding in halftone images with cooperating pair toggling human visual system. Int. J. Imaging Syst. Technol. **17**(6), 328–332 (2007)
11. Guo, J.M., Liu, Y.F.: Halftone-image security improving using overall minimal-error searching. IEEE Trans. Image Process. **20**(10), 2800–2812 (2011)
12. Guo, M., Zhang, H.: High capacity data hiding for halftone image authentication. In: Shi, Y.Q., Kim, H.-J., Pérez-González, F. (eds.) IWDW 2012. LNCS, vol. 7809, pp. 156–168. Springer, Heidelberg (2013). https://doi.org/10.1007/978-3-642-40099-5_14
13. Jarvis, J.F., Judice, C.N., Ninke, W.H.: A survey of techniques for the display of continuous tone pictures on bilevel displays. Comput. Graph. Image Process. **5**(1), 13–40 (1976)
14. Knuth, D.E.: Digital halftones by dot diffusion. ACM Trans. Graph. **6**(4), 245–273 (1987)
15. Lien, B.K., Lan, Z.L.: Improved halftone data hiding scheme using Hilbert curve neighborhood toggling. In: International Conference on Intelligent Information Hiding and Multimedia Signal Processing, pp. 73–76. IEEE (2011)
16. Lien, B.K., Pei, W.D.: Reversible data hiding for ordered dithered halftone images. In: IEEE International Conference on Image Processing, pp. 4237–4240. IEEE (2009)
17. Lin, C., Lu, W., Huang, X., Liu, K., Sun, W., Lin, H.: Region duplication detection based on hybrid feature and evaluative clustering. Multimedia Tools Appl. **78**, 20739–20763 (2019)
18. Lin, C., et al.: Copy-move forgery detection using combined features and transitive matching. Multimedia Tools Appl. **78**, 30081–30096 (2018)

19. Liu, A., Lin, W., Narwaria, M.: Image quality assessment based on gradient similarity. IEEE Trans. Image Process. **21**(4), 1500–1512 (2012)
20. Liu, X., Lu, W., Liu, W., Luo, S., Liang, Y., Li, M.: Image deblocking detection based on a convolutional neural network. IEEE Access **7**, 26432–26439 (2019)
21. Liu, X., Lu, W., Zhang, Q., Huang, J., Shi, Y.Q.: Downscaling factor estimation on pre-JPEG compressed images. IEEE Trans. Circ. Syst. Video Technol. **30**(3), 618–631 (2020)
22. Lu, W., He, L., Yeung, Y., Xue, Y., Liu, H., Feng, B.: Secure binary image steganography based on fused distortion measurement. IEEE Trans. Circ. Syst. Video Technol. **29**(6), 1608–1618 (2019)
23. Mannos, J., Sakrison, D.: The effects of a visual fidelity criterion of the encoding of images. IEEE Trans. Inf. Theory **20**(4), 525–536 (1974)
24. Mese, M., Vaidyanathan, P.P.: Optimized halftoning using dot diffusion and methods for inverse halftoning. IEEE Trans. Image Process. **9**(4), 691–709 (2000)
25. Wang, Z., Bovik, A.C., Sheikh, H.R., Simoncelli, E.P., et al.: Image quality assessment: from error visibility to structural similarity. IEEE Trans. Image Process. **13**(4), 600–612 (2004)
26. Xue, Y., Liu, W., Lu, W., Yeung, Y., Liu, X., Liu, H.: Efficient halftone image steganography based on dispersion degree optimization. J. Real-Time Image Process. **16**, 601–609 (2019)
27. Yeung, Y., Lu, W., Xue, Y., Huang, J., Shi, Y.Q.: Secure binary image steganography with distortion measurement based on prediction. IEEE Trans. Circ. Syst. Video Technol. **30**(5), 1423–1434 (2020)
28. Zhou, W., Zhang, W., Yu, N.: A new rule for cost reassignment in adaptive steganography. IEEE Trans. Inf. Forensics Secur. **12**(11), 2654–2667 (2017)

Halftone Image Steganography Based on Maximizing Visual Similarity of Block Units

Xiaolin Yin[1], Mujian Yu[1], Lili Chen[2], Ke Wang[1], and Wei Lu[1($\boxtimes$)] (iD)

[1] School of Computer Science and Engineering, Guangdong Key Laboratory of Information Security Technology, Ministry of Education Key Laboratory of Machine Intelligence and Advanced Computing, Sun Yat-sen University, Guangzhou 510006, China
{yinxl6,yumj8}@mail2.sysu.edu.cn, luwei3@mail.sysu.edu.cn
[2] Guangdong Science and Technology Innovation Monitoring and Research Center, Guangzhou 510033, China

Abstract. Steganography focuses on imperceptibility of both the human eyes but also to potential analyzers. Based on the human visual system (HVS) of halftone image, most previous visual quality measurements for multi-tone images can not be adopted to design the steganographic schemes. In this paper, we propose a halftone image steganographic scheme based on the maximizing visual similarity of block units aiming at improving the statistical security but also the image visual quality. First, the halftone HVS model is discussed. The similarity of a pixel and its neighboring regions (which are called block units) is an important factor for human eyes. Then the distortion score is designed based on the visual similarity for each pixel in an image. Several visual similarity scores owned by a pixel are obtained in different block units. In general, the maximal visual similarity score means that this pixel is optimal to embed data. Finally, these visual similarity scores are combined with a weight matrix, and the distortion score that measures the embedding distortion is sent into syndrome-trellis code (STC) to minimize the distortion. Experimental results demonstrate the proposed scheme preserves the visual quality and improves the statistical security.

Keywords: Halftone image steganography · Human visual system · Visual similarity · Syndrome-trellis code

1 Introduction

Digital images are widely used in data hiding [2,11,14,16]. In public channels, steganography [7,17,23] focuses on imperceptibility of both the hidden data and the act of data embedding, which is undetectable not only to human eyes but also to potential analyzers [20]. In addition, imperceptibility is the top property for steganography. Image steganalysis [3,7,21] detects the existing hidden data

© Springer Nature Switzerland AG 2021
X. Sun et al. (Eds.): ICAIS 2021, LNCS 12737, pp. 388–399, 2021.
https://doi.org/10.1007/978-3-030-78612-0_31

in stego images, and with the development of steganalysis, the statistical security of steganography has been threatened.

As one kind of the host image media, binary images play a significant role in the carriers of the steganography [25]. In contrast to multi-tone images such as gray-scale images and color images, binary images need only 1 bit per pixel (bpp) [22]. However, the smallest storage requirement of binary images leads to fewer embeddable bits to hide data. The embedding operation in steganography of binary images is flipping the pixel from '0' to '1' or from '1' to '0'. In addition, the embedding payload is limited, and the visual quality is decreasing while embedding more bits of secret messages by flipping pixels.

Ordinary binary images usually adopt the edge lines to express the image contents [24]. Halftone image, a special kind of binary image, can simulate the continuous-tone image by utilizing a low-pass filter based on human visual system (HVS) [12]. When viewed from a certain distance, halftone image resembles the continuous-tone image. Representing the brightness of an image, the average intensity of a local region is visually meaningful in halftone images.

In recent years, some data hiding schemes for halftone images are proposed [9,11,16,19,22]. Fu et al. [9] proposed a data hiding method to maintain the average intensity of the local region that achieves better visual quality by toggling the smart pair. When flipping a pixel, its neighboring pixel is taken into consideration as a smart pair to preserve the local intensity. Xue et al. [22] measures the intensity and complexity of the area texture in a halftone image. Lien et al. [16] utilize the Hilbert curve approach to select the most suitable pair of neighboring pixels to embed the secret messages, which improves the visual quality of the marked halftone image. It is still a challenging work for halftone image steganography to retain the demanded high image visual quality as well as statistical security.

In this paper, a halftone image steganographic scheme based on maximizing visual similarity of block units is proposed. Due to the special features in halftone images, the traditional steganographic methods on multi-tone images are not applicable to halftone images. Based on the HVS model, a visual distortion measurement considering the visual similarity is proposed especially for halftone images. Visual similarity is an evaluation of the visual changes in a block unit. For a pixel that is flipped individually, it is at the different locations of different block units, and a weight matrix is applied to evaluate the different visual effects of this flipped pixel. The similarity score of each pixel is obtained by measuring the sum of visual similarity in different block units. Utilizing the similarity score, the distortion map corresponding to all pixels in a halftone image is obtained. And the distortion map is used in syndrome-trellis code (STC) [8] for the embedding process. The measurement of visual similarity for halftone images is systematic analysis. While selecting the flippable pixels, our proposed scheme does not need a training process and statistical experiment on the whole image dataset. The experimental results demonstrate that while embedding the same secret messages, the proposed steganographic scheme can achieve good visual quality as well as high statistical security.

The rest of this paper is organized as follows. The HVS model for halftone image and the visual similarity of block units are discussed in Sect. 2. In Sect. 3, the proposed steganographic scheme is presented in detail. Section 4 discusses the experimental results and proves our proposed method achieves good visual quality and high statistical security. Finally, the conclusion is presented in Sect. 5.

2   The HVS Model for Visual Similarity of Block Units

2.1   The HVS Model for Halftone Images

In addition to statistical security, the visual quality of stego also plays an important role that the act of data embedding should be undetectable. To reduce the visual distortion, an HVS model for halftone images based on maximizing visual similarity is proposed. Halftone images resemble multi-tone images and preserve the visual similarity effect according to the density of binary pixels. A high density of white pixels in a region represents the bright region in the original image. To discuss the special features of halftone image, the HVS model based on visual similarity is proposed in this section.

(a)   (b)   (c)

Fig. 1. Example that different halftone images generated by different halftoning methods have a low PSNR = 8.0394 dB. (a) The original gray-scale image. (b) The halftone image generated by the dispersed ordered dither matrix [15] (c) The halftone image generated by the dither algorithm of MATLAB R2015b.

As halftone images have a similar vision with gray-scale images when they are viewed from a certain distance, the visual quality measurement is taken over first. Peak Signal to Noise Ratio (PSNR), common evaluation of the objective visual quality for gray images, measures directly according to the resultant mean square error (MSE). PSNR describes the visual similarity for gray-scale images but it is not suitable for halftone images. As halftone image is essentially a binary image with only 2 tones, the MSE virtually measures the number of different pixels from two halftone images. However, a large number of different pixels in stego do not mean a poor halftone image quality. In addition, halftone images which are converted from the same gray-scale image may have a low PSNR because of the different halftoning method. The halftoning process is shown in Fig. 1. The halftone image shown in Fig. 1(b) is generated by the dispersed ordered dither matrix [15] from the original gray-scale image shown in Fig. 1(a). The halftone image shown in Fig. 1(c) is generated by the dither algorithm of MATLAB R2015b from Fig. 1(a). When viewed from a far distance, Fig. 1(b) and (c) resemble the original gray-scale image Fig. 1(a), but the PSNR of these two halftone images is 8.0394 dB. It is indicated that PSNR is not applied to evaluating the visual quality of halftone images.

Furthermore, the perception of a flipped pixel is affected by its neighboring pixels. PSNR measures the MSE of pixels in an image, but the neighboring regions of these changed pixels are not considered. For the texture of a halftone image, there are complex regions and smooth regions. HVS is more sensitive to the changed pixels in the smooth regions than that in the complex regions. However, if the same number of pixels in two halftone images regardless of the regions are flipped, the PSNR is the same. For example, in Fig. 2, only one pixel is flipped respectively in cover 1 that is a complex region and cover 2 that is a smooth region. And the stego 1 and stego 2 are shown in Fig. 2(a) and (b). The PSNRs are the same for Fig. 2(a) and (b), but the visual distortion in stego 2 is more obvious than stego 1. In conclusion, PSNR cannot evaluate the similarity and visual distortion of halftone images.

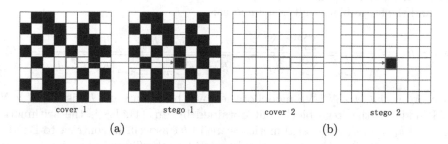

Fig. 2. Example of 2 regions for halftone image and the flipped pixel caused different visual distortion with the same PSNR. (a) The cover 1 and stego 1 which are in a complex region with PSNR = 66.1926 dB. (a) The cover 2 and stego 2 which are in a smooth region with PSNR = 66.1926 dB.

The similar structure for regions of halftone images is determined in visual quality rather than the same pixel value. As the regions where the flipped pixels exist in are more important in halftone image steganography, the HVS model based on the visual similarity of the regions is proposed instead of PSNR measurement.

2.2 Visual Similarity of Block Units

In general, the perception of space-frequency by human eyes is based on a band-pass filter. When viewing from a far distance, human eyes cannot distinguish the details of pixels. It is the same characteristic for human eyes and halftone images for resembling the natural images. For a halftone image, the texture and brightness are represented by the density of white pixels, and when viewing the halftone image, the details of pixels are not significant. Thus, a convolution filter for halftone images can simulate the vision of multi-tone images.

As the regions where the flipped pixels existing in are more important, the block unit is proposed to represent the changed region of halftone image. And we focus on the visual similarity of the changed block units. Assume an $M \times N$ block unit B is cropped from the halftone image. The $M \times N$ HVS model $h_{i,j}$ corresponding to the block unit B is denoted as:

$$h_{x,y} = \sum_{i=-\lfloor M/2 \rfloor}^{\lfloor M/2 \rfloor} \sum_{j=-\lfloor N/2 \rfloor}^{\lfloor N/2 \rfloor} f_{i,j} B_{x+i,y+j} \tag{1}$$

where x, y is the location of the HVS model for the block unit, and f is the visual response filter. The visual similarity of the block unit B is considered according to the HVS model $h_{x,y}$.

In halftone images, the embedding process is carried out by flipping pixels. A changed pixel affects the visual similarity of block units where it exists in. In a block unit B, after flipping a pixel, the visual similarity between the cover block unit and the stego block unit is defined as:

$$s(h_C, h_S) = \frac{\sum_{m=1}^{M} \sum_{n=1}^{N} (h_{C_{m,n}} - \bar{h_C})(h_{S_{m,n}} - \bar{h_S})}{\sqrt{(\sum_{m=1}^{M} \sum_{n=1}^{N} (h_{C_{m,n}} - \bar{h_C})^2)(\sum_{m=1}^{M} \sum_{n=1}^{N} (h_{S_{m,n}} - \bar{h_S})^2)}} \tag{2}$$

where h_C is the $M \times N$ HVS model of the cover block unit and h_S is the $M \times N$ HVS model of the stego block unit obtained by Eq. (1). $\bar{h_C}$ is the arithmetic means of h_C and $\bar{h_s}$ is the arithmetic means of h_S as well. In contract to PSNR, the visual similarity $s(h_C, h_S)$ not only considers the flipped pixel but also its neighboring pixel in the block units. Furthermore, the range of $s(h_C, h_S)$ is $[-1, 1]$ and the larger it is, the higher the visual similarity between C and S is. When $s(h_C, h_S) = 1$, the cover block unit is exactly the same as the stego block unit.

Based on the visual similarity between block units, the distortion score map of the whole image can be obtained. The visual similarity needs to be maximized, and the selection of flipped pixels has minimal visual distortion caused in all block units. If h_C in location (x, y) has the greatest the visual similarity $s(h_C, h_S)$, the pixel at (x, y) is an optimal flipped pixel. For example, in Fig. 3(a), a candidate of flipped pixel and its 3 block units with a size of 4×4 which are the visually affected regions are shown. In different block units, the flipped pixel is located differently, and the visual effect is distinct which is caused by the pixel flipping. The $P_{i,j}$ of visual similarity matrix $\mathbf{P}^{x,y}$ which measures the similarity $s(h_{C_{i,j}}, h_{S_{i,j}})$ of block units affected by the flipped pixel at (x, y) of image is denoted as:

$$P_{i,j} = s(h_{C_{i,j}}, h_{S_{i,j}}) \tag{3}$$

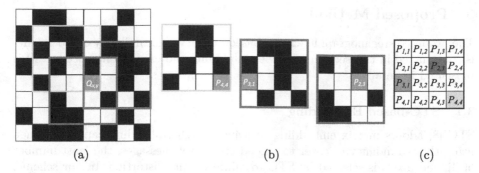

Fig. 3. Example of a candidate of flipped pixel and its 3 block units of all 16 block units with a size of 4×4 which are the visually affected regions and the visual similarity matrix for the candidate. (a) The joint visual similarity $Q_{x,y}$ and 3 block units of the candidate. (b) The 3 different block units of the flipped pixel located differently with distinct visual similarity $P_{i,j}$. (c) The visual similarity matrix $\mathbf{P}^{x,y}$ for the candidate in (x, y).

where $P_{i,j}$ is the visual similarity at (i, j) in matrix $\mathbf{P}^{x,y}$, $h_{C_{i,j}}$ means the cover block unit and $h_{S_{i,j}}$ means the stego block unit with flipped pixel at (i, j). The 3 block units are shown in Fig. 3(b) and the candidate is located in $P_{4,4}$, $P_{3,1}$ and $P_{2,3}$. The visual similarity matrix $\mathbf{P}^{x,y}$ of the candidate in (x, y) is presented in Fig. 3(c).

As the visual effect caused by the flipped pixel is distinct in different block units, the visual similarity $P_{i,j}$ should be distinguished with an affected weight. Lu et al. [13] proposed that the distance between two pixels plays a major role in their mutual interference perceived by human eyes for binary images. When the distance of two pixels is closed, the distortion caused by the flipped pixel when focusing on another pixel is large. Thus a visual affected weight matrix W with the same size of $M \times N$ as the visual similarity matrix $\mathbf{P}^{x,y}$ is designed. The weight matrix W measures the visual effect based on HVS. The joint visual similarity $Q_{x,y}$ of a flipped pixel in (x, y) is obtained by measuring all visual similarity $P_{i,j}$, denoted as:

$$Q_{x,y} = \sum_{m=1}^{M} \sum_{n=1}^{N} P_{m,n} W_{m,n} \qquad (4)$$

where $W_{m,n}$ is the visual affected weight in (m, n).

Obtaining the joint visual similarity $Q_{x,y}$ of a flipped pixel based on Eq. (4), a visual similarity score map is utilized to measure whether this pixel is suitable for flipping while maximizes the visual similarity in its block units.

3   Proposed Method

The proposed steganographic scheme based on the visual similarity of block units is constructed in this section, and the embedding and extraction procedures are presented in detail.

3.1   STC-based Embedding

STC [8] adopts matrix embedding to achieve high embedding capacity. When using the redundancy of cover to embed the secret messages, the least number of flipped pixels is selected by STC to minimize the distortion. In our scheme, the joint visual similarity $Q_{x,y}$ represents the visual similarity between the cover block units and stego block units after flipping a pixel. Due to $Q_{x,y}$ is in range of $[-1, 1]$, the maximal $Q_{x,y}$ indicates the maximal visual similarity and minimal visual distortion. The distortion map used in STC is obtained as:

$$D_{x,y} = 1 - (Q_{x,y} + 1)/2 \tag{5}$$

The distortion map D is applied in STC encoder to generate the bitstream with the lowest distortion to embed the secret messages.

3.2   Embedding Procedure

For a given cover halftone image I_C and the secret message sequence M_s, the embedding procedure includes the following steps:

1. Reshape I_C into a one-dimensional vector with a random scrambling, denoted as V_{I_C};
2. Calculate the visual similarity matrix $\mathbf{P}^{x,y}$ for all pixels of location (x, y) in the C according to Eq. (3);
3. Generate the joint visual similarity $Q_{x,y}$ based on the the visual similarity matrix $\mathbf{P}^{x,y}$ and the visual affected weight W according to Eq. (4);
4. Generate the distortion map D by Eq. (5);
5. Use a random scrambling to reshape D into a one-dimensional vector V_D;
6. Send V_{I_C}, V_D and the secret message sequence M_s to the STC encoder, and obtain the stego vector V_{I_S};
7. Obtain the stego image I_S by descrambling and reshaping V_{I_S} into the same size as the cover I_C.

3.3   Extraction Procedure

For a given stego image I_S, the length of the embedded message L_K and the same random scrambling seed in embedding procedure, the extraction procedure includes the following steps:

1. Obtain one-dimensional vector V'_{I_S} with the same random scrambling seed by reshaping stego image I_S.
2. Employ the STC decoder with V'_{I_S} and L_K, then extract the secret message sequence M_s.

4   Experimental Results

The experimental conditions are discussed in Sect. 4.1, including the image dataset and the design of convolution filter f, block unit B as well as the visual affected weight matrix W. The comparisons in both visual quality and statistic security are presented in Sects. 4.2 and 4.3.

4.1   Experimental Conditions

The halftone images dataset with the size 256×256 is converted from 10000 gray-scale images in BossBase-1.01 [1]. In [4,18], a 5×5 visual response filter is proposed to simulate the impulse response of a one-dimensional eye filter to a printed image with 300 dpi at a viewing distance of 30 in., shown as

$$f = \frac{1}{11.566} \begin{bmatrix} 0.1628 & 0.3215 & 0.4035 & 0.3215 & 0.1628 \\ 0.3215 & 0.6352 & 0.7970 & 0.6352 & 0.3215 \\ 0.4035 & 0.7970 & 1 & 0.7970 & 0.4035 \\ 0.3215 & 0.6352 & 0.7970 & 0.6352 & 0.3215 \\ 0.1628 & 0.3215 & 0.4035 & 0.3215 & 0.1628 \end{bmatrix} \tag{6}$$

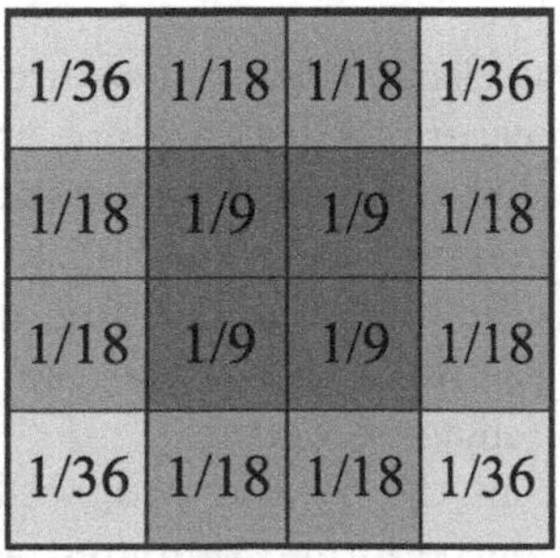

1/36	1/18	1/18	1/36
1/18	1/9	1/9	1/18
1/18	1/9	1/9	1/18
1/36	1/18	1/18	1/36

Fig. 4. The visually affected weight W with size 4×4 divided into 3 kinds of wights.

The size of the block unit in our experiments is set as a size 4×4, which means that there are 16 different block units of a flipped pixel and 16 different visual similarity $P_{i,j}$. Utilizing the filter f and the 4×4 block unit, the HVS model $h_{x,y}$ is obtained by Eq. (1) and visual similarity matrix $\mathbf{P}^{x,y}$ of this pixel is generated by Eq. (3). Considering the distance from the center of the block unit plays a significant role, the middle visual similarities are more important than edged ones. The 16 different locations for the flipped pixel in 16 block units are divided into 3 kinds of visually affected wights. As shown in Fig. 4, the red regions of visual similarity has the greatest weight as they are in the center. The blue regions own the second greatest weight and the yellow regions have the smallest weight because of the farther distance from the center in a block unit.

The weights of 3 regions are designed as 1/9, 1/18 and 1/36, which represents that the sensitiveness of human eyes is at a ratio of 4:2:1, shown in Fig. 4. The joint visual similarity score of a flipped pixel in the image can be obtained by Eq. (4) with the visually affected weight W.

Some halftone images data hiding schemes such as DHSPT [9], PTHVS [10], GIM [11] and DD [22] are employed in experiments with the proposed scheme.

Table 1. Average scores (S_1 to S_5) of various schemes on the halftone images dataset with 1024 bits embedded.

	S_1	S_2	S_3	S_4	S_5
Proposed	**82.8**	**302.4**	3.531	**67.1**	**219.5**
DD [22]	385.3	1160.9	**3.013**	269.6	803.2
PTHVS [10]	676.5	2371.5	3.441	533.7	1695.0
DHSPT [9]	786.9	2432.8	3.107	468.2	1645.9
GIM [11]	683.6	2198.5	3.216	398.3	1514.9

4.2 Comparison of Visual Quality

As discussed in Sect. 2.1, the visual quality measurements such as PSNR and structural similarity index measure (SSIM) are not applied for halftone images. In [9], Fu and Au proposed that the quantity and size of the "salt-and-pepper" clusters are determined to measure the visual distortion. They proposed the visual quality measurements S_1 to S_5 for halftone image. The fewer quantity and smaller size of clusters the image has while the smaller S_1 to S_5 are, and the visual quality of halftone image is better.

As shown in Table 1, except the S_3, our proposed method has the smallest visual quality measures and outperforms compared with other methods. Based on maximizing the visual similarity, our proposed method increases the imperceptibility of human eyes.

4.3 Comparison of Statistical Security

The statistical security is a top criterion for the performance of a steganography scheme. The performance of statistical security is measured by the decision error rate P_E that is defined as:

$$P_E = \frac{1}{2}(P_{FN} + P_{FP}) \tag{7}$$

where P_{FN} is the probabilities of false positive which detects cover as stego, and P_{FP} is false negative which detects stego as cover. The larger the P_E is, the higher the statistical security of the steganographic scheme is.

With the development of steganalysis, many steganalysis methods have been proposed focusing on halftone images. RLCM-100D [5] extracts the run length and co-occurrence as features. PMMTM-320D [6] considers the features of the texture structures. To construct the the steganalysis, the RLCM-100D [5] features and PMMTM-320D [6] features are as input of soft-margin SVMs utilizing an optimized Gaussian kernel.

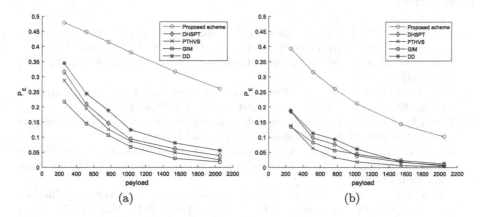

(a)   (b)

Fig. 5. The comparison of statistical security using different steganographic schemes under steganalysis methods. (a) RLCM-100D steganalysis [5]. (b) PMMTM-320D steganalysis [6].

The comparisons of statistical security are averaged over a half for training and a half for testing. The experiment result using RLCM-100D steganalysis [5] is shown in Fig. 5(a) and PMMTM-320D steganalysis [6] is shown in Fig. 5(b). While increasing the embedding payload, our proposed method outperforms with higher statistical security. Based on maximizing the visual similarity, our proposed method increases the imperceptibility not only to human eyes but also to potential analyzers as the statistical security is significantly improved.

5   Conclusions

In this paper, the visual similarity between the HVS model of halftone images is introduced to design our steganographic scheme. Considering the visual quality, the visual similarity is preserved in the block units affected by the flipped pixels. Based on maximizing the visual similarity, our proposed method is undetectable to the hidden data and the act of data embedding. Utilizing the STC-based embedding process under the distortion map calculated by the joint visual similarity, the objective visual quality and the statistical security are both improved. In the future work, improving statistical security is also a challenge while preserving the high visual quality and increasing the embedding payload. Herein, we will focus on achieving stronger statistical security in halftone image steganography.

Acknowledgements. This work is supported by the Key Areas R&D Program of Guangdong (No. 2019B010136002), the National Natural Science Foundation of China (No. U2001202, No. 62072480, No. U1736118), the National Key R&D Program of China (No. 2019QY2202, No. 2019QY(Y)0207), the Key Scientific Research Program of Guangzhou (No. 201804020068).

References

1. Bas, P., Filler, T., Pevný, T.: "Break our steganographic system": the ins and outs of organizing BOSS. In: Filler, T., Pevný, T., Craver, S., Ker, A. (eds.) IH 2011. LNCS, vol. 6958, pp. 59–70. Springer, Heidelberg (2011). https://doi.org/10.1007/978-3-642-24178-9_5
2. Cao, H., Kot, A.C.: On establishing edge adaptive grid for bilevel image data hiding. IEEE Trans. Inf. Forensics Secur. 8(9), 1508–1518 (2013)
3. Chen, J., et al.: Binary image steganalysis based on distortion level co-occurrence matrix. Comput. Mater. Continua 55(2), 201–211 (2018)
4. Cheung, S.M., Chan, Y.H.: A technique for lossy compression of error-diffused halftones. In: IEEE International Conference on Multimedia and Expo, vol. 2, pp. 1083–1086 (2004)
5. Chiew, K.L., Pieprzyk, J.: Binary image steganographic techniques classification based on multi-class steganalysis. In: Kwak, J., Deng, R.H., Won, Y., Wang, G. (eds.) ISPEC 2010. LNCS, vol. 6047, pp. 341–358. Springer, Heidelberg (2010). https://doi.org/10.1007/978-3-642-12827-1_25
6. Feng, B., Lu, W., Sun, W.: Binary image steganalysis based on pixel mesh Markov transition matrix. J. Vis. Commun. Image Represent. 26, 284–295 (2015)
7. Feng, B., Lu, W., Sun, W.: Secure binary image steganography based on minimizing the distortion on the texture. IEEE Trans. Inf. Forensics Secur. 10(2), 243–255 (2015)
8. Filler, T., Judas, J., Fridrich, J.: Minimizing additive distortion in steganography using syndrome-trellis codes. IEEE Trans. Inf. Forensics Secur. 6(3), 920–935 (2011)
9. Fu, M.S., Au, O.C.: Halftone image data hiding with intensity selection and connection selection. Sig. Process. Image Commun. 16(10), 909–930 (2001)
10. Guo, J.M.: Improved data hiding in halftone images with cooperating pair toggling human visual system. Int. J. Imaging Syst. Technol. 17(6), 328–332 (2007)
11. Guo, M., Zhang, H.: High capacity data hiding for halftone image authentication. In: Shi, Y.Q., Kim, H.-J., Pérez-González, F. (eds.) IWDW 2012. LNCS, vol. 7809, pp. 156–168. Springer, Heidelberg (2013). https://doi.org/10.1007/978-3-642-40099-5_14
12. Guo, Y., Au, O.C., Wang, R., Fang, L., Cao, X.: Halftone image watermarking by content aware double-sided embedding error diffusion. IEEE Trans. Image Process. 27(7), 3387–3402 (2018)
13. Lu, H., Kot, A.C., Shi, Y.Q.: Distance-reciprocal distortion measure for binary document images. IEEE Sig. Process. Lett. 11(2), 228–231 (2004)
14. Li, X., Li, B., Yang, B., Zeng, T.: General framework to histogram-shifting-based reversible data hiding. IEEE Trans. Image Process. 22(6), 2181–2191 (2013)
15. Lien, B.K., Lin, Y.M., Lee, K.Y.: High-capacity reversible data hiding by maximum-span pixel pairing on ordered dithered halftone images. In: International Conference on Systems, Signals and Image Processing, pp. 76–79 (2012)

16. Lien, B.K., Lan, Z.L.: Improved halftone data hiding scheme using Hilbert curve neighborhood toggling. In: Seventh International Conference on Intelligent Information Hiding and Multimedia Signal Processing, pp. 73–76 (2011)
17. Lu, W., He, L., Yeung, Y., Xue, Y., Liu, H., Feng, B.: Secure binary image steganography based on fused distortion measurement. IEEE Trans. Circ. Syst. Video Technol. **29**(6), 1608–1618 (2019)
18. Pan, J.S., Luo, H., Lu, Z.M.: Look-up table based reversible data hiding for error diffused halftone images. Informatica **18**(4), 615–628 (2007)
19. Pei, S.C., Guo, J.M.: Hybrid pixel-based data hiding and block-based watermarking for error-diffused halftone images. IEEE Trans. Circ. Syst. Video Technol. **13**(8), 867–884 (2003)
20. Shi, Y., Li, X., Zhang, X., Wu, H., Ma, B.: Reversible data hiding: advances in the past two decades. IEEE Access **4**, 3210–3237 (2016)
21. Wu, S., Zhong, S.H., Liu, Y.: Residual convolution network based steganalysis with adaptive content suppression. In: IEEE International Conference on Multimedia and Expo, pp. 241–246. IEEE (2017)
22. Xue, Y., Liu, W., Lu, W., Yeung, Y., Liu, X., Liu, H.: Efficient halftone image steganography based on dispersion degree optimization. J. Real-Time Image Process. **16**(3), 601–609 (2018). https://doi.org/10.1007/s11554-018-0822-8
23. Yeung, Y., Lu, W., Xue, Y., Huang, J., Shi, Y.: Secure binary image steganography with distortion measurement based on prediction. IEEE Trans. Circ. Syst. Video Technol. **30**(5), 1423–1434 (2020)
24. Yin, X., Lu, W., Liu, W., Zhang, J.: Reversible data hiding in binary images by symmetrical flipping degree histogram modification. In: Yang, C.-N., Peng, S.-L., Jain, L.C. (eds.) SICBS 2018. AISC, vol. 895, pp. 891–903. Springer, Cham (2020). https://doi.org/10.1007/978-3-030-16946-6_73
25. Zhang, J., Lu, W., Yin, X., Liu, W., Yeung, Y.: Binary image steganography based on joint distortion measurement. J. Vis. Commun. Image Represent. **58**, 600–605 (2019)

High Efficiency Quantum Image Steganography Protocol Based on ZZW Framework

Hanrong Sun[1] and Zhiguo Qu[1,2(✉)]

[1] School of Computer and Software, Nanjing University of Information Science and Technology, Nanjing 210044, P. R. China
[2] Jiangsu Engineering Center of Network Monitoring, Nanjing University of Information Science and Technology, Nanjing 210044, P. R. China

Abstract. This paper proposes an efficient quantum image steganography protocol based on Zhang Weiming, Zhang Xinpeng and Wang Shuozhong's steganography framework (ZZW). Based on the high embedding efficiency of the classical ZZW steganography framework, the new protocol combined with the quantum carrier, not only greatly improves the embedding efficiency of the existing quantum image steganography protocols, but also has high security. In order to reflect the practicability of the new protocol, we also designed dedicated quantum circuits to embed and extract secret information. In addition, the simulation results based on Matlab also show that the new protocol not only has good imperceptibility, but also has very high embedding efficiency.

Keywords: Quantum image steganography · ZZW steganography framework · Imperceptibility · Capacity · Embedding efficiency · Security

1 Introduction

Quantum image steganography is a significant branch based on quantum multimedia steganography. This steganography takes quantum image as the carrier of secret information transmission, so as to realize covert transmission of secret information. Currently, with the rapid development of quantum information technology, quantum image has multiple representation models, such as Qubit Lattice [1], Entangled Image [2], Flexible Representation of Quantum Images (FRQI) [3], Novel Enhanced Quantum Representation (NEQR) [4] and so on. According to these different representation models, many researchers have successively proposed various quantum image steganography protocols. For example, in 2015, Jiang et al. [5] first proposed two quantum image steganography protocols based on LSB. The first is to directly replace the LSB of the pixel with secret information value, and the second is to block the image and then embed secret information in the LSB of the pixel block. In 2018, Zhou et al. [6] also proposed a quantum image steganography protocol based on LSB. In this protocol, secret information image is scrambled firstly, then it is extended to the image of the same size as the carrier image and scrambled again. Finally, the disordered information image is embedded into the carrier image. Experimental analysis shows that the protocol not only has

© Springer Nature Switzerland AG 2021
X. Sun et al. (Eds.): ICAIS 2021, LNCS 12737, pp. 400–411, 2021.
https://doi.org/10.1007/978-3-030-78612-0_32

high security, but also the extracting process is very convenient. In 2019, Qu et al. [7], based on QUALPI model, proposed a quantum image steganography protocol by using quantum image extension technology and Grover search algorithm, which not only has good imperceptibility, but also has a large capacity. Based on the NEQR, Luo et al. [8] proposed a blind quantum steganoscopy protocol based on ASCII code in 2019. This protocol uses Gray code as the judgment condition to embed disordered quantum text into 8 carrier pixel blocks.

Since the embedding efficiency can better reflect the balance between imperceptibility and capacity of quantum steganography, the quantum image steganography protocol with high embedding efficiency has become a new development direction of quantum image steganography. In 2019, referring to the classic matrix encoding method, Qu et al. [9] proposed a quantum image steganography protocol based on matrix coding. This protocol uses quantum color images as a carrier and inherits the advantages of matrix coding's high embedding efficiency. This makes quantum image steganography gradually move towards the development direction of efficient coding steganography based on linear codes. In the same year, Qu et al. [10] proposed a quantum image steganography protocol based on Exploiting Modification Direction (EMD) [11], which improved the embedding efficiency and capacity again. However, it still had some shortcomings, such as not preprocessing the image before processing, which led to the possibility of pixel overflow in the actual embedding process and could not be modified. Aiming at the loophole in [10], Hu et al. [12] improved it and proposed a quantum image steganography based on modified EMD embedding, which realized embedding two quantum binary images into quantum color images of the same size. In summary, the efficient steganography of quantum image coding based on linear codes has been recognized by experts in the world, and it's developing rapidly in recent years. Learning from the development experience of classical steganography, the matrix coding framework based on linear codes has gone through three development stages, which are coding steganography oriented towards modification reduction, optional coding steganography for modified regions and coded steganography oriented to minimize steganography distortion. And the efficient steganography of quantum image coding based on linear codes is still in the first stage at present, so there is still a lot of room for development.

In order to further development of the efficient steganography of quantum image coding based on linear codes and continue to improve the embedding efficiency of quantum steganography protocol, this paper will make full use of the advantages of high embedding efficiency and high security of ZZW framework and puts forward a new quantum image steganography protocol based on ZZW framework (QIS-ZZW). The protocol is implemented on the basis of matrix embedding which is optional for the modified region. Compared with the matrix embedding in the first stage, ZZW framework not only has higher embedding efficiency, but also has higher security and better imperceptibility.

The rest of this paper is arranged as follows. Section 2 introduces ZZW steganography framework. Section 3 elaborates on the process of QIS-ZZW. Section 4 compares the performance of the new protocol with that of the existing protocols. In final, Sect. 5 concludes the paper.

2 ZZW Steganography Framework

The ZZW steganography framework is a double-layer matrix coding framework that combines wet paper code and hamming code proposed by Zhang et al. [13] in 2008. The framework effectively improves the security of steganography protocol by introducing wet paper codes. Furthermore, each pixel block of the double-layer matrix coding framework can embed secret information in two embedding channels with one modification, which greatly improves the embedding efficiency of the protocol. The main steps are shown as follows.

Step 1: Divide the carrier image into L disjoint blocks and each block contains 2^k pixels. Then the LSB block of the entire image can be expressed as Eq. (1).

$$(x_1, \cdots, x_{2^k}), \cdots, (x_{(L-1)2^k+1}, \cdots, x_{L2^k}) \tag{1}$$

Step 2: Compress the LSBs of each pixel block to one bit with $\oplus$ operations, as shown in Eq. (2) (i represents the i-th pixel block, and j represents the j-th pixel in the pixel block).

$$y_i = \bigoplus_{j=1}^{2^k} x_{i2^k+j}, \quad i = 0, 1, \cdots, L-1 \tag{2}$$

Step 3: Take $(y_0, \cdots, y_{L-1})$ as the first embedding channel, and then embed the channel in the manner of $SC(\frac{1}{2}, 1, 1)$, i.e., embed 1 bit secret information in each bit with a modification probability of $\frac{1}{2}$. Therefore, each pixel block has a probability of $\frac{1}{2}$ that needs to be modified. If no modification is needed, the pixel block can only embed the 1 bit secret information. If modification is needed, then go to **Step 4**.

Step 4: If the pixel block needs to be modified, the LSBs of the 2^k pixels of the pixel block are used as the second embedding channel, and the matrix coding embedding is performed in the first $2^k - 1$ pixels of the pixel block to determine which pixel is specifically modified. If the first $2^k - 1$ pixels do not need to be modified, then the LSB of the 2^k-th pixel is modified. Now, all secret information has been embedded, and the sender needs to send the position information of the modified pixel block as auxiliary information to the receiver.

Step 5: When extracting, firstly calculate the compression bit y_i of each pixel block according to Eq. (2) to extract secret information embedded in the first embedding channel. Secondly, secret information embedded in the second embedding channel can be extracted by using the matrix extracting method in the first $2^k - 1$ pixels of each modified pixel block according to the auxiliary information.

3 Quantum Image Steganography Protocol Based on ZZW Steganography Framework

This paper proposes a quantum image steganography protocol based on ZZW steganography framework. Compared with previous quantum image steganography protocols, the new protocol takes advantage of the high embedding efficiency of the classical

ZZW steganography framework, which not only greatly improves the embedding efficiency, makes the steganography protocol more efficient, but also has higher security. The framework of QIS-ZZW is shown as Fig. 1.

The flowchart of QIS-ZZW is shown as Fig. 2.

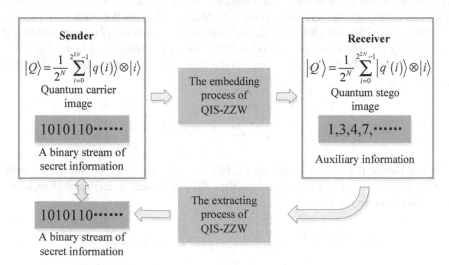

Fig. 1. The framework of QIS-ZZW

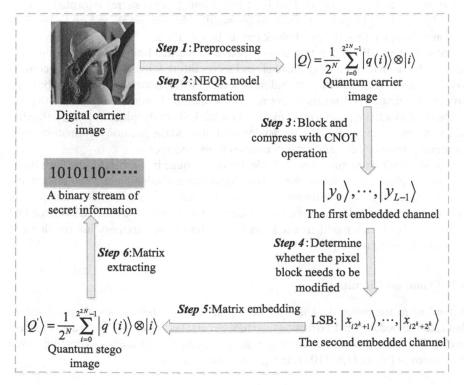

Fig. 2. The flowchart of QIS-ZZW

3.1 Specific Steps

***Step*1**: Image preprocessing. In order to avoid in the actual embedding process, the pixel value needs to be added or subtracted by 1 and the possible pixel value is close to saturation and cannot be modified. Therefore, the carrier image needs to be preprocessed before embedding. If the pixel gray value is 0, change it to 1; if the pixel gray value is 255, change it to 254. But usually because the probability that the pixel gray value is 0 or 255 is very low, the effect of preprocessing on the carrier image can be negligible.

***Step*2**: Convert the digital gray image to the quantum image of NEQR, as shown in Eq. (3).

$$|I\rangle = \frac{1}{2^N} \sum_{i=0}^{2^{2N}-1} |g(i)\rangle \otimes |i\rangle \tag{3}$$

***Step*3**: Divide the carrier image into L blocks and each block contains 2^k pixels. Then use the *CNOT* operation to compress the LSB of all pixels in each pixel block into one bit, as shown in Eq. (4).

$$|y_i\rangle = \overset{2^k-1}{\underset{j=1}{CNOT}}\left(\left|x_{i2^k+j}\right\rangle, \left|x_{i2^k+j+1}\right\rangle\right), \quad i = 0, 1, \cdots, L-1 \tag{4}$$

***Step*4**: By using $(|y_0\rangle, \cdots, |y_{L-1}\rangle)$ as the first embedding channel, L bits of secret information can be embedded. That is, if $|y_i\rangle$ is equal to the secret information to be embedded and the pixel block needs to be modified by one pixel, and go to ***Step*5**. If they are not equal, then the pixel block cannot be modified.

***Step*5**: The LSBs of the first $2^k - 1$ pixels of the pixel block to be modified are used as the second embedding channel, and secret information is embedded according to the quantum circuits of the embedding process of [9]. If during the matrix embedding process, the first $2^k - 1$ pixels do not need to be modified, then modify the 2^k-th pixel of the pixel block, i.e., perform X operation on the LSB of the pixel ($X|x_{i2^k+2^k}\rangle$). After secret information is embedded, the sender needs to send the position information of the modified pixel block as auxiliary information to the receiver.

***Step*6**: When extracting, firstly divide the stego image into L blocks and each block contains 2^k pixels. Then let extract secret information embedded in the first embedding channel according to the quantum circuit corresponding to Eq. (4). Secondly, secret information embedded in the second embedding channel can be extracted from the first $2^k - 1$ pixels of each modified pixel block according to the auxiliary information and the extracting circuits of [9].

3.2 Quantum Circuits

According to the embedding and extracting steps of the new protocol, we designed dedicated embedding and extracting quantum circuits (as shown in Figs. 3 and 4 respectively). Here, the quantum circuits of matrix embedding and matrix extracting haven been given in [9], and QC [10] is the quantum comparator.

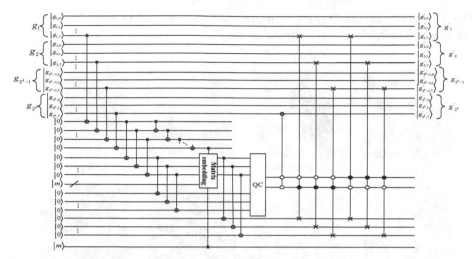

Fig. 3. Quantum circuit of QIS-ZZW's embedding process

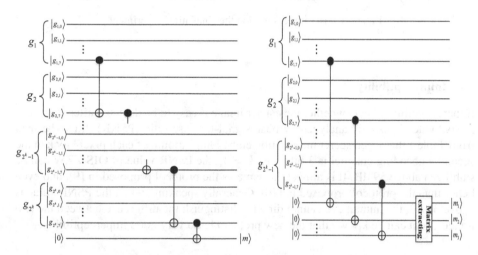

Fig. 4. Quantum circuit of QIS-ZZW's extracting process

4   Experimental Simulation and Performance Analysis

Imperceptibility, capacity, embedding efficiency and security have always been important parameters of steganography protocol. A good steganography protocol must have large capacity and embedding efficiency under the premise of good imperceptibility and high security. In order to analyze and highlight the performance advantages of the new protocol, this section will compare these parameters with previous quantum steganography protocols (such as Qu et al. [9], Qu et al. [10] and Hu et al. [12]). The simulation experiment in this section is based on the classic computer Matlab R2018b environment.

The selected pictures are *"Lena"*, *"Cameraman"*, *"Baboon"*, *"Airplane"*, *"Starfish"*, *"House"*, *"Butterfly"*, *"Rice"*, with the size of $2^8 \times 2^8$, as shown in Fig. 5.

(a) *Lena* (b) *Cameraman* (c) *Baboon* (d) *Airplane*

(e) *Starfish* (f) *House* (g) *Butterfly* (h) *Rice*

Fig. 5. Carrier images used in the simulation experiment

4.1 Imperceptibility

Imperceptibility reflects whether the carrier image is easy to be detected after steganography, which is usually analyzed by peak signal-to-noise ratio (PSNR). It can be seen from Table 1 that when secret information embedding amount of each pixel block in the second embedding channel is 3 bits (i.e., $k = 3$), the PSNR value of QIS-ZZW can be stabilized above 59 dB. It is almost the same as the protocol proposed in [9], and even better than the protocol proposed in [10]. Generally speaking, when the PSNR value is above 38 dB, the human eye cannot directly distinguish the difference between the two images, so it can be known that the new protocol has a very good imperceptibility.

Table 1. Comparison of PSNR values of different carriers for different protocols

PSNR	QIS-ZZW ($k = 3$)	Qu et al. [9] ($k = 3$)	Qu et al. [10]
Lena	59.2342	59.1441	56.5335
Cameraman	59.6661	59.5243	56.7256
Baboon	59.6426	59.2016	56.0156
Airplane	59.5104	59.6641	56.7264

(*continued*)

Table 1. (*continued*)

PSNR	QIS-ZZW ($k = 3$)	Qu et al. [9] ($k = 3$)	Qu et al. [10]
Starfish	59.6276	59.5367	56.5629
House	59.6492	59.1632	56.6317
Butterfly	59.6155	59.3426	56.1694
Rice	59.5589	59.2639	56.3269

4.2 Capacity

Capacity is a parameter that measures maximum amount of secret information that can be embedded in a carrier image, i.e., the ratio of the amount of secret information embedded in a unit pixel block to the amount of pixels contained in the unit pixel block. Generally speaking, the larger the capacity, the more secret information can be embedded in the carrier image.

For QIS-ZZW, the first embedding channel of a unit pixel block can embed 1 bit secret information on average, and the second embedding channel can embed k bits secret information with a probability of $\frac{1}{2}$. Therefore, the unit pixel block in QIS-ZZW can embed $1 + \frac{1}{2}k$ bits of secret information on average. So the capacity $(C_{QIS-ZZW})$ of QIS-ZZW is shown as Eq. (5).

$$C_{QIS-ZZW} = \frac{1 + \frac{1}{2} \times k}{2^k} = \frac{2 + k}{2^{k+1}} \; bits/pixel \tag{5}$$

According to the results of Matlab simulation experiment, we give a comparison curve of the capacity of the new protocol and the protocol proposed in [9], as shown in Fig. 6. It can be seen that the capacity of QIS-ZZW is slightly lower than that of the protocol proposed in [9].

4.3 Embedding Efficiency

Embedding efficiency is a parameter that measures the amount of secret information that can be embedded in a unit of modification, i.e., the ratio of the amount of secret information that can be embedded in a unit pixel block to the average amount of modification. Generally speaking, the better the imperceptibility of the steganography protocol, the lower the embedding capacity, which are two contradictory parameters. However, a good steganography protocol needs to have large embedding capacity as well as good imperceptibility. Therefore, we need to continuously optimize the relationship between the two to achieve the best balance, i.e., to continuously improve the embedding efficiency.

For QIS-ZZW, according to the embedding method of the first embedding channel, the probability that each pixel block needs to be modified is $\frac{1}{2}$, i.e., the average modification amount of the unit pixel block is $\frac{1}{2}$. If the pixel block needs to be modified, k bits secret information can also be embedded in the second embedding channel. Therefore, the average modification amount of the unit pixel block of QIS-ZZW is $\frac{1}{2}$, and the

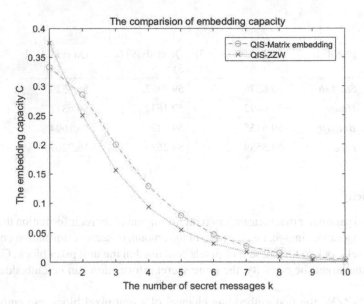

Fig. 6. Comparison of capacity of different protocols

average embedding capacity is $1 + \frac{1}{2}k$ bits. So the embedding efficiency of QIS-ZZW ($E_{QIS-ZZW}$) is shown as Eq. (6).

$$E_{QIS-ZZW} = \frac{1 + \frac{1}{2} \times k}{\frac{1}{2}} = 2 + k \tag{6}$$

Based on the results of Matlab simulation experiment, we give a comparison curve of embedding efficiency of the new protocol and the protocol proposed in [9], as shown in Fig. 7. It can be seen that the embedding efficiency of the new protocol is much higher than that of QIS-Matrix embedding, no matter how much secret information is embedded in the unit pixel block.

4.4 Security

Security also is a significant parameter that must be considered for performance of steganography protocol. High security can protect secret information and reduce the impact of external environment noises or eavesdropping attacks during the transmission process. From this prospective, security is one of the key factors to guarantee whether a steganography protocol can successfully transmit secret information or not.

On one hand, bit error rate (BER) refers to the ratio of the number of pixels that are changed due to external factors during the transmission process of the image to the entire image. It can be used to evaluate the security of the quantum image steganography protocol. The formula is shown as Eq. (7).

$$BER = \frac{1}{PSNR} \tag{7}$$

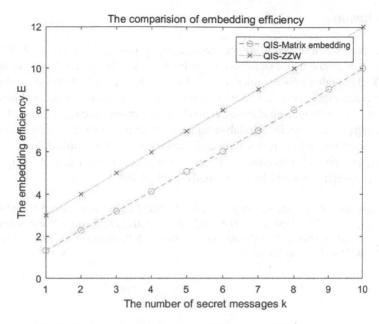

Fig. 7. Comparison of embedding efficiency of different protocols

Table 2 shows the comparison of the BER values of the new protocol and the protocol proposed by Hu et al. [12] under different salt-and-pepper noise densities. It can be seen that the BER values of these two protocols under salt-and-pepper noise are relatively small. When the salt-and-pepper noise density is 0.10 and 0.15, the BER values of the new protocol is even smaller than the protocol proposed in [12]. So it can be explained that QIS-ZZW have high security.

On the other hand, because the double-layer matrix coding framework combines the idea of wet paper code, it does not modify all pixel blocks, but selectively modify pixel blocks after embedding secret information in the first embedding channel. If a third party wants to extract secret information, it must have auxiliary information provided by the sender to extract it. Otherwise, all secret information cannot be extracted correctly. This also improves the security of the protocol to a certain extent.

Table 2. Comparison of BER values of different protocols under different salt-and-pepper noise densities

Stego image		Salt-and-pepper noise densities		
		0.05	0.10	0.15
Hu et al. [12]	*Lena*	0.0364	0.0727	0.1063
	Airplane	0.0372	0.0718	0.1057
QIS-ZZW	*Lena*	0.0552	0.0664	0.0753
	Airplane	0.0561	0.0670	0.0758

5   Conclusions

This paper proposes a quantum image steganography protocol based on ZZW framework. The new protocol is extended on the basis of the classic ZZW steganography framework. By combining wet paper code and hamming code, two embedding channels are constructed, respectively embedding secret information. In addition, combined with the quantum carrier image, we also designed dedicated quantum circuits for embedding and extracting process. Finally, Matlab simulation experiments show that the new protocol is not only better in imperceptibility and security, but also its embedding efficiency is greatly improved while its capacity is not much different from that of the quantum image steganography protocol based on matrix embedding.

Acknowledgments. This work was supported by the National Natural Science Foundation of China (No. 61373131, 61601358, 61303039, 61232016, 61501247), Sichuan Youth Science and Technique Foundation (No. 2017JQ0048), NUIST Research Foundation for Talented Scholars (2015r014), PAPD and CICAEET funds.

References

1. Venegas-Andraca, S.E., Bose, S.: Storing, processing and retrieving an image using quantum mechanics. In: Proceedings of SPIE Conference Quantum Information and Computation, vol. 5105, no. 1, pp. 137–147 (2003)
2. Venegas-Andraca, S.E., Ball, J.L.: Processing images in entangled quantum systems. Quantum Inf. Process. **9**(1), 1–11 (2010). https://doi.org/10.1007/s11128-009-0123-z
3. Le, P.Q., Dong, F., Hirota, K.: A flexible representation of quantum images for polynomial preparation, image compression, and processing operations. Quantum Inf. Process. **10**(1), 63–84 (2011)
4. Zhang, Y., Lu, K., Gao, Y.H., Wang, M.: NEQR: a novel enhanced quantum representation of digital images. Quantum Inf. Process. **12**(8), 2833–2860 (2013)
5. Jiang, N., Zhao, N., Wang, L.: LSB based quantum image steganography algorithm. Int. J. Theor. Phys. **55**(1), 107–123 (2015). https://doi.org/10.1007/s10773-015-2640-0
6. Zhou, R.-G., Luo, J., Liu, X., Zhu, C., Wei, L., Zhang, X.: A novel quantum image steganography scheme based on LSB. Int. J. Theor. Phys. **57**(6), 1848–1863 (2018). https://doi.org/10.1007/s10773-018-3710-x
7. Qu, Z.G., Li, Z.Y., Xu, G., Wu, S.Y., Wang, X.J.: Quantum image steganography protocol based on quantum image expansion and grover search algorithm. IEEE Access **7**(1), 50849–50857 (2019)
8. Luo, J., Zhou, R.G., Liu, X.A., Hu, W.W., Liu, G.Z.: A novel quantum steganography scheme based on ASCII. Int. J. Quantum Inf. **17**(4), 1950033 (2019)
9. Qu, Z.G., Cheng, Z.W., Wang, X.J.: Matrix coding-based quantum image steganography algorithm. IEEE Access **7**(1), 35684–35698 (2019)
10. Qu, Z., Cheng, Z., Liu, W., Wang, X.: A novel quantum image steganography algorithm based on exploiting modification direction. Multimedia Tools Appl. **78**(7), 7981–8001 (2018). https://doi.org/10.1007/s11042-018-6476-5
11. Zhang, X.P., Wang, S.Z.: Efficient steganographic embedding by exploiting modification direction. IEEE Commun. Lett. **10**(11), 781–783 (2006)

12. Hu, W.-W., Zhou, R.-G., Liu, X.-A., Luo, J., Luo, G.-F.: Quantum image steganography algorithm based on modified exploiting modification direction embedding. Quantum Inf. Process. **19**(5), 1–28 (2020). https://doi.org/10.1007/s11128-020-02641-5
13. Zhang, W., Zhang, X., Wang, S.: Maximizing steganographic embedding efficiency by combining hamming codes and wet paper codes. In: Solanki, K., Sullivan, K., Madhow, U. (eds.) IH 2008. LNCS, vol. 5284, pp. 60–71. Springer, Heidelberg (2008). https://doi.org/10.1007/978-3-540-88961-8_5

Halftone Image Steganalysis
by Reconstructing Grayscale Image

Junwei Luo[1], Cong Lin[2] , Lingwen Zeng[1], Jifan Liang[1], and Wei Lu[1(✉)] (iD)

[1] School of Computer Science and Engineering, Guangdong Province Key
Laboratory of Information Security Technology, Ministry of Education Key
Laboratory of Machine Intelligence and Advanced Computing, Sun Yat-sen
University, Guangzhou 510006, China
luojw8@mail2.sysu.edu.cn, luwei3@mail.sysu.edu.cn
[2] School of Statistics and Mathematics, Guangdong University of Finance
and Economics, Guangzhou 510320, China

Abstract. Utilizing some special pixels patterns constructing the steganalytic features is popular in binary image steganalysis, which could be
also used in halftone image. There is almost no specific image steganalysis for halftone image. In this paper, a halftone image steganalysis scheme
is proposed and achieves a satisfactory performance, which is totally different from the previous works focussing on some special pixels patterns.
Inspired by the fact that halftoning techniques based on the low-pass
characteristic of human visual system model (HVS model), the grayscale
image is considered reconstructing with a Gaussian filter. And the distortions caused by embedding secret messages will still exist. After that,
some common grayscale image steganalysis can be used for extracting
the steganalytic features. Furthermore, a series of experiments are conducted and the experimental results show that the proposed scheme is
effective on halftone image steganalysis.

Keywords: Data hiding · Steganalysis · Halftone image ·
Reconstructing grayscale image

1 Introduction

Steganography, as one of the branch of data hiding, aims at hiding secret messages inconspicuously into a special digital media. Generally, digital media are
digital files or data, such as image, video, text, and audio, and different characteristics are used to embed secret messages [6,23]. As an effective counter
technique of steganography, steganalysis is used to detect the existence of the
secret messages embedded by steganography. Researchers have shown a great
interest in steganalysis in the last decade, and numerous steganalysis schemes
have been proposed for different digital media [2,5,24,25]. Steganography and
steganalysis is an important topic in information security [6,15,16,18,19,26].

As a popular digital media, images have a high frequency of redundant data
which is able to conceal secret message. Binary images require only 1 bit per

© Springer Nature Switzerland AG 2021
X. Sun et al. (Eds.): ICAIS 2021, LNCS 12737, pp. 412–423, 2021.
https://doi.org/10.1007/978-3-030-78612-0_33

pixel, which make it suitable for processing and transmitting [18,26]. Generally, binary images can be divided into two kinds: ordinary binary images and halftone images. Halftoning techniques which are based on the low-pass characteristic of human visual system (HVS) model reduce visual reproductions and simulate continuous-tone image. Some common halftoning techniques include ordered dithering [22], error diffusion [7,27], dot diffusion [17,20] and direct binary search [12].

In previous works, some halftone image steganographic schemes have been proposed [9–11,19]. In [10], a data hiding scheme called Data Hiding by Smart Pair Toggling (DHSPT) is proposed, which is an improvement of Data Hiding Pair Toggling (DHPT) [9]. In DHSPT, a better visual quality is achieved by finding the toggling pair that selecting the slave pixel with minimum connectivity value. Guo [11] proposes a steganographic scheme named Pair Toggling with Human Visual System (PTHVS) which selects the slave pixels with the connectivity value along different directions. Considering the statistical security against steganalyzers, Lu et al. [19] propose a halftone image steganography based on pixel density transition, in which a pixel density histogram is constructed to select the appropriate blocks for embedding and minimizes the distortion of texture structure.

For ordinary binary image steganography, Feng et al. [6] propose a flipping distortion model (FDM), which minimizes the distortion on the texture by exploiting the texture property of binary images. Yeung et al. [26] propose a binary image steganography with Distortion Measurement based on prediction (PDM). The concept of "uncertainty" is introduced to evaluate pixels flippability and the embedding distortions. Although the representation of the texture of ordinary binary images are totally different from that in halftone images, the statistics-based FDM and PDM can be used to evaluate the distortion of halftone images.

With the aim at detecting the embedding secret messages, many steganalysis schemes have been developed in recent years [2,4,5,8,21]. For binary images steganalysis, Feng et al. [5] propose a steganalytic model called pixel mesh Markov transition matrix (PMMTM), which characterizes the distortion on the texture consistency by pixel meshes patterns to construct the steganlytic features. In [2], a binary images steganalysis scheme named LargeLTP utilizes a larger local texture pattern to construct the steganalytic feature. The size of local texture pattern is expanded to 5×5 which contains more information of region texture but causes the curse of dimensionality. Hence, Manhattan distance is employed to measure the inter-pixels correlation in the expanded LTPs and only some pixels with closely correlation to the center pixel are selected. Finally, 8192 types of LTPs are extracted to utilize as a 8192-dimensional steganalytic feature set. For grayscale images, a Subtractive Pixel Adjacency Matrix (SPAM) model [21] is proposed for steganalysis, in which local dependences are modeled as a Markov chain. Fridrich et al. [8] propose a general methodology for steganalysis based on a rich model consisting of 106 diverse submodels. In [4], a variant of the spatial rich model (MaxSRM) is proposed, which uses selection channel and achieves better performance. The steganalyzers can be trained by these steganalytic features with some machine learning method, such as SVM [3] and ensemble classifier (EC) [13,14].

In this paper, a halftone image steganalysis scheme is proposed, which is different from previous binary image steganalysis schemes focussing on some special patterns. There is almost no steganalysis method on halftone images. Hence, the binary image steganalysis schemes are used for halftone image steganalysis which never consider the characteristic of halftoning. Inspired by the fact that halftoning is based on the low-pass characteristic of HVS model, we consider reconstructing the grayscale image with a Gaussian filter. The distortion caused by embedding secret messages still exists in the reconstructed grayscale image. After that, the features of reconstructed grayscale image are extracted by grayscale image steganalysis schemes. Furthermore, many experiments are conducted when attacking different steganographic schemes. The experimental results show that the proposed scheme has an acceptable performance compared with the steganalysis schemes which is based on some special patterns.

The rest of this paper is organized as follows. In Sect. 2, the steganalysis schemes including PMMTM and LargeLTP are introduced in details. Both of them extract the features from some special patterns. The proposed scheme including reconstructing the grayscale image and extracting features will be discussed in Sect. 3. Finally, the experimental results and conclusions are described in Sects. 4 and 5, respectively.

2 Related Work

In this section, PMMTM [5] and LargeLTP [2] which can be used for halftone image steganalysis based on some special patterns are introduced.

2.1 PMMTM

PMMTM measures the embedding distortion on the texture consistency based on the high-order Markov chains of specific pixel meshes which are shown in Fig. 1. The Markov transition matrices $\{\mathbf{C}^{\leftarrow}, \mathbf{C}^{\rightarrow}, \mathbf{C}^{\uparrow}, \mathbf{C}^{\downarrow}, \mathbf{C}^{\searrow}, \mathbf{C}^{\nwarrow}, \mathbf{C}^{\swarrow},$ and $\mathbf{C}^{\nearrow}\}$ along 8 directions are calculated based on these specific pixel meshes. The pixel mesh can be denoted by a unique index t, which is calculated as

$$t = \sum_{k=0}^{k=N-1} I_k \times 2^k \tag{1}$$

where $k = 0, 1..., N-1$ correspond to the indices as shown in Fig. 1. I_k represents the value of k-th pixel. N is the number of valid pixel considered in the pixel mesh. For a halftone image with size $l_1 \times l_2$, the transition matrix $\mathbf{C}^{\rightarrow}$ along left-to-right direction from the pattern index t_1 to the pattern index t_2 is defined as

$$C_{t_1,t_2}^{\rightarrow} = Pr(t_2|t_1) = \frac{\sum\limits_{i=1}^{l_1} \sum\limits_{j=1}^{l_2-1} \delta(T_{i,j} = t_1) \cdot \delta(T_{i,j+1} = t_2)}{\sum\limits_{i=1}^{l_1} \sum\limits_{j=1}^{l_2-1} \delta(T_{i,j} = t_1)} \tag{2}$$

where

$$\delta(q) = \begin{cases} 1 & q \text{ is true} \\ 0 & q \text{ is false} \end{cases} \tag{3}$$

and $T_{i,j} = t_1$ represents that the index of the pixel mesh pattern located at (i, j) is t_1. The transition matrices along other directions can also be calculated. The feature in PMMTM is the aggregation of these eight directions

$$\mathbf{F} = \frac{1}{8}(\mathbf{C}^{\leftarrow} + \mathbf{C}^{\rightarrow} + \mathbf{C}^{\uparrow} + \mathbf{C}^{\downarrow} + \mathbf{C}^{\searrow} + \mathbf{C}^{\nwarrow} + \mathbf{C}^{\swarrow} + \mathbf{C}^{\nearrow}) \tag{4}$$

The flipped pixels could influence the transition probability of the pixel mesh, which can be captured by different directions transition matrices.

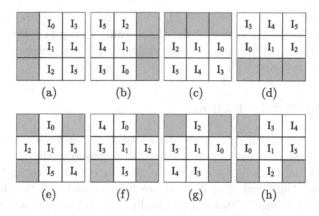

Fig. 1. The pixel meshes corresponding to different-directional Markov transition matrices. (a)–(h) correspond to $\mathbf{C}^{\rightarrow}$, $\mathbf{C}^{\leftarrow}$, $\mathbf{C}^{\downarrow}$, $\mathbf{C}^{\uparrow}$, $\mathbf{C}^{\searrow}$, $\mathbf{C}^{\nwarrow}$, $\mathbf{C}^{\swarrow}$, $\mathbf{C}^{\nearrow}$, respectively.

2.2   LargeLTP

LargeLTP based on local texture pattern extracts the histogram features to classify the cover and stego image.

Different from PMMTM [5], a larger pattern with size 5×5 is considered, which can capture the embedding distortion more exactly. The pattern with larger size causes the curse of dimensionality. Hence, only some pixels with closely correlation to the center pixel in the pattern are selected to construct the LTP structure, as shown in Fig. 2. The correlation between the pixel and the center pixel in the pattern is measured by the Manhattan distance. Totally 8192

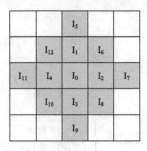

Fig. 2. The LTP structure in LargeLTP [2]

patterns are considered to construct the feature set. The features in LargeLTP [2] are extracted based on the frequency of occurrence of each pattern. F_i denotes the frequency of occurence of i−th pattern, which is denoted as

$$F_i = \sum_{k=1}^{M} \delta(T(k) = i) \tag{5}$$

where $T(k)$ is the k−th pattern and M is the number of patterns in an image. The index of specific pattern is calculated according to Eq. (1). The distribution of some patterns would be changed after embedding secret messages, which can be detected by the LargeLTP.

3   The Proposed Method

In this section, the proposed method will be introduced in details, which contains two processes. First, a Gaussian filter is used to reconstruct the grayscale image. The pixels from halftone image have only two states. After reconstructing the grayscale image, the number of pixel states is increased and the distortion by embedding secret messages still exists. Finally, the grayscale image steganalysis is applied to extract the feature.

3.1   Reconstructing Grayscale Image with Gaussian Filter

The halftone technique is based on the low-pass characteristic of HVS model. It is reasonable to use the low-pass filter to reconstruct the grayscale image.

Gaussian filter is a type of low-pass filter, which can be used to reconstruct the grayscale image. The coefficient of Gaussian filter is generated by a 2-D Gaussian distribution:

$$G(x, y) = \frac{1}{2\pi\sigma^2} e^{\frac{-x^2 - y^2}{2\sigma^2}} \tag{6}$$

where (x, y) is the coordinate with respect to the center and σ is the standard deviation of the Gaussian distribution. Suppose a Gaussian filter ω with size

$r \times p$ and a halftone image H with size $R \times P$, the reconstructed grayscale image G is calculated as

$$G = \sum_{i=1}^{R} \sum_{j=1}^{P} \left(\sum_{s=-r/2}^{r/2} \sum_{t=-p/2}^{p/2} \omega_{s,t} H_{i+s,j+t} \right) \tag{7}$$

After applied with a Gaussian filter, the grayscale image can be roughly reconstructed. Compared with halftone image, the number of pixel states of grayscale image is increased. Not only that, the distortion caused by the flipped pixels still exists in the reconstructed grayscale image as shown in Fig. 3. Hence, the original halftone image steganalysis can be converted to grayscale image steganalysis.

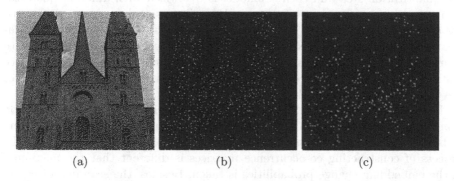

(a)   (b)   (c)

Fig. 3. (a) The cover halftone image. (b) The embedding changes between cover and stego halftone image which is applied PDHist [19]. (c) Applied with a Gaussian filter, the embedding changes between cover and stego reconstructed grayscale image.

3.2   Feature Extraction

As mention above, the distortions still exist in the reconstructed grayscale images. Hence, some common grayscale steganalysis including SPAM [21], SRM [8] and MaxSRM [4] can be considered extracting the steganalytic features.

SPAM exploits the independence of the stego noise and models the differences between adjacent pixels. With a reconstructed grayscale image with size $R \times P$, the difference array $\mathbf{D}$ can be computed along eight directions $\{\leftarrow, \rightarrow, \uparrow, \downarrow, \nwarrow, \searrow, \swarrow, \nearrow\}$. For a horizontal direction left to right, difference array $\mathbf{D}$ is computed as

$$\mathbf{D}_{i,j}^{\rightarrow} = G_{i,j} - G_{i,j+1} \tag{8}$$

where G is the reconstructed grayscale image, $i \in \{1, 2, 3, \ldots, R\}$, and $j \in \{1, 2, 3, \ldots, P-1\}$. And other directions can be obtained in the same manner. Using the difference array $\mathbf{D}$, a Markov chain is modeled and its transition probability matrix is used as the feature of steganalyzer. Finally, a second-order Markov procedure with 686-dimension features gets the best performance.

With the aim of detecting a wide spectrum of embedding algorithms, SRM is proposed as a general methodology for steganalysis based on a rich model including substantial diverse submodels that are formed from noise residuals which can be divided by two types: 'spam' and 'minmax'. In type 'spam', residual is computed as a linear high-pass filter of neighboring pixels, while 'minmax' residuals use more than one linear filters, and take the minimum or maximum of each filters' outputs. Non-linearity is contained in residual so that more different types of dependencies can be captured. To curb the range of residuals and make it more sensitive at edges, truncation and quantization are used for residuals which is shown in

$$\gamma^{qt} = trunc_T(round(\frac{\gamma}{t})) \tag{9}$$

where γ and γ^{qt} are the residuals and its quantized and truncated version. t is the quantization step and each submodel is quantized with different quantization step t to improve the performance. Four-dimensional co-occurrence matrices are constructed from γ^{qt} as steganalysis features. Considering the correlation between neighboring pixels, horizontal and vertical directions are chosen to form co-occurrences matrices but not diagonal directions. Besides, co-occurrence matrices' dimension is reduced by its symmetrization. Totally, the dimension of the union of submodels is 34671.

For further research, MaxSRM is proposed as a variant of SRM using selection channel, which is the probabilities with which the pixels are modified during embedding. The construction of feature set is similar to that in SRM but the process of constructing co-occurrence matrices is different that the maximum of the embedding change probabilities is taken. Besides, the scanning direction of the co-occurrence matrices is modified. Instead of using the horizontal and vertical scans, other four directions are considered.

4 Experimental Results

In this section, the experiment setup including the dataset, hyperparameters and evaluation criterion will be firstly introduced. In order to illustrate the validity of the proposed scheme, some comparative experiments with PMMTM and LargeLTP when attacking several steganographic schemes are conducted.

4.1 Experiment Setup

These experiments are conducted on BOSSbase 1.01 [1] containing 10000 grayscale images with size 512×512. Then the grayscale images are resized to 256×256 by `imresize` with default setting in Matlab. Finally, 10000 halftone images are generated by error diffusion [27] from these resized grayscale images. In our experiments, 5000 halftone images are randomly chosen as the training set, the rest 5000 halftone images are for the test set. The Gaussian filter with size 3×3 and $\sigma = 1.0$ is used to reconstruct grayscale images.

The average error rate P_E is used to measure the performance of steganalysis schemes calculated as

$$P_E = \frac{1}{2}(P_{FN} + P_{FP}) \tag{10}$$

where P_{FN} represents the false negative rate, P_{FP} represents the false positive rate, respectively.

4.2   Performance Comparison

In this section, many experiments are conducted in order to illustrate the effectiveness of the proposed scheme. The attacking steganographic schemes including PDHist [19], PDM [26], FDM [6], DHSPT [9], and PTHVS [11] are selected. There is almost no halftone image steganalysis schemes. Binary image steganalysis PMMTM [5] and LargeLTP [2] are compared, both of them are statistical models and can be also used for halftone images.

As for the steganographic schemes, PDM and FDM are applied syndrome-trellis codes (STC) to embedding messages, PDHist, DHSPT, and PTHVS are not. Yeung et al. [26] propose a prediction model by the "uncertainty" of a pixel in a local region. The pixels with high "uncertainty" which hardly distinguish the pixels black or white have a lower distortion. In FDM, a steganography based on the changes of the complement, rotation, and mirroring-invariant local texture patterns (crmiLTPs) is proposed. The distortion of flipped pixels is measured by the weight sum of crmiLTPs changes. PDHist constructs pixel density histogram model for halftone images, and embeds the messages through the pixel density transition. In DHSPT, the distortion is measured by the connectivity of master pixels with surrounding slave pixels. PTHVS proposed by Guo [11] considers the weights of pixel connectivity along different directions.

All these steganographic schemes have some parameters, different parameters mean different payloads. In PDM, DHSPT, and PTHVS, l_m represents the length of embedded secret messages. As for FDM, θ_c, θ_J, and θ_m represent the number of elements in cover vectors, the number of superpixel, and the number of message segment, respectively. l_{max} in PDHist means the max length of embedding secret messages.

The steganalysis schemes PMMTM and LargeLTP are introduced above. Local texture pattern (LTP) reflecting the texture property of image is used in LargeLTP, and PMMTM constructs a matrix which represents the second-order of it. For the proposed scheme, grayscale image is reconstructed for steganalysis, which is totally different from PMMTM and LargeLTP. The method of feature extraction of reconstructed grayscale image is selected MaxSRM, SRM, and SPAM which correspond to invh_MaxSRM, invh_SRM, and invh_SPAM. The experimental results are shown in Tables 1, 2, 3, 4, and 5. Among the proposed schemes, invh_MaxSRM outperforms the others. Invh_SRM and invh_SPAM are considered as the baseline of proposed scheme, which also have acceptable performances. When attacking PDM and FDM, invh_MaxSRM outperforms the other steganalysis schemes as shown in Tables 1 and 2. It is shown that the distortion

Table 1. Performance of different steganalysis schemes when attacking PDM [26]

l_m		256	512	768	1024	1280	1536
bpp		0.0039	0.0078	0.0117	0.0156	0.0195	0.0234
P_E	Invh_MaxSRM	**0.3587**	**0.2791**	**0.2164**	**0.1762**	**0.1447**	**0.1216**
	Invh_SRM	0.3918	0.3174	0.2572	0.212	0.1792	0.152
	Invh_SPAM	0.4631	0.4284	0.3976	0.3695	0.3413	0.3167
	PMMTM [5]	0.4458	0.4103	0.3821	0.3484	0.3233	0.3014
	LargeLTP [2]	0.4006	0.3365	0.2741	0.2285	0.1948	0.1623

Table 2. Performance of different steganalysis schemes when attacking FDM [6]

Parameters		$\theta_c = 8^2$ $\theta_\jmath = 5^2$ $\theta_m = 16$	$\theta_c = 8^2$ $\theta_\jmath = 4^2$ $\theta_m = 16$	$\theta_c = 8^2$ $\theta_\jmath = 5^2$ $\theta_m = 8$	$\theta_c = 8^2$ $\theta_\jmath = 3^2$ $\theta_m = 16$	$\theta_c = 8^2$ $\theta_\jmath = 4^2$ $\theta_m = 8$	$\theta_c = 8^2$ $\theta_\jmath = 3^2$ $\theta_m = 8$
bpp		0.0044	0.0078	0.0088	0.0121	0.0156	0.0243
P_E	Invh_MaxSRM	**0.2068**	**0.1417**	**0.1191**	**0.1123**	**0.073**	**0.054**
	Invh_SRM	0.2456	0.1763	0.1501	0.1446	0.0955	0.0731
	Invh_SPAM	0.3919	0.3429	0.3192	0.3135	0.2555	0.2193
	PMMTM [5]	0.3528	0.3099	0.2911	0.274	0.2253	0.1638
	LargeLTP [2]	0.2319	0.2071	0.1898	0.1834	0.1474	0.1022

Table 3. Performance of different steganalysis schemes when attacking DHSPT [9]

l_m		256	512	768	1024	1280	1536
bpp		0.0039	0.0078	0.0117	0.0156	0.0195	0.0234
P_E	Invh_MaxSRM	0.228	0.1123	0.0629	0.0406	0.0278	0.0203
	Invh_SRM	0.2771	0.1543	0.092	0.0595	0.0417	0.0301
	Invh_SPAM	0.3952	0.3105	0.2383	0.181	0.1399	0.1071
	PMMTM [5]	0.1801	0.0736	0.0423	**0.0268**	**0.0164**	**0.0113**
	LargeLTP [2]	**0.1753**	**0.059**	**0.0415**	0.0347	0.0293	0.0243

in the reconstructed grayscale images can still be detected effectively by the proposed scheme. Nevertheless, for the steganographic schemes PDHist, PTHVS, and DHSPT, the proposed scheme can not achieve a good performance, shown in Tables 3, 4, and 5. LargeLTP and PMMTM have a better performance in these steganographic schemes which are without STC. More specifically, the pair pixel toggling in PTHVS and DHSPT are sensitive in PMMTM and LargeLTP. With more embedded secret messages, the performance of invh_MaxSRM is closer to the performance of PMMTM and LargeLTP.

Table 4. Performance of different steganalysis schemes when attacking PTHVS [11]

l_m		256	512	768	1024	1280	1536
bpp		0.0039	0.0078	0.0117	0.0156	0.0195	0.0234
P_E	Invh_MaxSRM	0.1295	0.0488	**0.0259**	**0.0153**	0.0129	0.0089
	Invh_SRM	0.1604	0.0635	0.0337	0.0194	0.0161	0.0116
	Invh_SPAM	0.3622	0.2456	0.1629	0.1075	0.0844	0.0611
	PMMTM [5]	0.0971	0.0589	0.0308	0.017	**0.0114**	**0.0071**
	LargeLTP [2]	**0.0812**	**0.0399**	0.026	0.0177	0.0139	0.0111

Table 5. Performance of different steganalysis schemes when attacking PDHist [19]

l_{max}		256	512	768	1024	1280	1536
bpp		0.0039	0.0078	0.0117	0.0156	0.0195	0.0234
P_E	Invh_MaxSRM	0.3365	0.2411	0.20143	0.1936	0.19403	0.1955
	Invh_SRM	0.368	0.2767	0.234	0.2181	0.2158	0.2151
	Invh_SPAM	0.4539	0.3834	0.3451	0.3208	0.3094	0.3058
	PMMTM [5]	0.3120	0.2666	0.2307	0.217	0.2072	0.2068
	LargeLTP [2]	**0.2712**	**0.1814**	**0.1662**	**0.1643**	**0.1642**	**0.16**

5   Conclusions

In this paper, a new halftone image steganalysis scheme is proposed. Currently, there is almost no halftone image steganalysis scheme. Although the ordinary binary image steganalysis schemes which are based on some special patterns can be also utilized for halftone image, these schemes hardly considered the characteristic of halftoning. Considering the halftoning technique which is based on the low-pass characteristic of HVS, a Gaussian filter is used to reconstruct the grayscale image. The distortions by embedding the secret messages still exist in the reconstructed grayscale image. Then the grayscale image steganalysis schemes including SPAM, SRM, and MaxSRM are considered extracting the features. Many experiments are conducted to compare with other steganalysis schemes. The experiment results show the effectiveness of proposed scheme. More specifically, the grayscale image steganalysis MaxSRM has a satisfied performance. In the future work, we will study more deeply on the procedure of reconstructing grayscale images, which can preserve the embedding changes better. And the steganalysis on these reconstructed grayscale images can be improved.

Acknowledgements. This work is supported by the Key Areas R&D Program of Guangdong (No. 2019B010136002), the National Natural Science Foundation of China (No. U2001202, No. 62072480, No. U1736118), the National Key R&D Program of China (No. 2019QY2202, No. 2019QY(Y)0207), the Key Scientific Research Program of Guangzhou (No. 201804020068).

References

1. Bas, P., Filler, T., Pevný, T.: "Break our steganographic system": the ins and outs of organizing BOSS. In: Filler, T., Pevný, T., Craver, S., Ker, A. (eds.) IH 2011. LNCS, vol. 6958, pp. 59–70. Springer, Heidelberg (2011). https://doi.org/10.1007/978-3-642-24178-9_5
2. Chen, J., Lu, W., Fang, Y., Liu, X., Yeung, Y., Xue, Y.: Binary image steganalysis based on local texture pattern. J. Vis. Commun. Image Represent. **55**, 149–156 (2018)
3. Cortes, C., Vapnik, V.: Support-vector networks. Mach. Learn. **20**(3), 273–297 (1995). https://doi.org/10.1007/BF00994018
4. Denemark, T., Sedighi, V., Holub, V., Cogranne, R., Fridrich, J.: Selection-channel-aware rich model for steganalysis of digital images. In: IEEE International Workshop on Information Forensics and Security, pp. 48–53 (2014)
5. Feng, B., Lu, W., Sun, W.: Binary image steganalysis based on pixel mesh Markov transition matrix. J. Vis. Commun. Image Represent. **26**, 284–295 (2015)
6. Feng, B., Lu, W., Sun, W.: Secure binary image steganography based on minimizing the distortion on the texture. IEEE Trans. Inf. Forensics Secur. **10**(2), 243–255 (2015)
7. Floyd, R.W., Steinberg, L.: Adaptive algorithm for spatial greyscale. Proc. SID **17**, 75–77 (1976)
8. Fridrich, J., Kodovsky, J.: Rich models for steganalysis of digital images. IEEE Trans. Inf. Forensics Secur. **7**(3), 868–882 (2012)
9. Fu, M.S., Au, O.C.: Data hiding for halftone images. In: Security and Watermarking of Multimedia Contents II, vol. 3971, pp. 228–236. International Society for Optics and Photonics (2000)
10. Fu, M.S., Au, O.C.: Data hiding watermarking for halftone images. IEEE Trans. Image Process. **11**(4), 477–484 (2002)
11. Guo, J.M.: Improved data hiding in halftone images with cooperating pair toggling human visual system. Int. J. Imaging Syst. Technol. **17**(6), 328–332 (2007)
12. Guo, J.M., Liu, Y.F., Chang, J.Y.: High efficient direct binary search using multiple lookup tables. In: 19th IEEE International Conference on Image Processing, pp. 813–816. IEEE (2012)
13. Kodovsky, J., Fridrich, J., Holub, V.: Ensemble classifiers for steganalysis of digital media. IEEE Trans. Inf. Forensics Secur. **7**(2), 432–444 (2011)
14. Kodovský, J., Pevný, T., Fridrich, J.: Modern steganalysis can detect YASS. In: Media Forensics and Security II, vol. 7541. International Society for Optics and Photonics (2010)
15. Lin, C., Lu, W., Huang, X., Liu, K., Sun, W., Lin, H.: Region duplication detection based on hybrid feature and evaluative clustering. Multimedia Tools Appl. **78**(15), 20739–20763 (2019). https://doi.org/10.1007/s11042-019-7342-9
16. Liu, X., Lu, W., Zhang, Q., Huang, J., Shi, Y.Q.: Downscaling factor estimation on pre-jpeg compressed images. IEEE Trans. Circ. Syst. Video Technol. **30**(3), 618–631 (2020)
17. Liu, Y.F., Guo, J.M.: Dot-diffused halftoning with improved homogeneity. IEEE Trans. Image Process. **24**(11), 4581–4591 (2015)
18. Lu, W., He, L., Yeung, Y., Xue, Y., Liu, H., Feng, B.: Secure binary image steganography based on fused distortion measurement. IEEE Trans. Circ. Syst. Video Technol. **29**(6), 1608–1618 (2019)

19. Lu, W., Xue, Y., Yeung, Y., Liu, H., Huang, J., Shi, Y.: Secure halftone image steganography based on pixel density transition. IEEE Trans. Dependable Secure Comput. **18**, 1137–1149 (2019)
20. Mese, M., Vaidyanathan, P.P.: Optimized halftoning using dot diffusion and methods for inverse halftoning. IEEE Trans. Image Process. **9**(4), 691–709 (2000)
21. Pevny, T., Bas, P., Fridrich, J.: Steganalysis by subtractive pixel adjacency matrix. IEEE Trans. Inf. Forensics Secur. **5**(2), 215–224 (2010)
22. Ulichney, R.: Digital Halftoning. MIT Press, Cambridge (1987)
23. Yang, Z.L., Guo, X.Q., Chen, Z.M., Huang, Y.F., Zhang, Y.J.: RNN-stega: linguistic steganography based on recurrent neural networks. IEEE Trans. Inf. Forensics Secur. **14**(5), 1280–1295 (2019)
24. Yang, Z., Wang, K., Li, J., Huang, Y., Zhang, Y.J.: TS-RNN: text steganalysis based on recurrent neural networks. IEEE Sig. Process. Lett. **26**(12), 1743–1747 (2019)
25. Yang, Z., Yang, H., Hu, Y., Huang, Y., Zhang, Y.J.: Real-time steganalysis for stream media based on multi-channel convolutional sliding windows. arXiv preprint arXiv:1902.01286 (2019)
26. Yeung, Y., Lu, W., Xue, Y., Huang, J., Shi, Y.Q.: Secure binary image steganography with distortion measurement based on prediction. IEEE Trans. Circ. Syst. Video Technol. **30**(5), 1423–1434 (2020)
27. Zhou, B., Fang, X.: Improving mid-tone quality of variable-coefficient error diffusion using threshold modulation. In: ACM Transactions on Graphics, vol. 22, pp. 437–444. ACM (2003)

Halftone Image Steganography Based on Minimizing Distortion with Pixel Density Transition

Mujian Yu[1], Junwei Luo[1], Bozhi Xu[1], Guoliang Chen[2], and Wei Lu[1]([✉]) [iD]

[1] School of Computer Science and Engineering, Guangdong Key Laboratory of
Information Security Technology, Ministry of Education Key Laboratory of Machine
Intelligence and Advanced Computing, Sun Yat-sen University,
Guangzhou 510006, China
{yumj8,luojw8}@mail2.sysu.edu.cn, luwei3@mail.sysu.edu.cn
[2] Guangdong Science and Technology Innovation, Monitoring and Research Center,
Guangzhou 510033, China

Abstract. Many advanced halftone steganographic schemes focus only
on the distortion of human visual perception or the distortion according to statistics. In this paper, a halftone image steganography based
on minimizing distortion with density transition is proposed which aims
at utilizing the entropy model and pixel density to resist potential steganalysis. First, the entropy model is established on the image database
to describe the texture content and transformed to the preliminary distortion score map. Because the form of texture presentation is distinct
between halftone images and ordinary binary images, the feature of pixel
density is introduced to represent the local intensity in images. Then the
pixel density transition adjustment based on the entropy model is presented, which makes the distortion score more reliable. The final additive distortion map is generated by combining the entropy model and
the strategy of density transition. To play the advantage of distortion
measurement, syndrome-trellis code (STC) is applied with the distortion map to minimize the embedding distortions. Experimental results
demonstrate that compared with other halftone steganographic schemes,
the proposed method achieves high statistical security and great visual
quality with considerable embedding capacity.

Keywords: Halftone image steganography · Entropy model · Pixel
density transition · Syndrome-trellis code

1 Introduction

Data hiding is a scientific field integrating multiple studies and technologies.
As a branch of that, steganography aims at embedding secret messages into
host media such that only the sender and receiver can detect the existence of
the messages. Therefore, instead of fragileness, robustness or integrity of the

© Springer Nature Switzerland AG 2021
X. Sun et al. (Eds.): ICAIS 2021, LNCS 12737, pp. 424–436, 2021.
https://doi.org/10.1007/978-3-030-78612-0_34

host media, the imperceptibility, statistical security and capacity are taken into consideration in steganography.

Digital images are widely used in steganography because they are important and common in daily life, and as one kind of the host image media [1,6,22,23,33], binary images play a significant role as carriers of the steganography [5,8,10,26, 27,31,32]. Unlike grayscale images using 8 bit per pixel or RGB images using 24 bits per pixel, binary images require only 1 bit per pixel to present the image information, which need less storage space. Compared with modifying pixel value by ±1 in grayscale images, the unique embedding operation in binary images is flipping the pixel from '0' to '1' or from '1' to '0'. Since binary images' color is only constructed by black and white, flipping operations will cause more obvious distortion on visual quality and statistics and thus the embedding payload of cover images is limited when hiding information in binary images.

Binary images can be divided into ordinary binary images and halftone images according to the image binarization methods. Ordinary binary images usually adopt the edge lines to express the contents while halftone images simulate the grayscale effect of the continuous-tone images through the average pixel density of local regions when viewed at a certain distance by human eyes. This phenomenon depends on the low-pass filtering effect of the human visual system (HVS) [18]. For transforming continuous-tone images to halftone images, many halftoning methods [30] have been proposed, and the several popular ones are ordered dithering [3], error diffusion [19,29], dot diffusion [21] and direct binary search [20]. Based on when the secret messages are embedded into cover images, halftone steganographic schemes can be divided into 2 types. One carries out the steganography when the original images is converted to halftone images while the other one embeds the message on the generated halftone images. The first one can reach a high embedding capacity and great visual quality but it must analyze the original grayscale image and the halftoning methods which is not guaranteed in the embedding procedure. In daily life, the original images are usually missing. Even the grayscale images and the halftoning methods are learned, the security of the stego images can not be promised because there are other relative condition transformed in the common channel. From the perspective of university, our scheme focuses on the second type.

In recent years, some steganography schemes for ordinary binary images or halftone images are proposed. Fu et al. [15] proposed a straightforward data-hiding scheme called the Data Hiding Self Toggling (DHST). DHST [15] identifies a set of predefined pseudo-random locations and toggles pixels at the locations according to the secret messages. The random locations will decrease the visual quality dramatically for the reason that it never pays attention to the image content or the adjacent pixels. To improve the scheme, Fu et al. [14] proposed a method taking the pixel and its neighboring complementary pixel into consideration. If the pixel needs to be flipped, both pixels will be flipped simultaneously to maintain the average intensity of local regions. Yeung et al. [32] proposed a method called prediction distortion measure (PDM) which established a prediction model for ordinary binary images to represent the texture statistics. Based on that, Liu et al. [24]

consider both the statistic security and the HVS model, proposing the pair swapping (PS) scheme for halftone images. Lu et al. [27] pay more attention to the pixel density transition (PDT) in halftone images and design a pixel selecting strategy to locate the best position for embedding.

In this paper, a halftone steganography scheme based on minimizing distortion with density transition is proposed. To resist steganalyzers, an entropy model which makes a statistic for unit blocks is utilized to describe the uncertainty of different texture contents. In halftone images, the pixel density is as important as texture that can not be embodied in the entropy model [27]. Therefore, several blocks containing the center pixel is employed to generate the sum of density transition when the center pixel is flipped. Finally, the entropy model is combined with the density transition strategy and the result is converted into the distortion map corresponding to all pixels in a halftone image. The additive distortion map is used for embedding in syndrome-trellis code (STC) [11], which utilizes convolutional code with a Viterbi algorithm-based encoder to find a better path in an image for embedding secret messages and minimizing the image distortion. Synthesizing the features on the whole image database as well as a single image, the proposed scheme makes use of texture statistics and the pixel density in halftone images. The experimental results demonstrate that the proposed steganography scheme achieves high statistical security and great visual quality.

The rest of this paper is organized as follows. The entropy model and the strategy of density transition adjustment are presented in Sect. 2. The framework of the whole steganographic scheme is introduced in Sect. 3. Section 4 discusses the comparison experiments and results which proves that our method achieves high statistical security and great visual quality. Finally, conclusions are given in Sect. 5.

2   Entropy Model and Density Transition Adjustment

2.1   The Entropy Model on Halftone Images

Texture is a visual feature that reflects the homogeneity phenomenon in the image. It reflects the organization and arrangement of surface structure with slow or periodic variation. In grayscale images, the texture feature extraction methods based on statistics generally include gray level co-occurrence matrix, gray-scale travel statistics, gray-scale difference statistics, local gray-scale statistics and so on. However, in binary images, the texture representation is weaker than that in gray images because of the less bit planes, which means the statistic model mentioned above cannot be applied. Yeung et al. [32] establish an entropy model of the center pixel value in a 3 × 3 local region for ordinary binary image. Since the methods also reflect the statistics and relative characteristics of halftone images, the model based on the image database for ordinary binary images can be applied to halftone images.

Specifically, the local texture patterns (LTP) with size of 3 × 3 is introduced to express the texture structure. Pixels in each position in a block will be marked.

Let T denotes the texture of a block, which is defined as

$$T = \sum_{k=1}^{8} 2^k I_k \tag{1}$$

where $I_k \in \{0,1\}, k = 1,2...,8$ denotes the surrounding pixels and I_0 denotes the center pixel in a block. Black pixel value is assigned with '1' and the white one is assigned with '0'. T denotes the surrounding pixels' texture structure and it ranges from 0 to 511. On the condition that T is known, the probability of the center pixel is defined as follow:

$$p_0 = P\{c = 0|T = t\} \tag{2}$$

$$p_1 = P\{c = 1|T = t\} \tag{3}$$

where t is a specific example of T and c is the center pixel's value. p_0 and p_1 are the probabilities of whether the center pixel value is black or white and their sum is equal to 1. The closer the p_0 and the p_1 are, the more difficultly the center pixel value is judged according to the surrounding pixel texture. Thus, the information entropy is introduced as

$$H(c|T = t) = -[p_0 \log_2(p_0) + p_1 \log_2(p_1)] \tag{4}$$

When p_0 and p_1 are closer, H is larger, ranging from 0 to 1. Besides, the model should be expanded to multiple LTPs because there are inevitable effects between the center block and the neighboring blocks including the flipping pixel. There are four adjacent regions eventually taken to consideration because the correlations between neighboring pixels in the horizontal/vertical directions are usually judged stronger than those between neighboring pixels in the major/minor diagonal directions [9,12,25]. Therefore, the calculation of H is obtained by the conditional entropy, which is defined as

$$H(c) = \sum_{T_k \in \{T_U, T_D, T_L, T_R\}} H(c|T, T_k)/4 \tag{5}$$

where T_k denotes the LTP on the four directions. Then the entropy results are converted to distortion score. The flipping distortion score of a center pixel is denoted as

$$D(c_{i,j}) = 1 - H(c_{i,j}) \tag{6}$$

where $c_{i,j}$ is the pixel located on (i,j) in an image.

2.2 Density Transition Adjustment Based on the Entropy Model

Although the entropy model has described the texture structure and got high statistic security in ordinary binary images, it is inappropriate to apply it directly in halftone images. Texture contents are represented by edge lines in ordinary images where the smoothness and connectivity play an important role. While

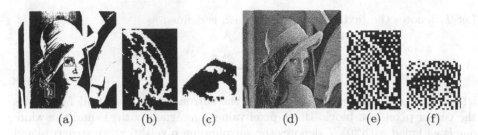

Fig. 1. Differences between the ordinary binary images and the halftone image. (a) and (d) are the ordinary binary image and halftone image of "Lena" respectively. (b) and (e) are the corresponding magnified red regions while (c) and (f) are the corresponding blue regions in (a) and (d) respectively. (Color figure online)

in halftone images, texture information is different from that in ordinary binary images. To simulate the continuous-tone images, halftone images focus on the average intensity of a local region instead of single pixel value [13,14,27]. When people are at a certain distance, due to the human low-pass filtered visual system, halftone images are usually regarded as grayscale images. As shown in Fig. 1, ordinary binary images maintain connectivity and smoothness of edge lines to construct the texture contents. But there is no the concept of edge lines in halftone images. Instead, the intensity of local area block is applied to simulate the gray level in grayscale images. Regions are irregular and noisy when we closely observe the halftone images.

Pixel density is a significant characteristic of halftone image blocks [27], which describes the intensity of blocks to some extent. The white pixel density is widely used in [4,28], which is defined as the ratio of white pixels to black pixels in a block. For the reason that black pixels usually have greater visual impact than white pixels in halftone images [27], the amount of black pixels in a block is defined as the block pixel density, which is replaced by pixel density in the following.

For a pixel in an image, the surrounding blocks which contain the pixel should be considered simultaneously because the embedding operation also influences the neighboring regions. The block size is fixed as 3×3 which is the same size as that in the entropy model construction. Apparently, the pixel density of a 3×3 block ranges from 0 to 9. As shown in Fig. 2, there are 9 surrounding blocks in total, from the top left to the bottom right, containing a marked red center pixel which locates on 9 different positions in different blocks respectively. In this method, the difference between the number of block with pixel density k in the 5×5 region is defined as

$$N_k = |n_k^{pre} - n_k^{after}| \tag{7}$$

where n_k^{pre} is the number of the block with pixel density k before flipping the red marked pixel and n_k^{after} is the one after flipping the red marked pixel. $| \bullet |$ is the absolute value operation.

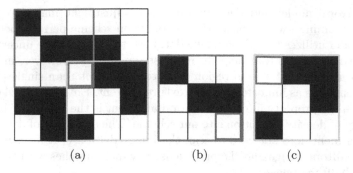

Fig. 2. An example when obtaining the sum of density transition. (a) The whole region including the flipping pixel. (b) The top left blocks including the flipping pixel. (c) The bottom right blocks including the flipping pixel. The pixel in red block is the flipping pixel which is contained by totally 9 surrounding blocks. The Block marked by blue and that marked by yellow are the top left one and right bottom one respectively. In this example, the sum of density transition is 12. (Color figure online)

Taking the top left block as an example, when the center pixel is flipped, the pixel density of this block changes from 3 to 4 which states that the flipping operation introduces 2 transformations in total: the amount of blocks with pixel density 3 is decreased by 1 and the amount of blocks with pixel density 4 is increased by 1. This calculation will be extended to other surrounding blocks and then the practical density transition is obtained as the adjustment scale. It is worth mentioning that despite there is 2 density changing for a single block, the final sum of density transition is not necessarily 18 for 9 surrounding blocks. For instance, considering the top left block and the bottom right block together, the sum of pixel density transition in the two blocks is not 4 but 2: the amount of blocks with pixel density 3 is decreased by 1 and the amount of blocks with pixel density 5 is increased by 1 while there is no change in the amount of blocks with pixel density 4. Therefore, the density transition adjustment scale for a pixel is defined as

$$S(c_{i,j}) = \sum_{k=0}^{9} N_k/18 \tag{8}$$

where $c_{i,j}$ is the center pixel located on (i, j) in an image. As shown in Fig. 2, the total sum of density transition is 12: the amount of blocks with pixel density 3 is decreased by 1; the amount of blocks with pixel density 4 is decreased by 5; the amount of blocks with pixel density 5 is increased by 4 and the amount of blocks with pixel density 6 is increased by 2. Therefore, its adjustment scale is 2/3. Based on the adjustment scale, the flipping distortion obtained by Eq. (6) is modified and the final distortion score is defined as

$$D'(c_{i,j}) = D(c_{i,j}) \times S(c_{i,j}) \tag{9}$$

The lower the distortion score is, the less distortion is caused when the corresponding pixel is flipped.

The entropy model and density transition adjustment make up for each other's shortcomings, which makes the combination scheme perform better. The entropy model utilizes the whole image database to generate the uncertainty of different texture blocks that helps to resist steganalyzers. However, in halftone images, the intensity of a local region is more significant than single pixel and the pixel density is as important as the texture content. Entropy model does not take the density property into consideration and that is the reason we introduce the strategy of density transition into our scheme. The operation of density transition adjustment does not need to scan the image database. It focuses more on the single halftone image and the pixel density, which matches with the characteristics of halftone images.

3   The Framework of the Proposed Method

The framework of the proposed steganographic scheme is discussed in this section and the embedding and extraction procedures will be presented in detail.

3.1   STC-Based Embedding

STC is proposed by Filler et al. [11], which adopts matrix embedding to achieve high embedding capacity with additive distortion which find a path that the distortion caused by flipping pixels is as less as possible. When utilizing STC to embed the secret messages, the additive distortion is arbitrary that the main task for us in the proposed scheme is to design the reliable distortion score maps for images. Distortion map D' according to Eq. (9) will be employed in STC encoder to generate bitstream with the lowest distortion.

3.2   Embedding Procedure

For a given cover halftone image $\mathbf{X}$ and the secret message sequence $\mathbf{M}$, the embedding procedure includes the following steps:

1. Scan the whole image database, generate the entropy model and obtain the preliminary score D for $\mathbf{X}$ according to Eq. (6);
2. Calculate the density transition adjustment map S by Eq. (8) and then generate the final distortion map D' by Eq. (9);
3. Reshape $\mathbf{X}$ and D' into two one-dimensional vectors, $V_{\mathbf{X}}$ and $V_{D'}$, with the same random scrambling seed $\mathbf{r}$;
4. Apply the STC encoder with $V_{\mathbf{X}}$, $V_{D'}$ and $\mathbf{M}$ to generate the stego vector $V_{\mathbf{Y}}$;
5. Descramble and reshape $V_{\mathbf{Y}}$ into the same size as $\mathbf{X}$, then obtain the stego image $\mathbf{Y}$.

3.3   Extraction Procedure

For a given stego image **Y**, the length of the embedded message l and the same random scrambling seed **r** used in the embedding procedure, the extraction procedure contains the following steps:

1. Reshape **Y** into a one-dimensional vector V_Y with the random scrambling seed **r**;
2. Employ the STC decoder with V_Y and l to generate the secret message **M**.

4   Experimental Results

In this section, the halftone image database will be introduced in Sect. 4.1. To reach the imperceptibility, a steganography should guarantee the visual quality and statistical security. The former one promise that the stego image can not be observed by human visual system, and the latter one is employed to judge the secure performance when the stego image is attacked by the steganalyzers. Thus the experiment results including the visual quality and statistic security are presented in Sect. 4.2 and Sect. 4.3 respectively, which shows the performance of the proposed scheme compared to other steganographic schemes in halftone images.

4.1   Experimental Conditions

The halftone images dataset is converted from 9000 grayscale images in BossBase-1.01 [2] by Floyd error diffusion-based method [29]. The other 1000 images in BossBase-1.01 are abandoned because in these halftone images, there are many uniform regions which are unsuitable for embedding. All the images in halftone images database are resized to 256 × 256.

Some state-of-the-art halftone images steganographic schemes presented in DHSPT [13], PTHVS [16], PS [24], PDT [27] are employed to compare with the proposed scheme. DHSPT [13] selects the master pixel and slave pixel for embedding which tends to preserve the local intensity. PTHVS [16] improves DHSPT and expands the local region to measure the candidate slave pixels from the perspective of visual distortion. PS [24] focuses on the human visual system to designs a pair swapping scheme based on prediction model. PDT [27] finds the blocks with medium pixel density where it utilizes PMMTM [9] to choose the best pixel flipping position.

4.2   Comparison of Visual Quality

Different from ordinary binary images, halftone images have various complex textures. To simulate the corresponding grayscale image through the low-pass filter effect on human visual system, a halftone image contains regular texture content and irregular texture content. For intuitively showing the steganography modification, a nature image with 1024 bits messages embedded as is taken as

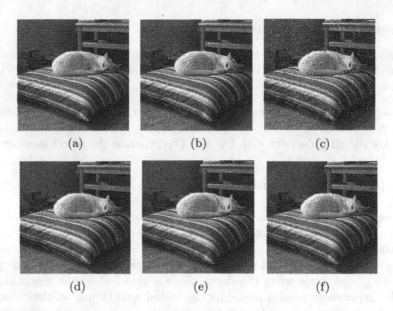

Fig. 3. Halftone Image visual quality comparisons of different steganographic schemes on an example image. (a) The original halftone image of size 256×256. (b)–(f) are the stego images with messages of 1024 bits embedded by DHSPT [13], PTHVS [16], PS [24], PDT [27] and the proposed scheme.

an example, which is shown in Fig. 3. Except for the stego image generated by PTHVS [16] is visually different from the cover image, there is no obvious noise in the other stego images including the one generated by the proposed scheme, which illustrates our method reach acceptable visual quality.

To further evaluate the visual quality of the stego images, a visual quality assessment method proposed in [13] which is widely used in halftone images [13,17,23] is employed in the comparison experiments. In the assessment method, the quantity and size of the salt-and-pepper clusters are significant measures. The 5 scores, S_1 to S_5, is mainly used to describe the amount of black and white pixels in bright and dark regions. In addition, the scores reflect the clusters of different region types in halftone images. The lower the scores are, the better the visual quality of the halftone images are.

As shown in Table 1, the average scores of the proposed scheme are lowest except for the S_3, which demonstrates that our method reaches greater visual quality in general. It is because that the proposed scheme considers the specific characteristic of the single halftone image. When embedding secret messages, our method will present a distortion map according to the single image, which states that the embedding position is adaptive according to different halftone images. Thus, our method achieves greater visual quality.

Table 1. The comparison of the Average S_1 to S_5 between different halftone stegano-graphic schemes on the halftone image database with 1024 bits messages embedded.

	S_1	S_2	S_3	S_4	S_5
Proposed	**222.9**	**987.4**	3.903	**232.8**	**668.7**
DHSPT [13]	786.9	2432.8	3.107	468.2	1645.9
PTHVS [16]	676.5	2371.5	3.441	533.7	1695.0
PS [24]	331.8	1129.8	3.405	246.2	806.4
PDT [27]	463.2	1346.2	**2.811**	264.0	880.0

4.3 Comparison of Statistical Security

The statistical security is a significant criterion to evaluate the performance of steganographic schemes. The detection performance is measured by the decision error rate P_E which is defined as follow

$$P_E = \frac{1}{2}(P_{FP} + P_{FN}) \tag{10}$$

where P_{FN} is the probabilities of false positive (detecting the cover images as the stego images) and P_{FN} is the probabilities of false negative (detecting the stego images as the cover images) respectively. The larger the P_E, the higher the statistical security of the steganographic scheme.

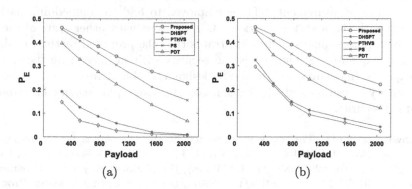

Fig. 4. The statistical security comparisons of different steganographic schemes when attacked by the steganalysis (a) PMMTM-320D [9]. (b) RLCM-1000D [7].

There are many effective steganalysis for halftone steganography. PMMTM-320D [9] captures the dependence on texture structures and RLCM-100D [7] employs the run length and co-occurrence as features. Based on these features, the soft-margin SVMs with an optimized Gaussian kernel are constructed as the steganalyzers.

The statistical security comparisons are averaged over 50 random training/testing divisions (half for training and half for testing) of the halftone image database containing 9000 images. Figure 4(a) and Fig. 4(b) show the experiment results on PMMTM-320D steganalysis [9] and RLCM-100D steganalysis [7] respectively. The proposed method applies the entropy model on the image database, which guarantee the statistical characteristics in steganography. Based on that, we modify the distortion map according to the pixel density transition of the single image. The final additive distortion map fits more for the cover image, which make it more difficult for steganalyzers to distinguish the difference between the cover image and stego image. Therefore, our method achieves high statistical security, and it performs better when the embedding capacity increases because the pixel density transition strategy begins to play its advantages on describing the changes of the single image's texture information.

The experimental results state that compare to other methods, the statistical security of the proposed scheme is higher. With the strategy of density transition adjustment based on the entropy model, our method achieves better visual quality and higher statistical security.

5   Conclusions

In this paper, the characteristic of density in halftone images is proposed to play a significant role as texture contents. Based on the entropy model established on the statistic of the image database, the pixel density transition adjustment on the single image is presented, which is utilized for adjusting the distortion score generated by the entropy model. For further taking the advantage of additive distortion measurement, STC is employed to find the embedding path in an image with the lowest distortions. Comparisons with other state-of-the-art halftone steganographic schemes illustrates that the proposed method achieves great visual quality and high statistical security without decreasing the embedding capacity. In future work, we aim to design a reliable strategy to describe the pixel density transition and a halftone image steganographic scheme for stronger statistical security.

Acknowledgements. This work is supported by the Key Areas R&D Program of Guangdong (No. 2019B010136002), the National Natural Science Foundation of China (No. U2001202, No. 62072480, No. U1736118), the National Key R&D Program of China (No. 2019QY2202, No. 2019QY(Y)0207), the Key Scientific Research Program of Guangzhou (No. 201804020068).

References

1. Arham, A., Nugroho, H.A., Adji, T.B.: Multiple layer data hiding scheme based on difference expansion of quad. Signal Process. **137**, 52–62 (2017)
2. Bas, P., Filler, T., Pevný, T.: "Break our steganographic system": the ins and outs of organizing BOSS. In: Filler, T., Pevný, T., Craver, S., Ker, A. (eds.) IH 2011. LNCS, vol. 6958, pp. 59–70. Springer, Heidelberg (2011). https://doi.org/10.1007/978-3-642-24178-9_5

3. Bayer, B.E.: An optimum method for two-level rendition of continuous tone pictures. In: IEEE International Conference on Communications, vol. 26 (1973)
4. Burrus, N., Bernard, T.M.: Adaptive vision leveraging digital retinas: extracting meaningful segments. In: Blanc-Talon, J., Philips, W., Popescu, D., Scheunders, P. (eds.) ACIVS 2006. LNCS, vol. 4179, pp. 220–231. Springer, Heidelberg (2006). https://doi.org/10.1007/11864349_20
5. Cao, H., Kot, A.C.: On establishing edge adaptive grid for bilevel image data hiding. IEEE Trans. Inf. Forensics Secur. 8(9), 1508–1518 (2013)
6. Cheddad, A., Condell, J., Curran, K., Mc Kevitt, P.: Digital image steganography: Survey and analysis of current methods. Signal Process. 90(3), 727–752 (2010)
7. Chiew, K.L., Pieprzyk, J.: Binary image steganographic techniques classification based on multi-class Steganalysis. In: Kwak, J., Deng, R.H., Won, Y., Wang, G. (eds.) ISPEC 2010. LNCS, vol. 6047, pp. 341–358. Springer, Heidelberg (2010). https://doi.org/10.1007/978-3-642-12827-1_25
8. Feng, B., Lu, W., Sun, W.: High capacity data hiding scheme for binary images based on minimizing flipping distortion. In: Shi, Y.Q., Kim, H.-J., Pérez-González, F. (eds.) IWDW 2013. LNCS, vol. 8389, pp. 514–528. Springer, Heidelberg (2014). https://doi.org/10.1007/978-3-662-43886-2_37
9. Feng, B., Lu, W., Sun, W.: Binary image Steganalysis based on pixel mesh Markov transition matrix. J. Vis. Commun. Image Represent. 26, 284–295 (2015)
10. Feng, B., Lu, W., Sun, W.: Secure binary image steganography based on minimizing the distortion on the texture. IEEE Trans. Inf. Forensics Secur. 10(2), 243–255 (2015)
11. Filler, T., Judas, J., Fridrich, J.: Minimizing additive distortion in steganography using syndrome-trellis codes. IEEE Trans. Inf. Forensics Secur. 6(3), 920–935 (2011)
12. Fridrich, J., Kodovsky, J.: Rich models for Steganalysis of digital images. IEEE Trans. Inf. Forensics Secur. 7(3), 868–882 (2012)
13. Fu, M.S., Au, O.C.: Halftone image data hiding with intensity selection and connection selection. Signal Proces. Image Commun. 16(10), 909–930 (2001)
14. Fu, M.S., Au, O.C.: Data hiding watermarking for halftone images. IEEE Trans. Image Process. 11(4), 477–484 (2002)
15. Fu, M.S., Au, O.C.: Data hiding for halftone images. In: Security and Watermarking of Multimedia Contents II, vol. 3971, pp. 228–236. International Society for Optics and Photonics (2000)
16. Guo, J.M.: Improved data hiding in halftone images with cooperating pair toggling human visual system. Int. J. Imaging Syst. Technol. 17(6), 328–332 (2007)
17. Guo, M., Zhang, H.: High capacity data hiding for halftone image authentication. In: Shi, Y.Q., Kim, H.-J., Pérez-González, F. (eds.) IWDW 2012. LNCS, vol. 7809, pp. 156–168. Springer, Heidelberg (2013). https://doi.org/10.1007/978-3-642-40099-5_14
18. Guo, Y., Au, O.C., Wang, R., Fang, L., Cao, X.: Halftone image watermarking by content aware double-sided embedding error diffusion. IEEE Trans. Image Process. 27(7), 3387–3402 (2018)
19. Jarvis, J.F., Judice, C.N., Ninke, W.: A survey of techniques for the display of continuous tone pictures on bilevel displays. Comput. Graphics Image Process. 5(1), 13–40 (1976)
20. Kim, S.H., Allebach, J.P.: Impact of HVS models on model-based halftoning. IEEE Trans. Image Process. 11(3), 258–269 (2002)
21. Knuth, D.E.: Digital halftones by dot diffusion. ACM Trans. Graph. 6(4), 245–273 (1987)

22. Liao, X., Qin, Z., Ding, L.: Data embedding in digital images using critical functions. Signal Proces. Image Commun. **58**, 146–156 (2017)
23. Lien, B.K., Lan, Z.L.: Improved halftone data hiding scheme using Hilbert curve neighborhood toggling. In: Seventh International Conference on Intelligent Information Hiding and Multimedia Signal Processing, pp. 73–76. IEEE (2011)
24. Liu, W., et al.: Secure halftone image steganography with minimizing the distortion on pair swapping. Signal Process. **167**, 107287 (2020)
25. Lu, H., Kot, A.C., Shi, Y.Q.: Distance-reciprocal distortion measure for binary document images. IEEE Signal Process. Lett. **11**(2), 228–231 (2004)
26. Lu, W., He, L., Yeung, Y., Xue, Y., Liu, H., Feng, B.: Secure binary image steganography based on fused distortion measurement. IEEE Trans. Circuits Syst. Video Technol. **29**(6), 1608–1618 (2019)
27. Lu, W., Xue, Y., Yeung, Y., Liu, H., Huang, J., Shi, Y.: Secure halftone image steganography based on pixel density transition. IEEE Trans. Dependable Secure Comput. (2019). https://doi.org/10.1109/TDSC.2019.2933621
28. Ren, Y., Liu, F., Lin, D., Feng, R., Wang, W.: A new construction of tagged visual cryptography scheme. In: Shi, Y.-Q., Kim, H.J., Pérez-González, F., Echizen, I. (eds.) IWDW 2015. LNCS, vol. 9569, pp. 433–445. Springer, Cham (2016). https://doi.org/10.1007/978-3-319-31960-5_35
29. Steinberg, R., Floyd, L.: An adaptive algorithm for spatial greyscale. Proc. Soc. **17**, 75–77 (1976)
30. Ulichney, R.: Digital Halftoning. MIT Press, Cambridge (1987)
31. Wu, M., Liu, B.: Data hiding in binary image for authentication and annotation. IEEE Trans. Multimedia **6**(4), 528–538 (2004)
32. Yeung, Y., Lu, W., Xue, Y., Huang, J., Shi, Y.Q.: Secure binary image steganography with distortion measurement based on prediction. IEEE Trans. Circuits Syst. Video Technol. **30**(5), 1423–1434 (2020)
33. Yi, S., Zhou, Y.: Separable and reversible data hiding in encrypted images using parametric binary tree labeling. IEEE Trans. Multimedia **21**(1), 51–64 (2019)

Research and Implementation of Medical Information Protection and Sharing Based on Blockchain

Wei Fang[1,2(✉)], Xuelei Jia[1], and Wei Jia[3]

[1] School of Computer and Software, Engineering Research Center of Digital Forensics, Ministry of Education, Nanjing University of Information Science and Technology, Nanjing, China
Fangwei@nuist.edu.cn
[2] Provincial Key Laboratory for Computer Information Processing Technology, Soochow University, Suzhou, China
[3] Information Center of the Second People's Hospital of Huai'an, Huai'an 223002, China

Abstract. Medical information data is showing massive growth. How to make good use of these medical data and realize data sharing and protection is a hot topic now. Based on the research of traditional medical information system and information security technology, this paper proposes a strategy of combining IPFS, Blockchain and Asymmetric Encryption to realize the protection and sharing of medical information. Since the data on the Blockchain and IPFS are immutable, the operation is traceable, and the encryption operation of Asymmetric Encryption will greatly protect the security of medical information and avoid malicious tampering and malicious denial of medical information problem. For the sharing of medical information, this paper proposes the use of ECC algorithm based on Asymmetric Encryption to realize the sharing of medical records. Through the experiment and test of protection and sharing strategy, we found that the transformation of the traditional medical information system by using Blockchain technology can well realize the security problem of medical information in the process of sharing, and ensure that the information after sharing is safe, credible and not tampered.

Keywords: Blockchain · IPFS · Asymmetric encryption · Sharing · Privacy protection

1 Introduction

At present, there are many challenges to the information sharing between medical institutions and the security of medical information itself [1]. First of all, patients are worried about the security of the shared medical data. After all, it is related to their own private data. Once these data are leaked, the consequences are unimaginable; Secondly, the data receiver will worry about whether the data has been tampered with and what they get is the tampered second-hand information, which will lose the value of the medical data; Finally, the traditional medical information system is only responsible for the maintenance of the medical information data of its own medical treatment. The patient's medical information is stored in the internal database. There is no data exchange with other hospitals. If a patient goes to a strange hospital for medical treatment, It also needs to register for consultation again, which not only repeats consumption, but also wastes time. In order to solve these problems that have existed for a long time and are difficult to solve, this paper designs a scheme for patients to realize data sharing while protecting their data privacy by virtue of the immutable and non-counterfeiting features of Blockchain [2–6] and Asymmetric Encryption technology. Since the Blockchain is a decentralized distributed ledger, and the data in the ledger cannot be changed, the authenticity of medical data is guaranteed first. However, using the Blockchain as a database does not have high storage efficiency. Therefore, this paper uses IPFS to store medical records. Only one Hash code that can be addressed on IPFS is stored on the Blockchain. It can not only improve the performance and storage efficiency of the Blockchain network, but also prevent someone from maliciously stealing data on the chain.

2 Related Work

The advent of Blockchain is destined to have its meaning. As early as 2016, a research team explored the combination of medical information data protection and Blockchain. After summarizing the traditional medical information system in 2016, the Asaph Azaria [7] team proposed the use of Blockchain to manage and control medical information. It was the first attempt of Blockchain in medical information security. The Ekblaw A [8] team implemented a medical management platform based on the Ethereum Blockchain in 2016, which made good use of the advantages of the Blockchain in the medical management platform, but it used Public Blockchain technology.The authorization authentication module was not very good, but it was also a genuine attempt of Blockchain in the field of medical information. The Jianghua liu [9] team analyzed that the medical privacy data in cloud storage may be used by third-party providers, which may lead to the leakage of data privacy. They proposed a ciphertext-based protection mechanism, which was very effective for cloud storage. Researchers such as Xia Qi [10] proposed a Blockchain-based data sharing framework in 2017. This framework was sufficient to solve the challenge of sensitive data access control in the cloud. It was a good way to integrate cloud storage and Blockchain. An attempt to fit together well. Liu Zhen's team [11] designed a Blockchain-based medical information sharing platform in 2020, which enabled cross-hospital authorized sharing of patient diagnosis and treatment information, electronic medical record sharing, and provides two-way referral function. Their design could transmit patient data in real time and achieve a leap from theoretical research of Blockchain technology in the field of medical information to actual projects. After summarizing the achievements and experiences of these scholars in the protection and sharing of medical information, we proposed a set of related technologies such as using Blockchain to protect and share medical information. The following are the techniques used in this article.

2.1 HyperLedger Fabric

Compared with Public Blockchains such as Ethereum, HyperLedger Fabric is a consortium chain that has an authorization mechanism for users to participate in the network, and not everyone can participate in the network. Because Fabric has made a certain transformation to the traditional fully decentralized Blockchain architecture. It provides a CA certification authority to register and review the identity of users who need to join the Fabric network, not anyone can be added to the network. This authentication mechanism also further improves the transaction efficiency of the Blockchain network [12].

2.2 IPFS

IPFS is a global distributed file system. Compared with traditional servers, the storage space is limited and long-term storage is limited. IPFS can make up for these shortcomings. It also incorporates cryptographic technology and can be based on content (file hash). Addressing to obtain the original file data [13].

The advantages of IPFS are as follows:

- Permanent, decentralized storage and sharing of files (storage DHTs in Blockchain mode).
- Peer-to-peer hypermedia: P2P saves various types of data (BitTorrent).
- Versioning: traceability of file modification history (Git-Merkle DAG Merkle Directed Acyclic Graph).
- Content addressable: Identify the file by generating an independent hash value through the content of the file, instead of identifying the location where the file is saved. Only one file with the same content will exist in the system, saving storage space [14].

2.3 Asymmetric Encryption

There are many Asymmetric Encryption algorithms [15], such as RSA, DSA, and ECC. In this paper, we use the ECC algorithm with high security and fast speed.

Asymmetric Encryption algorithm has two important properties. The first is that encryption is two-way. If the public key is used as the encryption key and the private

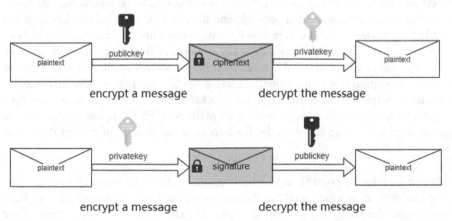

Fig. 1. Encryption and decryption of public and private keys

key is used as the decryption key, then the public key can be used to encrypt multiple pieces of information to obtain ciphertexts, which can only be carried out by the user who holds the private key. In this way, it can be used to encrypt data and communicate privately; it corresponds to signing with a private key and verifying the legitimacy of the signature with a public key.

The use of public and private keys (see Fig. 1).

3 Method

After analyzing the traditional medical information management system (HIS), we found that the medical information between hospitals is not shared, which results in the value of a lot of data not being used well. For example, if a patient is in hospital A, the medical records and other information will be stored in the HIS of hospital A; now the patient has a similar disease, but for some reason he went to hospital B for treatment. Hospital B performed repeated inspections on him, because Hospital B does not know much about the previous medical records, which will lead to repeated inspections and inaccurate and non-targeted analysis of the condition. If you want to use traditional software means to open the database between hospitals, once the database is not properly protected, the database will be leaked, and the patient's personal medical information and private information will be stolen. This will cause unimaginable consequences. How can we protect patients' medical information and share them reasonably?

This paper proposes a combination of Blockchain technology, IPFS and Asymmetric Encryption technology to realize the protection and sharing of medical information.

3.1 Methods of Sharing Medical Information

After adopting safe three-layer protection measures for the protection of medical information, the problem we need to solve is how to share medical information. In the process of sharing medical information, the method we use is Asymmetric Encryption. The premise of sharing is that the public key of each identity has been saved in the Blockchain. These public keys are synchronously uploaded to the Blockchain when the user registers into the Blockchain network, and the corresponding private key is stored securely in each identity device. If patient P wants to share his medical records with hospital B, he only needs to obtain the public key of hospital B from the Blockchain.Then he uses the public key of hospital B to encrypt his own IPFS Hash, and combines the username of hospital B with the ciphertext forms the key and puts it in the Blockchain. At this time, hospital B can retrieve it in the Blockchain according to its username, then decrypt it with its own private key to obtain the plaintext IPFS Hash, and finally perform content-based addressing based on the Hash to view the sharing of patient P Medical record.

- The sender selects a point G on an elliptic curve F(a,b) as the base point.
- The sender chooses a random R2 as the private key, and uses the formula $R1 = R2G$ to calculate the public key corresponding to the private key at the base point of the first step.

- The sender sends the curve F(a,b) and public key R1 to the receiver.
- After the receiver receives the message, it sends the plaintext code to the point M on the curve F (a, b) to generate a random integer r.
- The receiver uses two points C1 and C2. The generating formula of C1, C2 is shown in formula (1) and formula (2).

$$C1 = M + rR1 \tag{1}$$

$$C2 = rG \tag{2}$$

- The receiver sends C1 and C2 to the sender.
- The sender will calculate a formula (3):

$$C1 - R2C2 = m + rR2G - R2rG = M \tag{3}$$

- The sender will get the original plaintext by decrypting M.
  The attacker can only get the curve F(a,b), G, R1, C1, C2, but it is difficult to get M without the private key R2. So it is a good attempt to apply the ECC algorithm to the strategy of sharing medical records.

3.2 Description of the Overall Algorithm Flow

In this section, we will elaborate on the strategies used to protect and share medical information from an object-oriented perspective. In order to simulate the entire medical record protection and sharing process in our model, we set up one patient and two hospitals.

First, patient P, hospital A, and hospital B need to register on the DApp we designed. A pair of public and private key pairs will be generated when registering. The system will form a key-value pair of the user's account and public key into a block. Perform the operation on the chain. The public and private keys here are the key to our medical record sharing.

- Patient P enters the system, selects hospital A for the consultation operation, fills in the relevant medical information. After the doctor in hospital A logs into the system, he will diagnose and treat the condition of the patient who has just been asked for consultation, and return the result to the patient. The corresponding result is saved in the hospital's local database. At the same time, the doctor of hospital A forms the medical record information in the form of key-value (key: hospital name + patient name + patient social security account value: patient's medical record) and saves it in IPFS. IPFS will return a hash address of the medical record. Finally, the doctor of hospital A encrypts the Hash address of the medical record with the public key of patient P, and then performs the packing and chaining operation.
- After patient P completes the operation in hospital A, he can search in the Blockchain ledger based on his username, decrypt the search result with his private key, and view his own medical history.

- If patient P goes to hospital B for a consultation operation, and hospital B asks patient P for historical medical records, patient P can use the public key of hospital B to encrypt the historical medical record Hash and then take accounting operations. After getting the encrypted Hash from the blockchain, the doctor of hospital B can decrypt it with his own private key to obtain the Hash address. According to this Hash address, the patient's medical record can be viewed directly.

The entire process architecture diagram (see Fig. 2).

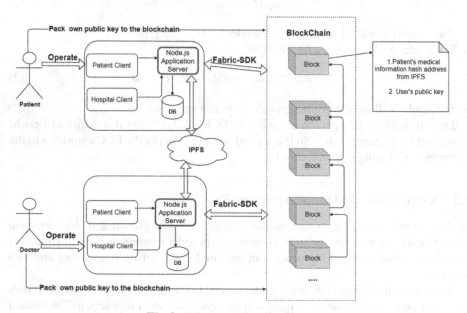

Fig. 2. Whole architecture diagram

3.3 Strategy Statement for Medical Information Protection

There are five main steps to realize the protection of medical information based on IPFS and Blockchain. First, the doctor needs to generate an electronic medical record. The second step is to save the electronic medical records in the hospital's self-built database for easy viewing in the future. The third step is to upload the electronic medical record to IPFS. Because the information on IPFS is unchangeable, medical information is well protected from malicious tampering. The fourth step is that the electronic medical records uploaded to IPFS will return a content-based hash address to the doctor. We all know that content-based Hash encryption, as long as the encrypted content changes, the encrypted hash code will change, so as long as the content is maliciously tampered with, it is impossible to get the content of the medical record with the existing Hash. Moreover, IPFS is not easy to tamper with, so we can safely store medical records in IPFS. The fifth step is to encrypt the returned Hash address with the patient's public key, and then perform the chain operation. At this point, our medical information protection process has been realized. The related steps (see Fig. 3).

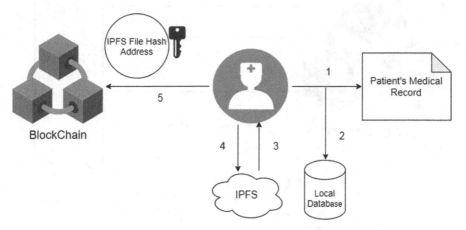

Fig. 3. Description of medical information protection

The steps of case record protection 1–5 in the figure are as follows:

- Diagnosis.
- Put patient's medical record into local database.
- Upload patient's medical record into IPFS.
- IPFS return IPFS file hash address.
- Use patient's public key encrypts the hash and upload it to the Blockchain.

In step 5 of the above figure, we used the public key encryption algorithm in Asymmetric Encryption to encrypt the IPFS address hash, and the implementation is shown in formula (4).

$$encrypt(PK, (hash)) - > encrypted(shash) \tag{4}$$

3.4 Strategies for Sharing Medical Information

In our strategy scenario, we set up one patient and two hospitals (patient P, hospital A, hospital B) in the entire system in order to facilitate the testing of the algorithm process. After the patient consults disease in hospital A, hospital A puts the medical record information to the Blockchain. At this time, the medical record Hash is encrypted and stored in the Blockchain. The patient can decrypt the IPFS hash of his medical record with his own public key. If B wants to view the patient's medical record, the patient can perform an authorization operation, encrypt it with the public key of hospital B, and then perform the chain operation. At this time, hospital B can perform decryption and viewing operations. Detailed description (see Fig. 4).

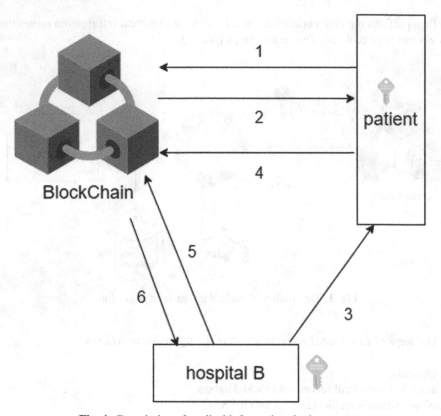

Fig. 4. Description of medical information sharing strategy

The steps for sharing 1–6 in the picture are as follows:

- View your own medical records on the Blockchain.
- Return the encrypted IPFS hash and decrypt it with your own private key.
- Hospital B submits a medical record visit to the patient.
- The patient agrees to the request and encrypts the medical record with the public key of hospital B on the chain.
- View patient's medical records on the Blockchain.
- Return the encrypted IPFS hash and decrypt it with hospital B 's private key.

In the above figure, we used the public key encryption and private key decryption strategy in the Asymmetric Encryption to realize the authorized sharing of medical data. The realization operation is shown in formula (5) (6).

$$encrypt(PKB, (hash)) - > encrypted(shash) \qquad (5)$$

$$decrypt(PrKB, (shash)) - > decrypted(hash) \qquad (6)$$

4   Experiment

4.1   Realization of Medical Information Protection

The key to realize the protection of medical information is to upload the medical record information to IPFS, and then encrypt the returned Hash to the Blockchain. This process is mainly performed on the hospital side. After the doctor enters the patient's name and ID, and the related medical record file, click on the data link operation to complete the medical record upload IPFS and Blockchain network.

In fact, we enter the patient's identity to get the patient's public key from the Blockchain, because the public key information of the identity in our entire Blockchain network is stored in the Blockchain, and we only need to use the user name You can get it.

See Table1 for the pseudo codes related to medical information protection.

Table 1. Pseudo code related to medical information protection

Medical Information Protection
BEGIN
1: GetFileObject->fileobj;
2: Change fileobj to Json;
3: GetFiledetail->filestr;
4: Upload file to IPFS->get IPFS file address hash;
5: Generate key->(hospital-patient-id);
6: Get public key from Fabric Network;
7: Use public key to encrypt IPFS file address hash;
8: Upload
END

The above code is mainly to upload the file to IPFS by getting the object of the local file. At the same time, IPFS will return a Hash, and system get the patient's public key from the Blockchain according to the patient's username. After the encryption process is completed, the encrypted medical record index will be packaged to the Blockchain.

4.2   Realization of Medical Information Sharing

In our strategic scenario, we realized the sharing of medical information between two different hospitals. The patient can first enter his name and ID in his system to form a query key, and then he can call the smart contract for on-chain query. What needs to be explained here is that when we share, we sometimes make some clever specifications on the key value of the information on the chain.

See Table2 for pseudo-codes related to medical information protection algorithms.

Table 2. Pseudo code related to medical information sharing algorithm

Medical information sharing algorithm pseudo code

```
Begin:
    1: get key = patient-id-hospital;
    2: get pubkey from Fabric network;
    3: encrypt(pubkey, IPFS)=>
        Get encode IPFS hash
    4: invoke tx(encode IPFS hash);
    5: if find(hospital) not null then
            Decrypt(privateKey,IPFS hash)
        endif
End
```

After the patient is authorized, we need to login to the client of hospital2 to view the authorized medical record information. We only need to enter the patient's name and ID to view it.

5   Comparison and Analysis

5.1   Comparison of Blockchain Platforms

Compared with Fabric, the Ethereum Blockchain used in Reference [8] does not highlight modularity, but focuses on providing a common platform for various transactions and applications. HyperLedger Fabric and Ethereum have great flexibility in different aspects. Ethereum is a powerful smart contract engine that can basically be used as a universal platform for any type of application. However, the unlicensed operation mode and full transparency of Ethereum comes at the expense of performance scalability and privacy. Fabric adopts an authorized operation mode that uses the PBFT consensus algorithm and fine-grained access control to solve the performance scalability and privacy issues. In addition, Fabric's modular architecture allows it to be customized for many applications. We can compare Fabric to a versatile toolbox. Therefore, we use Hyper-Ledger Fabric instead of Ethereum in the protection strategy of medical information, because Fabric can achieve fine-grained access control to solve the performance expansion and privacy issues. Table3 below summarizes the comparison between HyperLedger Fabric and Ethereum.

In addition, Ethereum's TPS is much lower than HyperLedger Fabric. The maximum number of transactions that can be processed per second in the Fabric network can reach 3000, while Ethereum has only 100, so the advantage of Fabric is very obvious.

5.2   Comparison of Sharing Algorithms

In our strategy for the protection and sharing of medical information, we use the ECC algorithm in Asymmetric Encryption for the sharing of medical information. In the The

Table 3. Comparison of HyperLedger Fabric and Ethereum

	HyperLedger Fabric	Ethereum [8]
Description of platfrom	Universal blockchain platform	Modular blockchain platform
Governance	Linux foundation	Ethereum developers
Currency	None	Ether
Consensus	Pluggable:PBFT	Proof of work
Network	Permissioned	Public or permissioned
State	Key-value database	Account data
Smart contracts	Yes	Yes
TPS	3000	100

most widely used is the RSA algorithm. In the literature [11], the RSA algorithm is used. In this study, we did not use the RSA algorithm. It is not that RSA is not good, but that compared with ECC, RSA has better efficiency and execution speed.

The main advantage of ECC is that in some cases it uses a smaller key (such as RSA) than other methods and provides a comparable or higher level of security [16]. Bilinear mapping has found a large number of applications in cryptography, such as identity-based encryption. However, one disadvantage is that the implementation of encryption and decryption operations takes longer than other mechanisms. ECC is widely regarded as the most powerful asymmetric algorithm for a given key length, so it can be very useful in connections with very tight bandwidth requirements. The comparison between ECC and RSA algorithms is shown in Table 4.

Table 4. Comparison of ECC and RSA

	ECC	RSA [11]
Maturity	Low	High
Security	High	High
Speed	Fast	Slow
Resource consumption	Small	Large

It can be clearly seen from the above table that ECC is significantly better than RSA in terms of speed and resource consumption.

6   Summary

This paper propose a Blockchain-based medical information protection and sharing strategy, using the decentralized, immutable mechanism of Blockchain and IPFS, which protects medical data well. Compared with the traditional storage of data in the cloud,

IPFS is much safer, because IPFS itself is actually a Blockchain. These three processes are like adding three locks to medical information data (IPFS, Asymmetric Encryption, Blockchain).

There are too few organizations and nodes in the Blockchain. There are three organizations, but there are definitely more than three in the actual business needs. Therefore, in the future, it is necessary to configure the organizations in the Blockchain to increase the traffic speed. Finally, there is the issue of encryption algorithms. We consider using the RSA and ECC random encryption strategy for encryption [17], and randomly select encryption algorithms for encryption before encryption. After plaintext encryption, the user inserts the selection code and other useful information into the original ciphertext bit by bit. This greatly increases the difficulty of decryption without the attacker knowing the encryption algorithm. Regardless of whether it is a brute force cracking method or a technical cracking method, even if an attacker obtains the ciphertext, the encryption algorithm cannot be judged, let alone the plaintext.

Acknowledgement. This work was supported by the National Natural Science Foundation of China (Grant No. 42075007), the Open Project of Provincial Key La-boratory for Computer Information Processing Technology under Grant KJS1935, Soochow University, and the Priority Academic Program Development of Jiangsu Higher Education Institutions.

References

1. Tang, H., Tong, N., Ouyang, J.: Medical images sharing system based on blockchain and smart contract of credit scores. In: 2018 1st IEEE International Conference on Hot Information-Centric Networking (HotICN), pp. 240–241, Shenzhen (2018)
2. He, P., Yu, G., Zhang, Y.-F., et al.: Survey on blockchain technology and its application prospect. Comput. Sci. (2017)
3. Tschorsch, F., Scheuermann, B.: Bitcoin and beyond: a technical survey on decentralized digital currencies. IEEE Commun. Surv. Tutorials, 2084–2123 (2016)
4. Nakamoto, S.: Bitcoin: a peer-to-peer electronic cash system (2009)
5. Fang, W., Pang, L., Yi, W.: Survey on the application of deep reinforcement learning in image processing. J. Artif. Intell. **2**(1), 39–58 (2020)
6. Fang, W., Zhang, F., Ding, S.Y., Sheng, T.J.: A new sequential image prediction method based on LSTM and DCGAN. Comput. Mater. Continua **64**(1), 217–231 (2020)
7. Azaria, A., Ekblaw, A., Vieira, T., Lippman, A..: MedRec: using blockchain for medical data access and permission management. In: 2016 2nd International Conference on Open and Big Data (OBD), Vienna, pp. 25–30 (2016)
8. Ekblaw, A., Azaria, A.: MedRec: medical data management on the Blockchain. Viral Commun. (2016)
9. Liu, J., Huang, X., Liu, J.K.: Secure sharing of personal health records in cloud computing: ciphertext-policy attribute-based signcryption. Future Gener. Comput. Syst. **52**, 67–76 (2015)
10. Qi, X., Emmanuel, S., Abla, S., et al.: BBDS:Blockchain-Based data sharing for electronic medical records in cloud environments. Information **8**(2), 44 (2017)
11. Liu, Z., Wang, W.Q.: Design and implementation of medical information sharing platform based on Blockchain. Med. Health Equip. **41**(08), 36–39 (2020)
12. Foschini, L., Gavagna, A., Martuscelli, G., et al.: HyperLedger fabric blockchain: chain-code performance analysis. In: ICC 2020 IEEE International Conference on Communications (ICC). IEEE (2020)

13. Kumar, R.: Implementation of distributed file storage and access framework using IPFS and blockchain. In: 2019 Fifth International Conference on Image Information Processing (ICIIP), pp. 246–251 (2019)
14. Sun, J., Yao, X., Wang, S., et al.: Blockchain-based secure storage and access scheme for electronic medical records in IPFS. IEEE Access **8**, 59389–59401 (2020)
15. Innokentievich, T.P., Vasilevich, M.V.: The evaluation of the cryptographic strength of asymmetric encryption algorithms. In: Russia and Pacific Conference on Computer Technology and Applications, pp. 180–183 (2017)
16. Chen, X.M., Zou, S.H.: A secure mobile payments protocol based on ECC. Software 519–520 (2013)
17. Zhang, S.: Research and design of random encryption scheme based on ECC and RSA. Inner Mongolia University (2015)

IoT Security

LoRa Network Security Schemes Based on RF Fingerprint

Siqing Chen[1], Yu Jiang[1,2(✉)], and Wen Sun[1]

[1] Southeast University, Nanjing, China
jiangyu@seu.edu.cn
[2] Purple Mountain Laboratories, Nanjing, China

Abstract. LoRa is widely used in the IoT due to its advantages of long distance and low power consumption. However, LoRa network has no reliable security scheme currently, making it unable to guarantee communication security. Therefore, based on the uniqueness and tamper-resistance of RF fingerprint, it is proposed to receive RF signals of the LoRa end nodes which request access, extract the fingerprints from it, mark it and match with the customized multi-scale security rules according to demands to decide whether the identities of the LoRa end nodes are safe, taking security measures accordingly. Based on this, our paper improves the original LoRa gateway and LoRa network architecture, designs new workflows, and proposes two LoRa network security schemes. The two LoRa network security schemes proposed in this paper implement identity authentication and access control of the LoRa end nodes from the physical layer. It is only needed to improve the original LoRa gateway in the LoRa network architecture and its workflow, which adds new security measures and guarantees for LoRa applications on the basis of not affecting the original LoRaWAN security mechanism, with no need to modify a huge number of LoRa end nodes. The security schemes we proposed have high practical value.

Keywords: RF fingerprint · Physical layer security · Access control · LoRa gateway · LoRa network security

1 Introduction

With the increasing popularity of Internet of Things (IoT), Low-Power Wide-Area Network (LPWAN) technology with properties of long distance and low power consumption emerges. As a representative of LPWAN, Long Range Radio (LoRa) adopts Chirp Spread Spectrum (CSS) and Forward Error Correction (FEC) coding and decoding technology. The advantages of wide range, long distance, low power consumption and high robustness of communication make LoRa valuable in practical application and widely concerned by domestic and foreign academia and industry [1].

Security is the basic requirement of any communication technology, and LoRa is no exception. LoRaWAN protocol, working in MAC layer, introduces the default security strategy adopted by LoRa [2]. The protocol stipulates that each LoRa end node has

© Springer Nature Switzerland AG 2021
X. Sun et al. (Eds.): ICAIS 2021, LNCS 12737, pp. 453–465, 2021.
https://doi.org/10.1007/978-3-030-78612-0_36

two 128-bit session keys generated by the exclusive AppKey: NwkSKey and AppSKey. NwkSKey is used to confirm the authenticity and integrity of packets in LoRaWAN. AppSKey provides end-to-end encryption to ensure the confidentiality of communication, preventing unauthorized devices from accessing the application data being transferred. In addition, LoRaWAN stipulates that a frame counter must be included in the data packet to prevent replay attacks [3]. Even so, There are still big security risks and loopholes in LoRa communication. It can be seen from the above that keys are the core of the entire LoRaWAN security strategy, which means LoRaWAN security is closely related to these keys and their management. Once attackers obtain these keys, LoRa network will have no secrets at all. In recent years, some studies have also shown that the existing LoRa security schemes lack protection of keys, which makes it easy for attackers to illegally crack LoRaWAN keys. LoRaWAN uses packet counters as input, and the possibility of reusing the keys stream after resetting is very high [4]. Also there is no periodic key update and management mechanism. Keys can only be updated through re-access or manual configuration each time, which is cumbersome and insecure [5]. LoRa end nodes do not have special secure storage module to store keys [6], and keys exchange between its MCU and wireless module can easily be intercepted by external hardware [7]. In addition, attackers can destroy the randomness of keys by adding high-power data packets to the LoRa network [8, 9]. In fact, in a network security system, link layer features such as keys and identities are easy to forge, meaning that security protection only in the data link layer is bound to be risky. End-to-end equipment authentication can effectively solve this problem, but at the same time original equipments must be modified, which prevents it from production practice. LoRa network security still lacks mature schemes.

Radio frequency (RF) fingerprint is the feature information of a RF equipment contained in its RF signal. The internal composition, the layout of the circuit, selection of the components, physical properties and even the aging condition of the RF equipment will cause it to have its own unique nonlinear deviations, which make the signal emitted by the RF equipment contains its unique physical layer (PHY) features [10]. RF fingerprints are unique that even the same batch of equipments produced in the same factory with the same equipment and process have slight differences caused by production standard tolerances, causing differences in RF fingerprints. The uniqueness and tamper-resistance of the RF fingerprint enables it to represent the identity of RF device, to effectively resist attacks such as forgery and tampering and to be a part of the PHY security [11].

This paper solves the identity authentication and access security problem of LoRa end nodes based on the RF fingerprint from PHY. Two LoRa network architecture security schemes with improved LoRa gateways are proposed, providing new thoughts to enhance the security of LoRa network.

2 Security Scheme I: LoRa Gateway Extension

2.1 Fingerprints Extraction

Working in the PHY, RF fingerprints are difficult to clone and tamper. Therefore, the RF fingerprints of LoRa end nodes can be identified and verified to achieve end nodes access control. This method is more secure than traditional wireless network authentication methods. The existing RF fingerprint extraction methods include fingerprint extraction based on transient fingerprint features, steady-state fingerprint features [12, 13], and constellation trace figures [14]. Among them, acquiring transient fingerprint features requires a higher signal-to-noise ratio of the received signal, while acquiring steady-state fingerprint features requires accurate frequency synchronization of the received signal. Acquiring fingerprint features based on constellation trace figures is relatively suitable for fingerprint extraction of LoRa end nodes. Constellation trace figure is a figure that the digital signal is drawn in the complex plane. The horizontal and vertical coordinates of the constellation trace figure are I channel and Q channel respectively. The signal component projected on the I channel is called the in-phase component, while the signal component projected on the Q channel is called the quadrature component. The amplitude and phase information of a digital signal is contained in their constellation trace figure. In digital communication, if the sampling rate of the receiver is higher than the transmitter, draw the oversampled signal in the complex plane so that we can get the constellation trace figure. Over-sampling enables constellation trace figure to display changes of sampling points, reflecting the signal features and their changing law, including many nonlinear deviation factors that cause the uniqueness of the RF fingerprint. Therefore, constellation trace figure can be chose to extract fingerprints. To draw a constellation trace figure, first perform pre-processing operations such as energy normalization on the signal, and then perform differential processing after I/Q delays to eliminate trajectory rotation caused by frequency deviation between transceivers to obtain a stable constellation trace figure.

Constellation trace figures drawn by different signals sent by different LoRa end nodes are not all the same, but trace figures belonging to the same end node are similar. The overall contour and shape of points distribution in the constellation trace figure, the density of the points in each region, etc. are unique with the end node, including the unique RF fingerprint features of each end node. According to the density of regional points distribution, K-means clustering algorithm in pattern recognition is used to calculate cluster centers to extract fingerprints. The specific process is: first evenly divide the drawn constellation trace figure into blocks, assign 1 or 0 to the block according to the number of trace points in each block, and then perform K-means clustering on blocks assigned 1 to obtain a specified number of cluster centers, which are set as one kind of RF fingerprints. Compare two fingerprints and calculate sum of the Euclidean distances between cluster centers of them. When the sum is less than a specified threshold, fingerprints are decided the same and belong to the same end node, otherwise they are decided to belong to different end nodes. The specific process of fingerprint acquisition and decision is shown in Fig. 1.

The number of constellation trace figure blocks, the threshold of 0/1 assignment, the number of cluster centers and the threshold of fingerprints decision are all determined according to specific requirements and type of the LoRa end node actually used. Also, the decision threshold can be improved by continuous training to make the accuracy of the decision results higher.

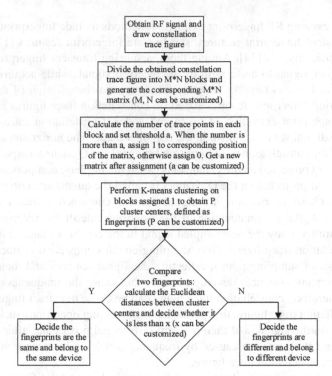

Fig. 1. Flow chart of fingerprint acquisition and discrimination

2.2 LoRa Gateway Extension

The standard LoRa network architecture specified in LoRaWAN protocol consists of four parts: LoRa end node, LoRa gateway, network server and application server, as shown in Fig. 2, in a star topology. LoRa end nodes are mostly sensor nodes composed of sensors. After collecting data, LoRa end node connects with LoRa gateway through single-hop LoRa wireless communication, and transmits data according to the LoRaWAN protocol. LoRaWAN protocol stipulates LoRa network has three working modes: Class A, Class B and Class C [15]. Class A is a necessary basic mode for all LoRa end nodes, which stipulates that end node is only allowed to open two downlink receive windows after each uplink transmission; Class B opens a downlink receive window periodically according to the Beacon sent by LoRa gateway in addition to the two receive windows of Class A; Class C always opens the downlink receive window when there is no uplink demand. Network server works at the MAC layer, relaying messages between LoRa gateway and application server. Also, network server processes messages including security checks, controls and regulates LoRa gateway and the communication network. Application server is the destination of data transmission in LoRa network architecture, manages network according to the data and provides application services.

In the entire LoRa network architecture, LoRa gateways are similar to general gateways, taking the responsibility of relaying and forwarding. LoRa gateway is the relay between LoRa end nodes and the cloud server in the LoRa network, receiving and

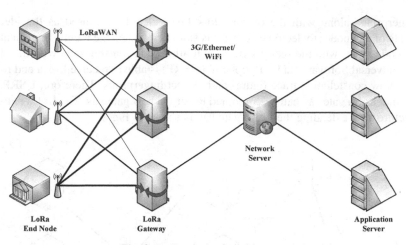

Fig. 2. LoRa network architecture

forwarding the communication data between them. During the whole process, LoRa gateway only converts data between LoRa communication and network communication without performing any additional processing on the data. It can be found from Fig. 2 that all data sent and received by LoRa end nodes must go through LoRa gateway if they want to reach the server. In other words, LoRa gateway is a must pass for data transmission of all LoRa end nodes, so it has the potential to manage communication links, control end nodes access, and maintain network architecture security.

The existing LoRa end node access authentication methods vary with activation methods. LoRaWAN stipulates that LoRa end nodes have two activation methods: Over-the-Air Activation (OTAA) and Activation by Personalization (ABP). In OTAA, a LoRa end node has a key shared only with the application server: AppKey, and two exclusive identifiers: DevEUI and AppEUI. AppKey can be used to generate session keys for encrypted communication: NwkSKey and AppSKey. DevEUI and AppEUI respectively identifies two communication parties: the LoRa end node and the server. LoRa end node performs access authentication based on the above-mentioned key and identifier. After confirming its identity is safe, the LoRa end node is allocated a network address and allowed access to the network. In ABP, LoRa end nodes directly configure keys and address required for secure communication with the specific LoRaWAN network, with no need to confirm identity security by access authentication [16]. However, these two LoRa end nodes access authentication methods have obvious security loopholes. In OTAA, the session key is only updated every time the LoRa end node reconnect to the network. In ABP, the update of the session keys even requires manual intervention by the manager. Failure to have a mechanism for periodic updates greatly increase the possibility of session keys leakage, making session keys lose the role of identity authentication and protecting session security. Also, once session keys are cracked, the content of the session will be exposed to the attacker for a period of time [17]. In summary, it is necessary to introduce a new LoRa end node access authentication method.

In our LoRa network security scheme, RF fingerprints are designed to be made of RF signals sent by LoRa end nodes at the LoRa gateway in the LoRa network architecture.

RF fingerprints, along with the original link layer identity, are used as the identity certificate of end nodes to decide whether it is safe. Only when the identity certificate of an end node meets with the security rules, is it allowed to transmit data with the cloud server. Universal Software Radio Peripheral (USRP) is able to receive LoRa end nodes signals, draw constellation trace figures and extract fingerprints. Therefore, USRP and the original LoRa gateway can be combined to form a new gateway. The LoRa network architecture after extending the LoRa gateway is shown in Fig. 3.

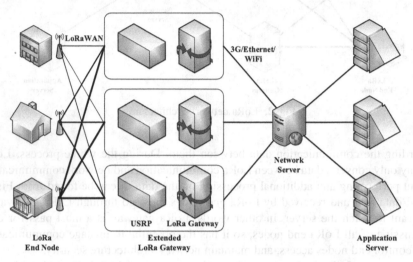

Fig. 3. LoRa network architecture after extending LoRa gateway

Working steps of the new LoRa gateway, which is the original gateway extended with USRP, are as follows:

(1) Store security rules in the original LoRa gateway in advance. The security rules include link layer identities of secure LoRa end nodes and the corresponding fingerprints. If new secure end nodes will access gateway in the future, their link layer identities and fingerprints can be extended to the security rules;

(2) Use USRP to obtain LoRa end node RF signal, extract fingerprint and LoRa end node link layer identity, send them to LoRa gateway together. LoRa gateway binds the end node fingerprint sent by the USRP with the corresponding link layer identity, marking it as a current online end node;

(3) Meanwhile, LoRa gateway also receives the end node signal and parses it into link layer data packets, extracts the link layer identity and compares it with the secure identity in the pre-stored security rules: if there is no matching result, it is decided that this LoRa end node identity is not secure, jump to (5); if it matches, jump to (4);

(4) LoRa gateway matches the link layer identity of LoRa end node it has extracted with the link layer identity sent by USRP, so that the link layer data packet parsed by LoRa gateway is bound to fingerprint. Then compare the fingerprint of this data

packet with the fingerprint corresponding to the link layer identity that matches pre-stored security rules in (3) to decide whether this LoRa end node data packet received by the gateway fully complies with security rules: If it does not match, decide that this LoRa end node is not secure, jump to (5); if it matches, then decide that this LoRa end node is secure, and LoRa gateway can forward the legal data packet to the network server;

LoRa gateway receives the downlink data from network server and parses it into link layer data packets, extracts the link layer identity and matches it with pre-stored security rules to obtain and bind legal end node fingerprint. Compare it with online LoRa end nodes: If fingerprints bound to the corresponding link layer identity do not match, this online LoRa end node with corresponding link layer is decided to be insecure and jump to (5); if it matches, this online LoRa end node is decided to be secure, and LoRa gateway is allowed to forward the network server data packet to the legal LoRa end node;

(5) LoRa gateway blocks data packets from unsafe LoRa end nodes and prevents unsecure LoRa end nodes from continuing accessing gateway.

The working flow chart of LoRa gateway extended with USRP is shown in Fig. 4.

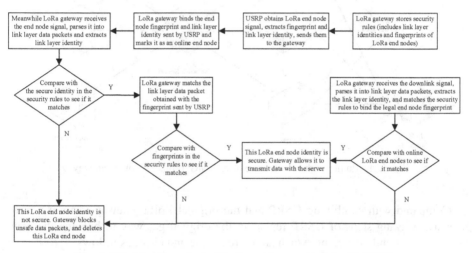

Fig. 4. Working flow chart of LoRa gateway extended with USRP

The new LoRa gateway controls LoRa end nodes access process at the PHY, rejecting requests from unsecure end nodes before their data are uploaded to the server or before the server data go down to end nodes, which greatly reduces hidden dangers. In this scheme LoRa gateway not only is an intermediate point for receiving and forwarding, but also takes important responsibilities in the LoRa network architecture to help maintain LoRa network security.

3 Security Scheme II: LoRa Gateway Replacement

To add RF fingerprint extraction function to the LoRa gateway to control LoRa end nodes access, apart from adding USRP to the LoRa network architecture and combining it with the original LoRa gateway together to form a new gateway, it is also feasible that USRP with the ability to extract fingerprints replaces the original gateway in the LoRa network. Just combining USRP and the original LoRa gateway to do simple addition will lose the simplicity of the original standard LoRa network architecture. USRP has the ability to acquire RF signals and make fingerprints of them, so it can be made to realize the relay and forwarding function of the original LoRa gateway to replace its position in the LoRa network without expanding the scale of the entire architecture. The LoRa network architecture obtained after USRP replaces the original gateway is shown in Fig. 5.

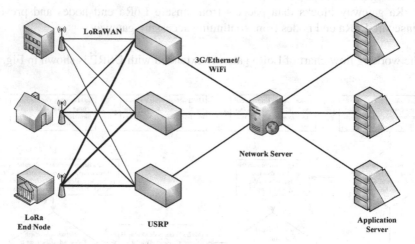

Fig. 5. LoRa network architecture after USRP replaces LoRa gateway

Compared with combining USRP and the original LoRa gateway to form a new gateway, working steps of USRP replacing the original gateway to become the new gateway are slightly different, which are more simple and clear, as follows:

(1) Store security rules in USRP in advance. The security rules include link layer identities of secure LoRa end nodes and the corresponding fingerprints. If new secure end nodes will access USRP in the future, their link layer identities and fingerprints can be extended to the security rules;

(2) Use USRP to obtain LoRa end node RF signal and extract fingerprint of it, parse it into link layer data packets and extract the LoRa end node link layer identity. Bind the end node fingerprint with the corresponding link layer identity, and mark it as a current online end node;

(3) USRP then compares the link layer identity and fingerprint above with the corresponding link layer identity and bound fingerprint in the pre-stored security rules

to determine whether the LoRa end node data packet received by USRP complies with the security rules: if it does not match, decide that this LoRa end node is not secure, jump to (4); if it matches, then decide that this LoRa end node is secure, and USRP can forward the legal data packet to the network server;

USRP receives the downlink data from network server and parses it into link layer data packets, extracts the link layer identity and matches it with pre-stored security rules to obtain and bind legal end node fingerprint. Compare it with online LoRa end nodes: If fingerprints bound to the corresponding link layer identity do not match, this online LoRa end node with corresponding link layer is decided to be insecure and jump to (4); if it matches, this online LoRa end node is decided to be secure, and USRP can forward the network server data packet to the legal LoRa end node;

(4) USRP blocks data packets from unsafe LoRa end nodes and prevents unsecure LoRa end nodes from continuing accessing USRP.

The working flow chart of USRP after replacing the original gateway to become the new LoRa gateway is shown in Fig. 6.

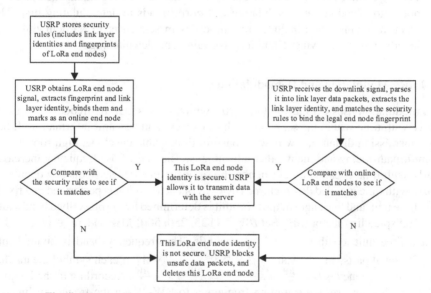

Fig. 6. The working flow chart of USRP after replacing LoRa gateway

Realizing the relay and forwarding function of the original gateway requires the complete realization of the LoRa PHY transceiver chain. Although the technical details of LoRa are proprietary and closed, a large amount of reverse engineering work and the corresponding Software Defined Radio (SDR) implementation in recent years have revealed many important details of the LoRa PHY [18, 19] and create possibilities of reproducing the LoRa PHY transceiver chain. GNU radio, as a partner of the hardware USRP, is an open source software system which can customize radio transceiver and create communication system. This article provides a GNU Radio SDR implementation of the LoRa PHY transceiver chain. It has all the necessary transmitting and receiving components, which enable the USRP to realize the transmitting and receiving of LoRa signals and achieve the purpose of replacing the original LoRa gateway.

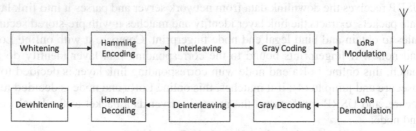

Fig. 7. LoRa PHY transceiver chain

As shown in Fig. 7, the LoRa PHY transmitting chain includes five modules in sequence: whitening, Hamming coding, interleaving, Gray coding and LoRa modulation. The receiving chain corresponds to the opposite of the transmitting chain, encoding first corresponds to decoding last, modulating last corresponds to demodulating first. The LoRa PHY receiving chain includes five modules in sequence: LoRa demodulation, Gray decoding, deinterleaving, Hamming decoding and dewhitening.

3.1 LoRa Modulation and Demodulation

LoRa modulation uses CSS technology [20], which means that the frequency changes linearly with time within the set bandwidth to express and transmit information. It has long transmission distance, low power consumption, stable envelope, high robustness, anti-multipath-fading and many other advantages. The one whose frequency increases linearly with time is called up-chirp, and the opposite one whose frequency decreases linearly with time is called down-chirp. The CSS of each symbol is performed in a fixed-length time unit, and the length of the time unit is determined by the prescribed bandwidth (BW) and spreading factor (SF). Set $BW \in \{125, 250, 500\}$ kHz and $SF \in \{7, \ldots, 12\}$ to get a time unit length of $T_s = \frac{2^{SF}}{BW}$ seconds. The frequency band is divided into $N = 2^{SF}$ equal parts, and the value $s \in S \triangleq \{0, \ldots, N-1\}$ of each symbol means that the starting frequency is $f_s = \frac{BW}{N} * s - \frac{BW}{2} = \frac{BW}{2^{SF}} * s - \frac{BW}{2}$. According to the Nyquist Sampling Theorem, set the sampling frequency to BW. When the frequency linearly rises with time to reach $\frac{BW}{2}$, it will flip to $-\frac{BW}{2}$, and then the frequency continues to rise. A LoRa modulation symbol can be represented as follows:

$$
x_s(t) = \begin{cases} e^{j2\pi(\frac{BW}{2T_s}t^2+(f_s)t)} & 0 \le t \le \frac{2^{SF}-s}{BW} \\ e^{j2\pi(\frac{BW}{2T_s}t^2+(f_s-BW)t)} & \frac{2^{SF}-s}{BW} \le t \le T_s \end{cases} \tag{1}
$$

Its discrete time expression is:

$$
x_s[n] = \begin{cases} e^{j2\pi(\frac{1}{2\cdot2^{SF}}(\frac{BW}{2f_s})^2 n^2+(\frac{s}{2^{SF}}-\frac{1}{2})(\frac{BW}{f_s})n)} & n \in \{0, \ldots, \frac{2^{SF}-s}{BW}f_s - 1\} \\ e^{j2\pi(\frac{1}{2\cdot2^{SF}}(\frac{BW}{2f_s})^2 n^2+(\frac{s}{2^{SF}}-\frac{3}{2})(\frac{BW}{f_s})n)} & n \in \{\frac{2^{SF}-s}{BW}f_s, \ldots, 2^{SF} - 1\} \end{cases} \tag{2}
$$

where f_s is the sampling frequency, $n = t \cdot f_s$. Since $f_s = BW$, the above equation can be simplified to:

$$x_s[n] = e^{j2\pi(\frac{n^2}{2 \cdot 2^{SF}}+(\frac{s}{2^{SF}}-\frac{1}{2})n)} \ n \in S \tag{3}$$

After passing through an Additive White Gaussian Noise (AWGN) channel, the LoRa signal received is given by:

$$y[n] = x_s[n] + z[n] \ n \in S \tag{4}$$

where $z[n] \sim CN(0, \sigma^2)$ is the AWGN. First multiply the received signal with the complex conjugate of the pure up-chirp signal $x_0[n]$ when $s = 0$, then do element-wise vector multiplication between $[y[0] \ldots y[N-1]]$ and $[x_0[0] \ldots x_0[N-1]]^*[0] \ldots x_0[N-1]]^*$, and calculate the DFT of the result as Y, finally estimate the result of LoRa demodulation, that is, the transmission symbol is $\hat{s} = \arg\max_{k \in S}(|Y[k]|)$.

3.2 Other Modules of LoRa PHY Transceiver Chain

Whitening XORs the message sequence with pseudo-random sequence to eliminate the DC bias in the transmitted message. The corresponding coding rate of the basic LoRa whitening matrix is $CR = \frac{4}{8}$, the rightmost column and the two rightmost columns of the basic matrix are removed to obtain the whitening matrix for $CR = \frac{4}{7}$ and $CR = \frac{4}{6}$. However, because the error correction coding technology used by LoRa changes from Hamming coding to parity check coding, for $CR = \frac{4}{5}$ the rightmost column of the whitening matrix was different from the corresponding one of basic whitening matrix. The detailed whitening matrix used by LoRa can be referred to [19]. It can be found that for $CR = \frac{4}{5}$ the parity bit of the matrix is calculated after first four bits are whitened, which means that whitening is the first module in the LoRa transmitting chain.

Error correction coding reduces the influence of channel noise by increasing code word redundancy and improves the robustness of communication transmission. In LoRa, redundancy is controlled by four types of coding rate, namely $CR \in \{\frac{4}{5}, \frac{4}{6}, \frac{4}{7}, \frac{4}{8}\}$. For $CR = \frac{4}{6}, \frac{4}{7}, \frac{4}{8}$, LoRa uses (k,n) Hamming coding, where $k = 4$ is the data length and $n \in \{6, 7, 8\}$ is the codeword length. The codewords of (4,7) Hamming coding and (4,6) Hamming coding are abbreviated versions of (4,8) Hamming coding with 1 bit removed and 2 bits removed respectively. Corresponding to the case of whitening module, the error correction coding technology used by LoRa for $CR = \frac{4}{5}$ is different from the other three types of coding rate. LoRa uses parity check coding instead of (4,5) Hamming coding. The detailed generation matrix and check matrix of error correction coding can be referred to [19].

Interleaving distributes the errors caused by noise and fading on multiple codewords, breaking the correlation between the error bits, thereby providing better anti-noise performance, which is not possible with error-correction coding designed to correct random errors in codewords. The interleaver used by LoRa is a diagonal interleaver, which can disperse a row of the input matrix to the diagonal of the output matrix. The diagonal interleaver used by LoRa can allocate at most SF error bits caused by symbol errors to multiple error correction codewords. Since most codewords only contain one error code, LoRa uses a combination of error correction coding and interleaving to ensure a high correct decoding rate.

Gray coding maps digital symbols into binary sequences. After mapping, binary sequences corresponding to the original adjacent symbols only differ by one bit. This feature is suitable for communication modulation techniques which are prone to have confusion errors between adjacent symbols in transmission. According to this, LoRa uses Gray coding to ensure that when adjacent symbols are confused, only one bit error will be generated after Gray mapping. Error correction coding with $CR = {}^4/_7$ and $CR = {}^4/_8$ can correct one bit error, which is suitable to be combined with Gray coding.

The above is a brief description of several modules of the LoRa PHY transmitting chain that USRP needs to replace the original LoRa gateway. Each module of the receiving chain corresponds to the transmitting chain and has certain similarities, so they won't be repeated here. It should be noted that in the LoRa PHY transceiver chain module on GNU Radio, parameters including SF, CR, BW, etc. can be selected according to needs.

Based on the above, USRP can realize the LoRa PHY transceiver function of the original LoRa gateway. combined with its ability to extract fingerprints from the constellation trace figures, USRP is very suitable as a new gateway to control LoRa end nodes access and is responsible for the security of the LoRa network architecture.

4 Conclusion

This paper aims at the weaknesses of the current LoRa network security scheme to introduce a PHY security concept of RF fingerprint. Based on the USRP ability of extracting RF fingerprints from received signals, the LoRa gateway is improved, and two new LoRa network security schemes are proposed, which are helpful to solve the identity authentication and access security problems of LoRa end nodes. The current security schemes only include two matching rules of link layer identity and RF fingerprint. Later the network layer address, transport layer port, and application layer identifier etc., of the link layer data load can be added to make multiple security standards and security schemes work together, to better protect the LoRa network security. In addition, the fingerprint algorithm and the reverse engineering work of LoRa PHY transceiver chain also need continuing research and improvement to cope with the complex and changeable communication conditions of the IoT, to understand the LoRa technology more effectively and to improve the security scheme pertinently.

Acknowledgement. This work was supported in part by Jiangsu key R & D plan BE2019109, the National Natural Science Foundation of China under Grant 61571110, 61601114, 61602113, 61801115, Natural Science Foundation of Jiangsu Province under Grant BK20160692, Key Laboratory of Computer Network Technology of Jiangsu Province, and Purple Mountain Laboratories (PML).

References

1. Neumann, P., Montavont, J., Noel, T.: Indoor deployment of low-power wide area networks (LPWAN): a LoRaWAN case study. In: IEEE International Conference on Wireless & Mobile Computing. IEEE (2016)
2. Silva, J.D.C., Rodrigues, J.J.P.C., Alberti, A.M., Solic, P., Aquino, A.L.L.: LoRaWAN—a low power WAN protocol for Internet of Things: a review and opportunities. In: International Multidisciplinary Conference on Computer and Energy Science (SpliTech 2017). IEEE (2017)
3. Santamaria, M., Marchiori, A.: Demystifying LoRaWAN security and capacity. In: 2019 29th International Telecommunication Networks and Applications Conference (ITNAC) (2019)
4. Yang, X., Karampatzakis, E., Doerr, C., Kuipers, F.: Security vulnerabilities in LoRaWAN. In: 2018 IEEE/ACM Third International Conference on Internet-of-Things Design and Implementation (IoTDI). IEEE (2018)
5. Sanchez-Iborra, R., Sánchez-Gómez, J., Salvador, P., et al.: Enhancing LoRaWAN security through a lightweight and authenticated key management approach. Sensors 18(6), 1833 (2018)
6. Butun, I., Pereira, N., Gidlund, M.: Security risk analysis of LoRaWAN and future directions. Future Internet 11(1), 3 (2018)
7. Aras, E., Ramachandran, G.S., Lawrence, P., et al.: Exploring the security vulnerabilities of LoRa. In: IEEE International Conference on Cybernetics. IEEE (2017)
8. Basu, D., Gu, T., Mohapatra, P.: Security issues of Low Power Wide Area Networks in the context of LoRa networks. arXiv, 2006 16554 (2020)
9. Chacko, S., Job, D.: Security mechanisms and vulnerabilities in LPWAN. In: 2018 IOP Conference Series: Materials Science and Engineering, vol. 396, p. 012027 (2018)
10. Danev, B., Zanetti, D., Capkun, S.: On physical-layer identification of wireless devices. ACM Comput. Surv. 45(1), 1–29 (2012)
11. Honglin, Y., Aiqun, H.: Fountainhead and uniqueness of RF fingerprint. J. Southeast Univ. 39(2), 230–233 (2009)
12. Frédéric, D., St-Hilaire, M.: Radiometric identification of LTE transmitters. In: Global Communications Conference. IEEE (2014)
13. Romero, H.P., Remley, K.A., Williams, D.F., et al.: Electromagnetic measurements for counterfeit detection of radio frequency identification cards. IEEE Trans. Microw. Theory Tech. 57(5), 1383–1387 (2009)
14. Peng, L.N., Hu, A.Q., Jiang, Y., Yan, Y., Zhu, C.M.: A differential constellation trace figure based device identification method for ZigBee nodes. In: International Conference on Wireless Communications & Signal Processing. IEEE (2016)
15. Cheong, P.S., Bergs, J., Hawinkel, C., et al.: Comparison of LoRaWAN classes and their power consumption. In: IEEE Symposium on Communications and Vehicular Technology (SCVT). IEEE (2017)
16. Behrad, S., Tuffin, S., Bertin, E., et al.: Network access control for the IoT: a comparison between Cellular, Wi-Fi and LoRaWAN. In: 22nd Conference on Innovation in Clouds, Internet and Networks (2019)
17. Sanchez-Iborra, R., Sanchez-Gomez, J., Perez, S., et al.: Internet access for LoRaWAN devices considering security issues. In: Global IoT Summit (GIoTS) (2018)
18. Ghanaatian, R., Afisiadis, O., Cotting, M., et al.: LoRa digital receiver analysis and implementation. arXiv, 1811 04146 (2018)
19. Tapparel, J.: Complete reverse engineering of LoRa physical layer. Technical report (2019). https://tcl.epfl.ch/resources-and-sw/lora-phy/
20. Vangelista, L.: Frequency shift chirp modulation: the LoRa modulation. IEEE Signal Process. Lett. 24(12), 1818–1821 (2017)

Smart Home Based Sleep Disorder Recognition for Ambient Assisted Living

Lulu Zhang, Shiqi Chen, Xuran Jin, and Jie Wan[⊠]

Nantong University, Nantong, China
`jiewan@ntu.edu.cn`

Abstract. As the age profile of many societies continues to increase, supporting health, both mental and physical, is of increasing importance if independent living is to be maintained. Sensing and, ultimately, recognising activities of daily living has been perceived as a prerequisite for detecting tasks that people avoid or find increasingly difficult to perform, as well as being indicators of certain illnesses. To date, extensive research efforts have been made in activity monitoring, recognition and assistance in indoor scenarios, frequently through smart home initiatives. Moreover, certain behaviours and activities may indicate certain disease especially for elderly people, such as sleep disorder. Thus this paper advocates a need for platforms that enable activity monitoring, in particularly, this sleep disorder, in home environment, thereby enabling the construction of more complex yet realistic activity models and behaviours patterns.

Keywords: Activity recognition · Healthcare · Ambient assisted living · Internet of Things (IoT)

1 Introduction

Population ageing is a global phenomenon and challenge; it is not a problem that is constrained to Asia, Europe, but rather affects all nations worldwide. A number of issues are significant contributors, including the decline of the fertility rate, together with a dramatically increased life expectancy. Therefore, along with the growth of the total population, the ratio of the working population to elderly and young population is projected to drop dramatically. In tandem with such demographic changes, another issue is emerging, that of the increasing proportion of people aged 65 and over who are living alone. This has a significant influence on the healthcare system, as some of these people may require 24 h professional healthcare or supervision as they age. A nursing home or hospital may eventually be required. From a technical point of view, AAL solutions embrace a heterogeneous set of disciplines, for example, sensors, microelectronics, human

This work is supported by NanTong Science and Technology Bureau under grant JC2018132 and National Natural Science Foundation of China under grant 62002179 within Nantong University China.

- computer interface, software, networking and so forth, all of which must be integrated into one system that empowers the user-cantered service. In recent years, IoT has been the emerging framework that integrates sensing, networking, data processing, artificial intelligence technologies etc., which has been widely embedded in many real-world scenarios, include healthcare [1]. In terms of activity recognition, machine learning techniques has been widely explored [2], many algorithms have been evaluated, such as SVM, Bayes, Neural Network and so on. Recently, deep learning-based approaches has been proved to be effective in many recognition tasks. Hence, this paper illustrates a home-based activity recognition solution, based upon IoT enabled smart home environment, and utilising learning based techniques. This paper is organised as follow: Sect. 2 discusses existing works, Sect. 3 illustrates a 5G Narrow-band internet of the things enabled sleep activity recognition framework. Then the sleep activity recognition approaches are described in Sect. 4, finally, this paper is concluded in Sect. 5.

2   Related Research

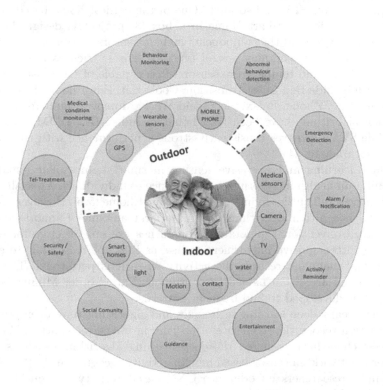

Fig. 1. IoT in healthcare, scenarios and applications

The establishment of the smart environment typically symbolises the procedure of design, identification and installation of a series of sensors, processors, actuators and smart devices. Sensors are the fundamental elements that are created to perceive the information about the environment and its occupiers, as is depicted in Fig. 1. A broad range of sensors are commonly installed. For example, the ambient environmental sensors include light, noise, temperature and so on. Moreover, action sensors are distributed within the home environment to detect action related events, including the magnetic contact sensors, motion sensors (usually of the PIR variety), RFID tags, liquid or water presence sensors and so forth.

In practice, a sensor itself does not provide sufficient memory and computational capacity; consequently, sensor data is often transmitted to a central server for further processing and storage. Sensor data can be transferred via either wired or wireless; the latter is more preferable in most cases. A number of wireless communication protocols have been embedded with many sensing devices. Such as Bluetooth, ZigBee, Wi-Fi, 4G, as well as recently introduced 5G, NB-IoT etc.

Home based activity recognition has been widely explored, many researchers focuses on recognising a number of home based activities, such as cooking, sleeping, eating, watching TV and so forth. One of the earliest home based activity recognition work is the Smart Home in a box [3] project is designed by the CASAS centre, where all the components include sensors, actuators, can be fitted in a small box. It contains several types of sensors such as motion, door, water, item, light, and temperature sensors. It is capable of recognising a set of ADLs, which include Bed-toilet Transition, Cook, Eat, Enter home, Leave home, Personal hygiene, Phone, Relax, Sleep, and Work. Moreover, numerous activity recognition algorithms have been tested that include NBC, HMM, SVM, and CRF, while SVMs achieves consistently stronger performance with the average weighted accuracy at 84%.

Machine learning and pervasive sensing in smart homes offer remarkable opportunities in health monitoring and assistance to individuals, especially those who experiences difficulties living independently at home [5,6]. However, most of the activity recognition algorithms demand a large amount of annotated training samples. Conventional annotation approaches are not effective for elderly and people with cognitive impairment to use, as it is not reasonable to expect the individual manually records the activity when it is performed. Therefore, an unsupervised algorithm named Discontinuous Varied-order Mining Method (DVSM) [4] is developed to find frequent patterns.

In recent years, deep learning techniques and algorithms have been proved in many situation recognition scenarios, especially in image recognition. However, many researchers have explored the deep learning algorithms, such as CNN, deep neural network, in sensor based human activity recognition [10–13]. A typical example, researchers introduced a CNN based activity recognition model utilising wearable sensor data [12].

However, most existing research focuses on the recognition of ADLs that are performed normally, but little attention is paid to the detection of illness and unexpected behaviour [9]. Given the smart home context, the detection of abnormal behaviour intensely relies on the domain knowledge, such as the abnormal time, duration, location and pattern during the occurrence of the ADLs. Some researchers [7] investigated utilising clustering techniques to detect abnormal behaviour, which formalised by three major rules. Firstly, data that reflects the regular or normal behaviour are grouped in clusters, while those data that do not fit in any clusters are treated as anomalies. Secondly, data that is near their closed cluster centroid are considered as normal data, while those located far away from the cluster centroid are measured as abnormal data. Thirdly, data in the large cluster are treated as normal data, while the smaller or sparse cluster may contain anomalies. Moreover, a number of clustering techniques are applied in this work, such as self-organising maps (SOM), K-means clustering and fuzzy C-means (FCM) [8].

Nonetheless, it is often difficult to recognise all type of activities or abnormal activities, hence some researchers focus on recognising very limited number of abnormal activities, such as sleep disorder recognition [14–20]. In order to detect sleeping quality, wearable sensors such as ECG is the most promising option [15,18,20]. As wearable sensors are often perceived as obtrusive where wearing them during the daily life, therefore, some researchers focus on ambient sensor enabled sleeping condition detection, such as utilising the uncontact pressure sensors [14,17]. Moreover, smart phones as the most commonly used devices for individuals daily life, which is also often adopted [16,19]. Therefore, in this paper, we introduced a smart home based activity and sleep disorder recognition approach. We mainly focused on the recognition of sleeping related activities include wake up, go to bed, wake up for toilet during the night sleep, wake up wandering during night sleep.

3 5G Narrow-Band Internet of Things Enabled Sleep Activity Recognition Framework

This paper introduced a sleeping activity recognition framework as is depicted in Fig. 2. Sensors are the key enabler for activity recognition, several categories of sensors are selected, which are described in the list below, whilst the sensor deployment map is illustrated in Fig. 3.

- Motion sensors usually refer to the Passive Infrared Sensors (PIR) that are designed for sensing the presence of any mobile object. PIR sensor allows the sensing range between 3 to 5 m.
- Magnetic contact sensors are typically designed to monitor the objects that are being contacted or touched during the occurrence of certain activities, for example, cabinets for cups/tea/sugar may be opened during the activity of making tea. Therefore, such sensor is often installed on the edge of the swing side of the door, to capture the maximum movement.
- Pressure sensors are attached on the bed.
- Environmental sensors such as temperature, humidity, light etc. are also deployed for general information observing.

Sensors are often designed with very limited storage and processing capacity, in this framework, sensor data are transmitted to a Cloud server for further analysing, via NB-IoT. NB-IoT is officially introduced by 3GPP whilst is initialised from the NB-M2M techniques that developed by Huawei Ltd. in 2014. NB-IoT is designed as a low power wide-area network solution that operates in licensed spectrum bands as part of the LTE standards, thereby, it can be benefited from the ecosystem offered by traditional LTE technology and existing mobile operators. NB-IoT promising a number of key features such as massive connection, low power consumption, extended coverage, low data rate, low complexity. NB-IoT devices can be heterogenous range from sensors, actuators, machines, vehicles and many other types.

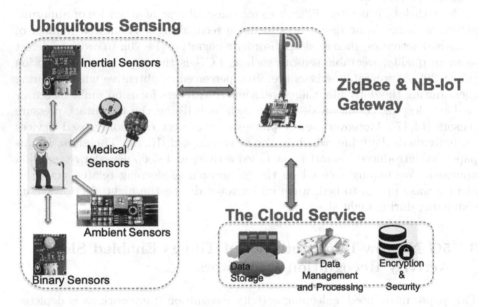

Fig. 2. The architecture of the NB-HIoT enabled sleeping activity recognition framework

4 Enabled Sleep Activity Recognition Approaches

4.1 Data Collection

To recognise the Sleeping based activities, machine learning based approaches are embedded, hence a relatively large amount of dataset is requisite. Hence, with the above-mentioned smart home environment (as is depicted in Fig. 3), a two-month experiment are conducted, and the example of dataset is illustrated in Fig. 4. As is demonstrated, the sensor data follows the template of <date, time, sensor ID, sensor value, activity label>. Figure 4 presents a brief sample

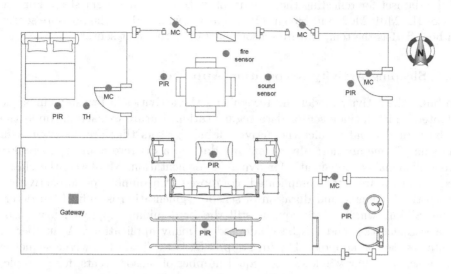

Fig. 3. The sensor deployment map of the NB-HIoT enabled sleeping activity recognition framework

2020-1-1, 21:07:05, M02, 1   go to bed
2020-1-1, 21:07:15, M02, 1
2020-1-1, 21:07:25, M01, 1
2020-1-1, 21:07:30, T01, 22.1
2020-1-1, 21:07:35, M01, 1
2020-1-1, 21:07:45, M01, 1
....
2020-1-1, 21:09:05, L01, 0.5
2020-1-1, 21:10:05, P01, 1
2020-1-1, 21:10:15, P01, 1
2020-1-1, 21:10:25, P01, 1
2020-1-1, 21:10:35, P01, 1
....
2020-1-1, 23:35:09, M01, 1   wake up during Sleep
2020-1-1, 23:35:19, M01, 1
2020-1-1, 23:35:29, M01, 1
2020-1-1, 23:35:25, M02, 1
2020-1-1, 23:35:35, M02, 1
2020-1-1, 23:35:25, M02, 1
2020-1-1, 23:35:25, P01, 0
2020-1-1, 23:35:35, P01, 1
2020-1-1, 23:36:55, M03, 1

Fig. 4. Sensor events exampLe from the NB-HIoT smart home environment

of the dataset for reflecting the activity of wake up during night sleep. For the sensor ID, M01, M02, and M03 are PIR sensors, while P01 is the pressure sensor on bed, T01 is the temperature sensor and L01 is the light sensor.

4.2 Sleeping Activity Recognition Approach

To build the activity model and recognising the activities, a few steps must be adopted which include sensor data segmentation, feature extraction, build the activity model and predict the activity label. Sensors that are distributed in the smart home are normally generating data in a discrete manner; therefore, this still remains problematic for dynamic segmentation. Moreover, the classified activities are often complicated, composed of a number of sub-activities, where the boundary and duration of sensor segmentation is difficult to determine. Sliding window technique is still the predominant approach for sensor data segmentation and has been adopted in many applications. A number of strategies can be adopted. The first approach is to divide the whole sequence into a set of sliding windows with equal number of sensor events, for example, every 20 sensor fires. The second approach is to split the whole sensor sequence into a set of sliding windows with an equal time interval, such as every 60 s. Such approaches are easier to implement, however, the disadvantages are that the real occurrence of the activities is not reflected, for example, sensor events that corresponding to one activity can be split into multiple sliding windows, or one sliding window may cover two or more activities. Consequently, a third approach is to segment the sensor events into chunks that are consistent with the incidence of each activity, such approach can correctly delineate the boundaries of the activity.

To build the activity model, a number of temporal features are extracted from the raw sensor data, which include:

- sensor frequency, which denotes the frequency of activation of a certain sensor within a time-window.
- activation length, which indicates the length of time a sensor has been active within the time-window.
- number of events within a time-window, which enables the combination of a multi-feature approach with a sliding-windowing technique to segment ongoing sensor events.

To build the activity model, a Logistic Regression model is embedded, the algorithm is described via Eq. (1). Logistic regression measures the relationship between the categorical dependent variable and one or more independent variables by estimating the probabilities using a logistic function. Logistic regression uses a cumulative normal distribution curve, and the conditional distribution $y \parallel x$ is a Bernoulli distribution. Predicted values are probabilities and are therefore restricted to (0, 1) through the logistic distribution; these represent the probability of a particular outcome, in this case, that of an activity label. The logistic function takes the values streamed from the sensor deployment as input;

the output can only take values between zero and one which is interpretable as a probability of the occurrence of a particular activity.

$$\delta(t) = \frac{e^t}{1 + e^t} = \frac{1}{1 + e^t} \tag{1}$$

To evaluate those above-mentioned activity recognition approaches and learning algorithms, a K-Fold Cross Validation strategy is accomplished, where K = 10. Moreover, two major evaluation criteria have been applied that can be explained as follows:

– Sensitivity (S) or Recall that corresponds to the correct classification rate relative to the ground truth is calculated via Eq. (2). It denotes the probability of correctly classified activities out of all true instances.

$$S = \frac{TruePositive(TP)}{TP + FalseNegative(FN)} \tag{2}$$

– Precision (P) or Positive Predictive Value (PPV), which measures the likelihood that a recognised instance corresponds to a real occurrence, and it is defined by Eq. (3).

$$P = \frac{TruePositive(TP)}{TP + FalsePositive(FP)} \tag{3}$$

As a result, the overall weighted accuracy of wake up is 98.9%, and the average weighted accuracy of go to bed is 99.4%. However, the overall weighted accuracy of wake up for toilet during night sleep is 90%, and the average weighted accuracy of wake up for wandering during night sleep is 89.3%. As for wake up and go to bed are easier to recognise, as it is an instantaneous activities, with relatively shorter duration and easy to segment. Whilst the recognition results for the activities of wake up for toilet and wandering during night sleep are less impressive, as such activities may always has different durations when the subjects taking such activities each time. Secondly, such activities have longer duration, which may result in false segmentation length. Thirdly, such activities have very few training examples.

5   Conclusion and Future Works

This paper presented a sleeping activity recognition model, which contains two major components. The first is the smart home based behaviour monitoring framework, and the second is the sleeping related activity recognition. The experiment results are also represented.

Acknowledgement. This work is supported by NanTong Science and Technology Bureau under grant JC2018132 and National Natural Science Foundation of China under grant 62002179 within Nantong University China.

References

1. Naresh, V.S., Pericherla, S.S., Sita, P., Reddi, S.: Internet of things in healthcare: architecture, applications, challenges, and solutions. Comput. Syst. Sci. Eng. **35**(6), 411–421 (2020)
2. Vincent, S.A.: Effective and efficient ranking and re-ranking feature selector for healthcare analytics. Intell. Autom. Soft Comput. **26**(2), 261–268 (2020)
3. Cook, D., Crandall, A., Thomas, B., Krishnan, N.: CASAS: a smart home in a box. Computer **46**(7), 62–69 (2013)
4. Rashidi, P., Cook, D., Holder, L., Schmitter-Edgecombe, M.: Discovering activities to recognize and track in a smart environment. IEEE Trans. Knowl. Data Eng. **23**(4), 527–539 (2011)
5. Akay, B.: Human activity recognition based on parallel approximation kernel k-means algorithm. Comput. Syst. Sci. Eng. **35**(6), 441–456 (2020)
6. Kabir, M.H., Thapa, K., Yang, J., Yang, S.H.: State-space based linear modeling for human activity recognition in smart space. Intelli. Autom. Soft Comput. **25**(4), 673–681 (2019)
7. Lotfi, A., Langensiepen, C., Mahmoud, S., Akhlaghinia, M.: Smart homes for the elderly dementia sufferers: identification and prediction of abnormal behaviour. J. Ambient. Intell. Humaniz. Comput. **3**, 205–218 (2012)
8. Pal, N., Bezdek, J.: On cluster validity for the fuzzy c-means model. IEEE Trans. Fuzzy Syst. **3**(3), 370–379 (1995)
9. Tran, A.C., Marsland, S., Dietrich, J., Guesgen, H.W., Lyons, P.: Use cases for abnormal behaviour detection in smart homes. In: Lee, Y., et al. (eds.) ICOST 2010. LNCS, vol. 6159, pp. 144–151. Springer, Heidelberg (2010). https://doi.org/10.1007/978-3-642-13778-5_18
10. Po, Y., et al.: Lifelogging data validation model for internet of things enabled personalized healthcare. IEEE Trans. Syst. Man Cybern. **48**(1), 50–64 (2018)
11. Ismail, W.N., Hassan, M.M., Alsalamah, H.A., Fortino, G.: CNN-based health model for regular health factors analysis in internet-of-medical things environment. IEEE Access. **8**, 52541–52549 (2020)
12. Zhou, Z., Yu, H., Shi, H.: Human activity recognition based on improved bayesian convolution network to analyze health care data using wearable IoT device. IEEE Access. **8**, 86411–86418 (2020)
13. Sundaravadivel, P., Kesavan, K., Kesavan, L., Mohanty, S.P., Kougianos, E.: Smart-log: a deep-learning based automated nutrition monitoring system in the IoT. IEEE Trans. Consum. Electron. **64**(3), 390–398 (2018)
14. Walsh, L., McLoone, S., Ronda, J., Duffy, J.F., Czeisler, C.A.: Noncontact Pressure-Based Sleep/Wake Discrimination. IEEE Trans. Biomed. Eng. **64**(8), 1750–1760 (2017)
15. Hachem, A., Ayache, M., El Khansa, L., Jezzini, A.: ECG classification for Sleep Apnea detection. In: 3rd Middle East Conference on Biomedical Engineering (MECBME) Proceddings, Beirut, pp. 38–41 (2016)
16. Montanini, L., Sabino, N., Spinsante, S., Gambi, E.: Smartphone as unobtrusive sensor for real-time sleep recognition. In: IEEE International Conference on Consumer Electronics (ICCE), Las Vegas, NV, pp. 1–4 (2018)
17. Waltisberg, D., Amft, O., Brunner, D.P., Trster, G.: Detecting disordered breathing and limb movement using in-bed force sensors. IEEE J. Biomed. Health Inform. **21**(4), 930–938 (2017)

18. Hahm, C., Lee, S., Shin, H.: Analysis of irregular breathing using respiration-induced intensity variations (RIIV) from photoplethysmography signals for sleep apnea. In: International Conference on Information and Communication Technology Convergence (ICTC), Jeju, pp. 52–55 (2016)
19. Montanini, L., Sabino, N., Spinsante, S., Gambi, E.: Smartphone as unobtrusive sensor for real-time sleep recognition. In: IEEE International Conference on Consumer Electronics (ICCE), Las Vegas, NV, pp. 1–4 (2018)
20. Bayatfar, S., Seifpour, S., Oskoei, M.A., Khadem, A.: An automated system for diagnosis of sleep apnea syndrome using single-channel EEG signal. In: 27th Iranian Conference on Electrical Engineering (ICEE), Yazd, Iran, pp. 1829–1833 (2019)
21. Wan, J., Li, M.S., OGrady, M.J., Gu, X., Alawlaqi, M.A.A.H., OHare, G.M.P.: Time-bounded activity recognition for ambient assisted living. IEEE Trans. Emerg. Top. Comput. 1 (1), 1–14 (2019)

Blockchain-Based Reliable Collection Mechanism for Smart Meter Quality Data

Liu Yan[1]($\boxtimes$), Zheng Angang[1], Shang Huaiying[1], Kong Lingda[1], Shen Guang[2], and Shen Shuming[3]

[1] China Electric Power Research Institute Co., Ltd., Beijing 100085, China
yanliu3@epri.sgcc.com.cn
[2] State Grid Zhejiang Electric Power Co., Ltd., Hangzhou 310007, China
[3] State Grid Zhejiang Electric Power Co., Ltd.,
Jiaxing Power Supply Company, Jiaxing 314000, China

Abstract. In terms of quality data collection of smart meters, there are still problems such as incomplete quality data collection, quality data loss, and difficulty in data sharing. In order to solve this problem, this paper adopts Hyperledger technology and proposes a blockchain-based trusted collection system architecture for smart meter quality data, including smart meters, edge computing nodes, blockchain, and data storage platforms. Secondly, the basic contract, identity contract, and data contract are designed in detail to realize the automation of data collection and improve the reliability of data collection. Finally, the four link mechanisms of smart meter winding and quality data collection strategy formulation, storage and use are designed. Through analysis from three aspects of execution speed, energy consumption, and security, the mechanism in this paper has a good performance.

Keywords: Smart meter · Quality data · Data collection · Blockchain

1 Introduction

Smart meters can achieve comprehensive and rapid collection of grid data, and are an important data source for grid companies to improve the quality of power services. Because the data collected by smart meters includes electricity consumption data and grid operation data, and smart meters are critical infrastructure, they play a very important role in national security [1]. The safe collection and management of smart meter data has become an important research content.

In order to improve the overall security capability of the power system, the literature [2] takes the data security management of the State Grid Sichuan Company as the research object and proposes a multi-dimensional data security management architecture, which comprehensively improves the power data security. In order to recover the damaged data, literature [3] proposed a missing data reconstruction algorithm based on a generative confrontation network. In order to improve the data security management ability from the daily operation of electric power companies, literature [4] studied the operation

© Springer Nature Switzerland AG 2021
X. Sun et al. (Eds.): ICAIS 2021, LNCS 12737, pp. 476–487, 2021.
https://doi.org/10.1007/978-3-030-78612-0_38

specifications of electric power big data and proposed a safe operation management system for grid data. Literature [5] applies quantum keys to the data security management system. Literature [6] applied the entropy weight-grey model to the early warning of power data security, which improved the early warning capability of data security events. In terms of data security for smart meter terminals, literature [7] proposes a blockchain-based terminal cross-domain authentication mechanism. Literature [8] improves the security authentication capability of mobile terminals based on biometric technology. Literature [9] proposes a terminal authentication and authorization mechanism based on SWP-SIM technology for the security of the SIM card of the mobile terminal.

From the existing research and analysis, we can see that more research results have been made in the safe collection of smart meter data. The quality data of smart meters plays a key role in the stable operation of smart meters. However, in terms of quality data of smart meters, there are still problems such as incomplete quality data collection, quality data loss, and difficulty in data sharing. To solve this problem, this paper adopts blockchain technology and proposes a reliable collection mechanism for smart meter quality data based on blockchain. Through the execution speed, energy consumption and safety analysis of the mechanism, the usability and practicability of the mechanism in this paper are verified.

2 System Architecture

Generally speaking, the quality data of a smart meter includes real-time data on the operation of the meter, data on the surrounding environment of the meter, and data on regular maintenance and inspection of the meter. The real-time acquisition of these data plays a very important role in the status of the power grid and the safe use of electricity by users. In order to realize the real-time and safe collection of smart meter data, this paper designs a reliable collection system architecture for smart meter quality data based on the hyperledger theory in blockchain technology.

2.1 Architecture

Hyperledger is the third version of blockchain technology that can implement distributed ledger functions. Different from other implementation versions of blockchain technology, Hyperledger mainly includes endorsement nodes, submission nodes, ordering service nodes, and smart contracts. Among them, the endorsement node mainly completes the signature function of the transaction content; the submission node realizes the creation and submission function of the blockchain node; the ordering service node realizes the ordering and packaging of multiple transaction contents; the smart contract executes the blockchain node according to the formulated instructions Create and manage.

In order to realize the reliable collection of smart meter quality data, this paper adopts the Hyperledger technology, and proposes a blockchain-based smart meter quality data trusted collection system architecture as shown in Fig. 1. It can be seen from the figure that the system architecture mainly includes four aspects: smart meters, edge computing nodes, blockchain, and data storage platforms.

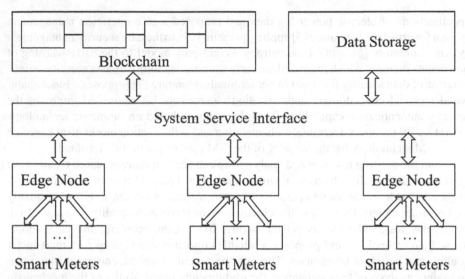

Fig. 1. Blockchain-based trusted collection system architecture of smart meter quality data

The smart meter is the producer of the quality data collected in this article. For the collector of smart meter quality data, it is generally necessary to collect smart meter production data, operation and maintenance data, and alarm failure data. In order to safely upload the quality data of the smart meter to the collector, it can be transmitted through a dedicated wireless network or a wired network. In order to save network resources, VPN encryption tunnel technology can be used to safely transmit data.

The edge computing node is the computing unit for data processing and submission in this article. Because the computing and storage capabilities of smart meters are limited, in order to ensure the reliability of smart meters, this paper uses edge computing technology and designs edge computing nodes. Server virtualization technology can be used to improve the scalability and reliability of edge computing nodes. In order to achieve reliable collection of smart meter quality data based on Hyperledger, the edge computing node has two functional modules: smart meter resource management and quality data collection strategy management. The smart meter resource management module includes an endorsement node and a submission node. The endorsing node is responsible for signing the identity and data of the smart meter, and the submitting node is responsible for submitting the quality data of the smart meter. According to the quality data collection requirements, the quality data collection strategy management module communicates with the smart meter to obtain designated quality data. The system service interface is based on RESTful technology, which can realize the secure access of multiple heterogeneous data platforms, edge computing nodes, and blockchain nodes.

Blockchain mainly includes three parts: consensus algorithm, ordering service node, and smart contract. The consensus algorithm adopts the PoA algorithm. After the ordering service node receives the request to link the smart meter from the edge computing node, it sorts the smart meter according to the smart meter's identity attributes, owner attributes and other information. Smart contracts are a key link in the reliable collection of smart meter quality data, including smart meter winding and data storage related strategies. The specific content is introduced below.

The data storage platform realizes the safe and reliable storage of smart meter quality data. In terms of safe storage, the dual mechanism of data encryption and identity authentication can be used to achieve data confidentiality and security. In terms of reliability storage, cloud computing technology is used to implement distributed redundant storage, thereby improving the reliability and integrity of data storage.

2.2 Smart Contract

Smart contracts can automatically execute blockchain instructions by setting trigger conditions to achieve various specific business requirements. Because smart contracts are safe, reliable, fast, and automatically executed, they have become an important part of blockchain technology. In this article, the smart contract can realize the automatic execution of smart meter on-chain and data collection. The smart meter quality data collection contract proposed in this paper includes three parts: basic contract, identity contract, and data contract. The specific structure is shown in Fig. 2.

Fig. 2. Smart contract for smart meter quality data collection

The main function of the basic contract is to manage the basic information of the smart meter, including the basic information contract and the identification public key contract. Among them, the basic information contract can obtain the attribute information and owner information of the smart meter. The identification public key contract can generate identification and public key information for smart meters that join the blockchain.

Identity contracts are mainly used for the creation and improvement of smart meter data identities, including identity creation voting contracts and identity reset contracts. The identity creation voting contract calls the basic information contract in the basic contract according to the identity creation rules to verify the information of the smart meter. After the verification is passed, each blockchain node will vote on identity creation, and according to the voting results, determine whether to create a new block. If you need to create a new block, you need to call the identification public key contract to create an identification and public key for the smart meter, which is used to create the identity of the smart meter. The identity reset contract updates the attribute information of the smart meter according to the request of the smart meter owner. In order to ensure the uniqueness and non-tampering of data, the identity reset contract can only reset the key information, location information and other auxiliary information of the smart meter, and cannot reset the unique information such as the identification of the smart meter.

The main function of the data contract is to safely store and trust the data of the smart meter, including data storage contracts, data sharing contracts, and permission control contracts. The data storage contract completes the two functions of data hash digest acquisition and data distributed storage. The data sharing contract provides data sharing functions for the verified data collectors based on the verification of the collector's identity information. The authorization control contract mainly includes the identity verification of the data collector and the data user. Only the relevant parties who have passed the identity verification can access and use the data.

3   Trusted Collection Mechanism

In order to satisfy the credible collection of smart meter quality data, it is necessary to complete the four links of smart meter winding, quality data collection strategy formulation, quality data storage, and quality data use. They are introduced separately below.

3.1   Smart Meter Registration Process

In the chain link of smart meters, it mainly completes the registration of smart meters on the blockchain, so as to realize the reliable collection and use of quality data of smart meters based on blockchain technology. After the edge computing node receives the smart meter registration request within its jurisdiction, it packs these requests and submits the request to the blockchain node through the system service interface. The registration process for smart meters to join the blockchain is shown in Fig. 3.

Step 1: The smart meter initiates a registration request to the edge computing node. The content of the registration request sent by the smart meter includes related information such as device ID, device attributes, and owner ID.
Step 2: The edge computing node performs verification and signature. The endorsement node in the edge computing node verifies and signs the registration data of the smart meter.
Step 3: The edge computing node sorts and packs all smart meter registration requests. The sorting node in the edge computing node sorts and packs the registration request data of all smart meters.
Step 4: The submitting node of the edge computing node submits the registration request package to the blockchain.
Step 5: Blockchain nodes create voting contracts. The blockchain selects the blockchain node closest to the edge computing node and creates a voting contract for the current request.
Step 6: Blockchain nodes vote. The voting contract sends the vote to all other blockchain nodes and receives the voting results.

Step 7: Create the identity of the smart meter and related contracts. When the received approval vote exceeds 1/3 of the total number of blockchain nodes, the smart meter's identity and related contracts are executed to create a new blockchain node for the smart meter.

Steps 8, 9: Return the smart meter identity. When the smart meter is successfully registered on the blockchain, the smart meter identity is returned for the edge computing node and the smart meter.

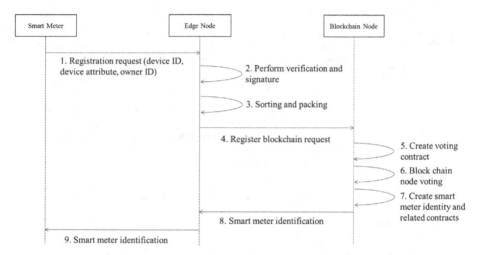

Fig. 3. The registration process for smart meters to join the blockchain

3.2 Quality Data Collection Strategy Management Mechanism

In the formulation of the quality data collection strategy, it is mainly to complete the implementation of the quality data collection strategy of the smart meter owner. According to business needs, the owner of the smart meter sets the content of the quality data collected by the smart meter, the collection method and other data attributes. At the same time, according to the business relationship, the user attributes of the quality data are set to complete the reliable and safe use of the quality data.

Step 1: The smart meter owner uploads the collection access policy. The collection strategy includes device attributes and requester attributes. Device attributes include device ID, collected data type, collection interval, and upload interval. The attributes of the requester include the attributes of the resource requester, the permission to use, the relationship with the resource owner, prerequisites, and the number of uses.

Step 2: Request the blockchain node to verify the owner's identity. The blockchain node compares the owner attributes of the smart meter and verifies the owner attributes.

Step 3: The verification is successful. After the identity of the smart meter owner is verified by the blockchain node, the verification result is returned to the edge computing node.

Step 4: Execute the collection strategy. The edge computing node issues the quality data collection strategy of the smart meter owner to the smart meter. The smart meter performs quality data collection according to the quality data collection strategy.

Step 5: Execute the access policy. The edge computing node requests the blockchain node to store the access policy, so that the resource requester can access and use the data according to the access policy of the smart meter owner.

Step 6: The execution is successful. The owner of the smart meter obtains the execution result of the collection access strategy (Fig. 4).

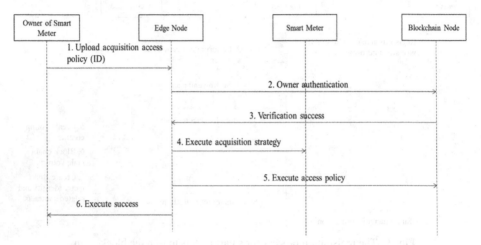

Fig. 4. Quality data collection strategy management

3.3 Quality Data Preservation Management Mechanism

In the storage of quality data, in order to ensure the safe and reliable storage of quality data of smart meters, a distributed storage platform is used to realize distributed redundant storage of quality data. The hash value (digest) of the data stored by the blockchain node.

Step 1: Collect data: The smart meter collects quality data according to the data collection strategy.

Step 2: Request data storage: The smart meter sends the data to be stored to the data storage platform according to the data storage strategy.

Step 3: Perform data storage and generate a data summary. The data storage platform stores the data of the smart meter, and uses a hash algorithm to obtain the hash value of the data.

Step 4: Request to store the data summary: The data storage platform sends the generated data summary to the blockchain node, and requests the blockchain node to store the data summary.

Step 5: Store the data summary: The blockchain node stores the data summary data in the block where it is located.

Step 6: Data storage is successful. After receiving the data summary of the blockchain, the data number of the current data in the blockchain is saved, which is convenient for the use and data sharing of the later data. And return to the smart meter a message that data storage is successful (Fig. 5).

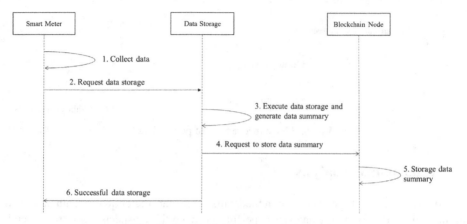

Fig. 5. Quality data storage management

3.4 Power Data Usage Mechanism

In the use of quality data, the data user submits a data use request to the blockchain based on the quality data attributes provided by the data owner, and the resource can be used after the blockchain is authenticated.

Step 1: The resource requester signs the identity ID and requested data. When the resource requester needs to obtain the data of the smart meter, the resource requester first uses his private key to sign his own identity and the data number to be obtained.
Step 2: Send the signature information. The resource requester sends the signature information to the blockchain node.
Step 3: Verify identity information. The blockchain node verifies the identity information of the resource requester according to the resource access strategy of the resource owner.
Step 4: Return a summary of the requested data content. After the blockchain node verifies the identity of the resource requester, according to the requirements of the requested data, it returns the summary information of the requested data content to the resource requester.
Step 5: Request data content. The resource requester submits a data content request to the data storage platform based on the summary information of the data content.
Step 6: Verify the data summary. The data storage platform verifies the data summary information.
Step 7: Return the data content. After passing the verification, the data storage platform returns the data content to the resource requester (Fig. 6).

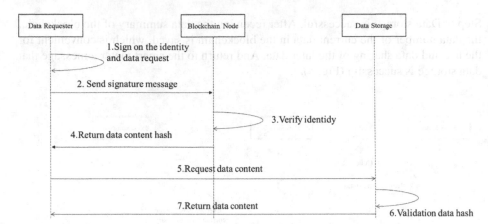

Fig. 6. Usage mechanism of power data

4 Performance Analysis

In order to verify the trusted collection mechanism of smart meter quality data proposed in this article, the following analysis is performed from three aspects: execution speed, energy consumption, and safety.

4.1 Perform Speed Analysis

The reliable collection mechanism of smart meter quality data proposed in this paper belongs to the field of IoT data security management. In the field of IoT data security management, the Fabric-iot mechanism is a relatively common security management mechanism. When using the Fabric-iot mechanism for IoT device management, it is necessary to obtain the IP address and MAC address of each IoT device, and manage the data of the IoT device based on the IP address and MAC address. Compared with the Fabric-iot mechanism, this article uses smart meter-based device ID and owner ID attributes to manage smart meters. In terms of acquisition speed, it is more convenient to acquire device ID and owner ID attribute information, so it can improve the execution efficiency of the quality data collection mechanism. Therefore, the execution speed of the mechanism in this article is faster.

4.2 Energy Consumption Analysis

Generally speaking, the quality data collection process of smart meters needs to include smart meters, data storage devices, and collection and management equipment. Compared with the general scheme, the edge computing node and blockchain in this scheme are equivalent to collection management equipment. Since the blockchain has the advantages of decentralization and non-tampering, compared with traditional solutions, the data collection mechanism in this article can significantly improve the security and reliability of quality data. Therefore, this article only achieves reliable collection of quality data by increasing the energy consumption of blockchain nodes.

4.3 Safety Analysis

Common security problems of data acquisition systems include single point of failure, data leakage, and data destruction. The following analyzes from these three aspects. In terms of single point of failure, the blockchain technology and distributed data storage technology in this article have the characteristics of redundant backup, which can effectively solve the problem of single point of failure. In terms of data leakage, because the data storage platform has features such as identity authentication and data encryption, it can effectively ensure data confidentiality. At the same time, since data users can access data storage resources only after obtaining the summary of the data through the blockchain node, the confidentiality of the data is further strengthened. In terms of data destruction, distributed data storage technology can effectively store multiple redundant copies of data. In addition, the summary information of the data is stored in the blockchain, which ensures that the summary information of the data cannot be tampered with, so that the summary information of the data can be used to verify whether the original data has been tampered with, which improves the reliability of the data.

5 Application Scenario

The blockchain-based reliable collection mechanism for smart meter quality data proposed in this paper is mainly used in the field of secure collection of smart meter quality data. Compared with the existing data collection scheme, the typical application scenario of this article is shown in Fig. 7. In order to use the mechanism of this article, it is necessary to add blockchain nodes to the existing scheme. The key points of the realization of each module are explained below to improve the application effect of the scheme. First of all, in terms of network security, it is necessary to ensure that the communication between each node is set from the two dimensions of channel security and data encryption. In terms of channel security, VPN technology or private network technology can be used to achieve effective isolation of network transmission media. In terms of data

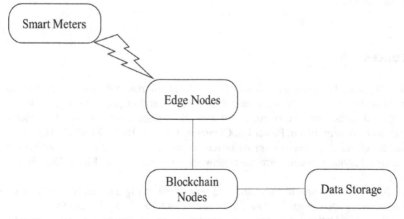

Fig. 7. Typical application scheme

encryption, traditional asymmetric encryption technology and digital signature technology can be used to achieve secure data transmission and security authentication. Second, in terms of the safety awareness of the personnel involved in the program, it is necessary to enhance the safety capabilities. Because of the security of the technical solution, data security can only be guaranteed from the dimensions of the physical environment. If account loss, misoperation, fire or flooding occurs within the relevant personnel of the scheme, it is easy to cause the loss and destruction of quality data. Therefore, it is of great value to strengthen the safety awareness of relevant implementation personnel of the plan.

6 Conclusion

Smart meters can achieve comprehensive and rapid collection of grid data, and are an important source of data support for grid companies to improve the quality of power services. However, in terms of quality data of smart meters, there are still problems such as incomplete quality data collection, quality data loss, and difficulty in data sharing. In order to realize the credible collection of smart meter quality data, this paper proposes a blockchain-based smart meter quality data credible collection system architecture, and designs the smart meter's chaining, quality data collection strategy formulation, quality data storage, and quality There are four mechanisms for the use of data. As smart meters are distributed in a wide area, in order to improve the efficiency of smart meter data collection, smart meters need to be managed in different regions based on regional characteristics. In the next step, based on the research results of this paper, smart meters will be managed in different domains, so as to solve the problem of reliable collection of smart meter quality data in large-scale environments.

Acknowledgment. This work is supported by the Science and Technology Project of State Grid Co., Ltd: Research and Application of Intelligent Electric Energy Meter Quality Analysis and Evaluation Technology Based on the Whole life Data -Topic 2: Research on the Technology of Collecting and Sharing Quality Data of the Whole Chain of Smart Energy Meters (5660-201955458A-0-0-00).

References

1. Kaikai, G., et al.: Design and implementation of handheld power data acquisition and analysis device based on mobile network. Power Syst. Prot. Control **46**(8), 110–116 (2018)
2. Fan, Y., et al.: Study on the construction of state grid sichuan electric power data asset security management system. Electr. Power Inf. Commun. Technol. **16**(1), 90–95 (2018)
3. Wang, S., et al.: A power system measurement missing data reconstruction method using an improved generative countermeasure network. Proc. Chin. Soc. Electr. Eng. **39**(1), 56–64 (2019)
4. Leng, X., et al.: Data specification and data processing of big data analysis system for smart grid monitoring and operation. Power Syst. Autom. **42**(19), 169–176 (2018)
5. Chen, Z., et al.: Optimal data protection model for power business based on quantum key. Autom. Power Syst. **42**(11), 115–121 (2018)

6. Li, W., et al.: Power data network risk prediction based on entropy weight-grey model (2018)
7. Zhou, Z., Li, L., Li, Z.: Efficient cross-domain authentication scheme based on blockchain technology. Comput. Appl. **38**(2), 316–320 (2018)
8. Xiang, M., Fugui, Z.: Multi-source biometric real-time identity authentication system for mobile internet terminals. Television Technology 4 (2017)
9. Tan, Z., Weixiong, L.: The realization method of mobile terminal identity authentication and authorization based on SWP-SIM technology. Sci. Technol. Innov. Appl. **9**, 21–22 (2018)

Power Blockchain Guarantee Mechanism Based on Trusted Computing

Yong Yan[1], Tianhong Su[2(✉)], Shaoyong Guo[2], and Song Kang[2]

[1] Electric Power Research Institute of State Grid Zhejiang Electric Power Company, Hangzhou 310009, China
[2] Beijing University of Posts and Telecommunications, Beijing 100876, China
sutianhong@bupt.edu.cn

Abstract. The power Internet of Things is an effective way to solve the inefficiency of traditional Internet of Things services in the era of big data. However, as the power Internet of Things is full of sensitive data, how to ensure the security of the information transmission and exchange process is an urgent problem in the power Internet of Things system. This paper combines the characteristics of blockchain and power Internet of Things to propose a power blockchain guarantee mechanism based on trusted computing for the above problems. The decentralized technology of the blockchain provides a reliable solution to the massive data and high concurrency problems in the power Internet of Things. The trusted platform module is added to the blockchain node server to ensure the credibility of the server operating environment. At the collection layer, the system designs an algorithm for real-time monitoring of malicious collection terminals based on reputation, which prevents malicious terminals from publishing malicious data. At the same time, the system detects the visitor's access authority through integrity certification and access policy verification, ensuring the credibility of the access terminal, maintaining the safe and reliable operation of the power blockchain system in all aspects, and protecting the private data in the power blockchain.

Keywords: Trusted computing · Blockchain · Privacy protection

1 Introduction

The concept of the Internet of Things was first proposed in 1999 by Professor Ashton of the Auto-ID Center. The Internet of Things is a giant network that uses the Internet as an information carrier to collect information about monitored objects in real time through information sensing equipment, and realize communication between people and things, and things and things. With the continuous development of the Internet of Things in smart cities, smart transportation and other fields, it has brought great convenience to people's lives. According to Gartner's report, the IoT market will grow to 5.8 billion endpoints by the end of 2020. There is a huge amount of private information in the Internet of Things. For example, wearable devices record the health of people, Internet of Vehicles systems record the daily trajectory of users, and user privacy data recorded

X. Sun et al. (Eds.): ICAIS 2021, LNCS 12737, pp. 488–501, 2021.
https://doi.org/10.1007/978-3-030-78612-0_39

in the Internet of Things. These private information will be recorded in the data center. if the central server is attacked by malicious users and causes privacy leakage, it will have an incalculable impact. Therefore, traditional IoT central nodes are faced with multiple challenges of high-concurrency and massive data processing against multiple attacks. Therefore, traditional IoT central nodes are faced with multiple challenges of high concurrent processing and malicious user attacks.

In the era of big data, massive high-concurrency data exchanges have brought great challenges to traditional networks with data centers as the computing core. The drawbacks of the traditional "collection + centralized" power service model are gradually emerging. There are many kinds of data in the traditional power service. Data collection and data status monitoring will consume huge human and financial resources, which cannot meet the demand of current power grid development. The power Internet of Things has become the first choice for improving the efficiency of power services and reducing costs. In 2019, the State Grid proposed the concept of ubiquitous power Internet of Things, aiming to provide a more efficient and flexible power Internet of Things.

Reliability and controllability are the top priorities for the development of the power Internet of Things system. It is necessary to ensure the service efficiency of the system under high concurrency and the security of user privacy. Therefore, it is necessary to ensure the security of collection, deployment, network and other aspects.

The power blockchain provides a reliable solution to the problem of excessive central pressure under the high concurrency of the power Internet of Things system, but the risk of privacy leakage still exists in the blockchain system working in the open environment. This paper proposed a power blockchain guarantee mechanism based on trusted computing that combines the advantages of the current power blockchain to jointly maintain the safe operation of the power blockchain system and the security of sensitive information in the system from the hardware and software levels, The system guarantees the credibility of the operating environment of the blockchain node through the TPM chip, and guarantees the credibility of the collection terminal and the collected information through the contract.

2   Key Concept

2.1   Trusted Computing

With the rise of emerging Internet computing models such as the Internet of Things and cloud computing, it has brought extremely serious security problems while facilitating people's lives. Trusted computing emerged as an effective solution.

Hardware-based trusted computing is an active defense technology. By adding a root of trust to the computing system and establishing the operating environment for isolated execution, and the trust relationship is extended from the bottom layer to the upper layer applications, thereby realizing hardware-based active protection. Trust means that the entity always proceeds towards the predetermined target result in a predetermined manner. The Trusted Computing Group (TCG) released the TPM2.0 specification in 2015, which further increased the authorization level and became an ISO/IEC standard.

2.2 Blockchain

Different from traditional centralized database, blockchain is in essence a decentralized distributed database technology. It maintains a chain structure of data blocks among participating nodes and maintains continuously growing and non-tamper able data records based on cryptography.

Each block can be logically divided into a block header and a block body. Each block is connected in series by the hash value of the block header, and each block header is associated with all transactions in the block through the Merkle root. The blockchain will synchronize transaction information to the entire network, and each client stores the latest transaction information, forming a decentralized storage method. When some nodes fail, it will not affect the operation of the entire system.

Consensus mechanism is the soul of blockchain. It is the core technology for blockchain to solve trust problem with decentralized idea. Its purpose is to maintain the consistency of blockchain system. The most common consensus mechanism is Proof of Work (PoW). Miners need to use their own computing power to calculate a hash problem, PoW mechanism is to use the solution of the problem to prove the credibility of the data, so that nodes get the right to keep accounts. This problem is computationally difficult but easy to verify. When a blockchain node wants to create a block, it must solve the problem and then broadcast it to other nodes. All nodes in the blockchain system will take the longest chain as the main chain of the system to complete the system consensus.

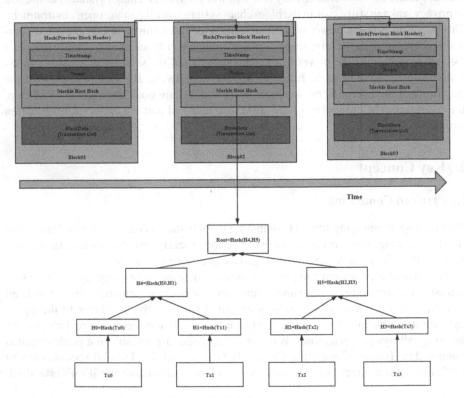

Fig. 1. Blockchain structure

A smart contract is composed of transaction processing and a state machine. It is a set of rules that are executed automatically by a computer system and needs to be jointly formulated by multiple participants. Smart contracts can make a set of complex and conditionally controlled rules execute in a pre-defined order. The smart contract defines trigger conditions. When the trigger conditions are met, the smart contract can be in the blockchain without human participation. The results of execution can be published in the blockchain network and added to the blockchain through the consensus mechanism. The bytecode of the smart contract is stored in each blockchain node, and the failure of one node does not affect the overall operation of the system. The scheduling process of the smart contract is also recorded and traceable by the blockchain, ensuring the safe operation of the smart contract (Fig. 1).

3   Related Works

The traditional Internet of Things system adopts the mode of central server-client terminal and connects to the Internet of Things devices through cloud computing. Due to the limitation of storage capacity of server and transmission bandwidth, it is easy to cause server paralysis under the scenario of high concurrency of mass terminals. Data centralization also brings security risks to user privacy. The decentralization, traceability and anti-tampering of the blockchain provide solutions to the hidden dangers of the Internet of Things [1]. However, as the blockchain works in an open environment and is vulnerable to malicious attacks. How to integrate the blockchain with the Internet of Things efficiently under the premise of ensuring privacy security has become a hot research topic at present.

Reference [2] proposes a scheme to guarantee the privacy of the Internet of Things based on block chain, which uses blockchain to solve the access control problem of distributed Internet of Things. Reference [3] uses the decentralization, non-tampering, and smart contract characteristics of the blockchain to combine blockchain technology and access control to design a smart contract-based access control system for the Internet of Things. Ding et al. proposed an attribute-based access control method for the Internet of Things, which simplifies the access control protocol of Internet of Things devices by storing attribute data through the blockchain and avoids illegal data tampering [4]. Liu proposed a blockchain-based distributed trusted network connection architecture (B-TNC), which builds a trusted blockchain network based on hardware [5]. Town Crier is an authenticated data feed scheme that uses Intel SGX as a trusted execution environment and uses trusted computing technology to ensure the credibility of external data used by smart contracts [6]. Zhang proposed a consensus mechanism based on integrity proofs to execute transactions, execute smart contracts, and protect sensitive data [7].

In summary, although blockchain IoT devices can be used to store access control strategies to ensure that access control can be traced and decision results cannot be tampered with, the privacy data protection and the efficiency of smart contract execution in blockchain are important factors that prevent the combination of the Internet of Things and the blockchain. Although the security of smart contracts can be enhanced by adding trusted computing technology, there are still limitations in security and efficiency. The Town Crier solution is only for external data and cannot guarantee the security of the smart contract execution environment. The blockchain body based on integrity proof weakens the decentralized characteristics of the blockchain, and there are still hidden dangers in high concurrency scenarios.

Based on the characteristics of power system service, this paper combines the power blockchain with trusted computing technology and proposed a trusted power blockchain system through Access Service Chain, Log Service Chain and Remote Proof Chain. The Access Service Chain (ASC) is a blockchain composed of multiple Certificate Authority (CA) and a high-performance trusted CA server. The trusted server has enough storage and computing power to support the operation of the system. The trusted server takes the TPM chip as the trust root, which can establish the trusted system [8] from the CPU instructions and execution links, build the trusted operating environment during the server operation, filter the illegal access, and dynamically defend the server in real time during the operation process. Log Service Chain (LSC) is a block Chain composed of high-performance trusted servers, which also integrates TPM as the trust root, and designs a malicious sensor detection scheme to monitor the security status of sensors in real time. Remote Proof Chain (ROC) records the link relationship between the TPM public and the TPM chip, which can provide remote proof and remote authentication functions to ensure the authenticity of the TPM and its key information. Through the integration of trusted computing and power blockchain, this paper jointly guarantees the credibility of the collection terminal and server in the power blockchain from both hardware and software aspects, ensuring the security of the privacy data of each user and the security of the smart contract execution environment in each blockchain node.

4 System Architecture

The decentralization characteristic of blockchain has made it very promising in the context of massive data such as the Internet of Things. The blockchain has been widely used in the Internet of Vehicles, smart home and other Internet of Things scenarios. This system combines power blockchain with trusted computing technology to maintain the security of the blockchain network and the security of private data in the blockchain node while ensuring the service efficiency of power blockchain.

The overall architecture of the power blockchain system based on trusted computing includes three blockchains, namely the access service chain, the log service chain, and the remote proof chain. Compared with the traditional blockchain, this system adds a trusted chip to each blockchain node, so that each blockchain node has strong identity authentication. The system creates a credible power Internet of Things working environment through trusted chips and malicious node detection mechanisms. The system requires that the access terminal contains a trusted chip, and the visitor needs to go through the double test of the access strategy and integrity certification when entering the network, which prevents malicious terminals from illegally accessing system resources and ensures the credibility of the network terminal.

The TPM chip integrates multiple cryptographic algorithms, encapsulates keys, and can provide multiple trusted computing functions, such as measuring platform integrity, verifying integrity information, encrypting sensitive messages, and signing. These functions can be implemented inside the TPM chip, separated from other parts of the system, so malicious code that tampered with the system cannot affect the execution environment inside the TPM.

TPM Remote Authentication: The system sets that all terminals requesting access to the system need to contain a TPM chip, and the signature verification key in each TPM chip is bound to the TPM chip and stored in a trusted third party (remote proof chain). The remote proof chain can verify the authenticity of the key.

TPM integrity measurement process is as follows:

When the system is initialized, TPM will perform a static integrity measurement on the system and generate an integrity value before all applications run. When the application starts to run, the integrity measurement program measures the running status of each application and module at the top and stores the generated integrity measurement value in the trusted register (PCR) in the TPM. Since PCR cannot be obtained from outside, the integrity value in PCR is considered safe. In order to verify the integrity measurement value, TPM records the PCR log, which records all the steps in the integrity measurement process. The verifier can quickly calculate the PCR value from the log and compare it with the original value to verify the legitimacy of the integrity certification process.

TPM can also provide remote integrity certification. The TPM contains a dedicated integrity message signature and signature verification key pair, which can be certified by the TPM authority. Because the key is stored in the hardware, the security of the key generation process is guaranteed. At the same time, external malicious users cannot steal the private key information in the hardware, which preventing signature forgery. The process of remote integrity certification is as follows:

The requester extracts the log information of the integrity measurement and signs it with the signature key to provide the verifier with the signed message.

$$ISM = Sign_{Isk}(M_{Log}, Pval) \tag{1}$$

In the message, ISM is the signed message, Isk is the signature key, M_{Log} is the partial integrity message in the TPM log, and Pval is the integrity measurement value of the requester. To ensure the real-time performance of the message, the requester needs to attach the timestamp information, and the final message sent is $\{ISM, Ts\}$.

After receiving the message, the verifier first verifies whether the message is real-time according to its own clock information, and the system sets a timeout threshold T_{res}. If $T - Ts < T_{res}$, is satisfied, the verifier starts the verification.

$$M_{Log}, Pval = Ver_{Ivk}(ISM) \tag{2}$$

Ivk is the verification key. The verifier uses the integrity verification module (IVM) to re- verify the integrity of the log message M_{Log} of the log requester.

$$Pval' = IVM(M_{Log}) \tag{3}$$

Compare whether $Pval'$ is consistent with the received $Pval$. If they are consistent, the verification is successful, otherwise the verification fails (Fig. 2).

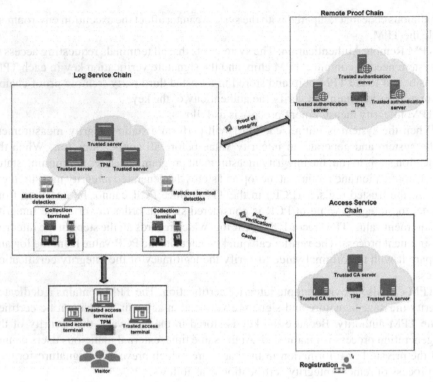

Fig. 2. System architecture

4.1 System Initialization

The system default asymmetric encryption algorithm is ECC algorithm, symmetric encryption algorithm is 128-bit AES algorithm, and signature algorithm is 256-bit ECDSA algorithm.

1) Each trusted server in the access service chain, log service chain and remote proof chain generates its own public and private key pair through the trusted chip and stores the public key information in the blockchain.
2) The access service chain selects nodes randomly to generate a blockchain master key pair ($ASCMPUK$, $ASCMPrK$) and synchronizes to the blockchain network. The log service chain and the remote proof chain respectively generate key pairs in the same way.($LSCMPUK$, $LSCMPrK$, $ROCMPUK$, $ROCMPrK$).
3) ASC needs to set the parameter L = (p, a, b, G, n) for the system to determine the elliptic curve E in the finite field GF(p). It is used to systematically encrypt communications.
4) ASC negotiates the session key with ROC and LSC.

Since the efficiency of symmetric encryption is much higher than that of asymmetric encryption, the communication between blockchains adopts symmetric encryption, which requires the exchange of keys before communication. The key negotiation process between ASC and LSC is as follows:

1) The access service chain selects the leader node, and the TPM of the leader node generates a random number A, Basic Key, and the timestamp information, which are encrypted with the private key *ASCMPrK* and sent to LSC. The randomness of A is guaranteed by timestamp information and TPM identification information.
2) LSC uses the ASC public key to verify the validity of the message after receiving the message. After successful verification, LSC stores the Basic Key, random number A, and generates random number B in the same way. and sends B to ASC after encryption with private key *LSC_{MPrK}*.
3) After receiving the message from LSC, ASC uses the public key *LSCMPUK* of LSC to decrypt the message and obtain the random number B. ASC uses TPM to combine random numbers A, B and Basic Key to generate the session key *SKAL*. At the same time, the session key is used to encrypt the negotiated message and send it to LSC.
4) LSC combines the random numbers A, B and Basic Key to generate the session key*SKAL'* using the same algorithm. After receiving the ASC message, LSC uses *SKAL'* to decrypt the message. If the decryption is successful, the key negotiation is completed. The LSC feeds back a message that the session key negotiation is successful to the ASC.
5) After ASC receives the message, the negotiation is completed.

The negotiation process between ASC and ROC is consistent with the above process.

4.2 User Registration

The terminal which the user used to access the IoT contains a TPM chip that can be verified on the remote proof chain. The TPM can provide functions such as secure storage, integrity measurement, and trusted password services.

1) The user encrypts the personal identity certificate and TPM public key information (*UTpmpuk*) with the ASC public key and sends it to the ASC. ASC examines user information and sends a remote public key verification request to a trusted TPM verification third party after successful review.
2) After the ROC receives the verification request, it will verify whether the public key is trustworthy, and the result will be signed with the master private key (*Rmprik*) and feed back to the ASC. To verify the real-time nature of the message, a timestamp information will be added after the message. The final message sent is Msg = {*Sign_{roc}*, *Ts_{roc}*} *Ts_{roc}* is the timestamp information.

$$\mathrm{Res_u} = Ver_{TPM}(UTpm_{puk}) \qquad (4)$$

$$\mathrm{Res_u} = Ver_{TPM}(UTpm_{puk}) \qquad (5)$$

3) After receiving the feedback result, the ASC verifies the real-time performance of the received message through its own timestamp information *Ts_{ASC}*, and discards the message if the message times out.

ASC uses the ROC public key to verify the ROC signature. If the verification is successful, it can prove that the user terminal contains a trusted TPM chip.

$$Res_{uASC} = Ver_{R_{mpub}}(sign_{roc}) \tag{6}$$

4) The system recognizes that the registered terminal is credible, and the TPM chip in the leader node generates a random number A by combining user identity information, and generates a credible key based on the random number A.

$$U_{pub}, U_{pri} = Gen(A) \tag{7}$$

After the user key is generated, the leader node generates a random integrity evidence (RIE) for the user to detect the integrity of the user's communication. The leader node signs the key and integrity evidence with its own private key (LN_{pri}) and then publishes them to the blockchain network.

5) After receiving the signature message of the leader node, other nodes of the blockchain verify the authenticity of the signature. After a certain number of nodes are successfully verified, the user key can be determined to be valid.

6) ASC sends the key information to users through secure channels.

A legal device owner can grant other legal users access to their own devices, ASC writes authorization rules into the blockchain to provide LSC with legal access policy authentication.

4.3 Malicious Node Detection

The system uses a combination of hardware and software to ensure the credibility of the operating environment of the power Internet of Things collection equipment. LSC adopts a malicious node detection technology based on smart contracts to conduct real-time credibility evaluation of terminals, and promptly investigate terminals with low credibility values to maintain the credibility of the system operating environment.

The structure of the smart contract is SC-ASC = (LS, ES, Sen, θ, P, σ, Loc, Time).

LS is the leading trusted server, responsible for issuing smart contracts. ES is the contract execution server, Sen is the collection terminals to be detected, σ is the evaluation index (PLR, MDR, CDR, HBRT), P is the credit score, and σ is the threshold. Loc is the position of the node to be detected.

The detailed process of malicious node detection is as follows:

ES first checks the timestamp information that detects whether the message forwarded by the terminal is out of date. And if the message is out of date, it will be dropped. The system records the number of timeout messages of each node. At the same time, the system sets the threshold σ_T. If the ratio exceeds the initial threshold σ_T, the node is directly judged as a malicious node. Then LS detects the location information in the message. If the location information is severely distorted, it directly determines that the current communication is malicious communication, records and discards the malicious data packet. The system also sets the threshold σLoc, when the ratio of the node's distorted location message exceeds the initial threshold σ_{Loc} in a certain period of time, the node is directly determined as a malicious node.

After verifying the time stamp information and location information, the system preliminarily determines that the current communication is normal communication, and then the system continues to receive data packets and calculates the credible score value of the current communication. The calculation standards are as follows:

Packet Loss Rate: Since malicious nodes and unreliable links will increase the node's packet loss rate, the packet loss rate can be used as one of the criteria for measuring malicious nodes.

$$PLR = 1 - \left(\frac{n_{recv}}{n_{send}}\right) \tag{8}$$

n_{recv} is the number of successfully received data packets, and nsend is the number of all the data packets sent in the current time interval.

Message Delay Rate: S Since malicious nodes will increase the delay when processing data, in order to ensure that the received data is valid, the system records the time taken by the current collection terminal from collecting data to forwarding data, and at the same time sets the time interval Td to calculate the message delay rate.

$$MDR = \begin{cases} (T_{sensor}/T_d)\ T_{sensor} < T_d \\ 1 \qquad\quad T_{sensor}{}^3 T_d \end{cases} \tag{9}$$

Communication Delay Rate: The response time of malicious nodes is longer than that of normal nodes. The system records the complete time from when the node to be detected receives the request to when the requester receives the response within a certain time interval. This delay is mainly for the messages on the communication link.

$$CDR = (T_{hd} + T_{td})/T_e \tag{10}$$

$$T_{td} = Ms/Nb + Pd/ts \tag{11}$$

Thd is the processing time, *Ttd* is the propagation time of message, Ms is the current size of message, Nb is the bandwidth of network, pd is the propagation distance, ts is the propagation speed, and *Te* is the preset time interval.

Historical behavior: Malicious nodes often communicate continuously within a certain interval. T The system calculates the ratio of malicious information to normal information of the node in a certain time interval as one of the reference standards for reputation value.

$$HBR_T = Num_{MB}/(Num_{NB} + Num_{MB}) \tag{12}$$

NumMB represents the number of malicious communications, *NumNB* is the number of normal communications, and T is the time interval.

The current communication score (Communication Score, CS) of the node is:

$$CS = \lambda_1 * PLR + \lambda_2 * MDR + \lambda_3 * CDR + \lambda_4 HBR_T \tag{13}$$

The ratio of each factor can be adjusted according to different scenarios, and it needs to satisfy $\lambda_1 + \lambda_2 + \lambda_3 + \lambda_4 = 1$. The system sets the threshold K. If CS $\leq$ K, the current communication is normal communication, otherwise it is malicious communication.

The total communication reputation P of the node to be detected is determined by the number of malicious communications (*NMB*) and the number of normal communications (*NNB*).

$$P = \frac{e^{N_{NB}}}{e^{N_{NB}} + e^{N_{MB}} + 1} \tag{14}$$

The system sets the threshold σ. The collection terminal is recorded as a malicious terminal when P ≤ σ. LS announces the information of malicious nodes to the entire network through the consensus mechanism and removes it from the trusted network.

4.4 Remote Access Policy Verification Mechanism

The Internet of Things has high requirements for the real-time nature of messages. The traditional blockchain uses a proof-of-work mechanism (PoW). Since the blockchain works in a completely open environment, the only way for an attacker to control the blockchain is to occupy with more than 51% of the entire network's computing power, and the cost of an attack is too high. What's more, the PoW mechanism requires a lot of computing power, which cannot meet the requirements in the power Internet of Things scenario. The server containing the TPM chip has a strong identity certificate that cannot be forged. The system has established a trusted verification chain (TVC) in the ASC that is specifically responsible for verification. Since each node in TVC is highly credible, the system can randomly assign accounting nodes without using the traditional consensus mechanism of proof-of-work, which improves the efficiency of the system. This paper designs a trusted verification mechanism based on a trusted server in the log record chain to efficiently verify user access rights and improve the system operating efficiency.

The system sets a parameter N. N is the number of trusted servers that need to participate in the verification, which can be adjusted according to different scenarios. N is set to 12 in this paper. To ensure the efficiency of verification, the TVC stores the cache of the verification strategy in the ASC.

The process of TVC trusted verification is as follows:

1) Randomly select a verification node from N nodes to establish communication with visitors. For example, assume that node 1 is selected
2) Set node 2 as the TVC accounting node at this time. Node 2 anonymizes the visitor's integrity information and verifies the authenticity of the integrity information with the ROC. If the ROC verification is unsuccessful, it rejects the visitor's access request. If successful, continue to step 3.
3) Node 2 verifies whether there are the visitor's access strategy and integrity evidence from the ASC cache. If the visitor's information does not exist in the cache, step 4 is executed. If it exists, go to step 5.
4) Node 2 requests ASC to update the cached data, and then queries again whether there is visitor's information in the blockchain, if it exists, execute step 5, if it still does not exist, then reject the visitor's access request.
5) Node 2 verifies whether the integrity evidence in the blockchain is the same as the evidence provided by the visitor. If they are the same, it proves that the information has not been modified, otherwise the verification fails.

6) Node 2 determines whether the visitor's access request meets the requirements according to the access policy in the ASC, and writes the judgment result into the blockchain system.

7) Node 2 returns the verification result to the visitor, and writes the verification process into the blockchain system for other verification nodes to check.

The Power Internet of Things is the application of the Internet of Things in the smart grid. The power system is realized the interconnection of everything in the power system and human- computer interaction with a smart service system with comprehensive status perception, efficient information processing, and convenient and flexible applications through the data collection, authority control, and status monitoring of key links in the power grid system such as power generation, transmission, transformation, distribution, and power consumption.

Through the data acquisition, access control, condition monitoring in the grid system's power generation, transmission, substation, power distribution process, power IoT realized the interconnection between all things in each step of the power system, human-computer interaction. Power IoT is an intelligence system which has the characteristics of state comprehensive perception, efficient information processing and convenient and flexible application.

The data collected by various smart meters in ASC is stored in the ASC blockchain. The trusted server can verify the reputation value of each terminal in real time, avoiding malicious terminals from uploading malicious data. The specific operation process of the trusted power Internet of Things system based on the blockchain is as follows:

1) If the visitor A wants to access the data in the power Internet of Things, the visitor terminal collects its own integrity status information through the TPM integrity collection module, The integrity status information, the requested access resource information (*Requ*), and RIE obtained at registration are packaged and encrypted with the private key and sent to the TVC.

TVC queries the visitor's public key information through the ASC cache and decrypts the visitor's request packet.

TVC randomly selects nodes to verify the visitor's access strategy and integrity through the trusted remote verification strategy, to determine whether the access terminal is credible and whether the access terminal has the legal access rights to the requested data.

If the verification is passed, LSC randomly selects the lead node to record the visitor's access behavior, and obtains the electricity data information requested by the visitor in the blockchain, uses the private key of blockchain to sign, and then uses the visitor's public key to encrypt the message and send to the visitors.

After receiving the message, the visitor uses his own private key to decrypt the message, and uses the blockchain public key to verify the authenticity of the source of the message.

The use of trusted computing combined with the power blockchain greatly reduces the risk of the paralysis of the central server and the leakage of privacy under high concurrency situations. The system separates each permission into different blockchains, solving the problem of excessive centralization of strategic decision-making in the traditional power blockchain system. Through trusted computing, the security of each blockchain server operating environment, power blockchain collection terminal, and power blockchain access terminal is guaranteed, which is more in line with the actual network operating environment.

5   Analysis

Anti-eavesdropping Attack: An eavesdropping attack means the attacker monitors the communication channel between the two parties to obtain unencrypted sensitive data from both parties. Although it will not affect the normal operation of the system, it will lead to the leakage of user privacy and cause serious consequences. The communication between the user and the blockchain is encrypted communication, which ensures that the information will not be eavesdropped by unauthorized users.

Anti-replay Attack: A replay attack refers to a malicious node republishing data packets in the previous system to the system, causing system performance degradation. This system includes timestamp information in all communication processes, and both parties in communication receive messages After that, first verify whether the difference between the synchronized clock information and the time stamp is less than the threshold THR, and only when the time difference is within the allowable range, the message is considered as a valid message.

Anti-witch Attack: A witch attack means that a single node has multiple identities and disrupts network behavior. Since the identities of users and blockchain nodes in the system are protected by trust, malicious nodes cannot forge identities.

Decentralized and Traceable: The system integrates each permission into three blockchains and greatly reduces the pressure on the central server by using the decentralized nature of the blockchain. At the same time, all operations in the blockchain will be recorded. It can be traced at any time, avoiding the problem that the traditional central server cannot supervise, and enhancing the user trust.

6   Summary

In the primary stage of power Internet of Things research, how to ensure the service efficiency of massive data under the high concurrency and the security of private data in the Internet of Things is particularly important. The power blockchain guarantee mechanism proposed in this paper combined the advantages of the trusted computing and the power blockchain, which not only removes the serious centralization problems of traditional power Internet of Things, but also guarantees the security of each blockchain node server through trusted computing. It solves the defect that blockchain nodes are vulnerable to be attacked in the open environment. Through remote integrity verification and policy verification, the system guarantees the security of networked terminals. At the same time, a reputation-based malicious node detection scheme is designed at the collection layer to monitor the status of each collection terminal in real time. It will find malicious terminals in time and remove the suspect terminals with low reputation from the network to guarantee the authenticity of the collection terminal and the information collected by the terminal. In summary, the power blockchain guarantee mechanism based on trusted computing greatly improves the security of system operation while ensuring the efficiency of power services.

Acknowledgment. This work is supported by Science and Technology Project of STATE GRID ZHEJIANG ELECTRIC POWER CO., LTD. (5211DS200002).

References

1. He, Z.Y., Duan, T.T., Zhang, Y., Zhang, H.W., Sun, Y.: The application and challenges of blockchain technology in the internet of things. J. Appl. Sci. **38**(01), 22–33 (2020)
2. Ouaddah, A., Elkalam, A.A., Ouahman, A.A.: Towards a novel privacy-preserving access control model based on blockchain technology in IoT. In: Rocha, Á., Serrhini, M., Felgueiras, C. (eds.) Europe and MENA Cooperation Advances in Information and Communication Technologies. Advances in Intelligent Systems and Computing, vol. 520, pp. 523–533. Springer, Cham (2017). https://doi.org/10.1007/978-3-319-46568-5_53
3. Zhang, J.H., Cui, B., Li, R., Shi, J.S.: Access control system of internet of things based on smart contract[J]. Comput. Eng. **47**(4), 21–31 (2021). https://doi.org/10.19678/j.issn.1000-3428.005 8302
4. Ding, S., Cao, J., Li, C.: A novel attribute-based access control scheme using blockchain for IoT. IEEE Access **7**, 38431–38441 (2019)
5. Liu, M.D., Shi, Y.J., Chen, Z.N.: Distributed trusted network connection architecture based on blockchain. J. Softw. **30**(8), 2314–2336 (2019)
6. Zhang, C., Truxen, A.: Trusted computing enhanced blockchain (2020). https://arxiv.org/abs/1904.08335
7. Zhang, F., Cecchetti, E., Croman, K.: Town crier: an authenticated data feed for smart contracts. In: Proceedings of the 2016 ACM SIGSAC Conference on Computer and Communications Security, Vienna, pp. 270–282 (2016)
8. Huang, J.H., Shen, C.X.: TPCM active defense trusted server platform design. J. Zhengzhou Univ. (Sci. Ed.) **51**(03), 1–6 (2019)

Analysis and Implementation of Distributed DTU Communication Method Based on DDS Protocol

Yonggui Wang$^{(\boxtimes)}$ (iD), Zhu Liu, and Lvchao Huang

State Grid Information and Telecommunication Group Co., Ltd., Beijing 100052, China

Abstract. In view of current problems of a wide variety, huge number, different specifications of different manufacturers, and low data real-time performance of distribution terminal unit (DTU), this paper proposes a distributed DTU communication method based on the data distribution service (DDS) protocol by comparing the characteristics of communication protocols used by the existing power distribution Internet of Things, and analyzes the function characteristics of the this protocol on distributed DTU. Based on modular design ideas, the software and hardware platforms are built to create a communication environment. The model files of the main control unit and interval unit of the distributed DTU are created and mapped to the message file of the DDS middleware. By setting the quality of service (QoS) required by publishers and subscribers, real-time efficient data transmission of master control unit and intervals unit is realized, and the data subscription and publishing functions of the terminal and the global data space are realized. The plug and play access method is studied to discovery automatically the complete Peer to Peer access node. The communication experiment was conducted, and the experiment show that the distributed DTU method based on the DDS protocol has the characteristics of high data throughput, low delay transmission, and custom priority.

Keywords: DDS protocol · Information model · Message mapping

1 Introduction

The distribution network is located at the end of the grid system and is a bridge connecting the grid and users. It is an important guarantee for the friendly access of distributed energy, the reliable bearing capacity of new loads, and the flexible satisfaction of the diverse energy demand of users. The aim is to realize the global identification of low-voltage equipment in the distribution network and the extensive interconnection of equipment by constructing a "cloud-pipe-side-end" distribution Internet of Things architecture, thereby promoting the "three streams" of energy flow, business flow, and data flow on the distribution side. Further, comprehensively improve the intelligent and digital level of the distribution network to meet the electricity demand of the people for a better life.

X. Sun et al. (Eds.): ICAIS 2021, LNCS 12737, pp. 502–513, 2021.
https://doi.org/10.1007/978-3-030-78612-0_40

In the power distribution Internet of Things architecture, the "edge" layer equipment integrates the core capabilities of network, computing, storage, and application, and realizes flexible function deployment and intelligent business processing through software-defined terminals and edge computing technologies. The "end" layer equipment integrates the core capabilities of sensing, communication, and execution, and realizes real-time collection and local control of the operation status, equipment status, and environmental status of the distribution network through ubiquitous perception, reliable communication and other technologies [1]. The DTU is an integrated edge-side and end-side device in the power distribution Internet of Things system architecture, and is widely deployed in power distribution switchgear, ring mains and other occasions. Complex functions lead to many problems in practical applications, such as large size, complicated wiring, insufficient scalability, and so on. Therefore, the concept of distributed DTU [2, 3] is proposed, which is divided into two parts: the main control unit and the interval unit. Compared with traditional distribution automation terminals, distributed DTU has the advantages of quickly and accurately locating fault points, automatic transfer of non-fault areas, and localization of processing. Although "side-end separation" reduces the complexity of DTU, it also introduces new problems: 1) There are many equipment manufacturers, and the communication interface and protocol between the main control unit and the interval unit are not unified, which increases the difficulty of application; 2) The main control unit and interval unit are changed from the original board bus "tightly coupled" to the information bus "loosely coupled", and the impact of communication delay on the delay-sensitive business of the distribution network needs to be considered; 3) New application requirements such as plug-and-play of power distribution Internet of Things terminal [4], rapid function iteration. Therefore, the current communication interface and protocol between the main control unit and the interval unit have become the focus of attention of all parties.

In recent years, DDS has been applied in many fields through the data-centric publish/subscribe transmission characteristics [5, 6]. Literature [7] introduces its application in traffic control system. Literature [8] proposes applications in the field of drones. Similarly, research and application exploration in the power industry have also emerged. Literature [9, 10] introduced the optimization of DDS to improve communication and control issues on the smart grid. Literature [11] proposed the application of DDS in the automatic demand response system to solve QoS requirements of the underlying data in the power demand response business. Florida International University has studied the use of DDS to design a new operating framework for the interoperability of the smart grid test basic platform, which is used to integrate data communication between devices with different protocols [12]. The current research has provided theoretical basis and practical exploration for the application of DDS in the field of power distribution Internet of Things [13].

This article aims to analyze and compare the applicability of mainstream communication protocols by studying the DTU "side-end" communication requirements under the power distribution Internet of Things architecture. It proposes a communication method for the main control unit and interval unit of the distributed DTU based on the DDS protocol, and carries out simulation verification for the industry's reference.

2   Characteristic Analysis of Distributed DTU Communication Protocol

2.1   Communication Protocol Comparison

The physical communication method between the main control unit and the bay unit generally recommends industrial Ethernet or broadband wireless, and usually uses a request/response mechanism or a communication protocol based on an intermediate agent-based centralized publish/subscribe mechanism, such as CAN, HTTP, MQTT, COAP, GOOSE et al. [14], as shown in Table 1 below.

Table 1. Comparison of commonly used communication protocols

Name	CAN	HTTP	COAP	MQTT	GOOSE
Mechanism	Request/response	Request/response	Request/response	Publish/subscribe	Publish/subscribe
Transport layer	No	TCP	UDP	TCP	No
Real-time	Limited to underlying communication				
Security	Verification algorithm, customizable encryption	Based on SSL and TLS	Supported DTLS encryption	Name/password authentication, SSL data encryption	Self-checking algorithm, customizable encryption

Common communication protocols of distribution Internet of Things are object-centric, and use a client/server model based on request/response mechanism to achieve data transmission. This method has transmission bottlenecks and it is difficult to ensure real-time data transmission. Analyze the common communication protocol between the main control unit and interval unit: 1) COAP protocol based on the request/response mechanism is widely used. The disadvantage is that it cannot be reversely controlled, and it does not response the types that are not supported. Data delay will cause the request and response channels to be blocked. 2) MQTT and GOOSE protocols adopt publish/subscribe communication architecture, but they are all object-centric. The former is only distributed communication based on the application layer and is still limited by the underlying hardware communication. The latter supports object-oriented features such as reuse and loose coupling. But it must be based on predefined data types, thereby limiting loosely coupled and self-registered connections of massive data types. 3) The CAN communication protocol uses request/response mechanism or broadcast for data communication, and has the characteristics of low-level, high reliability, and real-time. However, due to the limitation of the underlying communication, when the communication data volume is large and the transmission speed is high, the communication performance is reduced.

With the rapid development of distribution network technology and the wide application of distributed DTU, the transformation, upgrading and research of hundreds of millions of DTU equipment will become an important part in the construction of the distribution Internet of Things. Therefore, the communication protocol with the characteristics of strong flexibility, high real-time and low coupling will become the key needs of development of the distribution Internet of Things. To sum up, the current commonly used communication methods are limited by the underlying communication, and it is difficult to solve the problems of real-time data, diversity of data types, and rapid access to products of different manufacturers between distributed DTU. This paper introduces the Publish/Subscribe-based Data Distribution Service (DDS) protocol, builds a data-centric data communication model, realizes the loose coupling of communication between the main control unit and the interval unit, and solves the problem of distributed DTU communication mentioned in the above.

2.2 Principle of Distributed DTU Based on DDS Protocol

DDS is a middleware for data information publishing, using a publish/subscribe communication mechanism. Taking data as the center, it build a distributed real-time data transmission model in a heterogeneous environment and has the characteristics of loosely coupled structure of point-to-point transmission. It could realize the unified management of data based on the global data space, and the high real-time and reliable communication of distributed transmission.

In order to ensure the quality of communication data transmission, the DDS protocol provides as many as 22 QoS strategies to meet various demand services in the real-time transmission process as much as possible. Using these strategies, the optimal allocation of resources such as network bandwidth and memory space can be realized, and the lifetime of data can also be managed to ensure the reliability and real-time performance of data transmission. As a mature industry standard protocol, there have been various supplier implementation solutions, such as Connext DDS and OpenDDS implemented by RTI, OpenSplice from ADLink, Vortex from PrismTech, and ZRDDS from Zhenrong Technology.

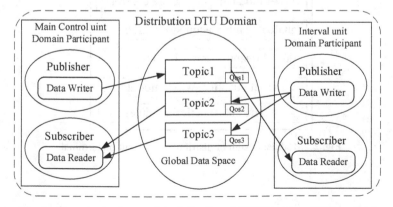

Fig. 1. Communication model of distributed DTU based on DDS protocol

Combining with the structural characteristics of DDS, distributed DTU provides a DDS protocol domain, and managed data with shared memory through global data space. The main control unit and the interval unit are domain participants in the protocol space domain, and include multiple publishers and subscribers. The publisher uses the data writer module to publish the topic, and the subscriber uses the data reader module to subscribe to the topic (see Fig. 1).

3   Key Point of Distributed DTU Based on DDS Protocol

According to the characteristics of DDS protocol and distributed DTU, the main key points are as follows: (1) Modular design of distributed DTU provide platform support for communication; (2) Information model mapping of main control and interval units solve the compatible interaction between different product communication protocols and DDS protocols, with less development workload and difficulty; (3) Plug and play access technology realize dynamic discovery and automatic communication between devices.

3.1   Modular Design of Distribution Terminal

Distributed DTU adopts modular design and is divided into power supply module, core control module, analog quantity acquisition module, digital quantity acquisition module, digital quantity switch module, information communication interface module and several sub-function modules according to function [15] (see Fig. 2). According to the combination of functional modules, the distributed DTU can be divided into a general-purpose main control unit and a customized interval unit. The main control unit and the interval unit transfer information model files, "three remote" (remote measurement, remote signaling, remote control) data and other type of information, and realize automatic registration and online operation.

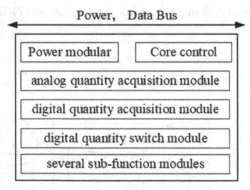

Fig. 2. Modular design of distributed distribution terminal

The core function of the interval unit is SCADA (Supervisory Control And Data Acquisition), which is used for AC sampling, data acquisition and processing, remote signaling and remote control, and troubleshooting, as shown in Table 2 below.

Table 2. Interval unit function information

Publish/subscribe information	Specification
Voltage and current sampling	Including 0.5-level accuracy of voltage and current acquisition, 1-level accuracy of active and reactive power, 0.5-level accuracy of active electrical energy, 2-level accuracy of reactive electrical energy, current and voltage loop power, etc.
Remote signaling, remote control	The remote signal voltage is 24V, the resolution is not more than 5 ms. The anti-shake time can be set by software, and the switch's opening and closing control can be realized by remote control. It has software and hardware anti-malfunction measures
Fault information	Fault recording and broadcasting information, self-diagnosis recovery and other alarm faults, etc.
Historical data	Record a certain amount of historical data as required

The key for the interval unit is current and voltage acquisition and processing. According to the standard requirements, the current and voltage sampling accuracy is 0.5-level, the sampling rate is not less than 4k Hz. Real-time acquisition of analog data volume is realized by selecting high-precision analog acquisition chip. According to the collected phase current, voltage or line current and voltage, the active power, reactive power and apparent power are calculated as follows.

$$P = 3U_P I_P \cos \phi \; or \; \sqrt{3}U_L I_L \cos \phi \tag{1}$$

$$Q = 3U_P I_P \sin \phi \; or \; \sqrt{3}U_L I_L \sin \phi \tag{2}$$

$$S = 3U_P I_P \; or \; \sqrt{3}U_L I_L \tag{3}$$

The main control unit and interval unit are connected through a data bus. This method can not only realize a one-to-one combined power distribution terminal, but also a one-to-many or many-to-many distributed connection combination. As the core unit of a distributed DTU, the main control unit is equipped with expandable NAND Flash, DDR, etc. to meet data management needs. In addition, it also has functions such as Ethernet, serial port, Bluetooth, wireless public network/wireless private network, etc. to realize multiple communication methods of interval unit and cloud master station.

3.2 Information Model Mapping

According to the smart terminal model specification of the distribution Internet of Things, the equipment information model suitable for the distribution Internet of Things includes basic equipment information, station topology, measurement data and asset information. Basic information composes of ID information, device name, manufacturer name, software and hardware version, and production date. Asset information includes equipment assets, asset maintainers, asset owners, and equipment manufacturers. The topology of the station area includes the topology information of the low-voltage primary equipment, and adopts the extended split-phase topology modeling method. The measurement data information of all equipment in the station area composes of analog, discrete, cumulative, control commands and configuration parameters, etc. [16–18].

As a data conversion site connecting the terminal equipment and the main control unit, the interval unit converts a large amount of various types of data into data types that can be directly read by the main control unit. Therefore, the interval unit is responsible for the precise collection and transmission of data and status, command reception and execution, and the function of recording equipment special status information. The interval unit exists as an "end point" of the main control unit, and the information model for creating the interval unit is shown in Fig. 3 below. For different interval unit functions, only need to add and delete the corresponding measurement equipment information to define different information models.

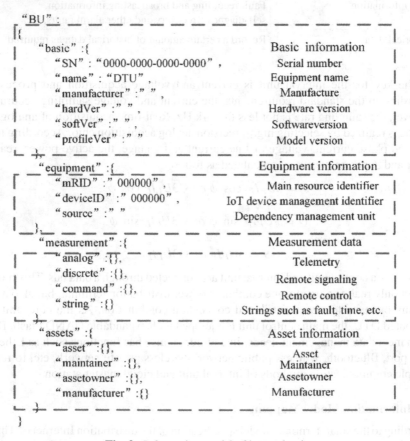

Fig. 3. Information model of interval unit

The main control unit participates in the data communication of the "cloud" and "end" devices. The information model of the main control unit include the data type communicated with the cloud master station in addition to the data type of the interval unit communication. When the interval unit is added or changed, the information model of the main control unit can be easily corrected.

The mapping relationship between the information model of the main control unit and the interval unit and the message type based on DDS is the key to ensure the correct transmission of data. The data type in the DDS is defined by a C++ style IDL file, which contains the data of publishing and subscription. The process is to map from the interval unit information model file based on xml or JSON format to the message file of the structure represented by C++. The mapping from the terminal information model file to the DDS middleware message type is to convert the message transmitted by the information model to a message type based on the DDS protocol, as shown in Fig. 4 below.

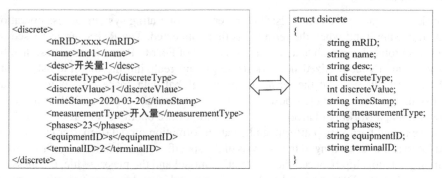

Fig. 4. Mapping of information model and DDS data type

The remote signaling 1 in Fig. 4 above is taken as an example. It is mapped to a structure message type conforming to the DDS middleware, and then corresponding publisher and subscriber programs are generated, and the publisher and subscriber of the associated data are discovered through the real time publish subscribe protocol (RTPS). For the switch status signal in the example, the reliability of message delivery is the key. The transmission strategy QoS of the publisher and subscriber is set to Reliability to ensure the orderly and complete delivery of data. For scenarios where transmission requirements are not strict, the publisher's transmission strategy QoS can be set to Best effort to ensure the real-time data transmission. The above introduces the intelligent terminal model specification based on the distribution of Internet of Things, and realizes the mapping between the information model and the DDS. For different communication protocols of other products, the mapping method is the same and converted into a structured file, as shown in Fig. 5 below.

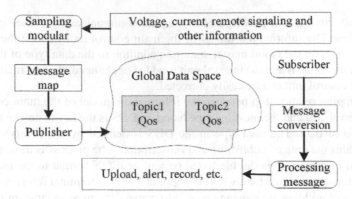

Fig. 5. Message mapping and conversion between different protocols based on DDS

3.3 Plug and Play Access

In order to maintain the entire distribution terminal operating system, access operation should be simplified when the terminal is first connected. The RTPS service based on the DDS protocol can realize automatic discovery of Peer to Peer access nodes, thereby constructing a decentralized network topology and realizing the data publishing and subscription functions of the terminal and the global data space. The plug-and-play access method of distributed power distribution terminal based on DDS protocol is shown. First, a working platform with DDS middleware operating environment is built on the existing hardware platform, and create information model of master control unit and interval unit according to the analysis of the specific realized functions. Through the mapping relationship between the information model and the message file, the message type based on the DDS protocol is directly generated, and the communication topic is registered. According to the analysis of functional requirements, create the main body of publishing and subscribing topics, and set the corresponding QoS to ensure that data transmission is performed. Finally, based on the RTPS protocol, the main control unit and interval unit are automatically associated according to the corresponding theme, the connection state is maintained through the heartbeat mechanism, and real-time data transmission is realized.

4   Experiment

In order to verify the feasibility of the application of the DDS protocol between the main control unit and the interval unit of the distributed power distribution terminal, the real-time data communication experiment is conducted. Using the middleware RTI DDS 6.0.1 of a mature commercial software company as the middle ware tool, the operating environment is configured on two laptops. The two devices are connected with a network cable to build a distributed power distribution terminal communication platform based on the DDS protocol. The UDP/IP protocol is used by the interval unit to send data in real time and test the main control unit receiving data.

To test the reliability of transmission at a fixed transmission speed, the interval unit selects three groups of data packets as 128 Byte, 512 Byte, and 1024 Byte commonly used in power distribution terminals and send 10,000 data packets. The number of data packets and total length of the data are calculated to illustrate the transmission rate at the current speed. Double verification was performed by program counting and the use of RTI's Monitor tool. Each experiment was repeated 10 times.

By calculating the ratio of the number of received packets, the total amount of data to the number of sent packets, and the total of data, the reliability of transmission is expressed. As shown in Table 3 below, it indicates that the DDS protocol-based operating software and hardware environment can meet basic requirements for data transmission reliability.

Table 3. Reliability test results

Classification	128 Byte	512 Byte	1024 Byte
Receive packet	10000	10000	10000
Total received data	1.28M	5.12M	10.24M
Transmission reliability	100%	100%	100%

The above experiments show that the distributed communication method based on the DDS protocol can complete data reception under reliable QoS, and meet the general reliable communication requirements. Next, by sending 10,000 data packets in increments of the data packet size through the interval unit, the change of communication throughput for different data packet sizes is calculated. In this experiment, both the main control unit and the interval unit use the Reliability strategy to publish/subscribe data packets. The experimental results are shown in Fig. 6 below, indicating that the throughput gradually increases as the data packet size changes. Similarly, due to the increase in the amount of data, the resulting delay results also show an increasing trend.

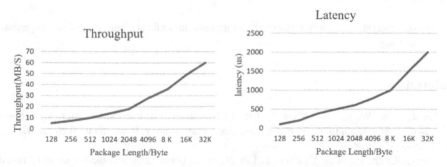

Fig. 6. Throughput and latency experimental test results

The DDS protocol provides many custom interfaces through QoS policies. The priority of sending and receiving data is set through DDS_TransportPriorityQosPolicy in the DDS_TopicQoS structure. The larger the data, the higher the priority. This experiment defines two pairs of publish/subscribe models, and set the parameter transport_priority to different values, indicating different transmission priorities. Experiments show that the received high-priority data is greater than the total amount of low-priority data, indicating that high-priority tasks can be received first in the process of receiving low-priority data. Because of the high real-time performance of DDS protocol data transmission, it is difficult to obtain the situation that low-priority data cannot be received completely, which also proves the effectiveness of DDS protocol transmission data priority setting.

The above experiments show that the distributed terminal communication method based on the DDS protocol can achieve the characteristics of high data throughput, low delay transmission, and custom priority, and realize real-time transmission of various data types of the distribution terminal communication.

5 Conclusion

Based on the analysis of data distribution services, this paper proposes a distributed DTU communication method based on the DDS protocol. First, build the software and hardware architecture of the distributed single terminal and configure the operating environment of the main control unit and the interval unit. Through the communication requirements of the main control unit and the interval unit, a corresponding information model is created. Through the communication requirements of the main control unit and the interval unit, a corresponding information model is created. On this basis, combining the characteristics of the subject and message of the DDS protocol, the mapping model from the information model to the subject message is studied to achieve efficient communication. By setting an experimental platform, the effectiveness and feasibility of the method is verified, and the plug-and-play between the main control unit and the interval unit of the distributed power distribution terminal and the real-time transmission of massive data types are realized.

Funding Statement. This work is supported by Science and Technology Project of the State Grid Corporation of China (No. 536800200021).

Conflicts of Interest. The authors declare that they have no conflicts of interest to report regarding the present study.

References

1. Lu, J., Luan, W., Liu, R., Wang, P., Lin, J.: Architecture of distribution internet of things based on wide spread sensing & software defined technology. Power Syst. Technol. **42**(10), 3108–3115 (2018)
2. Zhang, Z., Zhou, J., Cai, Y., Zhou, J., Liu, R., et al.: Distribution automation terminal based on modular configuration design. Autom. Electric Power Syst. **41**(13), 106–110 (2017)
3. Li, K., Wang, J., Fan, L., Huang, L., Chen, J., et al.: Novel distribution terminal based on separation design. Chin. J. Electron Devices **42**(6), 1435–1439 (2019)
4. Ying, J., Cai, Y., Liu, M., Du, H., Zhao, J., et al.: Adaptive access method of low voltage intelligent terminal for distribution internet of things. Autom. Electric Power Syst. **44**(2), 22–27 (2020)

5. Wang, X., Peng, H.: Research and implementation of message bus communication based on DDS. Wirel. Internet Technol. **24**, 1–10 (2019)
6. Lv, Y., Wang, X., Zhang, J.: Ship integrated platform management system based on DDS. Ship Sci. Technol. **33**(5), 47–52 (2011)
7. Almadani, B., Khan, S., Bajwa, M.N., et al.: AVL and monitoring for massive traffic control system over DDS. Mob. Inf. Syst. **2**(187548), 1–9 (2015)
8. Liu, J., Wang, Y., Liu, A.: Design of video acquisition and transmission architecture for UAV based on OpenCV and OpenDDS. New Product Tech **3**, 50–53 (2020)
9. Alaerjan, A., Kim, D.: Tailoring DDS to smart grids for improved communication and control. In: 5th Smart Greens, pp. 433–438 (2016)
10. Alaerjan, A., Kim, D.K., Ming, H., et al.: Using DDS based on unified data model to improve interoperability of smart grids. In: IEEE International Conference on Smart Energy Grid Engineering, pp. 110–114 (2018)
11. Li, B., Ye, Y., Qi, B., Zhang, J., Li, D.: Applicability analysis and prospect of DDS in automated demand response system. Power Syst. Technol. **44**(5), 1922–1930 (2020)
12. Youssef, T., Elsayed, A.T., Mohammed, O.: DDS based interoperability framework for smart grid testbed infrastructure. In: IEEE International Conference on Environment & Electrical Engineering, vol. 9 (2015)
13. Bi, Y., Jiang, L., Zhang, D., Wang, X., Cui, L.: Mapping of IEC 61850 to data distribute service for smart substation communication. Proc. CSEE **33**(7), 149–155 (2013)
14. Du, D., Ye, Z., Xu, Y.: A solution of integrated intelligent distributed feeder automation based on GOOSE. Power Syst. Prot. Control **44**(24), 183–190 (2016)
15. Li, Y., Shao, Q., Li, Y., Xu, K., Nie, M.: Research and application of intelligentmisoperation prevention technology for power grid operation. Inf. Technol. Inform. **1**, 65–68 (2018)
16. Xu, X., Mei, J., Qian, C., Zheng, J., Wang, Y., et al.: Research method for implementation of the self-describing function of distribution terminals based on the extended IEC 60870-5-104 protocol. Power Syst. Prot. Control **44**(7), 128–133 (2016)
17. Shen, B., Cai, Z., Dai, G., Guo, C.: Communication analysis of information collection services in smart distribution system towards ubiquitous power Internet of Things. Electric Power Constr. **40**(9), 27–34 (2019)
18. Wang, Y., Xu, X., Mei, J., Yu, J., Qian, C., et al.: Automatic recognition technology of distribution terminal based on IEC61850. Electr. Meas. Instrum. **6**, 32–36 (2016)

Sensor Failure Detection Based on Programmable Switch and Machine Learning

Xiaolong Zhang, Rengbo Yang, Guangfeng Guo, and Junxing Zhang(✉)

College of Computer Science, Inner Mongolia University, Hohhot 010021, China
junxing@mail.imu.edu.cn

Abstract. With the large-scale application of the Internet of Things, various sensors continue to produce new and various environmental data. Among them, there may be some failure data caused by environmental interference, device aging, etc., and these failure data are given to relevant scientific researchers and The Internet of Things system brings huge problems. We propose a new kind of Internet of Things nodes combined with programmable switches failure detection method. Different from the method proposed by the predecessors, we perform failure detection during the sensor data packet transmission. This method realizes the interaction between the programmable switch and the local controller. It can perform failure detection on a large amount of sensor data in real-time. Use the processing power of programmable switches to reduce the feature extraction time in machine learning algorithms. In this article, we reviewed the technical background of programmable switch The Internet of Things failure detection and explained its architecture. To prove the feasibility of the system, we implemented it on the bmv2 software switch. The prototype was verified through experiments, simulation evaluation was performed on the real data set, and the average time for the machine learning algorithm to classify each sensor data was 1.26 ms.

Keywords: Internet of Things · Wireless sensor networks · P4 · Software-defined networking · Fault detection · Fault diagnosis

1 Introduction

The Internet of Things (IoT) refers to systems that can be connected and communicate with the Internet without any human intervention. The system can be uniquely identified in the network and can transmit data without human interference. It has more advantages than other traditional network environments, mainly because of its non-interference, wider range and scalability [1]. The Internet of Things is now rapidly expanding. It is estimated that by 2025, the global economic impact will reach 11.1 trillion US dollars [2].

In a real environment, the sensors deployed in advance continuously collect and process a large amount of data. Thereby forming physical quantity data sets in various real environments. Literature [3] uses TelosB nodes to collect a labeled wireless sensor network data set from simple single-hop and multi-hop wireless sensor network

© Springer Nature Switzerland AG 2021
X. Sun et al. (Eds.): ICAIS 2021, LNCS 12737, pp. 514–525, 2021.
https://doi.org/10.1007/978-3-030-78612-0_41

deployments. The data includes humidity and temperature measurements collected at 5-s intervals over a 6-h period.

In 1999, IBM's Andy Stanford-Clark and Arlen Nipper introduced a messaging protocol called MQTT (i.e. message queue telemetry transmission). In 2013, MQTT became a standard protocol of the Organization for the Advancement of Structured Information Standards (OASIS). MQTT is considered to be the most advantageous connection protocol for Machine to Machine (M2M) and IoT. It uses the publish/subscribe model to provide simple implementation and flexible transition [4].

Programming Protocol-Independent Packet Processors (P4) [5] is a new domain-specific language that introduces programmability to the data plane of packet forwarding equipment that supports P4. Therefore, the behavior of the data plane can be described by the P4 program running on it, so that the network operator can continuously program and redeploy the behavior of the packet processing equipment. P4Runtime [6] extends P4 target devices to SDN controllers through API. So you can better monitor the operation of the P4 target device.

To detect data anomalies in IoT, various methods have been studied. According to the state of the sensor node to determine the location, it can be divided into the following three types [7]:

Geographically or logically centralized nodes are responsible for the failure management of the entire network. Lau et al. [8] proposed a centralized Naive Bayes detector, which classifies sensor nodes by analyzing the end-to-end transmission time collected at the receiving end. Yu et al. [9] proposed a new direction for the diagnosis of failed nodes. Their algorithm tried to reduce the failure information to reduce the diagnosis time. The article claims to use rough set (RS) theory to filter less important data and to establish a new simple data set for training SVM.

Each sensor node makes a corresponding decision according to its own level; the decision center is transferred from the receiving node to the public node. Babaie et al. [10] proposed a new method of self-diagnosis. This method reduces the influence of neighboring nodes and uses Petri nets and correlation graphs to analyze the behavior of sensor nodes. Panda and Khilar [11] proposed a distributed self-failure diagnosis (DSFD) algorithm to solve the failure diagnosis problem of large-scale WSN. This method can simultaneously diagnose hard and soft failures.

Between centralized and distributed methods, both the receiving end node and the public node have the right to determine the state of the node. Chanak et al. [12] proposed a distributed failure detection scheme based on mobile receivers, which can identify the operating status of each software and hardware component. In this algorithm, the mobile detector starts its failure diagnosis from the base station. When exploring each deployed node, you will get its operating status. Then, it uploads information from all nodes in the network. It completes its operation by returning to the base station.

Recently, deep learning methods have received widespread attention in the direction of failure detection. Chalapathy and Chawla [13] studied the application of deep learning methods in a wider field of anomaly detection.

Based on the above observations, the existing failure detection algorithms are generally divided into two categories: centralized failure detection and distributed failure detection. We propose a failure detection method that combines programmable switches and machine learning (ML). We combine ML and related MQTT data. Utilize the potential of the programmable switch to collect data packet information at the extreme speed of the data plane to reduce the related data packet transmission delay. So as to detect invalid data faster.

This method faces the following challenges:

In order to efficiently detect failures, how do we choose a fast and accurate ML method?

The matching-action table of programmable switches how should cooperate with the ML algorithm to improve the efficiency of failure detection.

This article, aiming at the widely used IoT application layer protocol MQTT. We have implemented the MQTT data packet format and the process of extracting the MQTT data packet header in the P4 program. We use real MQTT packet simulation traffic to compare different ML algorithms. Select the best algorithm among them and simulate online two scenarios. In this, we simulated the real-time execution of the failure detection algorithm in the ML-based module, which interacts through the interface of the programmable switch. Specifically, the main contributions of this article are as follows: We compared the accuracy and algorithm complexity of different ML algorithms for IoT failure detection, that is, the duration and prediction time of algorithm training.

We compared the accuracy and complexity of different ML algorithms for IoT failure detection, that is, the duration and prediction time of algorithm training.

To achieve a shorter detection delay, we use P4 language to carry out different forwarding strategies for related MQTT data packets on the programmable switch, namely, 1) packet mirroring, 2) payload data extraction.

In the MQTT data packet payload extraction part, we streamlined the data packet length, removed the TCP header and the IP header, and only retained the Ether header information and the payload part of the MQTT data packet to complete the forwarding.

The structure of this article is as follows: The first part is the introduction, which introduces the research background of this article, puts forward the research questions, and list the challenges and contributions of designing new solutions. The second part is the background of MQTT and P4. The third part puts forward the architecture of the IoT failure detection system based on programmable switches and the composition of each part. In the fourth part, we introduce the performance evaluation of the Mininet prototype. The fifth part is to use our new method to carry out related functional verification and result from the discussion. The sixth part is a summary.

2 Background

2.1 MQTT

The MQTT client includes Publisher and Subscriber, and they are mainly composed of programs or devices that use MQTT. The client always connects to the server through the network. The main functions of the client are as follows:

- Publish application messages to other related clients.
- Subscribe to request to receive related application messages.

- Unsubscribe to remove the request to accept application messages.
- Disconnect from the server.
- The client sends heartbeat messages to the server. The interval of heartbeat messages is 1 min by default, but it can also be modified by yourself.

  The MQTT server is called the Broker, which is mainly composed of a program or device. Its main function is to act as an intermediary between the client sending a message and the client requesting a subscription. The main functions of the server are as follows:
- Accept network connections from clients.
- Accept application messages published by the client.
- Handle the client's subscription and unsubscription requests.
- Forward application messages to eligible subscribed clients.

2.2 P4 Language

Figure 1 describes the core concepts and components of P4. The P4 program describes the entire behavior of the packet forwarding device. They are formulated for a specific P4 architecture. The P4 architecture defines the P4 programming model of the packet forwarding device. P4 programmable switch is a software or hardware data packet forwarding device that implements a specific P4 architecture. The P4 compiler designated by the programmable switch compiles the P4 program into binary code, which can be loaded on the P4 programmable switch. The core components of the programmable switch are as follows [14]:

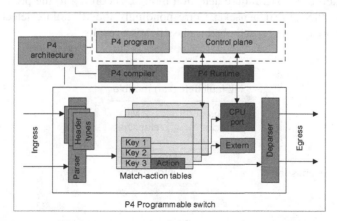

Fig. 1. The concept of P4$_{16}$: the interaction of P4 pipeline and control plane

- P4 packet header type: describes the format of the packet header through an ordered set of basic types. For example, the main data packet format in this article is MQTT connection request data packet, MQTT publishing message data packet and heartbeat data packet.

- P4 parser: It is a state machine that extracts data packet data by applying a predefined sequence, which is based on the type of P4 packet header to identify and extract data.
- P4 table: It is a matching and operation structure that maps user-defined keys to specific P4 operations that can manipulate packet data.
- P4 external function: It is a function provided by the P4 target (software or hardware) and can be used in the P4 program. The P4 external function has a predefined interface with a set of methods that can be used in the P4 program.
- P4 deparser: Assemble the header of the data packet into a complete data packet so that it can pass through the specific exit of the forwarding device.
- The P4Runtime framework provides APIs for controlling P4 target devices. Its operation is shown in Fig. 1. The function of P4Runtime is to manipulate matching and action tables through the control plane. In addition, it provides a CPU port for sending and receiving data packets. P4Runtime utilizes gRPC [15]. Optional client and server certificates can be used to protect the connection between the P4 target and the control plane through TLS for mutual authentication.

3 System Architecture and Components

This section introduces our proposed sensor failure detection system based on the programmable switch (P4). Figure 2 shows the system model described in this article. The ML failure detection module is mainly composed of two parts, namely 1) feature extractor and 2) ML classifier. Under normal circumstances, Publisher sends out MQTT message data packets, which are forwarded via P4 switch. On the P4 switch, we forward the data packet to the ML failure detection module according to the pre-set load data information or the entire data packet. Correspondingly, the ML failure detection module performs feature extraction and obtains classification results.

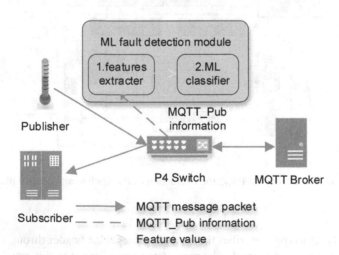

Fig. 2. Sensor failure detection based on programmable switch and machine learning system

To implement a classifier for IoT failure detection, we considered three different ML algorithms, namely stochastic gradient descent (SGD) [16], Multi-layer Perceptron (MLP) [17], and Support vector machines (SVMs) [18]. A comparison between various algorithms is carried out, and the best solution is expected according to the duration of the classification training and the prediction time.

4 System Prototype Implementation

We use Mininet [19] network simulator to build a test experiment platform for the prototype, bmv2 software switch [20] as a programmable switch, and run the ML failure detection module as a Python application. For testing, we ran 1 P4 switch and 3 Mininet network hosts in the system architecture. All test platform components are executed in Oracle VM virtualBox [21], which runs Ubuntu 16.04 with 4 CPU cores and 6 GB RAM. The host operating system of the hypervisor is Windows 10, with Intel Core i7 3770 CPU, 10 GB RAM, and 1TB SSD configuration.

We modified the P4Runtime of the P4 official website tutorial to run our specific topology and P4 program. First of all, we implemented the three types of MQTT packet headers, related parser parts, related forwarding settings, and MQTT packet cloning in the P4 program. In the MQTT data packet payload extraction part, we streamlined the data packet length and only retained the Ether header information to complete the forwarding. Second, we implement the interface with the local controller. It calls the P4Runtime API through gRPC and allows the local controller to read the counter readings in the P4 programmable switch.

We use the ML algorithm in Scikit learn [22] to implement it through a Python-based script, and we use tagged MQTT packet traces as input to illustrate actual traffic scenarios. We also used Eclipse Paho MQTT Python client [23] and Eclipse Mosquitto open-source message broker [24] as the implementation of the MQTT protocol.

5 Functional Verification and Result Discussion

We described the functional verification and results and discussion of this article, performed experiments on the test platform in Sect. 4, and reported the results.

This research uses a wireless sensor network data repository based on the tag released by the University of North Carolina at Greensboro in 2010. By using TelosB nodes, data is collected from simple single-hop and multi-hop WSN. Their data includes humidity and temperature measurements taken every 5 s for 6 h. They introduced hot water vapor to increase humidity and temperature. The purpose of their research is to divide the data into two categories: normal data and abnormal data. For our experiment, we only used indoor data collected from single-hop WSN. In order to evaluate our proposed method. Corresponding to the data set of temperature, humidity, and label, we extracted 4417 observation data, and first divided it into two parts. we use 4/5 with 1/5 The data are used as learning training data and verification data, and a total of 4417 pieces are used to evaluate test data. Then, test through the test platform in Sect. 4 for failure detection.

Now, we study the functional verification of the method proposed in this paper. As shown in Fig. 1, we created the corresponding topology in Mininet, which is composed of 3 PCs and a P4 switch, and they are in the same LAN. PC2 acts as the Broker and is mainly responsible for the transfer of MQTT messages. PC3 acts as the Publisher, sending 4417 MQTT messages to PC2 every 1 μs. PC1 runs the Python script of the ML failure detection module. First, we compile the P4 program and let it be injected into the P4 switch. Secondly, we run the local controller, let it inject forwarding rules, and prepare to read counter information. Once again, we open the MQTT server to provide the role of an intermediate communication server. Open the client Subscriber and initiate a message subscription. Finally, the client Publisher can continuously publish messages. Then the feature extractor module can continuously receive relevant humidity, temperature, and tag messages. After receiving 4417 related MQTT messages, the Ml classifier module can perform failure detection according to our pre-set ML algorithm.

5.1 ML Algorithm Performance Evaluation

To determine the most suitable solution for sensor failure detection based on programmable switches, we compared various algorithms in terms of classification accuracy and algorithm complexity (i.e. training duration and prediction time). For all ML algorithms, we use k-fold cross-validation (k = 5) to calculate the average classification accuracy and perform parameter selection. The parameter settings of the three ML algorithms are shown in Table 1.

Table 1. ML algorithm parameter settings

	Parameters	Values	Description
SGD	Penalty	'l2'	Penalty is the standard regularizer for linear SVM models
	Tol	1e−3	The stopping criterion
SVM	Kernel	'rbf'	Specifies the kernel type to be used in the algorithm
	Gamma	0.06	Kernel coefficient for 'rbf'
	Probability	True	Whether to enable probability estimates
MLP	Solver	'adam'	The solver for weight optimization
	Alpha	0.7	L2 penalty (regularization term) parameter
	Hidden_layer_sizes	(10, 10)	The ith element represents the number of neurons in the ith hidden layer

We compared 3 different ML algorithms and compared them with cross-validation time, failure detection accuracy, and test time respectively. In Fig. 3 we show the cross-validation time of the three algorithms in the case of five executions. This time is calculated and executed as 5-fold cross-validation. As expected, because the data set is relatively small. For SVM and MLP, they can quickly calculate the relevant data needed by the prediction model. And MLP is a neural network with 2 middle layers, and each middle layer contains 10 neurons. In order to determine the parameters of these 20 neurons, a certain amount of calculation is required. As shown in Fig. 5, we show the test time of the three algorithms in the case of five executions, that is, the time required to perform a test set classification (that is, the time of 1/5 of the data set). It can be clearly seen that the time spent by the SVM algorithm is about 4 times that of the other two. What we care most about is the accuracy of failure detection. As shown in Fig. 4, the failure detection accuracy of the three algorithms is shown in the case of five executions. The SGD algorithm is significantly better than the other two algorithms, but relatively speaking, MLP and SVM relatively stable. Considering these three algorithms comprehensively, we believe that SGD and SVM are more suitable for this data set and can provide higher detection accuracy. These two algorithms have also become good candidates for comparison experiments.

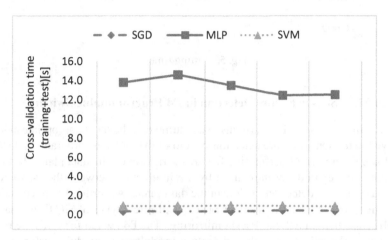

Fig. 3. Cross validation time

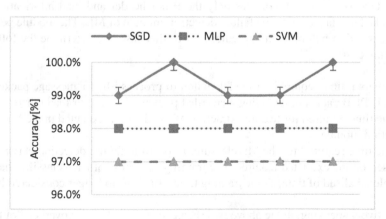

Fig. 4. Failure detection accuracy

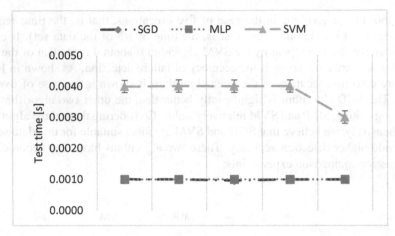

Fig. 5. Testing time

5.2 Real-Time Sensor Failure Detection in P4 Programmable Switch

After evaluating various ML algorithms, we assume that the most appropriate algorithm is deployed in the sensor failure detection system of the real-time programmable switch, and evaluate the impact of performing feature extraction on the data plane. To this end, we evaluated the extra delay introduced by the interaction between the P4 switch and the ML-based failure detection module in the data plane. Accordingly, we consider two different situations, where the P4 switch provides different types of MQTT message data to the ML classifier, namely: a) Packet mirroring: The P4 switch forwards the received data packet to the ML-based failure detection module, The module performs feature extraction before making predictions, b) Load mirroring: The P4 switch modifies the MQTT data packet, which contains only the Ether header and load information, and then sends the data packet to the failure detection module of ML, The module performs feature extraction before making predictions. In this case, we determine the following three delay costs:

- t_1: The total time required for the P4 switch to process MQTT message packets (i.e. MQTT_PUB packets). Including forwarded packet mirroring or load mirroring.
- t_2: The time required for feature extraction of the data set, executed in the ML failure detection module.
- t_3: The time required for the ML classifier to perform failure detection classification is based on the extracted features. The training operation of each classifier has been completed ahead of time, so the training time of ML is no longer considered here.

Intuitively speaking, in the above two scenarios a), b), the time overhead of t_3 does not change with different Ml algorithms. However, t_1 and t_2 may be different because of the more advanced packet processing operations performed in b). Figure 6 summarizes the time overhead in two different scenarios.

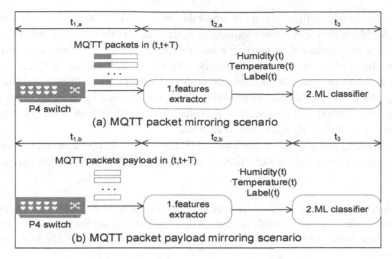

Fig. 6. Time consumption in different scenarios

To verify the sensor failure detection system of our programmable switch, we considered the SGD and SVM algorithms as described above. The numerical results are shown in Table 2. The result of the test is obtained by an average of several runs. As expected, for these two ML algorithms, when unnecessary packet header information is eliminated on the data plane through the P4 switch, t_2 time can be significantly reduced. We can also intuitively see that the extra time required to remove unnecessary packet header information on the P4 switch is negligible. Finally, as expected, the time contribution of classification (time contribution t_3) does not depend on different scenarios, but only depends on the ML algorithm used. Finally, through calculation, b) can reduce the prediction time of the 1.26 ms ML algorithm for each MQTT message packet.

Table 2. Time consumption in different scenarios

	SGD			SVM		
	t_1	t_2	t_3	t_1	t_2	t_3
Packet mirr.	109.75 s	11.38 s	0.99 ms	109.98 s	11.25 s	15.97 ms
Payload mirr.	109.91 s	5.67 s	0.99 ms	109.47 s	5.67 s	15.97 ms

6 Conclusion

In the environment of IoT, unpredictable situations occur at all times, which may cause our sensor data to become invalid. This phenomenon has brought great annoyance to the data statistics staff. In order to prevent this from happening, and timely detection fails. We propose a failure detection method for the Internet of Things based on programmable switches. Using this method, when the sensor data packet arrives at the P4 programmable switch, the ML failure detection module can determine whether it is failure data. So as to find the sensor failure data early. We use a wireless sensor network data repository based on the markers released by the University of North Carolina at Greensboro in 2010 to evaluate the performance of our proposed method. The results are shown in Table 2, which proves that the method has good performance in reducing time delay. The proposed method will reduce the eigenvalues in each MQTT message packet in the prediction time of the ML algorithm to 1.26 ms.

In the future, our goal is to implement ML algorithms in programmable switches, so as to perform faster failure detection. Our method can also be extended to other IoT protocols.

Acknowledgement. When the thesis is finished, I would like to thank my instructor, Junxing Zhang, for his warm care and careful guidance. In the process of writing the thesis, I also received valuable suggestions from Guangfeng Guo and Renbo Yang, and I would like to express my sincere thanks.

References

1. Roman, R., Zhou, J., Lopez, J.: On the features and challenges of security and privacy in distributed internet of things. Comput. Netw. **57**(10), 2266–2279 (2013)
2. Manyika, J., Chui, M., Bisson, P., et al.: The Internet of Things: mapping the value beyond the hype (2015)
3. Suthaharan, S., Alzahrani, M., Rajasegarar, S., et al.: Labelled data collection for anomaly detection in wireless sensor networks. In: 2010 Sixth International Conference on Intelligent Sensors, Sensor Networks and Information Processing, Brisbane, QLD, Australia, pp. 269–274. IEEE(2010)
4. Mqtt Homepage. https://mqtt.org/. Accessed 17 Jan 2021
5. Bosshart, P., Daly, D., Gibb, G., et al.: P4: Programming protocol-independent packet processors. ACM SIGCOMM Comput. Commun. Rev. **44**(3), 87–95 (2014)
6. P4 Runtime Spec. https://p4.org/p4-spec/docs/P4-16-v1.2.1.html. Accessed 17 Jan 2021
7. Zhang, Z., Mehmood, A., Shu, L., et al.: A survey on fault diagnosis in wireless sensor networks. IEEE Access **6**, 11349–11364 (2018)
8. Lau, B.C.P., Ma, E.W.M., Chow, T.W.S.: Probabilistic fault detector for wireless sensor network. Expert Syst. Appl. **41**(8), 3703–3711 (2014)
9. Yu, C.B., Hu, J.J., Li, R., et al.: Node fault diagnosis in WSN based on RS and SVM. In: 2014 International Conference on Wireless Communication and Sensor Network, Wuhan, China, pp. 153–156. IEEE (2014)
10. Babaie, S., Khosrohosseini, A., Khadem-Zadeh, A.: A new self-diagnosing approach based on petri nets and correlation graphs for fault management in wireless sensor networks. J. Syst. Architect. **59**(8), 582–600 (2013)
11. Panda, M., Khilar, P.M.: Distributed self fault diagnosis algorithm for large scale wireless sensor networks using modified three sigma edit test. Ad Hoc Netw. **25**, 170–184 (2015)
12. Chanak, P., Banerjee, I., Sherratt, R.S.: Mobile sink based fault diagnosis scheme for wireless sensor networks. J. Syst. Softw. **119**, 45–57 (2016)
13. Chalapathy R, Chawla S.: Deep learning for anomaly detection: A survey. arXiv preprint arXiv, 1901.03407, (2019)

14. P4 Homepage. https://p4.org/. Accessed 17 Jan 2021
15. Grpc. https://grpc.io/. Accessed 17 Jan 2021
16. Scikit-learn Stochastic Gradient Descentn. https://scikit-learn.org/dev/modules/sgd.html. Accessed 17 Jan 2021
17. Scikit-learn Multi-layer Perceptron. https://scikit-learn.org/dev/modules/neural_networks_supervised.html. Accessed 17 Jan 2021
18. Scikit-learn Support Vector Machines. https://scikit-learn.org/stable/modules/svm.html. Accessed 17 Jan 2021
19. Mininet Homepage. http://mininet.org/. Accessed 17 Jan 2021
20. BVM 2 Homepage. https://github.com/p4lang/behavioral-model. Accessed 17 Jan 2021
21. Virtualbox Homepage. https://www.virtualbox.org/. Accessed 17 Jan 2021
22. Pedregosa, F., Varoquaux, G., Gramfort, A., et al.: Scikit-learn: Machine learning in Python. J. Mach. Learn. Res. **12**, 2825–2830 (2011)
23. Paho-Mqtt Homepage. https://pypi.org/project/paho-mqtt/. Accessed 17 Jan 2021
24. Mosquitto Homepage. https://mosquitto.org/. Accessed 17 Jan 2021

A Solution to Reduce Broadcast Storm in VANET

Subo He, Lei Xiang[✉], Ying Wang, Minna Xia, and Yaling Hong

Hunan Automotive Engineering Vocational College, Zhuzhou 412000, China

Abstract. The rapid growth of global car ownership leads to energy shortage, environmental pollution, traffic congestion and frequent accidents. The development of intelligent connected vehicle is an effective way to solve the above problems, and it is also the future development direction of automobile. One of the key problems of intelligent network connection of automobile is how to build VANET. In the case of a large number of vehicles gathering, the frequent and intensive interaction of massive communication participants in VANET will inevitably produce broadcast storm, which will lead to network paralysis. To solve the above problems, in this paper, a periodically transmitted rpcm broadcast message forwarding control strategy was designed, and the effect of the forwarding control strategy was analyzed in three scenarios of intersection meeting, multi hop chain meeting and multi vehicle congestion. Simulation results show that the forwarding control strategy can greatly reduce the number of broadcast data packets and improve the effective throughput in large-scale VANET. Moreover, the wider the bandwidth, the higher the throughput performance. When forwarding packets to 32 nodes in 5 m bandwidth, the throughput performance is improved by more than 60%. It has obvious effect on suppressing broadcast storm.

Keywords: Forward · Broadcast storm · Node · VANET

1 Introduction

In order to improve road safety, VANET, as a new mode of intelligent transport system (ITS), emerge as the times require. In order to deal with this kind of problem better in VANET, a more mature wireless access protocol wave is proposed. In order to deal with this kind of problems better in VANET, a more mature wireless access protocol wave (wireless access in the vehicular environment) is proposed to adapt to the characteristics of relatively short transmission distance [1], relatively fast node moving speed and unstable network topology change in VANET. In recent years, some improvements have been made in this area. It included a protocol named Pro AODV proposed in [2], which uses information from AODV routing table to reduce congestion in VANET. The results of feedback congestion control (decentralized congestion control) and adaptive congestion control (limeric) were proposed and compared in reference [3]. Both methods adjusted and controlled secure message transmission according to channel load. The work in reference [4] was strengthened in reference [5]. It proposed a distributed algorithm, which uses the security type of transmission on each wireless link to calculate

© Springer Nature Switzerland AG 2021
X. Sun et al. (Eds.): ICAIS 2021, LNCS 12737, pp. 526–537, 2021.
https://doi.org/10.1007/978-3-030-78612-0_42

the information transmission probability of each node, so as to find a reasonable path. In reference [6], a machine learning congestion control (ml-cc) strategy, which consists of congestion detection, data control and congestion control, was proposed to solve the possible congestion problems. In reference [7], a distributed congestion control strategy for single channel inter vehicle communication was proposed, which shows that periodic broadcast is the main reason that affects whether the vehicle can quickly perceive the risk and give an alarm. In reference [8], an intelligent multi hop broadcast protocol was proposed, which uses fuzzy logic based method to determine the vehicles to relay or forward. In reference [9], a dynamic broadcast storm mitigation algorithm (dbsma) was proposed to mitigate the broadcast storm problem in vehicular network (VN). In this study, a broadcast forwarding control message (rpcm) is proposed to reasonably and efficiently control the broadcast forwarding of broadcast messages in the whole network, so as to greatly reduce the number of broadcast packets in the whole network, eliminate the broadcast storm caused by frequent broadcast of broadcast data packets, optimize the network capacity, and increase the effective data throughput by 60%.

2   Broadcast Forwarding Mechanism Based on Neighbor Discovery

In the existing VANET, each terminal node forwards the received user service broadcast message unconditionally until the TTL value of the broadcast message drops to 1. The initial TTL value of broadcast message is usually set to 50. In this way, when multiple vehicle terminals are connected to the network, the whole network may be filled with a large number of broadcast messages and form a broadcast storm, causing paralysis (see Fig. 1.

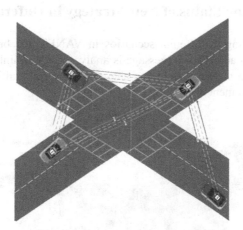

Fig. 1. Existing broadcast packet forwarding strategy.

To solve this problem, some researchers selected some nodes as transit nodes according to certain rules [7–9], which can significantly reduce the number of broadcast data packets. However, the actual effect is not good because the selection of nodes also requires resources.

In this study, a periodic rpcm broadcast message is designed. Rpcm broadcast message is not transmitted in the whole network, but only in the first hop. Therefore, through the interaction of rpcm messages, the MAC information carried by rpcm is used to determine other nodes within the scope of one hop around the node, so as to determine the network relationship between nodes and reduce the repeated broadcast. The simulation results are shown in Fig. 2.

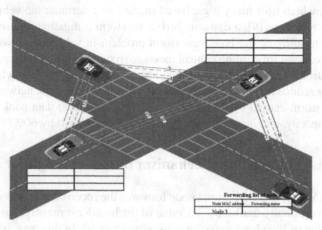

Fig. 2. RPCM node list.

3 Communication Status of New Strategy in Different Scenarios

In this paper, according to different scenarios in VANET, the broadcast forwarding situation of the newly added rpcm message is analyzed. It is mainly divided into three scenarios: intersection meeting, multi hop chain meeting and multi vehicle congestion to analyze the improvement of communication (Fig. 3).

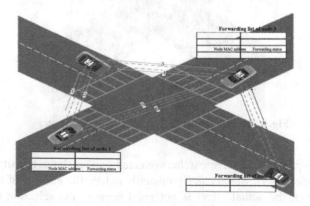

Fig. 3. Broadcast message forwarding status.

3.1 Intersection Meeting Scene

At the intersection, suppose there are four vehicular end nodes, node a, B, C three nodes two by two direct, node D can only directly with node C. Suppose node a sends a broadcast message with sequence number 10, Before optimization, the situation of receiving and forwarding broadcast message by each node is shown in Fig. 7. Nodes B, C and d all unconditionally forward a broadcast with the same sequence number, as shown in Fig. 4.

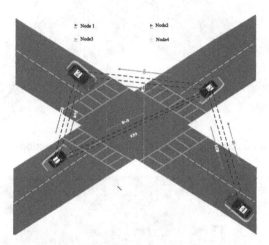

Fig. 4. Broadcast message forwarding under intersection meeting scenario before optimization.

When the broadcast message forwarding optimization is added, the broadcast message forwarding flag bits of each node are shown in Fig. 4. When nodes 2, 3 and 4 forward broadcast messages, they will judge whether to forward or not according to the forwarding flag bit of each node, as shown in Fig. 5.

It can be seen that only under the four nodes, after rpcm packet optimization, the number of broadcast packets forwarding has also changed from 8 to 5, reducing by 37.5%. However, in general V2V communication, if there are 20 nodes in the intersection, and all vehicles communicate in pairs, the broadcast forwarding will reach the peak value under 20 nodes, and it needs to forward 190 times. By using this strategy, when all vehicles communicate in pairs, the whole network will only forward 19 times, and the broadcast forwarding will be reduced by 90%. It can be seen that this method can well suppress broadcast storm.

3.2 Multi Hop Chain Meeting Scene

On the normal road, each vehicle end node forms a chain topology. Suppose there is a chain topology with 5 points and 4 hops, as shown in Fig. 6.

Before optimization, it is assumed that node 1 has an accident and sends out an alarm message. After adding RPCM message optimization, the broadcast message forwarding flag bit and broadcast message forwarding situation of each node are shown in Fig. 7.

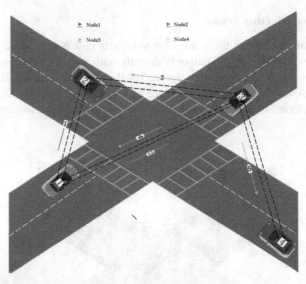

Fig. 5. Broadcast message forwarding under optimized intersection meeting scenario.

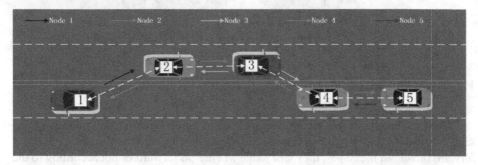

Fig. 6. Schematic diagram of multi hop chain meeting broadcast before optimization.

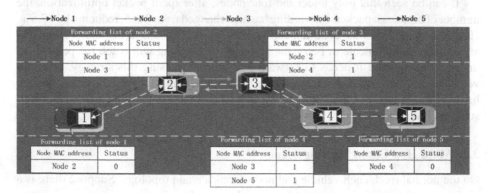

Fig. 7. Schematic diagram of optimized chain topology broadcast forwarding.

Compared with before optimization and after optimization, the number of broadcast forwarding is only reduced from 8 to 7, and the effect is not obvious, but this is based on the worst case of vehicle terminal in the road, and the distance between vehicles is often far. Generally, assuming that nodes 1, 2, 3 and 4 are very close and node 5 is far away, rpcm message optimization is used, and the results are shown in Fig. 8.

According to the analysis, in the scenario in Fig. 8, the broadcast message of node 1 needs to be forwarded 14 times. After optimization of RPCM message, it only needs to forward 7 times, and the broadcast message forwarding decreases by 50%. Therefore, in this scenario, broadcast data forwarding can still be reduced.

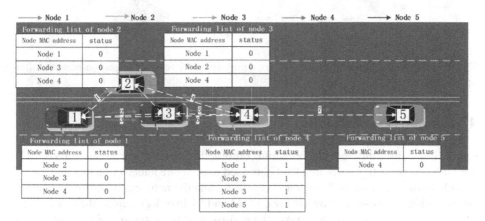

Fig. 8. Optimized vehicle forwarding on the same road.

3.3 Multi Vehicle Congestion Scenario

In VANET, the most important problem to be solved is the broadcast storm caused by sending broadcast messages in the case of vehicle convergence. As shown in Fig. 9, before optimization, five nodes form a ring topology network. By adding broadcast message forwarding optimization, each node in the network is two to two direct, so the broadcast message forwarding flag of each node is 0, and there is no need to forward, so the broadcast message only needs to be sent 4 times to complete the whole network broadcasting.

Broadcast packet forwarding optimization strategy can greatly improve the efficiency of the whole network forwarding, reduce the network overhead in the process of broadcast message transmission, and greatly reduce the broadcast data packets of the whole network in large-scale wireless network. The number of broadcast messages can be reduced to $\frac{n-1}{2C_n^2} * 100\%$ of the original. Therefore, it can effectively solve the problem of broadcast storm.

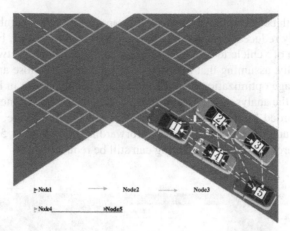

Fig. 9. Schematic diagram of broadcast forwarding in multi vehicle congestion scenario after optimization.

4   Comparison of Results

According to three different scenarios and combined with the characteristics of VANET, the OPNET simulation software [10–12] is used to simulate intersection meeting, multi hop chain meeting and multi vehicle congestion, and the networking test of 32 vehicle terminals is carried out. As shown in Figs. 11, 13 and 15. In order to ensure the consistency of test results, each group of tests takes the real-time dynamic throughput of node 1 and node 2 to consider the network performance status of VANET, and to see how the actual effective throughput is affected by the protocol and bandwidth.

4.1   Simulation Test of Intersection Meeting Scene

An intersection scene is designed in OPNET, which is distributed in a 650 m * 650 m rectangular simulation area, and the node movement is set as VANET_ move_ 1 mode, the communication coverage radius of the node is 50 m. Control the vehicles in each direction to gather at the intersection at the same time. When the North-South vehicles arrive at the intersection and stop waiting, the East-West vehicles pass through. The multi-directional vehicle aggregation scene is simulated, as shown in Fig. 10.

When there are few nodes in the network, there is little difference between using the new protocol and using the original protocol, but when a large number of nodes are gathered, the actual throughput will be greatly affected if the original protocol is used. But under the new protocol, the throughput change is not obvious.

4.2   Simulation Test in Multi Hop Chain Meeting Scenario

Node 1 and node 2 travel from both ends to the center. The other 30 nodes enter the communication range of node 1 and node 2 one by one with an interval of 5 s, forming a multi hop chain meeting scene, as shown in Fig. 12.

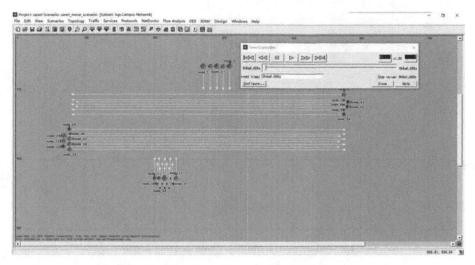

Fig. 10. Test chart of intersection meeting scene.

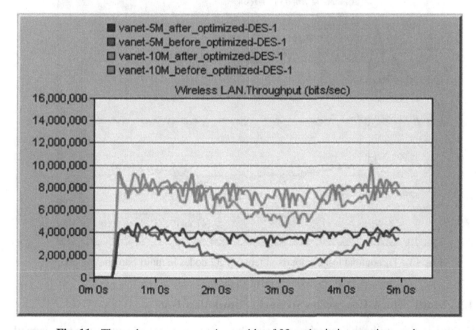

Fig. 11. Throughput test comparison table of 32 nodes in intersection mode.

Through the test, the throughput test results of node 1 and node 2 can be obtained, as shown in Fig. 13. It can be seen that the new protocol has good performance under the bandwidth of 5 m and 10 m. Especially when the bandwidth is low, it can effectively ensure greater communication capacity and eliminate broadcast storm. Experiments show that the effective throughput of the new protocol is about 60% higher than that of the original protocol in the chain meeting scenario with 5 m bandwidth.

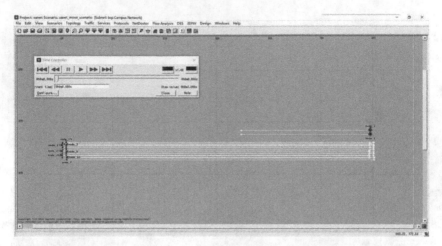

Fig. 12. Test chart of multi hop chain meeting scenario.

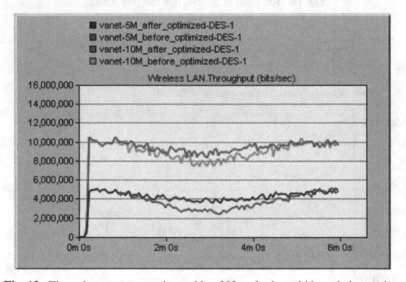

Fig. 13. Throughput test comparison table of 32 nodes in multi hop chain meeting.

4.3 Multi Vehicle Congestion Scenario Simulation Test

Finally, in this study, the experimental simulation of multi vehicle congestion is carried out, as shown in Fig. 14. In this experiment, 32 nodes are used to move to the other end one by one with 5 s interval. After excluding the data of the first 10 s, the throughput change between node 1 and node 2 is recorded in detail when each node is congested on the right side after the movement stops.

The test results are shown in Fig. 15. In the case of multi vehicle congestion, VANET is particularly prone to broadcast storm. In the case of using the new protocol, it can better alleviate this situation and ensure smooth communication.

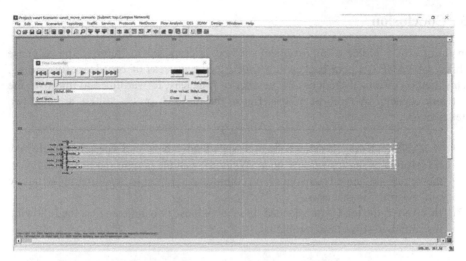

Fig. 14. Test chart of multi vehicle congestion.

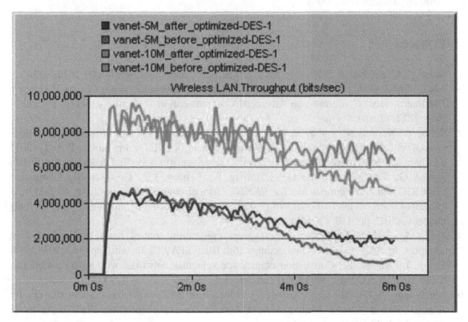

Fig. 15. Throughput test comparison table with 32 vehicles blocked together.

Through the simulation test, it can be found that the optimized rpcm packet can effectively reduce the bandwidth occupied by broadcasting and improve the actual effective throughput. Under the bandwidth of 5 m, 32 nodes forward data packets. Compared with the original protocol, the throughput of the optimized protocol increases by more than 60%.

5 Conclusion

In this study, a protocol improvement method is proposed to improve the response ability of VANET. Rpcm packets are added in the process of broadcast forwarding. This method effectively reduces the number of broadcast forwarding and improves the network capacity by more than 60%. But in the research process, there are also two deficiencies.

(1) In VANET, all vehicles may be in high-speed movement, and a certain vehicle may be selected as the forwarding node. When the vehicle is required to forward data, the vehicle has already run out of the communication range, resulting in the failure of forwarding in this area.
(2) In VANET, the load is unbalanced. In view of these two deficiencies, the following research will solve these problems.

Funding Statement. This research is supported by Scientific research project of Hunan Education Department (20C1000).

References

1. Saeed, R.A., Naemat, A.B.H., Aris AB.: Design and evaluation of lightweight IEEE 802.11p-based TDMA MAC method for roadside-to-vehicle communications. In: Chung, H-C. (ed.). The International Conference on Advanced Communication Technology, Seoul, pp. 1483–1488. IEEE (2010)
2. Kabir, T., Nurain, N., Kabir, M.K.: Pro-AODV (proactive AODV): simple modifications to AODV for proactively minimizing congestion in VANETs. In: Kuila, P. (ed.) 2015 International Conference, Networking Systems and Security (NSysS), Dhaka, pp. 1–6 (2015)
3. Bansal, G., Cheng, B., Rostami, A., Sjoberg, K., Kenney, J.B., Gruteser, M.: Comparing LIMERIC and DCC approaches for VANET channel congestion control. In: Gutierrez, J. (ed.) 2014 IEEE 6th International Symposium, Wireless Vehicular Communications (WiVeC), Vancouver, BC, pp. 1–7. (2014)
4. Zhang, L., Valaee, S.: Safety context-aware congestion control for vehicular broadcast networks. In: Srinivasan (ed.) Proceedings 15th IEEE SPAWC, Toronto, pp. 399–403 (2014)
5. Zhang, L., Valaee, S.: Congestion control for vehicular networks with safety-awareness. IEEE/ACM Trans. Netw. **99**(1), 1–1 (2016)
6. Taherkhani, N., Pierre, S.: Centralized and localized data congestion control strategy for vehicular ad hoc networks using a machine learning clustering algorithm. IEEE Trans. Intell. Transp. Syst. **99**(99), 1–11 (2016)
7. Chen, C., Li, Y., Pei, Q., Chen, C.: Avoiding information congestion in VANETs: a congestion game approach. In: Kang, S-K (ed.) 2014 IEEE International Conference, Computer and Information Technology (CIT), pp. 105–110 (2014)
8. Wu, C., Ji, Y., Chen, X., Ohzahata, S., Kato, T.: An intelligent broadcast protocol for VANETs based on transfer learning. In: Gencata, A. (ed.) 2015 IEEE 81st, Vehicular Technology Conference (VTC Spring), Glasgow, pp. 1–6 (2015)
9. Feukeu, E.A., Zuva, T.: DBSMA approach for congestion mitigation in VANETs. Procedia Comput. Sci. **109**(2), 42–49 (2017)

10. Akhtar, N., Ergen, S.C., Ozkasap, O.: Vehicle mobility and communication channel, models for realistic and efficient highway VANET simulation. IEEE Trans. Veh. Technol. **64**(1), 248–262 (2015)
11. Mukund, W.B., Gomathi, N.: Quantitative and qualitative correlation analysis of optimal route discovery for vehicular ad-hoc networks. J. Central South Univ. **25**(7), 1732–1745 (2018). https://doi.org/10.1007/s11771-018-3864-y
12. Sun, R., Ye, J., Tang, K.: Big data aided vehicular network feature analysis and mobility models design. Mob. Netw. Appl. **13**(6), 1–9 (2018)

A Vehicle Intrusion Detection System Based on Time Interval and Data Fields

Xun He[1] , Zhen Yang[2(✉)], and Yongfeng Huang[3]

[1] Tsinghua NGN Lab, Institute for Network Sciences and Cyberspace, Tsinghua University, Beijing 100084, China
[2] The School of Cyberspace Security, Beijing University of Posts and Telecommunications, Beijing 100876, China
yangzhenyz@bupt.edu.cn
[3] Tsinghua NGN Lab, Department of Electronic Engineering, Tsinghua University, Beijing 100084, China

Abstract. With the development of the Internet of Things and automobile technology, intelligent networked vehicles are becoming more and more mature. Automobile manufacturers have installed various entertainment and safety facilities for cars, such as remote access-controlling system, satellite navigation, and entertainment system. While improving the car driving experience, these facilities also increase the risk of remote attacks on the vehicle. Compared with traditional cars based on isolated embedded systems, intelligent networked cars have added many network devices for access to the Internet, causing vehicle components to be exposed to dangerous external network environments. These network interfaces may become potential entrances for hackers, causing vehicles to be illegally controlled and privacy leaked. For these dangerous situations, researchers have proposed many protective measures, however they cannot detect impenetrable intrusion well. In order to solve this defect, this paper proposed a vehicle intrusion detection system based on time interval and data field. By calculating the time interval of each packet, we can determine whether their sending frequency is normal and verify the source Electronic Control Units (ECU) of the packet. By analyzing the Manhattan distance of the data field to detect whether the content of the message has been tampered with. These extracted features will be as input feature vector of the decision tree, and obtain the detection result. In the experiment, we achieved a significant improvement and proved the superiority of this method.

Keywords: Intrusion detection · Vehicle · Time interval · Data field · Machine learning

1 Introduction

The Controller Area Network (CAN) bus is one of the most widely used vehicle buses and is a key target for hackers. With the vigorous development of the automobile industry, the safety of CAN bus communication in the car is facing more and more severe challenges.

X. Sun et al. (Eds.): ICAIS 2021, LNCS 12737, pp. 538–549, 2021.
https://doi.org/10.1007/978-3-030-78612-0_43

Malicious attacks penetrate directly into the vehicle CAN bus network through the external interface, seriously endangering the personal and property safety of drivers and passengers. In 2018, Tencent's Keen Lab achieved physical and remote attacks on various BMW vehicles [1]. Modern vehicles are becoming more intelligent. In order to provide users with a more comfortable driving experience, the number of automotive electronic control units (ECU) has increased year by year, and communication interfaces with the outside world such as 3G/4G and Bluetooth have become more abundant [2]. Improving the safety of CAN communication in the car is of great significance to ensure the driving safety of drivers and passengers.

The measurements to defend the danger of CAN bus include hardware protection and software protection. The hardware protection method is realized by adding encryption and decryption modules to the ECU. Although the CAN bus safety problem can be solved more comprehensively, the car's hardware settings will face great changes, such as a comprehensive upgrade of the existing ECU of the car, the addition of a gateway or a security chip, and etc. Some schemes need to modify the existing CAN protocol. For automobile manufacturers, it takes too much to upgrade the existing hardware. Therefore, it is impossible to fully promote the hardware means to ensure vehicle CAN bus safety in a short time. Software protection is achieved by adding firewalls and intrusion detection system (IDS) while keeping the existing bus configuration unchanged. Because this method has good scalability, it has been widely studied and applied in the industry [3, 4]. At present, the intrusion detection technology for the in-vehicle communication network is one of the most widely used technologies to ensure the safety of CAN communication in the vehicle. It monitors the message transmission on the CAN bus in real time and gives an alarm when abnormal messages are found. However, the research on the intrusion detection algorithm of the CAN bus is not mature enough, and the detection algorithm has problems such as misdetection.

The currently popular intrusion detection methods are based on statistics or machine learning [5]. The so-called statistics is to determine one or more statistical factors to measure the traffic, and obtain the threshold of these statistical factors through the study of the normal traffic. In the monitoring process, once the statistical factors exceed the threshold, it is determined that anomaly intrusion has occurred and an alarm is issued. Typical statistical intrusion detection methods applied to the vehicle CAN bus include intrusion detection algorithms based on time interval and intrusion detection algorithms using information entropy. The advantage of the method based on statistics is that the amount of calculation is small and does not require too much prior training process, but how to choose an appropriate threshold is the difficulty and defect of this method. The machine-based learning is to rely on inputting a large number of CAN bus messages to build an adaptive intrusion detection system, and the system is applied to determine whether the traffic is abnormal during detection. The advantages of machine learning-based methods are adaptive and predictive, but it requires quantities of prior knowledge for training.

In this paper, based on time interval and data field we designed an intrusion detection system to ensure vehicle safety. It extracts the time interval of each packet, the distance of the data field, and the packet identifier as features, with which the decision tree is trained. Finally, we will obtain a detector that can analyze traffic anomalies. The motivation for the method is that each ECU on the CAN bus has its own sending clock frequency, and the time interval between consecutive messages sent by the same ECU is theoretically the same. If the intruder disturbs the sending frequency of any message, it can be judged as abnormal. The content of the data field is also of interest to hackers. Usually hackers will forge or tamper with the data field of the message to achieve the purpose of intrusion. Therefore, the determination of the content of the data field is also one of the important ways to detect abnormal behavior. However, simply using statistics factors such as time intervals or data fields will cause a great false alarm rate. There is a legal threshold for them, and the traffic within the threshold is normal. Therefore, the determination of the threshold is very critical. Previous work failed to solve this problem well, which would result in a great false alarm rate. We introduced a machine learning method to get the most suitable threshold, based on its continuous learning ability.

The contributions of this paper are as follows: Verify the source ECU of each packet; A high-performance lightweight intrusion detection system; Cover all known attacks; No need to modify the current CAN bus, connected to the CAN bus in the form of a plug-in.

2 Related Work

There has been plenty of previous work under the research of vehicle intrusion detection. GIDS [6] performed one hot encoding of the CAN ID bit by bit to obtain a two-dimensional matrix, using GAN as the training model. Their another work [7] took out the CAN ID of 29 packets to form a 29 * 29 two-dimensional matrix, using CNN as a training model. DBN and decision tree [8] are used for feature extraction and classification. supervised learning [9] achieved promotion using real CAN logs collected from two passenger cars and open source CAN datasets collected from real scenes. General machine learning method requires a large amount of training data to get a better model. Through transfer learning [10], not only can the training of the model be accelerated, but also large amount of data is not required. Unsupervised learning [11] can also be used to learn the characteristics of messages sent on the CAN bus, and then to identify abnormalities.

Confirming the source ECU can detect specific attack. CIDS [12] proposed statistics-based methods, and it formed a fingerprint for the ECU through the clock cycle of each ECU. By recording the sender's information, the camouflage attack can be effectively located. Each ECU on the CAN bus has its own unique level signal when sending messages [13]. By analyzing these unique signals, each ECU can be marked a unique fingerprint to detect abnormal behavior. In order to be able to identify which ECU sent the message, the level signal information [14] on the CAN bus can be used to calculate the bit time of each ECU, so that each ECU can be uniquely identified.

Time interval is a popular statistics factor. It is effective to detect anomalies by measuring the sending interval of packets [15], and then comparing it with the normal sending frequency, especially when detecting injection attacks. Based on the analysis of the offset rate and time interval between requesting and answering messages in CAN [16], an intrusion detection method is proposed. On the CAN bus [17], ECUs with different identifiers perform different functions. They are all sending message periodically. If a hacker initiates an injection attack, the receiving interval of different identifiers will change. Many methods use the CAN bus message characteristic of time interval [18] for abnormal analysis and detection. Some intrusion detection mechanism [19] uses bloom filtering technology to calculate and analyze the period of the message identifier, so as to effectively detect potential suspension or injection attacks.

Electric signal and entropy are also introduced. Some work [20] analyzed the level signal transmitted on the CAN bus to authenticate different ECUs. By detecting this we can achieve the purpose of anomaly detection. There is a certain correlation between the signals sent by vehicles on the CAN bus because they convey the properties of the physical system [21]. Based on this principle, the shape (geometric and topological properties) of the CAN data can be used to identify attacks. Entropy [22] can also be used for data analysis on the CAN bus to achieve the purpose of identifying attacks.

The above methods have their own shortcomings. Deep learning methods will bring huge resource expenditure; using alone statistics factors, such as fingerprint of ECU, time interval as well as entropy will cause a greater false alarm rate. We proposed a CAN bus intrusion detection system based on time interval and data field, which can over-come the above problems.

3 Attack Defense

The ECU connected on the CAN bus will send two kinds of messages, one is a periodic message, which accounts for the vast majority, and the other is a non-periodic message. A periodic message is sent cyclically at a certain time. The time accuracy required for this type of message is high, guaranteeing reliability of the message. If the cycle is too short, the load on the bus may be too large and affect the quality of the network. There are two factors that influence frequency of the message. One is that the bus is busy, causing the current ECU cannot send data and is blocked. The other is that it takes time for the ECU to send message, and this process will cause time delay. The non-periodic messages are event-driven, and there is no sending cycle.

For different types of messages, hackers may adopt different attack methods. These attack methods can generally be divided into four categories, injection, suspension, camouflage and tampering attacks. An injection attack is to inject malicious messages into the CAN bus. Common injection attacks include deny of service (DoS) and replay attack. The DoS is to send a large number of high-priority messages to the CAN bus in a very short time, causing low-priority messages to not be processed in time. The replay attack is that a hacker first eavesdrops on and records a normal CAN message, and then replays the message at any other time. The suspension is to invade an ECU and stop its message sending. A camouflage attack is a hacker controlling two ECUs A and B. When stopping A's message sending, immediately ask B to send A's message in the same cycle, so that it will not be noticed that the sending source has been replaced. A tampering attack is an attacker invading the ECU to send a message with modified data field.

Injection and suspension would change the sending frequency of message. After the injection attack occurs, the sending frequency of the message will be increased to several times of the original frequency, especially the DoS attack which may be as high as a thousand times. When a suspension attack occurs, it will reduce the frequency of message transmission because it stops its sending. Therefore, these two types of attacks can be detected by analyzing the frequency of the message. Specifically, the frequency of each message has a legal range, and if exceeding this range, it will be abnormal. A camouflage attack is relatively difficult to detect, because the hacker controls two ECUs. When the source of the message is changed, the frequency does not change. To identify it, we must be able to perform source address verification on each ECU to ensure that each message is sent from the correct source. A tampering attack is to modify the data field of the message. If trying to identify it, we must analyze the content of the message. On the CAN bus, the functions performed by the same ECU remain basically unchanged, so the content of the message also has a high similarity. In order to measure this similarity, specific distance measurement methods can be introduced. The smaller the distance is, the higher the similarity is. If the distance is great, it will mean that the message content may have been tampered with.

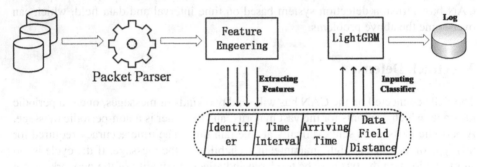

Fig. 1. Structure of the proposed IDS

4   The Proposed Model

In the previous section, we came to the conclusion that different features or statistical factors can be applied to identify different attacks. The proposed method can well detect four types of attack behavior: injection, suspension, camouflage and tampering. For the injection and suspension, the actual sending frequency of the packet can be determined by the time interval of adjacent packet to detect abnormalities. For camouflage, the source ECU of each packet can be verified to determine whether the sending source ECU is legal. For tampering attacks, we analyzed the Manhattan distance of the packet data field. Because the data field of packets with the same identifier is similar, the distance can be deployed as a basis for determining whether the packet content has been tampered. Therefore, we perform feature analysis and extraction for each attack behavior specifically, as shown in Fig. 1.

Identifier is unique for each message, so it can be extracted as a feature.

The sending frequency of normal messages has a legal range. To measure the frequency, we achieved the time interval in the transmission of adjacent messages. We know that the frequency of the message fluctuates. The specific analysis is as follows:

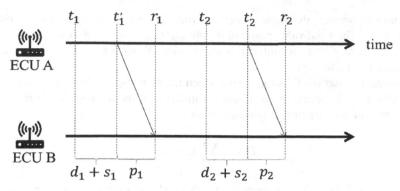

Fig. 2. Status of the sending message

We suppose A and B are two ECUs on the CAN bus shown in Fig. 2, and the inherent period of a message sent by A is T. A is ready to send two messages at t_1 and t_2. However, affected by the bus load and sending delay, the actual sending time is t_1' and t_2' respectively, the following sets of equations can be obtained:

$$t_1 + T = t_2 \tag{1}$$

$$t_1' = t_1 + d_1 + s_1 \tag{2}$$

$$t_2' = t_2 + d_2 + s_2 \tag{3}$$

$d_i(i = 1, 2)$ is the delay caused by bus load, and $s_i(i = 1, 2)$ is the delay caused by sending message. Therefore, the actual sending time interval between consecutive messages is:

$$t_2' - t_1' = t_2 - t_1 + d_2 - d_1 + s_2 - s_1 = T + \Delta \tag{4}$$

It can be seen from the above formula that the actual transmission time interval between messages mainly depends on Δ, and the legal value range of Δ is $[\Delta_{min}, \Delta_{max}]$. When Δ is the minimum value Δ_{min}, the sending time interval is the smallest, when Δ is Δ_{max}, the sending time interval is the biggest.

Now we consider the state of ECU B at the receiving end.

$$r_1 = t_1' + p_1 \tag{5}$$

$$r_2 = t_2' + p_2 \tag{6}$$

r_1 and r_2 respectively represent the actual time for ECU B to receive two messages, and p_1 and p_2 represent the transmission delay on the CAN bus. The receiving interval of consecutive messages is as follows:

$$r_2 - r_1 = t_2' - t_1' + p_2 - p_1 = T + \theta \tag{7}$$

In the above formula, the actual receiving time interval between messages mainly depends on θ. The legal value range of θ is $[\theta_{min}, \theta_{max}]$. When θ takes the minimum value θ_{min}, the receiving time interval is the smallest. When θ takes θ_{max}, the receiving time interval is the biggest.

In addition to statistical factors above, when facing non-periodic messages and tampering attacks, it is necessary to measure similarity of the data field. We introduced Manhattan distance, which is defined as follows:

$$Dis = \sum_{i=1}^{n} |x_i - y_i| \tag{8}$$

The Manhattan distance is a non-negative number and can be considered geometrically as the distance of steps between two points $A(x_1, x_2, \ldots, x_n)$ and $B(y_1, y_2, \ldots, y_n)$. the data field of each packet can be expanded into a vector, and the similarity between messages can be judged by calculating the Manhattan distance. Because the functions they control are basically similar, messages with the same identifier reflected high similarity in the data field. Obviously, due to the different execution functions, the messages of the same identifier are still different. The Manhattan distance used to measure the similarity also has a legal distance range $[D_{min}, D_{max}]$, and D_{min} and D_{max} represent the maximum distance and the minimum value respectively.

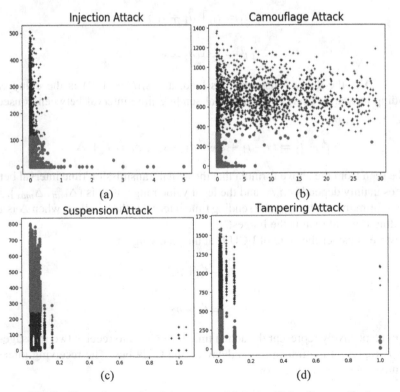

Fig. 3. Clustering results of the extracted features (Color figure online)

We combine the features above as a feature vector. In order to fully extract threshold information of these feature, we introduced lightGBM [23] as a model for training. Our purpose is to ensure that the classifier can maintain the best adaptability to the thresholds of the above features, improving the detection accuracy as well as reducing the false alarm rate.

5 Experiment and Evaluation

Based on the designed features above, we evaluated injection, suspension, camouflage, and tampering attacks.

Table 1. Description of datasets

Size of datasets	Normal message	Anomaly message
Injection	3,078,198	587,519
Camouflage	3,346,957	487,807
Suspension	823,943	164,874
Tampering	790,912	197,905

5.1 Dataset Process

The dataset includes four parts, and each part contains one attack, as shown in Table 1. The data of injection and camouflage are from another team [1], and we also compared with their work. Suspension and tampering attack are obtained through simulation. Suspension are caused by deleting random packets in normal traffic log. The tampering attack is obtained by modifying the data field of random packets in normal traffic log.

We extracted the frequency, source ECU sending time, the Manhattan distance of the message data field, and the identifier as a features vector of each packet, and mapped the vector in the coordinate system to get the following results. In the Fig. 3, the red dot and blue cross symbol represent normal messages and abnormal messages respectively. Using the feature vector we proposed for cluster analysis, there is a clear dividing line between the two types of data. Therefore, the features vector we proposed for CAN bus anomaly detection is in high suitability and superiority.

5.2 Hyperparameter Evaluation

In the training process of the lightGBM model, values of the hyperparameters will affect its performance, such as the learning rate and the number of leaf nodes. Especially the learning rate. In this section, we evaluated the impact of different sizes of learning rates on the detection results. We keep other conditions constant and get the result shown in Fig. 4 by changing the size of the learning rate. In (a) and (d), as the learning rate continues to increase, the detection rate of the model remains basically unchanged, which means that the two types of attack data are not sensitive to the selection of the learning rate. In (b) and (c), as the learning rate continues to increase, the detection rate of the model increases first and then maintains a stable state. Taking into account the above situation, we finally selected a learning rate of 0.02.

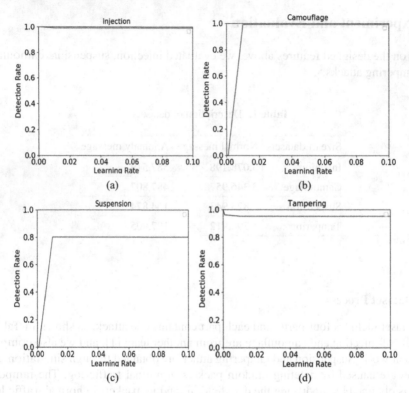

Fig. 4. Evaluation of learning rate

Table 2. Evaluation of different size of training set

Detection rate	Injection	Camouflage	Suspension	Tampering
1% of training set	3.53	97.16	82.57	81.98
10% of training set	99.78	98.17	83.28	92.70
100% of training set	100	99.98	85.31	95.42

Table 3. Experimental results of our method

		Precision	Accuracy	Recall	f-score
Injection	Ours	**100**	**100**	**100**	**100**
	GIDS[6]	96.8	97.9	99.6	–
Camouflage	Ours	**98.16**	**99.92**	**99.98**	**99.06**
	GIDS[6]	97.3	98.0	99.5	–

Table 4. Evaluation of suspension and tampering

	Precision	Accuracy	Recall	f-score
Suspension	99.01	97.08	85.31	90.49
Tampering	93.87	97.84	95.42	94.63

5.3 Performance Evaluation

We first evaluated the impact of the size of the training dataset on the model detection rate, as shown in Table 2. The performance of the model is positively correlated with the size of the training data. With the continuous increase of training data, the detection rate of the model on the four attack behaviors has gradually increased. On Injection, when the training data increases from 1% to 100%, the detection rate increases from 3.53% to 100%. Sufficient training data can ensure that the model is fully learned, improve its generalization ability, and achieve the purpose of increasing the detection rate.

For injection and camouflage, we compared the experimental results with GIDS [6]. As shown in Table 3, we conclude that our method has achieved better detection results regardless of injection or camouflage. We analyzed that GIDS only extracts the CAN identifiers of several consecutive messages as input features, and these few features extracted are very limited in attack detection. In our previous analysis in Sect. 3, each attack behavior has its own unique information. Only by making full use of this specific information can we better detect attacks. Obviously, our work is better in this regard. And in GIDS, they applied the deep learning network GAN as the classifier, which will generate greater resource overhead in training and detection. Our method uses a decision tree model with a simpler structure, which is more suitable for a resource-constrained scenario like the CAN bus.

In order to evaluate the comprehensiveness of our proposed method, we also conduct corresponding evaluation by simulating suspension and tampering attacks. The results are shown in Table 4. In general, our method is quite satisfactory in the detection of both attacks.

Through analysis of the detection of attack behavior above, we can conclude that the feature vector we proposed can identify and distinguish different traffic, which is very suitable for detecting abnormal behavior of CAN bus.

6 Conclusion

In this paper, we proposed a vehicle intrusion detection system based on time interval and data field. We designed different detection features based on the characteristics of different attack behaviors, and obtained a set of feature vector for CAN bus intrusion detection. We analyzed the effectiveness of the extracted features vector using a clustering algorithm, and proved that these feature combinations are very suitable for detecting abnormal traffic behavior on the CAN bus. We deployed LightGBM which is based on decision tree as the classifier, with the extracted feature vector as input, and compare the result with GIDS [6]. The experiment shows that our proposed method has high superiority compared with the previous method.

In addition to comparing with existing work, we also simulated suspension and tampering attacks to evaluate the comprehensiveness of our proposed method. In general, our method can detect these two attacks well. However, considering that suspension and tampering attacks have stronger concealment, it is more difficult for the system to detect them. Therefore, this direction is where we will continue to explore later.

Acknowledgement. The authors would like to thank the anonymous referees for their valuable comments and helpful suggestions.

Funding Statement. The work is supported by the National Natural Science Foundation of China (No. U1836204, No. U1936208, No. U1936216, No. 62002197).

Conflicts of Interest. We declare that there is no conflict of interests regarding the publication of this paper. We declare that we have no financial and personal relationships with other people or organizations that can inappropriately influence our work.

References

1. Greenberg, A.: Hackers remotely kill a jeep on the highway-with me in it. Wired **7**(2), 21–22 (2015)
2. SAE Vehicle Electrical System Security Committee. SAE J3061-cybersecurity guidebook for cyber-physical automotive systems. SAE-society of automotive engineers (2016)
3. Koscher, K., et al.: Experimental security analysis of a modern automobile. In: Proceedings of IEEE Symposium Security Privacy, pp. 447–462 (2010)
4. Checkoway, S., McCoy, D., Kantor, B.: Comprehensive experimental analyses of automotive attack surfaces. In: Proceedings of USENIX Security Symposium, pp. 1–16 (2011)
5. Hoppe, T., Kiltz, S., Dittmann, J.: Security threats to automotive CAN networks – practical examples and selected short-term countermeasures. In: Harrison, M.D., Sujan, M.-A. (eds.) SAFECOMP 2008. LNCS, vol. 5219, pp. 235–248. Springer, Heidelberg (2008). https://doi.org/10.1007/978-3-540-87698-4_21
6. Seo, E., Song, H.M., Kim, H.K.: Gids: Gan based intrusion detection system for in-vehicle network. In: 2018 16th Annual Conference on Privacy, Security and Trust (PST), pp. 1–6. IEEE (2018)
7. Song, H.M., Woo, J., Kim, H.K.: In-vehicle network intrusion detection using deep convolutional neural network. Veh. Commun. **21**, 100198 (2020)

8. Aloqaily, M., Otoum, S., Al Ridhawi, I., et al.: An intrusion detection system for connected vehicles in smart cities. Ad Hoc Netw. **90**, 101842 (2019)
9. Olufowobi, H., Young, C., Zambreno, J., et al.: Saiducant: Specification-based automotive intrusion detection using controller area network (can) timing. IEEE Trans. Veh. Technol. **69**(2), 1484–1494 (2019)
10. Tariq, S., Lee, S., Woo, S.S.: CANTransfer: transfer learning based intrusion detection on a controller area network using convolutional LSTM network. In: Proceedings of the 35th Annual ACM Symposium on Applied Computing, pp. 1048–1055 (2020)
11. Hanselmann, M., Strauss, T., Dormann, K., et al.: CANet: an unsupervised intrusion detection system for high dimensional can bus data. IEEE Access **8**, 58194–58205 (2020)
12. Cho, K.T., Shin, K.G.: Fingerprinting electronic control units for vehicle intrusion detection. In: 25th {USENIX} Security Symposium ({USENIX} Security 16), pp. 911–927 (2016)
13. Choi, W., Joo, K., Jo, H.J., et al.: Voltageids: low-level communication characteristics for automotive intrusion detection system. IEEE Trans. Inf. Forensics Secur. **13**(8), 2114–2129 (2018)
14. Zhou, J., Joshi, P., Zeng, H., et al.: Btmonitor: bit-time-based intrusion detection and attacker identification in controller area network. ACM Trans. Embed. Comput. Syst. (TECS) **18**(6), 1–23 (2019)
15. Song, H.M., Kim, H.R., Kim, H.K.: Intrusion detection system based on the analysis of time intervals of CAN messages for in-vehicle network. In: 2016 International Conference on Information Networking (ICOIN), pp. 63–68. IEEE (2016)
16. Lee, H., Jeong, S.H., Kim, H.K.: OTIDS: a novel intrusion detection system for in-vehicle network by using remote frame. In: 2017 15th Annual Conference on Privacy, Security and Trust (PST), pp. 57–5709. IEEE (2017)
17. Moore, M.R., Bridges, R.A., Combs, F.L., et al.: Modeling inter-signal arrival times for accurate detection of can bus signal injection attacks: a data-driven approach to in-vehicle intrusion detection. In: Proceedings of the 12th Annual Conference on Cyber and Information Security Research, pp. 1–4 (2017)
18. Gmiden, M., Gmiden, M.H., Trabelsi, H.: An intrusion detection method for securing in-vehicle CAN bus. In: 2016 17th International Conference on Sciences and Techniques of Automatic Control and Computer Engineering (STA), pp. 176–180. IEEE (2016)
19. Groza, B., Murvay, P.S.: Efficient intrusion detection with bloom filtering in controller area networks. IEEE Trans. Inf. Forensics Secur. **14**(4), 1037–1051 (2018)
20. Choi, W., Jo, H.J., Woo, S., Chun, J.Y., Park, J., Lee, D.H.: Identifying ECUs using inimitable characteristics of signals in controller area networks. IEEE Trans. Veh. Technol. **67**(6), 4757–4770 (2018). https://doi.org/10.1109/TVT.2018.2810232
21. Tyree, Z., Bridges, R.A., Combs, F.L., et al.: Exploiting the shape of CAN data for in-vehicle intrusion detection. In: 2018 IEEE 88th Vehicular Technology Conference (VTC-Fall), pp. 1–5. IEEE (2018)
22. Wang, Q., Lu, Z., Qu, G.: An entropy analysis based intrusion detection system for controller area network in vehicles. In: 2018 31st IEEE International System-on-Chip Conference (SOCC), pp. 90–95. IEEE (2018)
23. Ke, G., et al.: LightGBM: a highly efficient gradient boosting decision tree. NIPS 2017, 3146–3154 (2017)

An Authentication Mechanism for IoT Devices Based on Traceable and Revocable Identity-Based Encryption

Fei Xia[1], Jiaming Mao[1(✉)], Zhipeng Shao[2], Liangjie Xu[3], Ran Zhao[1], and Yunzhi Yang[3]

[1] State Grid Jiangsu Electric Power Co, Ltd. Information and Telecommunication Branch, Nanjing 210024, China
[2] Institute of Information and Communication, State Grid Key Laboratory of Information and Network Security, Global Energy Interconnection Research Institute, Nanjing 210003, Jiangsu, China
[3] Anhui Jiyuan Software Co. Ltd, SGITG, Hefei 230088, Anhui, China

Abstract. To solve low computing efficiency and high computational energy consumption in the traditional Public-key Infrastructure cryptosystem in the authentication of IoT devices, an authentication scheme for IoT devices based on the Identity-based Encryption is proposed in this paper, which is realized by introducing traceable and revocable mechanisms. The effective management of the secret key of the suspicious devices by the authentication center and the reasonable accountability of the dishonest private key generator (PKG) are realized. Finally, through the security proof, it is verified that the Identity-based Encryption designed in this paper can meet the security of the Chosen Ciphertext Attack (CCA), indicating that the scheme has high practicability and security.

Keywords: Identity-based encryption · Traceable · Revokable · Device authentication · CCA

1 Introduction

With the continuous development of the Internet of Things technology, more and more Internet of Things devices have gradually entered all aspects of production activities and human lives. The small Internet of Things devices represented by wearable smart monitoring devices have aroused the interest of the market and production companies, which has a broad market prospect. However, due to their storage and energy limitations, these small IoT devices cannot adapt to the current traditional Public Key Infrastructure (PKI) public-key encryption scheme based on digital certificates. These devices often need to process important privacy data of users or systems, so it is urgent to construct a lightweight authentication technology for small IoT devices.

The Identity-based Encryption is proposed by Shamir [1] that does not require a key authorization center to generate public-private key pairs and does not need to use a certificate to transfer the public key. Instead, it is a cryptosystem that uses user or device

© Springer Nature Switzerland AG 2021
X. Sun et al. (Eds.): ICAIS 2021, LNCS 12737, pp. 550–562, 2021.
https://doi.org/10.1007/978-3-030-78612-0_44

identification information as the public key and generates the secret key based on the system master key and user identification. Compared with the traditional PKI cryptosystem, this kind of cryptosystem has the characteristics of local and offline encryption and decryption, low management and operation cost, and high execution efficiency, which has received extensive attention and in-depth research from the academic field. Boldyreva et al. [2] proposed a revocable Identity-based Encryption scheme for the first time. They built a key update method that does not require time slices based on fuzzy IBE and binary tree structure, thus maintaining the efficiency of users. Au et al. [3] based on the standard traceable accountability Identity-based Encryption scheme, reducing the user's trust reliance on the private key generator and constructed a secure encryption mechanism, where the key can be traceable and revokable under the random language model. Xie et al. [4] proposed an efficient and secure identity-based aggregate signature scheme (EIAS) to provide data authenticity and integrity protection for WSNs. Ge et al. [5] proposed an Identity-based Proxy Re-encryption Scheme(IB-PRE), which allows a semi-trusted proxy to convert encryption under one identity to another without revealing the underlying message.

An authentication scheme is an important part of an IoT security protection system, which many scholars have paid attention to the correlational research [6–8]. Because of its simplicity, no certificate, and low computational cost, the Identity-based Encryption has been used in related research on constructing a lightweight security authentication architecture for the Internet of Things. Sankaran [9] proposed a lightweight hierarchical security architecture of the Internet of Things based on the Identity-based Encryption and further designed an identity-based secure communication protocol to meet the needs of lightweight authentication of the Internet of Things. Reddy et al. [10] designed a security protocol for identity verification between IoT gateways and mobile terminals based on a pseudo-identity encryption scheme. Experimental analysis shows that the protocol has high feasibility and robustness. Ullah et al. [11] proposed an identity-based signature authentication scheme for the Named Data Network (NDN) of the Internet of Things. This scheme is based on the hyperelliptic curve to achieve the same security level of bilinear pair and elliptic curve cryptosystem by using a smaller key length. Lavanya et al. [12] designed an identity-based revocable storage encryption method to transmit data to the client using IoT sensor nodes in a specific session time category. This method reduces the encryption complexity between the sensor node and the client and satisfies the needs of IoT security authentication. These studies have enriched the application research of the Identity-based Encryption in the security authentication of the Internet of things and improved the practicability of the Identity-based Encryption, which are of great significance to the research of the Identity-based Encryption. Among them, the Internet of Things security authentication process should be dynamic. For a terminal or user who has lost the system access qualification, the most effective method is to revoke it from the entire security authentication password system not to generate a valid private key. Meanwhile, because the Key Generation Center (KGC) in the Identity-based Encryption has a higher device private key generation permission, the system cannot guarantee the integrity of KGC, especially the key generation center is hacked by an adversary. If the adversary manipulates the key generation center to forge the user's key to perform illegal activities in the system, the user's rights protection and system account-ability are more difficult and costly. Therefore, a trustless and accountable Identity-based Encryption is important for IoT authentication systems. Unfortunately, the existing IoT security authentication mechanisms based on the Identity-based Encryption lacks applied research on the combination of revocability and accountability. To solve this problem, this paper will study the application of revocable and accountable Identity-based Encryption methods in IoT security authentication.

The structure of this paper is as follows. Sect. 2 introduces the basic knowledge related to the Identity-based Encryption of this paper; In Sect. 3 presents the design of an identity-based security authentication scheme for the Internet of Things; Sect. 4 describes the specific cryptographic scheme of this paper; Sect. 5 discusses the pro-posed cryptography. The scheme carries out safety proof and performance comparison; Sect. 6 summarizes the content of the paper and looks forward to the future development direction.

2 Preliminaries

This section will introduce the basic knowledge of the Identity-based Encryption involved in this paper.

2.1 Bilinear Map

We set G as a multiplication group of a large prime order p, g as the generator of G and $e : G \times G \to G_T$ as a bilinear map which satisfies the following properties:

(1) Bilinearity: $e(g^a, g^b) = e(g, g)^{ab}$ for all $a, b \in Z_N, g \in G$.

(2) Non-degeneracy: $e(P, Q) \neq 1$ for all $P, Q \in G$.

(3) Computability: There is an efficient algorithm to compute $e(X, Y)$ for all $X, Y \in G$.

2.2 IND-ID-CCA

We can say that under an identity attack challenge, if an adversary A cannot win the following game challenge with a non-negligible advantage, then the Identity-based Encryption scheme is an IND-ID-CCA secure scheme.

Setup: Challenger C inputs a security parameter k and generates the system public parameter pp and the system's main secret key msk.

Phase 1(Training): Adversary A executes queries $q_i, i \in [1, m]$, where q_i is one of the following queries: (1) querying for the user secret key with identity id_i, Challenger C executes the private key generation algorithm to generate the private key sk_i correspond-ing to id_i and sends it to Adversary A; (2) querying for the ciphertext of a user identified by id_i, Challenger C executes the private secret key generation algorithm to generate the private secret key sk_i corresponding to the id_i, then uses sk_i to decrypt the ciphertext C_i corresponding to id_i, and send the message to Adversary A.

Challenge: Adversary A outputs two messages m_0 and m_1, with the same length, a public key id that he wants to challenge, where the public key id needs to be restricted to appear in any private key queries in Phase 1. Challenger C randomly chooses a bit $b \in \{0, 1\}$ and uses the encryption algorithm to get the ciphertext C. Finally, Challenger C sends b and C to Adversary A.

Phase 2(Training): Adversary A executes other queries $q_i, i \in [m + 1, n]$, where q_i is one of the following queries: (1) querying for the user secret key with identity id_i, Challenger C executes the private secret key generation algorithm to generate the private key sk_i corresponding to id_i and sends it to Adversary A; (2) querying for the ciphertext of a user identified by id_i, Challenger C executes the private secret key generation algorithm to generate the private secret key sk_i corresponding to the id_i, then uses sk_i to decrypt the ciphertext C_i corresponding to id_i and sends the message to Adversary A.

2.3 Decisional Bilinear Diffie-Hellman (DBDH) Assumption

Let p be a prime, G and G_T be cyclic groups of order p, $e : G \times G \to G_T$ be a bilinear mapping. We randomly choose a generator $g \in G$ and four numbers $a, b, c, z \in Z_p$. For the given tuples $(g^a, g^b, g^c, e(g, g)^{abc})$ and $(g^a, g^b, g^c, e(g, g)^z)$, if an adversary can use algorithm S to determine whether these two tuples are equal, and output 1 when they are equal, otherwise output 0. Then the advantage of algorithm S to solve this assumption is shown as follows:

$$Adv = |\Pr[S(g^a, g^b, g^c, e(g, g)^{abc}] - \Pr[S(g^a, g^b, g^c, e(g, g)^z]| \qquad (1)$$

If A cannot distinguish the above two tuples with a non-negligible advantage in polynomial time, A cannot solve the DBDH assumption. We can say that the DBDH assumption holds in G.

3 Device Authentication Scheme

3.1 Overall System Architecture

The IoT authentication system designed in this paper is composed of IoT Device, Authentication Server (AS), Time Synchronization Server (TTS), and Key Generation Center (PKG). Its structure is shown in Fig. 1. The authentication server is responsible for verifying the public identification of the IoT access device, checking whether the identification is in the system's allowable access device identification list, and executing the accountability algorithm to account for dishonest components in the system. The time synchronization server is responsible for monitoring the time when the device is connected to the system authentication server and provides the time stamp information required for user key generation and update. The Key generation center executes key generation and update algorithms for IoT devices, and maintains the public and private keys of IoT devices. The IoT access devices encrypt their own authentication information according to the identification key created by the key generation center and complete the authentication verification function on the authentication server.

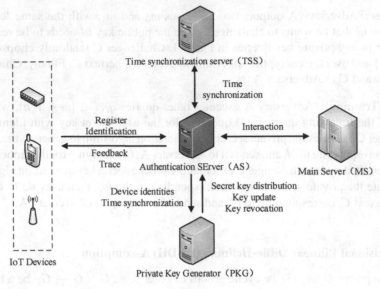

Fig. 1. Architecture diagram of IoT authentication

3.2 Authentication Protocol Based on Identity-Based Encryption

The interaction process between the system components is shown in Fig. 2.

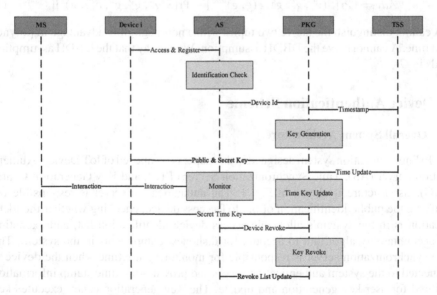

Fig. 2. IoT authentication architecture process

The specific steps are as follows:

(1) Devices access authentication.

Step 1: When the device is connected to the IoT system, the device's physical identification needs to be sent to the designated authentication server AS of the IoT authentication system. The AS compares the authorized device identity list. If the device's identification is in the list, it is allowed to access the system, otherwise be registered;

Step 2: The key generation center PSG executes the identity-based password initialization function $Setup(1^k) \rightarrow (pp, msk)$ to generate the public parameters pp and the master key msk of the cryptographic mechanism of the authentication system;

Step 3: The authentication server AS sends the physical identification i of the access device that is considered credible and unregistered. The time synchronization server TTS generates the device access timestamp t_j to the PSG. The PSG performs the bilinear calculation on the physical identification to generate the device's cryptographic public key, and then execute the private key generation algorithm to generate the device's revocable private key;

Step 4: PSG will send the generated public key to the access device, and the private key will be sent to the AS for escrow.

(2) Devices key update.

Step1: TTS monitors the access time of each access device in the system. After a specified time interval, TTS sends the current timestamp to the key authentication server of PSG;

Step2: PSG executes the key update algorithm $KeyUpdate(RL, id_i, t_{j'}) \rightarrow k_{t_{j'}}$ to update the time private key in the device private key.

(3) Devices revocation and Authentication accountability.

Step 1: If AS detects a suspicious adversary or dishonest device in the system, it can revoke and hold it accountable. AS will implement an accountability algorithm $Trace(id_i, ID, mpk) \rightarrow USR/PKG$ to trace the key's true generator, monitor whether the private key was generated illegally by PSG, and divide the responsibilities.

Step 2: When AS needs to revoke a suspicious adversary or dishonest device, it will send the public key id_i of the device i that needs to be revoked and a new revoked device list RL to the trusted PSG;

Step 3: PSG takes the public key id_i and revocation list RL as input, executes $Revoke(id_i, RL) \rightarrow RL'$, generates a new revoked devices list RL', and sends it to AS;

4 Proposed Cryptography Mechanism

This section builds a Traceable and Revocable Identity-based Encryption (TR-IBE) scheme. This scheme does not consider the problem of data tampering in the communication process, i.e., the communication content is complete during transmission in this paper. At the same time, it is assumed that the authentication server in the system is credible, and there is no illegal behavior.

We assume that k a security parameter represents the length of the private key in the system. It is a cyclic group with prime order p, and g is a generator of G. $e : G \times G \to G_T$ is a valid and computable bilinear mapping, identity $id \in ID$, where ID is the user identity space in the system.

1) Setup

The initialization algorithm $Setup(1^k) \to (pp, msk)$ is executed by the key generation center PKG, and the specific operations are as follows.

(1) Choose a cyclic group G and G_T with a large prime q, where g is the generator of G. Define the bilinear mapping $e : G \times G \to G_T$ on the group G and G_T. Randomly chooses $g_1 \in_R G$. Set ID. as the physical identification space of the system devices and K as the system keyspace;

(2) Define two strong collision-resistant hash functions $H_1 : \{0, 1\}^* \to ID$ and $H_2 : ID \to Z_q^*$.

(3) Randomly select the system master key $msk = s$, $s \in_R Z_q^*$, calculate the system public key $mpk = g_1^s$, and set the public parameters $pp = \{q, g, g_1, G, G_T, e, mpk, H_1, H_2\}$.

2) Key Generation

When PKG receives the request with the physical identification $i \in \{0, 1\}^*$ of the device sent by the certification center AS, it generates the corresponding public key and private key according to the request timestamp t_j recorded by TTS, where $\{0, 1\}^*$ represents a binary string of any length.

(1) PKG computes $id_i = H_2(H_1(i))$ and uses the physical identification of the device mapped by the hash function as the public key of the device in the system (i.e., $pk_i = id_i$) and sends it to the device.

(2) PKG computes and generates the private key of the IoT device. The private key is divided into two parts, i.e., the identity private key and the time private key. The device randomly generates $a \in Z_q^*$ and generates public parameter $P_i = g^a$. Then the device uses the private key agreement method based on zero-knowledge proof technology to compute the device identification private key $k_i = g^{s \cdot pk_i}$ and the timestamp private key $k_{t_j} = g_1^{a \cdot t_j}$, where the private key of the device can be expressed as $sk_i = (k_i, k_{t_j})$.

3) Encryption

When other devices or servers need to communicate with IoT devices i and transmit data required for authentication, a large number $r \in_R Z_q^*$ is randomly selected, an encryption algorithm is executed to encrypt the message, and the parameter p sent by the private key generation node is paired with the device public key pk_i are used to perform the Eq. (1) on the sent message.

$$C_1 = m \cdot e(g_1^r, g^a)^{t_j}, \quad C_2 = g^{a \cdot t_j}, \quad C_3 = g^r \tag{2}$$

Where m is the plaintext of the message to be transmitted, and the final ciphertext can be expressed as $C = \{C_1, C_2, C_3\}$.

4) Decryption

After the device i receives the ciphertext, it uses its private key to perform decryption operations. The decryption and transportation steps are as follows.

$$m = C_1 \frac{e(mps^{pk_i}, C_2)}{e(k_{t_j}, C_3 \cdot k_i)} \tag{3}$$

5) Revoke

PKG executes the revocation algorithm according to the device identity id_i to be revoked sent by the authentication server AS. PKG first checks the system identity revocation list RL. If the device identification is already in the list, it stops executing the revocation algorithm. Otherwise, it will add id_i to RL and update its corresponding key to an invalid key.

6) Key-ciphertext Update

When the time synchronization server TTS detects that the device's timestamp needs to be updated, the key generation center PSG first queries whether the device that needs the key is in the system identity revocation list RL. If it is not, it will update the private key of the device and the ciphertext transmitted to the device according to the new timestamp t_k; otherwise, it will stop executing the key update algorithm.

When the key generation center needs to update the device timestamp private key k_{t_j} of the device, the update method is as follows:

$$k_{t_k} = k_{t_j}^{t_k/t_j} \tag{4}$$

When the key generation center needs to revoke the private key of the device, the update method is as follows:

$$k_{revoke} = k_{t_j}^{0/t_j} = 1 \tag{5}$$

The key generation center sends the new timestamp to the device, and the device updates the ciphertext as follows:

$$C_1' = C_1 \cdot e(k_{t_j}, P_i)^{t_k - t_j}, \quad C_2' = C_2^{t_k/t_j} \tag{6}$$

7) Node Search Algorithm

This paper designs a tree structure for PKG to manage the time keys of different devices under the same timestamp and realizes the rapid search and update of the time stamp keys of the devices that need to be updated through the tree structure. The structure is shown in Fig. 3. The root node is a PKG that generates a device timestamp key; the second layer node is the timestamp that PKG received from TTS and TTS keeps the timestamp in its management, and the third layer is PKG generated according to the timestamp The device timestamp key.

This structure provides two update modes: timestamp update and device private key update.

(1) When PKG needs to update the timestamp private key of an individual device, PKG can search the tree structure according to the original timestamp provided by TTS and find the key that needs to be modified. After labeling the original key with the label that needs to be updated and revoking the key, PKG uses the new key generated by the new timestamp. If there is no new timestamp node in the tree, PKG creates a new timestamp node and its corresponding device key. Otherwise, PKG creates a key node under the existing new timestamp node.

(2) When PKG needs to update a certain timestamp, PKG finds the corresponding timestamp and marks the timestamp node that needs to be updated. After that, all the private keys of all connected devices are revoked and update under the new timestamp node.

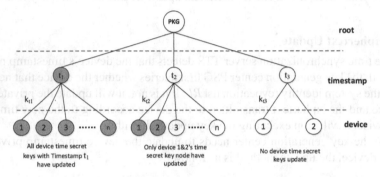

Fig. 3. The timestamp key retrieval structure diagram of PKG

8) Accountability

In the identification password scheme designed in this paper, PKG is curious, i.e., PKG may forge the device's private key and spy on message privacy. When the AS discovers a suspected untrusted terminal in the system, it needs to hold accountable and obtain evidence for the adversary's key generator. The AS uses the tree access structure according to the timestamp in TL to find out whether the device private key in the tree structure is illegally generated by the adversary or PKG, and arbitrates its responsibility. The method of accountability is as follows.

(1) AS needs to check whether the device's private key conforms to the form, i.e., judge $k_i? \in Z_q^*, k_{t_j}? \in G$. If the AS sends the private key that does not conform to the form, it can be determined that the device private key is forged by PKG or an adversary;

(2) The device i covertly transmits the identification of the private key k_i and the timestamp private key k_{t_j} to AS. The AS retrieves the timestamp t_j corresponding to the timestamp private key of the device i according to the key generation center device timestamp key. Finally, it calculates $e(k_i, k_{t_j})? = e(mpk, P_i^{pk_i \cdot t_j})$. If the equation does not hold, it can be determined that the PKG or the adversary forges the device's private key.

5 Scheme Analysis

This section will analyze the proposed TR-IBE scheme from the perspective of the cryptosystem's correctness and security.

5.1 Correctness Analysis

Encryption and decryption correctness:

$$C_1 \frac{e(mps^{pk_i}, C_2)}{e(k_{t_j}, C_3 \cdot g^{k_i})} = m \cdot e(g_1^r, g^a)^{t_j} \frac{e(g_1^{s \cdot id_i}, g^{a \cdot t_j})}{e(g_1^{a \cdot t_j}, g^r)e(g_1^{a \cdot t_j}, g^{s \cdot id_i})} = m \qquad (7)$$

The proposed decryption method can restore the ciphertext to the original plaintext, so the encryption and decryption method is correct.

Proof of correctness of key-ciphertext update:

$$k_{t_k} = k_{t_j}^{t_k/t_j} = g_1^{a \cdot t_k} \qquad (8)$$

$$C_1' = C_1 e(k_{t_j}, P_i)^{t_k - t_j} = m \cdot e(g_1^r, g^a)^{t_j} e(g_1^{a \cdot t_j}, g^a)^{t_k - t_j} = m \cdot e(g_1^r, g^a)^{t_k} \qquad (9)$$

$$C_2' = C_2^{t_k/t_j} = (g^{a \cdot t_j})^{t_k/t_j} = g^{a \cdot t_k} \qquad (10)$$

The correctness of the key-ciphertext update proves that the key-ciphertext update process's calculation result conforms to the new definition form. Hence, the proposed key update and revocation method is correct.

5.2 Security Analysis

Theorem: If the DBDH hypothesis is valid, then the proposed security model designed in Sect. 2.2 is IND-ID-CCA secure.

Proof: If there is a probabilistic polynomial-time advantage that adversary A can ignore the advantage ε to break this scheme, then adversary A can construct a probabilistic polynomial algorithm B and break the DBDH hypothesis with non-negligible advantage.

Challenger C sets up the cyclic groups G and G_T with the order of large prime q.

Initialization: Challenger C executes the initialization algorithm and extracts the challenge tuple (g, g^b, g^c, g^d, Z) of the DBDH hypothesis. Subsequently, challenger C sends the relevant system public parameters $pp = \{q, g, g_1 = g^b, g_2 = g^s, G, G_T, e, H_1, H_2\}$ to adversary A, where $H_1 : \{0, 1\}^* \rightarrow \widehat{ID}, H_2 : \widehat{ID} \rightarrow Z_q^*$ are two collision-resistant hash functions and s is the master private key;

Stage1: At this stage, adversary A can adaptively perform polynomial key generation and decryption queries.

Key Generation Query: For each user identity id_i, challenger C first selects a random number $a \in Z_q^*$ to generate the corresponding user private key $sk_i = (k_i, k_{t_j}) = (g_2^{pk_i}, g_1^{a \cdot t_j})$ and public parameters $P = g^a$.

Decryption Query: The adversary asks about the decryption of the identity and ciphertext (id_i, C). First, a key generation query is performed on the identity id_i to generate a private key sk_i corresponding to id_i, then run the decryption algorithm, encrypt the ciphertext with the private key, and send the response plaintext m to A.

Challenge: Adversary A submits a challenging identity id_i' and a challenging message m_0, m_1 of equal length. The challenger randomly selects $v \in \{0, 1\}$ and calculates the private key $sk_i' = (k_i', k_{t_j}')$ corresponding to the identity id' according to stage 1. Then A randomly selects a parameter to construct the corresponding ciphertext.

$$C_v' = (C_1', C_2', C_3') = (Zm_v, P^{t_j}, g^r) \tag{11}$$

If the input of challenger C is a DBDH tuple, i.e., $Z = e(g_1, g)^{bcd}$, the form of the ciphertext is

$$C_v' = (C_1', C_2', C_3') = (m_v e(g_1, g)^{bcd}, P^{t_j}, g^r) = (m_v e(g_1^b, g^c)^d, P^{t_j}, g^r) \tag{12}$$

Where C_v' is a valid encrypted ciphertext of the plaintext m_v.

Suppose the input of challenger C is a non-DBDH tuple, which Z is a random element in G_T. In this case, the output ciphertext of challenger C is an encrypted ciphertext of a random message.

Stage 2: Adversary A repeats the steps of querying the device key and ciphertext in stage1, and challenger C responds in the same way as stage1. However, in this stage, A cannot perform a key generation query on the challenge identity, nor can it perform a decryption query on the challenge identity and challenge ciphertext pair (id_i^*, C_v^*).

Guess: Finally, adversary A outputs a guess $v' \in \{0, 1\}$ on the random number v. If $v' = v$, then A successfully attacked.

Therefore, the advantage of adversary A to break through the cryptographic scheme designed in this article can be expressed as

$$Adv_A^{TR-IBE} = | \Pr[v' = v] - \frac{1}{2}| \tag{13}$$

Since this advantage cannot be ignored, it can be concluded that adversary A can distinguish the DBDH hypothesis with a non-negligible advantage. This contradicts the precondition that the known mathematical problems are indistinguishable, so the proposed scheme has the security of selecting ciphertext.

6   Conclusion and Future Work

This paper designs a lightweight device authentication scheme based on Identity-based Encryption. By introducing the revocable mechanism, the IoT authentication system implements the effective management of untrusted terminal keys. At the same time, to hold accountable the key generation center that may have forged the terminal secret key and maintain the terminal's legal rights in the system, accountability is also introduced in this paper. Compared with other Internet of Things authentication schemes based on the Identity-based Encryption, the proposed scheme is closer to the practical application scenario and satisfies the security of CCA. The future work would focus on the Identity-based Signature scheme based on non-bilinear mapping to improve the authentication scheme we designed in this paper, and make the corresponding security analysis be centered on non-malleability.

Acknowledgment. This work is supported by the Science and Technology Project of State Grid Jiangsu Electric Power Co., Ltd. under Grant No. J2020068.

References

1. Shamir, A.: Identity-based cryptosystems and signature schemes. In: Blakley, G.R., Chaum, D. (eds.) CRYPTO 1984. LNCS, vol. 196, pp. 47–53. Springer, Heidelberg (1985). https://doi.org/10.1007/3-540-39568-7_5
2. Boldyreva, A., Goyal, V, Kumar, V.: Identity-based encryption with efficient revocation. In: Proceedings of the 15th ACM conference on Computer and communications security, TaiPai Taiwan, pp. 417–426. ACM (2008)
3. Au, M.H., Huang, Q., Liu, J.K., Susilo, W., Wong, D.S., Yang, G.: Traceable and retrievable identity-based encryption . In: Bellovin, S.M., Gennaro, R., Keromytis, A., Yung, M. (eds.) ACNS 2008. LNCS, vol. 5037, pp. 94–110. Springer, Heidelberg (2008). https://doi.org/10.1007/978-3-540-68914-0_6
4. Xie, Y., Xu, F., Li, X., Zhang, S., Zhang, X., et al.: Eias: an efficient identity-based aggregate signature scheme for WSNS against coalition attack. Comput. Mater. Continua **59**(3), 903–924 (2019)
5. Ge, C., Xia, J., Fang, L.: Key-private identity-based proxy re-encryption. Comput. Mater. Continua **63**(2), 633–647 (2020)
6. Che, B., Liu, L., Zhang, H.: KNEMAG: key node estimation mechanism based on attack graph for IOT security. J. Internet Things **2**(4), 145–162 (2020)
7. Pan, X., Wang, Z., Sun, Y.: Review of PLC security issues in industrial control system. J. Cyber Secur. **2**(2), 69–83 (2020)
8. Choi, G.H., Jung, J.H., Moon, H.M., Kim, Y.T., Pan, S.B.: User authentication system based on baseline-corrected ECG for biometrics. Intell. Autom. Soft Comput. **25**(1), 193–204 (2019)
9. Sankaran, S.: Lightweight security framework for IoTs using identity based cryptography. In: 2016 International Conference on Advances in Computing, Communications and Informatics (ICACCI), Jaipur, pp. 880–886 (2016)
10. Reddy, A.G., Suresh, D., Phaneendra, K., et al.: Provably secure pseudo-identity based device authentication for smart cities environment. Sustain. Urban Areas **41**, 878–885 (2018)

11. Ullah, S.S., Ullah, I., Khattak, H., et al.: A lightweight identity-based signature scheme for mitigation of content poisoning attack in named data networking with Internet of Things. IEEE Access **8**, 98910–98928 (2020)
12. Lavanya, P., Sangeetha, A., Kumar, K.R.: A secure data getting/transmitting protocol for WSN in IoT using revocable storage identity based cryptography. In: 2018 3rd International Conference on Communication and Electronics Systems (ICCES), Coimbatore, India, pp. 1164–1170 (2018)

A Load-Balancing Algorithm for Power Internet of Things Resources Based on the Improved Weighted Minimum Number of Connections

Mingming Zhang[1], Jiaming Mao[1(✉)], Lu Chen[2], Nige Li[2], Lei Fan[1], and Leshan Shuang[3]

[1] State Grid Jiangsu Electric Power Co., Ltd., Information and Telecommunication Branch, Nanjing 210003, Jiangsu, China

[2] Institute of Information and Communication, Global Energy Interconnection Research Institute, State Grid Key Laboratory of Information and Network Security, Nanjing 210003, Jiangsu, China

[3] Engineering Research Center of Post Big Data Technology and Application of Jiangsu Province, Research and Development Center of Post Industry Technology of the State Posts Bureau (Internet of Things Technology), Broadband Wireless Communication Technology Engineering, Research Center of the Ministry of Education, Nanjing University of Posts and Telecommunications, Nanjing 210003, Jiangsu, China

Abstract. With the gradual increase of user visits in the power Internet of Things, load imbalances often appear, affecting server operation efficiency. This article is an improvement based on the weighted minimum number of connections algorithm. It sets weights for a group of servers and proposes two reference values: range and variance, and sets corresponding thresholds. Only the servers that exceed the threshold are used for the following operations. All data use re-hashing to deal with conflicts, and this process is repeated until an idle server is found to process the data. The simulation results show that the improved algorithm can effectively balance the user's task requests, realize the entire system's load balance, have good stability, and achieve the expected effect.

Keywords: Load balancing · Weighted least connection algorithm · Quicksort algorithm · Re-hashing

1 Introduction

1.1 Research Background

The power Internet of Things is the full application of modern information technologies and advanced communication technologies such as mobile Internet and artificial intelligence to realize the interconnection of everything in the power system [1], human-computer interaction, and create a network system with comprehensive status perception, efficient information processing, and convenient and flexible applications [2].

© Springer Nature Switzerland AG 2021
X. Sun et al. (Eds.): ICAIS 2021, LNCS 12737, pp. 563–574, 2021.
https://doi.org/10.1007/978-3-030-78612-0_45

In the face of different environments and real-time security incidents, security protection requirements are dynamically changing. Therefore, it is necessary to dynamically adjust security management and control strategies and cloud-side collaboration and dynamic linkage. At present, each core part of the existing network's business volume increases, and the amount of access and data traffic is also increasing rapidly. Its processing capacity and computing strength are correspondingly increased, making a single server device unable to afford it. The load balancing technology derived from this situation is a cheap, effective, and transparent method to expand the bandwidth of existing network equipment and servers, increase throughput, strengthen network data processing capabilities, and improve network flexibility and availability [3]. Load balancing is critical to the performance of large parallel applications [4].

1.2 Description of Research Status

At present, load balancing mainly includes the polling method, source address hashing method, weighted polling method, weighted random method, and weighted least connection (WLC) method.

Polling Method. The requests are distributed to the back-end servers in order, and it treats each back-end server in a balanced manner, regardless of the actual number of server connections and the current system load [5].

Source Address Hashing. The idea of source address hashing is to obtain a value calculated through a hash function based on the client's IP address and perform a modulo operation on the server list's size. The result is the serial number of the server that the client wants to access. Source address hashing is used for load balancing. Clients with the same IP address will map to the same back-end server for access whenever the back-end server list remains unchanged.

Weighted Polling Method. Different back-end servers may have different machine configurations and current system load, so their stress resistance capabilities are also different. Assign higher weights to machines with high configuration and low load to allow them to handle more requests, while machines with low configuration and high load are assigned lower weights to reduce their system load. Weighted polling works well. Deal with this problem carefully, and distribute the requests to the back-end in order and weight [6].

Weighted Random Method. Like the weighted round-robin method, the weighted random method assigns different weights according to the back-end machine's configuration and the system's load [7]. The difference is that it randomly requests back-end servers according to weight, not order.

Weighted Least Connection Method. The minimum number of connections algorithm's premise is that all servers in the system have the same performance. Whenever a new data processing task arrives, the task is always allocated to the server with the least number of connections [8]. Rather than saying that the number of connections to the Kth server at this time is the least, the new data processing task is assigned to the kth server for execution, and the number of connections to the server is updated at the same time; that is, the number of connections to the Kth server plus one. The minimum connection number algorithm uses the real-time connection number of each server to evaluate the server load. The minimum connection number algorithm is more flexible and intelligent. Since the back-end server's configuration is not the same, the request processing may be faster or slower [9]. It dynamically selects the server with the least number of backlog connections to process the current request according to the back-end servers' connection status, improves the utilization efficiency of the back-end services as much as possible, and distributes the responsibility to each server reasonably.

However, because the minimum connections algorithm does not consider each server's performance indicators when each server's performance differs significantly, it will affect load balancing. The weighted least connection algorithm is based on the least connection number algorithm, taking into account the performance differences of different servers, setting different weight values to identify server performance indicators, and assigning a larger proportion of activities to servers with larger weight values during task scheduling Connect [10]. Literature [11] proposed an algorithm to achieve load balancing with an adaptive weight minimum but did not consider the maximum load that the server can bear. The WLC algorithm is proposed in the literature [12] when a group of servers is assigned corresponding weights according to the nodes' performance. As the tasks increase, the servers' tasks with larger weights also increase. It will affect the performance of the server to a large extent. This paper proposes an improved power IoT resource load balancing algorithm based on the weighted minimum number of connections. It is an improvement to the WLC algorithm [13]. First, a set of server weights are calculated and analyzed. Two reference values are set: range and variance, set the corresponding threshold, only perform the following operations for the servers that exceed the threshold, apply re-hashing to all data to deal with conflicts, and loop this process until an idle server is found to process the data. This algorithm can effectively balance users' task requests, realize the load balance of the entire system, and have good stability, improving the server's processing efficiency.

2 Power Internet of Things Load Balancing Model

2.1 Power Internet of Things Load Balancing Model

As can be seen from Fig. 1, the control is divided into three layers in the vertical direction from the perspective of distributed control: management and application layer, network layer, and control target layer. Different functions are implemented horizontally, such as data perception and device control, but various data information exchanges and collaborative control exist between the horizontal layers. This article collects server weight values, calculates and processes them based on the management and application layers, classifies the data based on the processing results, and handles data conflicts.

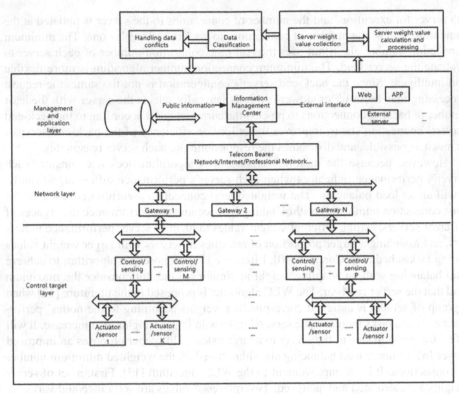

Fig. 1. Model architecture diagram.

2.2 Power IoT Resource Load Balancing Algorithm Based on the Improved Weighted Minimum Number of Connections

The WLC algorithm is a dynamic scheduling algorithm that calculates each node's number of connections in real-time and considers real servers' performance differences [14]. Although the WLC algorithm is widely used, there are still many problems: 1) The reasonableness and scientificity of the weight estimation need to be studied. The weight is an indicator that directly affects whether the system's nodes are balanced; 2) The weight configuration needs to be managed. It cannot be automatically and dynamically completed during system operation; 3) The dynamic weight of each node server cannot be estimated [15].

This article improves the weight part in response to the above problems. First, two reference data are proposed to judge whether a group of servers is load-balanced: the range value and the variance value. When the range of a data set is larger, the server with the larger weight is under excessive pressure, and the server with the smaller weight is still idle, which results in an unbalanced load. When the variance value is larger, the server weight value fluctuates greatly. The weight value difference between the servers is large, unstable, and load imbalance occurs.

Reference Data 1: Range Value. When load balancing allocates new connections to servers with a small number of active connections, the server weights are quickly sorted. Assuming that there are n servers, the weight values are $\{w_1, w_2, w_3, \ldots, w_n\}$, and the weight values of n servers are quickly sorted to obtain an increasing and orderly sequence of weight values.

The quicksort method [16] is an effective improvement to the bubble sort method. This sort of method was discovered by the British computer scientist Charles Anthony Richard Hall. At the same time, this algorithm is also the most extensive sorting algorithm in the world.

Split the data to be sorted into two independent parts by sorting. All the data in one part is smaller than all the data in the other part. Then according to this method, the two parts of data can be sorted quickly. The whole sorting process can be so that the entire data becomes an ordered sequence [17].

Quicksort algorithm process:

(1) Set two variables low and high, initialize the variables, low $= w_1$, high $= w_n$;
(2) Set the pivot, and the default first weight value W1 is the pivot. In the sorting process, the weight value smaller than the pivot is moved to the left of the pivot, and the weight value larger than the pivot is moved to the right of the pivot.
(3) Define two pointers i and j; i start from low (w_1) and search to the right; j starts from high+1 (w_{n+1}) and search to the left.
(4) i first search to the right from low (w_1) and compare the searched values with pivot. When it is less than the pivot, continue searching to the right until a record is greater than or equal to the pivot, The pointer i stop moving to the right.
(5) j search to the left from high+1 (w_{n+1}), and compare the searched values with the pivot in turn. When it is greater than the pivot, continue to search to the left until a record is less than or When it is equal to the pivot, the pointer j stops moving to the left.
6) Exchange the recorded values indicated by i and j.
(7) Continue to move the pointer i to the right, and stop moving when the pivot value is greater than or equal to the pivot. Continue to move the pointer j to the left, stop moving when it encounters a pivot less than or equal to the pivot, and exchange the record values pointed to by i and j.
(8) Repeat step 7 until the end when i is greater than or equal to j. At this time, j and pivot's record value is exchanged, and the quick sort ends.

In a set of increasing weight value sequences obtained by quick sorting, the maximum value is selected as w_{max}, the minimum value is selected as w_{min}, and the range is calculated, and the range is set as w_R.

$$w_R = w_{max} - w_{min} \tag{1}$$

The threshold is set to α, which represents a boundary value for the uneven distribution of the weight values of n servers. When the range w_R is less than the threshold α, it indicates that the weight values of n services are in a relatively average state, and the server distribution is relatively stable. When the range w_R is greater than or equal to

α, while the server with a larger weight is under excessive pressure, the server with a smaller weight is still idle, which causes a load imbalance.

Reference Data 2: Variance Value. Calculate the variance of the server's weight to determine the fluctuation of the weight of the server. The larger the variance of a set of data, the greater the server's weight fluctuation. The fluctuation refers to the deviation from the average. Assuming there are n servers, the weight values are $\{w_1, w_2, w_3, ..., w_n\}$.

First, find the average of the weights of n servers and set it as $\overline{w}$.

$$\overline{w} = \frac{(w_1 + w_2 + ... + w_n)}{n} \tag{2}$$

Then find the square of the difference between each weight value and the average value: $(w_1 - \overline{w})^2, (w_2 - \overline{w})^2, (w_n - \overline{w})^2$.

Finally, find the variance of the weight value and set it as s^2.

$$s^2 = \frac{(w_1 - \overline{w})^2 + (w_2 - \overline{w})^2 + ... + (w_n - \overline{w})^2}{n} \tag{3}$$

The threshold is set to β, which represents a boundary value for whether the weight value of n servers fluctuates sharply compared with the average value of all n servers. When the variance s^2 is less than β, it indicates that these n servers' weight value is relatively stable. When the variance s^2 is greater than or equal to β, it indicates that the server weight value fluctuates greatly. That is, the weight value difference between servers is large and unstable.

Handle Conflict. When the server weight value meets one of the above two conditions, the hash table is used to handle the conflict's re-hashing method. Each data is distributed on different nodes to achieve a balance of data and a balance of requests. When data is detected, find the corresponding server according to the data's attributes (size, function, type, urgency, etc.). Initially, the detection position is $H_0 = H_{key}\%m$ where i is the number of conflicts, initially 0.

When other data exists on the server, take $d_i = Hash_2(key)$ use.

$$H_1 = (H_0(key) + 1 * Hash_2(Key))\%m \tag{4}$$

Find a new address and place the data on the server corresponding to this address. If you find that the new address also has data, and the corresponding address is still not found to process the data, continue to re-hash function calculation, use

$$H_2 = (H_1(key) + 2 * Hash_2(Key))\%m \tag{5}$$

If the insertion position is still not found, continue to re-hash function calculation, use

$$H_i = (H_{i-1}(key) + i * Hash_2(Key))\%m \tag{6}$$

Processing data until the corresponding free address is found.

The algorithm steps are as follows:

Step 1: Assign weight values to all servers { $w_1, w_2, w_3, ..., w_n$}, quickly sort the weight values of n servers, and obtain an orderly increasing sequence of weight values.

Step 2: Select the maximum value w_{max}, select the minimum value w_{min}, calculate the range, and set the range as w_R.

Step 3: Determine whether the range value is greater than or equal to α. If yes, skip stepping 6. If no, the data enters the corresponding server and starts processing data.

Step 4: Calculate the average of all server weight values, and calculate the variance value s2 of this data set.

Step 5: Determine whether the variance value is greater than or equal to β. If yes, skip stepping 6. If no, the data enters the corresponding server and starts processing data.

Step 6: For all the data to be processed, find the corresponding server according to its own attributes, such as size, function, type, urgency, and other indicators.

Step 7: Determine whether the corresponding server is free. If so, the data enters the corresponding server and starts processing the data. If not, skip stepping 8.

Step 8: Apply a re-hash method to all the data to calculate the new server address, and skip to step 7.

The algorithm flow chart is shown as Fig. 2.

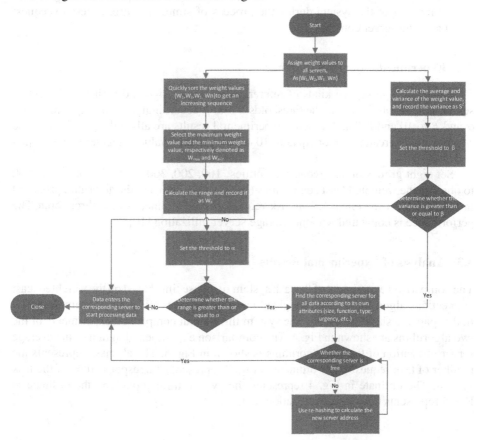

Fig. 2. Algorithm flow chart.

3 Experimental Analysis

3.1 Experimental Deployment

To verify and test the improved algorithm's effectiveness based on the weighted least connections (WLC) in the application of power Internet of Things cluster load balancing, this paper proposes three items: response time on the server, system throughput, and average server utilization. Indicators, and compared with the weighted least connection algorithm to judge the effect of the improved algorithm.

Experimental environment: The training and testing of the model are under Windows 10, using the VISIO platform to build the structural framework model, and using the LoadRunner system load testing tool for simulation testing.

Experimental deployment steps:

(1) Use IPVSADM software to deploy the improved algorithm based on the weighted least connections (WLC) proposed in this paper on the load balancing server [18];
(2) The LoadRunner system load testing tool is installed and deployed on the test client machine to record the average response time, system throughput, and average server utilization of the system during the process of simulating user access to request back-end server content [19].

3.2 Experimental Detailed Design

This article proposes two kinds of reference data: the range and variance of a set of server weight values and set the thresholds α and β accordingly. In this experiment, set α and β to 10 and 2. The following experimental results are all on the premise that the range value is greater than or equal to 10 or the variance value is greater than or equal to 2.

Set eight groups of task request quantities: 100, 200, 300, 400, 500, 600, 700, 800 to observe the weighted least connections (WLC) algorithm and the algorithm proposed in this article in the client, client task request response time, system throughput The performance is compared with the average server utilization [10].

3.3 Analysis of Experimental Results

The comparison experiment of the task system response time based on the weighted least connections algorithm and the weighted least connections (WLC) algorithm proposed in this paper is shown in Fig. 3. The system throughput comparison experiments of the two algorithms are shown in Fig. 4. The comparison experiment diagram of the average server utilization of the two algorithms is shown in Fig. 5. The abscissa represents the number of task requests. The ordinate in Fig. 3 represents the response time of the task system. The ordinate in Fig. 4 represents the system throughput, and the ordinate in Fig. 5 represents the average utilization rate.

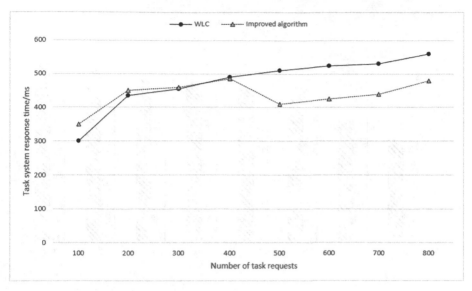

Fig. 3. Comparison diagram of response time experiment of the task system.

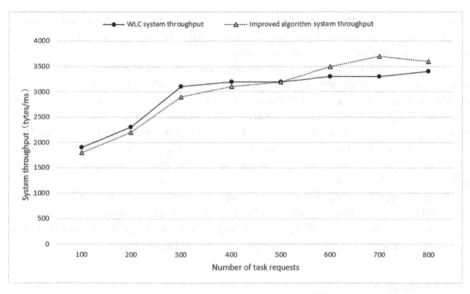

Fig. 4. Comparison of system throughput experiment.

It can be seen that when the number of task requests does not exceed 350, the task system response time of the WLC algorithm is shorter than the algorithm proposed in this paper. When the number of task requests does not exceed 500, the system throughput of the WLC algorithm is higher than the algorithm proposed in this paper. This is because the improved algorithm needs to perform quick sorting of server weights and compare

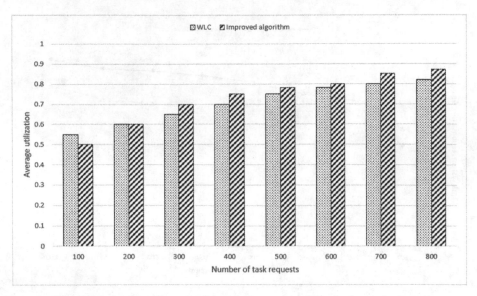

Fig. 5. Comparison diagram of the average server utilization rate experiment

with reference data before accepting task to judge the distribution of this set of server weights, which consumes a long time. The task system responds. The longer the time, the lower the corresponding system throughput.

However, when the number of task requests exceeds 350, the task system response time of the improved algorithm proposed in this article is shorter than that of the WLC algorithm. When the number of task requests does not exceed 500, the system throughput of the WLC algorithm is lower than the algorithm proposed in this article because of the previous period. The judgment of the weight value of a group of servers has classified this group of servers. The next task requests are targeted, thereby shortening the response time, making full use of system resources, increasing system throughput, and more effectively scheduled task requests.

It can be seen from Fig. 5 that the improved average server utilization based on the weighted least connections algorithm is better than the WLC algorithm.

In summary, the improved algorithm based on the weighted minimum number of connections proposed in this paper is better than the WLC algorithm.

4   Conclusion

This paper analyzes the existing load balancing algorithms and proposes an improved algorithm based on the minimum number of connections algorithm [20]. This method fully combines the outstanding advantages of multiple algorithms. It proposes an improvement in assigning new connections to the real server with the least number of active connections in the minimum connection algorithm. Two reference values are proposed: range and variance, and corresponding thresholds are set. The range and variance are calculated server's weight first to determine whether it exceeds the corresponding threshold. If the server weight value variance and range do not reach the threshold, it means that the server is relatively stable and relatively balanced. For these servers, the relevant data can be processed directly, which saves much work. You only need to perform the following operations on servers that exceed the threshold, apply re-hashing to all data to deal with conflicts, and loop this process until an idle server is found to process the data. This improved algorithm fundamentally improves the efficiency of load balancing in the data distribution to various servers.

Acknowledgment. This work is supported by the Science and Technology Project of State Grid Jiangsu Electric Power Co., Ltd. under Grant No. J2020068.

References

1. Jiang, L., Fu, Z.: Privacy-preserving genetic algorithm outsourcing in cloud computing. J. Cyber Secur. **2**(1), 49–61 (2020)
2. Sakhnini, J., Karimipour, H., Dehghantanha, A., Parizi, R.M., Srivastava, G.: Security aspects of Internet of Things aided smart grids: a bibliometric survey. Internet of things (2019)
3. Kumar, P., Kumar, R.: Issues and challenges of load balancing techniques in cloud computing: a survey. ACM Comput. Surv. (CSUR) **51**(6), 1–35 (2019)
4. Okhovvat, M., Kangavari, M.R.: Tslbs: a time-sensitive and load balanced scheduling approach to wireless sensor actor networks. Comput. Syst. Sci. Eng. **34**(1), 13–21 (2019)
5. Li-Yong, B., Dong-Feng, Z., Hong-Wei, D.: Research on load balance strategy of the double server in the synchronous dispatch mechanism of polling. J. Yunnan Univ. (Nat. Sci. Edn.) **31**(s1), 1–4+8 (2019)
6. Wachira, K., Mwangi, E.: A multi-variate weighted interpolation technique with local polling for bayer CFA demosaicking. In: 2015 International Conference on Information and Communication Technology Research (ICTRC), pp. 76–79, IEEE, Abu Dhabi (2015)
7. Xin, Y., Xie, Z.Q., Yang, J.: A load balance oriented cost efficient scheduling method for parallel tasks. J. Netw. Comput. Appl. **81**, 37–46 (2017)
8. Cheng-Yu, C., Yuan-Sheng, L., University, H.: Research on improved load balancing scheduling algorithm of weighted least-connection. J. Harbin Univ. Commer. (Nat. Sci. Edn.) **31**(1), 102–104 (2015)
9. Zhen-Bin, G., Ya-Chen, P., Zhong, H., Xiao-Hong, D., Dan, Z.: Improved load balancing algorithm based on weighted least-connections. Sci. Technol. Eng. **16**(6), 81–85 (2016)
10. Cheng, L., Kotoulas, S., Liu, Q.Z., et al.: Load-balancing distributed outer joins through operator decomposition. J. Parallel Distrib. Comput. **132**, 21–35 (2019)
11. Li, L., et al.: Load-balancing channel assignment algorithms for a multi-radio multi-channel wireless mesh networks. In: Proceedings of 2018 International Conference on Computer Modeling, Simulation and Algorithm (CMSA 2018), pp. 125–128. Atlantis Press, Beijing (2018)
12. Do, H.T., Shunko, M.: Constrained load-balancing policies for parallel single-server queue systems. Manag. Sci. **66**(8), 3501–3527 (2020)
13. Shi, X., Li, Y., Xie, H., Yang, T., Zhang, L., et al.: An openflow-based load balancing strategy in SDN. Comput. Mater. Continua **62**(1), 385–398 (2020)
14. She, P.: Research on LVS cluster weighted least connection scheduling algorithm. Comput. Digit. Eng. **47**(4), 794–798 (2019)

15. Meng, X.J., Zhang, C.Y.: An improved weighted least connection algorithm and its application analysis in CDN load balancing technology. J. Shandong Univ. Sci. Technol. (Nat. Sci. Edn.) **39**(1), 85–90 (2020)
16. Wang, H., Zhou, L., Zhao, G., Wang, N., Sun, J., et al.: PMS-sorting: a new sorting algorithm based on similarity. Comput. Mater. Continua **59**(1), 229–237 (2019)
17. Selvakumar, A., Gunasekaran, G.: A novel approach of load balancing and task scheduling using ant colony optimization algorithm. Int. J. Softw. Innov. (IJSI) **7**(2), 9–20 (2019)
18. Anitha, R., Vidyaraj, C.: An adaptive swarm optimization technique for load balancing and task scheduling in cloud computing. Indian J. Public Health Res. Dev. **10**(5), 955–965 (2019)
19. Zhang, X.Y.: Research on a quick sort algorithm based on element exchange. Gansu Sci. Technol. **47**(8), 1–3 (2018)
20. Khaliq, S., et al.: A load balanced task scheduling heuristic for large-scale computing systems. Comput. Syst. Sci. Eng. **34**(2), 79–90 (2019)

Research on Physical Layer Security Strategy in the Scenario of Multiple Eavesdroppers in Cognitive Wireless Networks Based on NOMA

Yuxin Du[✉], Xiaoli He[✉], Weijian Yang, Xinwen Cheng, and Yongming Huang

School of Computer Science, Sichuan University of Science and Engineering,
Zigong 643000, China

Abstract. In cognitive radio networks, signal transmission is easily attacked by eavesdroppers due to the broadcast characteristics of wireless media. The security of the network requires great attention. In the current research on cognitive wireless networks and NOMA, most people are separately studying the relevant characteristics of cognitive radio networks and the characteristics of wireless networks using non-orthogonal multiple access technology. Research on cognitive radio networks based on non-orthogonal multiple access technology is relatively lacking, especially from the perspective of the physical layer to analyze the security of cognitive radio networks based on non-orthogonal multiple access technology is extremely scarce. The thesis focuses on the scenario where there are multiple eavesdroppers in the NOMA-based cognitive wireless network, and analyzes the security of the secondary network and the entire network from the perspective of the physical layer. The security and rate of users in the network are the evaluation indicators of system security. By optimizing the secondary network and the power distribution algorithm of the entire network, better system security performance can be obtained, and spectrum utilization can be improved.

Keywords: Cognitive radio networks (CRN) · Non-orthogonal multiple access · Outage probability · Physical layer security

1 Introduction

The security of Cognitive Radio Networks (CRN) requires great attention. Non-orthogonal multiple access technology (Non-Orthogonal Multiple Access, NOMA) has become the key to 5G due to its excellent spectrum efficiency the multiple access technology [2]. The working principle of NOMA technology is that the sender sends information in a non-orthogonal manner, which actively introduces interference information, and the receiver uses serial interference cancellation (Success Interference Cancellation, SIC) technology to demodulate information correctly, which is essentially complicated by the receiving end. The increase in frequency has been exchanged for an increase in spectrum efficiency. The secondary users of the cognitive radio network can share the same spectrum resource with the primary users as long as they meet a certain interference power limit, while the NOMA technology introduces a power domain, which can introduce

© Springer Nature Switzerland AG 2021
X. Sun et al. (Eds.): ICAIS 2021, LNCS 12737, pp. 575–587, 2021.
https://doi.org/10.1007/978-3-030-78612-0_46

more users on the same frequency band, thus sharing the same frequency. A section of spectrum resources can be provided to more users at the same time, and is more suitable for large-scale networks.

Nowadays, there are many solutions for the physical layer security of cognitive radio networks, but there are few researches on the physical layer security of cognitive radio networks based on NOMA technology. This is one of the key points of this paper, and the in-depth physical layer security technology Research can further guarantee the high-quality and reliable transmission of communication networks in people's lives.

1.1 Related Work

How to ensure effectively the transmission reliability and security of cognitive wireless networks has always been the focus of CRN research [3–5]. When the channel performance of the system is weaker than the eavesdropping channel of malicious users, it will be insecure communication. Information leakage will lead to terrible consequences that cannot be estimated. Many current security studies on cognitive wireless networks have considered many scenarios and constraints. Literature [6] considered the analysis of the security capabilities of the network with two different user pairing methods in the network based on NOMA technology. Literature [7] considers the reliability of the system by obtaining the outage probability of the system under a large-scale cognitive wireless network. Literature [8] considers the MISO network, and every two users share the NOMA technology as a cluster. One of the users is a potential eavesdropper. In this case, the physical layer security of the network needs to be considered. In this paper, the safety rate of each cluster is calculated by reasonable power distribution to achieve the best system safety.

Due to different constraints, the capacity of the link (from the source node S to the destination node D) and the capacity of the eavesdropping link (from S to the eavesdropper E) are different. Literature [9] proved that if the capacity of the main link is smaller than the eavesdropping link, the eavesdropper can successfully intercept the signal transmission.

In order to improve transmission security and prevent eavesdropping attacks, it is very important to reduce interception incidents by improving security. However, in a multipath fading channel, the wireless security capacity is reduced. Therefore, people will work with relays to join the wireless network to overcome channel fading. Literature [9] proposed an optimal relay selection technology, which is some relay selection schemes under the AF and DF relay protocols to enhance wireless security capabilities.

The recent literature [10] research focuses on how to maximize the throughput of the secondary network under the premise of ensuring the QoS requirements of secondary users, and to solve the interference problem by introducing relevant multiple access technologies. It solves the transmission reliability of CRN in a single eavesdropping scenario, which is basically consistent with the research ideas of this paper. Document [11] studies the objective function of maximum security capacity, and proposes a joint relay and eavesdropper selection strategy (JRES) to solve the physical layer security problem. This is also similar to the research scenario of this article. In order to solve the physical layer security problem of cognitive wireless networks with multiple eaves-droppers, an effective iterative algorithm was developed in the literature using joint optimization technology.

1.2 Contribution

In the face of complex scenarios that have not been considered in the above literature. Firstly, this paper sets the performance such as secrecy sum rate, interruption probability as the measurement standards. Secondly, there are joint optimization methods such as convex optimization to solve the physics layer security issues in the complex environment with multiple eavesdroppers. This method not only guarantees the reliability and safety of the transmission of the cognitive wireless network based on NOMA technology, but also ensures the stability of the data transmission rate.

1.3 Organization of the Paper

The remainder of this paper is organized as follows. Section 2 presents the system model over Rayleigh fading channels. Section 3 formulates the optimization problem, including secrecy sum rate and the power allocation algorithm based on convex optimization. Numerical results are presented in Sect. 4. Finally, Sect. 5 concludes this paper.

2 System and Network Model

2.1 System Model

Let us now present our system model in Fig. 1. All nodes in this model are single antenna users, and the transmission of the secondary network follows the transmission principle of non-orthogonal multiple access. Assume that both the secondary base station SBS and the primary user transmitting end PT can estimate the CSI in the primary network and the secondary network through some calculations, and all CSI are accurate. In addition, in this network, the Eve may pretend to be a secondary user to eavesdrop and decode all legal information in the network. In this case, the secondary base station SBS can obtain the relevant CSI of the eavesdropper.

In this system model, it is assumed that all channel parameters obey a quasi-static Rayleigh distribution that is the channel coefficients are constant for each transmission slot, but vary independently between different slots.

Among them, a pair of primary users (PT, PR) communicate with each other, the transmitting end PT sends information 's' to the receiving end PR, and the secondary base station SBS broadcasts information S to each secondary user. The information broadcast by the base station SBS is definite. At the same time, Eve can eavesdrop on all relevant information in the network. Information X is a superimposed signal, and its specific representation is as follows:

$$X^{all} = \sqrt{p_1}x_1 + \sqrt{p_2}x_2 + \sqrt{p_3}x_3 + \ldots + \sqrt{p_n}x_n, (i = 1, 2, \ldots, n) \tag{1}$$

Multiple eavesdroppers in this model can eavesdrop on all signals and information in the auxiliary network and the main network. The information sent by the primary

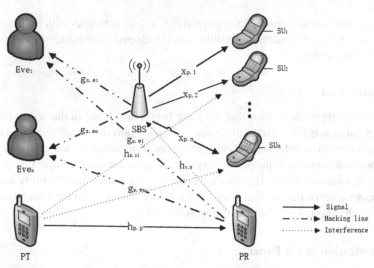

Fig. 1. NOMA-based cognitive radio network eavesdropping system model with multiple eavesdroppers

user transmitter PT to the PR is interference information to all secondary users in the secondary network. Therefore, the signal Y_e intercepted by the eavesdropper Eve is:

$$Y_e = f_{s,e_i}X^{all} + f_{p,e_n}s + \gamma_e \tag{2}$$

Where γ_e is the additive white Gaussian noise signal received by the eavesdropper Eve, with an average value of 0 and a variance of σ^2.

Similarly, the signal received by the primary user PR is expressed as follows:

$$Y_p = h_{s,p}X^{all} + h_{p,p}s + \gamma_p \tag{3}$$

The transmission power of all secondary users needs to meet a power threshold. Moreover secondary users in cognitive radio networks need to use the frequency bands of primary users, p_s needs to meet certain power constraints:

$$p_{s\,max} \geq \sum_{i=1}^{n} p_i \tag{4}$$

$$p_s = \min\left(\frac{I}{|h_{s,p}|^2}, p\right) \tag{5}$$

There is p_s the total transmission power that the secondary base station SBS can use. Among the formula (5), I is the maximum interference power that the primary user receiving end PR can accept, and p is the maximum transmission power of the secondary base station SBS.

In this model scenario, not only the channel gains of multiple eavesdroppers Even need to be considered, but also the channel gains of users in the secondary network need to be classified according to the ability of Rayleigh fading:

$$|h_{s,1}|^2 \geq |h_{s,2}|^2 \geq |h_{s,k_i}|^2 \geq |f_{s,e_i}|^2 \geq |h_{s,k_{i+1}}|^2 \geq \ldots \geq |h_{s,n}|^2 > 0 \tag{6}$$

It is assumed here that the numerical order of the secondary users is $1 \leq k < i < j$, and the i-th secondary user can decode the information of the k-th secondary user and treat the information of the j-th user as interference. Because the secondary base station SBS is not sure of the specific K value and all users in the secondary network use SIC technology.

The transmission rate R_{SU_i} of the secondary user SU_i is:

$$R_{SU_i} = \log_2(1 + SINR_{SU_i}) \tag{7}$$

$$SINR_{SU_i} = \frac{p_i |x_{p,i}|^2}{|x_{p,i}|^2 \sum_{m=1}^{i-1} p_m + \underbrace{p_t |h_{p,s_i}|^2}_{PT's \ \ interference \ \ to \ \ SU_i} + \gamma^2}, \ (1 \leq i \leq n) \tag{8}$$

Among them, p_i is the transmit power of the primary user's transmitting end PR.

What this paper considers is the worst case under the environment of eavesdropping, when any eavesdropper Eve eavesdropping on user SU_i's information, it can decode all previous secondary users' information, so the eavesdropper's eavesdropping rate is R_{e_i} for:

$$R_{e_i} = \log_2(1 + SINR_{e_i}) \tag{9}$$

$$SINR_{e_i} = \frac{p_i |f_{s,i}|^2}{|f_{s,i}|^2 \sum_{m=1}^{i-1} p_m + p_t |x_{p,i}|^2 + \gamma^2}, \ (1 \leq i \leq n) \tag{10}$$

Where $SINR_{e_i}$ represents the instantaneous signal-to-dry ratio, the eavesdropper Even tapped SU_i information.

In addition, the transmission rate $R_{p,p}$ at PR can be obtained from the above formula (3):

$$R_{p,p} = \log_2(1 + SINR_{p,p}) \tag{11}$$

$$SINR_{p,p} = \frac{p_t |h_{p,p}|^2}{\underbrace{\sum_{i=1}^{n} p_i |h_{s,p}|^2}_{SBS's \ \ interference \ \ to \ \ PR} + \gamma^2}, \ (1 \leq i \leq n) \tag{12}$$

Where $SINR_{p,p}$ is the instantaneous signal-to-dry ratio at the primary user PR.

2.2   Security Evaluation

We analyze the security of the secondary network in the cognitive wireless network of this model from the perspective of the physical layer, and mainly use the security accumulation rate [23] as a measure of system security performance, and improve the security accumulation rate of the network by optimizing power. When the security accumulation rate of users in the network increases, the security in the network becomes higher. From the definition of the security accumulation rate, the security rate is the difference between the mutual information between the message received by the legitimate user and the eavesdropping user and the original message, so the security rate R_{s_i} at the secondary user SU_i can be expressed as:

$$R_{s_i} = [I(x_i; y_i) - I(x_i; y_{e_i})]^+ = [R_{SU_i} - R_{e_i}]^+$$
$$= [R_{SU_i} - R_{e_{max}}]^+ \tag{13}$$

Here, I assume that $R_{e_{max}}$ is the eavesdropping channel with the largest channel capacity. Obviously, when $R_{s_i} > 0$, the secure communication between SBS and SU_i can be guaranteed; on the contrary, when $R_{s_i} < 0$, the channel condition of the eavesdropping channel is better than that of the legal channel, so there is no secure communication rate between SBS and SU_i. Sub-user information may cause information leakage. To ensure the best secure communication of the legal channel between the secondary user and the SBS, the best secure rate must be calculated.

Therefore, the safe accumulation rate R_s^{all} of all secondary users in the secondary network is expressed as follows:

$$R_s^{all} = \sum_{i=1}^{n} R_{s, i} \tag{14}$$

3 Optimization

This paper calculates the optimal proportion of the output power of each secondary user SU_i in the secondary base station SBS, so that the security of the secondary network under the environment of multiple eavesdroppers is improved. The secondary network power allocation algorithm proposed by the article [23], the algorithm can optimize the distribution of the transmission power pi of the secondary base station SBS to send different signals to the secondary user SU_i, at the same time, it can achieve the maximum value of the safety and rate of all secondary users in the secondary network. Therefore, the mathematical expression of the power distribution problem (P1) in the secondary network is P1:

$$\max_{\{p_i\}_{i=1}^{n}} R_s^{all}$$
$$\text{s.t.} \sum_{i=1}^{n} p_t \le p_s$$
$$R_{SU_i} \ge V_i, 1 \le i \le n \tag{15}$$

Where V_i is the minimum data rate required by the secondary user SU_i. Considering the environment of multiple eavesdroppers, we then specify the objective function in P1, and substituting formulas (7) and (9) into formula (16), we can get the specific expression of R_s^{all} as:

$$R_s^{all} = \sum_{i=1}^{n} R_{SU_i} - \log(|g_{s,e_{max}}|^2 \sum_{m=1}^{n} P_m + P_t|g_{p,e_{max}}| + \sigma^2)$$

$$= \log(|x_{s,1}|^2 \sum_{m=1}^{n} P_m + P_t|h_{p,1}|^2 + \sigma^2) - \sum_{i=1}^{2} \log(|g_{s,e_{max}}|^2 \sum_{m=1}^{n} P_m + P_t|g_{p,e_{max}}| + \sigma^2)$$

$$+ \sum_{i=2}^{n} [\log(|x_{s,i+1}|^2 \sum_{m=2}^{n} P_m + P_t|h_{p,i+1}|^2 + \sigma^2) - \log(|x_{s,i}|^2 \sum_{m=2}^{n} P_m + P_t|h_{p,i}|^2 + \sigma^2)]$$

$$(16)$$

Then, we define the following formula here:

$$\begin{cases} K_i = \sum_{m=i}^{n} P_m, (1 \le i \le n) \\ M_i = \begin{cases} |g_{s,e_{max}}|^2, & i = 1 \\ |x_{s,i}|^2, & 2 \le i \le n \end{cases} \\ N_i = \begin{cases} P_t|g_{p,e_{max}}|^2, & i = 1 \\ P_t|h_{p,i-1}|^2, & 2 \le i \le n \end{cases} \\ W_i = \log(M_{i+1}K_i + N_i + \sigma^2) - \log(M_iK_i + N_i + \sigma^2) \end{cases} \quad (17)$$

So, using the above definition formula, it can be simplified as:

$$R_s^{all} = \sum_{i=1}^{n} [W_i(K_i)] \quad (18)$$

From the perspective of the monotonicity of the function, the optimal optimization problem of the objective function $W_i(K_i)$ is analyzed, so the first derivative of $W_i(K_i)$ is expressed as:

$$\frac{d(W_i(K_i))}{d(K_i)} = \frac{(M_{i+1} - M_i)\sigma^2 + M_{i+1}N_i - M_iN_{i+1}}{(M_{i+1}K_i + N_{i+1} + \sigma^2)(M_iK_i + N_i + \sigma^2)\ln2} \quad (19)$$

It can be seen from the definition that secure transmission can only be achieved when the performance of the communication channel is greater than the performance of the eavesdropping channel. Therefore, where $c_i > b_i$, formula 1A is always greater than 0, and $W_i(K_i)$ is a monotonically increasing function. For 21B, it is obvious that it is impossible to accurately determine whether the value range is greater than 0. There are different situations. Therefore, first assume that the value of 21B is not less than 0. At this time, $W_i(K_i)$ is also a monotonically increasing function. In addition, substituting formula (7) into the constraint conditions of (17), the problem P1 can be transformed into P2:

$$\max_{p_j, 1 \le j \le n} K_i$$

$$\text{s.t.} \quad \sum_{j=1}^{n} p_j \leq P_s$$

$$p_j \geq A_j(B_j + |x_{p,j}|^2 \sum_{m=1}^{j-1} P_m) \tag{20}$$

Where $A_j = \frac{(2^{V_j}-1)}{|x_{s,j}|^2}$, $\quad B_j = \gamma^2 + p_1|h_{p,j}|^2$.

By analysis shows that P2 is a convex optimization problem. The following uses the Lagrangian multiplier method to solve the problem. First, write the Lagrangian function of the objective function in P2 under the inequality constraint:

$$L(p_j, \alpha, \beta_j) = -K_i + \alpha(\sum_{j=1}^{n} p_j - p_s) + \sum_{j=1}^{n} \beta_j(A_j(B_j + |x_{p,j}|^2 \sum_{m=1}^{j-1} P_m) - p_j) \tag{21}$$

Where a and b are Lagrange multipliers.

To solve (23), the following KKT constraints need to be met:

$$\begin{cases} \alpha \geq 0 \\ \beta_j \geq 0 \\ \frac{\partial L}{\partial p_j} = 0 \\ \alpha\left(\sum_{j=1}^{n} p_j - p_s\right) = 0 \\ \beta_j\left(A_j\left(B_j + |x_{p,j}|^2 \sum_{m=1}^{j-1} P_m\right) - p_j\right) \\ \sum_{j=1}^{n} p_j - p_s \leq 0 \\ A_j\left(B_j + |x_{p,j}|^2 \sum_{m=1}^{j-1} P_m\right) - p_j \leq 0 \end{cases} \tag{22}$$

Use $p_s - \sum_{l=1}^{j} p_l$ instead of $\sum_{m=1}^{j-1} p_m$ to get the relevant optimized solution of problem P2, which can be expressed as:

$$p_j = \frac{(2^{V_j} - 1)}{|x_{p,j}|^2 2^{V_j}}\left(\gamma^2 + p_t|h_{p,j}|^2 + |x_{p,j}|^2\left(p_s - \sum_{l=1}^{j} p_l\right)\right), 1 \leq j \leq i$$

$$= \frac{A_j}{2^{V_j}}\left(B_j + |x_{p,j}|^2\left(p_s - \sum_{l=1}^{j} p_l\right)\right) \tag{23}$$

From the above optimized solution, we find that when p_s and p_t are fixed, the only power distribution situation can be obtained, that is, the specific solution value of $\{p_i\}_{i=1}^n$.

4 Simulation Results and Analysis

The following analyzes the security of the system model proposed in this paper through a series of simulation experiments, and verifies the effectiveness of the secondary network power allocation algorithm in this paper. All channels in the simulation system are modeled as independent and identical distributed Rayleigh fading channels, assuming that the noise power density in the system is $N_0 = -50$ dBm.

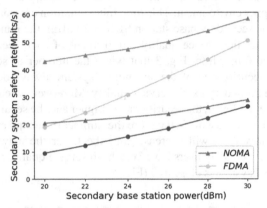

Fig. 2. Comparison of the safety rate of the secondary system under different transmission protocols.

Firstly, we compare the security capabilities of secondary systems using NOMA technology and FDMA technology under the same bandwidth. The simulation environment is set as the transmission power p_t at the primary user's transmitting end PT is 30 dBm, the number of secondary users $n = 6$, and the QoS requirement Vi of the transmission rate of each secondary user is 1bit/s/HZ ($1 \le i \le n$). Figure 1 shows the change of the safety rate of the secondary system with the power p_s of the secondary base station under different transmission protocols. Among them, the upper two lines of the chart are the channel bandwidth of 20 m, and the lower two lines are the channel bandwidth of 10 m. Obviously, as the ps increases, the security capabilities of the secondary systems using two different transmission technologies are improving, and the security capabilities will increase with the increase in bandwidth. However, under the same bandwidth, the security rate of the system using NOMA technology is significantly higher than that of the system using FDMA technology. It proves that the cognitive wireless network using NOMA technology is more secure.

Secondly, we analyzed the impact of the number of secondary users on the average network security rate. In this simulation environment, the total transmission power of the entire network is set to 30, 35, 40, 45, 50 dBm, the number of secondary users n is 4, 5, and 6, and the transmission rate QoS requirement of each secondary user is 1bit/s/HZ. It can be seen from Fig. 2 that in the case of different numbers of secondary users, the average safe rate of the network increases as the total power increases. This result proves that when more users are served in the network at the same time, even in an insecure environment with multiple eavesdroppers, the higher the spectrum utilization of the network using NOMA technology, the higher the spectrum efficiency, the higher the network safety.

In addition, we also studied the impact of the QoS requirements and number of secondary users' transmission rates on the sum of the secondary network security rates in a multi-eavesdropper environment. This time the simulation environment is set as the transmit power at the secondary base station SBS is 20 dBm, the number of secondary users n = 4, 5, 6, and the service quality requirement of each secondary user is 0-4 bit/s/HZ. It can be found from Fig. 3 that when the number of secondary users is different, the total security rate of the secondary system always decreases with the improvement of the secondary user's service quality. Moreover, when the transmission rate of secondary users is lower, the security rate is higher and the security of the network is higher. But with the increase of Vi, the more the number of secondary users, the faster the sum of its security rates will decrease, and the faster the network security will decrease; even if the secondary users have very high service quality requirements, The security of secondary system is close to 0 (Fig. 4).

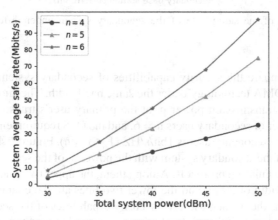

Fig. 3. Average secrecy sum rate of CRNs under different total system power

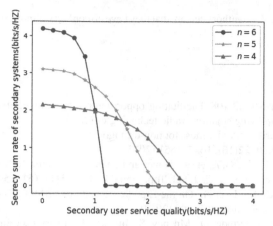

Fig. 4. Secrecy sum rate of secondary system under different service quality (Vi)

5 Conclusions

To sum up, this paper conducts in-depth research on the security performance of the multi-eavesdropper cognitive wireless network model based on NOMA technology. In this model, there are a pair of primary users, a secondary base station, multiple secondary users and two eavesdroppers. We analyzed in detail the security of user information transmission in the secondary network with NOMA technology to ensure the security of secondary network information transmission. After analyzing the transmission model of the system, promote the alternative expression of the incremental optimal power allocation, obtain the optimized transmission power of the secondary base station SBS to send different signals to the secondary users, and convert it into the safety and rate of the secondary system In order to obtain better security and confidentiality performance. The simulation experiment results show that the new cognitive wireless network model with NOMA technology proposed here can effectively improve the confidentiality performance of the system, and the security and confidentiality performance of the system is related to the number of users in the network and the quality of service of users. It is very important that better system security performance can be obtained by optimizing the algorithm, and at the same time, the utilization rate of the spectrum can be improved.

Acknowledgments. The authors would like to thank the anonymous reviewers for their selfless reviews and valuable comments, which have improved the quality of our original manuscript.

Funding Statement. This work was partially supported by the National Natural Science Foundation of China (No. 61876089, No. 61771410), by the Talent Introduction Project of Sichuan University of Science & Engineering (No. 2020RC22), by the Zigong City Key Science and Technology Program (No. 2019YYJC16), by the Horizontal Project (No. HX2017134, No. HX2018264), by the Enterprise Information and Internet of Things Measurement and Control Technology Sichuan Provincial Key Laboratory of universities (No. 2020WZJ02, No. 2014WYJ08), and by Artificial Intelligence Key Laboratory of Sichuan Province (No. 2015RYJ04).

Conflicts of Interest. The authors declare that they have no conflicts of interest to report regarding the present study.

References

1. FCC ET Docket No. 03-108. Facilitating opportunities for flexible, efficient, and reliable spectrum use employing cognitive radio technologies (2003)
2. Timotheou, S., Krikidis, I.: Fairness for non-orthogonal multiple access in 5G systems. IEEE Signal Process. Lett. **22**(10), 1647–1651 (2015)
3. Zhao, G., Yang, C., Li, G.Y., et al.: Power and channel allocation for cooperative relay in cognitive radio networks. IEEE J. Sel. Top. Signal Process. **5**(1), 151–159 (2011)
4. Qi, S., Han, S., Chilin, I., et al.: On the Ergodic capacity of MIMO NOMA systems. IEEE Wirel. Commun. Lett. **4**(4), 405–408 (2017)
5. Orumwense, E.F., Oyerinde, O., Mneney, S.: Impact of primary user emulation attacks on cognitive radio networks. Int. J. Commun. Antenna Propag. **4**(1), 1–26 (2014)
6. Ding, Z., Fan, P., Poor, H.V.: Impact of user pairing on 5G non-orthogonal multiple access. IEEE Trans. Veh. Technol. **65**(8), 6010–6023 (2014)
7. Liu, Y., Ding, Z., Elkashlan, M., et al.: Non-orthogonal multiple access in large-scale underlay cognitive radio networks. IEEE Trans. Veh. Technol. **65**(12), 10152–10157 (2016)
8. Li, Y., Jiang, M., Zhang, Q., et al.: Secure beam forming in downlink MISO non-orthogonal multiple access system. IEEE Trans. Veh. Technol. **66**(8), 7563–7567 (2017)
9. Zou, Y., Wang, X., Shen, W.: Optimal relay selection for physical-layer security in cooperative wireless networks. IEEE J. Sel. Areas Commun. **31**(10), 2099–2111 (2013)
10. Christian, I., Moh, S., Chung, I., Lee, J.: Spectrum mobility in cognitive radio networks. IEEE Commun. Mag. **50**(6), 114–121 (2012)
11. Zhang, L., Sun, J.: Channel allocation and power control scheme over interference channels with QoS constraints. In: IEEE International Conference on Control & Automation. IEEE (2017)
12. Li, Z., Jing, T., Cheng, X., et al.: Cooperative jamming for secure communications in MIMO cooperative cognitive radio networks. IEEE Wirel. Commun. Lett. **4**(4), 1 (2015)
13. Li, F., Wang, L., Hua, J., Meng, L., Zhang, J.: Power optimization for dynamic spectrum access with convex optimization and intelligent algorithm. Wireless Netw. **21**(1), 161–172 (2014). https://doi.org/10.1007/s11276-014-0775-1
14. Hu, H., Zhang, H., Yu, H.: Energy-efficient sensing for delay-constrained cognitive radio systems via convex optimization. J. Optim. Theory Appl. **168**(1), 1–22 (2016)
15. Devral,A.M., Sharma, M.K., Murthy, C.R.: Power allocation in energy harvesting sensors with ARQ: a convex optimization approach. In: Signal and Information Processing IEEE, pp. 208–212 (2014)
16. Chen, W.H., Lin, W.R., Tsao, H.C., Lin, C.: Probabilistic power allocation for cognitive radio networks with outage constraints and one-bit side information. IEEE Trans. Signal Process. **64**(4), 867–881 (2016)
17. Zou, Y., Wang, X., Shen, W.: Physical-layer security with multiuser scheduling in cognitive radio networks. IEEE Trans. Commun. **61**(12), 5103–5113 (2013)
18. Zhu, J., Zou, Y., Champagne, B., Zhu, W., Hanzo, L.: Security-reliability trade off analysis of multirelay-aided decode and forward cooperation systems. IEEE Trans. Veh. Technol. **65**(7), 5825–5831 (2016)
19. Xu, Y., Zhao, X.: Distributed power control for multiuser cognitive radio networks with quality of service and interference temperature constraints. Wirel. Commun. Mob. Comput. **15**(14), 1773–1783 (2015)

20. Zhao, N.: Joint Optimization of cooperative spectrum sensing and resource allocation in multi-channel cognitive radio sensor networks. Circuits Syst. Signal Process. **35**(7), 2563–2583 (2016)
21. Xu, D., Feng, Z., Li, Y., et al.: Fair channel allocation and power control for uplink and downlink cognitive radio networks.In: GLOBECOM Workshops, pp. 591–596. IEEE (2011)
22. Wang, X.: Computer Algorithm Design and Analysis, 4th edn, pp. 154–196. Publishing House of Electronics Industry,Beijing (2007). ISBN 9787121042782
23. Luwei Wei, F., Tao Jin, M.: A Physical Layer Security Scheme for NOMA-enabled Cognitive Radio Networks, 9 May 2019

Opportunistic Network Performance Optimization Model Based on a Combination of Neural Networks and Orthogonal Experiments

Zhihan Qi[1,2] , YunChao Pan[1,2], Hao Du[1,2], Na Zhang[1,2], ZongHan Bai[1,2], and Gang Xu[1,2(✉)]

[1] College of Computer Science, Inner Mongolia University, Hohhot 010021, China
[2] Inner Mongolia A.R. Key Laboratory of Wireless Networking and Mobile Computing, Hohhot, China
csxugang@imu.edu.cn

Abstract. Under the complex environmental conditions of remote geographic locations and fragmented network areas, sending data over traditional wired networks or wireless self. Organizing networks often results in connection interruptions, packet loss and other problems. In order to reduce the problem of data loss due to network disruptions, researchers have proposed a new network technology for cut networks, named opportunity Network. Opportunity network messages have a high rate of packet loss due to factors such as the small probability of node encounters and message lifetime limits. In order to reduce the packet loss rate, improve the success rate of message transmission and reduce the message transmission delay, the paper proposes a node message transmission performance optimization model based on the fusion of neural networks and orthogonal experiments. The experimental results show that the prediction model proposed in the paper for optimizing node message transmission performance can predict the packet loss rate more accurately, and it is found that node density, node rate, and node cache are the most important factors influencing the message packet loss rate of the opportunity network, and the optimal settings of these three factors are obtained to reduce the packet loss rate of message transmission and improve the message delivery efficiency.

Keywords: Opportunity network · Packet loss rate · Neural network · Orthogonal test

1 Introduction

Mobile opportunity networks originated from early studies of ICNs (intermittently connected networks) [1] and DTNs (delay-tolerant networks) [2]. In an opportunity network, the hop-by-hop forwarding of data packets between nodes is achieved in a "store-carry-forward" mode, usually when the nodes move into each others communication coverage, using the resulting communication opportunities for data

© Springer Nature Switzerland AG 2021
X. Sun et al. (Eds.): ICAIS 2021, LNCS 12737, pp. 588–600, 2021.
https://doi.org/10.1007/978-3-030-78612-0_47

transmission [3]. Because opportunity networks can deal with problems that are difficult to solve with existing wireless network technologies and can meet the needs of network communication under harsh conditions [4], the research on opportunity networks has become one of the hotspots in wireless mobile self-organizing networks. Currently message packet loss rate measurement is one of the most important performance measures in opportunistic networks [5]. The main causes of packet loss include congestion occurring at the nodes, lack of system resources, and large amount of storage space occupied by the nodes. The packet loss rate has a significant impact on the performance of opportunistic network routing algorithms [6]. In practical scenarios, existing opportunity network routing algorithms are focused on optimizing data transmission algorithms to achieve efficient data transmission. For example, predicting the packet loss rate before message delivery, combined with classical routing algorithms such as Epidemic [7], Prophet [8], SW (Spray and Wait) [9], CAR (Context-Aware Routing) [10], and so on, further reduces the packet loss rate and achieves a higher transmission success rate. Therefore, the study of packet loss rate prediction model is of great importance to improve the message delivery rate of opportunity networks.

In order to solve the problem of unpredictable packet loss rate in opportunistic network data transmission, the paper proposes a neural network-based packet loss rate prediction model for opportunistic networks. The model is capable of predicting packet loss rates in the environment required for practical use, and improving the efficiency and quality of data transmission in opportunistic network routing algorithms by optimizing the settings of node cache capacity, number of nodes, and node movement rate.

2   Related Works

Currently, in the field of research on opportunistic networks, there have been more studies on node message passing routing protocols and less studies on packet loss rate prediction.

The literature [11] addresses the prospect of application of opportunity networks in remote areas, constructs an application environment similar to remote areas, and analyzes typical routing protocols in opportunity networks to simulate the application of typical routing protocols in remote areas. And evaluate the routing algorithm in terms of four aspects: transmission success rate, routing overhead, average delay time, and average cache time. In this study, it is not considered to set the parameters in the current scenario to be optimal, resulting in a possible increase in the node packet loss rate.

The literature [12] proposes GAPR-based routing based on the laws of human activity, GAPR routing references contextual information to decide the path of message transmission. GAPR routing takes full advantage of the genetic algorithm and probabilistic routing characteristics. The path is searched by genetic algorithm, and a probabilistic mechanism is used to estimate the threshold value and select the optimal path to transmit the message. Although GAPR routing is effective in reducing message transmission latency and overhead, it does not analyze the impact of key parameters on routing performance.

The above algorithm is unable to discover the influential factors in data forwarding in opportunity networks because it does not analyze and predict the packet loss rate. Therefore, to address the shortcomings of the existing studies on the inadequate prediction of packet loss rate, this paper proposes a node message transmission performance optimization model based on the fusion of neural networks and orthogonal experiments to achieve packet loss rate prediction of data transmission, analyze the influencing factors of the opportunity network operation, and implement the optimal opportunity network factor setting model to improve the influencing factors of the opportunity network and improve the message forwarding message and quality.

3 Optimization Model for Node Message Transmission Based on Neural Networks and Orthogonal Experimental Algorithms

3.1 Relevant Definitions

To analyze the state of node forwarding data, the packet loss rate in different situations and scenarios. To complete the opportunity network message forwarding simulation experiments in one using Epidemic algorithm to obtain the data packet loss rate, the values of the variables *started*, *dropped*, and *delivery_prob* in the report are obtained from the generated *Message Stats Report*, where *started* is the total number of messages at start. *Dropped* is the number of lost messages and *delivery_prob* is the success rate of message delivery. The packet loss rate of the network is the ratio of the lost portion of the packet to the total number of transmitte data, which can be expressed as Eq. (1):

$$PacketLossProbability = \frac{dropped}{created + started} \tag{1}$$

3.2 Packet Loss Factor

In a real opportunistic network scenario, the different number of nodes in a region, the speed of node movement, and the size of the region's cache capacity all lead to changes in the message delivery rate, as shown in Table 1.

In Fig. 1, the packet loss rate shows a slow decrease in the overall trend as the number of nodes decreases. Figure 2, the message packet loss rate decreases as the node movement rate decreases. In Fig. 3, the packet loss rate decreases as the cache capacity increases.

In summary, the packet loss rate is closely related to the number of nodes, node movement rate and node cache capacity, and changes with the changes of these three factors. Based on the results of the above analysis, the paper proposes a neural network-based optimization model for node message transmission performance.

Table 1. Scenario setting.

Scenario 1: Network of Opportunity Scenario with Changing Number of Nodes	Node Cache Capacity	100M
	Node movement rate	100 m/s
	Number of nodes	1–100
Scenario 2: Opportunistic network Scenario with changing Node movement rate	Node Cache Capacity	100M
	Node movement rate	1 m/s–100 m/s
	Number of nodes	100
Scenario 3: opportunistic network Scenario with node Cache capacity change	Node Cache Capacity	1M-100M
	Node movement rate	100
	Number of nodes	100

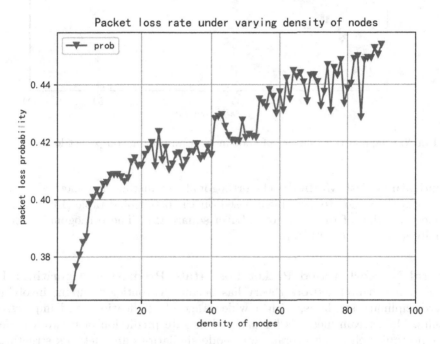

Fig. 1. Graph of the influence of node density change on packet loss rate.

3.3 Prediction Model with Fusion of Neural Networks and Orthogonal Experiments

Through experiments in different scenarios, different node densities, node movement rates, and node cache capacities have a significant impact on the success rate of message transmission in the opportunity network. In order to solve the problem of operating efficiency of the opportunistic network to the maximum extent possible, the paper applies the orthogonal test method to optimize the initial parameters of the opportunistic network and selects a set of better configurations with less number of tests.

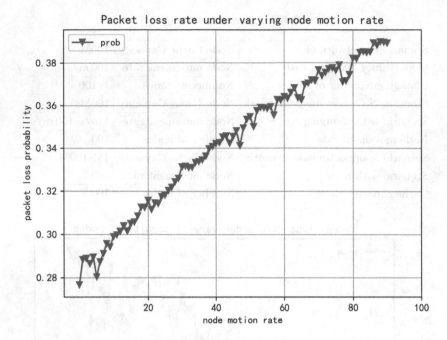

Fig. 2. Graph of the influence of node motion rate change on packet loss rate.

Quadrature Test Method: The orthogonal test method is a method to find the optimal solution to a problem based on the orthogonal table [13], which is a popularization of the orthogonal Latin square [14]. The orthogonal table is usually written as $L_a(t^9)$ [15].

Neural Network Based Packet Loss Rate Prediction Algorithm: In recent years, neural network theory has become a frontier discipline involving interdisciplinary synthesis, with a wide range of applications and impressive results. Mainstream methods for packet loss rate prediction of network nodes of opportunity often incorporate inter-node similarities and network structural features to accomplish packet loss rate prediction. These research methods ignore the historical information of network nodes in the time dimension. This paper based on the time-varying characteristics of opportunistic networks, the neural network algorithm extracts the key features of the packet loss rate variation of opportunistic networks based on the temporal information during the evolution of opportunistic networks and the correlation between the time dimension of nodes and historical information, so as to achieve the prediction of packet loss rate.

The criterion for judging the performance optimization model in an opportunistic network based on neural networks and orthogonal testing is the Mean-Square Error (MSE). It represents the mean value of the sum of squares of the errors corresponding to the predicted data and the original data, which is often

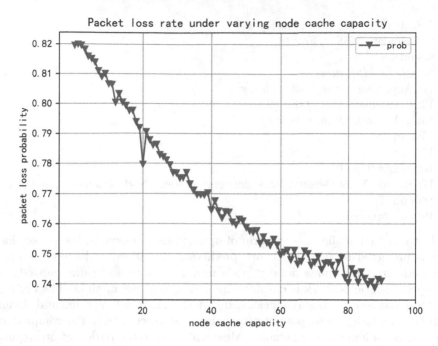

Fig. 3. Graph of the influence of node cache capacity change on packet loss rate.

used to judge the performance of the model. The calculation method is as shown in Eq. (2).

$$MSE = \frac{1}{n} \sum (y_i - f_i)^2 \tag{2}$$

In Eq. (2), n denotes the number of data, y1, y2 ... yn denotes n expected output values, i.e., actual values, and f1, f2, ..fn denotes n network predicted values. From the abovel formula, the smaller MSE indicates that the predicted value is closer to the actual value, so a smaller MSE is desired during the experiment.

Algorithm 1: Neural network based computational algorithm for packet loss rate prediction

Require:
   1: where there is a total number of samples p, where the number of samples ranges from 1-p and the number of training sessions is q
   2: Initialized weights w Deviation v, q=1
   3: Node Density, Node Movement Rate, Node Cache Capacity

Ensure: Packet loss rate

   4: function PACKET LOSS RATE PREDICTION:
   5: for $p=1;p_iP;p++$ do
   6: $q=q+1$

7: Calculate output of each layer
8: Calculate MSE //Eq.(2.)
9: end for
10: *MSE=MSE_min*
11: Adjusting the w, v of each layer
12: Recalculate MSE //Eq.(2.)
13: if *MSE=MSE_min* then
14: end
15: else
16: *MSE=0, p=0*
17: Retype Node Density, Node Movement Rate, Node Cache Capacity
18: end if
19: end function

In the actual application scenario of opportunistic networks, the packet loss rate is predicted by neural network prediction algorithm, and then the optimal configuration of node density, node movement rate and cache capacity in the opportunistic network is obtained by orthogonal test method. The orthogonal test method is a highly efficient, fast and economical experimental design method, in which some representative points are selected from the comprehensive test according to orthogonality. Meanwhile, the combination of orthogonal test method and neural network can reduce the number of calculations for the optimal settings of the number of nodes, node motion rate and cache capacity, and improve the efficiency of the model to find the optimal parameter settings in time [16].

Optimization Model for Predicting Routing Conditions for Opportunistic Networks Based on the Fusion of Neural Networks and Orthogonal Experiments: The optimal configuration in unfamiliar environments is analyzed by combining the predicted packet loss rate and orthogonal experiments. A total of 200, 000 data are trained. The node density, node movement speed and node cache capacity range from 1 to 100, 1 m/s to 100 m/s, 10M to 100M, respectively. Orthogonal experiments are conducted in this range, and the test factors are node density, node movement rate, node cache capacity, node density of 10, 100, 1000 nodes, and node cache capacity. The motion rate is 5 m/s, 50 m/s, and 500 m/s, and the node cache capacity is chosen to be 10M, 100M, and 1000M. Based on the above information, a factor level table is obtained, as shown in Table 2.

Because there are three levels and three factors, we choose $L_9(3^4)$ orthogonal test table. And calculate the packet loss rate of each scheme through the packet loss rate prediction model. As shown in Table 3.

Carry out orthogonal test, and get the intuitive analysis table of experiment, as shown in the following Table 4. Through visual analysis, the range of node density is 0.203, the range of node cache capacity is 0.138, and the range of node motion speed is 0.439. The larger the range, the more important the

Table 2. Orthogonal test factor level table.

Level factors	Node density	Node motion rate	Node cache capacity
1	10	5 m/s	10M
2	100	50 m/s	100M
3	1000	500 m/s	1000M

Table 3. Packet loss rate prediction results.

Proposal factors	Node density A	Node motion rate B (m/s)	Node cache capacityC (M)	Packet loss rate
1	1(10)	1(5)	1(10)	0.8887
2	1(10)	2(50)	2(100)	0.2419
3	1(10)	3(500)	3(1000)	0.3639
4	2(100)	1(5)	2(100)	0.6808
5	2(100)	2(50)	3(100)	0.2192
6	2(100)	3(500)	1(10)	0.2954
7	3(1000)	1(5)	3(1000)	0.4172
8	3(1000)	2(50)	1(10)	0.2087
9	3(1000)	3(500)	2(100)	0.2612

corresponding factors are. It can be seen that the node motion speed has the greatest influence on packet loss rate.

The orthogonal test effect curves were obtained from the experimental results, as shown in Fig. 4.

It can be seen from the figure that the packet loss rate reaches the minimum value when the node density is the largest, the node motion rate is 50 m/s, and the node buffer capacity is the largest. Therefore, when the node density is set to 100, the motion rate is set to 50 m/s, and the node buffer capacity is set to 100M, it is the optimal packet loss rate within this range.

4 Experimental Results and Analysis

4.1 Experimental Environment Settings and Performance Indicator

In order to detect the effect of node selfishness on opportunistic social network routing, the ONE1.4.0 (Opportunistic Network Environment) simulation environment platform is used, which is used to evaluate the correctness and validity of the proposed model and algorithm. The experimental environment parameter settings are shown in Table 5 to analyze the performance of the node identification model proposed in the paper under different environments.

Performance evaluation indexes include the success rate of message transmission, and the extreme difference of orthogonal test.

Table 4. Experimental visual analysis table.

Row	1	2	3	4	
Factors	Node density	Node motion rate	Node cache capacity		Experimental results
1	1(10)	1(5)	1(10)	1	0.8887
2	1(10)	2(50)	2(100)	2	0.2419
3	1(10)	3(500)	3(1000)	3	0.3639
4	2(100)	1(5)	2(100)	3	0.6808
5	2(100)	2(50)	3(100)	1	0.2192
6	2(100)	3(500)	1(10)	2	0.2954
7	3(1000)	1(5)	3(1000)	2	0.4172
8	3(1000)	2(50)	1(10)	3	0.2087
9	3(1000)	3(500)	2(100)	1	0.2612
Mean1	0.498	0.662	0.464	0.456	
Mean2	0.398	0.223	0.395	0.318	
Mean3	0.295	0.307	0.333	0.417	
Range	0.203	0.439	0.131	0.138	

Table 5. The settings of simulation experiment parameters.

Parameter	Value
Size of experimental area	$4000 * 3000\,\mathrm{m}^2$
Number of experimental areas	4–6
Node movement model	Shortest Path Map
	Based Movement (SPBM)
Node density	10/100/1000
Node movement speed	$1\,\mathrm{m/s}$
Node Cache Capacity	10M
Node communication radius	$50\,\mathrm{m}$
Experimental simulation time	$24\,\mathrm{h}(6400\,\mathrm{s})$

Theorem 1. *Message Delivery Success Rate: dprob is the ratio of the Number of successfully delivered messages Numd to the total messages Num generated in the network.*

Theorem 2. *Extreme Range: first calculate the large K value: emphK$_i$ means the sum of the corresponding test results when the horizontal number on any column is i. Secondly, calculate the small k value, as shown in Eq. (3).*

$$k_i = \frac{K_i}{s} \tag{3}$$

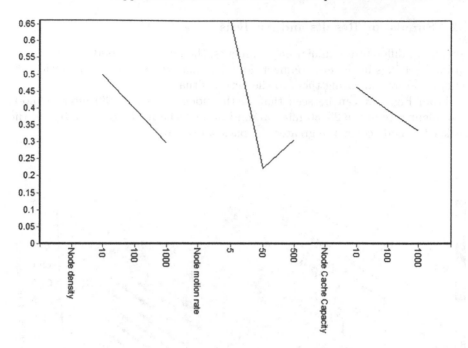

Fig. 4. Orthogonal test effect curves.

In which s is the number of occurrences of each level in any column, and ki in the experiment is mean 1, mean 2 and mean 3 respectively. Finally, calculate the range R, as shown in Eq. (4).

$$R = max\{k1, k2, k3\} - min\{k1, k2, k3\} \tag{4}$$

Based on the number of extreme differences, the influence of each factor on the experimental results can be judged. The principle of judgment is: the greater the extreme difference, the more important the corresponding factor is; from this, the order of the primary and secondary factors can be determined. Based on the size of the average value of the results of the indicators corresponding to each level of each factor, it can be determined what level is better for each factor. The principle of determination is: if the smaller the indicator is required, the level corresponding to the smallest average value is taken; if the larger the indicator is required, the level corresponding to the largest average value is taken.

4.2   Simulation Results and Analysis

Setting up different unfamiliar environments, the model was used to analyze the optimal settings in the environment, and the analyzed settings were verified to be optimal by comparing them to the actual situation.

From Fig. 5, it can be seen that in the node density 25–30 interval, node movement rate in the 25–30 interval, and node cache in the 50–70 interval, the darker the node color, the greater the packet loss rate.

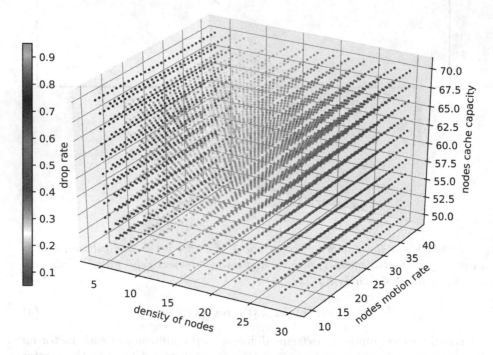

Fig. 5. Scatterplot of the three-factor packet loss rate for the 200 * 200 scenario.

In the 200 * 200 scenario take out the number of nodes, node movement rate, node cache capacity five groups of random configuration and a set of model prediction optimal configuration, compare the predicted packet loss rate and the actual value, from Fig. 6 shows that in the random configuration model prediction and the actual value of the accuracy of 75%, and the optimal configuration prediction is accurate, the difference between the prediction and the actual value, respectively, 0.06.

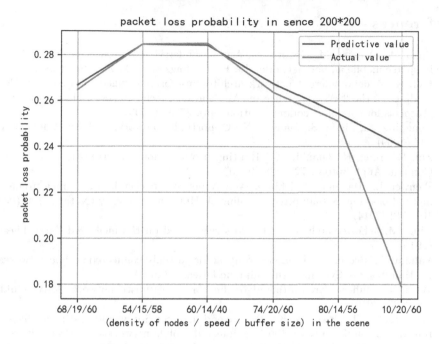

Fig. 6. Packet loss rate for 200 * 200 scenario.

5 Conclusion

This paper is based on the fusion of neural network and orthogonal test to predict the optimization model of routing conditions in opportunistic networks, and this paper predicts the packet loss rate of node transmission by neural network algorithm, and uses orthogonal test method to obtain the optimal parameter settings of node density, node movement rate, and cache capacity in real opportunistic networks, which significantly reduces the number of times to find the optimal parameter settings and improves the operation efficiency of the whole system. The actual packet loss rate in different scenarios is compared with an accuracy of more than 75%. The experiments prove that the proposed neural network- based prediction model for node message transmission in opportunistic networks can predict the packet loss rate in different application scenarios and find the optimal value of each environmental variable, effectively solving the parameter setting problem in real opportunistic networks. Provide support.

Acknowledgement. This work was partially support by the National Natural Science Foundation of China under Grant 62061036, 61841109 and 61661041, Naturel Science Foundation of Inner Mongolia under Grand 2019MS06031, in part by the CERNET Innovation Project under Grant NGII20170622.

References

1. Zhao, W., Ammar, M., Zegura, E.: A message ferrying approach for data delivery in sparse mobile ad hoc networks. In: Proceedings of ACM Mobihoc (2004)
2. Fall, K.: A delay-tolerant network architecture for challenged internets. In: Proceedings of the 2003 conference on Applications, technologies, architectures, and protocols for computer communications, pp. 27–34 (2003)
3. Yongping, X., Limin, S., Jianwei, N.: Opportunity network. J. Softw. **20**(1), 124–137 (2009)
4. Zhi, R., Yong, H., Qianbin, C.: Routing protocols for opportunistic networks. J. Comput. Appl. **30**(03), 723–728 (2010)
5. Wenwei, L., JIanguo, C., Zhimin, W.: A network packet loss rate measurement method based on self-adaptive sampling. J. Hunnan University (Nat. Sci.) **41**(03), 107–112 (2014)
6. Ting, M.: The research on packet loss rate based on the measured data. Thesis (2015)
7. Vahdat, A., Becker, D.: Epidemic routing for partially-connected ad hoc networks. In: Handbook of Systemic Autoimmune Diseases (2000)
8. Weijie, C.: Buffer aware routing algorithm for opportunistic network. Softw. Guide **7**, 80–83 (2019)
9. Spyropoulos, T., Psounis, K., Raghavendra, C.S.: Spray and wait: an efficient routing scheme for intermittently connected mobile networks. In: Proceedings of the 2005 ACM SIGCOMM Workshop on Delay-Tolerant Networking, pp. 252–259 (2005)
10. Musolesi, M., Hailes, S., Mascolo, C.: Adaptive routing for intermittently connected mobile ad hoc networks, pp. 183–189 (2005)
11. Dinghai, G., Xiaohang, H., Songhe, T.: Simulation studies of opportunity network applications in remote areas. J. HeChi Univ. **34**(05), 66–71 (2014)
12. Ping, Z., Zhidong, Z., Shengzheng, W.: Packet forwarding protocol in coal mine opportunistic networks based on terminal attribute. China Sci. Paper **13**(14), 1669–1673+1678 (2018)
13. Luquan, R.: Test Optimization Design and Analysis. Higher Education Press (2003)
14. Ruhe, D., Bihua, X., Yongshui, F.: Optimization test design method and data analysis, vol. 06, pp. 103–106. Chemical Industry Press (2004)
15. Haijun, G., Xingqi, H., Ming, D., Yaowen, Z.: Two indexes of design and analysis of orthogonal experiments about a novel phosphorus free builder. Comput. Appl. Chem. **03**, 481–484 (2004)
16. Xiaolin, W., Bingjun, W., Qiang, Z.: Theoretical analysis methods and applications of quadrature test design. J. Anhui Inst. Archit. **27**(03), 95–99 (2010)

Security Analysis of Measurement Automation System Based on Threat Intelligence

Shaocheng Wu[1], Tao Liu[1], Jin Li[2(✉)], Hefang Jiang[1], Xiaowei Chen[1], and Xiaohong Cao[1]

[1] Shenzhen Power Supply Bureau Co. Ltd., Shenzhen 518001, Guangdong, China
[2] Beijing University of Posts and Telecommunications, Beijing 100876, China
li_jin@bupt.edu.cn

Abstract. With the development of artificial intelligence, the network space is characterized with more features such as openness, heterogeneity, mobility, dynamics, security. In this diverse cyberspace, the security defense technology based on threat intelligence, is more suitable for advanced persistent threats compared with traditional security protection and plays an important role in the network security of measurement automation system. According to the characteristics of measurement automation system, this paper summarizes threat information platforms provided by information security government organizations and unit. And based on the risk impact factors existing in current measurement automation system, we comprehensively analyze its security problems. Finally, aims at the problem that current risk warning models do not consider warning storms and management costs when the network is much larger, we propose adding the priority evaluation of nodes into the model when it carries out correlation analysis. The proposed model improves execution efficiency and realizes the lightweight.

Keywords: Measurement automation · Network security · Correlation analysis

1 Introduction

1.1 A Subsection Sample

As the large data and artificial intelligence develop fast, the data needs to be processed in the field of information security also grows rapidly and network space appears many new features such as openness, heterogeneity, mobility, dynamic, security and so on. Under this environment, security risk issues are particularly prominent. Traditional security protection only relies on firewalls, intrusion detection systems, intrusion prevention systems and other security devices deployed at the boundary or special nodes for static control. This kind of passive defense is no longer applicable to the protection of new network security such as advanced persistent threats. In order to maximize the security of core system assets, it is urgent to optimize and improve the traditional security defense methods, forming a diversified and sustainable threat defense system [1]. Therefore, security defense technology based on threat intelligence emerges. Threat intelligence

X. Sun et al. (Eds.): ICAIS 2021, LNCS 12737, pp. 601–610, 2021.
https://doi.org/10.1007/978-3-030-78612-0_48

perception and analysis technology can collect large-scale fragmented anomalous data with a variety of technical means, and concentrate on deep mining, refining and fusion to form a threat clue collection, then use machine learning, semantic analysis, correlation analysis and other technical analysis to predict the invasion or future threat situation [2].

However, in the current measurement automation system, most of the network fault management level is still relatively backward, and fault management is very passive. Network administrators can discover and troubleshoot failures only after a network failure occurs. But due to the complexity and logical relevance of the network itself, a single failure may trigger a large number of warnings [3]. Therefore, the first problem of network fault management is to carry out alarm association analysis, which combines multiple alarms into one alarm with more information to help network administrators analyze fault information and locate faults quickly. In the measurement automation system, if all the alarm information in the system is processed, it will bring great problems to the maintenance and management cost of the automation system.

Therefore, according to the characteristics of measurement automation system, combined with information security threat intelligence and vulnerability information at home and abroad, this paper summarizes threat intelligence platforms provided by international and domestic information security government organizations and units. This paper also analyses the risk impact factors of measurement automation system, integrates the environmental, hardware, software risk problems, and improves the existing risk warning model. Based on the early risk warning model, we join the priority evaluation of nodes to lighten the task of association analysis. Then, according to the overall design idea, the network topology structure is designed and the rationality of this model is verified by experimental simulation.

2   Related Work

Measurement automation system transmits meter data to the power system based on digital communication technology. After the related information is collected by the power system, the corresponding calculation and analysis are carried out. As the core business system in electric power communication, measurement automation system is making more changes to electric power enterprises with its huge influence, greatly reducing labor costs, promoting the intellectualization and data of power networks, and profoundly embodying the key of automated power networks. Therefore, the construction of measurement automation system plays an important role in the service quality of power enterprises.

2.1   Platforms of Threat Intelligence

At present, threat intelligence driven information security defense has become the recognized direction of information security development in the future. Threat intelligence system construction has been incorporated into security strategic planning by many government organizations and units supporting information security. In 2015, the U.S. House of Representatives passed the Cybersecurity Information Sharing Act, which calls for enhanced information sharing between businesses and governments to improve the country's decision-making ability in responding to cybersecurity incidents. Some platforms in our country also provide platforms for collecting and sharing threat intelligence [2]. This paper summarizes the existing threat intelligence acquisition source platforms at home and abroad, as shown in Table 1.

Table 1. Summary of threat intelligence acquisition sources

From	Platform	
Abroad	Fire Eye	Core Security
	Crowd Strike	Webroot
	Unit42	Looking Glass Cyber
	FOX IT	Infoblox
	NetScout	Securosis
	Vera Code	Recorded Future
Domestic	Threat Book	Ti Qian Xin
	360net-lab	Venus Eye
	IBM X-Force Exchange	Alien Vault

2.2 Architecture of Measurement Automation System

The measurement automation system mainly consists of application functions such as collection and maintenance, data management, business application and system management, as well as various application servers, network devices and user-side measurement terminals, as shown in Fig. 1.

In daily operation practice, with the help of functions such as abnormal alarm function, load analysis and power analysis of power measurement automation system, power inspectors and metering personnel can timely and effectively monitor and analyze the power abnormalities in their jurisdiction. By fully grasping the power and load of customers, power inspectors can lock abnormal operating equipment in time, which improves the quality of anti-theft ultimately [4]. Among the functions of measurement automation system, the most important one is low-voltage meter reading management. In the past meter reading operations, although it requires a lot of people and costs much material resources, the efficiency of meter reading is much low. After the application of measurement automation system, by strengthening the monitoring and maintenance of related data, managers can find the fault in time. The accuracy of information can be improved at large. Finally, it realizes real-time data review, and can also improve the quality of data accounting [5].

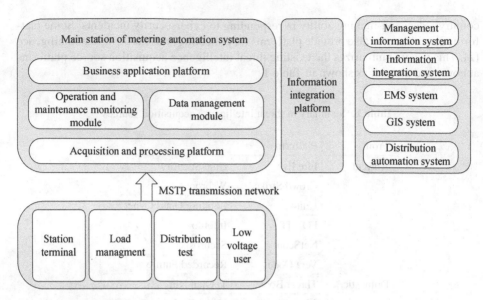

Fig. 1. Summary of threat intelligence acquisition sources

2.3 Security Analysis of Measurement Automation System

As a typical industrial production control system, the safety protection and operation of measurement automation system are important cornerstones ensuring the safe and stable operation of power network. The fast development of the Internet put forward higher requirements for the smooth and safe operation of power automation system. It is necessary to comprehensively analyze its risk impact factors, build a complete security protection system, and ensure the validity of power network operation. This paper summarizes the three aspects that affect the safety of measurement automation system as follows.

First, environmental risks. The environmental risk factors for the operation of power measurement automation system are mainly from three aspects. One is the personnel factor of power measurement automation system. Because the large number of human and machine, the efficient operation environment of equipment is hard to be guaranteed. And human neglect can easily cause the system paralysis, which threaten the safe operation of power measurement automation system. The second is the equipment power supply maintenance of power measurement automation system. The power supply of power measurement automation system is very vital for the whole system, but the maintenance and maintenance of power supply often lack corresponding attention. Third, the defects of the power grid measurement automation system itself make it vulnerable to external environment attacks. Once the system attacked, many data and information will be damaged, which will have great adverse impact on the company and power grid measurement automation system [6].

Second, hardware risks. The metering automation system needs to run for a long time, so its internal hardware often fails. Common failures are manifested as defects or errors in the data display. Generally, when the current is unstable in transmission, it is easy to cause the internal components of the metering automation system to fail due to the unstable voltage, which will lead to abnormal operation of the hardware in metering automation system.

Third, network security risks. The existing power metering automation system is not strong enough to resist network risks. As a complete information security defense system has not yet been established, the vulnerability of the measurement automation system is the inherent reason for the existence of network security risks and security risks. Direct connection to the local data network without safe and effective isolation will threaten the safety of the system. Strengthening the safety and reliability of the power metering automation system is the main task of the current power metering automation system [7].

3 Risk Warning Model of Metering Automation System

3.1 System Introduction of Risk Warning Model

From the second part of this article, we know that compared with the other two security risks existing in metering automation systems, network security risks have greater damage intensity and broader damage scope. Therefore, it is of great significance to design a reasonable security warning model based on network security risks. For the measurement automation system, the risk early warning model can specifically involve three parts: alarm information acquisition, alarm information format standardization, and transaction correlation analysis [8].

Firstly, acquire alarm information. In the metering automation system, the channels for obtaining alarm information mainly come from host equipment, network switches and routers. The host equipment includes these types of data source entities: bastion machine, front collector, database server, interface server, report server, production and release data equipment and database equipment. Security equipment mainly includes hardware firewalls, IDS, network acces, security isolation arrays, and encryption authentication devices. Network equipment mainly includes application system servers such as libraries and workstations. The sources of alarm information obtained from the above security devices, network devices, hosts and other security protection systems mainly include security logs, network traffic, device operating status and configuration information, security alarm logs, security vulnerabilities and virus logs [9].

Secondly, standardization of alarm information format. The security warning model needs to extract key warning information from different devices. Then the data preprocessing module needs to collect, filter, merge and analyze the data. Data preprocessing extracts intuitive, effective and standardized data sources for the safety early warning system. The system log collector collects key hosts, security equipment and other system logs. The collected log information mainly includes key host logs, firewall logs, switch logs, bastion machine logs, and other logs. These logs can be divided into Textual and protocol-based. There are two ways to deal with the standardization of the alarm information format, one is based on network protocol-based exchange device log analysis, and the other is based on network security device log. The former log is generated by network devices such as switches, routers, etc., and the log is forwarded through the protocol. The second type of security device logs mainly involves security logs generated by firewalls and intrusion detection systems. Since the IDS system has not yet formed a unified standard format, such logs are output as standardized data based on XML attributes [10].

The last step is alarm information correlation analysis. Most of the current network fault management levels are still relatively backward, and fault management is very passive. Only after the network fails, the network administrator can discover and eliminate the fault based on the fault alarm. However, due to the complexity and logical correlation of the network itself, the single failure may cause a large number of alarms. The primary problem of network fault management is to perform alarm correlation analysis. To consolidate and transform alarms, merge multiple alarms into one alarm with more information, helping network administrators analyze fault information and quickly locate faults [11]. Apriori algorithm is a classic association rule mining algorithm. It aims at obtaining frequent item sets and strong association rules in the data. First scan the database, get the item set and calculate the support. Then set the support threshold, pruning the item sets smaller than this value, and meeting the requirements is the frequent items. Then the frequent item sets are formed into a new set and rescanned to obtain a larger frequent itemset until all frequent item sets that meet the requirements are found. Finally, the high-frequency k-item group of the previous step is used to generate rules. Under the threshold of the minimum reliability, if the reliability obtained by a rule meets the minimum reliability, this rule is an association rule [12].

3.2 Improved Risk Warning Model

The correlation analysis of alarm information based on data mining can finally find the strong correlation rules between risky transactions, revealing the valuable strong correlation attributes existing in each transaction. However, if all the alarm information in the system is processed and the alarm correlation analysis is performed, it will bring much pressure to the maintenance and cost of the automation system. Therefore, in this paper, we propose that in the metering automation system, corresponding strategies should be adopted for these main important nodes. By improving the reliability of the entire system, reducing the probability of network abnormalities, save costs, and achieve lightweight models ultimately.

First, calculate the importance of the metering automation system node according to the network topology [13]. For the measurement automation system network, the better the connection, the higher the reliability of the network, and the stronger the survivability of the network system. Define the cut point weight as $T(i)$, shows in equation Eq. (1) and Eq. (2). For a network with m nodes, where $i = 1, 2, \ldots, m$, and any vertex is $X(i)$, then the set of all vertices in the network is denoted as $X = \{X_i\}$. Define the cut point set $V_{deg} = \{v_i\}$, v_i is the cut point in the network, where c_i is the weight of each edge, and the total number of cut points in the network is defined as $N = sum\{v_{dge}\}$.

$$T(i) = \begin{cases} f_{id}(i) \cdot \left(1 - \frac{c_{min}}{c_{max}}\right) & c_{min} \neq c_{max} \\ f_{id}(i) & c_{min} = c_{max} \end{cases} \tag{1}$$

$$f_{id}(i) = \begin{cases} 1 + \frac{1}{N} & X_i \in V_{dge} \\ 1 & X_i \notin V_{dge} \end{cases} \tag{2}$$

Second, the importance of network nodes is distinguished based on the types of services carried by the metering automation system. From the power business level to determine the importance of the corresponding node, this part includes the following three steps:

(i)   Define node importance based on power indicators. Select several main power indicators that affect the importance of nodes: load level, load flow, node type, and voltage level. The sum of the expert's evaluation value of the power index in the power communication network and the weight of the power index in the communication network is defined as the node importance, denoted as $PI(i)$.

(ii) Node importance based on power business. The evaluation indicators adopt the following four types: transmission delay, bit error rate, bandwidth level, and bearing mode. The score of each index of each power business and the corresponding evaluation index weight are weighted and calculated, and the calculated weighted sum of each power business is log-normalized to obtain the importance of each business. For each node, take the value of the highest business importance on the communication link directly connected to the node as the node importance of the node based on power services, denoted as $PB(i)$.

(iii) Node importance based on failure probability. Compared with nodes with low failure probability, nodes with high failure probability have a more important impact on the normal operation and planning of the metering automation system, and the importance of their nodes should be slightly higher than nodes with low failure probability. The node importance based on the probability of failure is recorded as $PR(i)$. λ and μ are the failure rate and repair rate of the node respectively, and the reliability of each node can be used as a node importance index to measure the failure probability, where $PR(i) = 1 - e^{\lambda t}$.

Therefore, the importance of any node in the metering automation system is $ID(i) = T(i) * PI(i) * PB(i) * PR(i)$.

4 Simulation and Analysis

According to the improved risk warning model in this paper, this part simulates the topology of the metering automation system, and the reconstruction of the network topology is shown in Fig. 2.

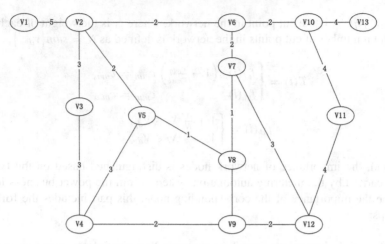

Fig. 2. Topology of metering automation system

Consider the node distribution of network topology connection, power business, power index, and failure probability. The value between nodes is the link weight between these two nodes. The improved model of this paper is used to calculate the importance of 13 nodes, and then the key nodes of the system are sorted and then analyzed.

Table 2. Weighting factor of power service

Index	Transmission delay	Bit error rate	Bandwidth level	Carrying method
Weight	0.62	0.20	0.12	0.04

Based on the analytic hierarchy process, the power business distribution and index weights are constructed as shown in Table 2. First, from a purely mathematical level, the importance of network nodes is calculated according to T. Secondly, this article sets up the business-level parameters of each node in gradients. Among them, nodes 3, 5, and 7 are defined as provincial regulation points, the voltage levels of nodes 1, 2, 4, and 9 are 220 kV, and the rest are 500 kV.

As shown in Fig. 3, it is the execution efficiency before and after the model is improved. The orange line shows the execution efficiency of the correlation analysis algorithm after the model is improved, and the blue line shows the execution efficiency before improved. According to the above images, compared with the original risk warning model, the improved model in this paper has significantly improved execution efficiency of the model algorithm, which verifies the rationality of the model studied in this paper.

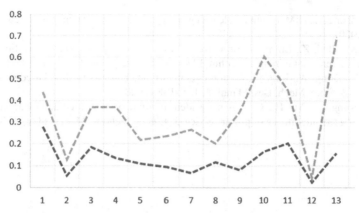

Fig. 3. The execution efficiency of mode

5   Conclusion

In the measurement automation system, if all the alarm information in the system is processed and the alarm correlation analysis is carried out, it will bring great pressure to the maintenance and cost of the automation system. Therefore, this paper joins the evaluation of the priority of the nodes, adding the priority evaluation of nodes into the model when it carries out correlation analysis. Based on this, certain improvements are made to the risk warning model. Then, according to the overall design ideas, the network topology is designed to illustrate the design of each node function module. Finally, the rationality of the model in this paper is verified through experimental simulation.

References

1. Li, J.: Overview of the technologies of threat intelligence sensing, sharing and analysis in cyber space. Chin. J. Netw. Inf. Secur. **2**(2), 16–29 (2016)
2. Jia, F.: Threat intelligence in the era of big data. Libr. Inf. Serv. **6**, 15–20 (2016)
3. Li, G., Chen, Y., Huang, P., Li, Y., Xue, H.: Research on information communication network security early warning based on log analysis. Electric Power Inf. Commun. Technol. **16**(12), 1–8 (2018)
4. Wen, C.: Application of measurement automation system in electric power marketing management. Sci. Technol. **27**(2), 137 (2020)
5. Li, G., Jiang, Z., Yu, X.: Study on electronic energy meter failure power calculation based on metering automation systems. In: MATEC Web of Conferences, vol. 260, no. 02009, pp. 1–4 (2019)
6. Guo, X., Wang, P., Zhou, J.: Research on risk analysis of safe operation of power grid dispatch automation system. Silicon Valley **7**(19), 148–152 (2014)
7. Cheng, J.: Analysis and processing of abnormal data collected by measurement automation system. China High-Tech Zone **12**, 53 (2018)
8. Qian, B., Cai, Z., Xiao, Y.: Network security situational awareness of measurement automation system based on fuzzy reasoning. China Southern Power Grid Technol. **13**(2), 51–58 (2019)
9. Wang, B., Zhang, W., Fang, X.: Explore ways to optimize warning information of integrated power dispatching and monitoring system. Electron. World **09**, 178–179 (2020)

10. Yue, P., Zhang, L.: BIM log mining: learning and predicting design command. Autom. Constr. (112) (2020)
11. Zhang, X., Zhai, Z., Li, Y.: Alarm correlation analysis of power communication network based on incremental mining algorithm. Electron. Des. Eng. **16**(10), 67–68 (2008)
12. Zhang, L., Dong, W., Kan, W.: Customer demand data analysis method based on improved Apriori algorithm. Mech. Des. Manuf. **5**, 185–188 (2020)
13. Li, C., Kang, Z., Yu, H.: Critical node identification of power communication network considering the importance of power service. J. Electr. Technol. **34**(11), 2384–2394 (2019)

A MOEA-D-Based Service Quality Matching Optimization Algorithm in Electric Power Communication Network

Qinghai Ou[1], Yanru Wang[1], Yongjie Li[2], Jizhao Lu[2], Hongkang Tian[3], Wenjie Ma[1(✉)], and Hui Liu[1]

[1] Beijing Fibrlink Communications Co., Ltd., Beijing 100070, China
mawenjie@sgitg.sgcc.com.cn
[2] State Grid Henan Information & Telecommunication Company (Data Center), Zhengzhou 450052, China
[3] Beijing University of Posts and Telecommunications, Beijing 100876, China

Abstract. In the smart grid scenario, this article proposes a blockchain-based smart grid service system based on the alliance chain established by power plants, distribution network operators, energy storage operators, and power companies as nodes. Each node can flexibly change its role according to its own needs, and can be used as a service provider or as a user requesting service. In this service system, users and service providers store business data and transaction data through the blockchain, and match services through smart contracts. On this basis, this paper establishes a mathematical model of power business service quality, abstracts the user matching power business process as a service composition problem under the constraint of service quality, and uses the multi-objective optimization algorithm MOEA/D as the basis, based on price, time delay, Service quality indicators such as bandwidth are analyzed and optimized for optimization goals. On the one hand, in the smart grid scenario, it has achieved decentralization, improved power data security, and user privacy security. On the other hand, multi-objective optimization algorithms are used to optimize the different needs of users to improve the service quality of the smart grid system. The results of calculation examples verify the validity and rationality of the proposed framework.

Keywords: Smart grid · Blockchain · Alliance chain · Multi-objective optimization · Service quality

1 Introduction

As a new generation of power transmission network, smart grid is based on the physical power grid and integrates wireless sensor network and Internet of Things technology. It covers the six major links of generation, transmission, transformation, distribution, utilization and dispatch. A large amount of business data passes through the smart grid. Communication network for transmission. As an emerging information technology, blockchain technology can provide important support for the realization of digital smart

© Springer Nature Switzerland AG 2021
X. Sun et al. (Eds.): ICAIS 2021, LNCS 12737, pp. 611–621, 2021.
https://doi.org/10.1007/978-3-030-78612-0_49

grid business systems. On the one hand, the smart grid is a huge business management system. In order for the business to operate normally, a third-party supervision agency needs to be introduced. The intervention of a third party will greatly increase operating costs. The use of blockchain technology can achieve decentralization. Reduce operating costs; on the other hand, the blockchain records the transaction information of each transaction participant in a chain structure, and uses cryptographic algorithms to store the information in the form of blocks, which ensures the integrity of the information and cannot be tampered with. Security of business data.

There are already many applications of blockchain in smart grids. Li, Z. proposed a secure P2P energy trading system based on alliance chain, which consists of small-scale consumers, industrial consumers, electric vehicles, etc. [1, 2]. Nodes can flexibly choose their own roles and initiate transactions as buyers or sellers according to their own needs, which improves the transaction security of P2P energy transactions; Kang, J. proposed a blockchain-based PETCON system, which can not only Resist network security attacks, and can also optimize costs for multiple nodes to achieve secure electricity transactions [3, 4]; Guan, Z. proposed a blockchain-based data aggregation and privacy protection scheme, which solves the problem of users' use of smart meters the problem of leaking private information [5]; By integrating blockchain into the power generation system, it helps to solve the problem of grid data being manipulated by cyber attackers, and even causing regional power outages [6]; In the smart grid equipment maintenance system, the introduction of blockchain technology reduces maintenance time and is not affected by regional restrictions [7]. The above are the applications of blockchain in the smart grid scenario, which solves the security problems in various scenarios in the smart grid.

This article focuses on the service quality of smart grid business. Due to the complexity of smart grid business, the requirements for service quality are obviously higher. When the number of participants increases, both service quality and security will be greatly reduced, and blockchain can solve this problem. In the smart grid scenario, this paper proposes a smart grid service system based on the alliance chain, in which the alliance chain is established with power plants, distribution network operators, energy storage operators, and power companies as nodes, and each node can be based on You can change your role flexibly according to your needs, and you can act as a service provider or as a user requesting service. Under this service system, a mathematical model of power business service quality is established, the power business matching problem is abstracted as a service composition problem based on service quality constraints, and the model is simulated using a decomposition-based multi-objective optimization algorithm (MOEA-D) analysis.

2   Smart Grid Service System Based on Alliance Chain

2.1   Smart Grid Alliance Chain Structure

The core of the smart grid service system proposed in this paper is an alliance chain established by power plants, distribution network operators, energy storage operators, and power companies as nodes. As shown in the figure below, power plants provide power supply services and distribution network operators Provide power distribution services, energy storage operators provide electric energy resale services, and power companies provide lease line services, power transmission services, and meter lookup services. In the traditional smart grid service system, transactions between various entities usually require a third-party agency for supervision. This centralized transaction method allows transaction data to be stored centrally. Once attacked, it will cause irreversible losses, and data privacy of each subject also has great hidden dangers. This article builds a smart grid service system based on the alliance chain to realize decentralization and ensure the security of transaction data and the privacy of data.

In this service system, the major transaction entities are semi-open local nodes, responsible for uploading business data and transaction data provided to public nodes. The public node is any non-specific node in the alliance chain, which is dynamically generated by the local node [16], thus realizing the distributed storage of data in the alliance chain. In the consortium chain, on the one hand, the major entities act as service providers and upload their available business information to public nodes for storage, so that other entities or users can query and retrieve the target service; on the other hand, the major entities will also act as Users request services and search the blockchain to find the services they need. The following is a smart grid service framework based on this alliance chain (Fig. 1).

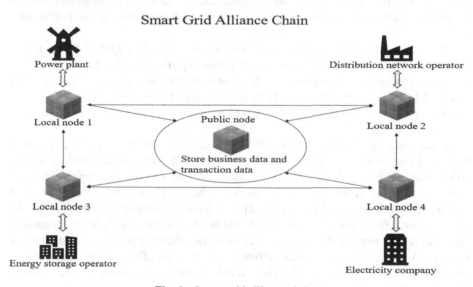

Fig. 1. Smart grid alliance chain.

2.2 Smart Grid Service Framework Based on Blockchain

The alliance chain composed of various entities in the smart grid scenario has been proposed above. On this basis, this section proposes a blockchain-based smart grid service framework. Which defines the main process and functional modules for generating power business. As shown in the figure, the main roles involved include: users, service providers, blockchain, and smart contracts. The smart contract is composed of four functional modules.

Service providers: This article abstracts several entities that provide power services in the alliance chain as service providers. The service providers first upload the types of power services they can provide and the service quality indicators of the services to the blockchain, and users can pass Blockchain accesses different types of power services and the service quality information of the power services. Service quality indicators include price, response time, bandwidth, and so on. It is assumed here that the service quality indicators of various types of power services provided by service providers are true and credible, and the impact of unstable power service quality is ignored. Among them, the same type of power business may be provided by different service providers, and the corresponding service quality will be different.

User: There are two types of users, one is ordinary users who only request services; the other is the role played by the major entities in the alliance chain when seeking the power business they need. Users can retrieve all types of power services that have been connected to the chain through the blockchain, so as to know the existing services that can be provided. When a user requests a service, he first sends a service request to the blockchain. A service request may include multiple power service types, and each service type can choose different service providers, and different service providers will obviously also To provide different service qualities, it is necessary to use smart contracts for multi-objective optimization to generate a combined business with the best service quality.

Blockchain: Blockchain mainly stores two types of data. One type of data is power business data, which mainly includes power business type information and corresponding service quality index information, which are uploaded by service providers; the other type of data is Transaction data mainly includes various transaction records. Both types of data are stored in the Merkle tree in the form of hash values under the operation of the encryption algorithm.

Smart contracts: Smart contracts call blockchain nodes to interact with blockchain data blocks to complete data verification and storage. Smart contracts mainly receive service requests from two parties. On the one hand, they receive service requests from users and screen matching services for users; on the other hand, they receive on-chain requests from service providers and upload power business types and service quality indicators to blockchain nodes. After the smart contract receives the user's service request, it first analyzes the request, designs the structure of the combined service according to the user's service needs, and determines the functional attributes of each atomic service; then searches all existing power service types on the blockchain that meet the user's needs; After the search is completed, multi-objective optimization is performed on all combined businesses to obtain the combined business with the best service quality. Finally, the combined power business is deployed and transactions are generated, where the service quality level of each atomic service of the combined business is clearly described by the service provider (Fig. 2).

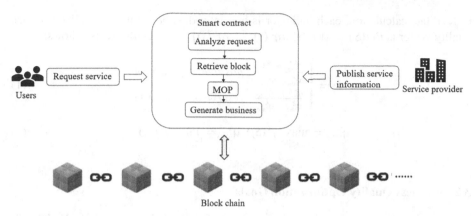

Fig. 2. Smart grid service framework.

3 Formal Description of Power Business

This section describes the mathematical description of the service quality indicators of the power business, and gives a detailed introduction to the multi-objective optimization process in the process of generating the power business.

3.1 Service Quality Indicators

Suppose S is a set of power business types, combined business $CS = \{S_1, S_2, ..., S_m\}$, which $S_i \in S$, $1 \leq i \leq m$. Every S_i both represent an abstract business with specific functions. Every abstract business S_i can be provided by different power service providers, which has n different implementations, $S_i = (S_{i1}, S_{i2}, ..., S_{in})$. Each specific business s_{ij} (among them $s_{ij} \in s_i$, $1 \leq i \leq m$, $1 \leq j \leq n$) has same business function but may have different service quality. So combined business CS has n^m plans at most.

The quality of service of each specific business s_{ij} is described by k quantifiable indicators, such as price, throughput, response time, etc., the vector $Q(S) = \{q^1(s), q^2(s), ..., q^k(s)\}$ is used to represent the quality of service of business S.

For each combined business CS, the service quality is calculated by comprehensive calculation of the service quality of each specific business, and different indicators have different calculation methods. Accumulate indicator price and response time, assume that $q^k(CS)$ is the service quality of CS under index k for combined service, $q^k(CS) = \sum_{i=1}^{m} q^k(S_i)$. For throughput, $q^k(CS) = \min_{1 \leq i \leq m} q^k(S_i)$. This article takes the minimum throughput. Multiplying for effectiveness, $q^k(CS) = \prod_{i=1}^{m} q^k(S_i)$. Among the optimization indicators, throughput and effectiveness optimization are positive, that is, the greater the throughput, the better; while the price and response time optimization is the reverse, that is, the lower the price, the shorter the response time, the better. In order to facilitate calculation, each indicator is normalized, suppose the normalized service quality vector is $RQ(S) = \{rq^1(s), rq^2(s), ..., rq^k(s)\}$. The details are as follows:

$$rq^k(s) = \begin{cases} \frac{q_{max}^k - q^k(s)}{q_{max}^k - q_{min}^k}, & positive \text{ optimization,} \\ \frac{q^k(s) - q_{max}^k}{q_{max}^k - q_{min}^k}, & reserve \text{ optimization,} \end{cases} \tag{1}$$

$$q_{max}^k = \max_{1 \leq i \leq m} q^k(S_i), q_{min}^k = \min_{1 \leq i \leq m} q^k(S_i). \tag{2}$$

3.2 Business Quality Optimization Goals

This article sets three service quality indicators for power business: price V, delay T, bandwidth B. In order to achieve the best service quality, the price and delay need to be minimized and reverse optimized; bandwidth is the maximum value, and Forward optimization. So the three indicators are normalized separately:

$$\begin{cases} RV(S) = \frac{V(S) - V_{max}}{V_{max} - V_{min}} \\ RT(S) = \frac{T(S) - T_{max}}{T_{max} - T_{min}} \\ RB(S) = \frac{B_{max} - B(S)}{B_{max} - B_{min}} \end{cases} \tag{3}$$

After normalization, we get $RV(S), RT(S), RB(S)$. Since the three are processed separately according to the different optimization directions, the optimization direction after normalization is all forward optimization, and the optimal value can take the maximum value, then the objective function is:

$$\max Q(CS) = \sum_{i=1}^{m} V(S_i) + \sum_{i=1}^{m} T(S_i) + \min_{1 \leq i \leq m} B(S_i), 1 \leq i \leq m \tag{4}$$

Then for a combined service, the optimization objective is to take the maximum value of the objective function, and the constraint conditions are:

$$\begin{cases} V_{min} \leq V(S) \leq V_{max} \\ T_{min} \leq T(S) \leq T_{max} \\ B_{min} \leq B(S) \leq B_{max} \\ RV(S) - RT(S) \geq g_{vt} \\ RV(S) - RB(S) \leq g_{vb} \end{cases} \tag{5}$$

Among the above constraints, g_{vt} and g_{vb} are adjustment parameters that takes into account the actual situation. Since the input data is a randomly generated data set, considering the situation that may be greatly different from the actual situation, such as a certain service price is very low. Latency and bandwidth performance are very good, in order to avoid this situation, set g_{vt} and g_{vb}. $RV(S), RT(S), RB(S)$ are all normalized service quality indicators.

3.3 Multi-objective Optimization Based on MOEA-D

When the user's service request contains multiple power services, each power service can be regarded as an atomic service. For each atomic service, there may be different service providers competing with each other and different service quality levels to choose from, and the choices are different. Different service providers and service quality levels will get different power business combination plans. Therefore, the service quality of the combined business depends on the choice of service providers and service quality levels. Service providers need to choose the best according to the user's service quality requirements Therefore, this paper abstracts the user matching service problem as a multi-objective optimization problem under service quality constraints, and uses the MOEA-D algorithm as the core algorithm of the mechanism.

The main idea of MOEA-D is to decompose the multi-objective optimization problem into a series of single-objective optimization sub-problems, and use the evolutionary algorithm to optimize the above sub-problems simultaneously according to the information of the adjacent problems, and finally obtain a set of Pareto optimal solutions [17]. For MOEA-D, the core of the algorithm is the selection of decomposition strategies and the calculation of uniform distribution weights. For m objective functions, the multi-objective optimization problem can be abstracted as:

$$
\begin{cases}
\max F(x) = [f_1(x), \cdots, f_m(x)] \\
s.t.\ x \in \Omega
\end{cases}
\tag{6}
$$

$f_1(x), \cdots, f_m(x)$ are optimization objective functions. X is a set of variables, and a set of constraints. The algorithm flow is as follows:

(1) Initialize the optimal solution set POS, set the number of populations (that is, the number of scalar optimization sub-problems after decomposition) to N, and each population contains the service quality index information of the power business type. According to the initial population, various groups are obtained Objective function value, referred to as FV^i, $i = 1, 2, \cdots, m$. And get the initial reference point $z = [z_1, \cdots, z_i, \cdots], i = 1, 2, \cdots, m$. z_i is the current optimal value of objective function $f_i(x)$.

(2) Randomly select N sets of vectors from C_{H+m-1}^{m-1} sets of uniformly distributed weight vectors $\lambda^1, \lambda^2, \cdots$. Calculate the Euclidean distance between any two weight vectors. $\lambda^{j1}, \lambda^{j2}, \cdots \lambda^{js}$ are the S weight vectors closest to λ^s. S is the number of neighbors of each weight vector.

(3) Randomly select sequence numbers a and b from neighbors, use genetic operators to generate a new solution y, and modify y to obtain y′ so that its size is within the constraints. The crossover and mutation methods use binary crossover and polynomial mutation respectively.

(4) Solve using y′ to get a $f_i(y')$. If $z_i > f_i(y')$, then update the value of z_i, $z_i = f_i(y')$.

(5) If $g^{te}(y') \leq g^{te}(x^k)$, then $FV^i = F(y'), g^{te}(x^k) = \max_{1 \leq i \leq m} \lambda_i |f_i(x^k) - z_i|$.

(6) Remove the vector dominated by a in the optimal solution set POS and update POS.
(7) Let the number of iterations K = K + 1, if $K \leq K_{max}$, go to step (3). Otherwise, the algorithm terminates and outputs the optimal solution set POS.

4 Experiment Method and Analysis

4.1 Experimental Method

According to the common business types of smart grids, this article sets up five business types, power purchase business, line lease business, power transmission business, power transformation business, and table lookup business. Each business has three service quality indicators, price and time delay. And bandwidth, where the constraints are 1000 $\leq$ V $\leq$ 20000 yuan, 1 $\leq$ T $\leq$ 200 ms, 100 $\leq$ B $\leq$ 2000 people (the upper limit of the number of people that can be served at the same time for each power business). Because the real available large-scale power data is difficult to obtain. The experiment was completed on a comprehensive data set generated randomly. The algorithm was implemented in the Matlab environment, the running environment was Windows 10 Home Chinese operating system, and the hardware environment was Intel i5-9300H CPU and 16 GB RAM memory.

In order to solve the simulation system of the example system, set the maximum number of iterations of MOEA-D $K_{max} = 250$, the number of populations N = 100, and the required uniform distribution weight vector is randomly selected. The number of neighbors of the weight vector S = 20, crossover and mutation Binary crossover and polynomial mutation are used respectively, $g_{vt} = 0.5$, $g_{vb} = 0.2$. The crossover probability is 1%, and the mutation probability is 5%. The entire example uses Matlab software for programming and debugging.

4.2 Experiment Analysis

The multi-objective optimization is performed with the best of each service quality index as the constraint condition, and the obtained Pareto optimal scatter plot is shown in the following figure. It can be seen that there are conflicts between the service quality indicators. After one party is optimized, the other party is bound to Will be affected. For example, when the price is reduced, the delay will increase, and the bandwidth will decrease. The best advantages of the examples in this paper under different constraints are shown in the following table. This paper finally selects a set of constraints with the optimal bandwidth as the target. The solution is used as an optimized solution. At this time, the price, delay and bandwidth are 2041 yuan, 52.88 ms, and 1662 people (the maximum number of people who can be served at the same time). This experiment simulates the power business matching process and successfully uses MOEA/D to get the optimal service combination is verified, and the validity and rationality of the proposed framework are verified (Figs. 3, 4 and 5).

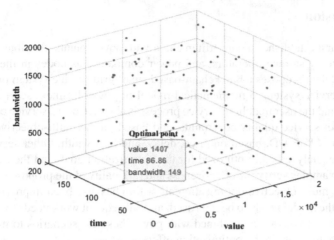

Fig. 3. Price constraint graph.

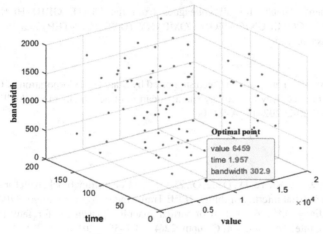

Fig. 4. Time constraint graph.

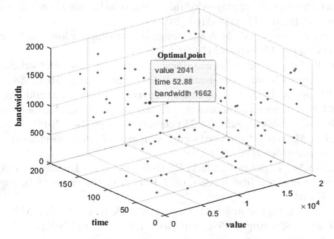

Fig. 5. Bandwidth constraint graph.

5 Conclusion

This article first establishes a consortium chain with power plants, distribution network operators, energy storage operators, and power companies as nodes in the smart grid scenario, and then proposes a blockchain-based smart grid service system on this basis. Under this service system, a mathematical model of power business service quality is established, and the user matching service process is abstracted as a service combination problem under service quality constraints, and based on the multi-objective optimization algorithm MOEA/D, based on price, delay, and bandwidth. Other service quality indicators are analyzed and optimized for the optimization goal, and the results of the calculation examples verify the effectiveness and rationality of the proposed framework.

Since the multi-objective optimization algorithm has also been improving, the performance of the model needs to be improved, and subsequent work needs to try different multi-objective optimization combined with power business scenarios to make further improvements to improve the optimization effect.

Acknowledgement. Thanks for all colleagues from the STATE GRID HENAN INFORMATION & TELECOMMUNICATION COMPANY (DATA CENTER) and Beijing Fibrlink Communications Co., Ltd.

Funding Statement. This work has been supported by State Grid Corporation of China science and technology project "Key technology and application of new multi-mode intelligent network for State Grid" (5700-202024176A-0-0-00).

References

1. Li, Z., Kang, J., Yu, R., Ye, D., Deng, Q., Zhang, Y.: Consortium blockchain for secure energy trading in industrial internet of things. IEEE Trans. Ind. Inform. **14**, 3690–3700 (2017)
2. Chen, X., Jiang, J.H.: A method of virtual machine placement for fault-tolerant cloud applications. Intell. Autom. Soft Comput. **22**(4), 587–597 (2016)
3. Kang, J., Yu, R., Huang, X., Maharjan, S., Zhang, Y., Hossain, E.: Enabling localized peer-to-peer electricity trading among plug-in hybrid electric vehicles using consortium blockchains. IEEE Trans. Ind. Inform. **13**, 3154–3164 (2017)
4. Ali, L., Sidek, R., Aris, I., Ali, M.A.M.: Design of a testchip for low cost IC testing. Intell. Autom. Soft Comput. **15**(1), 63–72 (2009)
5. Guan, Z., et al.: Privacy-preserving and efficient aggregation based on blockchain for power grid communications in smart communities. IEEE Commun. Mag. **56**, 82–88 (2018)
6. Singh, K., Choube, S.: Using blockchain against cyber attacks on smart grids. In: Proceedings of the 2018 IEEE International Students' Conference on Electrical, Electronics and Computer Science (SCEECS), Bhopal, India, 24–25 February 2018, pp. 1–4 (2018)
7. Zhang, X., Fan, M.: Blockchain-based secure equipment diagnosis mechanism of smart grid. IEEE Access **6**, 66165–66177 (2018)
8. Nichols, K., Blake, S., Baker, F., Black, D.: Definition of the Differentiated Services field (DS field) in the IPv4 and IPv6 headers. IETF RFC 2474, December 1998. http://www.ietf.org/rfc/rfc2474.txt
9. Sklower, K., Lloyd, B., McGregor, G., Carr, D., Coradetti, T.: The PPP Multilink Protocol (MP). IETF RFC 1990, August 1996. http://www.ietf.org/rfc/rfc1990.txt

10. Deshpande, J.G., Kim, E., Thottan, M.: Differentiated services QoS in smart grid communication networks. Bell Labs Tech. J. **16**(3), 61–81 (2011). https://doi.org/10.1002/bltj. 20522
11. Musleh, A.S., Yao, G., Muyeen, S.M.: Blockchain applications in smart grid-review and frameworks. IEEE Access **7**, 86746–86757 (2019). https://doi.org/10.1109/ACCESS.2019. 2920682
12. Li, M., Hu, D., Lal, C., Conti, M., Zhang, Z.: Blockchain-enabled secure energy trading with verifiable fairness in industrial Internet of Things. IEEE Trans. Ind. Inf. **16**(10), 6564–6574 (2020). https://doi.org/10.1109/TII.2020.2974537
13. Ward, S., Higinbotham, W., Duvelson, E., Saciragic, A.: Inside the cloud—network communications basics for the relay engineer. In: Proceedings of 61st Annual Conference for Protective Relay Engineers, College Station, TX, pp. 273–303 (2008)
14. United States, Department of Energy, National Energy Technology Laboratory: Specification for North American SynchroPhasor Initiative (NASPI): attachment A—statement of work, May 2008.
15. Szigeti, T., Hattingh, C.: End-to-End QoS Network Design: Quality of Service in LANs, WANs, and VPNs. Cisco Press, Indianapolis (2005)
16. Kang Jiawan, Y., Rong, H.X., et al.: Enabling localized peer-to-peer electricity trading among plug-in hybrid electric vehicles using consortium blockchains. IEEE Trans. Ind. Inf. **13**(6), 3154–3164 (2017)
17. Qingfu, Z., Hui, L.: MOEA/D: a multiobjective evolutionary algorithm based on decomposition. IEEE Trans. Evol. Comput. **11**(6), 712–731 (2008)

Abnormal Traffic Detection of Industrial Edge Network Based on Deep Nature Learning

Qi Liu[1,2], Bowen Zhang[2,3], Jianming Zhao[2,3], Chuanzhi Zang[2,3(✉)], Xibo Wang[1], and Tong Li[4]

[1] School of Information Science and Engineering, Shenyang University of Technology, Shenyang 110870, China
[2] Shenyang Institute of Automation, Chinese Academy of Sciences, Shenyang 110016, China
zangcz@sia.cn
[3] Institutes for Robotics and Intelligent Manufacturing, Chinese Academy of Sciences, Shenyang 110169, China
[4] State Grid Liaoning Electric Power Research Institute, Shenyang 110004, China

Abstract. In view of the network and application security risks in the field of industrial Internet edge computing, a method for classifying abnormal traffic of industrial edge network based on Convolution Neural Network (CNN) is presented, which is designed by using feature self-learning through analyzing the substantial flow content and protocol hierarchy characteristics of edge network packets. Authors present an abnormal traffic detection model for industrial edge network based on CNN, by using the preprocessed raw traffic data as sample data to directly learn features. The experimental results show that the average accuracy of the trained and optimized model is 98.76%, which can meet the practical application standard of the industrial edge network anomaly traffic detection task.

Keywords: Industrial edge network · Abnormal flow detection · Deep learning · Convolutional Neural Network

1 Introduction

As a product of the deep integration of the new generation of Internet technology with industrial enterprises and industrial manufacturing industry, industrial internet is the key technical support to achieve the integration. It is widely recognized as an important cornerstone of the development of China industry 4.0 and the fourth industrial revolution.

In recent years, attackers attacking the industrial Internet are becoming more specialized and organized, and their attacking behaviors are also upgrading. At present, they have gradually changed from traditional attacking methods to more advanced attacking forms such as 0-day vulnerability utilization, nested attacking, Trojan horse latent implantation, etc. These behaviors utilize a large number of AI projects, intelligence projects, evasion projects, social engineering and other disturbing factors [1]. Similarly, the security threat of the Internet has penetrated into the industrial field. As the relatively closed production environment in the traditional industrial field is connected to the relatively open Internet, resulting in more attack paths, diverse network attacks will directly

X. Sun et al. (Eds.): ICAIS 2021, LNCS 12737, pp. 622–632, 2021.
https://doi.org/10.1007/978-3-030-78612-0_50

invade the production line, making the security potential risk of industrial production more serious.

As the core part of the industrial Internet, edge computing can transfer, store, compute and optimize critical data locally before key data is transferred to the central data processing center or cloud repository and integrated with the cloud platform. Large data analysis can be used to enable production to bring the actual value of industrial data into play. Therefore, the security protection of industrial Internet focuses on the edge side protection, that is, the comprehensive security protection of Industrial Edge Network (IEN).

As one of the core technologies of industrial security, anomalous traffic detection technology (intrusion detection technology) is a kind of technology that ensures the security of network environment by means of monitoring and anomaly alarm [2, 3]. By collecting the traffic information in IEN and analyzing and identifying the collected data, it can judge whether there are anomalous conditions in the network. Therefore, as an active network security risk detection technology, anomalous traffic detection method can effectively make up for the shortage of traditional network security protection technologies such as firewalls, and realize IEN global real-time anomaly detection.

In the artificial intelligence environment, deep learning technology is one of the most widely used technologies. It is mainly used in computer vision, image processing, natural language processing and other fields, and has achieved good results [4]. In recent years, deep learning technology has been widely used in the field of intrusion detection, and has achieved some results. Document [5] presents an intrusion detection model based on deep neural network to verify the possibility of deep learning technology in the field of intrusion detection. Document [6] presents a multi-class SVM intrusion detection method based on deep belief network to solve the classification problem that traditional machine learning methods cannot effectively process large amounts of data. Document [7] shows that the application of recurrent neural network in intrusion detection is superior to other classical machine learning methods. Document [8] presents a network protocol identification method based on stacked auto-encoder, and uses the original traffic data to achieve high accuracy. In many deep learning models applied to anomaly detection, the various features of the dataset are generally analyzed, summarized and extracted by extracting the features. The normal and malicious activities with a large number of normal and attack networks and various response events are learned by self-learning, and then the extracted features are compared by classification.

Through the analysis of the above research methods, it is found that although deep learning technology greatly promotes the development of anomaly detection technology, the common problem of most methods is that they use similar manual feature extraction datasets such as KDD99 dataset [9] or NSL-KDD dataset [10] as input and the accuracy of artificial feature extraction has a great impact on the effectiveness of the algorithm. The KDD99 datasets are used in document [11, 12], and the accuracy is 96.53% and 95.75%; document [13–15] use NSL-KDD datasets and the accuracy of those are 91.7%, 83.34%, 88.39%, the results are lower than those presented in this paper, so it does not fully take advantage of deep learning technology.

This paper holds that the advantage of deep learning technology is that it can directly extract some features from the input information, train the model to achieve the purpose of feature self-learning, and finally output the results. This paper is based on convolution neural network method, which is good at image classification technology, to learn the spatial characteristics of network packets, so as to classify and detect abnormal traffic.

The remainder of this article is structured as follows. Section 2 introduces the selection standard of traffic granularity and packet level in industrial edge network. The IEN anomaly detection model and the whole process are introduced in Sect. 3. Section 4 carries out experiments and analysis, and evaluates the performance of the model, and finally, conclusions are drawn in Sect. 5.

2   Related Works

In industrial edge networks, for both network security and application security risks, it is necessary to determine the acquisition and representation of IEN traffic data, and anomaly traffic detection based on deep learning requires that the collected continuous traffic data be divided into several discrete packets, and each packet can also be divided into several levels according to the OSI architecture. The following describes the method of segmenting traffic packets and OSI architecture level selection.

2.1   Flow Granularity

IEN traffic granularity is divided into TCP connections, one-way streams, sessions (two-way streams), services, and hosts [16]. The original traffic is processed in different ways to get different traffic units. The datasets composed of different traffic units are also very different. A large amount of data is interactively transmitted in IEN, which results in a large number of two-way interactive traffic. Therefore, this paper uses the session (two-way flow) currently adopted by most researchers.

If P is used to represent the collection of all data packets of the original traffic, and q^i represents each of the data packets, then $P = \{q^1, q^2 ... q^n\}$; if x represents the quintuple information of the data packet, l represents the length of each data packet in bytes, and t represents the time when the data packet starts to be sent, then $q^i = (x^i, l^i, t^i)$, where $i = 1, 2, ...n$, $l^i \in (0, \infty)$, $t^i \in (0, \infty)$. After the original traffic is segmented according to the one-way flow segmentation method, the set P will be divided into multiple subsets according to the characteristics of the five-tuple information, that is, $P = \{q^1 = (x^1, l^1, t^1), ..., q^n = (x^n, l^n, t^n)\}$; the data packets inside each subset are stacked in time series, that is, $t^1 < t^2 <, ..., < t^n$; if f represents a unidirectional flow, then $f = (x, l, d, t)$, where x is the same 5-tuple, that is, $x = x^1 = ... = x^n$; l is the sum of the lengths of all data packets in the subset, that is, $l = \sum_1^n l^i$; d is the duration of all data packets, ie $d = t^n - t^1$; t is the initial transmission time of the data packet, namely $t = t^1$. Based on the above method, the entire original data flow can be converted into a one-way flow $= \{f^1, ..., f^n\}$, and a two-way flow can be obtained after the source and destination of the one-way flow are interchanged.

Session lengths are different after slicing, and the length of data required by the CNN model must be uniform. To solve this problem, only the first 784 bytes of the session are selected in this paper. A reasonable explanation is that the header of each layer of the conversation contains a large number of traffic characteristics, which can make better use of deep learning techniques for feature learning.

2.2 Packet Level

There are seven layers in the OSI model: physical layer, data link layer, network layer, transport layer, session layer, presentation layer and application layer. Each traffic data generated by IEN passes through each protocol layer of the OSI to generate information that reflects traffic characteristics, such as port information and flags in the transport layer, connection-oriented and connectionless services in the network layer, full-duplex or half-duplex communication protocols in the session layer, and several separate user generic service protocols in the application layer. But looking at the seven-tier communication benchmark of OSI model, the main characteristics of traffic are mainly in the application layer, such as DNS domain name system, FTP file transfer protocol, Telnet remote landing protocol, etc. Based on the above analysis, this paper chooses two data packet levels as the feature collection areas of traffic data: All-Layers (hereinafter referred to as A) and Application Layers (App-Layers, hereinafter referred to as P). It is important to emphasize that the information such as IP address and physical address held by various traffic in the source dataset will affect the feature extraction process. To avoid these factors causing or minimizing the impact, the special information of traffic data needs to be cleaned to remove noise data and unrelated data, i.e. to randomize [17].

Through the analysis of traffic granularity and packet level, the IEN traffic data representation in this paper is identified as Session-A under all layers and Session-P under application layer. Experiments show that these two representations can effectively summarize the actual situation of various types of traffic data in IEN to deal with network security risks and application security risks in IEN.

3 An Abnormal Flow Detection Method for IEN Based on Deep Nature Learning

Based on what has been described above, the IEN anomaly traffic detection method is proposed in this chapter is shown in Fig. 1.

3.1 Data Preprocessing

Data preprocessing is to unify induction, conversion and processing of related data collected in IEN, so that the format of traffic data conforms to the standard format of CNN model, so as to conduct in-depth learning model training tests, and further complete the related work of anomaly detection. To achieve the experimental results that match the real environment, the data collected in SWaT is in the original format of pcap, instead of using CSV data which has been manually selected as features.

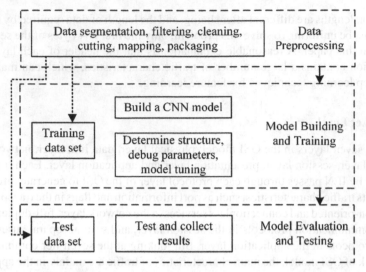

Fig. 1. Flow chart of abnormal traffic detection method

The standard input data format of CNN model is idx [18, 19], so the purpose of this section is to preprocess the original data collected from real environment as pcap to idx format, which includes the following stages: traffic slicing, traffic cleaning, picture conversion, IDX file generation. The whole process is shown in Fig. 2.

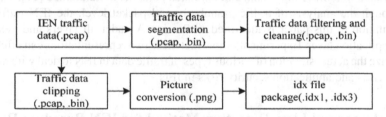

Fig. 2. Data preprocessing flowchart

Traffic slicing: According to the analysis in Sect. 3.1, the collected traffic data is divided into granular, hierarchical slicing, and a set of data is divided into several groups. The traffic data input format is pcap, the output format of Session-A is pcap, and the output format of Session-P is bin.

Traffic filtering and cleanup: Incomplete packets and duplicate files are filtered out of the traffic data in the two output forms after segmentation, and the address information highlighted in Sect. 2.2 that will affect feature extraction is anonymized and randomized. Both input and output formats are pcap and bin.

Traffic clipping: Files that have been filtered and cleaned are clipped as required in Sect. 2.1, that is, take the first 784 bytes of each packet file, and add 0×00 after the file if it is less than 784 bytes. The length of all the cut packet files is the same. The same input format and output format are pcap and bin.

Picture conversion: The clipped package file has a uniform size and length of 784 bytes. By getting the matrix in the pcap file, each byte is converted to a grayscale pixel value, where black corresponds to 0×00 and white corresponds to $0 \times ff$. All bytes are converted to grayscale pixel values to form a grayscale picture with a size of 784 bytes and an aspect ratio of 28 * 28. The input format is pcap and bin, and the output format is png.

Idx file generation: each picture set can generate an idx3 file and an idx1 file, which contains the pixel information and label information of this picture set. The statistics in idx1 correspond to the pixel information in the idx3 file. Idx file is a common data input format in CNN.

3.2 Design of Deep Nature Learning Model Structure

The deep nature learning model uses CNN multilayer structure, which is composed of input layer, convolution layer, pooling layer, full connection layer and so on [20, 21]. The structure design of the model is shown in Fig. 3.

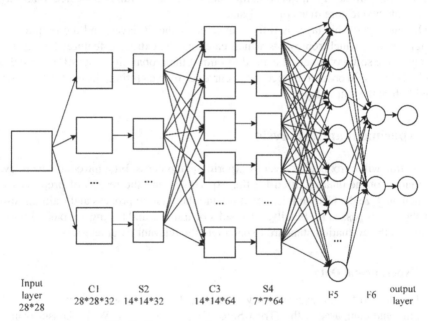

Fig. 3. Deep nature learning model structure

There are eight layers in the model structure, each containing trainable parameters.

Input layer: Read a picture valued 28 * 28 pixel from the preprocessed IDX file into the CNN, and normalize each pixel value before convoluting, converting from 0–255 to 0–1.

Layer C1: This layer is the first convolution layer. 32 convolution cores of 5 * 5 size are used to convolute the input pixel value pictures, and then complete them. The size of the feature map is 28 * 28 and the output number is 32.

Layer S2: This is the first pooling layer (also known as the down-sampling layer). The maximum pooling operation (max_pool), the pooled size is set to 2 * 2, so the output feature map size is 14 * 14, and the number is 32, which serves as the input for the next layer of neurons.

Layer C3: This layer is the second convolution layer. Sixty-four different convolution cores of size 5 * 5 are used to convolute the output feature maps of the previous layer. It is important to note that each feature map in C3 is a weighted combination of all 32 or any of the feature maps in S2. The output feature maps have a size of 14 * 14 and the number is 64.

Layer S4: This layer is the second pooling layer, which still uses the maximum pooling operation of size 2 * 2. Finally, 64 7 * 7 feature maps are output, and the number of neurons is reduced to 64 * 5 * 5 = 1600.

Layer F5: This layer is the first fully connected layer, it continues to convolute the output of layer S4 with a 5 * 5 convolution core, increasing the number of convolution cores to 1024, so that the output picture size of layer F5 is 1 * 1, the final output will be 1024 1 * 1 features.

Layer F6: This layer is the second fully connected layer, fully connected to F5 Layer, and outputs two feature maps of 1 * 1 size.

Output Layer: This layer is fully connected to the F6 layer, and the output length is a tensor of 2, which represents which category the extracted features belong to. In this layer, the softmax function is used to output the probability values for normal and attacked classes. In order to reduce the occurrence of over-fitting, dropout technology is added before the output layer.

4   Experiment and Analysis

This section will introduce the overall experimental process. First introduce the relevant information of the data required for the experiment and the results of preprocessing, and then analyze the CNN model structure and the training process and training results after the data is passed in. Finally, the results of training and testing are passed into the formula of the evaluation standard to calculate the relevant parameters.

4.1   Experimental Data

The data needed for the experiment was in pcap format and was not processed. After screening and comparison, the iTrust Safe Water Treatment (SWaT) dataset from the Network Security Research Center of the University of Science and Technology Design (SUTD) of Singapore was selected. The dataset has been updated five times so far, and this article selected a set of attacking datasets collected in December 2019. This dataset records a number of malicious software infection attacks, including historical data disclosure attacks and process interruption attacks, on the SWaT project master site. This includes three hours of normal operation with six attacks per hour [22, 23]. The dataset is divided into two parts, Normal and attack, with sizes of 2.66 GB and 2.64 GB, respectively, which are collectively referred to as N-a datasets.

A total of 119546 pieces of data were generated by preprocessing operations such as segmentation, filtering, cleaning, cropping and so on. The statistical results are shown in Table 1.

Table 1. Data preprocessing results

Data set	Representation	After splitting	After filtering and cleaning	After cropping
Normal	Session-A	31158	30043	30043
	Session-P	30549	29781	29781
Attack	Session-A	30752	29994	29994
	Session-P	30655	29728	29728
Total	–	123114	119546	119546

The clipped data is 784 bytes in size, which is then batched by Python code into pictures in PNG format. Each byte corresponds to a grayscale pixel value. The final visualization is a 28 * 28 PNG grayscale picture. The number of pictures corresponds to the number of clipped data, i.e. 119546 pictures.

Pictures generated by random sampling are packaged into test sets and training sets at a scale of 2:8 for model training and testing.

4.2 CNN Model Training and Testing

The CNN model is the core part of the whole anomaly detection mechanism. It trains the preprocessed N-a dataset to form a CNN architecture and obtain a precise training model. In terms of experimental configuration, Lenovo X3650M server is used, two CPUs are Intel Xeon E5-2620v4 2.10 GHz with 2-core 8 threads, 64 GB of memory, Nvida GeForce RTX 2080s as GPU accelerator, Tensorflow + CUDA + CUDNN [24] as software framework, and the operating system is Windows Server 2016. The processed training dataset is passed into the CNN model, the bitch size is adjusted to 50, the loss function uses cross-entropy function, the learning rate is 0.001, and the training model is completed 40 times by setting epoch = 40.

The task of CNN is to classify the data, extract the feature values of the test set, and then use the prediction function to verify which type of classification result the feature data belongs to, which is Normal or attack in this experiment. After judging, we get the y value of the corresponding model, use the np.argmax function to calculate the y value to get the maximum index value, and use the np.argmax function to extract the final label of the test set. By evaluating the calculation accuracy of the function np.average, the confusion matrix method is used to calculate the precision and recall.

4.3 Evaluation Standard

This part adopts the more authoritative evaluation methods in the field of deep learning: Accuracy, Precision, Recall, F1-Score [25], namely accuracy, precision, recall and F1 score. Among them, Accuracy evaluates the overall effect of the model, and Precision, Recall and F1-Score evaluate the identification and detection effect of a certain traffic type. The formula is shown below.

$$A - Accuracy = \frac{TP + TN}{TP + FP + FN + TN} \tag{1}$$

$$P - Precision = \frac{TP}{TP + FP} \tag{2}$$

$$R - Recall = \frac{TP}{TP + FN} \tag{3}$$

$$F1 - Score = \frac{2 * Precision * Recall}{Precision + Recall} \tag{4}$$

TP indicates the number of target type traffic data detected correctly, TN indicates the amount of other types of traffic data detected correctly, FP indicates the number of target type traffic data detected by error identification, and FN indicates the number of target type traffic data that has not been successfully identified.

4.4 Analysis and Comparison

This article conducted two experiments to evaluate and test the two data flow representations of Session-A and Session-P. The evaluation results are shown in Fig. 4 and Fig. 5.

Figure 4 shows how the accuracy of the model changes during the training process.

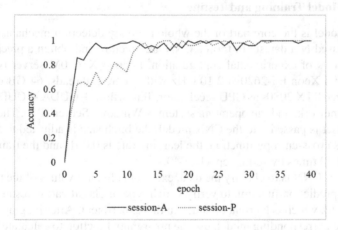

Fig. 4. Model training accuracy changes

Figure 5 shows the precision, recall, and F1 values of the Normal part and the attack part of the N-a data set in Session-A and Session-P, and the overall accuracy. Since all layer traffic data contains more key information, the accuracy of some parameters is higher than that of application layer traffic data. In the two experiments, the comprehensive accuracy rate of the CNN model corresponding to the traffic data of Session-A and Session-P reached 99% and 98.5%.

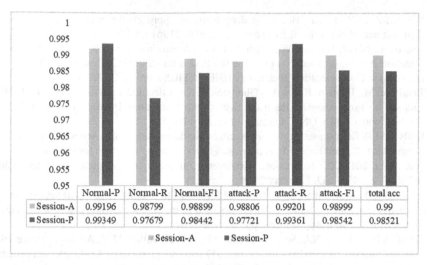

	Normal-P	Normal-R	Normal-F1	attack-P	attack-R	attack-F1	total acc
Session-A	0.99196	0.98799	0.98899	0.98806	0.99201	0.98999	0.99
Session-P	0.99349	0.97679	0.98442	0.97721	0.99361	0.98542	0.98521

■ Session-A   ■ Session-P

Fig. 5. Model evaluation index summary

5 Conclusion

Aiming at the edge computing field in the industrial Internet, this paper studies the abnormal traffic classification and detection method based on Convolutional Neural Network. By analyzing the characteristics of the flow granularity and data packet level in the industrial edge network, the representation of the collected flow is set, and pre-processing is performed on the basis of the original flow, which further reduces the error caused by artificial labeling. Convolutional neural network technology is used to make full use of its high performance and high accuracy in the field of image recognition to provide strong support for anomaly detection in industrial edge networks.

According to the experimental results, this method has high feasibility and can protect the normal communication of the industrial edge network to a certain extent, so as to ensure the transmission of industrial data, the operation of industrial production, etc., and meet the accuracy requirements of actual industrial deployment.

References

1. Venkatraman, S., Alazab, M.: Use of data visualisation for zero-day Malware detection. Secur. Commun. Netw. **2018** (2018). https://doi.org/10.1155/2018/1728303
2. Buczak, A.L., Guven, E.: A survey of data mining and machine learning methods for cyber security intrusion detection. IEEE Commun. Surv. Tutor. **18**(2), 1153–1176 (2016)
3. Bhuyan, M.H., Bhattacharyya, D.K., Kalita, J.K.: Network anomaly detection: methods, systems and tools. IEEE Commun. Surv. Tutor. **16**(1), 303–336 (2014)
4. LeCun, Y., Bengio, Y., Hinton, G.: Deep learning. Nature **521**(7553), 436 (2015)
5. Jin, K., Shin, N., Jo, S.Y., Kim, S.H.: Method of intrusion detection using deep neura network. In: 2017 IEEE International Conference on Big Data and Smart Computing, February 2017
6. Gao, N., He, Y.-Y., Gao, L.: Deep learning method for intrusion detection in massive data. Appl. Res. Comput. **35**(4), 1197–1200 (2018)

7. Yin, C., Zhu, Y., Fei, J., He, X.: A deep learning approach for intrusion detection using recurrent neural networks. IEEE Access. **5**, 21954–21961 (2017)
8. Javaid, A., Niyaz, Q., Sun, W., Alam, M.: A deep learning approach for network intrusion detection system. In: Proceedings of the 9th EAI International Conference on Bio-Inspired Information Communcation Technology (BIONETICS), pp. 21–26 (2016)
9. Tavallaee, M., Bagheri, E., Lu, W., Ghorbani, A.A.: A detailed analysis of the KDD CUP 99 data set. In: Proceedings of the IEEE Symposium Computing Intelligent Security Defense Applicatipon, Ottawa, ON, Canada, pp. 1–6, July 2009
10. UNB. NSL-KDD Dataset. https://www.unb.ca/cic/datasets/nsl.html. Accessed: 10 May 2020
11. Farahnakian, F., Heikkonen, J.: A deep auto-encoder based approach for intrusion detection system. In: 2018 20th International Conference on Advanced Communication Technology (ICACT), pp. 178–183, February 2018
12. Al-Yaseen, W.L., Othman, Z.A., Nazri, M.Z.A.: Multi-level hybrid support vector machine and extreme learning machine based on modified K-means for intrusion detection system. In: Expert Systems with Applications, pp.296–303 (2017)
13. Yusof, A.R.A., Udzir, N.I., Selamat, A., Hamdan, H., Abdullah, M.T.: Adaptive feature selection for denial of services (DoS) attack. In: 2017 IEEE Conference on Application, Information and Network Security (AINS), pp. 81–84 (2017)
14. Yousefi-Azar, M., Varadharajan, V., Hamey, L., Tupakula, U.: Autoencoder based feature learning for cyber security applications. In: 2017 International Joint Conference on Neural Networks (IJCNN), pp. 3854–3861 (2017)
15. Javaid, A., Niyaz, Q., Sun, W., Alam, M.: A deep learning approach for network intrusion detection system. In: Proceedings of the 9th EAI International Conference on Bio-inspired Information and Communications Technologies (formerly BIONETICS), pp. 21–26 (2016)
16. Dainotti, A., Pescape, A., Claffy, K.C.: Issues and future directions in traffic classification. IEEE Network **26**(1), 35–40 (2012)
17. Koukis, D., Antonatos, S., Antoniades, D., Markatos, E.P., Trimintzios, P.: A generic anonymization framework for network traffic. In: IEEE International Conference on Communications, pp. 2302–2309 (2006)
18. Vilasini, M., Ramamoorthy, P.: CNN approaches for classification of Indian leaf species using smartphones. Comput. Mat. Continua **62**(3), 1445–1472 (2020)
19. Liu, P., Ren, H., Shi, X., Li, Y., Cai, Z., et al.: Motransframe: model transfer framework for CNNS on low-resource edge computing node. Comput. Mat. Continua **65**(3), 2321–2334 (2020)
20. Chen, R., Pan, L., Li, C., Zhou, Y., Chen, A., et al.: An improved deep fusion CNN for image recognition. Comput. Mat. Continua **65**(2), 1691–1706 (2020)
21. Zhao, Y., Cheng, J., Zhan, P., Peng, X.: ECG classification using deep CNN improved by wavelet transform. Comput. Mat. Continua **64**(3), 1615–1628 (2020)
22. Goh, J., Adepu, S., Junejo, K.N., Mathur, A.: A dataset to support research in the design of secure water treatment systems. In: The 11th International Conference on Critical Information Infrastructures Security
23. Taormina, R., Galelli, S., Tippenhauer, N.O., et al.: The battle of the attack detection algorithms: disclosing cyber attacks on water distribution networks. J. Water Resour. Plann. Manage. **144**(8) (2018)
24. Abadi, M., et al.: Tensor-flow: large-scale machine learning on heterogeneous distributed systems. arXiv preprint arXiv:1603.04467 (2016)
25. Nguyen, D.L.H., Do, D.T.T., Lee, J., Rabczuk, T., Nguyen-Xuan, H.: Forecasting damage mechanics by deep learning. Comput. Mat. Continua **61**(3), 951–978 (2019)

Recent Development, Trends and Challenges in IoT Security

Morteza Talezari[1], Shanshan Tu[1(✉)], Sadaqat ur Rehman[1,2], Xiao Chuangbai[1], Basharat Ahmad[3], Muhammad Waqas[1,4], and Obaid ur Rehman[5]

[1] Research Center of Intelligent Perception and Autonomous Control, Faculty of Information Technology, Beijing University of Technology, Beijing 100124, People's Republic of China
sstu@bjut.edu.cn
[2] Department of Computer Science, Namal Institute, Mianwali 42250, Pakistan
[3] Department of Electronic Engineering, Tsinghua University, Beijing, China
[4] Department of Computer Science and Engineering, Ghulam Ishaq Khan (GIK) Institute of Engineering Sciences and Technology, Topi 23460, Pakistan
[5] Department of EE, Sarhad University of Science and IT, Peshawar, Pakistan

Abstract. A large amount of data that IoT applications deal, is users' Private data, and their privacy is a significant issue. However, if users are not sure about the security of their data, they will not desire to use such applications. The goal of this study is to improve the security and privacy of users in the Internet of Things (IoTs) setting. Since, the application of IoT technology is growing day by day. Also, the importance of users' data security is always top of the list and difficult to achieve. In this study, we studied latest development in the security of Internet of Things (IoTs) so that we can use it to investigate its challenges and advantages.

Keywords: IoT security · Architecture improvement · Recent development in IoT

1 Introduction

The Internet of Things is an emerging technology that represents a major milestone in the evolution of cyberspace. These technologies are actually a network of objects that communicate with other objects via the Internet. Each of these smart objects has a unique address to identify on the network. In fact, this technology is a new model that integrates the Internet and physical objects, which aims to integrate the two physical and digital worlds into a single ecosystem, creating a new smart age of the Internet. The number of devices connected to the Internet that have digital identities is increasing day by day. But the biggest concern after the arrival of objects in organizations, homes, and private companies is the issue of privacy and information security, which has challenged the spread of the Internet of Things with the intensification of information theft from users by hackers. And the concern of data insecurity at all levels of the IoT model is the most important research issue. Increasing IoT security is an important and challenging issue

© Springer Nature Switzerland AG 2021
X. Sun et al. (Eds.): ICAIS 2021, LNCS 12737, pp. 633–646, 2021.
https://doi.org/10.1007/978-3-030-78612-0_51

today, as the widespread use of this technology and its continued use by large numbers of users endanger privacy and create shortcomings.

Now, decreasing energy consumption and improving the efficiency of the Internet of Things is an essential and challenging problem. Because the extensive existence of this technology and its constant use by a large number of users increases energy and expenses and creates difficulties.

Information security indicates the protection of information and information systems from illegal activities. These activities involve accessing, using, disclosing, reading, copying, or recording, destroying, modifying, and manipulating.

Zhang et al. [1] maintain that the value of information security in these units is indisputable, given the structure of large industrial units as well as the nature of competition between commercial centers. In general, information security in each set is measured by three factors:

1. Confidentiality: Blocking the exposure of information to unapproved persons.

2. Accessibility: Information should be accessible when required by authorized individuals.

3. Integration: stopping the unauthorized change of data and identifying the change in case of unauthorized manipulation of data.

The rest of the article is described as: In Sect. 2, comparisons are made to the reviewed articles according to the purpose of the article, their advantages and disadvantages, and their chosen algorithm. In Sect. 3, the IoT architecture, its hardware will be fully discussed, and existing security problems. Section 4 gives a detail discussion on open research gaps and challenges in IoT security. Finally, Sect. 5 gives concluding remarks.

2 Comparison

The following table covers comparisons between the work done to investigate the benefits and weaknesses of different methods.

Table 1 summarizes the studied articles, which examines them in terms of purpose of use, advantages and disadvantages of each of them, as well as the method and algorithm used by each of the articles along with evaluation parameters for comparisons and experiments.

Table 1. An overview of the articles studied

Evaluation Parameters	Advantages and Disadvantages	Method used	Target	Year of Publication
Accuracy Performance	+Increase privacy security −Decreased accuracy	Machine learning	Security and privacy in decentralized business	2018

(continued)

Table 1. (*continued*)

Evaluation Parameters	Advantages and Disadvantages	Method used	Target	Year of Publication
Speed Energy	+Check a smart home −Reduce Speed	Blockchain	Increase IoT security and privacy	2017
Time Speed	+Improved blockchain performance −Increase latency and time	Blockchain	Improve security and performance	2016
Time	+Improved digital storage −Increase processing time	Combination of two processing algorithms	Digital storage of documents	2018
Accuracy Processing Time	+Provide lightweight IoT +Increase Accuracy −Reduce speed	Provide a new security framework	Improve IoT information sharing security	2019
Performance	+Improve the performance of IoT security model	Blockchain	IoT security model	2018
Accuracy	+Describe the promotion of functions and benefits of blockchain in IoT and IioT OS −Decreased Accuracy	Use of China Blockchain security tools and technology	Improve IoT	2019
–	+Highlight the main requirements of implementing the China Block in IoT	–	Comparison, security needs and challenges for IoT	2019
Speed	+Improved Privacy −Increased latency	Blockchain	Improve IoT security	2019
Speed Reliability	+Increased security −Reduced speed	Blockchain	Create IoT security	2019

(*continued*)

Table 1. (*continued*)

Evaluation Parameters	Advantages and Disadvantages	Method used	Target	Year of Publication
Reliability	+Increased accuracy	Set of China Blockchain technologies	Improve accuracy and performance	2020
Speed Reliability	+Consider distribution +Increased accuracy −Reduced speed	Introducing a new protocol	Improve IoT security	1397
−	+Check the types of attacks +Check the types of solutions	Provide potential machine learning-based solutions for IoT security	Investigate the IoT architecture and the importance of machine learning	2020
−	+Mention important challenges, types of attacks, MQQT-based authentication, access control and data security −Lack of real world reviews	Examine the security aspects of the various protocols used to establish MQTT communications	Technology 4.0 Review, Impact of IoT on Technology 4.0, MQTT Protocol	2020
−	+Different approaches offered against attacks of two wireless technologies (WSN, RFID)	Introduces a detailed three-tier security architecture	Compare different solutions against IoT attacks	2020
−	+Clarify future research paths towards research in the field of 5G systems	Investigating the role of emerging paradigms including IoT, fog calculations and blockchain	Review existing 5G security and privacy solutions	2020
−	+Categorize potential privacy threats	Using a set of appropriate technologies	Provide a privacy framework	2020

3 IoT Architecture

The Internet of Things does not simply mean consumer devices connected to the Internet. In fact, the Internet of Things is a technology that can create systems capable of sensing and responding to real-world stimuli without human intervention. Therefore, it is necessary to develop a process flow for a specific framework on which IoT solutions are created. The IoT architecture generally consists of 4 different levels:

Level 1: Sensors / Operators: An object within the IoT framework must be equipped with sensors and operators to be able to propagate, receive, and process signals.

Level 2: Data Acquisition Systems: The data obtained from the sensors are first in analog form, which needs to be aggregated and converted into digital streams for further processing. Data acquisition systems handle this aggregated data and conversion functions.

Level 3: Edge Analysis: This IoT step is where the digitized and collected data, which needs further processing, is sent before entering the data center.

Level 4: Cloud Analysis: At the last level of the Internet of Things, data that needs deeper processing is sent to physical data centers or cloud systems.

3.1 IoT Hardware

First, we need sensors that understand the environment. Then you need a remote dashboard to control the output and display it more clearly. Finally, we will need a device with routing capabilities. The key task of this system is to identify specific conditions and take action based on them. The most important thing is to keep the connection between the devices and the dashboard secure. We are surrounded by some sensors such as accelerometers, temperature sensors, proximity sensors, optical gyroscopes, acoustic sensors, pressure sensors, gas pressure sensors, humidity sensors and small current sensors. Today we also have many consumer devices such as smartwatches, shoes and 3D glasses. This is the best example of a smart solution. 3D glasses adjust the brightness and contrast of the TV according to your eyes, and a smartwatch to track your daily activities and fitness.

3.2 Security Problems

The Internet of Things connects billions of devices to the Internet and involves the use of billions of data points, all of which must be secured. Given the level and type of hacker attacks, IoT security and the privacy of IoT devices are major concerns [46].

Because IoT devices are interconnected, all a hacker has to do is enter the network from a weak point and disrupt the system. If digital device makers do not update IoT devices on a regular basis, they are more likely to have their system hacked.

However, hackers are not the only threat to the Internet of Things; Privacy is another major concern for IoT users. For example, companies that manufacture and distribute consumer IoT devices can use these devices to access and sell users' personal information [47].

In addition to leaking users' personal data, IoT mismanagement can jeopardize critical infrastructure, including electricity, transportation, and financial services.

In this section, we first introduce the three layers of IoT architecture for the intelligent system with the aim of establishing security, namely the perception layer, the network layer and the application layer.

- Application layer: Remote cloud-based that includes various IoT applications (e.g., smart home, diagnostics, smart healthcare) [48].
- Network layer: establishes the connection between the perception layer and the application layer, which includes routers, gateways, and other network devices. This device can connect the mobile device to the application layer and transfer the application layer instructions to the perception layer [49].
- Perception layer: includes various measuring devices. IoT devices connect to the remote cloud via the network layer, allowing users to transfer data to the remote cloud for analysis. After analysis, the remote cloud gives the users feedback on the results. In addition, when IoT is applied to smart health care, computing can be used to reduce user service delays. This is because the edge border is usually closer to the user through a hop [50].

In addition to smart healthcare, IoT has a wide range of applications in all dimensions. Therefore, with the development of measuring devices, especially smartphones, IoT has created many suitable applications in people's daily lives. However, in addition to convenience, the IoT also brings with it many security and privacy issues. The next section will introduce security issues at three levels in the IoT.

Application layer security problems: The application layer is mainly located in the remote cloud, which can support a variety of services such as smart city, smart home, smart health care and smart transportation. These various services require different user data. In the case of smart health care, users have to collect different types of services. However, the data collected belongs to the user's privacy data, and medical service providers must use this data for analysis to provide appropriate services to users. Therefore, if this data is not properly protected, users' privacy will be exposed. Therefore, three security issues must be considered at the application layer, namely the protection of user data privacy, the analysis of data encrypted in the remote cloud, and secure computing. Authentication is usually required when mobile devices access services remotely from the cloud. This is because if there is no reasonable authentication technology, it can lead to malicious terminals for receiving services. In addition, when malicious users launch DoS or DDoS attacks, it reduces the requests of legitimate users to request normal services due to low security. Although the remote cloud can use its computing and storage resources to provide authentication from a large number of IoT devices, it makes sense to design a reasonable authentication mechanism because the number of devices is so large. In addition, with the advent of mobile technology, users can use mobile devices to connect to the IoT, which may require a dynamic authentication mechanism to authenticate a large number of dynamic mobile devices.

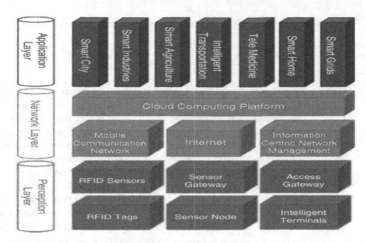

Fig. 1. IoT Architecure [7]

Network layer security problems: Perception layer devices can access the application layer via cellular network or WiFi. In the network layer, with the continuous development of the 5G network, the network layer generally adopts the standard communication protocol. Therefore, in this dissertation, security problems due to communications are not considered.

Perception layer security problems: The IoT perception layer connects to the application layer via the network layer. For example, in the field of smart health care, the user transmits data collected by smart clothing via the mobile network or WiFi to the remote cloud.

There are two types of security threats that the perception layer faces:

- Many terminals, ports or insecure services open, and there are many vulnerabilities that allow unauthorized access. There are often threats that hackers can exploit these vulnerabilities to launch large-scale DDoS attacks.
- Many terminals can be connected to the gateway via Zigbee, Bluetooth and WiFi, but the security mechanism of these telecommunication protocols is weak in itself and these devices are protected against hacking.

Table 2 lists the attacks on the various layers of the IoT and the solutions proposed for each.

Table 2. Classification of attacks and solutions in IsoT layers [7]

Layer/Component	Attacks	Solutions
a. Perception Layer		
Perception Nodes RFID	Tracking, DoS, repudiation, spoofing, eavesdropping, data newness, accessibility, self-organization, time management, secure localization, tractability, robustness, privacy protection, survivability, and counterfeiting [8]	Access control, data encryption which includes non-linear key algorithms, IPSec protocol utilization, cryptography techniques to protect against side channel attack [9,10], Hashed-based access control [11], Ciphertext re-encryption to hide communication [16], New lightweight implementation using SHA-3 appointed function Keccak-f (200) and Keccak-f (400) [12]
Sensor nodes	Node subversion, node failure, node authentication, node outage, passive information gathering, false node message corruption, exhaustion, unfairness, sybil, jamming, tampering, and collisions [13, 14]	Node authentication, Sensor Privacy
Sensor Gateways	Misconfiguration, hacking, signal lost, DoS, war dialing, protocol tunneling, man-in-the-middle attack, interruption, interception, and modification fabrication [15]	Message Security, Device Onboard Security, Integrations Security [16]
b. Network Layer		
Mobile Communication	Tracking, eavesdropping, DoS, bluesnarfing, bluejacking, bluebugging alteration, corruption, and deletion [17, 18]	Developing secure access control mechanisms to mitigate the threats by employing biometrics, public-key crypto primitives and time changing session keys
Cloud Computing	Identity management, heterogeneity which is inaccessible to an authentic node, data access controls, system complexity, physical security, encryption, infrastructure security and misconfiguration of software [19]	Identity privacy – Pseudonym [20–22], group signature [23], connection anonymization [24] Location privacy – Pseudonym [25], one-way trapdoor permutation [26] Node compromise attack – Secret sharing [27–29], game theory [30], population dynamic model [31] Layer removing/adding attack – Packet transmitting witness [32], aggregated transmission evidence [33] Forward and backward security – Cryptographic one-way hash chain [34] Semi-trusted/malicious cloud security – (Fully) homomorphic encryption [35], zero knowledge proof [36]

(continued)

Table 2. (*continued*)

Layer/Component	Attacks	Solutions
Internet	Confidentiality, encryption, viruses, cyberbullying, hacking, identity theft, reliability, integrity, and consent [38]	Identity Management for confidentiality [37], Encryption schemes for confidentiality of communication channels [39], Cloud based solutions to establish secure channels based on PKI for data and communication confidentiality [39]
c. Application Layer		
	Data privacy, Tampering Privacy, Access control, disclosure of information [40]	Authentication, key agreement and protection of user privacy across heterogeneous networks [41], Datagram Transport Layer Security (DTLS) for end-to-end security [42], Information Flow Control [42]

4 Current Challenges and Open Research Gaps in IoT Security

The digital world is saturated with personal and shared data, which raises concerns about the security and protection of personal information. Problems with the transmission and processing of unwanted data have caused concern among users [6].

With the rapid growth of IoT applications, security implications are emerging that raise concerns about privacy and the inability of people to control their personal lives. If people's daily activities are monitored and they produce information outputs, political, economic and social activities are affected. IoT benefits are diminished in the event of a security breach, an attack, or a malfunction. In the near future, a large amount of information will be received and sent by connected devices and management systems.

Information is constantly moving and moving, and with the advent of IoT, the approach to this movement will be very different from the current state. IoT security will be completely different from current trends by connecting all devices to each other. Therefore, we must pay attention to the connection and communication points of our information transfer between all devices and clouds and networks and create security there [3].

Sopho Security Center, one of the largest security product support banks, has started forecasting security threats in 2015. Sopho believes that in 2015, software vulnerabilities will be reduced. Due to the reduction in the number of software vulnerabilities, few vulnerabilities will be used extensively. The Internet of Things seems to be the biggest security concern of 2015. This nascent technology has paid close attention to security at birth. Google, Samsung, Sony and other tech giants that have somehow contributed to the development of this technology have made safety one of the basic principles of work, but experts believe that the Internet of Things has moved from "safe" to "safe". "Dangerous at work" will come, and no doubt the real deal with malware will change the situation in another way [4].

Network and information security are measured by the components of identification, confidentiality, integrity and undeniable. IoT is used in the global economy and in medical services, healthcare, smart transportation and many other areas, so security requirements are very important. With the Internet of Things, it can be predicted that cybercriminals will initially attack the hotspots, command centers, hotspots, and network intrusions, and that protection must be provided. Heterogeneity of protocols and devices makes the development of high-error security services a difficult task [5].

The IoT faces many challenges. In terms of scalability, IoT applications require a large number of devices that are difficult to implement due to time, memory, and processing constraints. For example, calculating daily temperature changes within a country requires many devices and requires a lot of data management [43–45].

Figure 2 shows the essential security requirements for the Internet of Things. As you can see, privacy and security are needed as key technical building blocks.

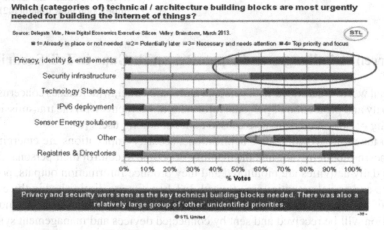

Fig. 2. IoT security requirements [7]

One of the security mechanisms in IoT is the use of an appropriate architecture and design. The IoT architecture has four levels. Figure 3 shows the four IoT levels, on the left and on the right, of the security requirements of each layer, to familiarize them with the architectural layers of the technology and the mechanisms of each layer. The discussion of how these four layers work and their security systems requires a separate topic that is not covered in this article.

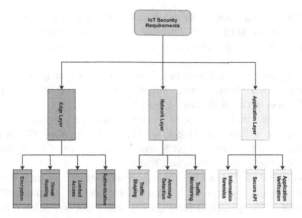

Fig. 3. IoT security architecture and security requirements at each layer [2]

5   Conclusion

With the growing development of IoT technology, users can operate in many areas, such as smart homes, smart transportation, and so on. This growth has also created inherent security risks. As the number of mobile devices progresses, more devices connect to the IoT. Accordingly, obtaining traditional business-based security management is not hard. The purpose of the study was to make a comparison and review among articles and researchers in this domain. By examining them, we realized their benefits and disadvantages.

Also, a decentralized blockchain-based security design was explored that identifies and reduces security attacks in the IoT ecosystem. This architecture has formed three new steps in IoT security. In the first stage, the proposed architecture performs the task of continuous monitoring and analysis of traffic data throughout the IoT ecosystem. Hence, it overcomes the problem of lack of data access in security detection and optimal defense presentation. Second, the architecture uses Blockchain technology, which supports decentralized attack exposure, to overcome the inherent failure in a centralized and distributed design. Ultimately, the architecture relies on a layered composition where attacks are seen at the fog node and finally reduced at the edge node. This helps to decrease the time spent recognizing and reducing attacks. In fact, this design can be deployed as a security detection component that is identified and reduced by monitoring and examining traffic data of the entire IoT ecosystem.

References

1. Zhang, Y., Wen, J.: An IoT electric business model based on the protocol of bitcoin. In: 2015 18th International Conference on Intelligence in Next Generation Networks (ICIN), pp. 184–191. IEEE (2015)
2. Gubbi, J., Buyya, R., Marusic, S., Palaniswami, M.: Internet of Things (IoT): A vision, architectural elements, and future directions. Futur. Gener. Comput. Syst. **29**(7), 1645–1660 (2013)

3. Khoo, B.: RFID - from tracking to the Internet of Things: a review of developments. In: Proceedings of the IEEE/ACM International Conference on Green Computing and Communications & International Conference on Cyber, Physical and Social Computing (2010)
4. SY, P.: Defending Privacy e Dark Side of IoT. Automating Crypt. (2015)
5. Jing, Q., Vasilakos, A.V., Wan, J., et al.: Security of the internet of things: perspectives and challenges. Wireless Netw. **20**(8), 2481–2501 (2014)
6. Weis, S., Sarma, S., Rivest, R., Engels, D.: Security and privacy aspects of low-cost radio frequency identification systems. In: Hutter, D., Müller, G., Stephan, W., Ullmann, M. (eds.) Security in Pervasive Computing. LNCS, vol. 2802, pp. 201–212. Springer, Heidelberg (2004). https://doi.org/10.1007/978-3-540-39881-3_18
7. Kavun, E., Yalcin, T.: A lightweight implementation of keccak hash function for radio-frequency identification applications. In: Ors Yalcin, S.B. (ed.) RFIDSec 2010. LNCS, vol. 6370, pp. 258–269. Springer, Heidelberg (2010). https://doi.org/10.1007/978-3-642-16822-2_20
8. Zhang, Y., Shen, Y., Wang, H., et al.: On secure wireless communications for IoT under eavesdropper collusion. IEEE Trans. Autom. Sci. Eng. **13**(3), 1281–1293 (2015)
9. Massis, B.: The internet of things and its impact on the library. New Libr. World **117**(3/4), 289–292 (2016)
10. Liu, Y., Cheng, C., Gu, T., et al.: A lightweight authenticated communications scheme for a smart grid. IEEE Trans. Smart Grid **7**(3), 1304–1313 (2016)
11. Kumar, T., Porambage, P., Ahmad, I.: Securing gadget-free digital services. Computer **51**(11), 66–77 (2018)
12. Alaba, F., Othman, M., Hashem, I., Alotaibi, F.: Internet of things security: a survey. J. Netw. Comput. Appl. **88**, 10–28 (2017)
13. Jurcut, A.D., Liyanage, M., Chen, J., et al.: On the security verification of a short message service protocol. Presented at the 2018 IEEE Wireless Communications and Networking Conference (WCNC), Barcelona, Spain (2018)
14. Horrow, S., Anjali, S.: Identity management framework for cloud based internet of things. In: Proceedings of the First International Conference on Security of Internet of Things, SecurIT 2012, pp. 17–19. ACM, Kollam (2012)
15. Lin, X., Sun, X., Wang, X., et al.: TSVC: timed efficient and secure vehicular communications with privacy preserving. IEEE Trans. Wireless Commun. **7**(12), 4987–4998 (2008)
16. Lin, X., Li, X.: Achieving efficient cooperative message authentication in vehicular ad hoc networks. IEEE Trans. Veh. Technol. **62**(7), 3339–3348 (2013)
17. Zhou, J., Dong, X., Cao, Z., et al.: 4S: a secure and privacy-preserving key management scheme for cloud-assisted wireless body area network in m-healthcare social networks. Inf. Sci. **314**, 255–276 (2015)
18. Sen, J.: Privacy preservation technologies in internet of things. In: Proceedings of International Conference on Emerging Trends in Mathematics, Technology, and Management, pp. 18–20 (2011)
19. Zhou, J., Dong, X., Cao, Z., et al.: Secure and privacy preserving protocol for cloud-based vehicular DTNs. IEEE Trans. Inf. Forensics Secur. **10**(6), 1299–1314 (2015)
20. Roman, R., Alcaraz, C., Lopez, S.N.: Key management systems for sensor networks in the context of the internet of things. Comput. Electr. Eng. **37** (2), 147–159 (2011)
21. Zhou, J., Cao, Z., Dong, X., et al.: TR-MABE: white-box traceable and revocable multi-authority attribute-based encryption and its applications to multi-level privacy-preserving e-heathcare cloud computing systems. IEEE INFOCOM (2015)
22. Lu, R., Lin, X., Zhu, H., et al.: Pi: a practical incentive protocol for delay tolerant networks. IEEE Trans. Wireless Commun. **9**(4), 1483–1492 (2010)

23. Paillier, P.: Public key cryptosystems based on composite degree residuosity classes. In: Eurocrypt 1999 Proceedings of the 17th International Conference on Theory and Application of Cryptographic Techniques, pp. 2–6. ACM, Prague (1999)
24. Groth, J., Sahai, A.: Efficient non-interactive proof systems for bilinear groups. In: Smart, N. (ed.) EUROCRYPT 2008. LNCS, vol. 4965, pp. 415–432. Springer, Heidelberg (2008). https://doi.org/10.1007/978-3-540-78967-3_24
25. Akhunzada, A., Gani, A., Anuar, N.B., et al.: Secure and dependable software defined networks. J. Netw. Comput. Appl. **61**, 199–221 (2016)
26. Miorandi, D., Sicari, S., De Pellegrini, F., Chlamtac, C.: Internet of things: vision, applications and research challenges. Ad Hoc Netw. **10**(7), 1497–1516 (2012)
27. Porambage, P., Okwuibe, J., Liyanage, M., et al.: Survey on multi-access edge computing for internet of things realization. IEEE Commun. Surv. Tutorials **20**(4), 2961–2991 (2018)
28. ur Rehman, S., et al.: Deep learning techniques for future intelligent cross-media retrieval. arXiv preprint arXiv:2008.01191. 2020 July 21
29. Zhong, N., et al.: Research challenges and perspectives on Wisdom Web of Things (W2T). J. Supercomput. **64**(3), 862–882 (2013)
30. Lai, C., Lu, R., Zheng, D., Li, H., Shen, X.: Toward secure large-scale machine-to-machine communications in 3GPP networks. IEEE Comm. Mag. Suppl. (2015)
31. Tiburski, R.T., Amaral, L.A., de Matos, E., Hessel, F.: The importance of a standard security architecture for SOA - based IoT middleware. IEEE Commun. Mag. (2015)
32. Valerie Aurora, "Lifetimes of cryptographic hash functions" (2012). http://valerieaurora.org/hash.html
33. ETSI TR103 167 v0.3.1: Machine to Machine Communications (M2M); Threat Analysis and Counter Measures to M2M Service Layer (2011)
34. International Workshop on Big Data and Data Mining Challenges on IoT and Pervasive Systems (BigD2M 2015), New Security Architecture for IoT Network (2015)
35. Geneiatakis, D., Kounelis, I., Neisse, R., Nai-Fovino, I.: Security and privacy issues for an IoT based smart home. In: 2017 40th International Convention on Information and Communication Technology, Electronics and Microelectronics (MIPRO), pp. 1292–1297. IEEE Conference Publications (2017)
36. J. Comput. Commun. **3**, 164–173 (2015). Published Online May 2015 in SciRes. http://www.scirp.org/journal/jcc https://doi.org/10.4236/jcc.2015.35021
37. Source: Cisco IBSG projections, UN Economic & Social Affairs. http://www.un.org/esa/population/publications/longrange2/WorldPop2300final.pdf
38. NIST Selects Winner of Secure Hash Algorithm (SHA-3) Competition, 2 October 2012. http://www.nist.gov/itl/csd/sha-100212.cfm
39. Ur Rehman, S., Bilal, M., Ahmad, B., Yahya, K.M., Ullah, A., Ur Rehman, O.: Comparison based analysis of different cryptographic and encryption techniques using message authentication code (MAC) in wireless sensor networks (WSN). arXiv preprint arXiv:1203.3103 (2012)
40. Ur Rehman, S., Tu, S., Huang, Y., Yang, Z.: Face recognition: a novel un-supervised convolutional neural network method. In 2016 IEEE International Conference of Online Analysis and Computing Science (ICOACS), pp. 139–144. IEEE (2016)
41. ur Rehman, O., Yang, S., Khan, S., Ur Rehman, S.: A quantum particle swarm optimizer with enhanced strategy for global optimization of electromagnetic devices. IEEE Trans. Mag. **55**(8), 1–4 (2019)
42. Tu, S., Huang, Y., Liu, G.: CSFL: a novel unsupervised convolution neural network approach for visual pattern classification. AI Commun. **30**(5), 311–324 (2017)
43. ur Rehman, S., Tu, S., Huang, Y., Ur Rehman, O.: A benchmark dataset and learning high-level semantic embeddings of multimedia for cross-media retrieval. IEEE Access **6**, 67176–67188 (2018)

44. Ur Rehman, S., Tu, S., Ur Rehman, O., Huang, Y., Sarathchandra Magurawalage, C.M., Chang, C.-C.: Optimization of CNN through novel training strategy for visual classification problems. Entropy **20**(4), 290 (2018)
45. Ur Rehman, S., et al.: Unsupervised pre-trained filter learning approach for efficient convolution neural network. Neurocomputing **365**, 171–190 (2019)
46. ur Rehman, S., Huang, Y., Tu, S., ur Rehman, O.: Facebook5k: a novel evaluation resource dataset for cross-media search. In: Sun, X., Pan, Z., Bertino, E. (eds.) ICCCS 2018. LNCS, vol. 11063, pp. 512–524. Springer, Cham (2018). https://doi.org/10.1007/978-3-030-00006-6_47
47. ur Rehman, S., Huang, Y., Tu, S., Ahmad, B.: Learning a semantic space for modeling images, tags and feelings in cross-media search. In: U., L.H., Lauw, H.W. (eds.) PAKDD 2019. LNCS (LNAI), vol. 11607, pp. 65–76. Springer, Cham (2019). https://doi.org/10.1007/978-3-030-26142-9_7
48. Tu, S., et al.: ModPSO-CNN: an evolutionary convolution neural network with application to visual recognition. Soft Comput., 1–12 (2020)
49. ur Rehman, S., et lal.: Deep learning techniques for future intelligent cross-media retrieval
50. Tu, S., et al.: Optimisation-based training of evolutionary convolution neural network for visual classification applications. IET Comput. **14**(5), 259–267 (2020)

Energy Optimization for Wild Animal Tracker Basing on Watchdog Technology

Zhenggang Xu[1,2,3,4], Wenhan Zhai[2], Chen Liang[2], Yunlin Zhao[3], Tian Huang[1,4], Minghui Zhou[4], Libo Zhou[1,4], Guiyan Yang[2], and Zhiyuan Hu[1(✉)]

[1] School of Material and Chemical Engineering, Hunan City University, Yiyang 413000, China
[2] Country College of Forestry, Northwest A & F University, Yangling 712100, China
[3] Key Laboratory of Forestry Remote Sensing Based Big Data & Ecological Security for Hunan Province, Central South University of Forestry and Technology, Changsha 410004, China
[4] Engineering Research Center for Internet of Animals, Changsha 410000, China

Abstract. Wild animal tracker, as an important IoT device terminal, can collect animal's position information and movement information in real time. The analysis based on the above big data provides us with a new perspective on recognizing animal behavior. It is useful in scientific research and animal management, while the device is always limited by energy. In order to develop the tracker device and enhance the energy supplying, wild animal tracker module including solar energy module, Maximum Power Point Tracking module, lithium battery, energy module, communication module, Global Positioning System module, data management module, stability controlling module, and ephemeris backup module etc. was designed in the study to optimize energy. Circuits for watchdog, energy management, solar energy protective were also designed in the novel tracker. Solar utilization efficiency and energy conversion efficiency have been enhanced after the energy optimization based on watchdog technology. The novel trackers were applied in many wild animals. Tests showed that the positioning accuracy, energy supplying, data collection all had been improved effectively. The tracker also proper worked in many harsh environments, such as desert and so on. The novel wild animal tracker can not only connect wild animals and the natural environment, but also human activities. There is also a huge market prospect, especially with the development of IoT technology and big data technology.

Keywords: Watchdog technology · Solar energy · Animal tracker · Energy optimization

1 Introduction

Data collection terminal is the foundation of IoT and big data. Wild animal tracker, as a important mobile terminal, is considered as an useful tool for animal research and animal management. It can supply footstep information of wild animal which is always difficult to get without the device. Positioning is always basing on radio or Global Positioning System (GPS) for the wild tracker device [1, 2]. More details have been gotten in many filed such as ecology, animal behavior, environment field and so on. Eastern palearctic

© Springer Nature Switzerland AG 2021
X. Sun et al. (Eds.): ICAIS 2021, LNCS 12737, pp. 647–655, 2021.
https://doi.org/10.1007/978-3-030-78612-0_52

flyway of tundra swan in Japan have been identified based on satellite tracking [3, 4]. Foraging behaviour and fuel accumulation of capital breeders have also been understood from a combination of satellite and ground-based observations [5]. Movement model and software about tracking data have been develop in recent year [6–9]. As we all known that wild animals always live in different environment such as forest, wetland, desert and so on, energy supplication is one of the key factors for wild animal tracker device. Lithium batter was used in wild animal tracker in the past, while the tracking process was interrupted quickly. Then solar module was application into the device and the work time become longer than before [10]. However the energy is still can't fulfill the application of animal tracker. The longer the device works, the more data is collected. We also know and get more details about wild animal. It's necessary to increase effectiveness of energy utilization of the device. Some algorithms, such as Maximum Power Point Tracking (MPPT), were be used to manage energy of wild animal tracker [11] and more researcher focus on the energy optimization.

Paying attention on energy management, increasing utilization of solar and decreasing energy loss is the only way to extend working time of the animal tracker because the work environment is so different. Watchdog technology that increase the safety for systems designed with traditional microcontrollers or with modern dual core safe ones is used in many instrument, such as architecture [12], pulse diagnosis instrument [13], computer [14] and so on. Besides of hardware equipment, there is software algorithm to implement watchdog. Watchdog algorithm is employed to monitor uses of nuclear energy or detection in Heterogeneous Sensor Networks [15, 16]. There is no application case for watchdog technology in device of wild environment. In order to develop the wild animal tracker and make sure it can work longer in wild, study introduced watchdog technology into the animal device based on novel tracker designed. Hardware and software module are designed to optimized energy of wild animal tracker. The study is meaning not only for the tracker but also for other subjects.

2   Experiments Design

2.1   Wild Animal Tracker Module Design

Research on design of wild animal tracker puts microprocessor at the core, including solar energy module, MPPT (Maximum Power Point Tracking) module, lithium battery, energy module, communication module, GPS module, data management module, stability controlling module, and ephemeris backup module etc. (Fig. 1). By solar energy module, the tracker absorbs solar energy, and by MPPT module, it can monitor the generating energy of solar cell, track the highest voltage and current value. Meanwhile, to utilize the lithium battery energy more efficiently, we designed a energy module to manage lithium battery energy. Communication module and GPS module is interactive with microprocessor. On the one hand, communication module sends back positioning information and other information, and microprocessor can control satellite positioning frequency remotely. The research designed data management module and stability control module to verify receiving data of microprocessor and ensure the data being accurate and timely. Ephemeris backup module ensures to read back normal data of the device about the extreme environment condition. The microprocessor puts MSP43F2419 as core control component, has ultra-low power consumption and integrates double serial ports internally, which can meet design requirement better (Fig. 2).

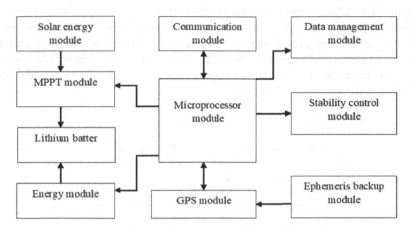

Fig. 1. The framework of wild animal tracker module

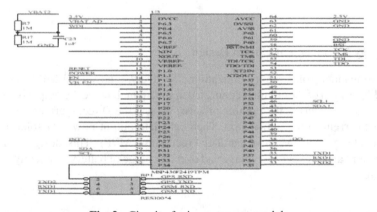

Fig. 2. Circuit of microprocessor module

2.2 Watchdog Electric Circuit Design

Power supply monitor system was design on watchdog. Hardware was designed to come true watchdog technique and monitor the system running. Watchdog circuit can be seen in Fig. 3. Giving watchdog a figure, once the application runs, the watchdog starts countdown. If it runs normally, the microprocessor will give an order to make watchdog reset after a while, then it restarts to countdown. If it reduces to zero, the procedure is regarded as not working properly, the system is forced to reset. On the other hand, watchdog circuit ensures the system electricity reset effectively and monitors working voltage of the system. It combines with real-time clock, monitors and controls the system to ensure the system never fail. Among them, Watch Dog Timer (WDI) is a feeding-dog signal of watchdog chip. When the program "runs away" or crashes in single-chip software and it can't "feed dog" in time. The "watchdog" will produce a low level so that the single-chip can't reset. When the Manual-Reset (MR) of watchdog chip is in low level, RESET (RST) generates a reset signal, and single-chip will be forced to reset automatically. In addition, the software technology is set to monitor system, which ensure the normal running of watchdog.

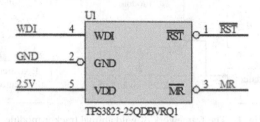

Fig. 3. Circuit of watchdog module

2.3 Energy Management Circuit Design

In order to manage solar energy utilization effectively, a advanced MPPT circuit was designed. The input of the circuit is connected to solar panel, while the output is connected to lithium battery. During the running process, we test the Direct Current (DC) voltage and output current in the major loop. Then calculate output power of solar array and achieve tracking about Massive Parallel Processing (MPP). This design can protect lithium battery and prevent overcharge and over discharge of battery efficiently, to extend battery life.

2.4 Solar Energy Protective Circuit

The core and key of wild animal tracker is energy problem. How to ensure the energy supply of the device for a long time in the wild is always the technique bottleneck. To make certain the energy supply, "increase income and reduce expenditure" is necessary. The mature technology of solar energy charging offers a solution of "increase income" of device energy supply. To make certain the energy supply system of wild animal tracker, we studies technology of solar energy charging and protection of lithium battery. 4.5V series voltage reference is made up by 2.5VLM4040 voltage regulator tube and 2.0VLM4040 voltage regulator tube. Then in parallel with series circuit which is composed by Schottky diode of 0.3V voltage drop and lithium battery. The accumulator is charging by solar cells (Fig. 4). When the voltage of point a is lower than 4.2V, the lithium battery is charged by solar cell in forward direction; when the voltage is higher than 4.2V, the voltage regulator tube is reserve breakdown, and forms short-circuited circuit, which is efficiently prevent lithium overcharging and achieves the aim of protecting lithium battery. This technical design is relatively simple to attain its goal only in two voltage regulator tube and one Schottky diode. It improves solar cell's charging efficiency and sharply reduces the volume and weight of the device. Meanwhile, during the solar cell output process, there are less losses which greatly increase the solar energy charging efficiency.

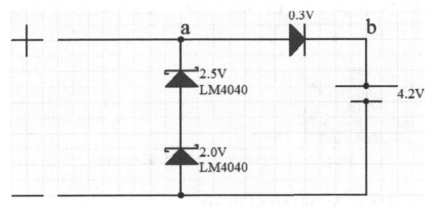

Fig. 4. Circuit of solar energy protection

3 Result

3.1 Wild Animal Tracker Dimensions

Wild animal tracker designed in this research can adopt multi-positioning methods, including monolithic System-on-a-Chip (SOC) integrated measurement which adopts a 4 mm * 4 mm chip and bases on new Always Locate Mode, advanced anti-interference countermeasure to make sure that the GPS can be achieved in severe environment, and generate and extend ephemeris automatically. The ephemeris data which is derived from broadcast cooperates with embedded system, which can reduce the start time to 3s during three days. Moreover, the self accessibility function can be lengthened to 14 days, and the 90 percent of hot start time can be shortened. The research tests positioning accuracy of wild animal tracker in different directions, and it considers that the positioning accuracy is relatively high in different direction, and the reliability is over 90% (Fig. 5).

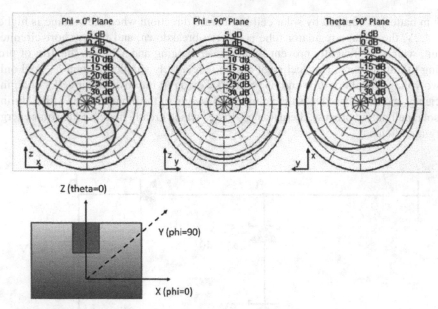

Fig. 5. Positioning accuracy test of wild animal tracker

3.2 Use of Energy for Wild Animal Tracker

Through energy optimization based on watchdog technology and other energy management measures, energy consumption of wild animal tracker is improved effectively (Table 1). Solar utilization efficiency is measured and the energy utilization is enhanced obviously. Before energy optimization, the solar utilization efficiency is only $10.3 \pm 1.2\%$, while the solar utilization efficiency increase to 12.2 ± 1.3 ($p < 0.05$). Besides from solar utilization efficiency increasing, energy conversion efficiency is also developed by watchdog technology. Energy conversion efficiency is 60.1 ± 5.2 before energy optimization, and energy conversion efficiency increase to 65 ± 3.4 after energy optimization. Energy conversion efficiency is improved significantly basing the study ($p < 0.05$).

Table 1. Compare of energy utilization efficiency for animal tracker before and after energy optimization

	Before energy optimization (%)	After energy optimization (%)	p value
Solar utilization efficiency	10.3 ± 1.2	12.2 ± 1.3	$p < 0.05$
Energy conversion efficiency	60.1 ± 5.2	65 ± 3.4	$p < 0.05$

3.3 Application of Wild Animal Tracker

The research applied the wild animal tracker on *Cygnus columbianus*, *Ardea cinerea*, swan goose, gray goose, *Elaphursu davidianus*, white crane and so on. In accordance with wild animal tracking case, we found that the device can work well in multi-environment like desert, virgin forest and plateau etc. (Fig. 6).

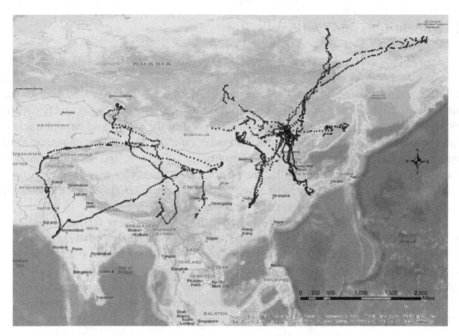

Fig. 6. Positioning point of wild animal tracker in the wild

The electric quantities, GPS positioning data and GIS map were overlaid to explore the result of energy optimization. The result showed that wild animal tracker could get extremely supply energy in more than 95% of the time. At the same time, the electric quantities maintained at over 3.9V, the maximum working voltage is 4.4V and the minimum working voltage is 3.5V. And at 3.9V, the battery life of such tracking device can still keep in about 30 days without sunlight. And the number of locations is also stable. The number of points send-back everyday except lack of locates in very few non GPS signal areas (Fig. 7, Fig. 8).

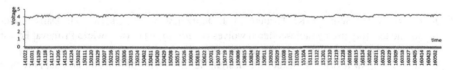

Fig. 7. Voltage change of animal tracker while working continuous

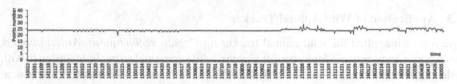

Fig. 8. Locations number of animal tracker change while working continuous

4 Conclusions and Outlook

Wild animal tracker module including solar energy module, MPPT module, lithium battery, energy module, communication module, GPS module, data management module, stability controlling module, and ephemeris backup module etc. was designed in the study based on designing of energy optimization. Circuits for watchdog, energy management, solar energy protective were also designed in the novel wild animal tracker. Solar utilization efficiency and energy conversion efficiency have been enhanced after the energy optimization based on watchdog technology. The novel tracker was applied in many wild animals. Tests showed that the positioning accuracy, energy supplying, data collection all had been improved effectively. The animal tracker also proper worked in many harsh environments, such as desert and so on.

The wild animal tracker is useful to promote the development of related disciplines. We may know more details about relationship between animal behavior and environment, animal reaction to global climate change, the spread of disease and so on. Besides the scientific research, there is a huge market potential in other fields. The tracker device can play an important role in livestock tracking and management, avian game and so on. More other novel technology should be introduced into wild animal tracker research process.

Funding Statement. This research was supported by the National Natural Science Foundation of China (U20A20118 to X.Z.), Natural Science Foundation of Hunan Province (2019JJ40012, 2019JJ50027 to H.T. and X.Z.), Key Technology R&D Program of Hunan Province (2016TP2007; 2016TP1014; 2017TP2014 to Z.Y.) and College Students' Innovative Entrepreneurial Training Plan Program of Shannxi Province (S202010712295 to L.C.).

Conflicts of Interest. The authors declare that they have no conflicts of interest to report regarding the present study. The authors declare that they have no conflicts of interest to report regarding the present study.

References

1. Jedrzejewski, W., Schmidt, K., Theuerkauf, J., Jedrzejewska, B., Okarma, H.: Daily movements and territory use by radio-collared wolves (*Canis lupus*) in Bialowieza Primeval Forest in Poland. Can. J. Zool. **79**(11), 1993–2004 (2001)
2. Cordier, J.A.: An investigation into the design, development, production and support of a wildlife tracking system based on GSM/GPS technologies. Master dissertation, North-West University, South African (2006)

3. Chen, W.: Migration of tundra swans (*Cygnus columbianus*) Wintering in Japan using satellite tracking: identification of the eastern palearctic flyway. Zool. Sci. **33**(1), 251–277 (2016)
4. Shimada, T., et al.: Satellite tracking of migrating whooper swans *Cygnus* wintering in Japan. Ornithol. Sci. **13**(2), 67–75 (2015)
5. Chudzińska, M.E., Nabe-Nielsen, J., Nolet, B.A., Madsen, J.: Foraging behaviour and fuel accumulation of capital breeders during spring migration as derived from a combination of satellite- and ground-based observations. J. Avian Biol. **47**, 563–574 (2016)
6. Avgar, T., et al.: Space-use behaviour of woodland caribou based on a cognitive movement model. J. Anim. Ecol. **84**(4), 1059–1070 (2015)
7. Kuhn, C.E., Johnson, D.S., Ream, R.R., Gelatt, T.S.: Advances in the tracking of marine species: using GPS locations to evaluate satellite track data and a continuous-time movement model. Mar. Ecol. Prog. **393**(6), 97–109 (2009)
8. Aing, C., Halls, S., Oken, K., Dobrow, R., Fieberg, J.: A Bayesian hierarchical occupancy model for track surveys conducted in a series of linear, spatially correlated, sites. J. Appl. Ecol. **48**(6), 1508–1517 (2011)
9. Jerde, C.L., Visscher, D.R.: GPS measurement error influences on movement model parameterization. Ecol. Appl. **15**(3), 806–810 (2008)
10. Butler, M.D: Solar Powered Animal Tracking Tags with GSM Telemetry. M.S., University of Otago, USA (2015)
11. Kunamneni, R., Vijay, B.A.R., Suman, S.: Solar Energy Harvester Using MPPT Tracker. LAP LAMBERT Academic Publishing, Saarbrücken (2012)
12. Scherer, B., Horvath, G.: Trace and debug port based watchdog processor. In: Conference Record-IEEE Instrumentation & Measurement Technology Conference, Piscataway, N.J. (2012)
13. Yongqi, Q.I.: Study on watchdog technology of pulse diagnosis instrument. Hydromecha-tronics Eng. **41**(6), 74–77 (2013)
14. Ling, Y.: The application of watchdog technology in MCS-51 single-chip computer control system. J. Hunan Metall. Prof. Technol. Coll. **4**(4), 303–305 (2004)
15. Prokoski, F.: Watchdog for nuclear development: technology can help monitor civilian uses of nuclear energy while discouraging military applications. IEEE Spectr. **18**(7), 51–55 (1981)
16. Makwana, N.P., Jayesh, S.K.V., Dhanesha, D.: Intrusion detection-watchdog: for secure AODV routing protocol in VANET. Int. J. Eng. Trends Technol. **4**(5), 2151–2157 (2013)
17. Atluri, S.N., Shen, S.: Global weak forms, weighted residuals, finite elements, boundary elements & local weak forms. In: The Meshless Local Petrov-Galerkin (MLPG) Method, 1st ed., Henderson (2004)

Performance Comparison of Curve Fitting and Compressed Sensing in Channel State Information Feature Extraction

Xiaolong Wang, Xiaolong Yang[(⊠)], Mu Zhou, and Liangbo Xie

Chongqing University of Posts and Communication, Chongqing 40065, China
yangxiaolong@cqupt.edu.cn

Abstract. Various commercial Wi-Fi based applications have been proposed, such as indoor positioning, indoor tracking, behavior recognition, gesture recognition, etc. These applications need to use the channel state information (CSI) fed back by Open-Source wireless network card devices, but without prior compression, the CSI feedback overhead is huge, which is not conducive to practical applications. Therefore, in order to promote the application of commercial Wi-Fi, CSI compression plays a key role. In this paper, we compare two compression methods. One is a novel curve fitting method, which can compress CSI by fed back the fitting parameters of CSI curve. The other one is the classical compressed sensing method, which can restore the original signal from a small number of measurements by using the sparsity of the signal specific domain. Using the CSI data collected from commercial Wi-Fi devices, we test the effect of the two compression methods, and compare the effects of the two compression methods on feature extraction with the same CSI feedback overhead. The experimental results show that the compression scheme is feasible.

Keywords: Compressed sensing · Curve fitting · Wi-Fi · CSI

1 Introduction

Channel characteristics of wireless communication link are usually measured by Channel State Information (CSI). In the indoor Wi-Fi link, multipath effect and random noise will cause changes in CSI [1], which can reflect the characteristics of things or persons. As shown in Fig. 1, the movement of an object will cause changes in the propagation delay and amplitude of the signal, and the channel state information can record these changes. Through some algorithms, we can extract the movement rules of objects or people hidden in CSI, so as to realize passive perception. Before 2011, it is difficult to obtain the CSI information of Wi-Fi, which limits the application of commercial Wi-Fi in indoor scenes. However, in 2011, Halperin et al. [2] found that 30 subcarriers of CSI can be obtained by modifying the driver of wireless network card. Since then, many scholars have also carried out relevant research using the CSI information of Wi-Fi, and achieved fruitful results, such as indoor positioning [3], indoor tracking [6–8], behavior recognition [9], gesture recognition [12], etc. However, most applications using indoor

© Springer Nature Switzerland AG 2021
X. Sun et al. (Eds.): ICAIS 2021, LNCS 12737, pp. 656–666, 2021.
https://doi.org/10.1007/978-3-030-78612-0_53

Wi-Fi are based on full feedback CSI. For wireless network card using IEEE 802.11n protocol, a link contains complex numbers [13], while the wireless network card using IEEE 802.22ac protocol has complex numbers [14]. This is only in the case of single snapshot. In practical applications, such as indoor tracking, gesture recognition, indoor positioning etc., it is impossible to achieve by single snapshot, so it is crucial to adopt appropriate compression methods.

This paper compares the compression effect of two compression methods on CSI. One is a novel curve fitting method [15], which obtains the coefficient solution of sinusoids by fitting the CSI curve, and then feeds back the coefficient to achieve the purpose of compression; the other is the classical compression sensing method [16], which is widely used in MIMO [17], the original signal is transformed into the sparse domain through a sparse transformation matrix, and then the measurement matrix is used to obtain less measured values, and the receiver restores the original signal from the less measured values to achieve the less CSI feedback overhead. In addition, the angle of arrival (AOA) and time of flight (TOF) extracted from CSI are selected as the comparison parameters to test effect of compression [18].

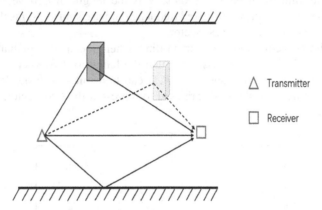

Fig. 1. Illustration of the multipath effect of wireless signals.

2 Compression Methods

In this section, two compression methods are introduced. One is a new curve fitting method, which has low computational complexity and good compression performance. Its principle is to get the coefficient solution of the sinusoidal signal by fitting the CSI curve, and then feedback a small number of coefficients to achieve the purpose of compression. The other is the classical compressed sensing method, which is widely used in Massive MIMO. Firstly, the original signal is represented by the product of sparse matrix and sparse coefficient, and then the dimension of the original signal is reduced by using the measurement matrix; finally, the receiver uses convex optimization algorithm to recover the original signal from the low dimension measurement value with high probability. Meanwhile, the feasibility of the compression method is verified by simulation data.

2.1 Curve Fitting

Curve fitting is a method of approximating discrete data with analytic expression, which can be used to describe the functional relationship between CSI subcarriers index and CSI value. In the problem of CSI curve fitting, a set of data pairs (j, c_j) of CSI subcarrier index and CSI value are collected by Intel 5300 wireless network card, where $j = 1, 2, .., N$, and N is subcarrier index. We use complex exponential function $c_j = f(j; \Lambda)$ to fit the relationship between j and c_j. In general, $f(j; \Lambda)$ is fitting model and $\Lambda = (\alpha_1, \alpha_2, ..., \alpha_P)$ is undetermined parameter. Specifically, CSI vector is approximated as the linear combination of base sinusoids at a constant frequency, and the complex coefficient of base sinusoids are used as the compressed CSI [19]. The complex coefficient of base sinusoids can be obtained by minimizing following formula:

$$J = \sum_{j=1}^{N} \left| \sum_{k=1}^{P} \alpha_k e^{iif_k} - c_j \right|^2 \tag{1}$$

where, P is the number of base sinusoids, N is the length of CSI vector, α_k is the coefficient to be calculated, f_k is the fixed frequency of base sinusoids, i is the imaginary unit, and c_j is the jth element of CSI vector.

Figure 2 shows the feasibility of curve fitting, where it can be seen that the raw CSI vector has some level of noise. Assuming that the length of CSI vector is N and the number of base sinusoids is P and $N > P$, it can transmit $\frac{N-P}{N}100\%$ less CSI data. Obviously, the more base sinusoids are used to represent the CSI vector, the less CSI can be lost.

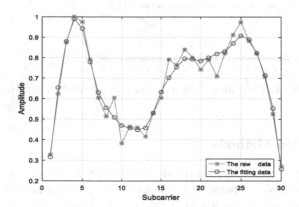

Fig. 2. Fitting diagram of original data

2.2 Compressed Sensing

Compressed sensing can be divided into three steps. Firstly, the signal is expressed as the product of the sparse matrix and the sparse coefficient vector. Here, it is very important to select the appropriate sparse matrix for signal reconstruction, because different sparse matrix has different sparse effect. Under the effect of the sparse matrix, the less the non-zero value of the sparse coefficient vector, the higher accuracy of signal reconstruction; then, the Gaussian random observation matrix is used to reconstruct the original signal; finally, greedy algorithm or convex optimization algorithm is used to recover the original signal. According to the theory of compressed sensing, as long as any signal itself is sparse or the corresponding sparse representation space is found, the effective compressed sampling can be carried out, and the original signal can be recovered efficiently by reconstruction algorithm.

If the signal $x \in R^{N \times 1}$ is sparse, compressed sensing can recover the original signal through the observation value $y \in R^{M \times 1}$, where M is much less than N and it can transmit $\frac{N-M}{N} 100\%$ less CSI data.

In many practical applications, however, the signal $x \in R^{N \times 1}$ does not show sparsity, which needs to be transformed in a certain transform domain:

$$s = \Psi x \tag{2}$$

where s is the sparse representation of the signal x and $\Psi \in R^{N \times N}$ is the sparse matrix. This transformation is usually orthogonal:

$$x = \Psi^T s \tag{3}$$

where $(\cdot)^T$ denotes the matrix transpose.

The compressed signal can be reconstructed by the following formula:

$$\min \|s\|_{l_1} \ s.t. \ y = \Phi \Psi^T s \tag{4}$$

where the $\Phi \in R^{M \times N}$ is measurement matrix, $\Psi \in R^{N \times N}$ is sparse matrix, and the elements in Φ are random variables generated according to the distribution such as Gauss or Bernoulli. In order to reconstruct x from the measured values y, because there are more unknowns than equations, it is necessary to solve underdetermined linear equations. This problem can be expressed as the l_1 norm minimization problem of sparse signal s, which can be solved by optimization algorithm. In the paper, OMP (orthogonal matching pursuit) algorithm is used [20].

The Signal Itself is Sparse. Figure 3(a) shows the original sparse signal, where it can be seen that most elements are equal to 0 except that a small number of elements are not 0. This kind of signal does not need sparse transformation, which is equivalent to the sparse matrix of the signal as the unit matrix. For a strictly sparse signal, compressed sensing theory can compress and reconstruct the signal without losing any precision. Figure 3(b) is a diagram of sparse signal reconstruction, where it can be seen that there is no difference between the reconstructed signal and the original signal.

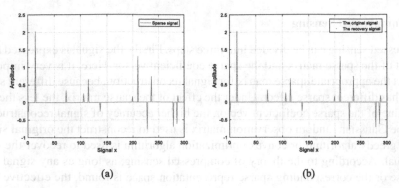

Fig. 3. Original sparse signal and reconstructed sparse signal. (a) Original sparse signal. (b) Reconstructed sparse signal.

The Signal Itself is Not Sparse. In practical application, it is difficult to find a strictly sparse signal. As shown in Fig. 4(a), the signal is generated by superposition of several sinusoids with the frequency 25, 50 and 100 Hz. Obviously, the most element in the sinusoids signal are not zero.

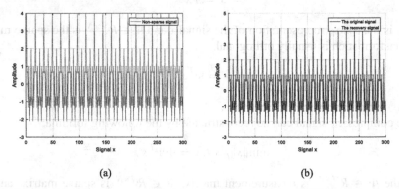

Fig. 4. Original signal and reconstructed signal. (a) Original signal. (b) Reconstructed signal.

The signal shown in Fig. 4(a) cannot be measured directly because the signal itself is not sparse. However, the FFT transform domain of signal shown in Fig. 5 is sparse, which has only a few peaks in the Fourier transform domain. As shown in Fig. 4(b), although the signal itself is not sparse, the signal is sparse in the Fourier transform domain, so the compressed sensing theory can be applied to it.

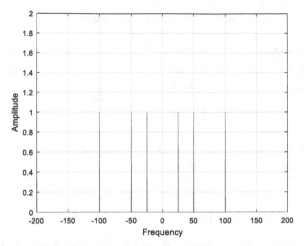

Fig. 5. FFT transform of the signal

3   Experiments Results

In this section, the experiment configuration and experimental results of the two compression methods are given, and the AOA and TOF parameters are selected as the performance comparison of different compression methods. For curve fitting, we test the AOA estimation error and TOF estimation error when the CSI overhead is reduced by 60%, 70% and 80%; for compressed sensing, we compare the sparse coefficients of the original CSI signal in different sparse basis, and give the AOA estimation error and TOF estimation error when the CSI overhead is reduced by 33%.

3.1   Experimental Platform and Data Acquisition

In our experimental platform, the transmitting and receiving devices of signal are equipped with commercial Intel 5300 wireless network card and an open source csi-tool toolkit that can measure the channel state information. We use the mini-pc with the type of Probox23 equipped with the Ubuntu 14.0 operating system as the transmitter. The transmitter works in the monitor mode under the IEEE 802.11n protocol, and the frequency is 5.745 GHz. The receiver is also equipped with the same operating system and mini-pc type.

During the measurement, the transmitter is equipped with a directional antenna, while the receiver is equipped with three antennas. The receiver receives data packets from the transmitter and stores them in name.dat format. Since the Intel 5300 wireless network card can only reflect the amplitude and phase data of 30 subcarriers, the CSI packet dimension extracted from the received packets by the receiver is $1 \times 3 \times 30$. We set the transmitter to the Injection mode to send packets, and the receiver to the monitor mode to monitor the wireless channel and collect CSI. Meanwhile, in order to avoid packet loss in 2.4 GHz wireless channel, we set the working frequency to 5 GHz. In addition, our packet delivery rate is 400 packet/s. Table 1 shows the specific parameter configuration of the transmitter and receiver.

Table 1. Parameter configuration

Parameter	Transmitter	Receiver
Model	Injection	Monitor
Bandwidth	40 MHz	
Packet delivery rate	400 packet/s	
Subcarrier	30	
Index	[−58, −54... −2, 0, 2... 54, 58]	
Power	15 dBm	

3.2 Test Curve Fitting Algorithm

In the curve fitting method, we first use the music algorithm to estimate the AOA and TOF parameters of the original CSI data, and then use the reconstructed CSI data to estimate the AOA and TOF parameters. Taking the AOA and TOF parameters estimated from the original CSI data as the standard, the AOA and TOF parameter errors estimated from the reconstructed CSI data can be obtained. Meanwhile, the cumulative distribution function (CDF) of the reconstructed CSI data parameter estimation error (AOA and TOF) is given. Figure 6(a) and (b) show the AOA estimation error and TOF estimation error when CSI overhead is reduced 60%, 70% and 80%, respectively.

As can be seen from Fig. 6, the more CSI overhead is reduced, the greater the estimation error of AOA and TOF. In the case of 80% less feedback overhead of CSI, the AOA estimation error is less than 5° and the TOF estimation error is less than 5ns of 67% reconstructed data.

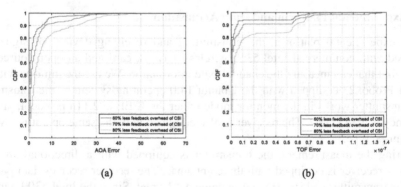

(a)   (b)

Fig. 6. AOA and TOF error in curve fitting. (a) AOA estimation error. (b) TOF estimation error.

Table 2 shows the average error of AOA and TOF estimation under different feedback overhead. From the experiment results in Table 2, with the increase of CSI overhead, the performance of parameter estimation of compressed data decreases sharply.

Table 2. Average error of AOA and TOF estimation

Parameter	Overhead		
	60%	70%	80%
AOA error	1.927°	3.384°	6.31°
TOF error	4.676 ns	8.136 ns	12.692 ns

3.3 Test Compressed Sensing Algorithm

In the compressed sensing method, AOA and TOF parameters are estimated using the original CSI data and the reconstructed CSI data, respectively, and then the cumulative error distribution of the parameter estimation errors (AOA and TOF) of the reconstructed data is given. Figure 7 shows the real part amplitude and imaginary part amplitude of CSI signal and their sparse representation under FFT sparse matrix and DCT sparse matrix, respectively.

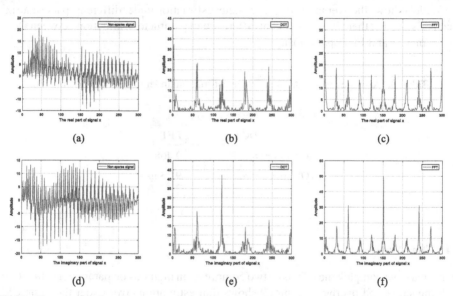

Fig. 7. The raw signal and its sparse representation. (a) The real part of signal. (b) The real part in DCT domain. (c) The real part in FFT domain. (d) The imaginary part of signal. (e) The imaginary part in DCT domain. (f) The imaginary part in FFT domain.

Figure 7 shows that the original signal is not sparse and its corresponding matrixes under FFT and DCT are sparse. According to the theory of compressed sensing, we can compress and reconstruct the signal. Figure 8 shows the CDF of parameter estimation error under different sparse matrix when the CSI overhead is reduced by 33%.

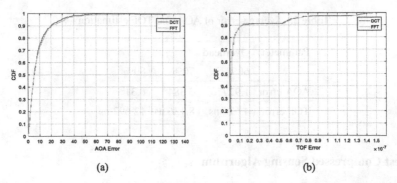

Fig. 8. The signal under sparse matrix. (a) AOA estimation error. (b) TOF estimation error.

As shown in Fig. 8, the estimation errors of FFT sparse matrix and DCT sparse matrix are similar. When the CSI overhead is reduced by 33%, the AOA estimation error is less than 8° and the TOF estimation error is less than 3ns of 67% reconstructed data compared with the original CSI data parameter estimation.

Table 3 shows the average error of parameter estimation under different sparse matrix. It can be seen that there is no significant difference in parameter estimation between DCT sparse matrix and FFT sparse matrix.

Table 3. Average error of AOA and TOF estimation under different sparse matrix

Parameter	Sparse matrix	
	DCT	FFT
AOA error	8.608°	9.408°
TOF error	9.528 ns	9.23 ns

3.4 The Contrast

In this part, we compare the effects of two compression methods on parameter estimation with the same CSI overhead. Figure 9 shows that estimation error under the same CSI overhead. As shown in Fig. 9, the AOA estimation error is less than 8° and the TOF estimation error is less than 3 ns of 67% for compress sensing, while the AOA estimation error is less than 1.6° and the TOF estimation error is less than 1.5 ns of 67% for curve fitting.

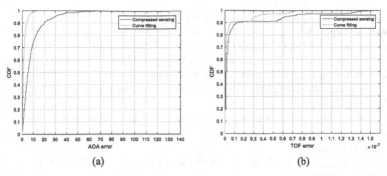

Fig. 9. Performance comparison of two compression methods. (a) AOA estimation error. (b) TOF estimation error.

4 Conclude

In this paper, we introduce two compression methods to solve the problem of huge overhead of CSI. First of all, we introduce the basic principles of the two compression methods. The curve fitting can compress CSI through feedback fitting coefficient, while compressed sensing can restore CSI through a small number of measured values. On the one hand, we use the simulation data to prove the feasibility of the compression method; on the other hand, we use the measured CSI information extracted from commercial Wi-Fi, and select typical parameters (AOA and TOF) to measure the effect of algorithms. The experimental results show that the AOA estimation error is less than 8° and the TOF estimation error is less than 3 ns of 67% for compress sensing, while the AOA estimation error is less than 1.6° and the TOF estimation error is less than 1.5 ns of 67% for curve fitting at the same CSI feedback overhead. In the future work, we will test the impact of compressed CSI on the accuracy of device-free passive sensing system (such as behavior recognition, gesture recognition and indoor location).

Acknowledgement. This research was supported in part by the National Natural Science Foundation of China (61771083, 61704015), Science and Technology Research Project of Chongqing Education Commission (KJQN201800625) and Chongqing Natural Science Foundation Project (cstc2019jcyj-msxmX0635).

References

1. Fang, S.H., Hau, S., Wang, C.H.: A novel fused positioning feature for handling heterogeneous hardware problem. IEEE Trans. Commun. **63**(7), 2713–2723 (2015)
2. Halperin, D., Hu, W., Sheth, A., Wetherall, D.: Predictable 802.11 packet delivery from wireless channel measurements. ACM SIGCOMM Comput. Commun. Rev. **40**(4), 159–170 (2010)
3. Ma, L., Wang, S.T., Ma, D.C.: CSI localization method based on sparse representation. J. Softw. **27**(1), 21–27 (2016)
4. Wu, K., Xiao, J., Yi, Y., Gao, M., Ni, L.M.: FILA: fine-grained indoor localization. In: Proceedings of IEEE INFOCOM, Orlando, FL, USA, pp. 2210–2218. IEEE (2012)

5. Nannuru, S., Li, Y., Zeng, Y., Coates, M., Yang, B.: Radio-frequency tomography for passive indoor multitarget tracking. IEEE Trans. Mobile Comput. **12**(12), 2322–2333 (2013)
6. Bocca, M., Kaltiokallio, O., Patwari, N., Venkatasubramanian, S.: Multiple target tracking with RF sensor networks. IEEE Trans. Mobile Comput. **13**(8), 1787–1800 (2014)
7. Bahl, P., Padmanabhan, V.N.: RADAR: an in-building RF-based user location and tracking system. In: Proceedings of IEEE International Conference on Computer and Communications, pp. 775–784 (2000)
8. Qian, K., Wu, C.S., Yang, Z., Liu, Y.H., Jamieson, K.: Widar: decimeter-level passive tracking via velocity monitoring with commodity Wi-Fi. In: Proceedings of MobiHoc, New York, NY, USA, pp. 1–10 (2017)
9. Gillian, N., Paradiso, J.A., Harras, K.: The gesture recognition toolkit. J. Mach. Learn. Res. **15**(1), 3483–3487 (2014)
10. Wang, Y., Liu, J., Chen, Y., Gruteser, M., Yang, J., Liu, H.: E-eyes: device-free location-oriented activity identification using fine-grained WiFi signatures. In: Proceedings of ACM 20th Annual International Conference on Mobile Computing and Networking, pp. 617–628 (2014)
11. Wang, W., Liu, A.X., Shahzad, M., Ling, K., Lu, S.: Understanding and modeling of WiFi signal based human activity recognition. In: Proceedings of the 21st Annual International Conference on Mobile Computing and Networking, Paris, France, pp. 65–76 (2015)
12. Virmani, A., Shahzad, M.: Position and orientation agnostic gesture recognition using WiFi. In: Proceedings of MobiSys, New York, NY, USA, pp. 252–264 (2017)
13. Hajlaoui, N., Jabri, I., Benjemaa, M.: Experimental study of IEEE 802.11n protocol. In: Proceedings of WiNTECH, New York, NY, USA, pp. 93–94 (2012)
14. Karmakar, R., Chattophyay, S., Chakraborty, S.: Channel access fairness in IEEE 802.11ac: a retrospective analysis and protocol enhancement. In: Proceedings of MobiWac, New York, NY, USA, pp. 51–58 (2016)
15. Mukherjee, A., Zhang, Z.: Fast compression of OFDM channel state information with constant frequency sinusoidal approximation. In: Proceedings of GLOBECOM, Singapore, SG, pp. 1–7 (2017)
16. Donoho, D.L.: Compressed sensing. IEEE Trans. Inf. Theory **52**(4), 1289–1306 (2006)
17. Lu, W., Liu, Y., Wang, D.: Efficient feedback scheme based on compressed sensing in MIMO wireless networks. Comput. Electr. Eng. **39**(6), 1587–1600 (2013)
18. Kotaru, M., Joshi, K., Bharadia, D., Katti, S.: SpotFi: decimeter level localization using WiFi. ACM SIGCOMM Comput. Commun. Rev. **45**(4), 269–282 (2015)
19. Mukherjee, A., Zhang, Z.: Channel state information compression for MIMO systems based on curve fitting. In: Proceedings of SECON, London, UK, pp. 1–9 (2016)
20. Pati, Y.C., Rezaiifar, R., Krishnaprasad, P.S.: Orthogonal matching pursuit: recursive function approximation with applications to wavelet decomposition. In: Proceedings of ACSSC, California, CA, USA, pp. 40–44 (1993)

Dynamic Time Warping Based Passive Crowd Counting Using WiFi Received Signal Strength

Min Chen, Xiaolong Yang[✉], Yue Jin, and Mu Zhou

School of Communication and Information Engineering, Chongqing University of Posts and Telecommunications, Chongqing 40065, China
yangxiaolong@cqupt.edu.cn

Abstract. In the current era, the Internet of Things is developing rapidly. The increasing number of persons pay attention to personnel information in an area. Crowd counting is favored by many researchers. It can be applied in many people-centric scenarios, such as the smart home and supermarket energy management. In this paper, we only use a pair of transceivers, relying on the Received Signal Strength Indicator (RSSI) information of the commercial WiFi signal to count the crowd without requiring the people carry any device. We first model the received signal into three parts, which are the Line-of-Sight (LoS) path blockage effect, Multipath (MP) effect on the received signal, and the multipath effect resulting from signal reflection by the fixed objects. Then, we analyze the Probability Density Function (PDF) of the received signal based on the characteristic function and then combine two different distributions to characterize the relationship between the number of persons and the PDF of the received signal amplitude. Finally, we use the Dynamic Time Warping (DTW) algorithm for crowd counting. We validate the performance of the approach in an outdoor environment, and the experimental results show that our approach can count four persons with an average accuracy of 96.25%.

Keywords: Crowd counting · WiFi signal · Dynamic time warping · Passive recognition · Characteristic function

1 Introduction

Monitoring the number of people in a given area plays a critical role in many scenarios, such as smart guiding in museum, energy management of supermarket, and evacuation of people in crowded areas in emergency situations. Specifically, in a retail store, lighting and air conditioning can be automatically adjusted according to the crowd density in each area. In addition, analyzing the consumption habits and preferences of consumers based on the distribution of the number of consumers in each area, and adjusting sales strategies timely or providing consumers with better services and guidance has become the most important part of the shopping experience. While reducing the cost of market management, it also improves consumer satisfaction. In places with heavy traffic such as subway stations, railway stations and squares, the passenger flow can be channeled in

© Springer Nature Switzerland AG 2021
X. Sun et al. (Eds.): ICAIS 2021, LNCS 12737, pp. 667–677, 2021.
https://doi.org/10.1007/978-3-030-78612-0_54

time according to the crowd density in the area to improve travel efficiency and prevent the occurrence of stampede due to excessive concentration of people. The "Parade of Love" in Germany [1] and the Turin stampede [2] are typical examples of crowd disasters.

Since the importance of crowd counting, researchers have invested a lot of time and cost in it in recent years, and it has been implemented in many applications. The traditional method of crowd identification is mainly based on computer vision [3–5] and Radio Frequency Identification (RFID) system. The method based on computer vision is accurate. However, it needs a huge amount of calculation and is easily affected by lighting conditions. More importantly, setting a camera in a certain place may be banned, mainly for privacy concerns. An RFID-based crowd counting system requires everyone to have radio frequency identification, which not only requires considerable deployment costs, but also requires the cooperation of the monitored object. Wireless signals are ubiquitous, simple to deploy and low cost. Therefore, an increasing number of researchers have used wireless signals to count crowd density [6, 7] in recent years.

The crowd counting based on wireless signals is mainly divided into two categories, one is based on channel state information (CSI), and the other is based on RSSI. CSI-based crowd counting, the PHY layer information provided by commercial WiFi devices is used to perceive the number of people in the environment. However, CSI is difficult to extract in commercial WiFi devices. RSSI-based crowd counting, due to unknown radio path loss factors, multipath effects, hardware differences, etc., received signal strength (RSS) is not considered the best choice for crowd counting, but it does provide some useful crowd related information.

Based on the above analysis, this paper uses a probability statistical model to propose a method for estimating the number of people based on RSSI, and everyone does not carry any devices (that is, passively). The method is divided into two stages: offline training and online detection. In the offline training phase, we collect the original RSSI sequences in the WiFi signal, filter the sequences through outliers removal, then calculate the coefficient of variation of different RSSI sequences, and select the RSSI sequence with the largest coefficient of variation for counting in online phase; in the online detection stage, the experimental PDF is first displayed, then the curve is matched with the theoretical PDF of different people, and finally the estimated number of people is calculated by using the DTW algorithm. In order to verify this method, we conducted four persons experiments in an outdoor environment. The experimental results show that the approach we proposed is accurate and acceptable for counting the number of people.

The rest of this paper is organized as follows: Sect. 2 discusses the related work to crowd counting; Sect. 3.1 introduces data preprocessing and Sect. 3.2 introduces the influence of people on the received signal, and Sect. 3.3 introduces a mathematical model of crowd counting; The fourth section is experimental verification. First, we describe the experimental setup, and then the experimental results obtained by using the DTW algorithm are shown; finally, we summarize the full text in the fifth section.

2 Related Work

There are a lot of works in the literature on crowd counting. This paper divides them into two categories: video-based crowd density estimation and RF-based crowd counting methods.

Camera-based Approachs: Traditional solutions mainly rely on surveillance cameras for crowd counting, such as [8–10]. In [8] the system combined closed circuit elevision cameras (CCTV) to use regression technology to count crowd density, and used The University of California (UCSD) and the Peds2 datasets for experimental verification. The system is in the mean absolute error (MAE) and mean squared error (MSE) has achieved good performance. Reference [9, 10] is dedicated to using deep learning algorithms to improve the robustness of crowd counting algorithms. However, there are some drawbacks for most of the video-based methods of crowd counting mentioned above. First of all, the overlap of blind spots and targets will cause inaccurate counting results. The second is that when a large coverage area is required, multiple cameras need to be used, which will bring a lot of work and pre-calibration.

RF-based Approaches: As for RF-based crowd counting methods, we classify them into two categories: device-based active methods and device-free passive methods. The device-based active method relies on the radio frequency signals emitted by the devices carried by people in the area to evaluate the crowd density [11–13]. However, these methods require all persons in the area to carry wireless devices, which limits their applicability and high cost. On the other hand, the deviceless passive radio frequency method uses different wireless signals for crowd counting, such as WiFi and ultra-wideband radar. Since the presence of the human will affect the propagation of wireless signals in the air, there is no need to attach any devices to the human body to achieve crowd counting. In this way, user privacy can be protected and deployment cost is low. The existing work mainly uses the RSS of the wireless signal or the CSI amplitude to characterize the relationship between the number of people moving and changes in wireless signals. In [14], the researchers deployed wireless sensor networks and estimated rough crowd density based on RSS using clustering algorithms. In [15], the researcher's RSSI measurements of several WiFi connections were used to track up to 4 people walking in the same area. Xi et al. [16] found a monotonic relationship between the amplitude of CSI measurement and the "number of people moving in a certain area", and used the gray Verhulst model to count crowd. However, these methods rely on a large amount of pre-calibration, and the training overhead is greatly increased.

3 Our Approach

In this section, we propose a approach to estimate the total number of people in an area, using only a pair of WiFi links. More specifically, we first remove outliers in the RSSI sequences collected in the offline phase, and calculate the coefficient of variation for RSSI sequences selection, and then analyze the effects of persons on the received signal. Finally, we will use a theoretical model to capture the relationship between the number of people in the area and the amplitude of the received signal.

3.1 Data Preprocessing

Outlier Removal. In the offline stage, when we collect RSSI data, due to the influence of environmental noise, outliers may appear in the RSSI measurements. Because this paper estimates the number of people based on a kind of distribution, such outliers will have a great impact on the performance of crowd counting, so it needs to be filtered before estimating the number of people. Through the observation of a large amount of silent measurements (i.e., no one in the area), we found that the fluctuation is below-30 dBm. When people move around in the area, the collected received signal strength measurements will drop obviously, so we remove the deviation measurements greater than-30 dBm. This method does not change the distribution of received signal strength measurements, but improves the matching accuracy of the predicted number of people.

RSSI Sequence Selection. When a person walks in an area, because the person's walking speed is different, and the signal is random, the degree of fluctuation to each RSSI sequence is different, which causes some RSSI sequences are not sensitive to the number of people, so the RSSI sequence collected cannot accurately reflect the actual number of people. Based on the above analysis, this paper estimates the number of people based on the matching degree of the theoretical distribution curve and the experimental distribution curve. Therefore, when estimating the number of people in the online phase, the selection of the RSSI sequence will have a great impact on the performance of crowd counting. With different numbers of people, we first collect RSSI sequences $[s_1, s_2, \ldots, s_m]$, where m represents the number of RSSI sequences. Then calculate the coefficient of variation of each RSSI sequence:

$$c_m = \frac{\sigma_m}{\mu_m} \tag{1}$$

where σ_m and μ_m represent the standard deviation and mean of the m - th RSSI sequence respectively. After obtaining the coefficient of variation of each RSSI sequence, we select the RSSI sequence with the largest coefficient of variation as the crowd counting, which further improves the fit between the experimental distribution curve and the theoretical curve.

3.2 Effect of Persons on Received Signal in an Area

Overview of RSSI. RSSI is obtained by monitoring changes in the received signal strength caused by human movement. If someone walks between transceivers, the RSSI value will drop. As the number of people increases between the transceivers, human has a greater influence on the received signal, and the RSSI declines will be more serious.

The following formula is the Friis transmission equation. Let c [m/s] be the speed of light, f [Hz] be the frequency, R [m] be the distance between a pair of transceivers, G_T [dBi] and G_R [dBi] be the absolute gain of the transmitter and receiver antenna respectively, P_T [W] be the power of the transmitting antenna. Then, the electric power of the receiver P_R [W] is defined by:

$$P_R = \frac{P_T G_T G_R c^2}{(4\pi R)^2 f^2} \tag{2}$$

We can calculate RSSI by:

$$RSSI = 10 \log_{10} \left(\frac{P_R}{1mW} \right) \tag{3}$$

Effect of Persons on Received Signal. People in the area mainly affect the received signal in two ways: one is the link Line-of-Sight blocking effect and the other is the multipath effect. More specifically, when a person blocks the LoS link, the received signal strength drops significantly, which we call the line-of-sight blocking effect. On the other hand, when the person moves near the LoS but does not block the LoS path, the signal is reflected by the person from the transmitter to the receiver. This phenomenon is called multipath fading. Of course, other fixed objects in the area will also reflect the transmitted signal and then reach the receiver. Here, we consider a simple three-path model to analyze the effect of the person on the received signal, as shown in Fig. 1.

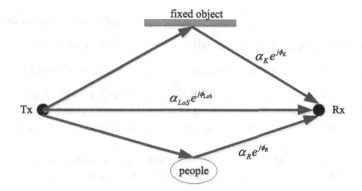

Fig. 1. Components of the received signal

According to Fig. 1, the received signal can be expressed as:

$$H = \alpha_{LoS} e^{j\phi_{LoS}} + \sum_{R=1}^{N} \alpha_R e^{j\phi_R} + \sum_{K=1}^{M} \alpha_K e^{j\phi_K} \tag{4}$$

where α_{LoS} and ϕ_{Los} represent the amplitude and phase of the LoS path respectively, α_R and ϕ_R represent the amplitude and phase of the path resulting from the signal reflected by a person respectively, α_K and ϕ_K are the amplitude and phase of the reflected path caused by fixed object in the area. When the number of fixed objects increases and there is more than one person in the area, formula (4) can be extended to:

$$H = \alpha_{LoS} e^{j\phi_{LoS}} + \sum_{R=1}^{N} \alpha_R e^{j\phi_R} + \sum_{K=1}^{M} \alpha_K e^{j\phi_K} \tag{5}$$

where N represents the total number of people in the area, and M is the number of fixed objects in the area.

3.3 Theoretical Model

In this section, we mainly derive the PDF of the received signal amplitude. This function contains information about the number of people.

According to formula (5), we can know that the received signal is mainly composed of three components: blocking the LoS path, reflection as people walk, signals reflected by fixed objects in the area. For the convenience of subsequent analysis, formula (5) can be writed as:

$$
\begin{aligned}
H &= \alpha_{LoS} e^{j\phi_{LoS}} + \sum_{R=1}^{N} \alpha_R e^{j\phi_R} + \sum_{K=1}^{M} \alpha_K e^{j\phi_K} \\
&= \alpha_0 e^{j\phi_0} + \sum_{R=1}^{N} \alpha_R e^{j\phi_R} \\
&= H_{LoS,FX} + H_{MP}
\end{aligned}
\tag{6}
$$

where $H_{LoS,FX} = \alpha_{LoS} e^{j\phi_{LoS}} + \sum_{K=1}^{M} \alpha_K e^{j\phi_K} = \alpha_0 e^{j\phi_0}$ represents the summation of people blocking the LoS path component and MP effects due to the fixed objects in the area, $H_{MP} = \sum_{R=1}^{N} \alpha_R e^{j\phi_R}$ represents the multipath effect due to people walking. In practice, the WiFi link is configured to operate in a sub-channel of the 2.4 GHz wireless frequency band, so the phase $\phi_R(R = 1, 2, \ldots, N)$ and $\phi_K(K = 1, 2, \ldots, M)$ are assumed to be uniformly distributed in $[0, 2\pi]$ [17]. α_R and α_S are considered to be independent for $R \neq S$.

Through understanding the relationship between characteristic function and probability density function, we next derive the PDF expression of the received signal [17]:

$$
\begin{aligned}
p_H(Z) &= \frac{1}{4\pi^2} \int_{|T|=0}^{\infty} \int_{\angle T=0}^{2\pi} e^{-jT \cdot Z} C_H(T) |T| d|T| d\angle T \\
&= \frac{1}{4\pi^2} \int_{|T|=0}^{\infty} \int_{\angle T=0}^{2\pi} e^{-j|T||Z|\cos\left(\angle T - \angle Z\right)} C_H(T) |T| d|T| d\angle T \\
&= \frac{1}{2\pi} \int_{|T|=0}^{\infty} |T| J_0(|T||Z|) \left(\prod_{R=1}^{N} E_{\alpha_R}(J_0(\alpha_R|T|)) \right) E_{\alpha_0}(J_0(\alpha_0|T|)) d|T| \\
&= \frac{1}{2\pi} \int_{|T|=0}^{\infty} |T| J_0(|T||Z|) \left(\prod_{R=1}^{N} E_{\alpha_R}(J_0(\alpha_R|T|)) \right) \\
&\quad \times \sum_{k=0}^{N} \binom{N}{k} p_1^k (1-p_1)^{N-k} J_0(|T|B_k) d|T|
\end{aligned}
\tag{7}
$$

where $C_H(T)$ represents the characteristic function of the received signal, T is the corresponding variable of the characteristic function. J_0 represents the zero-order Bessel function of the first kind, $E_\alpha(\cdot)$ represents expectations with respect to α. $p_{\alpha_R} = \frac{2}{a\Gamma(v)} \left(\frac{\alpha}{2a}\right)^v K_{v-1}\left(\frac{\alpha}{a}\right)$ is the PDF of α_R, and K_{v-1} is the modified Bessel function of the second kind, and a is the scaling factor, v is the shape parameter. p_1 is the probability of a person blocks the LoS path within one time step. In this paper, we assume it to be 0.16. B_k is the received signal power when there are k persons in the area walking along the LoS path.

Every person in the area can be regarded as a scatterer. Since the scatterers are independent and identically distributed [17], and H contains the information of $|H|$ and $\angle H$, the PDF of the received signal amplitude can be found as:

$$p_{|H|,N}(Z) = \int_{\angle H=0}^{2\pi} p_H(Z)d\angle H$$

$$= \int_{|T|=0}^{\infty} |T| J_0(|T||Z|) \left(E_{\alpha_R}(J_0(\alpha_R|T|)) \right)^N \sum_{k=0}^{N} \binom{N}{k} p_1^k (1-p_1)^{N-k} J_0(|T|B_k)d|T|$$

$$(8)$$

4 Experimental Results

In this section, before reporting our experimental results, we describe our experimental setup, and then conduct experiment in an outdoor area to verify and evaluate the performance and effects of the proposed approach.

We use 4×8 square meters (i.e., the width is 4 m, the length is 8 m) for experiments in an outdoor area, as shown in Fig. 2. The transceivers are placed at both ends of the area and are stationary. We use D-Link router as transmitter, and it is equipped with two antennas, and a Samsung GT-S7568 mobile phone as receiver. When people are walking in the area, we use the signal collection software developed on our mobile phones to collect the original RSS data sent by the transmitter. The WiFi link is configured to operate in a sub-channel of the 2.4 GHz wireless frequency band. The receiver collects data at the rate of 1 sample/s, collecting data for 10 min each time. We performed experiments with 1, 2, 3, 4 people in the area. People were told to walk casually in the area and need to return when they approached the boundary of the area. It should be noted that for mathematical modeling and number estimation, we assume that everyone in the area walks at a speed of 1 m/s, but there is no limit to their speed in practice.

It can be seen from formula (8) that in order to calculate the theoretical PDF of the received signal amplitude, we need to estimate B_k a priori. In order to obtain this value, we performed pre-measurements when k number of people were walking along the LoS path. In addition, it can be seen from Eq. (8) that we also need to know the prior estimatation of a and v to get the distribution. We first let a person walk in the area without crossing the LoS path, and then the PDF of the collected received signal power convolutionally match with the PDF of the MP part and the PDF of the LoS path when there is no person around in (11) to find a and v are the best fit. In order to obtain these two values more accurately, we performed three sets of experiments, and finally took the average of the three groups of values as the estimatation of a and v.

Since the DTW algorithm can evaluate the similarity of two sequences with different lengths, we next estimate the number of people by minimizing the DTW distance between the experimental and theoretical PDFs:

$$N_{est} = \arg\min_{S} DTW\left(p_{\exp}, p_{|H|,S}\right) \tag{9}$$

where $p_{\exp}$ represents the PDF of the measured received signal amplitude. Figure 3 shows the DTW distance between the experimental PDF when there are two persons in

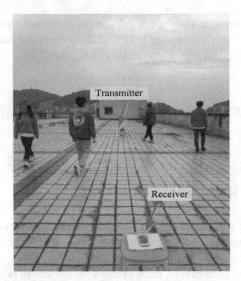

Fig. 2. Experimental scene in an outdoor area

the area and the theoretical PDF with other people. It can be seen that the calculated DTW distance is similar, but the curve is minimized at $N = 2$. Therefore, when there are two people walking in the area, the obtained PDF matches the theoretically calculated PDF of the two people best, which means $N_{est} = 2$. Obviously, the total number of people can be accurately estimated with our approach.

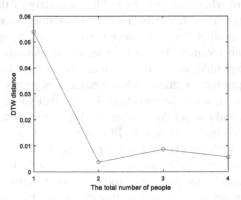

Fig. 3. The DTW distance between the experimental PDF for the case of N = 2 and the theoretical PDF of other people

Figure 4 compares the best fit between the experiment and the theoretical PDF for different people. It can be seen that the method we proposed can show good performance under different people. Therefore, the theoretical curve is very close to the experimental curve, and as the number of people increases in the area, the experimental curve is getting fatter.

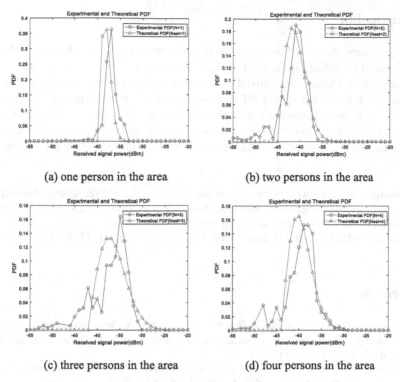

(a) one person in the area

(b) two persons in the area

(c) three persons in the area

(d) four persons in the area

Fig. 4. A comparison of experimental PDF and theoretical PDF

For different samples of people, we performed a lot of experiments in an outdoor area. Figure 5 is a confusion matrix of the results of crowd counting. It can be seen that the average accuracy of our proposed method is 96.25% for crowd counting, which is a good accuracy.

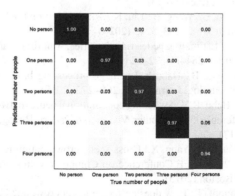

Fig. 5. Confusion matrix shows accuracy of crowd counting

5 Conclusion

This paper proposes a method to passively estimate the number of persons through the analysis of the RSSI information of the commercial WiFi signal. More specifically, we use a probability statistical model to mathematically describe the amplitude of the received signal, which carries key information about the number of persons and then use the DTW algorithm to estimate the number of persons. We conduct an experiment in the scenario with four persons in an outdoor area, with an average estimation accuracy of 96.25%, which demonstrates that our method can achieve passive crowd counting accurately.

Acknowledgement. This work is supported in part by the Science and Technology Research Program of Chongqing Municipal Education Commission (KJQN201800625, KJZD-K202000605), the Chongqing Natural Science Foundation Project (cstc2019jcyj-msxmX0635, cstc2020jcyj-msxmX0842), and the National Natural Science Foundation of China (61771083, 61771209).

References

1. Cardone, G., Cirri, A., Corradi, A., Foschini, L., Ianniello, R., Montanari, R.: Crowdsensing in urban areas for city-scale mass gathering management: geofencing and activity recognition. Journal **14**(12), 4185–4195 (2014)
2. Shiwakoti, N., Xiaomeng, S., Zhirui, Y.: A review on the performance of an obstacle near an exit on pedestrian crowd evacuation. Journal **113**, 54–67 (2019)
3. Wang, L., Yung, N.H.C.: Crowd counting and segmentation in visual surveillance. In: IEEE International Conference on Image Processing, pp. 2573–2576. IEEE, Cairo (2009)
4. Pham, V., Kozakaya, T., Yamaguchi, O., Okada, R.: COUNT forest: CO-Voting uncertain number of targets using random forest for crowd density estimation. In: 2015 IEEE International Conference on Computer Vision, pp. 3253–3261. IEEE, Santiago (2015)
5. Idrees, H., Saleemi, I., Seibert, C., Shah, M.: Multi-source multi-scale counting in extremely dense crowd images. In: 2013 IEEE Conference on Computer Vision and Pattern Recognition, pp. 2547–2554. IEEE, Portland (2013)
6. Wang, F., Zhang, F., Wu, C., Wang, B., Liu, K.J.R.: Respiration tracking for people counting and recognition. Journal **7**(6), 5233–5245 (2020)
7. Kurkcu, A., Ozbay, K.: Estimating pedestrian densities, wait times, and flows with WiFi and bluetooth sensors. Journal **2644**(1), 72–82 (2017)
8. Al-Zaydi, Z., Vuksanovic, B., Habeeb, I.: Image processing based ambient context-aware people detection and counting. Journal **8**(3), 268–272 (2018)
9. Sam, D.B., Surya, S., Babu, R.V.: Switching convolutional neural network for crowd counting. In: 2017 IEEE Conference on Computer Vision and Pattern Recognition, pp. 4031–4039. IEEE, Honolulu (2017)
10. Zhang, C., Li, H., Wang, X., Yang, X.: Cross-scene crowd counting via deep convolutional neural networks. In: 2015 IEEE Conference on Computer Vision and Pattern Recognition, pp. 833–841. IEEE, Boston (2015)
11. Prasertsung, P., Horanont, T.: How does coffee shop get crowded? Using WiFi footprints to deliver insights into the success of promotion. In: Proceedings of the 2017 ACM International Joint Conference on Pervasive and Ubiquitous Computing, pp. 421–426. ACM, Maui (2017)

12. Weppner, J., Lukowicz, P.: Bluetooth based collaborative crowd density estimation with mobile phones. In: 2013 IEEE International Conference on Pervasive Computing and Communications, pp. 193–200. IEEE, San Diego (2013)
13. Ni, L.M., Liu, Y., Lau, Y.C., Patil, A.P.: LANDMARC: indoor location sensing using active RFID. Journal 10, 701–710 (2004)
14. Yuan, Y., Qiu, C., Xi, W., Zhao, J.: Crowd density estimation using wireless sensor networks. In: 2011 Seventh International Conference on Mobile Ad-hoc and Sensor Networks, pp. 138–145. IEEE, Beijing (2011)
15. Bocca, M., Kaltiokallio, O., Patwari, N., Venkatasubramanian, S.: Multiple target tracking with RF sensor networks. Journal 13(8), 1787–1800 (2014)
16. Xi, W., et al.: Electronic frog eye: counting crowd using WiFi. In: IEEE Conference on Computer Communications, pp. 361–369. IEEE, Toronto (2014)
17. Depatla, S., Muralidharan, A., Mostofi, Y.: Occupancy estimation using only WiFi power measurements. Journal 33(7), 1381–1393 (2015)

Wi-Fi Indoor Positioning Using D-S Evidence Theory

Zhu Liu[✉], Yong Wang, Yuexin Long, Yaohua Li, and Mu Zhou

School of Communication and Information Engineering, Chongqing University
of Posts and Telecommunications, Chongqing 400065, China

Abstract. The Wi-Fi indoor positioning method is one of research hot-spots in
the field of mobile computing. However, the existing methods rarely consider the
impact of the diversity of the Received Signal Strength (RSS) on the performance
of the signal propagation distance estimation, resulting in the low positioning
accuracy and the poor system robustness. In response to this problem, this paper
proposes an information fusion-based Wi-Fi indoor positioning method by using
the Dempster-Shafer evidence Theory (DST). First of all, the heuristic distribution
model is used to establish the mathematical relationship between the RSS data
from each Wi-Fi Access Point (AP) and the signal propagation distance. Second,
the Gaussian kernel density estimation method is applied to estimate the signal
propagation distance distribution. Third, the multi-source RSS information is fused
according to DST synthesis rules, and the trust function synthesized by the DST
is used to select matching Reference Points (RPs). Experimental results show
that the proposed method has higher positioning accuracy and stronger system
robustness compared to the existing methods.

Keywords: Indoor positioning · Wi-fi RSS · Dempster-Shafer evidence Theory ·
Information fusion · Gaussian kernel density estimation

1 Introduction

In recent years, with the increasing demand for Location-Based Service (LBS), indoor
positioning technology plays an indispensable role in many technical fields, such as
pedestrian navigation or tracking in large airports, shopping supermarkets, underground
garages and other scenes. The satellite signals of the Global Positioning Since system
(GPS) are not continuously and stably captured in indoor environments, GPS is difficult to meet the positioning accuracy requirements of most indoor LBS. At the same
time, positioning systems such as Bluetooth [1], Infrared Ray (IR) [2] and ZigBee [3]
often require additional infrastructure, which greatly limits their application scope. In
comparison, Wi-Fi [4] network has the advantages of wide coverage, low deployment
cost and no need for special hardware equipment. Therefore, Wi-Fi positioning based
on RSS has gradually become the mainstream of indoor positioning technology. For the
diversity of indoor signals, commonly used probability estimation methods [5] are inconvenient to deal with incomplete and inaccurate RSS information, and it is not easy to

© Springer Nature Switzerland AG 2021
X. Sun et al. (Eds.): ICAIS 2021, LNCS 12737, pp. 678–687, 2021.
https://doi.org/10.1007/978-3-030-78612-0_55

distinguish the contribution of RSS information from different APs to ranging accuracy. For example, the signal is usually affected by environmental noise with the increase of the propagation distance, which increases the uncertainty factors contained in the RSS information [6], resulting in the decrease of the positioning accuracy. Therefore, this paper proposes a Wi-Fi indoor positioning method based on DST information fusion, which has the following characteristics. According to the heuristic distribution model, the mathematical relationship between the signal propagation distance of different APs and RSS is established, and estimate the signal propagation distance distribution by Gaussian kernel density estimation method. At the same time, the normalized signal propagation distance distribution estimation is used as the basic probability assignment of DST, and merge multi-source RSS information through DST synthesis rules. Finally, the k-nearest neighbors (KNN) [7] of the matching RPs is treated as target position.

The structure of this paper is as follows. Section 2 describes the construction method of the signal propagation distance distribution model. Section 3 gives the specific steps of Wi-Fi indoor positioning method based on DST information fusion. Section 3 verifies the effectiveness and robustness of the method proposed in this paper through experiments. Section 4 summarizes the full text and gives the next steps.

2 Distance Distribution Model Construction

2.1 Distance Distribution Characteristics

Considering the signal diversity characteristics caused by environmental noise such as indoor complex, time-varying signal occlusion, multi-path effect, etc. Using the traditional signal propagation model shown in formula (1) [6] to locate the target will produce a large distance deviation.

$$d(v) = d_{fs} + X = \left(\frac{c_1}{10^v}\right)^{\frac{1}{c_2}} + X \tag{1}$$

where, $d(v)$ and d_{fs} respectively represent the target ranging results when RSS is v in the actual environment and free space. X represents the distance deviation caused by actual environmental noise, and represent model parameters introduced by hardware conditions such as signal transmission power and antenna gain.

Due to the presence of indoor environmental noise, the traditional signal propagation model [8] cannot accurately describe the true distribution of the signal. Therefore, this article uses three common heuristic distribution models F1: $d(v) = c_1 e^{\lambda_1 v} + c_2 e^{\lambda_2 v}$ [9], F2: $d(v) = b_0 + b_1 v + b_2 v^2$ [10] and F3: $d(v) = \left(l_1/10^v\right)^{1/l_2}$ [11] to fit the mean, maximum and minimum of the signal propagation distance with RSS. Then, a heuristic distribution model with minimum fitting error was selected to establish the mathematical relationship between RSS from different APs and the signal propagation distance. Verified by experiment, F1 has the minimum average fitting error, so a signal propagation model about the average, maximum, and minimum values of the signal propagation distance are established as Average $d(v) = c_1 e^{\lambda_1 v} + c_2 e^{\lambda_2 v}$, Maximum $d_u(v) = c_{u,1} e^{\lambda_{u,1} v} + c_{u,2} e^{\lambda_{u,2} v}$, Minimum $d_l(v) = c_{l,1} e^{\lambda_{l,1} v} + c_{l,2} e^{\lambda_{l,2} v}$.

2.2 Distance Distribution Characteristics

Due to the complexity of indoor environment, it is difficult to fit the distance distribution of different RSS values with a single type of distribution function (such as Gaussian function [12], inverse segmentation function [13], etc.). Therefore, the Gaussian kernel density estimation method is used to estimate the distance distribution. Specifically, let $d_1, \cdots, d_l$ denote l signal propagation distances randomly selected when the RSS is v, and construct the corresponding Gaussian kernel density estimation function for signal propagation distance distribution.

$$p(d|v) = \frac{1}{lh} \sum_{i=1}^{l} K\left(\frac{d - d_i}{h}\right) \tag{2}$$

where $K(\cdot)$ represents the kernel function[1], h represents the bandwidth. Under the condition of Epanechnikov kernel function selected in our paper, where $h_{MISE} \approx 2.345\sigma l^{-0.2}$, σ is the standard deviation of the signal propagation distance d. By normalizing the formula (3), we can obtain the normalized signal propagation distance density distribution estimate when the RSS is v.

$$\hat{p}(d|v) = \frac{p(d|v)}{\max\limits_{d \in [d_l(v), d_u(v)]} \{p(d|v)\}} \tag{3}$$

3 Localization Approach Based on DST

Based on the advantages of DST in processing incomplete and inaccurate RSS information, this paper estimates the target location by constructing a trust function based on multi-source RSS information fusion. Specifically, first, construct the relationship state set of each RP and the target position, and use the boundary error test method to correct the RSS sample mean. Secondly, the normalized signal propagation distance distribution estimation is used as the basic probability assignment of DST to establish the initial trust of the relationship between each RP and the target position. Thirdly, according to the DST synthesis rules, the multi-source RSS information is fused to obtain a comprehensive trust estimate for each RP, and the trust function synthesized by DST is used to select the matching RP.

Step 1: Construct the relationship state set $H = \{I, N, \Theta\}$ of each RP (ie $p_i(i = 1, \cdots, n)$, n represents the number of RP) and the target, where I and N indicate that the target is at and not at p_i respectively, $\Theta(= I \text{ or } N)$ indicates the uncertain state of the target position, and from this, the corresponding basic probability assignment m_j (that is, the mapping of H to $[0, 1]$) for the j - th AP is established:

$$\begin{cases} m_j(\phi) = 0 \\ \sum\limits_{A \subseteq H} m_j(A) = 1 \end{cases} \tag{4}$$

---

[1] Since the type of kernel function has little effect on performance, the Epanechnikov kernel function [14] is selected in this paper.

where ϕ is the empty set. Based on this, the trust function $Bel_j(I)$ and the likelihood function $Bel_j(I)$ of the target with respect to p_j are defined:

$$\begin{cases} Bel_j(I) = \sum_{B \in I} m_j(B) = m_j(I) + m_j(\Theta) \\ Pl_j(I) = \sum_{B \cap I = \phi} m_j(B) = m_j(N) \end{cases} \qquad (5)$$

Let the ratio of the number of singular RSS samples to the total number of samples be a, then the probability of the uncertain state and the determined state of the target position are $p(\Theta) = a$ and $p(I) + p(N) = 1 - a$, respectively. Furthermore, the boundary error test method is used to eliminate singular RSS samples to modify the RSS sample mean. The algorithm description of this process is shown in Algorithm 1.

Algorithm 1 RSS sample mean correction algorithm based on boundary error test

---

Input: $X_j = \{x_{j,1}, \ldots, x_{j,s}\}$ (The collection of RSS samples from the j-th AP collected at the target, where s is the total number of samples); $d_j(v)$ (The fitting function of the mean value of the signal propagation distance of the j-th AP); $d_{j,l}(v)$ (The fitting function of the minimum value of the signal propagation distance of the j-th AP); $\varepsilon(=0)$ (RSS singular sample number initial value)

    Output: $\bar{x}'_j$ (Corrected value of RSS sample mean); a (Probability of uncertain state of target position).

1: Calculate the average $\bar{x}_j$ of RSS samples in X_j;

2: Calculate $d_{j,l}(\bar{x}_j)$ and $d_{j,u}(\bar{x}_j)$;

3: **for** $k = 1 : s$ **do**

4:     **if** $d_{j,l}(\bar{x}_j) \leq d_j(x_{j,k}) \leq d_{j,u}(\bar{x}_j)$ **then**

5:         $\varepsilon \leftarrow \varepsilon + 1$;

6:         Remove $x_{j,k}$ from X_j to get a new RSS sample set $X'_j = X_j - x_{j,k}$;

7:     **else**

8:         **Continue;**

9:     **end if**

10: **end for**

11: Calculate $a = \varepsilon / s$;

12: Calculate the RSS sample mean $\bar{x}'_j$ in X'_j and let it be the correction value of the RSS sample mean.

Step 2: Based on the normalized signal propagation distance density distribution estimation shown in formula (10), the initial trust $\{m_j(I), m_j(N), m_j(\Theta)\}$ of the relationship state between p_i of the j - th AP and the target position was established.

$$
\begin{cases}
m_j(I) = \hat{p}\left(d_{ij}\middle|\overline{x}_j'\right) \\
m_j(N) = 1 - \hat{p}\left(d_{ij}\middle|\overline{x}_j'\right) \\
m_j(\Theta) = a_j
\end{cases}
\tag{6}
$$

where $\hat{p}\left(d_{ij}\middle|\overline{x}_j'\right)$ is the normalized density of distance d_{ij} when RSS is $\overline{x}_j'$, d_{ij} is the distance between the i - th reference point and the j - th AP, a_j represents the probability of an uncertain state about the target position of the j - th AP.

Step 3: According to DST synthesis rule [17], the basic probability assignment of m APs is used to fuse multi-source RSS information to obtain a comprehensive trust estimate for each RP. The algorithm description of this process is shown in Algorithm 2.

Algorithm 2 RP Comprehensive trust estimation algorithm based on DST synthesis rules

---

Input: m_j ($j = 1, L, m$) (Basic probability assignment of m APs); $H = \{I, N, \Theta\}$ (Relationship state set).

Output: $\{m(I), m(N), m(\Theta)\}$ (Comprehensive trust estimation).

1: Initialize $m(I) = m_1(I)$, $m(N) = m_1(N)$, $m(\Theta) = m_1(\Theta)$;

2: Calculate $d_{j,l}\left(\overline{x}_j\right)$ and $d_{j,u}\left(\overline{x}_j\right)$;

3: **for** $j = 2 : m$ **do**

4:     Calculate $m(I) = \dfrac{m(I)m_j(\Theta) + m(\Theta)m_j(I)}{1 - m(I)m_j(N) - m(N)m_j(I)}$;

5:     Calculate $m(N) = \dfrac{m(N)m_j(\Theta) + m(\Theta)m_j(N)}{1 - m(I)m_j(N) - m(N)m_j(I)}$;

6:     Calculate $m(I, N) = \dfrac{m(\Theta)m_j(\Theta)}{1 - m(I)m_j(N) - m(N)m_j(I)}$;

7: **end for**

From Algorithm 2, the trust estimates $m(I)$ and $m(N)$ of the target's two determined states and a trust estimate $m(\Theta)$ of uncertain state about p_i can be obtained. At this time, when relationships $m(I) > m(N)$ and $m(I) > m(\Theta)$ are satisfied, p_i is defined as an ideal RP. In general, we take the k-nearest neighbors [7] of the position of the first three matching RPs as the target position.

4   The Experimental Results

The experimental environment selected in this paper is shown in Fig. 1. All experimental tests are conducted on the same floor, and the size of the experimental environment is 56.93 m × 20.08 m. 9 APs (D-Link DAP-2310 AP, recorded as AP1, …, AP9 respectively) are randomly deployed in the environment and 143 reference points and 20 test points (Test Point, TP) are evenly marked. The black circle represents the RP, and the red triangle represents the test point. At each RP and TP, 200 RSS samples from all APs are collected for testing (where the RSS sampling frequency is 1 Hz).

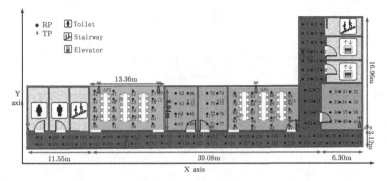

Fig. 1. Structure diagram of the experimental environment.

4.1   Effect of RSS Sample Number on Ideal Matching RP

Figure 2 shows the variation of the number of ideal matching RP with the number of AP and the number of RSS samples. It can be seen from the Fig. 2, in the case of a small number of APs, the increase in the number of APs can significantly reduce the number of ideal matching RPs, thereby reducing the probability of the uncertain state of the target position. However, the impact of changes in the number of RSS samples on the number of ideal matching RP is not obvious. The reason is that the increase in the number of RSS samples has little effect on the correction of the RSS sample mean, so that the trust of the ideal RP will not change significantly.

4.2   Performance Comparison of Different Wi-Fi Indoor Positioning Methods

Figure 3 shows the variation of average positioning error[2] with the increase of AP number. It can be seen from the figure that as the number of APs increases (that is, the dimension of the basic probability assignment increases), the average positioning error shows a downward trend overall. However, due to the redundancy of positioning information, the average positioning error tends to be stable with a larger number of APs.

---

[2] For a given number of APs, the average positioning error is the average of all possible AP deployment methods.

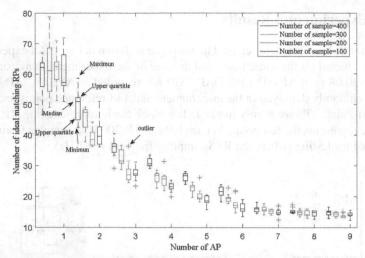

Fig. 2. The variation of the number of ideal matching RP with the number of AP and the number of RSS samples

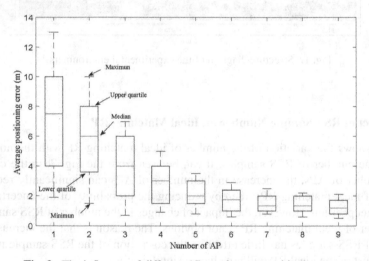

Fig. 3. The influence of different AP numbers on positioning error.

4.3 Performance Comparison of Different Wi-Fi Indoor Positioning Methods

In order to further verify the effectiveness of the proposed method, Fig. 4 compares the average positioning error(i.e. the average positioning error of all TPs) using maximum likelihood estimation, APIT, Bayesian estimation and the method of this paper under the same experimental environment(as shown in Fig. 1) and test data. It can be seen from the figure that, the proposed method in our paper show poor positioning performance when the number of APs is less than 3. The reason is that the dimension of the basic probability assignment at this time is low, and the trust degree of the ideal matching

RPs cannot be guaranteed. When the number of APs is greater than 3, the positioning performance of the method in this paper will be significantly improved, and the maximum error under the same number of APs is lower than other methods. The reason is that as the number of APs increases, the uncertainty factors contained in the RSS information increase. Therefore, through the processing of incomplete and inaccurate RSS information by the DST adopted in this paper, RSS information from different APs can be fully utilized for positioning. While ensuring higher positioning accuracy, the system has strong positioning robustness.

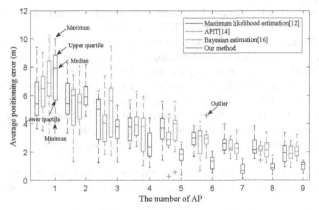

Fig. 4. Performance comparison of four Wi-Fi indoor positioning methods under different numbers of AP

5 Conclusion

Aiming at the problems of low positioning accuracy and poor system robustness of the existing Wi-Fi indoor positioning methods, this paper proposes a Wi-Fi indoor positioning method based on information fusion by using the DST. First of all, the normalized distribution density of the signal propagation distance estimated by the Gaussian kernel density estimation method is selected as the basic probability assignment of the DST. Second, the multi-source RSS information is merged according to DST synthesis rules, and based on the decision function, the ideal matching RP is used for positioning. Finally, the impact of the number of RSS samples and the number of APs on positioning performance is discussed through experiments. The performance comparison with other three existing indoor Wi-Fi positioning methods proves the superiority of our method. However, although the DST has certain advantages in processing the incomplete and inaccurate RSS information, how to guarantee its effectiveness in the case of a small number of APs will form an interesting work in future.

Acknowledgement. This work was supported in part by the Science and Technology Research Project of Chongqing Education Commission (KJZD-K202000605, KJQN202000630, KJQN201800625, KJQN201900603), the Chongqing Natural Science Foundation Project (cstc2020jcyj-msxmX0842, cstc2020jcyj-msxmX0865, cstc2019jcyj-msxmX0635, cstc2019jcyj-msxmX0742, cstc2019jcyj-msxmX0108), and the National Natural Science Foundation of China (61771083, 61901076, 61704015).

References

1. El-Kafrawy, K., Youssef, M., El-Keyi, A., et al.: Propagation modeling for accurate indoor WLAN RSS-based localization. In: IEEE Vehicular Technology Conference, Ottawa, Canada, pp. 1–5 (2010)
2. Wu, N., Wang, X., Hu, Q.: Multiple LED based high accuracy indoor visible light positioning scheme. J. Electron. Inf. Technol. **37**(3), 727–732 (2015)
3. Baha aldin, N., Erçelebi, E., Aykaç, M.: Advanced boundary virtual reference algorithm for an indoor system using an active RFID interrogator and transponder. Analog Integr. Circ. Sig. Process **88**(3), 415–430 (2016). https://doi.org/10.1007/s10470-016-0789-y
4. Yin, F., Zhao, Y., Gunnarsson, F., et al.: Received-signal-strength threshold optimization using Gaussian processes. IEEE Trans. Sig. Process. **65**(8), 2164–2177 (2017)
5. Cho, H., Kang, M., Park, J., et al.: Performance analysis of location estimation algorithm in ZigBee networks using received signal strength. In: International Conference on Advanced Information Networking and Applications Workshops, Niagara Falls, Canada, pp. 302–306 (2007)
6. Vaughan, R., Bach-Andersen, J.: Channels, Propagation and Antennas for Mobile Communications. Bibliovault OAI Repository, pp. 156–158. The University of Chicago Press (2003)
7. Yu, J., Liu, J.: A KNN indoor positioning algorithm that is weighted by the membership of fuzzy set. In: IEEE International Conference on Green Computing and Communications and IEEE Internet of Things and IEEE Cyber, Physical and Social Computing, Beijing, pp. 1899–1903 (2013)
8. Kwon, H., Kim, Y., Lee, B.: Characteristics of radio propagation channels in tunnel environments: a statistical analysis. In: IEEE Antennas and Propagation Society Symposium, Monterey, CA, USA, vol. 3, pp. 2995–2998 (2004)
9. Chu, Y., Tzeng, J., Cheng, Y., et al.: Density-adaptive range-free localization in large-scale sensor networks. In: International Conference on Parallel Processing, Pittsburgh, USA, pp. 488–495 (2012)
10. Luo, R., Hsiao, T.J.: Dynamic wireless indoor localization incorporating with an autonomous mobile robot based on an adaptive signal model fingerprinting approach. IEEE Trans. Ind. Electron. **66**(3), 1940–1951 (2019)
11. Jung, S., Lee, C.O., Han, D.: Wi-Fi fingerprint-based approaches following log-distance path loss model for indoor positioning. In: IEEE MTT-S International Microwave Workshop Series on Intelligent Radio for Future Personal Terminals, Daejeon, South Korea, pp. 1–2 (2011)
12. Chuku, N., Pal, A., Nasipuri, A.: An RSSI based localization scheme for wireless sensor networks to mitigate shadowing effects. In: IEEE Southeastcon, Jacksonville, USA, pp. 1–6 (2013)
13. Graefenstein, J., Ebouzouraa, M.: Robust method for outdoor localization of a mobile robot using received signal strength in low power wireless networks. In: IEEE International Conference on Robotics and Automation, Pasadena, USA, pp. 33–38 (2008)
14. Stefanski, L.A., Carroll, R.J.: Deconvoluting kernel density estimators. Statistics **21**(2), 169–184 (1990)
15. Ahmad, I.A., Fan, Y.: Optimal bandwidths for kernel density estimators of functions of observations. Stat. Prob. Lett. **51**(3), 245–251 (2001)

16. Arabsheibani, R.G., Rees, H.: On the weak vs strong version of the screening hypothesis: a re-examination of the P-test for the U.K. Econ. Educ. Rev. **17**(2), 189–192 (1998)
17. Fan, X., Ming, J.Z.: Fault diagnosis of machines based on D-S evidence theory. Part 1: D-S evidence theory and its improvement. Pattern Recogn. Lett. **27**(5), 366–376 (2006)

A Hybrid Localization Algorithm Based on Carrier Phase Ranging in UHF RFID System

Zengshan Tian, Xixi Liu[✉], Kaikai Liu, and Liangbo Xie

School of Communication and Information Engineering, Chongqing University of Posts and Telecommunications, Chongqing 400065, China

Abstract. In this paper, we present a solution to locate the targets with tags in an ultrahigh-frequency (UHF) radio frequency identification (RFID) system, which achieves centimeter level localization accuracy. Many prior works use the Newton iteration method based on Least squares method (LS-Newton) to solve the coordinate of the target for accurate indoor localization, and the performance depends on an initial guess. However, it is difficult to get a good initial value close to the true value. In order to solve the problem, we propose a hybrid localization algorithm, which can effectively solve the initial guess problem and realize a good localization accuracy. First, we establish the objective localization equations and convert them into an LS problem. Second, we transform the LS problem into Semi-Definite Programming (SDP) problem by adopting the semidefinite relaxation technique (SDR). Third, we obtain a coarse coordinate estimate of the target by solving the SDP problem. In the end, we input this estimate into the LS-Newton method for iterative calculation and obtain high localization accuracy. Our experiments are conducted in a multi-static transceiving system with 1 transmitter and 3 receivers using the software-defined platform and commercial reader Impinj R420. The comprehensive test in indoor environments indicates that our proposed algorithm can solve the initial guess problem of the LS-Newton method, ensure the convergence of the algorithm, and finally achieve a probability accuracy of 95% when the localization error is less than 50 cm.

Keywords: RFID · Ranging system · Indoor localization · Iteration · SDP · Initial value

1 Introduction

Global Positioning System (GPS) can achieve the most basic target localization in the outdoors environment, but in the indoor environment, GPS will be unavailable. With the development of personal mobile devices, domestic and foreign scholars have launched research on indoor localization technology. At present, the most commonly used indoor localization technologies include infrared localization technology, WiFi localization technology, ultrasonic localization technology and RFID localization technology. Infrared localization technology uses infrared sensors for distance measurement and angle measurement to achieve target localization. Literature [1] proposes the Active

© Springer Nature Switzerland AG 2021
X. Sun et al. (Eds.): ICAIS 2021, LNCS 12737, pp. 688–699, 2021.
https://doi.org/10.1007/978-3-030-78612-0_56

Badge system which can achieve simultaneous localization of multiple targets. However, infrared rays cannot penetrate obstacles and have a short propagation distance, so this method can only achieve target localization within the line of sight (LoS). Ultrasonic localization technology does not require strict synchronization between systems and can achieve high localization accuracy. Literature [2] proposes the first ultrasonic localization system Active Bat which deploys a large number of transponders, with a 95% probability of achieving localization accuracy within 9 cm. However, ultrasonic localization system requires large-scale layout with many of hardware devices, and the localization result is very sensitive with the environment. Due to the low cost and the ease installation of access points, indoor localization based WiFi [3] signal strengths are becoming increasingly popular. However, due to the abundant multipath in the indoor environment, WiFi has a low localization precision. In RFID localization system, the tag is attached to the object and the radio frequency signal from the reader is modulated by the tag and returned to the reader, then the information of the returned signal is processed to realize the target localization. In recent years, RFID technology has been used in warehouse management, service industries, smart home, logistics and transportation, automated office and other aspects. RFID [4] plays an irreplaceable role in indoor localization due to its low cost, strong anti-interference ability, battery-free, fast identification, etc.

In this context, it is particularly important to improve the distance estimation accuracy of RFID ranging [5] technology. The RFID ranging methods based on the radio frequency (RF) signals can be divided into two categories: received signal strength (RSS) and phase. Based on the RSS-distance estimation model, RSS [6] suffers from poor accuracy and reliability due to multi-path interference. And the method still needs a mass of reference tags or off-line RSSI fingerprint databases. The phase-based method has high sensitivity to distance, but the method based on the time difference of arrival (TDOA) [7, 8] is limited due to the narrow available bandwidth. Another typical method based on phase is based on the angle of arrival (AOA) [9]. Due to the phase ambiguity, the AOA-based method requires that the distance between adjacent antennas is less than half of the wavelength, which is impractical for the directional antennas used in RFID systems.

In order to improve localization accuracy in complex environments, the localization technology based on time sum of arrival (TSOA) has been widely used. TSOA [10] is usually done by measuring the sum of arrival times of signals at the same time by multiple stations. TSOA appears as an ellipse in space, and the target position is obtained by the intersection of several ellipses. Due to the pseudo-linearity of the measurement equation, many scholars have carried out related research. The most classic methods are the classic Newton iteration algorithm (Newton) and the least square (LS) method. The least squares algorithm is applied to multi-station passive localization. The algorithm first converts the nonlinear observation equation into a pseudo-linear observation equation, then constructs an augmented matrix, and performs singular value decomposition of the matrix to estimate the target position, so there is no need to iteratively calculate or obtain a coarse estimate of the target position. However, the LS is susceptible to measurement errors, resulting in a poor localization accuracy. Newton converges fast, and an accurate solution can be obtained quickly in the iterative process, but the convergence problem of Newton is often relying on the selection of initial values. Literature [11] proposed a joint localization algorithm using LS and Newton, but the LS is greatly affected by the ranging error. When the ranging error is large, this algorithm is not applicable.

Based on the above issues, the main contributions of this paper are as follows:

- We design a RFID localization system which uses frequency hopping technology to expand the bandwidth and improve the resolution. Then we use the phase information to achieve the high accuracy ranging.
- We propose a hybrid localization algorithm to solve the local convergence problem caused by the Newton iteration method based on Least squares (LS-Newton). We utilize the semidefinite programming (SDP) algorithm to provide initial values, and then use LS-Newton to complete target localization. The proposed method can effectively solve the initial valve problem and ensure the convergence of the LS-Newton algorithm, as well as improve the convergence speed of iterative algorithm. The experimental result shows that the hybrid localization algorithm has higher localization precision, better algorithm stability and faster convergence speed.

The rest of this paper is organized as follows. Section 2 mainly shows the experimental platform, distance estimation model and target localization model. Section 3 is the experimental analysis and performance comparison of the proposed algorithm. Finally, Sect. 4 provides the conclusion.

2 System Design

Figure 1 shows the system localization architecture, which mainly contains two modules: the distance estimation system and the target localization system. The testing platform is primarily composed of readers, passive tags, and RFID antennas. The two readers are Impinj R420 reader for activating the tag and USRP N210 as transmitter and receiver. As shown in Fig. 1, the Impinj R420 reader transmits a high-power signal to activate the tag. One USRP N210 transmitter sends low power signals, and three USRP N210 receivers receive signals reflected by tags. The RFID antennas we use are directional antennas. Literature [12] shows that directional antennas used at the receiver may help reduce the multipath in the channel as opposed to using omnidirectional antennas. Passive tags have a specific identification number. After the tag is activated, the stored ID information is sent to the receivers through backscatter modulation.

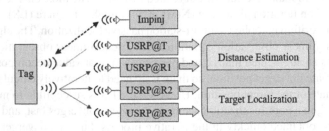

Fig. 1. System localization frame

After the receiver receives the signal, the CFR is obtained through channel estimation. The phase information can be extract from CFR to complete distance estimation [13] and target localization.

2.1 Carrier-Phase Based Distance Estimation

The system emulates a large virtual bandwidth on RFIDs through frequency hopping technology [14, 15] and transmits signals at 20 frequency points, such as 730 MHz–920 MHz with 10 MHz interval.

The phase information can be extract from CFR [16] according to the Eq. (1):

$$\phi = angle(h) \tag{1}$$

where h is the CFR. Due to the frequency points may be lost during the process of collecting data, we use linear interpolation method to compensate the phase information and finally obtain the phase information ($\varphi = [\varphi_1, \varphi_2, ..., \varphi_{20}]$) of the full frequency in 730 MHz–920 MHz. The clock of transmitter and receiver is synchronous, the inherent error generated by the equipment can be eliminated by making a phase difference with the reference point. Assuming the phase of the reference point is $\varphi' = [\varphi'_1, \varphi'_2, ..., \varphi'_{20}]$, then the phase difference between the target point and the reference point can be expressed as:

$$\theta = \varphi - \varphi' = [\varphi_1 - \varphi'_1, \varphi_2 - \varphi'_2, ..., \varphi_{20} - \varphi'_{20}] \tag{2}$$

The channel state information (CSI) can be reconstructed by leveraging the phase difference of Eq. (2):

$$CSI = e^{-j\theta} = \left[e^{-j(\varphi_1 - \varphi'_1)}, e^{-j(\varphi_2 - \varphi'_2)}, ..., e^{-j(\varphi_{20} - \varphi'_{20})} \right] \tag{3}$$

Literature [17] shows that the frequency domain zero padding is performed by adding zeros to a border of data record prior to the inverse fast Fourier transform (IFFT). The IFFT result of the zero-padded signal is viewed as the time sampled version of discrete Fourier transform (DFT) with a finer sampling interval. To obtain more accurate time domain information, the CSI after frequency domain zero-padding is:

$$CSI' = \left[e^{-j(\varphi_1 - \varphi'_1)}, e^{-j(\varphi_2 - \varphi'_2)}, ..., e^{-j(\varphi_{20} - \varphi'_{20})}, 0, 0, ..., 0 \right] \tag{4}$$

The time-domain information after IFFT is:

$$f(t) = IFFT(CSI') \tag{5}$$

where t is the time-of-flight (ToF) of the path. To do this, the coarse distance estimate can be solved by leveraging that: among all the paths of the wireless signal, the direct path is the shortest. Therefore, the ToF of the direct path is the time corresponding to the first peak in the time domain spectrum of Eq. (5). Due to the multipath interference, the coarse distance estimate has the low precision, so we use the multipath suppression method in [18] for multipath suppression, and finally utilize the phase after multipath suppression combined with the Chinese remainder theorem (CRT) [19, 20] to achieve the distance estimation.

2.2 Target Localization Model

Figure 2 is a propagation process of useful signals. Supposing the tag coordinate is (x, y), the transmitter coordinate is (x_0, y_0), the receiver coordinate is (x_i, y_i) $(i = 1, 2, 3)$. The total distance of the target tag is $d_i = r_0 + r_i (i = 1, 2, 3)$, where r_0 is the distance from the tag to the transmitter, and $r_i (i = 1, 2, 3)$ is the distance from the tag to the receiver. $\hat{d}_i = d_i + v_i (i = 1, 2, 3)$ is the measurement total distance containing the distance estimation errors, where $v_i (i = 1, 2, 3)$ is the distance estimation error of each receiver.

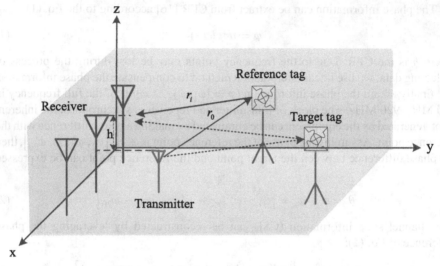

Fig. 2. Propagation process of useful signals

According to the ellipse localization algorithm, the distance error equation is:

$$\begin{cases} \sqrt{(x - x_0)^2 + (y - y_0)^2 + h^2} + \sqrt{(x - x_1)^2 + (y - y_1)^2} = \hat{d}_1 + v_1 \\ \sqrt{(x - x_0)^2 + (y - y_0)^2 + h^2} + \sqrt{(x - x_2)^2 + (y - y_2)^2} = \hat{d}_2 + v_2 \\ \sqrt{(x - x_0)^2 + (y - y_0)^2 + h^2} + \sqrt{(x - x_3)^2 + (y - y_3)^2} = \hat{d}_3 + v_3 \end{cases} \quad (6)$$

where h is the height difference between the transmitter and receiver, and the height of the receiver is the same as the tag.

Obtaining Initial Value of Iteration. LS-Newton method has the fast convergence speed and the algorithm can save much time under the condition of certain localization accuracy. But how to make the LS-Newton method converge is still a problem, which is often associated with the selection of initial values. Solving the initial value problems is the premise of high accuracy of LS-Newton method. We will introduce the SDP estimate value as the initial value of LS-Newton method for iteration calculation, which can realize the optimization of the algorithm.

First, we obtain the initial value of iteration through the SDP algorithm. Without considering the distance estimation error, Eq. (6) can be expressed as:

$$\hat{d}_i = d_i = \sqrt{(x - x_0)^2 + (y - y_0)^2 + h^2} + \sqrt{(x - x_i)^2 + (y - y_i)^2} \tag{7}$$

The matrix form can be obtained by simplifying the Eq. (7) combined with the equations $x - x_i = (x - x_1) - (x_i - x_1)$, $y - y_i = (y - y_1) - (y_i - y_1)$:

$$Az = l \tag{8}$$

where

$$A = \begin{bmatrix} x_1 - x_0 & y_1 - y_0 & -\hat{d}_1 \\ x_2 - x_0 & y_2 - y_0 & -\hat{d}_2 \\ x_3 - x_0 & y_3 - y_0 & -\hat{d}_3 \end{bmatrix} \tag{9}$$

$$l = \frac{1}{2} \begin{bmatrix} (x_1 - x_0)^2 + (y_1 - y_0)^2 - \hat{d}_1^2 - h^2 \\ (x_2 - x_0)^2 + (y_2 - y_0)^2 - \hat{d}_2^2 - h^2 \\ (x_3 - x_0)^2 + (y_3 - y_0)^2 - \hat{d}_3^2 - h^2 \end{bmatrix} \tag{10}$$

$$z = \begin{bmatrix} x - x_0 \\ y - y_0 \\ r_0 \end{bmatrix} \tag{11}$$

Considering the measurement error, Eq. (8) can be expressed as:

$$Az = l - V \tag{12}$$

where $V = [v_1, v_2, v_3]^T$ is measurement error.

The least-square solution of Eq. (12) can be expressed as:

$$z = \arg\min(Az - l)^T(Az - l) \tag{13}$$

$$\text{Subject to } (x - x_0)^2 + (y - y_0)^2 + h^2 = r_0^2 \tag{14}$$

Therefore, the localization process can be modeled into the quadratic constrained quadratic programming problems. In order to linearize the constraint function and objective function, we introduce the redundant variables $Z = zz^T$. However, the rank of the redundant variable is 1, it is not a convex optimization problem. Thus, the LS problem can be transformed into the following convex optimization problem by slacking the rank constraints:

$$\min_{Z,z} tr\left\{ \begin{bmatrix} Z & z \\ z^T & 1 \end{bmatrix} \begin{bmatrix} A^T A & -A^T l \\ -l^T A & l^T l \end{bmatrix} \right\}$$

$$subject\ to \left\{ \begin{bmatrix} Z & zl \\ z^T l & l^2 \end{bmatrix} \Sigma \right\} = 0$$

$$\begin{bmatrix} Z & zl \\ z^T l & l^2 \end{bmatrix} \geq 0$$

$$\begin{bmatrix} Z & z \\ z^T & 1 \end{bmatrix} \geq 0$$

(15)

where $\Sigma = diag(1, 1, -1, 1)$.

The initial localization result can be obtained by Eq. (15). Due to the initial localization result is close to the true values but has low accuracy, we can use it as the initial value of the LS-Newton algorithm for obtaining the optimal solution.

Target Localization. According to Eq. (15), the initial value of iteration can be obtained, assuming that the initial value is (x', y'). We leverage Tylor expansion and omit the quadratic term and above to linearize Eq. (6). The linearized equation is expressed in matrix form as:

$$A'z' - l' = V'$$

(16)

The matrix shown in Eq. (16) is expanded into the following form:

$$\begin{bmatrix} A'_{x1}, & A'_{y1} \\ A'_{x2}, & A'_{y2} \\ A'_{x3}, & A'_{y3} \end{bmatrix} \times \begin{bmatrix} z_x \\ z_y \end{bmatrix} - \begin{bmatrix} l_1 \\ l_2 \\ l_3 \end{bmatrix} = \begin{bmatrix} v_1 \\ v_2 \\ v_3 \end{bmatrix}$$

(17)

where,

$$A'_{xi} = \frac{x'-x_0}{\sqrt{(x'-x_0)^2+(y'-y_0)^2+h^2}} + \frac{x'-x_i}{\sqrt{(x'-x_i)^2+(y'-y_i)^2}}$$

$$A'_{yi} = \frac{y'-y_0}{\sqrt{(x'-x_0)^2+(y'-y_0)^2+h^2}} + \frac{y'-y_i}{\sqrt{(x'-x_i)^2+(y'-y_i)^2}}$$

$$l_i = \hat{d}_i - \left(\sqrt{(x'-x_0)^2 + (y'-y_0)^2 + h^2} + \sqrt{(x'-x_i)^2 + (y'-y_i)^2} \right)$$

$$z_x = x - x'$$

$$z_y = y - y'$$

(18)

According to Eq. (16), we can obtain the least square estimation by Eq. (19):

$$z' = \arg\min_z (V^T V)$$

(19)

By giving an upper threshold ε, the final localization result $[x, y] = [x' + z_x, y' + z_y]$ can be obtained by solving Eq. (19) when the condition $|z_x| + |z_y| < \varepsilon$ is satisfied. The system localization process is shown in Fig. 3.

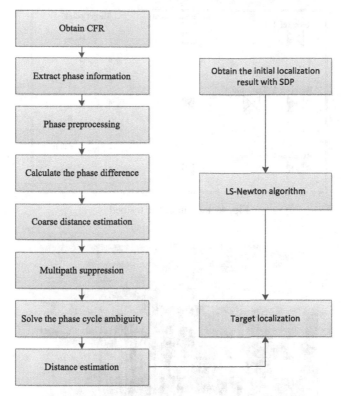

Fig. 3. Flowchart of the localization system

3 Evaluation Measurement Results

We design RFID system on four USRP N210 software radios which are all synchronized, three of them are used as receiver and the rest one is used as transmitter. Due to the low power of the transmitter which cannot activate the tag to communicate with the readers, another commercial reader Impinj R420 is adopted. We conduct experiment in a small and empty room with a size of 5×5 m^2. Figure 4 shows the layouts of the testbed. Figure 5 shows the test prototype in an empty room.

As shown in Fig. 4, three receivers are placed in a row, and we mainly complete distance estimation and localization for 21 target points. The coordinates of the three receivers are (35 cm, 0 cm), (35 cm, 75 cm), (35 cm, 150 cm), the coordinate of the transmitter is (66 cm, 75 cm), the coordinates of the reference points are (0 cm, 150 cm), (75 cm, 150 cm), (150 cm, 150 cm). Among them, the reference point of known information is used to eliminate the inherent error between the devices. According to the distance estimation process, we can get the distance estimation result of each receiver for each position. Figure 6 is the CDFs of the distance estimation error.

As shown in Fig. 6, three receivers can achieve the median ranging accuracy are 3 cm, 5 cm and 1.5 cm, respectively. Although the clocks between the receivers are synchronized, there are still errors between the devices. And in actual measurement

	Reference point	Target point
Receiver 3 ⋈	⊠ 3	⊠ 7 ⊠ 14 ⊠ 21
		⊠ 6 ⊠ 13 ⊠ 20
		⊠ 5 ⊠ 12 ⊠ 19
Receiver 2 Transmitter ⋈ ⋈	⊠ 2	⊠ 4 ⊠ 11 ⊠ 18
		⊠ 3 ⊠ 10 ⊠ 17
		⊠ 2 ⊠ 9 ⊠ 16
Receiver 1 ⋈	⊠ 1	⊠ 1 ⊠ 8 ⊠ 15

Fig. 4. Layout of the testbed

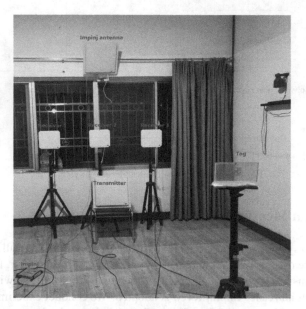

Fig. 5. Prototype of the test

environment as shown in Fig. 5, there is a table and other debris placed on the left of receiver 1, which causes serious multipath interference. On the right side of the receiver 3, there are no other obstacles except the wall, and the effect of multipath interference on the receiver 3 is small, so the receiver 3 has better ranging accuracy than the receiver 1. For the receiver 2, it can be found in Fig. 5 that the signals emitted by the Impinj antenna and the transmitter will affect the receiver 2, resulting in a decrease in ranging accuracy. In addition, the phase center of the directional antenna used in the system cannot be determined, which will lead to equipment measurement deviations and a decrease in ranging accuracy.

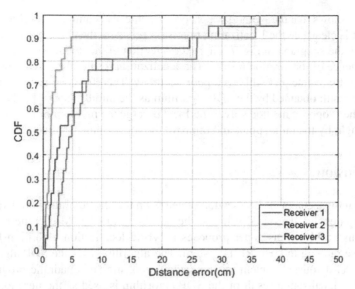

Fig. 6. CDFs of the ranging error

As shown in Fig. 4, the relative position between the tag and the receiver will also affect the ranging results. For example, the target position in the corner tends to have a poor ranging accuracy due to its lower signal-to-noise ratio, such as position 18 and position 21. Using the ranging result for target localization, the localization result is shown in Fig. 7.

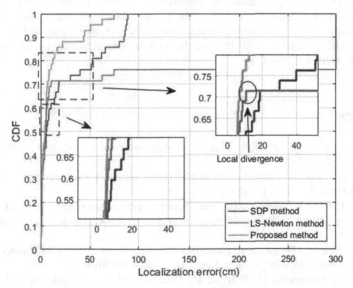

Fig. 7. CDFs with different localization algorithm

Figure 7 shows that the method we proposed achieves centimeter-level localization accuracy. It is clear that the localization precision relies on the choice of initial points. As shown in the subgraph in Fig. 7, improper selection of the initial point will result in local divergence of localization results. The localization result of the SDP algorithm is closer to the true value, but still has a poor accuracy. Therefore, we can use the initial localization result obtained by the SDP algorithm as the initial value of LS-Newton. As expected, the proposed method solves the local divergence problem of the localization results brought by the initial point and improve the localization accuracy.

4   Conclusion

The localization accuracy of LS-Newton depends on the choice of the initial value. LS-Newton requires that the initial value of the iteration must be close to the true value. To solve this problem, this paper proposes a hybrid localization algorithm based on carrier phase ranging in UHF RFID system. The algorithm uses the SDP algorithm to convert the least square problem into a quadratic constrained quadratic programming problem. The localization result of the SDP algorithm is used as the iteration's initial coordinates to complete the final target localization. Experimental results show that in this system, the average ranging error of the three receivers is less than 10 cm with a probability of 84%, and the final localization error is less than 50 cm with a probability of 95%. Compared with other algorithms, the proposed hybrid localization algorithm has better convergence performance. In addition, this paper solves the initial point selection problem of the LS-Newton method, and realizes the optimization of the algorithm.

Acknowledgment. This work was supported in part by the Science and Technology Research Project of Chongqing Education Commission (KJZD-K202000605, KJQN202000630, KJQN201800625, KJQN201900603), the Chongqing Natural Science Foundation Project (cstc2020jcyj-msxmX0842, cstc2020jcyj-msxmX0865, cstc2019jcyj-msxmX0635, cstc2019jcyj-msxmX0742, cstc2019jcyj-msxmX0108), and the National Natural Science Foundation of China (61771083, 61901076, 61704015).

References

1. Want, R., Hopper, A., Falcao, V., et al.: The active badge location system. ACM Trans. Inf. Syst. **10**(1), 91–102 (1992)
2. Harter, A., Hopper, A., Steggles, P., et al.: The anatomy of a context-aware application. Wireless Netw. **8**(2), 187–197 (2002)
3. Kotaru, M., Joshi, K., Bharadia, D., et al.: Spotfi: decimeter level localization using wifi. In: Proceedings of the 2015 ACM Conference on Special Interest Group on Data Communication, pp. 269–282 (2015)
4. Zhou, C., Griffin, J.D.: Accurate phase-based ranging measurements for backscatter RFID tags. IEEE Antennas Wirel. Propag. Lett. **11**(2), 152–155 (2012)
5. Arnitz, D., Muehlmann, U., Witrisal, K.: Characterization and modeling of UHF RFID channels for ranging and localization. IEEE Trans. Antennas Propag. **60**(5), 2491–2501 (2012)

6. Ouyang, R.W., Wong, A.K.S., Lea, C.T.: Received signal strength-based wireless localization via semidefinite programming: noncooperative and cooperative schemes. IEEE Trans. Veh. Technol. **59**(3), 1307–1318 (2010)
7. So, H.C., Chan, Y.T., Chan, F.K.W.: Closed-form formulae for time-difference-of-arrival estimation. IEEE Trans. Sig. Process. **56**(6), 2614–3262 (2008)
8. Bard, J.D., Ham, F.M.: Time difference of arrival dilution of precision and applications. IEEE Trans. Sig. Process. **47**(2), 521–523 (1999)
9. Kulakowski, P., Alonso, J.V.: Angle-of-arrival localization based on antenna arrays for wireless sensor networks. Comput. Electr. Eng. **36**(6), 1181–1186 (2010)
10. Zheng, X., Hua, J., Zheng, Z., et al.: Wireless localization based on the time sum of arrival and Taylor expansion. In: 2013 19th IEEE International Conference on Networks, pp. 1–4. IEEE (2013)
11. Lv, J., Yao, J.: Aerial target localization based on least squares and Newton iterative algorithm. Microelectron. Comput. **28**(9), 108–110 (2011)
12. Dabin, J.A., Haimovich, A.M., Grebel, H.: A statistical ultra-wideband indoor channel model and the effects of antenna directivity on path loss and multipath propagation. IEEE J. Sel. Areas Commun. **24**(4), 752–758 (2006)
13. Tamura, T., Kumar, S.: Evolutionary distance estimation under heterogeneous substitution pattern among lineages. Mol. Biol. Evol. **19**(10), 1727–1736 (2002)
14. Liang, W., Liu, S., Yang, Y., Li, S.: Research of adaptive frequency hopping technology in WIA-PA industrial wireless network. In: Wang, R., Xiao, Fu. (eds.) CWSN 2012. CCIS, vol. 334, pp. 248–262. Springer, Heidelberg (2013). https://doi.org/10.1007/978-3-642-36252-1_23
15. Cormio, C., Chowdhury, K.R.: Common control channel design for cognitive radio wireless ad hoc networks using adaptive frequency hopping. Ad Hoc Netw. **8**(4), 430–438 (2010)
16. Zaghloul, H., Morrison, G., Fattouche, M.: Frequency response and path loss measurements of indoor channel. Electron. Lett. **27**(12), 1021–1022 (1991)
17. Shin, J.G., Kim, J.W., Lee, J.H.: Accurate reconstruction of digital holography using frequency domain zero padding. In: 25th International Conference on Optical Fiber Sensors, pp. 1–4. OFS, Korea (2017)
18. Ma, Y., Selby, N., Adib, F.: Minding the billions: ultra-wideband localization for deployed RFID tags. In: the 23rd Annual International Conference, pp. 248–260. MobiCom (2017)
19. Yen, S.M., Kim, S., Lim, S., et al.: RSA speedup with Chinese remainder theorem immune against hardware fault cryptanalysis. IEEE Trans. Comput. **52**(4), 461–472 (2003)
20. Li, X., Liang, H., Xia, X.G.: A robust Chinese remainder theorem with its applications in frequency estimation from undersampled waveforms. IEEE Trans. Signal Process. **57**(11), 4314–4322 (2009)

Multimedia Forensics

Trusted Digital Asset Copyright Confirmation and Transaction Mechanism Based on Consortium Blockchain

Shaoyong Guo[1], Cheng Huang[1(✉)], Yong Yan[2], Liandong Chen[3], and Sujie Shao[1]

[1] State Key Laboratory of Networking and Switching Technology, BUPT, Beijing 100876, China
makoto@bupt.edu.cn
[2] Zhejiang Electric Power Corporation, Hangzhou 310014, China
[3] Hebei Electric Power Corporation, Shijiazhuang 050022, China

Abstract. Aiming at the problems of low transaction efficiency, digital asset copyright and transaction privacy in traditional digital asset trading platforms, based on alliance chain technology, this paper proposes a decentralized digital asset trustworthy copyright confirmation and transaction mechanism, which combines The common digital watermark technology in the field of traditional digital asset copyright confirmation and the common homomorphic encryption technology in the field of cloud computing solves the problem of user data privacy protection in the process of embedding digital watermark on the chain. And combined with smart contract technology to solve the problem of security and credibility of digital assets in the process of confirming the chain and transactions, realizing the confirmation of digital copyright and the traceability of transactions on the chain. Finally, experimental simulations prove that the reform mechanism can stably handle the copyright confirmation of digital asset transactions under normal circumstances, and basically meet the digital asset transaction needs of users.

Keywords: Consortium blockchain · Digital asset transaction · Credible confirmation of copyrights · Smart contract

1 Introduction

Now that we are in an information society, both companies and individuals may generate electronic data related to themselves in their daily production and life. As a kind of invisible asset, these data were often not fully managed and utilized in the past. In fact, through the use of scientific digital asset management methods, the potential value of digital assets can be maximized. In recent years, there have been researches on digital asset management and trading. As a kind of sensitive data, a centralized system can guarantee the security and reliability of them. However, in terms of digital asset trading, traditional digital asset trading platforms inevitably suffer from various problems in terms of system closure, difficulty in expansion, credible data, privacy protection, and transaction efficiency due to their centralization. As a new technology that is transparent,

© Springer Nature Switzerland AG 2021
X. Sun et al. (Eds.): ICAIS 2021, LNCS 12737, pp. 703–714, 2021.
https://doi.org/10.1007/978-3-030-78612-0_57

open, credible and decentralized, blockchain has gradually been used in the construction of digital asset trading platforms [1, 2].

The existing digital asset trading platform projects based on the public chain are restricted by factors such as increasing block size, too long data confirmation time, and too low block transaction frequency, and cannot serve the management of digital asset transactions well. Related applications. Therefore, it is necessary to combine the consortium blockchain technology to design a trusted transaction mechanism of digital assets based on the consortium blockchain, and rely on the weak centralization of the consortium blockchain to solve the problems of the public chain system in terms of digital asset transaction efficiency and consensus efficiency.

At the same time, digital assets are a commodity in the transaction process. If the ownership of rights cannot be determined, digital asset transactions cannot be conducted normally. Existing digital copyright protection methods are centralized registration, and there are problems of difficulty in confirming rights, serious piracy, poor publicity, and high cost of rights protection. Therefore, it is necessary to combine consortium blockchain technology to design a credible digital asset based on consortium blockchain. The copyright confirmation mechanism realizes the protection of the ownership, possession, use and income rights of digital assets.

This paper proposes a trustworthy copyright confirmation and transaction mechanism for digital assets based on the consortium blockchain, which combines traditional digital asset copyright confirmation methods with consortium blockchain technology to solve the security and credibility issues in the digital asset transaction process, and finally realize Centralized, transaction traceable and efficient digital asset credible copyright confirmation and transaction. Digital assets are actually all digitizable assets, including Bitcoin, digital intellectual property, digital equity, digital income rights, and various digital currencies. The most important point for digital assets to be tradable is digital identity. Blockchain is driven by algorithms and naturally supports the digitization of assets.

2 Related Work

2.1 Digital Asset Trading Platform

Digital assets are actually all digitizable assets, including Bitcoin, digital intellectual property, digital equity, digital income rights, and various digital currencies. The most important point for digital assets to be tradable is digital identity. Blockchain is driven by algorithms and naturally supports the digitization of assets [3, 4].

Among the digital asset applications, the most familiar one is digital money. Digital money is also called Ecash or Emoney, which is regarded as a simulation of real currency, involving users, merchants and Centralized bank or third-party payment institution. Bubi Company released the Bumeng digital asset platform in 2016. At present, the platform only provides services such as the issuance, transfer, and query of digital assets for enterprises and developers, and cannot customize the development of the basic blockchain platform, and the specific performance of the system lacks authoritative data. In 2017, ZhongAn Technology launched a digital asset platform called "Extreme Line" to circulate digital assets such as commercial points, coupons, and electronic insurance policies through the blockchain. At present, the platform only provides enterprises with application access functions.. It can be seen from this that blockchain technology has already had a certain application in the field of digital asset trading. Therefore, this article uses blockchain technology as the basis to design a credible trading mechanism for digital assets.

2.2 Homomorphic Encryption

In recent years, cloud computing has received widespread attention, and one of the problems encountered in its implementation is how to ensure the privacy of data. Fully homomorphic encryption can solve this technical problem to a certain extent [5].

Specifically, homomorphic encryption refers to an encryption function that performs addition and multiplication operations on the plaintext and then encrypts it, and performs corresponding operations on the ciphertext after encryption, and the result is equivalent. Because of this good nature, people can entrust an untrusted third party to process data without revealing information. Therefore, homomorphic encryption has important applications in cloud computing and e-government [6, 7].

Fully homomorphic encryption provides a theoretical solution for the privacy and security of computing on the consortium blockchain. It can complete the processing of ciphertext without revealing sensitive information, and has inherent protection of user data security and privacy The feature of, to a large extent solves the data security problem in the calculation of the consortium blockchain. Simply put, the user can encrypt the data and save it in the consortium blockchain in a secret form. Unless the private key of the encryptor is obtained, no one can obtain the plaintext. But the consortium blockchain can perform meaningful operations on the ciphertext on the chain. Fully homomorphic encryption allows reasonable use of such encrypted data without affecting user privacy.

2.3 Digital Watermarking Technology

Digital watermarking refers to embedding identification information into the data carrier to achieve the purpose of version protection, confidential communication, document authenticity identification and product identification. The embedded information does not affect the use of the data carrier and cannot be easily extracted or modified. Once ownership disputes occur, the watermark can be extracted for testing to prove the ownership of the copyright. In the digital asset transaction scenario, digital assets are transmitted in the form of data throughout the transaction process, so digital watermarking technology can be used to achieve effective protection of the copyright of digital assets [8].

At the same time, in view of the user data privacy protection problem when watermarking is embedded in the consortium blockchain, the digital watermarking scheme based on fully homomorphic encryption can effectively resist this attack [9–11]. This scheme first uses a fully homomorphic encryption system to encrypt the watermark signal and the original carrier, and then embeds the encrypted watermark into the original carrier. Before the user detects the watermark, the carrier containing the watermark must be homomorphically decrypted to ensure that there is no obvious correlation between the decrypted watermark signal and the watermarked carrier [12–14]. After decrypting the watermarked carrier, the correlation between the decrypted carrier and the watermark signal can be calculated to determine the existence of the watermark and then extract the watermark.

3   System Structure

The main purpose of this system is to realize the issuance and copyright confirmation of digital assets, the storage of copyright confirmation information and the functions of asset trading. Since the transaction is only visible to the accessing user, and the transaction process is completely executed inside the system, the system adopts the consortium blockchain model with authority control. In order to realize the credible copyright confirmation mechanism of digital assets on the basis of the consortium blockchain and comprehensively analyze actual needs, it is necessary to make detailed designs for the issuance and copyright confirmation of digital assets, the storage of copyright confirmation information on the chain, and the asset copyright confirmation and transaction mechanism. The overall model of the digital asset copyright confirmation and transaction system based on the consortium blockchain is shown in Fig. 1.

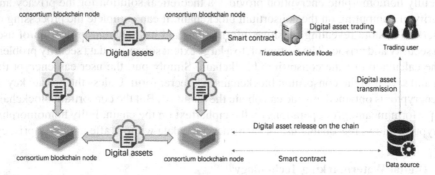

Fig. 1. System model diagram

The trusted copyright confirmation and transaction model of digital assets based on the consortium blockchain is divided into three parts: consortium blockchain nodes, data sources and transaction users. The data source first prepares the digital assets to be put on the chain, and then sends the digital asset copyright confirmation request to the consortium blockchain node, and then the digital asset completes the digital watermark generation and digital watermark embedding processes on the chain, and finally the digital asset related information is uploaded to the consortium blockchain and stored together to ensure the credibility and non-tampering of the digital asset copyright confirmation results. The transaction service node is responsible for receiving the data asset transaction request from the transaction user. After receiving the request, the transaction service node will call the corresponding smart contract to complete the transaction process on the chain and return the result to the user. The transaction user completes the digital asset transaction transmission process by interacting with the digital asset data source server after receiving the necessary information for the transaction returned by the transaction service node. The consortium blockchain node mainly completes core business processing in the entire system model, calls smart contracts to complete the generation and embedding of digital watermarks, digital asset copyright confirmation and transactions, and package copyright confirmation and transaction results into blocks, which are written after consensus Consortium chain ledger. The consortium blockchain device node is jointly maintained by different institutions in the digital asset trading system to form a distributed and credible consortium blockchain server network.

Transaction authentication and data credible storage are the basic features of the consortium blockchain technology, which can ensure that the data information and transaction records stored on the chain cannot be tampered with, and provide a guarantee for the credible storage of digital asset information and the traceability of digital asset transactions. Therefore, we can base on the two basic functions of transaction consensus authentication and data credible storage, combined with smart contract technology, to support the various functions required by the entire system, including the realization of digital asset copyright confirmation, transaction user management, and digital watermark management As well as digital asset transactions and other functions, and finally with the support of these contract functions, the entire digital asset trust copyright confirmation and transaction mechanism is realized. The specific process will be described in detail in the next chapter.

4 Trusted Copyright Confirmation and Transaction Mechanism of Digital Assets

In order to be able to effectively confirm rights during the use of digital assets and safeguard the interests of digital asset providers, we use digital watermarking technology to solve the problem of copyright protection of digital assets. Considering that there are multiple storage forms of digital assets such as text, audio, video, and images, a single digital watermark embedding algorithm is difficult to meet the needs of actual use. At the same time, the current digital watermark embedding algorithms for various carrier media are very mature. Therefore, we choose not to pay attention to the specific watermark embedding algorithm design in this article, and focus on the overall process design. The process of credible copyright confirmation of digital assets is shown in Fig. 2.

4.1 The Process of Digital Asset Encryption and Release on the Blockchain

In the consortium blockchain system, the CA node is responsible for the access authentication and identity certificate issuance of the node in the system, so we can consider the CA node to be absolutely credible. In order to solve the problem of data privacy in the process of digital asset transaction, when both parties of the transaction access the consortium blockchain system for the first time, the CA node will distribute the various keys needed for encryption and decryption in the entire process according to its identity.

In the entire transaction process, the storage of digital assets and the generation and embedding of watermarks are performed on the chain, which can effectively prevent data sources from tampering with digital assets on the chain and embedding illegal watermarks. In view of the data leakage and data privacy protection issues faced in the process of storage and watermark embedding on the digital asset chain, we chose to

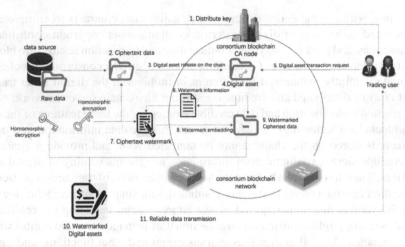

Fig. 2. Digital asset copyright confirmation and transaction flow chart

use homomorphic encryption technology to encrypt digital assets before they are on the chain, and adopt homomorphic encryption watermark embedding technology to ensure On the premise that data privacy is not leaked, it is ensured that the encrypted data after the watermark embedding can be successfully restored. The specific algorithm flow of digital asset on-chain processing is as follows:

Algorithm1 Digital Asset Encryption

Input : DA(digital asset) , DSI(data source info)

Output : EDA(encrypted digital asset) , DAD(digital asset description)

1: DSI send to CA

2: Key ← CA.generateKey(DSI)

3: Key send to DS

4: EDA ← DS.HomomorphicEncryption(DA, Key)

5: DAD ← DS.GenerateDescription(DA, DSI)

6: Return EDA,DAD

When a data source accesses the consortium chain system for the first time, it needs to submit the identity information DSI to the CA node to complete identity authentication. The CA node generates and distributes the key required for homomorphic encryption after confirming the identity of the data source. After the data source receives the key, the digital asset DA on the chain is encrypted to obtain the ciphertext data EDA. Finally, the data source also needs to generate description information of the digital asset, including but not limited to digital asset type, digital asset size, complete data HASH value, transaction pricing and other information. After completing the above operations, the data source calls the smart contract interface of digital asset copyright confirmation on-chain to complete the asset on-chain operation. The specific flowchart is shown in Fig. 3.

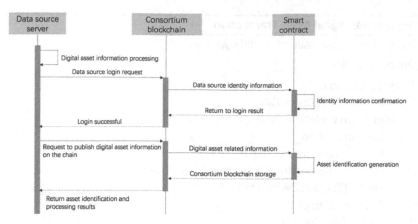

Fig. 3. Flow chart of digital asset release on the chain

From the figure, we can see that the data source server will initiate a login request and a request for digital asset information on the chain to the consortium blockchain platform after completing the homomorphic encryption processing of the digital asset and the integration of the description information. After the consortium chain completes the verification of the identity information of the data source, the process of digital asset copyright confirmation and chaining is completed through smart contracts.

4.2 Trusted Transaction Process of Digital Assets

After the digital asset completes the process of confirming the rights and going on the chain, it can be retrieved by the users on the chain. Transactions on the consortium blockchain rely on smart contracts. Smart contracts may require customized operations in the face of different transaction needs of both parties to the transaction. Therefore, after both parties send a transaction request to the consortium blockchain, they need to confirm the transaction contract. If the existing contract If the demand cannot be met, it needs to initiate a request to establish a transaction contract to the consortium blockchain. After establishing a transaction contract that meets the needs, call it to finally complete the digital asset transaction process. The key operations in the process will complete the consensus certification in the consortium blockchain. The consortium blockchain consensus adopts the PBFT fault-tolerant mechanism. The research on the reform mechanism is now very comprehensive, so we will not repeat it here.

In the process of calling the digital asset transaction contract, the user first needs to authenticate the identity information at the transaction service node, and then the transaction service node forwards the transaction request to the consortium blockchain node. The consortium blockchain node processes the transaction contract and broadcasts the transaction completion consensus, and finally returns the transaction result to the transaction user. The flow of digital asset trading algorithm is shown in the figure below.

Algorithm2 Digital Asset Transaction

Input : DAI(digital asset info) , BI(buyer info)

Output : result

1: DAI,BI send to CB
2: price ← CB. PriceCheck(DAI)
3: wallet ← CB.WalletCheck(BI)
4: **if** wallet>price **then**
5:      EDA ← CB.RetrieveData(DSI)
6:      DWM ← CB.GenerateWatermark(EDA, BI, timestamp)
7:      DSI ← CB.QueryOwner(DAI)
8:      DWM send to DS
9:      Key ← DS.QueryKey
10:     EDWM ← DS.HomomorphicEncryption(DWM, Key)
11:     EWDA ← CB.WatermarkEmbed(EDWM, EDA)
12:     EWDA, BI send to DS
13:     DSI send to Buyer
14:     CB.WalletDeduction(wallet, price)
15:     CB.TransactionRecord(BI, DAI, timestamp)
16:     Return result ← Successful transaction
17: **else**
18:     return ← false with Insufficient wallet balance

Transaction users initiate digital asset transactions by submitting identity information BI and the digital asset information DAI that they intend to trade to the Consortium
Blockchain (CB). The smart contract confirms that the price of the digital asset is less
than the user's wallet balance and enters the digital asset transaction process, otherwise
the transaction failure result is returned. After entering the transaction process, the smart
contract first extracts the encrypted digital asset ciphertext data EDA according to the
digital asset information DAI. After that, the smart contract combines the ciphertext
data EDA, transaction user information BI, and timestamp to generate a unique digital
watermark DWM (digital watermark). Then the smart contract extracts the data source
information DSI (data source info) based on the digital asset information DAI, and
sends the digital watermark DWM to the data source DS (data source) to complete the
homomorphic encryption operation to obtain the encrypted digital water mark EDWM
(encrypted digital water mark). Finally, the data source DS returns the encrypted digital
watermark EDWM to the smart contract. The smart contract uses a digital watermark
embedding algorithm based on homomorphic encryption to watermark the cipher text
data EDA to obtain the encrypted watermarked digital asset EWDA (encrypted watermarked digital asset) and Return it to the data source DS along with the purchase user
information BI. After completing the above whole process, the smart contract calculates
and records the transaction, and returns the transaction result and data source information
to the buyer.

5   Simulation Results and Analysis

This system builds the consortium blockchain test environment by arranging 6 virtual machines with the same configuration. The basic configuration of each virtual machine is: single-core CPU, 2G memory, ubuntu16.04 LTS operating system. The entire experiment was carried out in a local area network environment, using the PBFT consensus mechanism to exclude the influence of network bandwidth and consensus mechanism on the experimental results. Among the six virtual machines, in order to ensure the minimum fault tolerance of the PBFT consensus mechanism, we choose four virtual machines as the consortium blockchain nodes, one virtual machine as the consortium blockchain CA node, and one virtual machine as the transaction service node.

In the experiment, we take the system transaction processing rate and the average transaction delay during concurrent transactions as the main indicators to evaluate the transaction performance of the system. The specific calculation formulas of these two indicators are as follows:

Average transaction delay = total transaction delay/number of transactions.

Transaction processing rate = number of normally processed transactions/total number of transactions.

The experimental results obtained when a single transaction data is 100 bytes are shown in Fig. 4:

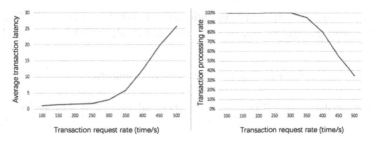

Fig. 4.   Graph of transaction performance experiment results

As can be seen from the figure, in a distributed network composed of 4 consortium blockchain nodes, when the PBFT consensus mechanism is adopted, the average transaction delay gradually increases with the increase of the transaction request rate. When the transaction request rate reaches 350 transactions/s, The average transaction latency began to increase significantly. At the same time, the transaction processing rate can be maintained at the highest level of 100% when the transaction request rate is low, and it starts to gradually decrease when the transaction request rate is higher than 300 transactions/s. Comprehensive analysis of the two indicators shows that when the transaction request rate received by the system is below 350 transactions/s, it has a better operating effect.

The comparison between the results of this experiment and traditional centralized systems is shown in Table 1 (traditional centralized systems have relatively single transaction functions, so you can choose a single transaction data size of 100 bytes as a reference):

Table 1. System comparison

System features	Digital asset transaction based on consortium blockchain	Centralized point exchange platform
System structure	Distributed	B/S, C/S
Data storage method	Data blockchain storage	Central database storage
Transaction processing capacity	350 times/s	100 times/s
Average response delay	3.5 s	5–7 s
System fault tolerance	Fault tolerant	No fault tolerance
Inter-agency transactions	Support	Not support

It can be seen from the table that the performance of the trustworthy copyright confirmation transaction mechanism of digital assets based on the consortium blockchain is superior to that of the traditional centralized digital asset trading platform. It has corresponding fault tolerance according to the number of nodes in the consortium blockchain, and it also has cross-institutional capabilities. The ability to trade can meet the needs of small and medium-sized alliances for cross-institutional digital asset trustworthy transactions.

At the same time, using the same evaluation criteria as before, in the case of increasing the size of a single transaction data, the experimental results in Table 2 can be obtained.

Table 2. Transaction performance comparison

Single transaction data volume (byte)	Optimal transaction rate (time/s)
100	350
200	220
300	150
400	90

It can be seen that the amount of data in a single transaction also has a significant impact on the transaction rate. However, in actual use, the ability of consortium blockchain nodes to process high concurrent transactions is also closely related to their own hardware configuration. Using methods to appropriately increase CPU performance and memory size, and improve network conditions can effectively improve consortium blockchain nodes. Transaction processing capabilities. Therefore, we can think that the credible copyright confirmation and transaction mechanism of digital assets based on the consortium blockchain can meet the normal use needs.

6 Conclusion

This paper aims at the copyright protection, transaction credibility, privacy protection and other issues in the traditional digital asset transaction system. Based on the consortium blockchain technology, it adopts the method of combining the traditional digital watermark and the consortium blockchain to realize the digital assets on the chain after the transaction. Effective and credible copyright confirmation of rights, and finally designed a credible copyright confirmation transaction mechanism for digital assets. After the simulation test of the reform mechanism, it can be seen that the mechanism can achieve the design goal, realize the efficient and reliable transaction of digital assets on the chain, and has the ability of inter-agency transactions that the traditional centralized platform does not have, but the current system Simulations were performed only in the environment of four consortium blockchain nodes and the amount of data was relatively small. It has not been confirmed whether the consensus mechanism and complex network conditions have a significant impact on transaction efficiency under large-scale experiments. Therefore, in the future work, further research and optimization will be made on the consortium blockchain consensus mechanism and network communication mechanism, so that the mechanism can achieve better transaction processing capabilities.

Acknowledgement. First of all, I would like to extend my sincere gratitude to my supervisor, Shaoyong Guo, for his instructive advice and useful suggestions on my thesis. I am deeply grateful of his help in the completion of this thesis. I am also deeply indebted to all the other tutors and teachers in Translation Studies for their direct and indirect help to me. Special thanks should go to my friends who have put considerable time and effort into their comments on the draft. Finally, I am indebted to my parents for their continuous support and encouragement.

Funding Statement. This work is supported by:
1. National Key R&D Program of China (2018YFB1402704)
2. the National Natural Science Foundation of China (62071070)
3. Test bed construction of industrial Internet platform in specific scenes (new mode)

Conflicts of Interest. The authors declare that they have no conflicts of interest to report regarding the present study.

References

1. Zhu, Y., Qin, Y., Zhou, Z., Song, X., Liu, G., Chu, W.C.: Digital asset management with distributed permission over blockchain and attribute-based access control. In: 2018 IEEE International Conference on Services Computing (SCC), San Francisco, CA, pp. 193–200 (2018)
2. Chomsiri, T., Pansa, D.: JSP digital asset trading system. In: 2019 23rd International Computer Science and Engineering Conference (ICSEC), Phuket, Thailand, pp. 255–260 (2019)
3. Zheng, J., Dong, X., Liu, Q., Zhu, X., Tong, W.: Blockchain-based secure digital asset exchange scheme with QoS-aware incentive mechanism. In: 2019 IEEE 20th International Conference on High Performance Switching and Routing (HPSR), Xi'An, China, pp. 1–6 (2019)

4. Takeuchi, T., Shimizu, T., Kamakura, K., Shimoyama, T., Tsuda, H.: A limited-use asset management system on the blockchain platform with an extended open assets protocol. In: 2017 23RD Annual International Conference in Advanced Computing and Communications (ADCOM), Bangalore, India, pp. 1–7 (2017)
5. Mahmood, Z.H., Ibrahem, M.K.: New fully homomorphic encryption scheme based on multistage partial homomorphic encryption applied in cloud computing. In: 2018 1st Annual International Conference on Information and Sciences (AiCIS), Fallujah, Iraq, pp. 182–186 (2018)
6. Song, X., Wang, Y.: Homomorphic cloud computing scheme based on hybrid homomorphic encryption. In: 2017 3rd IEEE International Conference on Computer and Communications (ICCC), Chengdu, pp. 2450–2453 (2017)
7. Kangavalli, R., Vagdevi, S.: A mixed homomorphic encryption scheme for secure data storage in cloud. In: 2015 IEEE International Advance Computing Conference (IACC), Banglore, pp. 1062–1066 (2015)
8. Chen, N., Zhu, J.: A multipurpose audio watermarking scheme for copyright protection and content authentication. In: 2008 IEEE International Conference on Multimedia and Expo, Hannover, pp. 221–224 (2008)
9. Lin, C., Liu, J., Shih, C., Lee, Y.: A robust watermark scheme for copyright protection. In: 2008 International Conference on Multimedia and Ubiquitous Engineering (MUE 2008), Busan, pp. 132–137 (2008)
10. Dhar, P.K., Echizen, I.: Robust FFT based watermarking scheme for copyright protection of digital audio data. In: 2011 Seventh International Conference on Intelligent Information Hiding and Multimedia Signal Processing, Dalian, pp. 181–184 (2011)
11. Xuehua, J.: Digital watermarking and its application in image copyright protection. In: 2010 International Conference on Intelligent Computation Technology and Automation, Changsha, pp. 114–117 (2010)
12. Al-Afandy, K.A., Faragallah, O.S., EL-Rabaie, E.M., El-Samie, F.E.A., ELmhalawy, A.: Efficient color image watermarking using homomorphic based SVD in DWT domain. In: 2016 Fourth International Japan-Egypt Conference on Electronics, Communications and Computers (JEC-ECC), Cairo, pp. 43–47 (2016)
13. Singh, J., Kaur, P.: Digital image watermarking of homomorphic encrypted images: a review. In: 2016 International Conference on Electrical, Electronics, and Optimization Techniques (ICEEOT), Chennai, pp. 1790–1793 (2016)
14. Khare, P., Srivastava, V.K.: Image watermarking scheme using homomorphic transform in wavelet domain. In: 2018 5th IEEE Uttar Pradesh Section International Conference on Electrical, Electronics and Computer Engineering (UPCON), Gorakhpur, pp. 1–6 (2018)

Automatic Source Camera Identification Technique Based-on Hierarchy Clustering Method

Zhimao Lai[1(✉)], Yufei Wang[2], Weize Sun[3], and Peng Zhang[3]

[1] China People's Police University, Guangzhou 510663, China
[2] Sino-Singapore International Joint Research Institute, Guangzhou 510700, China
[3] Shenzhen University, Shenzhen 518000, China

Abstract. Many existing source camera identification technique depend on a set of images of known origins to train a classifier or to acquire the reference pattern noise of camera, and match the being tested images. However, it is hard to get the natural images which are the same type of tested image as training image library in our actual applications. In this work, we propose the automatic source camera identification technique based-on Hierarchy Clustering method, which can formulate the classification task without any training image library. Experimental results have verified the validity and practicality of the proposed approach at last.

Keywords: Source camera identification · Image sensor · Hierarchy clustering · Correlation-based detection

1 Introduction

In recent years, the digital camera is becoming more and more convenient for photo acquisition, and digital images are wildly used in daily life. As a result, the use of digital images in forensic investigations becomes more frequent and important [1–4]. The source camera identification [5–8] is one of the most techniques for image forensics, which has become a hot research area and attracted a lot of attention from researchers.

The most common usage of source camera identification is link digital images to an exact camera. Different camera model produced by different manufacturer usually uses different lenses and sensors. Moreover, they also use different signal post-processing methods, including demosaicing, gamma correction, color correction, white balance, compression, and so on. When different cameras capture the same scene to generate digital images, the style and the quality of the images will be different though they have the same content. By extracting and analyzing the features from the images, source camera identification can be carried out. By using the technique of source camera identification, the images generated by the same camera can be grouped from a large set of images, and the relevance between an exact image and an exact camera can be proved.

The existing techniques for source camera identification can be grouped into 3 types [9]. The first type extracts the statistical features from color, quality, wavelet coefficients,

© Springer Nature Switzerland AG 2021
X. Sun et al. (Eds.): ICAIS 2021, LNCS 12737, pp. 715–723, 2021.
https://doi.org/10.1007/978-3-030-78612-0_58

lens distortion, and so on [10, 11]. The second type extracts features from the pattern noise caused by the hardware of the camera, and confirms the source camera by comparing the correlation between the features [12, 13]. The third type uses the periodic statistical features from images caused by the color filter array interpolation [14, 15].

Kharrazi et al. [16] proposed a source camera identification method based on supervised learning. A feature vector represents an image is extracted from each image training sample, then a Support Vector Machine (SVM) for multiple classification is trained. After training, the SVM can be used to classify the images to the cameras which provide the training samples. Geradts et al. [17] analyzed the defects of the pixels in the images, and used the pattern of the hot pixels and dead pixels for source camera identification. Lukas et al. [18] proposed a method to use the pattern noise of the sensors as the fingerprint to identify the type and model of the camera. The pattern noise is caused by the photo response non-uniformity (PRNU) of the sensor. In order to obtain the fingerprint of an exact camera, a large set of images captured by the camera need to be used. The images are denoised and the pattern noise of each image is extracted. The average of the pattern noise is computed to get the individual fingerprint of the camera. The pattern noise fingerprint can be treated as a spread spectrum watermarking. By using a correlation detector, one image can be connected with the exact camera which generates the image.

The biggest challenge in the existing source camera identification methods is that their performance rely on the training samples. If the testing samples are similar to the training samples, the performance of the source camera identification methods can be very well. However, it is difficult to build the training dataset containing the samples similar to the query samples in practice. In order to solve this problem, we propose an automatic source camera identification method based on hierarchy clustering. For a set of query images, our method uses the denoising filter to process each image and get their pattern noise fingerprint. Then a hierarchy clustering method is used based on the correlation between the pattern noise fingerprints, to make the images from the same camera divided in the same group. The proposed source camera identification method is an unsupervised learning method and does not rely on the training samples.

The rest of this paper is organized as follows. In Sect. 2 the proposed method will be introduced in detail. Section 3 will show the experimental results and the discussion. The conclusion will be made in Sect. 4.

2   The Proposed Method

In this section, the detail of our propoesd method will be elaborated, including the way of extracting pattern noise fingerprint, and the procedure of hierarchy clustering.

2.1   Image Pattern Noise Obtaining

The image acquisition process of an ordinary digital camera is shown in Fig. 1 [19]. For two cameras in the same model, their lens, anti-aliasing filter, CFA and sensors are usually the same type, and the demosaicing method and post-processing method are always the same, so the pattern noise fingerprints for the same model cameras are

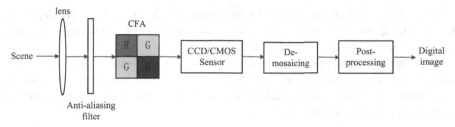

Fig. 1. The image acquisition process of an ordinary digital camera.

usually similar. However, due to the condition of lenses and sensors are different in each camera, the pattern noise fingerprint can be used to distinguish individual camera.

The way to extract the pattern noise fingerprint from an image is shown as follows [13].

$$\mathbf{W} = \mathbf{I} - F(\mathbf{I})$$ (1)

In Eq. (1), $\mathbf{I}$ is the original image, $\mathbf{W}$ is the residual noise, and F is the context based spatially adaptive wavelet denoising function introduced in Reference [20]. The method introduced in Reference [21] is used to extract the pattern noise, because the method can avoid the influence from other noise, such as the noise from circumstance and JPEG compression. The process of pattern noise extraction from the testing images is shown in Fig. 2.

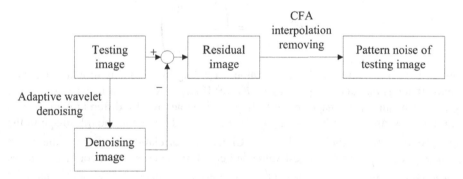

Fig. 2. The process of image pattern noise extraction.

Assume that the number of the testing images is n, and the pattern noise of the ith image $\mathbf{F}_i$ can be obtained by the method shown in Fig. 2. The pattern noise of all testing images constitute a set of pattern noise $D = \{\mathbf{F}_i | i = 1, 2, \cdots, n\}$.

The correlation coefficient between pattern noise of two images can be calculated as follows.

$$corr(\mathbf{F}_i, \mathbf{F}_j) = \frac{(\mathbf{F}_i - \bar{\mathbf{F}}_i) \cdot (\mathbf{F}_j - \bar{\mathbf{F}}_j)}{\left\| \mathbf{F}_i - \bar{\mathbf{F}}_i \right\| \left\| \mathbf{F}_j - \bar{\mathbf{F}}_j \right\|}$$ (2)

In Eq. (2), $\bar{\mathbf{F}}_i$ denotes the mean of the pattern noise $\mathbf{F}_i$, $\mathbf{X} \cdot \mathbf{Y} = \sum_{i=1}^{n} \mathbf{X}[i]\mathbf{Y}[i]$, and $\|\mathbf{X}\| = \sqrt{\mathbf{X} \cdot \mathbf{X}}$. By using Eq. (2), the correlation coefficient of pattern noise between each two images in the testing set can be obtained.

When the judgement of whether two images are from the same camera is needed to be determined, a special threshold T_ρ can be used. If the correlation coefficent of pattern noise between two images larger than the threshold, these two images can be regarded as generated by the same camera.

2.2 Hierarchy Clustering

The clustering method will make the objects with similar properties as one group, and divide the objects with different properties into different groups. Based on the similarity, the objects can be divided into groups with different levels. In our method, the hierarchy clustering is used to make the images captured by the same camera into one group, and make the images generated by different cameras into different groups, which achieve the target of source camera identification.

The procedure of hierarchy clustering in the propoesed method is shown as follows.

Step 1: Calculate the correlation coefficient of pattern noise between each two images in the testing set, record the correlation coefficent value in an upper triangular matrix, which is shown in Eq. (3). The element ρ_{ij} in the ith row and the jth column of the matrix denotes the correlation coefficient of pattern noise between the ith and the jth image sample. Then a threshold K_1 is selected.

$$R^0 = (\rho_{ij}) = \begin{pmatrix} 1 \cdots \rho_{1n} \\ \vdots \ddots \vdots \\ 0 \cdots 1 \end{pmatrix} \tag{3}$$

Step 2: Find the element with largest value excluding the elements in main diagonal, assume that it is ρ_{pq}, and compare it with K_1. (a) If $\rho_{pq} < K_1$, each image forms a group itself, that means each image in the testing set is generated by different camera, and then the clustering is finished. (b) If $\rho_{pq} \geq K_1$, make the pth and the qth image in the same group, represent the group by $G_1^{(1)}$. Check the correlation coefficient value in set $\{\rho_{pi} | i \neq p, i \neq q\}$, find the largest value and check if the correlation coefficient values between this sample and samples in $G_1^{(1)}$ are all not lower than K_1. If so, add it into $G_1^{(1)}$ and check the second largest value in the set. Repeat this process until no sample can be added into $G_1^{(1)}$.

Step 3: Remove the row and the column containing the elements in $G_1^{(1)}$, then do the same process as Step 2, to find whether the rest samples can be grouped under the threshold K_1. At last, we get the 1st level groups $G_1^{(1)}, G_2^{(1)}, \ldots, G_{l_1}^{(1)}$, under the threshold K_1.

Step 4: Calculate the correlation coefficient of pattern noise between each two 1st level groups as follows.

$$\rho_{G_i^1 G_j^1} = corr(G_i^{(1)}, G_j^{(1)}) = corr(\frac{1}{n_i^{(1)}} \sum_{u=1}^{n_i^{(1)}} \mathbf{F}_{iu}, \frac{1}{n_j^{(1)}} \sum_{v=1}^{n_j^{(1)}} \mathbf{F}_{jv}) \tag{4}$$

In Eq. (4), $n_i^{(1)}$ and $n_j^{(1)}$ are the number of samples in $G_i^{(1)}$ and $G_j^{(1)}$ respectively, and $\mathbf{F}_{iu}$ means the pattern noise of the uth image in $G_i^{(1)}$. After obtaining the correlation coefficent between each two 1st level groups, an upper triangular matrix $R^1 = (\rho_{G_i^1 G_j^1})$ is formed.

Step 5: Select a new threshold K_2, where $K_2 < K_1$, and then follow the steps above to get 2nd level groups $G_1^{(2)}, G_2^{(2)}, ..., G_{l_2}^{(2)}$, under the threshold K_2.

Step 6: Repeat the steps above, until all element value in the matrix R^m are lower than the threshold K_{m+1}, then the clustering is finished.

An example of hierarchy clustering following the procedure introduced above is shown in Fig. 3. After that, we can determine which images in the testing set are produced by the same camera.

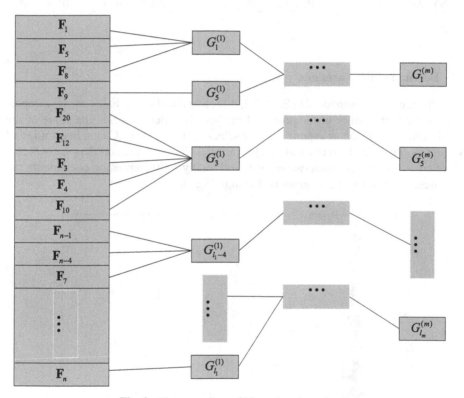

Fig. 3. The procedure of hierarchy clustering.

3   Experimental Results

In order to evaluate performance of the proposed method, we collect 6 camera models, the detail of the experimental camera models are shown in Table 1. The all images are croped into 1024 × 1024 resolution at the center. The 300 images constitute the testing set in the experiments.

Table 1. The detail of the experimental camera models

Model	Sensor	Resolution	Format
Canon Eos 450D	22.2 × 14.8 mm CMOS	4272 × 2848	JPEG
Canon PowerShot A40	1/2.7-in. CCD	1600 × 1200	JPEG
Canon PowerShot A620	1/1.8-in. CCD	3072 × 2304	JPEG
Nikon CoolPix L3	1/2.5-in. CCD	2592 × 1944	JPEG
SONY DSC-T10	1/2.5-in. CCD	3072 × 2304	JPEG
SONY DSC-W90	1/2.5-in. CCD	3264 × 2448	JPEG

3.1 Decision of the Threshold

From the procedure introduced in Sect. 2.2, it is clear that the thresholds are very important for the performance of the proposed method. In order to decide the value of the thresholds, we carry out an experiment. We select the images from Canon Eos 450D and Nikon CoolPix L3, which are 100 images in total. Calculate the correlation coefficent of pattern noise between each two images, and totally 4950 correlation coefficients can be gotten. The statistical histogram is shown in Fig. 4.

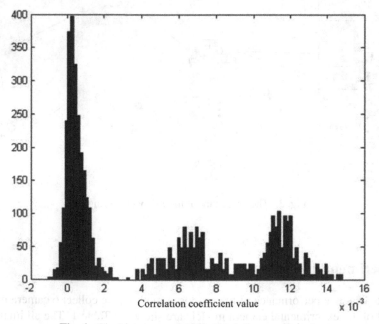

Fig. 4. The histogram of 4950 correlation coefficients.

From Fig. 4 we can see that in the left part of the figure, the correlation coefficients with samll value are calculated between images generated by different cameras, and in the right part of the figure, the correlation coefficients with large value are calculated between images generated by the same camera. In our proposed method, after finishing the clustering in one level, we need to calculate the center of each group to get a better pattern noise fingerprint, so we need to set the threshold based on the number of samples. We take the images captured by Canon Eos 450D as an example, examine the average correlation coefficient value between the elements and the center of the group, which is shown in Fig. 5.

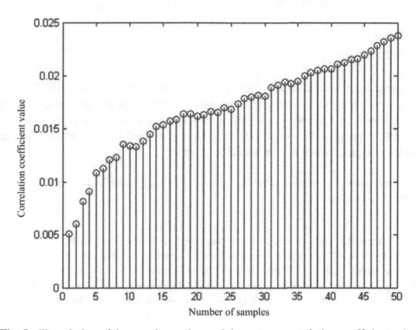

Fig. 5. The relation of the sample number and the average correlation coefficient value.

According to Fig. 5, we set the threshold based on the sample number n as follows.

$$K(n) = -0.000004059n^2 + 0.0004998n + 0.0077 \tag{5}$$

By using Eq. (5), we can choose a suitable threshold according to the number of images needed to be processed.

3.2 Detection Results

The proposed method is used to cluster the 300 images in the testing set, and the results are shown in Table 2.

The results in Table 2 show that the source camera identification accuracy of our method is 96.3%. The results demonstrate that the proposed method can finish the source camera identification tasks automatically, and it also has good performance without the help of training datasets, which is valuable in practice.

Table 2. The testing results of the proposed method

Model	A	B	C	D	E	F
A: Canon Eos 450D	47	0	2	0	1	0
B: Canon PowerShot A40	0	49	0	1	0	0
C: Canon PowerShot A620	0	0	50	0	0	0
D: Nikon CoolPix L3	0	2	2	46	0	0
E: SONY DSC-T10	0	1	1	0	48	0
F: SONY DSC-W90	0	1	0	0	0	49

4 Conclusion

In this article, we proposed an automatic source camera identification method based on hierarchy clustering. For a testing set of images, we extract the pattern noise fingerprint from each image, and use the correlation coefficient between fingerprints to carry out the hierarchy clustering. The proposed method has good performance and does not need the training samples, which is very useful in practice.

Acknowledgement. The authors would like to thank Professor Yongjian Hu from South China University of Technology.

Funding Statement. This work is partially supported by Young Teachers Program of Scientific Innovation Project from China People's Police University (ZQN2020028), Key Research Project from China People's Police University (2019zdgg012), Sino-Singapore International Joint Research Institute (206-A017023, 206-A018001), Science and Technology Project of Hebei Education Department (QN2021417) and Natural Science Foundation of Shenzhen (JCYJ20190808122005605).

References

1. Van Lanh, T., Chong, K.S., Emmanuel, S., et al.: A survey on digital camera image forensic methods. In: Proceedings of IEEE International Conference on Multimedia and Expo, Beijing, China, pp. 16–19 (2007)
2. Chen, Y., Kang, X., Shi, Y.Q., Wang, Z.J.: A multi-purpose image forensic method using densely connected convolutional neural networks. J. Real-Time Image Proc. 16(3), 725–740 (2019). https://doi.org/10.1007/s11554-019-00866-x
3. Gloe, T., Kirchner, M., Winkler, A., et al.: Can we trust digital image forensics? In: Proceedings of the 15th ACM International Conference on Multimedia, Augsburg, Germany, pp. 78–86 (2007)
4. Fridrich, J.: Digital image forensics. IEEE Signal Process. Mag. 26(2), 26–37 (2009)
5. Freire-Obregón, D., Narducci, F., Barra, S., et al.: Deep learning for source camera identification on mobile devices. Pattern Recogn. Lett. 126, 86–91 (2019)
6. Yang, P., Ni, R., Zhao, Y., et al.: Source camera identification based on content-adaptive fusion residual networks. Pattern Recogn. Lett. 119, 195–204 (2019)

7. Chen, L., Li, A., Yu, L.: Forensic technology for source camera identification. In: Sun, X., Wang, J., Bertino, E. (eds.) ICAIS 2020. CCIS, vol. 1254, pp. 466–477. Springer, Singapore (2020). https://doi.org/10.1007/978-981-15-8101-4_42

8. Sarkar, J., Naskar, R.: A curve fitting thresholding approach for forensic source identification of JPEG compressed images. In: Proceedings of 7th International Conference on Computing for Sustainable Global Development, New Delhi, India, pp. 22–28 (2020)

9. Hu, Y., Liu, B., He, Q.: Survey on techniques of digital multimedia forensics. J. Comput. Appl. **30**(3), 22–28 (2010)

10. Choi, K.S., Lam, E.Y., Wong, K.K.: Source camera identification using footprints from lens aberration. In: Proceedings of SPIE, vol. 6069, pp. 172–179 (2006)

11. Van, L.T., Emmanuel, S., Kankanhalli, M.S.: Identifying source cell phone using chromatic aberration. In: Proceedings of IEEE International Conference on Multimedia and Expo, Beijing, China, pp. 883–886 (2007)

12. Goljan, M., Chen, M., Fridrich, J.: Identifying common source digital camera from image pairs. In: Proceedings of IEEE International Conference on Image Processing, San Antonio, USA, pp. 14–19 (2007)

13. Chen, M., Fridrich, J., Goljan, M., et al.: Determining image origin and integrity using sensor noise. IEEE Trans. Inf. Forensics Secur. **3**(1), 74–90 (2008)

14. Popescu, A.C., Farid, H.: Exposing digital forgeries in color filter array interpolated images. IEEE Trans. Signal Process. **53**(10), 3948–3959 (2005)

15. Swaminathan, A., Wu, M., Liu, K.J.R.: Nonintrusive component forensics of visual sensors using output images. IEEE Trans. Inf. Forensics Secur. **2**(1), 91–106 (2007)

16. Kharrazi, M., Sencar, H.T., Memon, N.: Blind source camera identification. In: Proceedings of IEEE International Conference on Image Processing, Singapore, pp. 709–712 (2004)

17. Geradts, Z., Bijhold, J., Kieft, M., et al.: Methods for identification of images acquired with digital cameras. In: Proceedings of SPIE, Enabling Technologies for Law Enforcement and Security, Boston, USA, pp. 505–512 (2000)

18. Lukas, J., Fridrich, J., Goljan, M.: Digital camera identification from sensor pattern noise. IEEE Trans. Inf. Forensics Secur. **1**(2), 205–214 (2006)

19. Swaminathan, A., Wu, M., Liu, K.J.R.: Digital image forensics via intrinsic fingerprints. IEEE Trans. Inf. Forensics Secur. **3**(1), 101–117 (2008)

20. Chang, G., Yu, B., Vetterli, M.: Spatially adaptive wavelet thresholding with context modeling for image denoising. IEEE Trans. Image Process. **9**(9), 1522–1531 (2000)

21. Hu, Y., Yu, B., Jian, C.: Source camera identification technique using large components of imaging sensor pattern noise. J. Comput. Appl. **30**(1), 31–35 (2010)

A Fast Tongue Image Color Correction Method Based on Gray World Method

Guojiang Xin[1,2], Lei Zhu[1,2], Hao Liang[1,2], and Changsong Ding[1(✉)]

[1] Hunan University of Chinese Medicine, Changsha 410208, China
dingcs1975@hnucm.edu.cn
[2] TCM Big Data Analysis Laboratory of Hunan, Changsha 410208, China

Abstract. In traditional Chinese medicine (TCM), tongue diagnosis is an important way of disease diagnosis. In the study of intelligent tongue diagnosis, due to various reasons, the color distortion of tongue images will affect the accuracy of tongue diagnosis results. Therefore, it is necessary to correct the color of tongue images. In this paper, a fast color correction method for tongue image based on gray world method is proposed. Firstly, the image dimension is reduced twice to remove the unnecessary information in the image which makes the image data reduced to 3.6% of the original image and reduces the operation time for the image analysis. Then, the equivalent circle method is used to detect the color deviation of the image to check the degree of color distortion. Finally, the gray world method is used to correct the color of the image. Through the experimental comparison, it is found that the method proposed in this paper can greatly reduce the data amount of the image, and effectively improve the effect of color correction.

Keywords: Tongue diagnosis · Dimension reduction · Color correction · Gray world method

1 Introduction

"Inspection, listening and smelling, inquiry, pulse reading and palpation" are four ways of Chinese medicine to diagnose diseases, of which tongue diagnosis is one way of "seeing diagnosis". Chinese medicine believes that some internal diseases of the human body are reflected in the tongue image, and doctors can judge the patient's disease by observing the tongue image. At the same time, since tongue diagnosis is not harmful to the human body, it occupies a very important position in the diagnosis process of Chinese medicine.

At present, with the help of modern information technology and methods to study the inheritance and innovation of traditional Chinese medicine and the modernization of traditional Chinese medicine has gradually become a hot spot, among which the intelligent tongue diagnosis has become the focus and research direction of many experts and scholars.

The intelligence of tongue diagnosis mainly uses tongue image acquisition equipment to digitize the tongue image, and then uses information technology and methods to

© Springer Nature Switzerland AG 2021
X. Sun et al. (Eds.): ICAIS 2021, LNCS 12737, pp. 724–735, 2021.
https://doi.org/10.1007/978-3-030-78612-0_59

process and analyze it to assist doctors in disease diagnosis. Wang developed a complete tongue image analysis system that can obtain high-quality tongue diagnosis images and control the error within a range that is difficult to identify with the naked eye [1].

In the process of digital collection of tongue images, the color of the collected tongue images is often distorted due to the complicated and diversified collection conditions, non-standardized light collection, and non-standard posture of the person being collected [1]. The distorted tongue image will cause the computer to give wrong results during analysis. Therefore, after the tongue image is collected, the color cast detection and color correction must be performed first.

In practical applications, color correction of images is a very widely used research field, such as underwater image color correction [2], facial image color correction [4], tongue image color correction [3–5], Foggy day image color correction [5], night image color correction [6], plant image color correction [7], endoscopic image color correction [8], remote sensing image color correction [9], etc.

In terms of tongue image color correction, Xu [11] proposed to convert the tongue image collected under natural light conditions to the Lab color model to correct the chromatic aberration of the tongue image and achieved good results. Cao [10] proposed a color correction algorithm based on the ICC standard to improve the color reproduction of the tongue image. Xu [12] proposed two improved gray-scale world color correction algorithms based on standard deviation weighting and image entropy constraints, and achieved good correction results. Aiming at the problem of color deviation in the acquisition of TCM tongue images in natural environments, Liu [15] proposed a block color correction algorithm that combines an improved gray world method and a mirror method, and the color correction results are more in line with actual needs.

Among the image color correction methods, neural network method [12, 13], support vector machine method [14], white balance method [6, 8, 12] and so on are commonly used. Neural network method and support vector machine method need a certain number of samples for training, and the calculation process is relatively complicated. White balance methods are mainly divided into two categories: 1) based on hypothetical statistics, such as gray world method and mirror method; 2) based on sample learning, such as Regression Tree algorithm, CCC algorithm, etc. Among them, the method based on hypothetical statistics requires the image color distribution to meet certain premise assumptions, otherwise it will affect the accuracy and effect of the correction; the method based on sample learning is generally slow and requires a large number of samples for long-term learning [8].

The tongue images processed in this paper were collected by the TFDA-1 tongue and surface diagnostic instrument provided by Shanghai University of Traditional Chinese Medicine, and the equipment is shown in Fig. 1. When collecting images, the person is required to put his(her) face in the device, stick out his(her) tongue, close his(her) eyes, and then turn on the device's lights for collection. So far, we have collected thousands of tongue images. The collected tongue surface image is shown in Fig. 2. The middle part of the image is the human tongue surface, and the two sides are the equipment wrapping parts. The resolution of the collected images is uniformly set to 3712 * 5568, and the image size is about 10 MB.

Before post-processing and analysis of the self-collected images, color correction is first required. Based on the characteristics of the collected images, this paper proposes a fast color correction method based on the gray world method. The algorithm first reduces the dimensionality of the collected image twice, reducing the amount of image data to 3.6% of the original image, which can reduce the subsequent processing time. Then the color cast detection is performed on the reduced image. For images with color deviations, based on the principle of color constancy, the gray-scale world method is used for color correction. Through the analysis of subjective and objective evaluation criteria and comparing with other algorithms, the method proposed in this paper can well solve the problem of color correction of the collected images, the correction effect is good, and it can meet the needs of subsequent processing and analysis.

   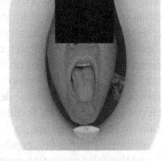

Fig. 1. Image acquisition equipment   **Fig. 2.** The acquisited tongue image

Before the images analysis, color correction should be done to make the analysis result more accurate. Based on the characteristics of the acquired images, we proposes a fast color correction method based on the equivalent circle method and gray world method. Firstly, the image data is reduced to 3.6% of the original image by reducing the image dimension twice. Then, the color deviation of the reduced image is detected by the equivalent circle method. Then, for the image with color deviation, the gray world method is used to correct the color. Through the analysis of subjective and objective evaluation standards, compared with other algorithms, the method proposed in this paper can correct the color of the acquired images, and the correction effect is good, which can meet the needs of subsequent processing and analysis.

2 Algorithm Description

Because the acquired image is a high-dimensional image, half of the information (equipment package part) in the image is useless for the image analysis. In order to reduce the processing time of the color correction, the image dimension is reduced first, then the color deviation detection is carried out, and finally the color correction is done. The flow chart of color correction algorithm is shown in Fig. 3.

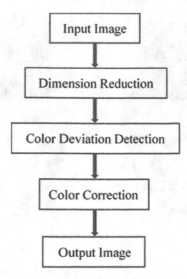

Fig. 3. The algorithm flowchart

2.1 Image Dimension Reduction

There are many methods to reduce the dimension of high-dimensional image. According to the characteristics of the image to be processed, we adopt two methods to reduce the dimension. At first, image cutting dimension reduction is used to remove the useless part for post-processing; then, the remaining part is reduced by pyramid down-sampling to further reduce the data amount of the image.

Image Cutting Dimension Reduction. Because the two side part with equipment package in the image is useless for the post-analysis, it can be removed totally. A threshold segmentation method is used to cut the part to reduce the dimension. The cutting function is shown in Eq. (1), where $g(x, y)$ is the image pixel after cutting, $f(:, y)$ represents the pixels in the Y column of the image, and T is the segmentation threshold.

$$g(x, y) = \begin{cases} f(x, y) & f(:, y) < T \\ 0 & f(:, y) \geq T \end{cases} \tag{1}$$

Through the data analysis, the pixel values of the equipment package part in the image are all greater than 160, so the segmentation threshold T is set to 160. Then scan the left and right sides of the image column by column to find the pixel value which is equal to the threshold T in th left and right columns. Set these two columns as the segmentation lines, keep the middle part surrounded by the left and right segmentation lines, and remove the white parts on both sides of the left and right segmentation lines. The cutting dimension image is shown in Fig. 4, the image dimension becomes 3712 * 3219, and the data amount is reduced to 58% of the original image.

Image Dimension Reduction by Pyramid Down-Sampling. The left part of the image by cutting dimension reduction contains the human face, which is useful for

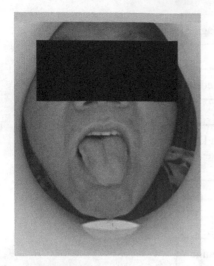

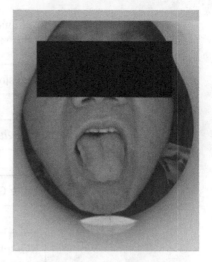

Fig. 4. The image with dimension reduction   **Fig. 5.** The image with down-sampling

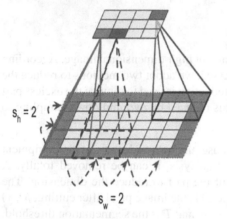

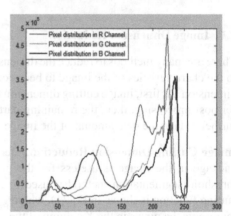

Fig. 6. The pyramid down-sampling   **Fig. 7.** Pixel distribution

the subsequent analysis. However, it is still a high-dimension image and needs further dimension reduction. The pyramid down-sampling method is used to reduce the dimension, The sampling pattern is shown in Fig. 6. The sampling formula is shown in Eq. (2), where I' represents the image after dimension reduction, I represents the image before dimension reduction, s represents the down sampling multiple, M and N represent the number of rows and columns of the image after dimension reduction. Here, we set $s = 4$. After down sampling got the image is shown in Fig. 5, the image dimension is reduced to 928 * 805, and the image data amount is reduced to 3.6% of the original image. At the same time, the image quality is still good.

$$I' = I\left(\frac{x}{s}, \frac{y}{s}\right) \quad x \in [1, M], \quad y \in [1, N] \tag{2}$$

2.2 Color Deviation Detection

Generally, for the color devition detection, there are many methods, such as histogram statistical method, gray balance method, white balance method and so on. These methods generally calculate the average value of RGB color channels of the image, and determine the degree of color deviation by analyzing the average characteristics and variance. However, the color deviation of color image is not only related to the average value of color, but also to the distribution characteristics of brightness and chroma. Based on this, Xu Proposed a color detection method of equivalent circle based on Lab color space [9]. The method first transforms the image from RGB color space to lab color space, and then calculates the characteristics of lab color space. The formula is shown in Eq. (3) (4) (5).

$$D = \sqrt{\left(\frac{\sum_1^M \sum_1^N a}{M * N}\right)^2 + \left(\frac{\sum_1^M \sum_1^N b}{M * N}\right)^2} \tag{3}$$

$$E = \sqrt{\left(\frac{\sum_1^M \sum_1^N (a - \sum_1^M \sum_1^N a/(M * N))^2}{M * N}\right)^2 + \left(\frac{\sum_1^M \sum_1^N (b - \sum_1^M \sum_1^N b/(M * N))^2}{M * N}\right)^2} \tag{4}$$

$$K = D/E \tag{5}$$

Among them, D is the distance from the center of the equivalent circle to the origin of the neutral axis of a-b chromaticity plane (a $= 0$, b $= 0$). The larger D is, the larger the average chromaticity of the image is; M is the radius of the equivalent circle; the smaller M is, the more concentrated the color distribution in the image; K is the chromatic aberration factor; and the larger K is, the more serious the color deviation is.

In this paper, the equivalent circle color detection method is used to detect the color deviation of the image. The color deviation factor K of the experimental image is calculated.

2.3 Color Correction

Among the commonly used color correction algorithms, white balance method is one of the popular methods, which includes gray world method and mirror method. These two methods are based on some assumption of image content, and can get better correction results without the help of standard color card.

Based on the white object, the mirror method adjusts the maximum point to white point by linear transformation of RGB color channels, so as to do the color correction of the whole image. However, when there is no white object in the image, the mirror method may make error correction. When the maximum point in the image is a white point, the mirror method may be unuseful.

Gray world method is based on von kries diagonal theory for color correction. The algorithm assumes that for any image, when it has enough color changes, the average value of RGB components in the image will tend to be equal. Color correction is done by adjusting the mean value of RGB color channels to the same state. When there are large single colors in the image, the gray world algorithm will produce over correction, because the image no longer meets the "gray world" hypothesis.

The pixel distribution of the image in the RGB color channels is shown in Fig. 7. It can be seen that the pixels of the RGB color channels are widely distributed, covering the whole color range. Therefore, the reduced image meets the hypothesis of gray world method, and the gray world method can be used for the color correction of the image.

The correction formula of gray world method is shown in Eq. (6) (7), where K is the correction coefficient, $\bar{R}$, $\bar{G}$ and $\bar{B}$ are the mean values of RGB color channels, R1, G1 and B1 are the pixel values of the image before correction, and R2, G2 and B2 are the pixel values of the image after correction.

$$K = (\bar{R} + \bar{G} + \bar{B})/3 \qquad (6)$$

$$R_2 = \frac{K}{\bar{R}}R_1 \quad G_2 = \frac{K}{\bar{G}}G_1 \quad B_2 = \frac{K}{\bar{B}}B_1 \qquad (7)$$

3 Experimental Results Analysis

The experiment compares the mirror method (method 1), the block color correction algorithm (method 2) which combines mirror method and gray world method. Through subjective and objective analysis, and the operation time of the algorithm analysis. It is found that the correction result of the proposed algorithm is better than the other algorithms, and the operation time of the algorithm is also the least.

3.1 Evaluation Criteria for the Color Correction

Usually, there are two standards to evaluate the effect of color correction: subjective evaluation standard and objective evaluation standard [4]. The subjective evaluation standard is to use the observer's visual experience to evaluate the color quality and analyze the correction effect. The objective evaluation standard is to use some evaluation indexes to calculate the color quality of the image, analyze the calculation results, and evaluate the correction effect.

Subjective Evaluation. The experiments were carried out on a large number of images, and some correction results are shown in Fig. 8. From the subjective evaluation standard, the correction effect of method 1 is not obvious which has a slight change; method 2 is over correction, and the image is over blue-green; for the proposed method, the image color is corrected to the normal color, and the correction effect is better.

Objective Evaluation. At present, there are not many objective evaluation methods for color correction effect, one of which is based on the principle of color constancy by calculating Euclidean distance. Firstly, the image is converted to the lab color space, and the color center of the image in the lab space is calculated. Then, the Euclidean distance between the color center of two images (standard image and the image to be evaluated) is calculated. The larger the difference is, the larger the color difference is, and the smaller the difference is. The smaller the color difference is, the better the correction effect is [10]. The calculation formula is shown in Eq. (8).

$$\Delta E_{ab} = \sqrt{\left(\bar{L}_1 - \bar{L}_2\right)^2 + (\bar{a}_1 - \bar{a}_2)^2 + (\bar{b}_1 - \bar{b}_2)^2} \qquad (8)$$

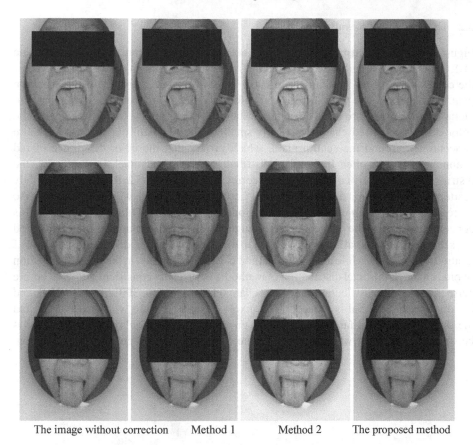

| The image without correction | Method 1 | Method 2 | The proposed method |

Fig. 8. The correction results of three methods (Color figure online)

Among them, ΔE_{ab} stands for color difference, $\bar{L}_1, \bar{a}_1, \bar{b}_1$ represents the color center value (mean value) of the image to be evaluated in lab space, $\bar{L}_2, \bar{a}_2, \bar{b}_2$ represents the color center value of standard image in lab space.

In order to comprehensively evaluate the correction effect, a judgment method is defined in RGB color space. Based on the principle of color constancy and Macbeth standard color card, the Euclidean distance of RGB color of two images is calculated to obtain the color difference. The formula is shown in Eq. (9).

$$\Delta E_{RGB} = \sqrt{(\bar{R}_1 - \bar{R}_2)^2 + (\bar{G}_1 - \bar{G}_2)^2 + (\bar{B}_1 - \bar{B}_2)^2} \qquad (9)$$

Where ΔE_{ab} represents the color difference between the standard image and the image to be evaluated, $\bar{R}_1, \bar{G}_1, \bar{B}_1$ is the color center value (mean value) of the image to be evaluated, $\bar{R}_2, \bar{G}_2, \bar{B}_2$ is the center value of the standard image. The smaller the difference is, the smaller the color difference is, and the better the correction effect is.

3.2 Experimental Results Analysis

Figure 9 is a pixel distribution map drawn according to the chromatic difference value of RGB channels calculated by formula (9). The black point in the center represents the center value of the standard color card. First, in the red channel pixel distribution map, for method 1, the pixel distribution before correction are basically consistent. For method 2, the pixels are more clustered around the center pixel, which proves that the color difference of red channel pixels is smaller. The pixels in our method are more concentrated around the central pixel, which proves that the color difference of red channel pixels is smaller. In the pixel distribution of green channel, for method 1, the distribution is basically consistent before correction. For method 2, the pixels are widely scattered. The pixel distribution range is between [-50, 300], which proves that the correction of the green channel has deviation. The pixel distribution of our method is concentrated around the central point, although the distribution map is similar to method 1, its distribution interval has been reduced to a certain extent. The distribution interval of method 1 is [0, 250], while that of our method is [0, 220]. Finally, in the pixel distribution of blue channel, the pixel distribution of method 1 is basically consistent with that before correction, but the distribution range has changed from [−100, 300] to [−50, 250], and the distribution interval is reduced. The pixels of method 2 are widely scattered, and there are many pixels far away from the central point. The pixel distribution range is between [−100, 300], which proves that the correction of blue channel has deviation.

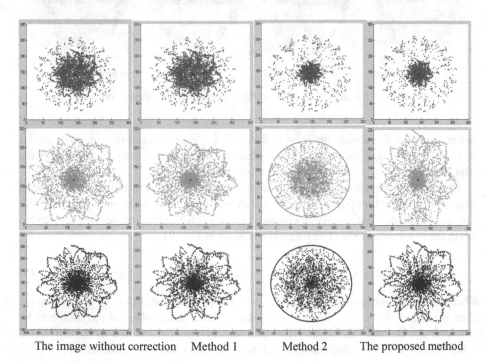

The image without correction　　Method 1　　　Method 2　　　The proposed method

Fig. 9. The pixel distribution of RGB color channel (Color figure online)

The distribution shape of our method is similar to the original image and method 1, but the range of the distribution interval is effectively reduced to $[-50, 250]$.

Comprehensive analysis shows that the overall pixel distribution of method 1 has no significant change, and the corresponding correction image has no obvious change. The overall distribution of pixels in method 2 has changed greatly. The red pixels are clustered obviously, while the green and blue pixels do not form a good clustering effect. From the correction results, we can see that the correction image of method 2 is blue-green and over corrected. The pixels of our method are well distributed in RGB color channels, and gather to the central point, and the corresponding correction image is also the best.

Table 1. Color difference value of Lab

Image	Method			
	Image before correction	Method 1	Method 2	Our method
Image 1	29.2771	27.7231	46.3660	**21.7215**
Image 2	27.8823	26.6383	44.8961	**18.6441**
Image 3	28.2776	27.1687	43.6007	**21.8398**

Table 2. Color difference value of RGB

Image	Method			
	Image before correction	Method 1	Method 2	Our method
Image 1	48.4181	45.8701	115.1929	**37.7455**
Image 2	36.0237	33.3821	100.5738	**19.6148**
Image 3	41.6546	39.1541	108.4912	**28.9196**

Table 3. The running time (s)

Image	Method		
	Method 1	Method 2	Our method
Image 1	**30.945995**	37.311376	31.308276
Image 2	34.793932	40.938870	**34.546873**
Image 3	34.914189	39.711651	**33.920882**

While analyzing the pixel distribution map, we will display the specific value list of the color difference results of the three selected experimental images, as shown in Table 1 and Table 2. Table 1 shows the lab color difference value, and Table 2 shows the RGB color difference value. From the data in the two tables, we can see that the color difference value of method 1 is slightly reduced, the value of method 2 is significantly increased, and the value of our method is smallest, it shows that the color of the image after correction is closest to the standard color, and the correction effect is the best.

The correction effect of different algorithms is analyzed, and the running time of the algorithm is also analyzed. The experimental environment (computer configuration) is as follows: memory: 4 GB, operating system: win10, CPU: Intel Core I3. Table 3 shows the running time of the three algorithms. It can be seen that the time of method 1 is basically the same as that of our method. Our method takes a little less time, while the method 2 takes more time.

4 Conclusion

Color correction is a necessary step in the analysis of tongue diagnosis image. Aiming at the tongue image acquisited by ourselves, a fast color correction algorithm based on gray world method is proposed to correct the color. The algorithm firstly reduces the dimension of the image, then uses the equivalent circle method to detect the color deviation, and finally uses the gray world method to correct the color. Through the experimental comparative analysis, compared with the block correction algorithm of mirror method, mirror method and gray world method, we can see that our method is more suitable for self-acquisited images, with fast correction speed and better correction effect, and reduces the data amount of the image which can save time for subsequent analysis and processing.

5 Fund Statement

Support foundation: National Key Research & Development Plan (2017YFC1703306), Natural Science Foundation of Hunan Province (2018JJ2301), Key Research & Develop Plan of Hunan Province (2017SK2111), Key Project of Hunan Provincial Department of Education (18A227), Key Project of Hunan Provincial Traditional Chinese Medicine Research Plan (2020002), School Level Project of Hunan University of Chinese Medicine (2018GL01).

References

1. Wang, X., Zhang, D.A.: New tongue color checker design by space representation for precise correction. IEEE J. Biomed. Health Inf. **17**(2), 381–391 (2013)
2. Meng, H., Yan, Y., Cai, C., Qiao, R., Wang, F.: A hybrid algorithm for underwater image restoration based on color correction and image sharpening. Multimedia Syst. 1–11 (2020). https://doi.org/10.1007/s00530-020-00693-2
3. Tu, L.P., Xu, J.T., Zhang, Z.: Application of color calibration methods for the tongue-color images under nature indoor light. J. Nanjing TCM Univ. **27**(1), 15–18 (2011)
4. Niu, J., Zhao, C., Li, G.-Z.: A comprehensive study on color correction for medical facial images. Int. J. Mach. Learn. Cybern. **10**(5), 935–947 (2018). https://doi.org/10.1007/s13042-017-0773-6

5. Xiao, C., Zhao, H.Y., Yu, J.: Traffic image defogging method based on WLS. Infrared Laser Eng. **44**(3), 1080–1084 (2015)
6. Chen, G.H., Zhang, L.: Research and realization of white balance algorithm for night image. Microelectron. Comput. **35**(3), 33–36+41 (2018)
7. Xu, Z.H., Zhang, L.E.: White balance processing of cucumber leaf image in greenhouse. Trans. Chinese Soc. Agric. Mach. **38**(11), 189–191 (2007)
8. Xu, M.F., Wang, L.Q., Yuan, B.: Auto white-balance algorithm of high-definition electronic endoscop. Infrared Laser Eng. **43**(9), 3110–3115 (2014)
9. Zhu, S.J., Lei, B., Wu, Y.R.: Automatic color correction for remote sensing optical image based on dense convolutional Networks. J. Univ. Chinese Acad. Sci. **36**(1), 93–100 (2019)
10. Xu, X.Z., Cai, Y.H., Liu, C.: Color cast detection and color correction methods based on image analysis. Meas. Control Technol. **27**(5), 10–12 (2008)
11. Cao, M.L., Cai, Y.H., et al.: ICC-based color correction in a new type instrument for tongue image analysis. Meas. Control Technol. **26**(5), 23–25 (2007)
12. Dong, C., Loy, C.C., He, K., Tang, X.: Learning a deep convolutional network for image super-resolution. In: Fleet, D., Pajdla, T., Schiele, B., Tuytelaars, T. (eds.) ECCV 2014. LNCS, vol. 8692, pp. 184–199. Springer, Cham (2014). https://doi.org/10.1007/978-3-319-10593-2_13
13. Wang, X., Zhang, D.: A comparative study of color correction algorithms for tongue image inspection. In: Zhang, D., Sonka, M. (eds.) Medical Biometrics. ICMB 2010. Lecture Notes in Computer Science, vol. 6165. Springer, Heidelberg (2010). https://doi.org/10.1007/978-3-642-13923-9_42
14. Zhang, H.Z., Wang, K.Q., Jin, X.S., et al.: SVR based color calibration for tongue image. In: Proceedings of 2005 International Conference on Machine Learning and Cybernetics, pp. 5065–5070. IEEE, Guangzhou (2005)
15. Wang, F., Wang, W.: An automatic white balance method via dark channel prior. Opto-Electron. Eng. **45**(1), 1–7 (2018)
16. Cheng, D.L., Price, B., Cohen, S., et al.: Effective learning-based illuminant estimation using simple feature. In: Proceedings of 2015 IEEE Conference on Computer Vision and Pattern Recognition, pp. 1000–1008 (2015)
17. Wang, X.Z., Zhang, D.: An optimized tongue image color correction scheme. IEEE Trans. Inf. Technol. Biomed. **14**(6), 1355–1364 (2010)
18. Xu, X.Z., Cai, Y.H., Liu, X.M.: Improved gray-scale world color correction algorithm. Acta Photonica Sinica **39**(3), 559–564 (2010)
19. Liu, Q., Huang, X.Y., Wang, B.L.: Color deviation detection and color correction method of tongue diagnostic image in natural environment. J. Xiamen Univ. (Nat. Sci.) **55**(2), 278–284 (2015)
20. Li, L., Wang, H.G., Liu, X.: Underwater image enhancement based on improved dark channel prior. Acta Photonica Sinica **37**(12), 1–9 (2017)
21. Qu, D., Chen, Y.B., Liao, F.: Improving precision and accuracy of skin color measurement by using image analysis methods with individual image color correction algorithms. Chinese J. Aesth. Med. **26**(8), 93–96 (2017)
22. Zhao, X.M., Zhang, Zh.P., Yu, Y.C.: Color correction algorithm of tongue diagnosis image based on CS-BP neural network. J. Guizhou Univ. (Nat. Sci.) **36**(5), 82–87 (2019)
23. Liu, Q., Huang, X.Y., Wang, B.L., et al.: A method for color cast detection and color correction of tongue inspection images under natural environment. J. Xiamen Univ. (Nat. Sci.) **55**(2), 278–284 (2015)

Evaluation of RGB Quantization Schemes on Histogram-Based Content Based Image Retrieval

Ezekiel Mensah Martey[1]([⊠]), Hang Lei[1], Xiaoyu Li[1], Obed Appiah[2], and Nicodemus Songose Awarayi[2]

[1] University of Electronics Science and Technology of China, Chengdu 611731, China
martey003@std.uestc.edu.cn
[2] University of Energy and Natural Resource, P.O. Box 214, Sunyani, Ghana

Abstract. Colour feature indexing for images has seen several approaches such as Conventional Colour Histogram, Colour Coherent Vector, Colour Moment and Colour Correlogram. These approaches for indexing images have proven to be fast, simple, and retrieve images from database with satisfactory results. The strength of these approaches however is based on the colour space and quantization schemes employed for the indexing of images. Various works have explored colour spaces and quantization for CBIR applications and have reported that the RGB colour space for CBIR sometime suffers some inefficiencies in retrieval accuracies. Interestingly, almost all the experiments used images that were converted from RGB colour space. Mathematical formulas were used to perform this conversion of RGB colour space to the other spaces. This suggests that RGB colour space may not necessarily be a poorer colour space for CBIR application, but the choice of quantization affects its performance with CBIR task. This work therefore evaluated various quantization schemes (uniform and non-uniform) to determine which of the schemes perform best for histogram based CBIR application. Results show that CBIR developers can opt for RGB quantization schemes in the combination of 4s and 8s bins on each of the colour channel or band for optimum retrieval.

Keywords: CBIR · Colour quantization · RGB quantization · Colour histogram · RGB quantization schemes

1 Introduction

Colour is considered as one of the important and prominent features for Content Based Image Retrieval (CBIR) or Query by Image Content (QBIC). It is normally categorized as low-level visual features and the human eye can differentiate between images on the basis of colours. Colour features for CBIR or QBIC therefore continue to be a primary feature for most image retrieval applications today [1]. The colour features together with image texture and shapes have been widely used with significant retrieval accuracies [2]. However, colour features extraction may not be necessary for most medical imagery applications since most images in the domain are grayscale images [3]. Colour features

© Springer Nature Switzerland AG 2021
X. Sun et al. (Eds.): ICAIS 2021, LNCS 12737, pp. 736–747, 2021.
https://doi.org/10.1007/978-3-030-78612-0_60

generally help minimize the problem of semantic gap which continue to be a major challenge in the domain of CBIR making the domain an active one over the last three decades [4].

Colour feature indexing for images has seen several approaches such as Conventional Colour Histogram (CCH), Colour Coherent Vector (CCV), Colour Moment (CM), and Colour Correlograms (CC). CCH have proven to be fast and simple to index, and retrieve images from a database with satisfactory results [5, 6]. Again various colour spaces such as RGB, HSV, L * a * b, YCbCr, and XYZ have also been implemented with various degrees of successes [7–9] however the RGB colour spaces has been used extensively in literature for indexing images using colour features [9–14].When comparing a query image with target images in a database, the images' signature vectors or index files are used. This is done by using a similarity metrics such as Euclidean Distance between the two vectors and the smaller distances considered as best matches [15].

In order to extract colour features such as CCH from an image, colour quantization must be performed first. The quantization of colours in an image helps reduce natural colours to finite number for easy comparison. Again, sub quantization further reduces the number of colours to make it even simpler for storing and manipulating images. The technique primarily assigns an integer number to a range of colours in the visible spectrum of the electromagnetic waves, making it a crucial stage in Computer Vision (CV) applications. Improper quantization seriously affects the performance of CV applications, and especially CBIR.

This paper primarily evaluates the effect of RGB quantization approaches (uniform and non-uniform) on the performance of colour histogram based CBIR task. The paper offers CBIR developers a comprehensive overview of quantization for histogram generation that can be used for indexing images for effective retrieval.

The rest of the paper is structured into four sections. Section 2 deals with some related works and current limitations in colour histogram CBIR systems. Section 3 describes the methodology and experimental concepts. Section 4 presents and discusses the results of this study. Finally, the last section concludes this paper.

2 Related Works

Several approaches of using colour feature or information have been proposed for indexing images. These methods or algorithms have been used since the 1980s and have generated satisfactory results [18, 20, 21]. Colour Histogram, Colour Coherent Histogram, and Colour Vector are various means of indexing images using colour features [9, 11, 12]. Colour histogram approach is still common today because developers of CBIR believe that similar images would contain similar proportions of certain values [7]. Colour spaces, colour histograms, histogram distance measurements, and quantization play an important role in retrieving images based on similarities [22]. This section reviews recent works that explored the effectiveness of colour spaces and quantization on CBIR performance.

[22] evaluated the effect of various colour spaces on CBIR recall precision. The colour spaces of HSV, YCbCr and YIQ were used in their experiment and various quantizations of $4 \times 8 \times 8$, $8 \times 8 \times 8$, $12 \times 12 \times 12$, and $16 \times 16 \times 16$ were used to

represent colour images. The paper concluded that Histogram Euclidean Distance (HED) produce better results than Histogram Intersection Distance (HID), and again HSV colour space gives better precision than the YIQ and YCbCr colour spaces. However, the work generally used uniform bins for all the components of the colour spaces. The RGB colour space as well as the non-uniform bins for histogram generation was not generally considered in their work.

[8] explored the number of intensities most appropriate for a colour quantization for image retrieval or CBIR application. The paper used RGB, HSV and XYZ colour spaces. Quantization of each channel or component of the colour spaces started from 2 to 254 with step of 8. Quantizations of $2 \times 2 \times 2$, $10 \times 10 \times 10$, $18 \times 18 \times 18$, etc. were used to represent images. Optimal precision of the various quantizations was reached with a quantization scheme of ($12 \times 12 \times 12$). The work generally contributes to the need for appropriated quantization schemes in CBIR systems that use colour histograms. However, the work basically used uniform number of bins for each component or axis of the colour spaces applied. This again may not reflect the true performance of a particular colour space against another, since non-uniform quantization was omitted for their experiment.

A study of colour histogram based image retrieval by [23] acknowledged the limitation of colour histogram algorithms being their inability to easily incorporate the spatial characteristics of the colours in the image. [12] therefore attempted solving the issue by implementing vector quantization technique that inherently integrates spatial distribution as seen in Colour Coherent vector (CCH). In their work, 48 bins normalized histograms for each of the RGB components images are saved as signature for each image. Thus, each image will have a signature that is made up of 3 histograms each representing one of the colour channels of the RGB colour space. This indexing approach is different from the traditional quantization of colour image but has been used with satisfactory results for CBIR works [23].

According to [24] colour information of an image can be represented with small amount of colours. The number of colours in an image is used to determine the number of bins when a histogram is to be generated from the image. The higher the number of colours in an image, the higher the number of bins that will be required to generate the histogram. Global Colour Histogram (GCH) and Local Colour Histogram (LCH) approaches are also common means of indexing files [24]. [24] indicates that the effectiveness of which type of histogram used is largely dependent on the kind of quantization used. In this work, largely uniform quantization is used for the experiment conducted and again leaves some gaps for the non-uniform bins histogram approach.

The choice of quantization scheme may increase the space required to store histogram generated for indexing of images in a database. For example, an RGB image of size 64×64 may require 12,288 bytes to store while indexing with $32 \times 32 \times 32$ quantization scheme may require 131,072 bytes making the index file far larger than the original size [11, 25, 26]. This curse of dimensionality associated with colour quantization led to an alternative approach for indexing files proposed by [16]. In [16], the mean, standard deviation and skewness colour moments are used instead of the traditional histogram and they proved to be efficient and effective in representing colour distribution of an image. However, Fig. 1 will still generate same mean, deviation and skewness which make the approach performing same as split-channel colour histogram. The strength of the proposed method by [16] is based on the fact the signature files are very small in sizes and therefore the running time required to retrieve images is reduced drastically, but the effect of quantization is still inherent in the approach.

[26] reiterated the challenge of quantization and its effects on the space required to store signature of images and eventually the running time of algorithm that search for similar image in a database. [26] proposed a method that computes feature vectors for global descriptor which uses less space for storing signature files of images as compared to using the histogram approach. The paper achieved good results with respect to running time but the challenge of spatial representation of pixel is not necessary addressed by this approach. Again the split approach of RGB used may also exhibit the challenges illustrated earlier when images with different colour having the same colour histogram.

The paper [20] also demonstrated the effect of colour spaces and quantization on image retrieval systems or CBIR applications. The paper presented an efficient quantization of HSV colour space and similarity measure by using the vector Cosine Angle distance between image. Again, the work also demonstrated the effects of image's size on accuracy of retrieval as well as running time. Images of sizes $256 \times 256, 128 \times 128, 64 \times 64, 32 \times 32, 16 \times 16$ and 8×8 were used for the experiment and HSV colour quantization (2, 5, 10) with Histogram Vector Cosine Angle distance under uniform size of 8×8 pixels gave better results. The work however focused only on HSV image space for retrieval which is not the only colour space used for indexing or generated signature files for images. RGB is still common image space and extensive work on its performance can aid developers to select appropriate space for effective performance.

Work by [6] discussed Content-Based Image Retrieval (CBIR) Methods from various dimensions. Various forms of colour feature indexing were discussed including CH and CCV. The paper concluded that each of the CBIR methods have their own advantages and disadvantages. The paper did not do extensive work in order to validate the reliability and efficiency of each of the method. It was observed that, per the kind of application, one method may do better than the other. The same can be said about colour space and quantization of colours for histogram generation. Each approach may have its own advantages and disadvantages. Various colour space experiments for CBIR applications have concluded that RGB colour spaces suffers some level of inefficiencies when compared with other colour spaces, however RGB colour space continue to be prominent in the CBIR domain due to its simplicity. Extensive work on RGB quantization (uniform and non-uniform) and histogram generation (Split-Channel and 3D) for CBIR has not been evaluated as suggested by literature so far [6]. This paper therefore offers wider dimension of quantization and histogram generation in order to significantly help developer select an effective approach for CBIR applications.

3 Methodology

There are two main approaches in generating CH for indexing images in a database and this work employed both methods on all the images in an identified image database.

Two main experiments (Experiment 1 and Experiment 2) are conducted in this work to evaluate the performance of various quantization schemes on the recall precision of CH based CBIR. 3D-Histogram and Split-Channel-Histogram are used to index the various images in the database. The Euclidean distance is used to estimate the similarity between the query image(histogram) and the target images (histograms) in the database. Experiment 1 used the 3D-Histograms of images for indexing, while that of Experiment 2 used Split-Channel Histogram.

3.1 D-Histogram

The steps to generate the 3D-Histogram can be outline as follows:

- Create a three (3) dimensional array to store the histogram of an image.
- Separate the colour bands or channels of the image (Red, Green, Blue). This separation will lead to three (3) primary colours or matrix each representing a component of the colour space.
- For each pixel, use the first channel value for first subscript value, second channel value as second subscript and third channel's value as third subscript to generate histogram

  $H_{(x, y, z)}\ H_{(x, y, z)} + 1$

  for an RGB image:

  x : Red channel

  y : Green channel

  z : Blue channel
- Reshape the 3D histogram into a 1D histogram by using Row major or Column Major.
- Normalize the vector
- Save the normalized vector as signature file.

3.2 Split-Channel Histogram

The steps to generate the 3D-Histogram can be outline as follows:

- Separate the colour bands or channels of the image (RGB). This separation will lead to three (3) primary colours or matrix each representing components of the colour space.
- Generate histogram for each of the separated channels.
- Concatenate the three (3) histograms to get a 1D Vector
- Normalize the vector.
- Save the normalized vector as signature for the image.

Table 1 presents all 64 RGB quantization schemes that were used for the experiments. Both the 3D-Histogram and the Split-histogram used the same quantization schemes for the experiments. Various ratios of bins along each of the channels were used to evaluate the performance of colour histogram for CBIR task. The format of quantization scheme is R × G × B where R, G, and B values represent the number of bins along each of the channels or colour band.

Table 1. Quantization used for generating colour histogram

Seq.	Ratio of Bins on each Channel			RGB Histogram Quantization			
	R	G	B	A	B	C	D
1	1	1	1	$2 \times 2 \times 2$	$4 \times 4 \times 4$	$8 \times 8 \times 8$	$16 \times 16 \times 16$
2	1	1	2	$2 \times 2 \times 4$	$4 \times 4 \times 8$	$8 \times 8 \times 16$	$16 \times 16 \times 32$
3	1	2	1	$2 \times 4 \times 2$	$4 \times 8 \times 4$	$8 \times 16 \times 8$	$16 \times 32 \times 16$
4	2	1	1	$4 \times 2 \times 2$	$8 \times 4 \times 4$	$16 \times 8 \times 8$	$32 \times 16 \times 16$
5	2	2	1	$4 \times 4 \times 2$	$8 \times 8 \times 4$	$16 \times 16 \times 8$	$32 \times 32 \times 16$
6	2	1	2	$4 \times 2 \times 4$	$8 \times 4 \times 8$	$16 \times 8 \times 16$	$32 \times 16 \times 32$
7	1	2	2	$2 \times 4 \times 4$	$4 \times 8 \times 8$	$8 \times 16 \times 16$	$16 \times 32 \times 32$
8	1	1	4	$2 \times 2 \times 8$	$4 \times 4 \times 16$	$8 \times 8 \times 32$	$16 \times 16 \times 64$
9	1	4	1	$2 \times 8 \times 2$	$4 \times 16 \times 4$	$8 \times 32 \times 8$	$16 \times 64 \times 16$
10	4	1	1	$8 \times 2 \times 2$	$16 \times 4 \times 4$	$32 \times 8 \times 8$	$64 \times 16 \times 16$
11	4	4	1	$8 \times 8 \times 2$	$16 \times 16 \times 4$	$32 \times 32 \times 8$	$64 \times 64 \times 16$
12	4	1	4	$8 \times 2 \times 8$	$16 \times 4 \times 16$	$32 \times 8 \times 32$	$64 \times 16 \times 64$
13	1	4	4	$2 \times 8 \times 8$	$4 \times 16 \times 16$	$8 \times 32 \times 32$	$16 \times 64 \times 64$
14	1	2	4	$2 \times 4 \times 8$	$4 \times 8 \times 16$	$8 \times 16 \times 32$	$16 \times 32 \times 64$
15	2	4	1	$4 \times 8 \times 2$	$8 \times 16 \times 4$	$16 \times 32 \times 8$	$32 \times 64 \times 16$
16	4	1	2	$8 \times 2 \times 4$	$16 \times 4 \times 8$	$32 \times 8 \times 16$	$64 \times 16 \times 32$

3.3 Test Dataset

Corel100 database (http://www.ci.gxnu.edu.cn/cbir/Dataset.aspx- Corel10K) was used for the testing of the various histograms used for indexing. The database contains 10,000 images that have been categories into 100 types. We experimented with 10 categories of images from the database of which each is made up of 100 images. Twenty (20) images were used for testing each of the quantization schemes. The first and second images in each category are selected as query images (20 images in all) for evaluating the quantization schemes presented in Table 1.

3.4 Similarity Measures

Similarity measure for CBIR task is done with distance metrics. Distance metrics include the sum of absolute difference (SAD), the sum of squared of absolute differences (SSAD), Euclidean distance, city block distance, Canberra distance, maximum value metric and Minkowski distance [27]. Query images are compared with targets images in the database to help retrieve relevant images from the database. The CH descriptor of the query images is compared with the CH descriptor of the images that were stored in the signature files. Images with similar colour distribution should have similar descript to aid the retrieval process. To check this similarity for this paper, the Euclidean distance similarity measure is used because of its robustness. The vectors of the images with small Euclidean distances are most similar to the query images. The distance can simply be described as the ordinary distance between two values. It is given in Eq. 1 below:

$$dist = \sqrt{\sum_{k-1}^{n} (p_k - q_k)^2} \tag{1}$$

Where:

$dist$ = distance measure
P_k = target image
q_k = query image

3.5 Performance Evaluation

20 images were selected as query images for each quantization scheme and the least 30 distances from the 1000 images were selected to be the retrieved images. The precision for each query instance is estimated and the average of the best 10 precision values for each quantization scheme selected for analyses. The recall and precision formula are illustrated in Eq. 3 and 2 respectively and have been effectively used by a lot of works to evaluate the performance of CBIR task.

$$\text{Precision} = \text{RR} / \text{TR} \tag{2}$$

$$\text{Recall} = \text{RR} / \text{RD} \tag{3}$$

$$Precision = (Relevant\ Images\ Retrieved\ in\ top\ T\ Returns)/(T) \tag{4}$$

Where:

- RR = Number of Relevant Images Retrieved
- TR = Total Number of Images Retrieved
- RD = Number of Relevant Images in the Database

4 Results and Discussion

This section presents the results of the experiments conducted in this work. We first start by presenting the results of Experiment 1 followed by Experiment 2. The discussions on each of the experiments follow immediately after the results are presented.

4.1 Results for Experiment 1

Figure 1 presents the precision percentages of the various quantization schemes used for the 3D Histograms indexing performances. The highest precision value was recorded by the quantization scheme of $4 \times 4 \times 8$ with 77% precision while the least was recorded by $64 \times 16 \times 64$ with 45% precision value.

Table 2. Quantization with precision above 70% for 3D Histogram

Seq.	RGB Quantization	No. of Bins	Precision
1	4 × 4 × 4	64	0.75
2	4 × 4 × 8	128	0.77
3	4 × 8 × 4	128	0.74
4	2 × 4 × 4	32	0.70
5	4 × 8 × 8	256	0.72
6	4 × 16 × 4	256	0.72
7	2 × 4 × 8	64	0.74
8	4 × 8 × 16	512	0.73

Table 2 presents the best 8 performing quantization schemes for the 3D-Histogram. The best performing 3D histograms generally had the number of bins between 64 and 256. From the results, quantization schemes having the combinations of 4 s and 8 s bins along the colour channels generally produced excellent precision results.

Table 3 presents the worst 10 performing quantization schemes. The quantization 8 × 2 × 2 is the only scheme among the worst performing schemes with very small number of bins of 32. The rest of the worst performing quantization schemes have number of bins above 4,000.

Table 3. Quantization with worst performance for 3D Histogram

Seq.	RGB Quantization	No. of Bins	Precision
1	64 × 16 × 64	65536	0.45
2	64 × 16 × 32	32768	0.49
3	32 × 64 × 16	32768	0.50
4	32 × 32 × 16	16384	0.52
5	8 × 2 × 2	32	0.52
6	64 × 64 × 16	65536	0.52
7	16 × 64 × 64	65536	0.52
8	32 × 8 × 32	8192	0.53
9	32 × 16 × 16	8192	0.55
10	16 × 16 × 16	4096	0.55

The results from the experiment indicate that high quantization does not necessarily result in better retrievals. This may be due to the rigid matching of images as the number of colour in images increase.

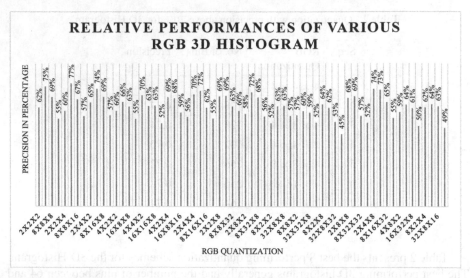

Fig. 1. General performance of all the 64 quantization schemes used for 3D-Histogram

4.2 Results for Experiment 2 (Split-Histogram)

Figure 2 presents the precision percentages of the various quantization schemes used for the Split-Channel Histogram for indexing. The highest precision value was recorded by the quantization scheme of $2 \times 4 \times 8$ with 66% precision while the least was recorded by $16 \times 64 \times 64$ with 53% precision value.

Table 4 presents the best 10 performing quantization schemes recorded by this Experiment 2. The best performing Split histograms generally have the number of bins between 10 and 20. From the results, quantization schemes having the combinations of 4 s and 8 s

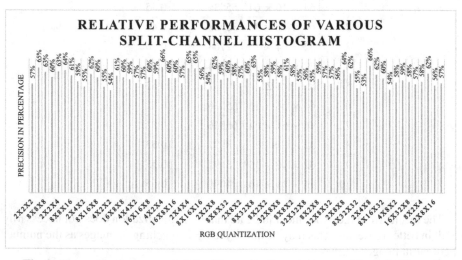

Fig. 2. General performance of all the 64 quantization schemes used for Split Channel

Table 4. Quantization with precision above 63% for Split-Channel Histogram

Seq.	RGB Quantization	No. of Bins	Precision
1	2 × 4 × 8	14	66%
2	4 × 2 × 4	10	66%
3	4 × 4 × 4	12	65%
4	2 × 4 × 4	10	65%
5	4 × 8 × 8	20	65%
6	2 × 8 × 8	18	64%
7	4 × 4 × 8	16	64%
8	2 × 2 × 4	8	63%
9	8 × 8 × 8	24	63%
10	8 × 32 × 8	48	63%

Table 5. Quantization with worst performance for Split-Channel Histogram

Seq.	RGB Quantization	No. of Bins	Precision
1	16 × 64 × 64	144	53%
2	4 × 2 × 2	8	54%
3	16 × 32 × 32	80	54%
4	16 × 32 × 64	112	54%
5	8 × 32 × 32	72	55%
6	64 × 64 × 16	144	55%
7	16 × 64 × 16	96	55%
8	16 × 32 × 16	64	55%
9	2 × 4 × 2	8	55%
10	16 × 16 × 4	36	55%

bins along the channels generally produced best precision results for the split histogram as well.

Table 5 presents the worst 10 performing quantization schemes. The quantization 4 × 2 × 2 and 2 × 4 × 2 are the only schemes among the worst performing schemes with very small number of bins of 8. The rest of the worst performing quantization schemes have the number of bins above 36.

Again, the results from the experiment 2 also indicate that higher quantization does not necessarily results in better precision value. This may be due to the rigid matching of images as the quantization of images increase.

5 Conclusion

This paper evaluated the effect of RGB quantization and histogram generation approach on the performance of CBIR. Uniform and non-uniform quantization for 3D histogram as well as Split-Channel histogram was used for the work. For 3D histogram, the highest precision value was recorded by the quantization scheme of $4 \times 4 \times 8$ with 77% recall precision, while the least value was recorded by $64 \times 16 \times 64$ with 45% recall precision. Generally, it was observed that quantization schemes with the combinations of 4s and 8s bins along the colour channels produced excellent recall precision results for the 3D histogram. The Split-Channel histogram also recorded better performances with quantization schemes having the combination of 4s and 8s bins along the various channels. It was observed that 3D histogram could register 77% recall precision, while the split-channel histogram recorded 66%. 3D colour histogram therefore performs better than Split-Channel histogram and in the situation where by histograms are to be deployed by any CBIR task, 3D histogram with the total number of bins between 64 to 256 as well as channels or bands bins in the order of 4s and 8s can be deployed for optimum results.

Acknowledgement. This work is supported by the National key Research & Development Program of China, Grant No. 2018YFĂ703.

Declaration of Competing Interest. The authors declare that they have no known or potential competing financial interests that could have appeared to influence the work reported in this paper.

References

1. Mustikasari, M., Madenda, S., Prasetyo, E., Kerami, D., Harmanto, S.: Content based image retrieval using local color histogram. Int. J. Eng. Res. **3**(8), 507–511 (2014)
2. Lin, C.H., Chen, R.T., Chan, Y.K.: A smart content-based image retrieval system based on colour and texture feature. Image Vis. Comput. **27**, 658–665 (2009)
3. Müller, H., Michoux, N., Bandon, D., Geissbuhler, A.: A review of content-based image retrieval systems in medical applications—clinical benefits and future directions. Int. J. Med. Informatics **73**(1), 1–23 (2004)
4. Kakade, V.M., Keche, I.A.: Review on Content Based Image Retrieval (CBIR) Technique. Int. J. Eng. Comput. Sci. **6**(3), 20414–20416 (2017)
5. Huang, J., Ravi, S.K.: Image indexing using colour correlograms. In: Proceedings of the IEEE Conference, Computer Vision and Pattern Recognition, vol. 8(3), 233–254 (1997)
6. Olaleke, J.O., Adetunmbi, A.O., Ojokoh, B.A., Olaronke, I.: An appraisal of content-based image retrieval (CBIR) methods. Asian J. Res. Comput. Sci. 1–15 (2019)
7. Jain, A.K., Vailaya, A.: Image retrieval using color and shape. Pattern Recogn. **29**(8), 1233–1244 (1996)
8. Meskaldji, K., Boucherkha, S., Chikhi, S.: Color quantization and its impact on color histogram based image retrieval accuracy. In: 2009 First International Conference on Networked Digital Technologies, pp. 515–517. IEEE (2009)
9. Pass, G., Zabih, R.: Refinement histogram for content-based image retrieval. In: IEEE Workshop on Application of Computer Vision, pp. 96–102. IEEE (1996)
10. Stricker, M., Dimai, A.: Colour indexing with weak spatial constraints. In: IS&T/SPIE Conference on Storage and Retrieval for Image and Video Databases IV, vol. 2670, pp. 29–40 (1996)
11. Pass, G., Zabih, R.: Comparing images using joint histograms. Multimedia Syst. **7**(3), 234–240 (1999)

12. Pass, G., Zabih, R., Miller, J.: Comparing images using color coherence vectors. In: Proceedings of the Fourth ACM International Conference on Multimedia, pp. 65–73. ACM (1997)
13. Liua, Y., Zhanga, D., Lua, G., Wei-Ying, M.: A survey of content-based image retrieval with high-level semantics. Pattern Recogn. **40**, 262–282 (2007)
14. Marín-Reyes, P.A., Lorenzo-Navarro, J., Castrillón-Santana, M.: Comparative study of histogram distance measures for re-identification. arXiv preprint arXiv:1611.08134 (2016)
15. Tyagi, V.: Content-Based Image Retrieval. Springer, Singapore (2017)
16. Afifi, A.J., Ashour, W.M.: Image retrieval based on content using color feature. In: International Scholarly Research Notices (2012)
17. Gaddam, C.S.: Drawing Color Histograms and Color Clouds. https://www.mathworks.com/matlabcentral/fileexchange/20757-drawing-color-histograms-and-color-clouds. Accessed 18 Mar 2020
18. Song, Y.J., Park, W.B., Kim, D.W., Ahn, J.H.: Content-based image retrieval using new color histogram. In: Proceedings of 2004 International Symposium on Intelligent Signal Processing and Communication Systems, pp. 609–61. IEEE (2004)
19. Mark, R.: RGB2Lab. https://www.mathworks.co/matlabcentralfileexchange/24009-rgb2lab. Accessed 23 Mar 2020
20. Niranjanan, S., Gopalan, S.R.: Performance efficiency of quantization using HSV colour space and vector cosine angle distance in CBIR with different image sizes. Int. J. Comput. Appl. **64**(18), 39–47 (2013)
21. Smith, J.R., Shi-Fu, C.: Tools and techniques for color retrieval. In: Symposium on Electronic Imaging: Science and Technology - Storage & Retrieval for Image and Video Databases IV, San Jose, pp. 1–12 (1996)
22. Girgis, M.R., Reda, M.S.: A study of the effect of color quantization schemes for different color spaces on content-based image retrieval. Int. J. Comput. Appl. **96**(12), 1–8 (2014)
23. Chakravarti, R., Meng, X.: A study of color histogram based image retrieval. In: Sixth International Conference on Information Technology: New Generations, pp. 1323–1328. IEEE (2009)
24. Latif, A., et al.: Content-based image retrieval and feature extraction: a comprehensive review. Math. Probl. Eng. **2019**, 1–21 (2019)
25. Mensah, M.E., Li, X., Lei, H., Obed, A., Bombie, N.C.: Improving performance of colour-histogram-based CBIR using bin matching for similarity measure. In: Sun, X., Wang, J., Bertino, E. (eds.) ICAIS 2020. LNCS, vol. 12239, pp. 586–596. Springer, Cham (2020). https://doi.org/10.1007/978-3-030-57884-8_52
26. Rawat, P.S., Jaikaran, S.S.: Efficient CBIR using color histogram processing. Signal Image Process. Int. J. **2**(1) (2011)
27. Malik, F., Baharudin, B.: Analysis of distance metrics in content-based image retrieval using statistical quantized histogram texture features in the DCT domain. J. King Saud Univ.-Comput. Information Sci. **25**(2), 207–218 (2013)

Correction to: A Container-Oriented Virtual-Machine-Introspection-Based Security Monitor to Secure Containers in Cloud Computing

Zhaofeng Yu(iD), Lin Ye, Hongli Zhang, Dongyang Zhan, Shen Su, and Zhihong Tian

Correction to:
Chapter "A Container-Oriented Virtual-Machine-Introspection-Based Security Monitor to Secure Containers in Cloud Computing" in: X. Sun et al. (Eds.):
Artificial Intelligence and Security, **LNCS 12737,**
https://doi.org/10.1007/978-3-030-78612-0_8

The original version of this chapter was revised. Shen Su and Zhihong Tian have been added as co-authors and their affiliation have been added, as they made important contributions to the paper.

The updated version of this chapter can be found at
https://doi.org/10.1007/978-3-030-78612-0_8

© Springer Nature Switzerland AG 2021
X. Sun et al. (Eds.): ICAIS 2021, LNCS 12737, p. C1, 2021.
https://doi.org/10.1007/978-3-030-78612-0_61

Author Index

Printed in the United States
by Baker & Taylor Publisher Services